A STAR TO STEER HER BY

A
STAR TO
STEER
HER BY

A Self-Teaching Guide to Offshore Navigation

By Edward J. Bergin

CORNELL MARITIME PRESS

Centreville, Maryland

Library of Congress Cataloging-in-Publication Data

Bergin, Edward J.,
   A star to steer her by.

   1. Navigation.   I. Title.
VK555.B494   1983   623.89   83-71313
ISBN 0-87033-309-7

Manufactured in the United States of America
First edition, 1983; fifth printing, 2000

To Jane Louise Roberts-Bergin

I must down to the seas again, to the
          lonely sea and the sky,
And all I ask is a tall ship and a star to
          steer her by . . .

—John Masefield, *Sea Fever*

Contents

Contents

Preface

A major boating magazine a few years ago published an article that said celestial navigation would soon go the way of the saber-toothed tiger. According to this article, the development of sophisticated electronic navigation systems would soon make celestial navigation obsolete.

Recently, a serious navigation error in a United States Navy Pacific Fleet maneuver was caused by reliance on electronic navigation equipment. As a result, the Navy ships fired their missiles from a point sixty-eight miles away from where they should have been. In the entire fleet, no one had bothered to take out a sextant to check the accuracy of the satellite navigation or LORAN fixes.

A February, 1980 government study concluded that the Navy should place greater emphasis on celestial navigation. If the United States Navy, with all its sophisticated electronic equipment, has decided to "go back to basics," the rest of us should take heed. Anyone who has spent much time offshore will tell you that electronics are fine when they work. They'll also tell you "the stars don't lie."

The major reason more people don't know and use celestial navigation has little to do with the electronics industry and a lot to do with the philosophy by which celestial navigation has been communicated. The truth of the matter is anyone who can look up numbers in a phone book, keep a dead reckoning plot, use the sextant, and add and subtract can learn how to solve celestial navigation problems.

Once the barnacles are scraped from the subject, it can be understood in eight to ten hours. That is exactly how much time it took my partner Jack Buchanek and me to teach newcomers in our "Celestial in a Day" workshops.

The essence of our training philosophy was to concentrate on the "need to know" areas avoiding nonessential, highly technical background information.

All the important concepts—including the how and why—were stated in simple, everyday language. The speed and accuracy of the process were improved through the use of special worksheets which not only organize data but give the student instructions on where to find it and what to do with it.

Traditional approaches to teaching celestial navigation are based on the outdated philosophy that students must understand complex theory, derive equations, and mathematically solve the problems. The development of precomputed tables, such as H. O. 229, make it possible for the first time to solve celestial navigation problems without a knowledge of spherical trigonometry and higher mathematics. However, the books and instruction methods were never revised to take full advantage of the breakthrough represented by the tables.

To this day most books and courses in celestial navigation continue to be based on theory, astrophysics, terrestrial spheres, and higher math. The actual process of solving problems, however, requires only the ability to understand and follow a set of rules and conventions for getting into, and out of, the almanac and sight reduction tables. Much of what is available on the subject of celestial navigation, therefore, bears little relation-ship to the steps by which problems are actually solved. For that reason, celestial navigation continues to be a difficult subject for instructors to teach and students to learn.

The mismatch between the materials and the methods also means that those few who do memorize the rules and learn the conventions often forget them after a short time and are then unable to review the subject on their own and regain proficiency.

I know from experience, that once people have the ability and confidence to work out their sights, they will practice and improve their skills with the sextant.

Some readers—like some of our students—may be skeptical that they can understand the process of celestial navigation after only eight hours of study. I ask that you give me eight hours of your time. Read the chapters in sequence, work the practice problems, and you'll soon find that celestial navigation—the mystical, mysterious skill of finding your way with the sextant, watch, almanac, and table—is within your grasp.

Acknowledgments

I would like to thank Jack Buchanek, my colleague at the Navigation Institute, who has worked with me over the last six years to develop the workforms, concepts, and principles we used to teach navigation. I would also like to thank Dolores Buchanek who supplied many of the drawings, Rear Admiral Thomas D. Davies, USN (Ret), Aaron Bodin, Ethan Bodin, Elena Hernandez, and Roger H. Jones who read the manuscript and offered many useful suggestions.

A STAR TO STEER HER BY

Introduction: Getting Organized

Before we start the clock, let's take a little time out to get organized. The materials you will need to learn celestial navigation using the concepts in this book include:

Pencils. Several, number 2, sharpened, with erasers.

Workforms. Make your own or order preprinted forms from a nautical supply store. (See list of suppliers below.)

TR 1210 training chart. The standard U.S. training chart 1/80,000 scale covering Martha's Vineyard to Block Island. This chart, which is used to review piloting and dead reckoning, is available at navigation supply stores or from local Power Squadrons.

Universal Plotting Sheet VP-OS X001. Available in pads of 50 at navigation supply stores.

Starfinder, 2102-D. A base plate with plastic discs that help identify stars. The book also shows you how the H. O. 229 table can be used to identify stars and planets. This item is optional.

Parallel plotter or parallel rules. A basic plotting tool used to transfer direction on a chart.

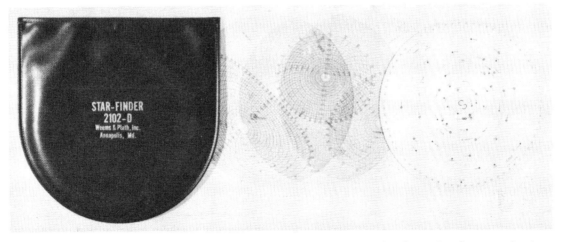

The starfinder is a base plate and a series of plastic discs which are used to determine the approximate sextant angle and direction of the 57 navigation stars. Courtesy Weems & Plath, Inc.

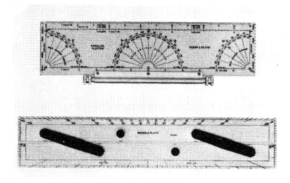

The parallel plotter, *top*, or parallel rules, *bottom*, help the navigator transfer direction lines on the chart. The parallel plotter is particularly useful for constructing celestial lines of position. Courtesy Weems & Plath, Inc.

Dividers. A tool used to measure distances and locate positions on a chart.

Volume III of H. O. 229. Selected excerpts from Volume III have been reprinted as Appendix 3 so you can work the example problems with the information in this book. To work practice problems, however, you will need Volume III.

Nautical Almanac for 1983. Excerpts of the 1983 almanac have been reprinted as Appendix 2. You can work all of the example and practice problems using the almanac data supplied with this book.

An accurate timepiece, like this Tamaya MQ-Z quartz crystal chronometer, is essential for celestial navigation. This chronometer is accurate to with +/− 4.5 seconds per month. Courtesy Tamaya, Ltd., Tokyo.

Once you finish the book and begin to practice celestial navigation you will need some additional equipment including:

Nautical Almanac for the current year.

Charts of the area in which you are sailing.

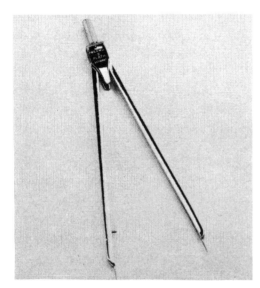

Dividers measure distance on a nautical chart. They are also useful in determining the latitude and longitude of a point on a chart, given its coordinates. Courtesy Weems & Plath, Inc.

A handbearing compass is useful not only in piloting but also for celestial navigation. In celestial navigation, the handbearing compass is used to obtain the approximate direction of stars. Courtesy Weems & Plath, Inc.

An accurate timepiece.

Radio receiver or RDF which can pick up time signals.

Handbearing compass.

Knotmeter and distance log.

Choosing a Sextant

The most expensive—and important—piece of gear needed for celestial navigation is the sextant. The sextant is used to measure the angle between the celestial body and the edge of the sea.

In selecting a sextant, the first decision you must make is whether to buy a plastic or metal one.

The advantages of plastic sextants are low cost and light weight. On the negative side, plastic sextants are less accurate and less durable than metal sextants. But how accurate must a sextant be? How much must you spend to get an instrument that will get you close enough to find a lighthouse or an island?

Top quality metal sextants have instrument certificates guaranteeing that they are within + or − 10″ (10 seconds) of arc, meaning for all practical purposes they are error free.

While plastic sextants do not come with instrument certificates, some I have tested gave results within + or − 2.0′ (2 miles) of the best metal sextants. The Davis Mark 25 plastic sextant is rated as the best plastic sextant on the market. It is also the only plastic sextant that I would recommend as an alternative to a metal sextant. Since the average yachtsman will have observer errors due to sextant misalignment, wave action, and motion on the order of 5 to 8 miles, a plastic sextant that is accurate to within 1 to 2 miles is acceptable.

There are three things to remember about plastic sextants.

A reliable distance log, like this Walker KDO Knotmaster Log for boats up to 40 feet, helps the offshore navigator maintain an accurate dead-reckoning position. Courtesy Weems & Plath, Inc.

1. The working parts involve plastic rubbing against plastic. Over time, this causes wear and adversely affects the accuracy of the instrument.

2. Plastic—much more than metal—is affected by changes in temperature. A plastic sextant left on deck in direct sunlight may give you a different reading than the same instrument which wasn't heated by the sun.

3. Plastic sextants go out of adjustment more easily than metal sextants. Therefore, the mirrors on a plastic sextant should be adjusted each time the instrument is used. This is no problem, really, but you must remember to check the mirror alignment frequently.

When you buy a sextant you are buying two systems. The mechanical system consists of a frame, index arm, release clamp, micrometer drum, and worm gears. The optical system consists of the shade glasses, mirrors, and scope. The mechanical system should operate smoothly. When you release the clamp, the gears should click solidly in place. There should be little or no movement in the index arm when the release clamp and gears are engaged.

Good sextants have optical quality shades, mirrors, and scopes. This eliminates light distortion and improves accuracy. You should look for a sextant with large index and horizon mirrors. These admit more light and help you obtain sights in difficult conditions.

A wide range of shade glasses is useful. The standard sextant comes with four shades on the index mirror and three shades on the horizon mirror. A sextant with variable density shades is a better choice than one fitted with a single polarizing filter. If you try to use a polarizing filter on a pitching, rolling boat, the movement of the vessel changes the angle of the filter which affects the amount of light that comes to your eye.

A sextant should feel comfortable in your hand. It should be well balanced, with the handle angled slightly to fit your grip. Since sextants come in a variety of weights, you can choose one to suit your liking. A sextant that is too light may not be steady enough. One that is too heavy can cause fatigue. Metal sextants now come in lightweight aluminum alloys as well as the heavier traditional brass.

These photos illustrate the wide range of choices you have when considering a sextant. The Weems & Plath metal sextant, *top*, has a 4 × 40 scope and whole horizon mirrors. The Davis Mark 25 plastic sextant, *bottom*, has a 3-power scope and whole horizon mirror. Courtesy Weems & Plath, Inc. and Davis Instruments.

Once you have made your decision about plastic versus metal, you have to decide on the following features: type of mirrors; type of scope; lighted or unlighted arc and drum; and whether or not you want a prism level.

Metal sextants, like this Cassens & Plath, have instrument certificates mounted inside the lid of the sextant case.

Whole horizon versus half-silvered mirrors: The new whole horizon mirror superimposes both the horizon and the celestial body on the entire mirror. This gives you the whole viewing surface of the mirror to work with.

Traditional sextants show the celestial body through a half-silvered mirror while viewing the horizon through the clear half. As a result, you end up working with about half the viewing surface of the horizon mirror.

Whole horizon sextants use specially coated optics to obtain their effect. The coating reduces by a small amount the light coming through the horizon mirror. Traditional sextants with an uncoated horizon glass transmit a bit more light but give you less viewing area. I've used both, and give a slight nod to the whole horizon sextants. The larger viewing surface makes it easier to find stars and

planets and helps you bring the body tangent to the horizon.

Whole horizon mirrors are available as original equipment on new plastic or metal sextants or as conversion kits for metal sextants. The whole horizon feature goes by several different trade names, depending on the sextant manufacturer: Weems & Plath call it Fulvew; Tamaya calls it Univision; C. Plath calls it Transflex; and Davis Instruments calls it the Beam Converger.

Type of Scope: For all-around use, a 4 × 40 scope is excellent. This scope has a large objective lens and admits a great deal of light. The four power magnification helps locate stars and keep them in view. This scope can also be used for sun and moon sights. Some navigators like a 6 × 30 or 7 × 35 monocular for sun sights because the increased magnification helps determine the point where the

Prism levels. The one above is for use with a plastic sextant; the one below for use with a metal one.

sun's edge is tangent to the horizon. The increased magnification, however, makes finding and holding sights more difficult on a pitching deck.

Lighted arc and drum: Some sextants are fitted with a tiny light that illuminates the arc and the micrometer drum. This is a very useful option, since many of your sights will be taken at twilight when it is really difficult to read the sextant. A button on the handle activates the light.

Prism level: This is an optional, clip-on device that can be fitted to plastic sextants and most metal sextants. Invented by retired Admiral Thomas D. Davies, this device can significantly reduce observer error by making it easier to line up the body, the sextant, and the horizon correctly. The prism level optically moves a section of the horizon up or down as the sextant is tilted. When the sextant is correctly lined up, the horizon shows as an unbroken line.

Nautical Equipment Suppliers

Weems & Plath
214 Eastern Avenue
Annapolis, Maryland 21403
    Navigation tools, instruments, charts, and
    books.

Baker, Lyman & Company
3220 S I 10 Service Road West
Metairie, Louisiana 70001
    Nautical instruments, sextants, calculators,
    plotting tools, navigation books, compasses,
    charts, plotting sheets.

Davis Instruments
3465 Diablo Avenue
Hayward, California 94545
    Plastic sextants, handbearing compasses,
    plotting tools, and workforms.

Kelvin Hughes Limited
New North Road
Hainault, Ilford, Essex IG6 2UR
England
    Charts, nautical publications, sextants, bin-
    oculars, navigational instruments, British
    Admiralty charts and publications.

Waterway Guide
6151 Powers Ferry Road, N.W.
Atlanta, Georgia 30339
    Cruising guides to the East and Gulf Coasts
    plus the Bahamas in three volumes. Distrib-
    utor of NOAA charts.

1

Piloting and Dead Reckoning
(Time: 45 minutes)

A solid foundation in piloting and dead reckoning (DR) is essential for celestial navigation. Many skippers today use chartbooks and cruising guides with preprinted magnetic courses and distances, and as a result, their piloting skills become rusty. When you sail offshore, you will have to keep a detailed log, maintain a dead-reckoning position, calculate time, speed, and distance problems, and make conversions from true to compass and compass to true.

You will have to locate a position on the chart by given coordinates, and determine the coordinates of objects on the chart, take bearings and plot lines of position, and know how to use the parallel plotter or parallel rule and dividers. You should know how to set up a Universal Plotting Sheet to keep a record of the DR track and record fixes without unnecessarily marking up your charts.

The dead-reckoning position is the starting point for celestial navigation. Celestial navigation will, of course, still work if your DR position is uncertain. However, you'll feel more confident at sea if your DR track stays fairly close to the fixes you obtain with the sextant.

The Navigator's World

The navigator's world is a sphere 6,888 nautical miles in diameter. A system of coordinates called latitude and longitude was developed in order to locate any point on the globe. Every point on the earth's surface has a unique latitude and longitude. Given a set of latitude and longitude coordinates, you can locate a specific point on the earth's surface.

Latitude refers to the left to right or horizontal coordinates and marks the distance north or south of the equator. Figure 1-1 shows the equator is in the middle of the earth and forms the base line from which all coordinates of latitude are given. Figure 1-2 shows two parallels of latitude circling the earth. Notice how they stay the same distance apart and do not meet each other.

Longitude refers to the earth's north-south or vertical coordinates and marks

Figure 1-1. Latitude starts at the equator, which is zero degrees, and marks the distance north or south. (Reprinted from Bowditch).

the distance east or west of the zero, or prime, meridian of longitude that runs through Greenwich, England. Figure 1-3 shows two meridians of longitude. Notice that they converge at both the North and South poles and the distance between the meridians of longitude gets smaller as the lines approach the North and South poles.

Figure 1-2. Latitude lines circle the earth and remain the same distance apart. (Reprinted from Bowditch).

Figure 1-4 shows the latitude and longitude numbering system. The latitude coordinates start at zero, the equator, and move north or south to a maximum of 90° at the poles. The South Pole is 90°S and the North Pole is 90°N. Latitude cannot exceed 90°.

The longitude coordinates start at zero, the Greenwich meridian, and move

east or west to a maximum of 180°. Longitude cannot exceed 180°E or 180°W.

Degrees, Minutes, and Tenths

Each degree of latitude or longitude contains 60 minutes. Each minute is further divided into ten-tenths. The correct way to record coordinates of latitude is to write the whole degrees first, then the minutes/tenths, and then indicate whether the latitude is north or south, with the symbol N for north and S for south. For example, thirty-eight degrees, fifty-four minutes, four-tenths north latitude would be written as: 38°54.4′N.

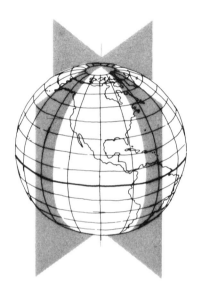

Figure 1-3. Longitude lines run north and south and get closer together as you near the poles. (Reprinted from Bowditch).

The correct way to record a coordinate of longitude is to write the whole degrees first, then the minutes/tenths, and then indicate whether the longitude is west or east with the symbol W for west and E for east. For example, seventy-six degrees, thirteen minutes, one-tenth west longitude would be written as 76°13.1′W. When giving coordinates, give the latitude first followed by the longitude.

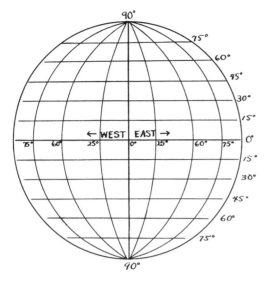

Figure 1-4. The earth's system of coordinates.

Longitude and Distance

Figure 1-5 shows how the distance represented by a degree of longitude changes based on your location. At the equator, 60′ of longitude equals 60 nautical miles. At 30° north latitude, however, 60′ of longitude covers a distance of only 52 nautical miles. At 60° north latitude 60′ of longitude covers 30 miles. There are always 60′ of longitude in a degree, but the distance represented by a degree of longitude shrinks as you get closer to the poles. For this reason you cannot use the longitude scale to measure distances on a chart. The longitude scale can be used only to measure longitude.

Latitude and Distance

The latitude lines, however, are evenly spaced throughout the world. This means that a degree of latitude represents the same distance no matter where you are. The distances represented by degrees, minutes, and tenths of latitude are equivalent to the distances represented by nautical miles. Therefore a degree of latitude which has 60′ is equal to 60 nautical miles. One minute of latitude equals one nautical mile.

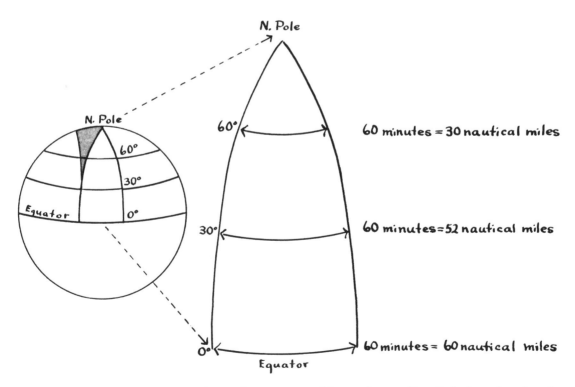

Figure 1-5. The distance on the earth's surface represented by one degree of longitude depends on how far you are from the equator.

Nautical Charts

In the sixteenth century, Dutch mapmaker Gerhard Mercator developed the technique for projecting the earth's round surface on a flat chart in such a way that navigators could use the latitude scale as an accurate measure for nautical miles. That's why almost all nautical charts are known as Mercator projections.

A chart contains information on the water depth, aids to navigation, dangers, and the contours of the shorelines. The longitude scale is at the top and bottom margins while the latitude scale is along the left and right hand margins.

True and Magnetic Compass Roses

Most charts, including TR 1210, have dual compass roses. The zero degree mark of the true compass rose is lined up with the earth's geographic North Pole. The zero degree mark of the magnetic compass rose is oriented to the earth's magnetic north. On TR 1210 the difference between true north and magnetic north is 14°45′ west. This tells you that the earth's magnetic field in this part of the world will deflect your boat's compass 14°45′ west of true north. The deflection of the ship's compass due to the earth's magnetic field is called variation.

The variation of the magnetic compass differs depending on where you are in the world. Information about the local variation is given inside the dual compass rose, or on ocean sailing charts on the chart itself.

In addition to the earth's magnetic field, objects on your boat such as the engine, keel, or anchors, can affect the compass. The deflection of the ship's compass due to the boat's own magnetic properties is called deviation.

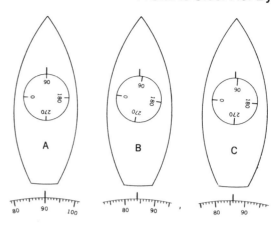

Figure 1-6. Variation and deviation deflect a ship's compass from its intended course. (Reprinted from Bowditch).

Figure 1-6 shows three boats with compass cards inside. At the bottom of each boat is a partial view of the compass card showing the direction or heading of the boat. Boat A is in a part of the world where there is no variation and the boat has no deviation on this heading. Therefore, the compass and compass card remain at 90° true. Boat B is in a part of the world where there is 6°E variation so the compass card points to 84°. Boat C is also in a part of the world where there is 6°E variation, but the boat's own magnetic influences deflected the compass 2°W. The combined forces result in the compass card pointing to 86°.

Deviation and variation are called compass errors. The mathematical process of removing errors—going from compass to true—is called correcting. When correcting, easterly errors are added and westerly errors are subtracted.

Example: Your compass reads 108°. The charted variation is 7°W and the deviation from the deviation table is 2°E. What is the true direction? *Solution:* 103° true.

The mathematical process of adding errors to the true course to obtain the compass course is called uncorrecting. When uncorrecting, easterly errors are subtracted and westerly errors are added.

Example: The true course is 39°. The variation is 9°E and the deviation is 1°W. What is the compass course? *Solution:* 31°.

PRACTICE PROBLEMS

1. The true course to your destination is 143°, the variation is 3°E, there is no deviation. What is the compass course?

2. The compass course is 54°, the variation is 7°W and the deviation is 2°W. What is the true course?

3. The compass course is 291°, variation is 8°W and deviation is 3°W. What is the true course?

4. The true course is 34°, the deviation is 2°E, variation is 2°W. What is the compass course?

5. The true course is 121°, variation is 4°E, deviation is 2°W. What is the compass course?

ANSWERS

1. 140° 2. 45° 3. 280° 4. 34° 5. 119°

Measuring Distances on a Chart

Distances on a chart are measured by using dividers. If the distance is small, the dividers are simply spread between the two objects on the chart. The distance is read either on the distance scale or on the latitude scale.

If the distance is longer than the span of the dividers, the dividers are first set for a convenient distance—say five miles—and then walked between the two points.

PRACTICE PROBLEMS *(Use TR1210)*

1. What is the distance between Point Judith Light (41°21.6'N; 71°28.8'W) and R"2" Fl. 10 sec. Whistle (41°20'N; 71°28.5'W)?

2. What is the distance between Point Judith Light and Schuyler Ledge Buoy R"2" Bell (41°27.4'N; 71°11.6'W)?

ANSWERS

1. 1.7 miles 2. 13.8 miles

Determining the Latitude and Longitude of Charted Objects

Dividers can also be used to determine the latitude and longitude of any charted object, or any point on a chart. To use dividers this way, locate the meridian of longitude or latitude that is closest to but not greater than the latitude or longitude of the object. These become your reference meridians. Place one point on the reference meridian and the other on the charted object. Then move the dividers up or down, or left or right along the reference meridian until you reach the scale. The desired latitude or longitude is the reference meridian plus the increment showing along the scale.

PRACTICE PROBLEMS *(Use TR1210)*

Use the dividers to locate the latitude and longitude of the following charted objects:

1. Buzzard's Horn Light.
2. Brenton Reef Light.
3. Elisha Ledge (buoy).

ANSWERS

1. 41°23.8'N; 71°02.0'W.
2. 41°25.6'N; 71°23.3'W.
3. 41°26.7'N; 71°09.4'W.

Direction on a Chart

Parallel rules or parallel plotters are used to determine or transfer directions on a chart. The parallel rule is used by lining up the straight edges with the charted objects and then "walking" the rule to a convenient compass rose. The parallel plotter is used the same way except you press down on the trailing edge of the knurled rollers to keep the plotter from shifting out of alignment as you move it to the compass rose. Whichever

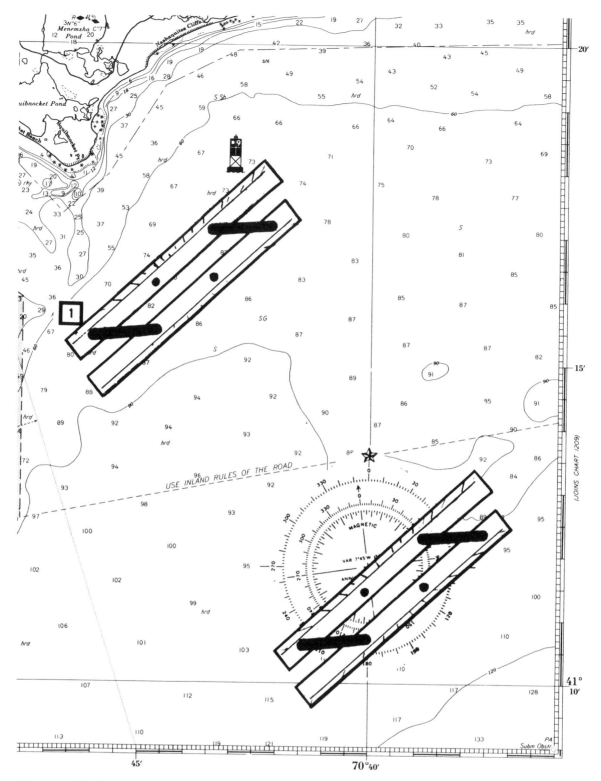

Figure 1-7. To determine course between charted objects line up objects with edge of parallel rule then slide rule to convenient compass rose. Edge of rule must go through center of compass rose. Directions are read at outer edge of compass rose.

instrument you use, when you get to the compass rose, the edge must pass through the center of the compass rose.

If you already know the course you want to transfer, set the parallel plotter or rule to the course using a convenient compass rose. You then walk or glide the plotter or rule to the buoy or spot on the chart where you wish to transfer the direction.

Figure 1-7 shows how the parallel rules were used to determine the course between two charted objects, daymark number "1" and "9."

When you look at the compass rose, you'll see that the parallel rule cuts through both the true and magnetic compass roses. Therefore you can, at a glance, determine the true and magnetic directions between the buoys.

If you were at buoy "1" and wanted to sail to buoy "9" you would read the direction from the right side of the compass rose, in this case 48° true or 56° magnetic. If you were at buoy "9" and wanted to sail to buoy "1" you would take the direction from the left side of the compass rose, in this case 228° true or 236° magnetic. Using the compass rose and parallel plotter or rule to draw lines toward or away from a given direction will play a major role later in constructing celestial lines of position.

PRACTICE PROBLEMS (Refer to TR 1210)

1. What is the magnetic course from Buzzard's Horn (41°23.7′N; 71°02.0′W) to the Red "2" S&P Bell Buoy off the end of Sow and Pig's Reef (41°23.9′N; 70°58.9′W)?

2. What is the magnetic course from the Red "2" S&P Bell Buoy to Buzzard's Horn?

3. Draw a line from Brenton Reef light in a direction of 220° magnetic for a distance of 4 miles. What charted object is passed close by?

ANSWERS

1. 104° 2. 284° 3. W or "H" Fl. 2 Sec. Bell

Locating a Point Given Its Latitude and Longitude

In celestial navigation you often have to locate a point on a chart given its coor-dinates of latitude and longitude. If you use your dividers and parallel rules together, this job is fast and easy.

Let's assume that you need to locate 41°11.1′N; 70°43′W on TR 1210. Look at the chart to see in what general area the coordinates are located. Figure 1-8 shows how the dividers and parallel rules are used to find the position.

PRACTICE PROBLEMS (Use TR 1210)

1. What charted object is located at 41°17.6′N; 71°00.1′W?

2. What charted object is located at 41°21.8′N; 70°51.8′W?

3. What charted object is located at 41°15.8′N; 70°46.3′W?

ANSWERS

1. BW Whistle
2. "29" Fl. 10 sec. gong
3. "1" Fl. G 5 Sec. Bell

Time, Speed, Distance

When you are sailing offshore, you need to update your DR position from the time of the last fix. This requires the ability to solve time, speed, distance problems.

Since the *Nautical Almanac*, as well as the tide tables, use the 24-hour military time system, so will we. In this system the hours from midnight to 12 noon are the same as the familiar 12-hour system. For times after noon, you simply add 12 hours. For example, 8:30 A.M. is recorded the same way in both the 12- and 24-hour systems; 8:30 P.M. in the 24-hour system is obtained by adding 12 hours to get 2030 hours. In piloting and figuring your DR track, you should keep time to the nearest hour and minute. In celestial navigation, though, you will time the sextant observations to the nearest hour, minute, and second.

Speed refers to the movement or velocity of the boat. Speed at sea is calculat-

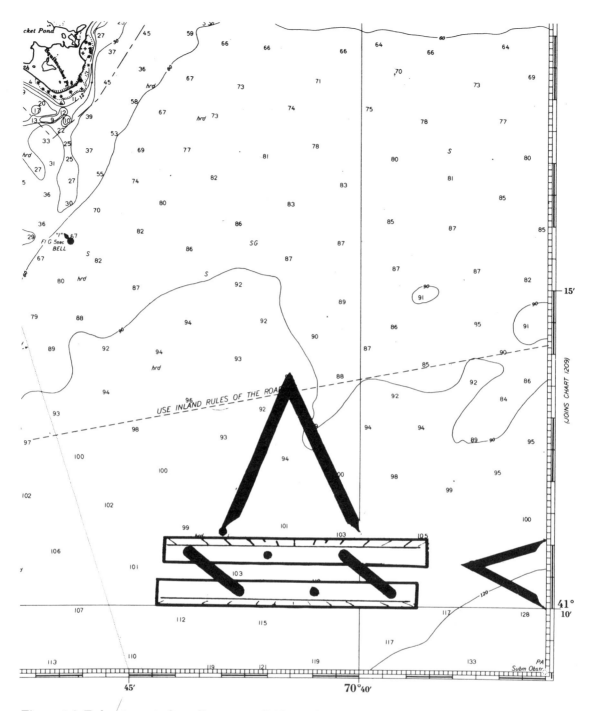

Figure 1-8. To locate a set of coordinates, use dividers to locate desired latitude; then use dividers, parallel rule, and pencil to mark dotted latitude line through area of chart in vicinity of desired longitude. Set dividers to desired longitude, and mark off this distance on latitude line to find desired location.

ed in knots. A knot means nautical miles per hour. The speed should be kept in knots and tenths.

In piloting, distance means the straight line between two points on a chart. (Of course, we all know that when you travel very long distances, a curved line called a great circle course is the shortest distance.) Distances will be calculated in nautical miles and tenths of miles. The latitude scale or distance scale can be used to measure distance.

Examples: When the distances are in miles, time in hours, and speed in knots, the following formulae can be used.

$$\text{Distance} = \text{speed} \times \text{time}$$

A boat travels 7.6 knots for 4 hours 20 minutes. What is the distance? Since there are 60 minutes in an hour, convert the 20 minutes to decimal hours by dividing 20/60 to obtain .33. The distance, rounded, is, therefore, 7.6 times 4.33 or 32.9 nautical miles.

$$\text{Speed} = \frac{\text{distance}}{\text{time}}$$

A boat traveled 11.4 miles in 1 hour 12 minutes. What was the speed? Twelve minutes is converted to decimal hours by dividing 12/60 to obtain .2. The speed equals 9.5 knots.

$$\text{Time} = \frac{\text{distance}}{\text{speed}}$$

A boat traveled 21.8 miles at a speed of 5.6 knots. How much time did it take? Time for the run was 3.9 hours.

Sometimes, you must solve time, speed, distance problems when the time is in minutes, not hours. The following formulae and examples show how these problems are solved.

$$\text{Distance} = \frac{\text{speed} \times \text{minutes of time}}{60}$$

A boat is making 11.3 knots, how far will it travel in 28 minutes? It will travel 5.3 miles.

$$\text{Speed} = \frac{60 \times \text{distance}}{\text{time}}$$

Recently, it took you 41 minutes to run between two buoys 4.4 miles apart. How fast were you going? The speed was 6.4 knots.

$$\text{Time} = \frac{60 \times \text{distance}}{\text{speed}}$$

You need to cover 6.2 miles to return to your dock. Your top cruising speed is 14.7 knots. How long will it take to run this distance? It will take 25.3 minutes.

PRACTICE PROBLEMS

1. Your boat traveled 5.3 knots for 2 hours 10 minutes. How far did it go?

2. A boat traveled 6.7 miles in 1 hour 36 minutes. What was its speed?

3. A boat traveled 13.2 miles at a speed of 4.6 knots. How much time elapsed?

4. Your boat is making 5.9 knots. How far will it go in 36 minutes?

5. It took 19 minutes to run between two buoys 2.6 miles apart. What speed were you making?

6. It is 7.1 miles to your destination. The knotmeter indicates you are making 8.3 knots. How long will it take you?

ANSWERS

1. 11.5 miles
2. 4.2 knots
3. 2.9 hours or 2 hrs. 54 mins.
4. 3.5 miles
5. 8.2 knots
6. 51.3 minutes or 51 mins. 18 sec.

Dead Reckoning

Dead reckoning—frequently abbreviated as DR—is the process of keeping track of a boat's estimated position on a chart based on the courses steered and speed through the water. Since dead reckoning does not generally take into account currents, wave action, leeway, or windage on the hull, the DR position should be considered an approximate position. It is your best estimate of where you think your boat is located.

In keeping the DR, the boat's position is recorded by drawing lines on the chart or Universal Plotting Sheet that represent the progress of the voyage. Navigators have adopted a system of useful symbols to record information on the chart. Figure 1-9 illustrates how these symbols are used.

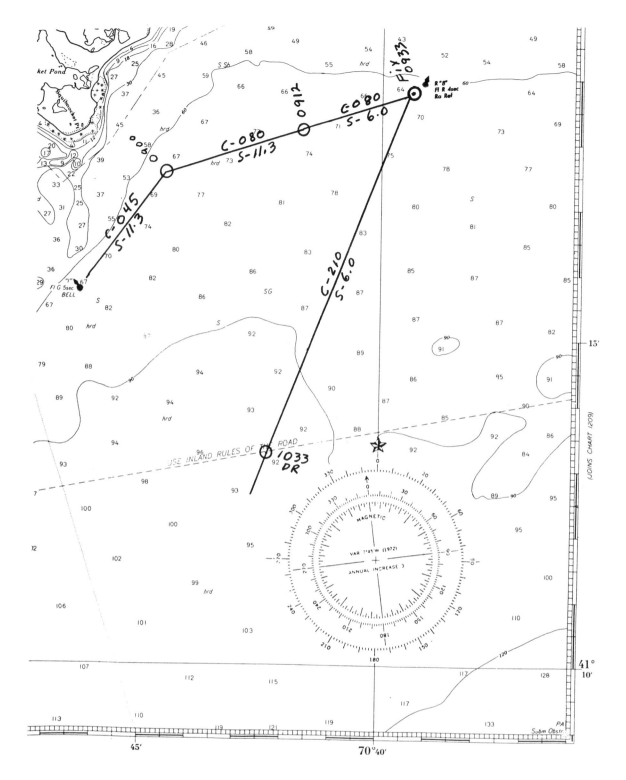

Figure 1-9. The DR starts at a known position. The course is written above the line, the speed underneath. A new DR is plotted for every change of course or speed. A circle with a dot is used to indicate a fix. A DR is plotted at least every hour.

A DR plot always starts from a known position, such as the boat's point of departure or a buoy. In maintaining the DR, the boat's distance is a function of the speed of the boat through the water multiplied by the time.

A new DR plot is started whenever you obtain a fix. A DR position, with the

time, is recorded whenever there is a
change of course or change of speed. The
DR position should be kept up-to-date. In
heavily traveled pilot waters, this could
mean every fifteen minutes. On a long
offshore passage, you could update the
DR position every four hours as the crew
changes watches. When keeping the DR,
take the time to be neat and erase all
unnecessary lines.

Before leaving port, you should use
your dividers, plotters, and charts to plan
ahead the courses and distances to be
sailed. This plan should include information about buoys, lighthouses, and other
aids to navigation that will be passed and
can be seen along your course.

After you're underway, keep a written log—called a rough log—with all the
information needed to construct the DR
position on the chart. *The Offshore Log*
developed by author-yachtsman Earl R.
Hinz, available from navigation supply
stores, organizes passage information in
a concise and orderly manner.

Bearings and Lines of Position

The handbearing compass plays an
important role in coastal piloting. You
will see how it can also help identify stars
by obtaining the approximate direction
of the star you observed with the sextant.

Figure 1-10. Handbearing compass is used to determine 240° bearing on water tank.

Figure 1-10 shows how a handbearing compass was used to take a bearing
on a water tank. Figure 1-11 shows the
difference between the boat's heading
and a bearing.

One bearing on a charted object or
point of land enables you to draw one line
of position on a chart. To construct a line
of position from a bearing use the parallel
rules or plotter to transfer the direction of
the bearing from the compass rose to the
charted object. The bearing line is drawn
beginning from the charted object. Figure 1-12 shows how the compass rose was
used to construct a line of position from
the bearing on the water tank. In this
case the 240° bearing represents the direction from the boat to the charted object. You cannot draw the line of position
starting from the boat because you do not
know the exact location of the boat on the
chart.

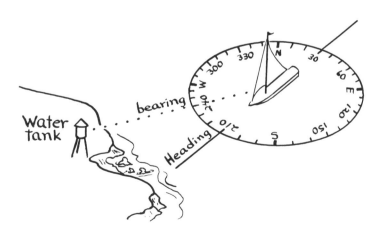

Figure 1-11. Ship's course or heading is 210° while bearing of water tank is 240°.

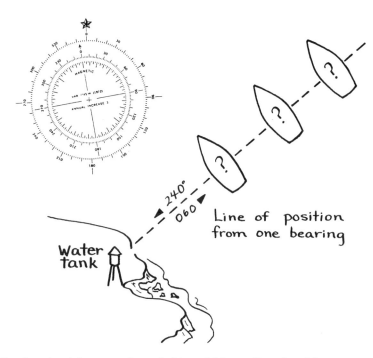

Figure 1-12. One bearing taken on a charted object yields one line of position.

Since you know the location of the water tank on the chart, draw a line from the tank to the boat. This line will be drawn the opposite way from 240° which in this case is 60°. The mark on the opposite side of a compass rose from an indicated direction is called the reciprocal. The 60° mark is the reciprocal of 240°. The bearing line is always drawn on the chart as a dotted line and labelled with the bearing not the reciprocal.

In piloting, it takes two or more lines of position from bearings on two charted objects to produce a fix. In celestial navigation it takes at least two observations of celestial bodies to produce a fix.

Figure 1-13 shows how bearings from two charted objects intersect. The intersection of the two lines of position is a fix.

Figure 1-14 shows how lines of position from bearings taken on three objects intersect to form a triangle. When this happens, the center of the triangle is taken as the fix. In celestial, the three star fix will produce three lines of position that intersect in the form of a triangle.

When taking bearings, it is important to locate charted objects or points of land that are separated by at least 30°. Bearings on objects that are not adequately

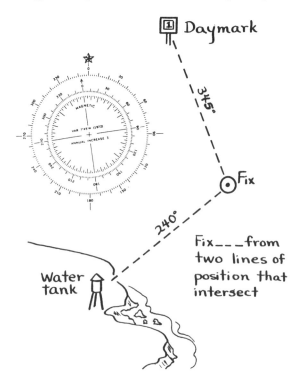

Figure 1-13. Two bearings taken on charted objects that intersect produce a fix.

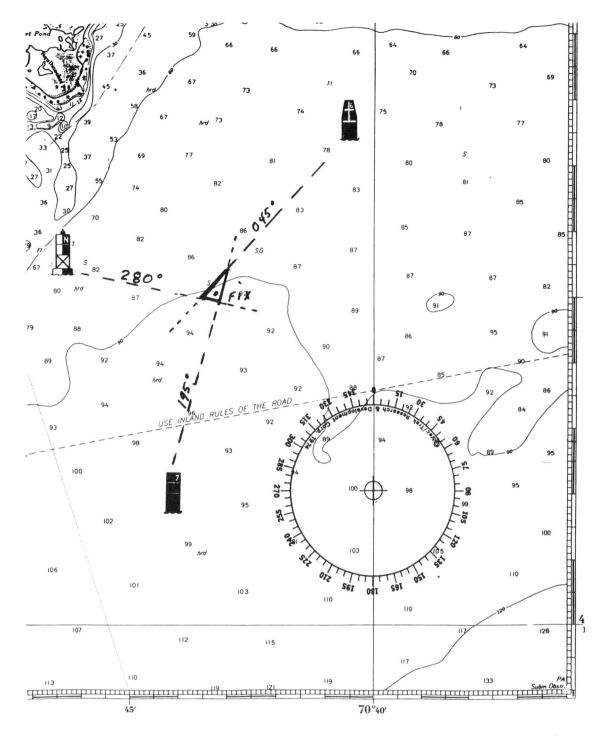

Figure 1-14. Three lines of position taken from bearings on charted objects can intersect to form a triangle. The fix is the center of the triangle.

separated produce lines of position too close together to give you an accurate fix.

Running Fixes

Sometimes a navigator needs to fix his position when the distance between two charted objects prevents him from taking bearings on them at the same time. This is done by using a technique called the "running fix." A running fix is the method used to combine the results of two bearings taken on different objects at different times so they produce a fix.

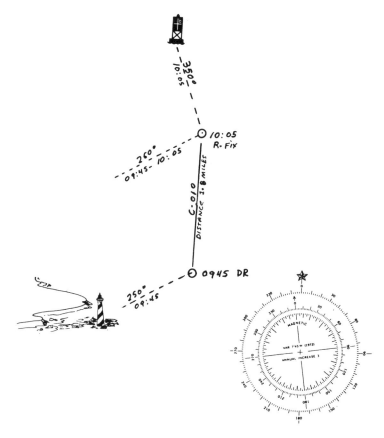

Figure 1-15. A running fix combines the results of two observations on different charted objects taken at different times in such a way that they yield a fix. To do this the line of position from the first bearing is advanced to account for the movement of the boat between the first and second bearings.

Figure 1-15 illustrates the concept of a running fix. To plot a running fix you must advance the earlier line of position to account for the movement of the boat during the time that elapsed between the first and second bearing. A bearing of 250° magnetic was obtained on the lighthouse at 0945. A distance of 1.8 miles later, at 1005, a bearing of 350° magnetic was obtained on the buoy. To obtain a running fix, first construct and label the 0945 lighthouse LOP. Maintain your DR track and log, so you know the course and distance sailed between the first and second bearings. When you obtain the second bearing, construct and label it, and then "advance" the earlier line of position to account for the movement of the boat between bearings. The boat moved 1.8 miles along the course line of 10° mag-

netic, so the lighthouse LOP was "advanced" or moved forward in this direction (10° magnetic) and for this distance (1.8 miles). The fix should be labelled as a running fix to distinguish it from simultaneous fixes.

Running fixes are not as accurate as fixes obtained from objects observed at the same time.

Circles of Position

A line of position (LOP) is a series of possible places along one line where the boat might be. It is also possible to have a circle of position. In Figure 1-16 a boat is approaching a lighted buoy at night. The maximum range of the light, assuming good visibility, is six miles. If the light is observed resting on the horizon, the navi-

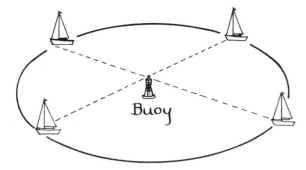

Figure 1-16. A circle of position is a series of possible places the boat can be at a given distance from a charted object.

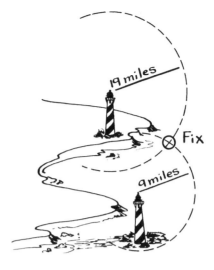

Figure 1-17. Two circles of position that intersect produce a fix. Celestial navigation is based on this principle.

gator would know that he is somewhere on the edge of a circle with a radius of six miles from the light. If he obtained a bearing on the buoy, he could fix his position by constructing a line of position which intersected the circle of position. Figure 1-17 shows how a navigator along the coast used the arc of visibility from two lighthouses to obtain two circles of position and a fix.

Celestial navigation is based on these same principles. The lighthouses, however, will not be along a rocky coast. They

will be the stars, sun, moon, and planets. Your observations will be taken with the sextant, not the handbearing compass.

One observation of a celestial body with a sextant will give you a circle of position. It requires two or more circles of position that intersect to obtain a fix.

2

Understanding Celestial Navigation
(Time: 1 Hour)

How Celestial Navigation Works

The sextant is really a sophisticated protractor. It measures angles. In celestial navigation, the sextant is used to measure the vertical angle between the horizon and a heavenly body.

In piloting, lines of position are based on bearings taken on charted objects. One bearing enables you to construct one line of position. Two lines of position that cross produce a fix. You can also obtain a running fix from observations of charted objects taken some time apart.

It is almost the same with celestial navigation. One observation of a celestial body with the sextant will give the information needed to construct one line of position on a chart. You need two observations of celestial bodies that produce lines of position that intersect to fix your position. You can also obtain a running fix from lines of position based on observations of heavenly bodies taken several hours apart.

In addition to measuring the angle (or altitude) of the body, the sextant also measures the distance from your location to the point on the earth directly under the star. A sextant reading of 90° would

mean the star is directly above your head. If the star moved 10° away from you, the angle measured by the sextant would be 90° − 10° or 80° as Figure 2-1 indicates.

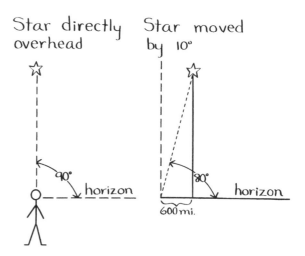

Figure 2-1. If the sextant angle was 90°, the star is directly overhead. If the sextant angle is 80°, the position on the earth under the star is 10° times 60′ or 600 nautical miles from the observer.

The relationship between the sextant and distance is one of the most important concepts in celestial navigation. One minute of arc measured by the sextant equals one nautical mile on the earth's surface. Since each degree on a sextant contains 60 minutes, each degree of arc on the sextant is equal to 60 nautical miles. Therefore, when the star moved from directly overhead, a 90° angle, to 80° the spot on the earth under the star is 90° − 80° or 10° away from you. Since there are 60′ in a degree, and since a minute equals one nautical mile, we know that the spot on the earth under the star is now 60′ × 10° or 600 nautical miles from the observer.

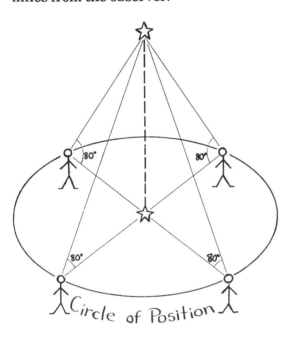

Figure 2-2. There are a number of places on the earth where an observer could obtain the 80° angle of the star with the sextant. When you know your distance from the spot on the earth under a star, you have a large circle of position.

Even if you know the distance you are from the spot on the earth under the star, you still do not know exactly where you are. As Figure 2-2 shows, there is a very large 600 mile circle of position on the earth where you could be and still obtain that same 80° reading with the sextant.

The spot on the earth directly under the celestial body is called the geographic position or GP. This is the "splash down" position on the earth's surface where the

celestial body would land if it fell from the sky and headed directly toward the center of the earth. Like any position on the earth, the GP can be located by a set of coordinates. The coordinates of the GP of celestial bodies are similar to latitude and longitude.

The "longitude" measurement of the GP is called the Greenwich Hour Angle (GHA) and the "latitude" measurement of the GP is called the Declination (Dec.). As Figure 2-3 indicates, the GHA shows how far west of the Greenwich meridian the GP of the body is located while the Declination indicates how far north or south of the equator the GP is located. The *Nautical Almanac*, issued every year by the U. S. government, is a compilation of the GP's of all the important celestial bodies for every day, hour, minute, and second of one year. If you know the date, and the exact time you observed a celestial body, you can look up the GP in the Almanac.

Once you know the GP of a celestial body for the exact time you observed it with a sextant, it is possible to use the H. O. 229 table to find two things:

1. What the sextant angle would have been if the observation had actually been taken from the DR position (or a DR position rounded off to get into the table). This angle is called the computed angle or computed altitude.
2. The true direction of the GP of the celestial body from the DR position. This is called the azimuth. This information is then used to help you construct a line of position on the chart.

To begin the process of celestial navigation, measure the angle between the horizon and a celestial body with the sextant and correct the sextant reading for several factors. Look up the GP of the body for the exact time of the observation in the *Nautical Almanac*.

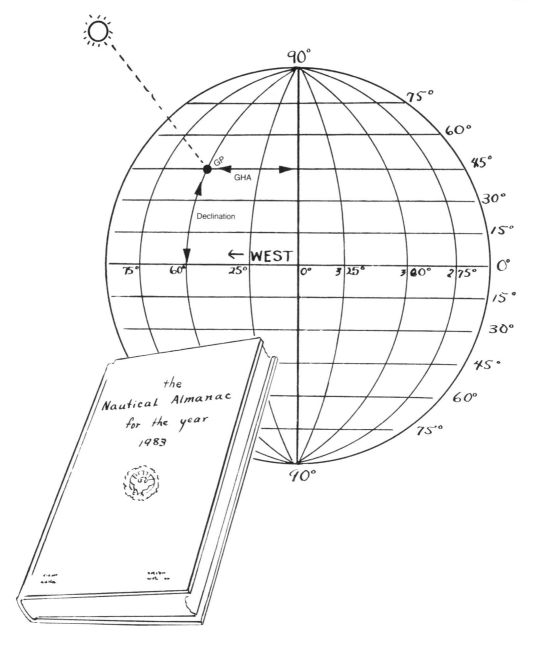

Figure 2-3. The *Nautical Almanac* lists the geographical positions of celestial bodies. The longitude or GHA of the GP of the sun is 60° while the latitude, or declination, is 45° north.

The sextant angle subtracted from the "overhead angle" of 90° represents the distance the GP of the celestial body is from the observer. Since you could obtain this same sextant angle from a number of places, all of which are the same distance from the GP, the sextant has given you a very large circle of position, like the one shown in Figure 2-4.

If there was a convenient way to locate the GP of the body on a chart covering thousands of miles, and if we had plotting instruments capable of drafting huge circles on the charts, we could plot the circle of position directly. The sextant angle subtracted from the 90° overhead angle would be used.

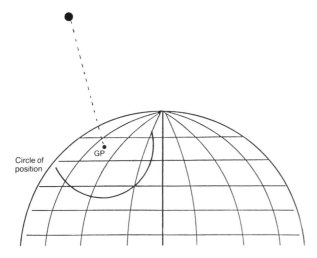

Figure 2-4. Since the sextant angle can be used to calculate the distance of the observer from the GP of a celestial body, one observation yields a large circle of position.

If you could plot the circles resulting from two celestial observations, as Figure 2-5 shows, you could fix your position at the point where the two circles intersected. Since it is impossible to plot circles this large, navigators developed a way to solve the problem. It is called the altitude-intercept method.

In this method, the H. O. 229 tables are used to compute the angle the sextant would have read if the sight had been taken at the DR position. The computed angle, then, gives you a circle of position which runs through the DR position. Fig-

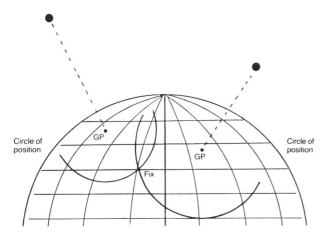

Figure 2-5. The intersection of two circles of position yields a fix.

ure 2-6 shows the only two possibilities. The DR position can either lie outside the sextant circle (case 1) or it can lie inside the sextant circle (case 2). (While it is extremely unlikely, your DR position could also be on the sextant circle.)

If the DR lies outside the sextant circle, the computed angle will be smaller than the sextant angle. If the DR lies inside the sextant circle, the computed angle will be greater than the sextant

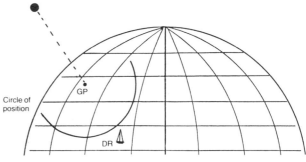

Case 1: DR lies outside circle of position.

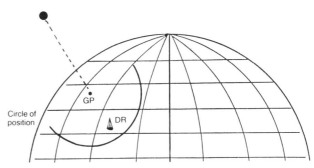

Case 2: DR lies inside circle of position.

Figure 2-6. There are only two possibilities. *Top*, the DR lies outside the circle of position measured by the sextant, or *bottom*, the DR lies inside the circle of position measured by the sextant.

angle because the larger the angle, the closer you are to the GP, and the smaller the circle will be. The smaller the angle, the farther away from the GP you are, and the larger the circle.

Navigators have developed a handy way to remember this: Coast Guard Academy stands for C-G-A or Computed, Greater, Away. If the computed angle is

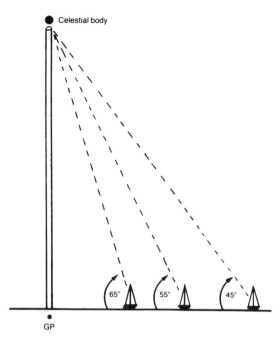

Figure 2-7. The smaller the angle, the farther the observer is away from the GP of the body. The smaller the angle, the larger the circle of position will be.

greater than the angle measured by the sextant, then the line of position is farther away from the GP than the DR position. If the computed angle is less than the angle measured by the sextant, then the line of position lies closer to the GP than the DR position.

Figure 2-7 shows how this works. Consider the star as the top, and the GP as the bottom, of a giant maypole. Three observers on the earth measured the same star with a sextant and obtained readings of 45°, 55°, and 65°. You can see that the smaller angles place the observer farther away from the base of the maypole. You can also see that the smaller angles produce larger circles of position. This is the basis for the Computed, Greater, Away.

If the computed angle is 65° and the observed angle 55°, the observer is farther away from the GP. A line drawn from the DR position on the 65° circle to the observer at the 55° circle would have to be drawn away from the GP.

If the observed angle is 65° and the computed angle 55°, then the observer is closer to the GP. A line drawn from the DR position on the 55° circle to the observer on the 65° circle would have to be drawn toward the GP.

Now we are working with two angles and two circles of position. The "real" angle and the "real" circle of position are given by the sextant. The "computed" angle and the "computed" circle are given by the H. O. 229 tables. The difference between the two angles is equal to the distance in nautical miles between the two circles.

The difference between the two angles is called the intercept. The intercept represents the distance, in nautical miles, the "real" circle of position is from the "computed" circle that goes through the DR position.

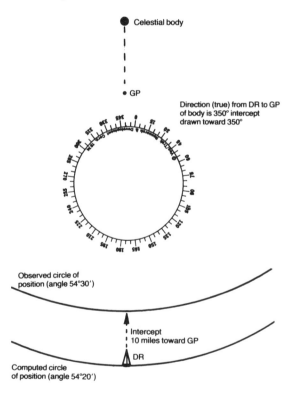

Figure 2-8. When the computed angle is less than the observed angle, the observed circle of position is reached by marking off the 10′ difference in the angles toward the GP of the body. The direction of the GP from the DR position is the azimuth. Here, it is 350°.

The H. O. 229 tables also compute the true direction from the DR to the GP of the body. This direction is called the azimuth.

Once you have the azimuth and intercept, you can readily solve the problem of plotting the circles of position.

Figure 2-8 shows the computed angle of 54°20′ obtained from H. O. 229 was less than the sextant angle of 54°30′. The difference in the angles is 10′ and one minute equals one nautical mile. Therefore, the intercept, distance between the circles, is ten miles.

The H. O. 229 tables show that the true direction or azimuth of the GP from the DR position is 350°. Since the computed angle is smaller than the sextant angle, the "real" circle of position lies closer to the GP than the DR position. Therefore, the navigator begins at the DR position and marks off the dotted intercept line 10 nautical miles toward 350°. At the end of the dotted intercept line, a solid perpendicular line is constructed. The perpendicular line is really a portion of the huge circle of position measured by the sextant. For practical purposes, however, we know that a straight line can represent a small segment of a very large circle.

Figure 2-9 shows that the computed angle of 54°30′ was greater than the sextant angle of 54°20′. The intercept or difference in the angles is still 10′ or ten nautical miles. Since the sextant angle is smaller than the computed angle the "real" circle of position is farther away from the GP of the body than the DR position. Therefore, mark off the dotted intercept line beginning at the DR position 10 miles away from 350°. To do this, take the reciprocal of 350° which is the direction exactly opposite 350° on the compass rose. The parallel rules cut the compass rose in half anyway, so you can set the rules for the azimuth of 350° and

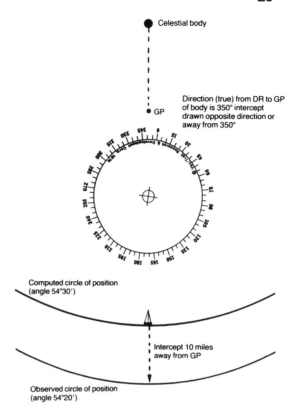

Figure 2-9. When the computed angle is greater than the observed angle, the observed circle of position is reached by marking off the difference in the angles away from the GP of the body. Here, the 10′ distance is marked off away from 350° by using the reciprocal of 350° which is 170°.

without moving the rules draw the line the opposite way.

At the end of the dotted intercept line, draw a straight perpendicular line. This represents a portion of the large circle of position measured by the sextant. Intercept lines should be dotted lines so they do not become confused with the solid lines of position. The line of position should be labelled with the name of the body and the time of the observation.

In actual practice, no one draws circles of position on a chart or plotting sheet. The "computed" circle is represented in plotting only by the DR position which, after all, is a point through which the computed circle of position passes.

The intercept is drawn as a dotted line starting from the DR position either toward or away from the azimuth depending on whether the computed or observed angle was greater. Since the azimuth is always a true direction, you must use the true compass rose when plotting celestial lines of position. At the end of the dotted intercept line, a solid, straight, perpendicular line is constructed. This solid line is the celestial line of position. The line of position is one segment of the large circle of position measured by your sextant.

The intersection of the intercept and the perpendicular line of position is not a fix. A celestial observation yields a line of position. The boat is somewhere along the line of position but you do not know exactly where. It takes two lines of position that cross to obtain a fix.

In the very rare instance where the computed angle is the same as the sextant angle, there is no difference in the angles, no intercept, and the celestial line of position is drawn right through the DR position. In other words, this can only happen if where you think you are (the DR position) and where you really are (the sextant position) are the same.

Figure 2-10 shows how a celestial fix is plotted on TR 1210 from the following information: DR 41°10′ N; 70°40′ W. Star 1, azimuth 150°, intercept 2 miles away. Star 2, azimuth 50°, intercept 1 mile toward. The fix is located at 41°12.1′ N; 70°40.6′ W.

PRACTICE PROBLEMS (Use TR 1210)

1. Locate 41°20′N; 71°W on TR 1210. Label as DR position. Set parallel rules for azimuth or true direction of 090°. Transfer direction to DR position and draw dotted intercept line 2 miles in length toward 90°. At end of intercept construct solid perpendicular line. Set parallel rules for azimuth of 030°, transfer direction to DR position and draw dotted intercept line one mile away from 030°. At end of dotted line, draw solid perpendicular line. What is the latitude and longitude of the intersection of the solid perpendicular lines?

2. Locate a DR of 41°14′N; 70°40′W. When you solved star sight 1 you obtained an azimuth of 180° and an intercept of 2.5 miles away. When you solved star sight 2 you obtained an intercept of 1.5 miles toward and an azimuth of 240°. What is the latitude and longitude of the celestial fix?

3. The sextant reading (fully corrected) is 61°49.8′. The computed angle from H. O. 229 is 61°58.0′. The azimuth is 281°. What is the intercept? Do you draw it toward or away from the azimuth?

4. The sextant reading (fully corrected) is 37°28.7′. The computed angle from the H. O. 229 table is 37°08.4′. The azimuth is 218°. What is the intercept? Do you draw it toward or away from the azimuth?

ANSWER

1. 41°17.7′ N; 70°57.3′ W.
2. 41°16.5′ N; 70°44.3′ W.
3. Intercept is 8.2 miles. It is drawn away.
4. Intercept is 20.3 miles. It is drawn toward.

Plotting Celestial Lines of Position

There are three ways to plot celestial lines of position. You can draw them directly on a chart, you can use preprinted plotting sheets with latitude and longitude lines already on them, or you can construct them on the universal plot sheet.

If you construct your LOP's on a chart you'll clutter the charts which are expensive. Further, the scale of most ocean sailing charts does not permit convenient, accurate plotting given the rather small distances involved in most celestial intercepts.

Preprinted plotting sheets are almost as expensive as charts, and if you are traveling a long distance you would need a variety because they are only scaled for

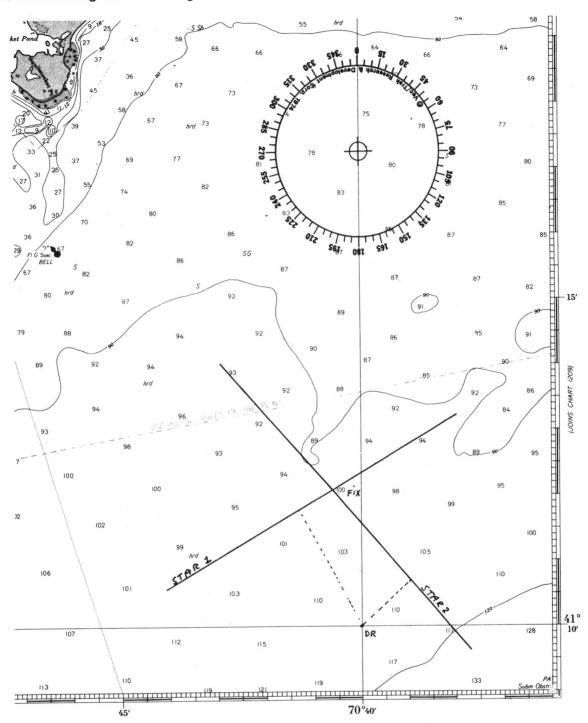

Figure 2-10. When plotting celestial lines of position, use the true compass rose for direction and the latitude scale for distance.

certain areas. Preprinted plotting sheets are also cumbersome, since many of them are almost as large as a chart.

Using the Universal Plotting Sheet (UPS) VP-OS is the answer. These inexpensive sheets, available in pads of 50, can be customized to fit any area of the world. The scale is large enough for accurate plotting and yet small enough to enable you to record several day's DR progress. They are also sized right for most navigation stations.

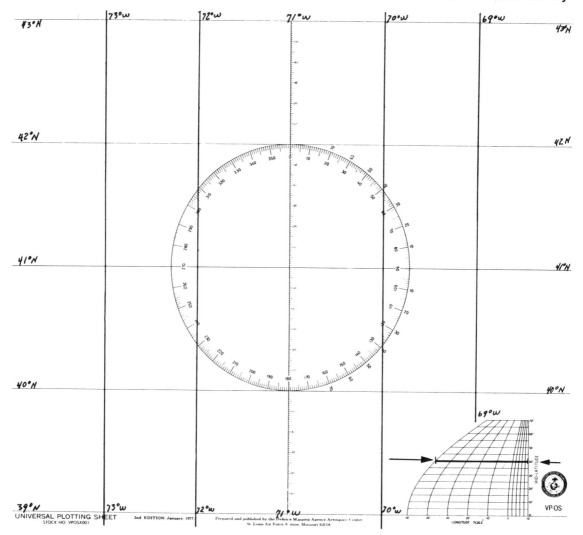

Figure 2-11. Universal Plotting Sheet laid out for midlatitude of 41°N and a midlongitude of 71°W.

On a recent round trip cruise from the Chesapeake Bay to the Bahamas six UPS sheets saved over $300 worth of charts from ruinous navigational scratchings.

Use the UPS to record all your day's work, the DR position, lines of position, and fixes on the plotting sheet. Transfer significant events, such as the day's progress, to the main sailing chart.

Setting Up the Universal Plotting Sheet

The UPS is essentially a blank-form chart which you can quickly and easily customize for the area in which you are sailing. A plotting sheet has the latitude

lines already drawn (See Figure 2-11). The latitude scale is in the middle, between the latitude lines. The latitude lines are already on the plot sheet because the distance represented by a degree of latitude stays the same everywhere in the world.

The UPS also has a true compass rose printed in the center. Use the degree markings inside the circle and ignore the degree notations outside since they are used with an alternative method of setting up the plot sheet, not for direction.

The longitude lines on the earth get closer as we leave the equator and move north or south toward the poles. That's why the UPS has a variable longitude

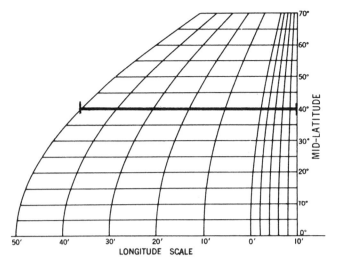

Figure 2-12. The variable longitude scale on the UPS can be used to determine the distance between longitude lines anywhere in the world.

scale in the bottom right hand corner. This scale can be used to determine the distance represented by a degree of longitude anywhere from the equator to 70° north or south latitude. Figure 2-12 shows the UPS longitude scale.

When you prepare a UPS for use, you should always have both the UPS and the chart available at the same time because you must see which way the longitude and latitude numbers are increasing. For example, if you are anywhere in the lower 48 states, latitude increases as you go north and longitude increases as you go west. However, in other areas of the world this may not be the case.

Constructing a UPS

If you learn to construct a UPS for the TR 1210 training chart, these same principles can be used to set up plotting sheets for any charted area. TR 1210 covers an area from 41°09′N to 41°45′N and from 70°36′W to 71°35′W. After studying the chart, you can see that the most useful midlatitude for setting up the UPS is 41°N. This latitude permits you to record the boat's movement north or south of the 41st parallel.

Because the latitude lines are already printed on the form, you have only to fill in the missing latitude degree notations along the left and right hand margins. As you write in the latitude values, remember that here latitude increases as you go north and decreases as you go south. This completes the latitude labelling portion of the UPS.

On the UPS you'll see that one longitude line—the midlongitude or center line—already has been drawn on the chart. Refer to TR 1210 and you'll see that it is appropriate to label the midlongitude line as 71°. Notice that longitude increases as you move west (left) and decreases as you move east (right) from the midlongitude line.

To determine the distance apart to place the other longitude lines look at the UPS longitude scale in Figure 2-12. On the scale, the length of a degree of longitude varies depending on your latitude. Because this UPS is being laid out for a midlatitude of 41°, locate and make a mark by the closest printed midlatitude value on the right hand margin of the variable longitude scale. Because 40° is so close to 41° midlatitude, you can safely use 40° as the midlatitude point on the scale. (If our midlatitude was 43° we could interpolate on the scale by marking a point halfway between 40° and 45°. In this case, since 40° is so close to 41°, interpolation is not necessary. In Figure 2-12 a solid line has been drawn from left to right along the longitude scale at the 40° midlatitude point. This solid line is the distance represented by one degree of longitude for this charted area. The solid line is drawn to remind you that this is the only part of the variable longitude scale you should use from now on.

For example, if you constructed a UPS for a midlatitude closer to the equator—say 25°—you would draw the line along the 25° area of the scale. Use dividers and the variable longitude scale to determine how much greater the length of one degree of longitude is at 25° than it is at 40°.

To finish the longitude portion of the UPS, set the dividers for the distance represented by the solid line at your particular midlatitude. In this case it is the 40° line. Use parallel rules and a pencil to construct and label the rest of the longitude lines on the UPS. The distance between the longitude lines on the UPS should equal the spread of the dividers on the variable longitude scale at a midlatitude of 40°.

Latitude measurements on a UPS are easy because the scale is printed in the middle right on the plotting sheet. Remember, the latitude scale on the UPS is used both for latitude and distance.

Longitude measurements on the UPS are a bit more involved but once you understand them you'll have no trouble.

Study the variable longitude scale in Figure 2-12 and you'll see that this scale is really two scales in one. There is a zero to 50 minute scale that moves to the left of the zero mark in 10 minute increments. There is also a zero to 10 minute scale that moves to the right in two minute increments.

If you require a longitude measurement rounded to the nearest 10 minutes, put the right divider pointer on zero and the left pointer on whatever value is needed: 10, 20, 30, 40, or 50 minutes. If you need to find an intermediate value such as 48 minutes, put the left pointer of the dividers on 40° then move the right pointer four "ticks" to the right of zero, because each line to the right of zero is equal to two minutes of longitude. When obtaining longitude measurements, make sure you stay along the solid line you have drawn on the scale because this is the only part of the scale you can use for your sailing latitude.

PRACTICE PROBLEMS

The following exercises will help you become familiar with the UPS. Check your work by comparing the width of your dividers with the length of the lines under each question. Remember, use the longitude scale for longitude only. Use the latitude scale for distance and latitude. If you do not have a UPS handy, use Figure 2-12 as the longitude scale.

1. Use the latitude scale to measure 60 minutes.

_____

2. Use the longitude scale to measure 60 minutes if the midlatitude is 20°.

_____

Use the longitude scale to measure 60 minutes if the midlatitude is 45°.

_____

Use the longitude scale to measure 60 minutes if the midlatitude is 65°.

_____

Notice that 60 minutes of longitude can represent a different distance. The same 60 minutes of longitude covers a greater distance as you near the equator and represents a smaller distance as you get into the higher latitudes nearer the poles.

3. What is the distance in nautical miles represented by the line below?

_____

Answer: 33 nautical miles

4. What is the distance in nautical miles represented by the line below assuming the midlatitude is 30°?

_____

Answer: 33 nautical miles

5. Use the longitude scale to set your dividers for 60 minutes, assuming a midlatitude of 40°.

_____

6. With midlatitude of 40° set your dividers for 50 minutes of longitude.

_____

7. With midlatitude of 40° set your dividers for 8 minutes of longitude.

———

8. With midlatitude of 40° set your dividers for 58 minutes of longitude.

————————————

18 minutes of longitude.

—————

22 minutes of longitude.

—————

33 minutes of longitude.

——————

9. If your midlatitude is 35° how many nautical miles apart will your longitude lines be placed on the universal plot sheet?

——————————

10. At midlatitude 35° you must advance the DR position a distance of 18 miles. Set your dividers for this distance.

————

Assumed Positions and Plotting

When you use H. O. 229, you will have to "round off" your DR position to enter the sight reduction tables. You must round the latitude to the nearest whole degree, and select a longitude that's within 30′ of your DR longitude. Later, in Chapter 6 detailed instructions for developing the assumed position are given. This is done so you obtain the solution from the table closest to your DR position. Then, you'll have relatively short intercept lines to draw.

The "rounded off" position is the position from which the celestial problem is solved. Therefore, the answer must be plotted from the rounded off position and not the DR position. The rounded off position is called the assumed position. The assumed position, or AP is the rounded latitude and the assumed longitude.

Figure 2-13 shows how a single line of position is plotted. The steps in plotting a celestial LOP are:

1. Mark and label the DR position for the time of the sight.
2. Mark the assumed position (AP) and label it as the AP.
3. Find the azimuth using the true compass rose and set the parallel plotter or rule for this direction. Transfer the direction to the AP.
4. Draw the dotted intercept line the required length and direction. If the computed angle is greater than the observed angle, draw the intercept away from the azimuth. If the observed angle is greater than the computed angle, draw the intercept toward the azimuth.
5. At the end of the dotted intercept line draw a solid perpendicular line and label it with the name of the body and the time of the observation.

Figure 2-14 shows how two celestial lines of position based on observations taken at nearly the same time intersect to form a fix. Even though the DR position was the same for both sights, notice the AP's are different. To enter the H. O. 229 table, as you will see in Chapter 6, you must take into account the GP's of the celestial bodies which are different.

The most accurate fixes result from the intersection of three or more celestial lines of position which usually form a triangle. The center of the triangle is taken as the fix. Figure 2-15 shows how a three star fix based on observations taken at nearly the same time is plotted.

The Running Fix

In celestial navigation, as in piloting, it is sometimes useful to obtain a fix from sights taken several hours apart.

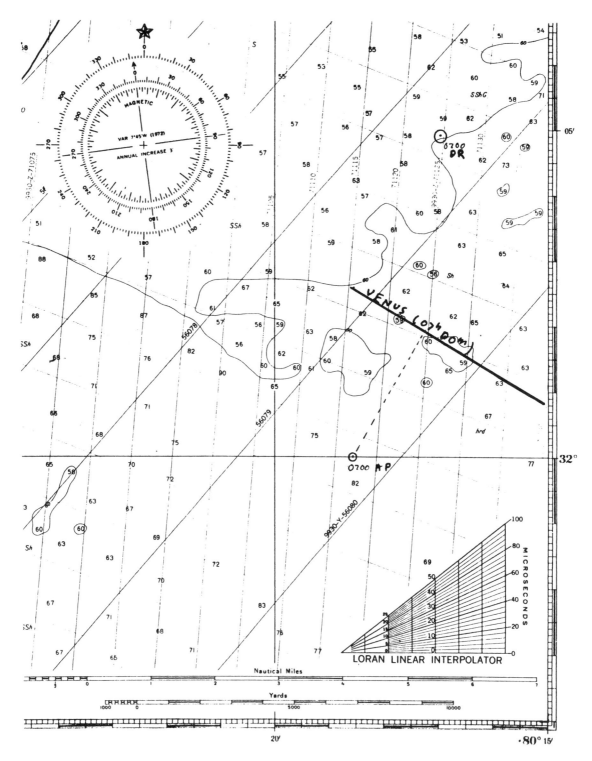

Figure 2-13. Single line of position showing DR and AP.

In many sailing latitudes most of the time you can obtain a running fix from observations of the sun, taken at various times during the day. You could take the first sight around 1000 hours local time and a second observation around 1300 hours local time. By advancing the line of position from the first sight and combining it with the line of position from the second sight you obtain a running fix. You can also obtain a running fix from the sun by using the 1300 local time ob-

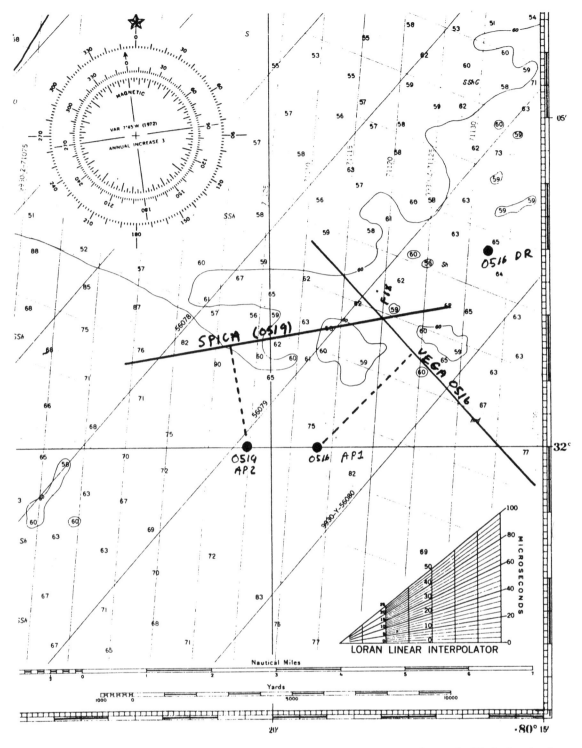

Figure 2-14. Two lines of position taken at nearly the same time intersect to form a fix. Notice how each body is labelled with the name of the star and the time of observation.

servation and combining it with one taken around 1500 local time. Use the time interval when taking running sun fixes, to permit the sun's azimuth or direction to change so the LOP's when combined will form lines that intersect at navigationally useful angles.

At sea, nearly 60% of all fixes obtained by yachtsmen will be running fixes on the sun. They are an important part of celestial navigation.

A running fix allows you to obtain a fix from two sights taken several hours

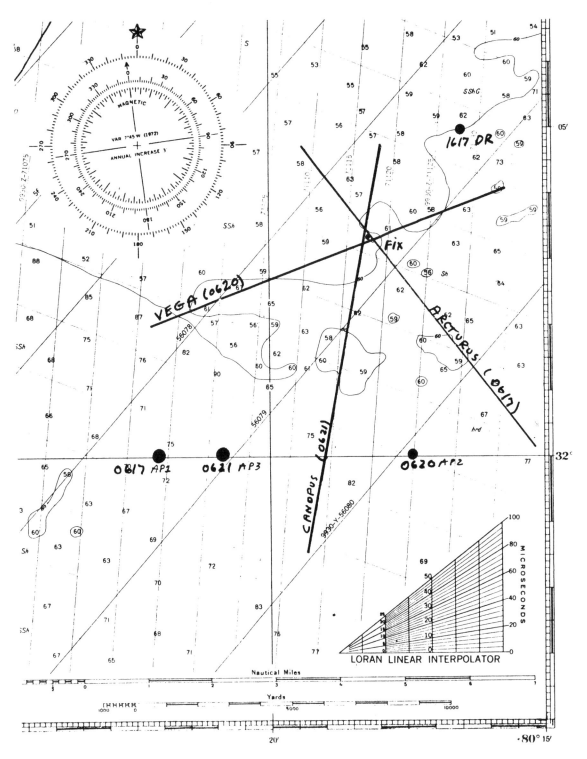

Figure 2-15. Three celestial lines of position intersect to form a triangle. The center of the triangle is used as the fix.

apart. Take the first sight of a running fix and plot it from the AP for that sight. Then carefully maintain the DR track, updating the DR position to account for the movement of the boat, including speed and course changes.

When the second sight is obtained, bring the DR position up-to-date for that time and plot the second sight from the AP for that sight.

Then, advance the AP for the first sight to account for the movement of the

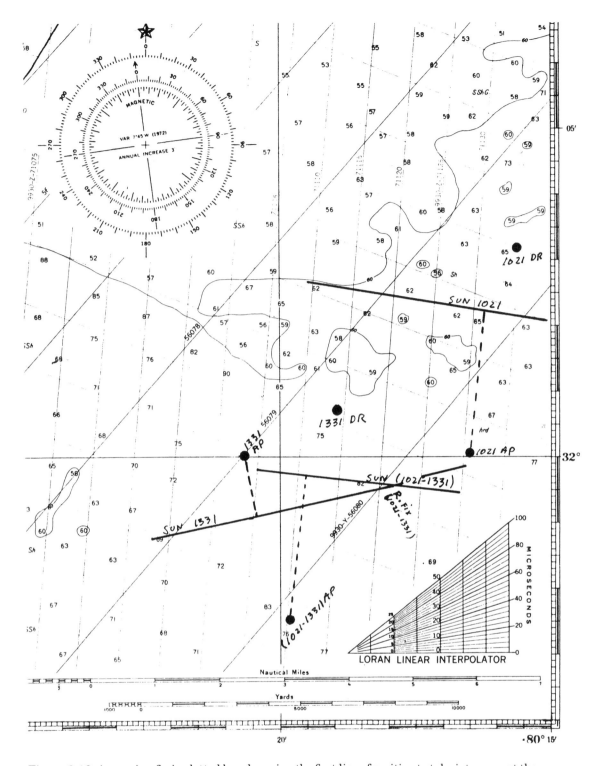

Figure 2-16. A running fix is plotted by advancing the first line of position to take into account the movement of the boat during the time interval between the sights. The fix is labelled as a running fix and the time of the earlier and later sight.

boat during elapsed time between sights. The direction and distance the AP is advanced is obtained from the chart or plotting sheet by determining the direction and distance between the DR positions for the two sights.

Finally, replot the first sight from the advanced AP using the original azimuth and intercept. The running fix is given by the intersection of the second LOP and the first LOP as replotted from the advanced AP. Figure 2-16 shows how a running fix was plotted.

You should always be attentive when calculating navigation problems but pinpoint accuracy is unobtainable. On a chart or UPS the width of a pencil is nearly a mile. With care, you can work the practice problems to within +/− 2 minutes of latitude or longitude.

PRACTICE PROBLEMS *(Use TR 1210 and UPS Sheets)*

Set up a UPS for the TR 1210 area with 41°N as midlatitude and 71°W as midlongitude.

You are finishing an ocean passage and returning to Newport, Rhode Island with your destination Brenton Reef Light. Locate Brenton Reef Light on the UPS at 41°25′N; 71°23′W. Label this position as Brenton Reef Light.

Your DR at 0105 GMT is 39°18′N; 72°20′W when you obtain a two star fix with the following results:

Arcturus (name of star)
Assumed position: 39°N; 72°37.1′W Azimuth: 340° Intercept: 14 miles toward

Vega (name of star)
Assumed position: 39°N; 72°41.5′W Azimuth: 200° Intercept: 26 miles away

1. What is the latitude and longitude of the two star fix?

2. What is the course (true) and distance to Brenton Reef Light from the fix?

At 1312 GMT your DR is 39°58′N; 71°42′W when you obtain a line of position from an observation of the sun. Your assumed position for this sight is 40°N; 71°04.6′W. The azimuth is 21° and the intercept 12.1 miles away. Later that day, at 1539 GMT your DR is 40°12′N; 71°33′W when you obtain another sight of the sun. Your assumed position for the second sun sight is 40°N; 71°56.3′W. The azimuth is 342° and the intercept 14.1 miles toward. Your log indicated that the boat moved 15.6 miles on a course of 26° true during the 2 hours 27 minutes between the two sun sights. Use this information to plot a running fix.

3. What is the latitude and longitude of the running sun fix?

4. What is the course (true) and distance from the fix to Brenton Reef Light?

ANSWERS

1. 39°21′N; 72°17′W
2. Course, 19° true, distance 131 miles.
3. 40°17′N; 71°50′W
4. Course, 17° true, distance 71 miles.

Celestial Timekeeping
(Time: 30 minutes)

The development of quartz crystal watches and chronometers has greatly simplified celestial timekeeping. These new timepieces are many times more accurate than even the finest jeweled movement chronometers of a few years ago. The ideal timepiece is a quartz watch that displays 24-hour digital time which can be set to keep the time and date for any place on the earth.

Celestial navigation requires that you know the Greenwich, England date and time of your sextant observation. The time should be accurate to the nearest second, since an error of four seconds means that your line of position will be off by one minute of longitude.

Time Signals

Navigators use time signals from radio station WWV, Fort Collins, Colorado to set their chronometers or watches to Greenwich time. These signals are broadcast continuously on 2.5, 5, 10, 15, and 25 megahertz throughout the North Atlantic. WWVH transmits time signals throughout the Pacific on the same frequencies except for 25 megahertz. The radio broadcasts refer to Greenwich Mean Time (GMT) as Coordinated Universal Time (UTC). Many radio direction finders and radio receivers include the time signal frequencies. In the United States you can also obtain a time check from WWV by calling the station on 303-499-7111.

It is a good idea to check out your navigation timepiece several weeks before leaving to ascertain the daily rate it is gaining or losing time. That way, if it becomes impossible to obtain regular time checks, you can still add or subtract the amount the watch is gaining or losing.

Watch error is the difference between your watch time and the reference time given by the radio signal. To obtain the corrected GMT, you subtract errors that are fast and add errors that are slow.

Greenwich time uses six digits.

The first two record the hours, 0 through 23 in the day.
The second two record the minutes, 0 through 59 in an hour.

The third two record the seconds, 0 through 59 in a minute.

Every correctly written GMT will contain six digits. When you have values with only one digit, fill in the missing zeroes.

Example: How would you record as GMT the time of one hour, three minutes, seven seconds past midnight? *Solution:* 01 hours, 03 minutes, 07 seconds.

GMT follows the standard 24-hour military time system. If your watch or chronometer has a 12-hour dial, 12 hours must be added to all P.M. readings. One hour, thirteen minutes, seven seconds after noon would be recorded as: 13^h 13^m 07^s.

Figure 3-1, a table adapted from Bowditch, can be used to convert local or zone time to Greenwich. To convert from zone to Greenwich time, in an area in the United States keeping daylight saving time, subtract one hour from the hours you would add according to the table. When using the table follow these rules:

Table for Conversion of Zone Time to GMT

If your Longitude is Greater Than	Less Than	West Longitude from Zone Time to GMT Add	East Longitude from Zone Time to GMT Subtract
0°	7½°	0	0
7½°	22½°	+ 1 hr.	− 1 hr.
22½°	37½°	+ 2 hrs.	− 2 hrs.
37½°	52½°	+ 3 hrs.	− 3 hrs.
52½°	67½°	+ 4 hrs.	− 4 hrs.
67½°	82½°	+ 5 hrs.	− 5 hrs.
82½°	97½°	+ 6 hrs.	− 6 hrs.
97½°	112½°	+ 7 hrs.	− 7 hrs.
112½°	127½°	+ 8 hrs.	− 8 hrs.
127½°	142½°	+ 9 hrs.	− 9 hrs.
142½°	157°	+10 hrs.	−10 hrs.
157½°	172°	+11 hrs.	−11 hrs.
172½°	180°	+12 hrs.	−12 hrs.

Figure 3-1. This table is used to convert local time to Greenwich Mean Time. In west longitude times are added to local time to obtain GMT and in east longitude times are subtracted from local time to obtain GMT.

1. If you obtain a GMT total hours greater than 24, subtract 24 hours.
2. If you ever obtain a negative time value, add 24 hours.

If you live in the continental United States you can obtain GMT by adding the following number of hours to the time on your watch:

Your Time Zone	To Obtain GMT	Daylight Saving Time
Eastern standard	add 5 hours	add 4 hours
Central standard	add 6 hours	add 5 hours
Mountain standard	add 7 hours	add 6 hours
Pacific standard	add 8 hours	add 7 hours

Example: You live in San Francisco, California and plan to sail to Hawaii. You are not on daylight saving time and want to know how many hours you should add or subtract from local time to obtain GMT. *Solution:*

Longitude of San Francisco:	122°25′ West
Hours added or subtracted according to the table:	+8 hours

In addition to setting the GMT hours, and obtaining the correct minutes, and seconds from the time tick on the radio, you must make sure the date on the watch is correct for Greenwich.

Time Diagrams

A time diagram is a sketch which indicates the relationship of time to longitude and helps you set the Greenwich date on your timepiece. Depending on your location, the date at Greenwich can be the same, a day ahead, or a day behind your local date.

To work with time diagrams you have to understand the time/longitude relationship. The distance on the earth that the sun covers in one hour as it moves westward is equal to 15 degrees of longitude. During a day, the sun moves all the way around the world covering 360° of longitude. Thus you can determine how many hours you are ahead of or behind Greenwich by dividing your local longitude by 15°. If you are east of Greenwich, the sun will reach you before it reaches Greenwich and you are in a time zone ahead of Greenwich. If you are west of Greenwich, the sun reaches you after it has passed Greenwich and you are in a time zone later than Greenwich.

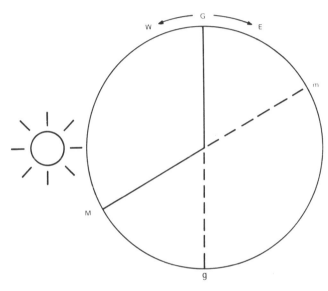

Figure 3-2. Time diagram with Greenwich date same as local date.

Navigators graphically represent these relationships by drawing a time diagram like Figure 3-2. The circle represents the path the sun makes around the world in a day. Mentally divide the circle into hourly time increments like a 24-hour clock face. The G (capital) located at the top of the circle represents the longitude of the Greenwich meridian. The arrows at the top indicate east and west longitude. When the sun is overhead at G, it is noon at Greenwich. When the sun reaches g (lower case), located at the bottom of the circle, it is midnight at Greenwich. Therefore, when the sun passes g, a new day starts at Greenwich. Draw a solid line from G to the center of

the circle, to represent noon. Draw a dotted line from the center of the circle to represent midnight. The solid and dotted lines are reminders of the two major events, noon at G and midnight at g.

In the time diagram, M represents the longitude of the observer. The placement of M on the circle represents your own time-longitude relationship to Greenwich. To locate M, determine the number of hours ahead of or behind Greenwich you are, then multiply the hours times the 15° the sun moves per hour.

The following time diagrams illustrate the three possibilities.

1. Greenwich date same as local date: (Refer to Figure 3-2) If you were in San Francisco, where the sun reaches you 8 hours after it passes Greenwich, you would locate M 8 hours × 15° or 120° west of G. When the sun is directly over M, it is noon in San Francisco. On the other side of the world from M, mark a lower case m to indicate where the sun will be when it is midnight at San Francisco. When the sun passes m on that side of the world, a new day starts for you at M. Draw a solid line from M to the center of the circle and a dotted line from the center to m. Let's assume that it is 1000 local time in California and the local date is March 1. You are not on daylight saving time. You need to set your watch to the GMT time and date. From the table you know you must add 8 hours so the GMT time will be 1800.

To determine the GMT date place the sun in the time diagram according to the local time. Since the sun always moves in a westerly direction, it must still travel two more hours before it will be noon at M. The sun is therefore located 2 hours × 15° or 30° before M. The completed time diagram shows that the Greenwich date is the same as the San Francisco date. The date at Greenwich will not change

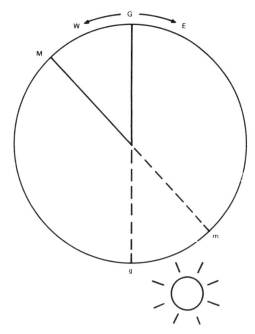

Figure 3-3. Time diagram with Greenwich date one day ahead of local date.

until the sun moves all the way around to g.

2. Greenwich date one day ahead of local date: (Refer to Figure 3-3) You are at Nanortalik, Greenland, 45°15′W keeping local time of 2200 hours on March 2. What is the Greenwich time and date?

The table shows you must add three hours to local time to obtain Greenwich time. Therefore GMT equals 2500 hours. Since there cannot be more than 24 hours in a day we follow the rule and subtract 24 hours giving us a GMT time of 0100 hours.

To set the date, consult the time diagram which shows M 45° west of Greenwich and m on the opposite side of the world. If it is 2200 hours in Greenland, then the sun has 2 hours of time or 2 × 15°, or 30°, to move before it reaches m when it will be midnight in Greenland.

When the sun passed g a new day started at Greenwich. The sun has not yet reached m where a new day would start at Greenland. Therefore, the date at Greenwich is March 3, one day ahead of the date in Greenland.

3. Greenwich date one day behind local date: (Refer to Figure 3-4) You are in the East Indian Ocean at Ile Aux Cochons, 50°10′E keeping local time of 0200 hours, July 3. What is the Greenwich time and date?

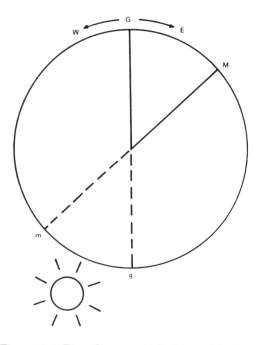

Figure 3-4. Time diagram with Greenwich date one day behind local date.

The conversion table indicates you must subtract 3 hours from Indian Ocean time to obtain Greenwich time. When you subtract 0300 hours from 0200 hours you end up with a −0100 hours. Since you cannot have a negative time value, follow the rule and add 24 hours to the −0100 hours to obtain 2300 hours GMT.

The time diagram shows M located 50° east of Greenwich and m on the other side of the world. Since it is 0200 where you are, the sun is placed 2 hours × 15°, or 30°, past m. This locates the sun 2 hours past m which represents midnight at the East Indian Ocean. The sun has just passed m, so a new day, July 3 has started at Ile Aux Cochons. However, the sun has not reached g where the new day starts at Greenwich, so the date at Greenwich is still July 2nd.

By studying the three time diagrams you will see:

When the sun is outside the two dotted lines, the Greenwich date is the same as the local date. When the sun is any where on the diagram except between m and g the date is the same where you are as it is at Greenwich.

When the sun is inside the two dotted lines, the Greenwich date is one day different from your local date. When the sun has passed g and is moving toward m then the date at Greenwich is one day more than the local date. If the sun has passed m and is moving towards g then the local date is one day more than the date at Greenwich.

PRACTICE PROBLEMS

1. You are at the Mikomoto Jima Light near Japan, 138°57′E. The local date is February 2 and the local time is 15 hours 34 minutes 12 seconds. You need to set your watch to the Greenwich time and date. How many hours do you add or subtract? What is the Greenwich date?

2. You are in Trabzon, Turkey, 39°46′E, keeping local time of 07 hours 12 minutes 03 seconds. The local date is June 14. How many hours do you add or subtract to obtain GMT? What is the Greenwich date?

3. You are in the Azores, 31°07′W on August 1 keeping local time of 23 hours 01 minutes 04 seconds. How many hours do you add or subtract to obtain GMT? What is the Greenwich date?

ANSWERS

1. Subtract 9 hours; February 2.
2. Subtract 3 hours; June 14.
3. Add 2 hours; August 2.

Workforms

Workforms are most helpful to beginning students of celestial navigation. There are too many calculations and too many things to remember to try and work problems without them. A good workform should not only organize information, it should guide you through the steps.

Figures 3-5 and 3-6 are examples of well organized workforms. These forms were designed to help you learn navigation. When the steps have been committed to memory, you can shorten the forms or dispense with them entirely.

There is one workform for the sun, moon, planets, and another similar workform for the stars. Each has two major sections. The left hand side of the form organizes the information you need to work out a sight. This includes general data such as the name of the body, the watch time, GMT, and the DR position.

The sextant corrections part is used to record the sextant reading and apply corrections to the reading. At the top of the workform is a diagram similar to the time diagrams. This will be used to show the relationship between our DR longitude and the longitude of the celestial body.

The right hand side of the workform uses information from the left column to enter H. O. 229, obtain the information you need to find the computed altitude, and compare the computed altitude with the corrected sextant reading to obtain the intercept and the azimuth.

The right hand side is organized into steps. The first step guides you through the process of adjusting the information from the left hand column to get the most convenient solution from the H. O. 229 table. Steps two and three are used to enter the main body of the H. O. 229 table and obtain a computed altitude and a number later converted to the azimuth. Step four adjusts the answers you got in steps two and three to make them more precise. Step five converts the number from the table to a true azimuth. Step six is the Coast Guard Academy calculation

Item   General Data

1. Name of Body

2. Limb (Upper/Lower)

3. Date (G)

	Hrs	Min	Sec
4. Watch Time (G)			
5. Watch Error (+ if slow − if fast)			
6. GMT (six digits)			

	Deg	Mins	Tenths
7. DR Latitude .N/S)			
8. DR Longitude (E/W)			

Sextant Corrections —general

	Deg	Mins	Tenths
9. Sextant Reading (Hs)			
10. Instrument Corr. (+ or −)			
11. Index Correction (+ or −)			
12. Dip Correction for___feet −)			
13. Total (Items 9-12) is Apparent Altitude (Ha).			

Sextant corrections from inside front/back covers of Almanac

	Deg	Mins	Tenths
14. Altitude Correction (+ or −)			
15. Venus, Mars only, add'l correction (+ or −)			
16. Moon only, Corr. for daily page HP: (+)			
17. Moon only, if *upper* limb −30'			
18. Non-Standard conditions only, add'l Corr.			
19. Total (Items 13-18) is Observed Altitude (Ho)			

GHA—from Nautical Almanac

DAILY PAGES

	Deg	Mins	Tenths
20. GHA of body, whole hours ● "v" value, planets moon, + unless shown otherwise "v"			

YELLOW PAGES

	Deg	Mins	Tenths
21. Increments, (+) minutes and secs., from sun/planets or moon column.			
22. Moon, planets, "v" correction for "v" value above, use same sign			
23. Total GHA (items 20-21 & 22) ● if over 360° subtract 360°			

Declination—From Nautical Almanac

DAILY PAGES

	Deg	Mins	Tenths
24. Declination, whole hour, (N/S)			
● "d" value, (+ if Dec. increasing, − if Dec. decreasing) "d"			

YELLOW PAGES

	Deg	Mins	Tenths
25. "d" correction for "d" value above, use same sign			
26. Total Declination (items 24-25) (N/S)			

LHA Diagram

W G e

Step 1: Computing LHA:

West Longitude	East Longitude
deg min tenths	deg min tenths

. Enter GHA (#23).....

deg min tenths

. Enter DR Long (# 8) range── −30' / +1°

. Enter Assum. Long.....   − / +

. Total is LHA (+360 if neg; − 360 if over 360)   0 0.0 / 0 0.0

Step 2: Enter HO-229 With: Degrees

. LHA (from Step 1) ......
. DR Lat (#7) rounded....   N   S   (same or
. Dec. (#26) degrees......   N   S   contrary)

Step 3: Extract from HO-229:
Hc (tab) _____ d* (tab) + − _____ *   Z(tab) _____
                                        *Zbelow _____
                    d* diff. _____ *Zdiff. _____
                                        (inc; dec.)

Step 4: Corrections from Interpolation Table:
. Enter with Dec. Increment (#26) of _____.

	mins	tenths

. d (tab) from Step 3   Deg min tenths
  (   ) tens........... corr. + −
  (   ) units (   )dec. corr. + −
. d*, enter DSD table with d.diff....corr. +
. Enter Hc (tab) from Step 3.............+
. Total is Computed Altitude, Hc.........

	Degrees	tenths

. Enter Z (tab) from Step 3.............
. Z (diff) from Step 3
  (   ) units (   )dec. corr.(+Inc,
                              − Dec.)
. Total is Z.(Azimuth Angle)

Step 5: Compute Zn. (True Azimuth):

North Latitude		South Latitude	
LHA greater than 180°	LHA Less than 180°	LHA greater than 180°	LHA less than 180°
000°.0	360°.0	180°.0	180°.0

. Enter Z.   + /   / − / +
. Total is Zn.

Step 6: Compute Intercept:

Deg min tenths

. Enter Ho (#19)........ +
. Enter Hc from Step 4... −
. Difference is Intercept   A T
  (Hc greater, away)

Step 7: Plotting Data:

. Assumed Longitude (Step 1) _____ W E
. Latitude (rounded) (Step 2) _____ N S
. Azimuth (Step 5).......... _____
. Intercept (Step 6)........ _____ A T

Weems & Plath
Education Division
In Association with Navigation Institute
COPYRIGHT 1980 by   NI, Inc.

Figure 3-5. H.O. 229 Celestial Workform: Sun, Moon, Planets

Item General Data

1. Name of Star

2. Date (G)

	Hrs	Mins	Secs

3. Watch Time (G) (six digits)

4. Watch Error (+ if slow − if fast)

5. GMT

	Deg	Mins	Tenths

6. DR Latitude (N/S)

7. DR Longitude (E/W)

Sextant Corrections—general

	Deg	Min	Tenths

8. Sextant Reading (Hs)

9. Instrument Corr. (+ or −)

10. Index Correction (+ or −)

11. Dip Correction for ___ feet (−)

12. Total (Items 8-11) is Apparent Altitude (Ha)

Sextant corrections from inside front cover of Almanac

13. Altitude Correction (+ or −)

14. Additional Correction for Non-Standard Conditions

15. Total (Items 12-14) is Observed Altitude (Ho)

GHA—from Nautical Almanac

DAILY PAGES

	Deg	Mins	Tenths

16. GHA of Aries, whole hours

17. SHA of Star, list of stars (+)

YELLOW PAGES

18. Increments, minutes & secs., aries column (+)

19. Total GHA (items 16, 17, 18) • If over 360° subtract 360°

Declination—from Nautical Almanac

DAILY PAGES

	Deg	Mins	Tenths

20. Declination, list of stars (N/S)

Direction of Star—use with star ID only

A. Handbearing compass direction _____ degrees

B. Variation from chart (+E; −W) _____ degrees

C. Deviation (if known) (+E; −W) _____ degrees

21. True Direction (Total, A, B, C) _____ degrees

LHA Diagram

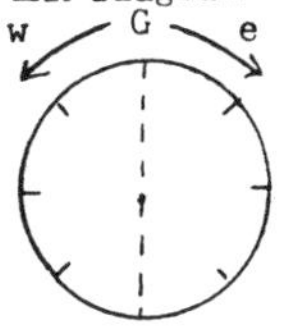

Step 1: Computing LHA:

West Longitude — deg min tenths

East Longitude — deg min tenths

. Enter GHA (#19)......

. Enter DR Long (# 7) —30'
range +1°

. Enter Assum. Long.....

. Total is LHA (+360 if neg; − 360 if over 360)

West: − ... 0 0.0
East: + ... 0 0.0

Step 2: Enter HO-229 With: Degrees

. LHA (from Step 1) ......
. DR Lat (#6) rounded..... N S (same or
. Dec. (#20) degrees...... N S contrary)

Step 3: Extract from HO-229:
Hc (tab) _____ d* (tab) + − _____ * Z(tab) _____
                                          *Zbelow _____
                    d* diff. _____ *Zdiff. _____
                                     (inc; decr.)

Step 4: Corrections from Interpolation Table:
. Enter with Dec. Increment (#20) of _____.

| | mins | tenths |
| | Deg | min tenths |

. d (tab) from Step 3
  (   ) tens............ corr. + −
  (   ) units (   )dec. corr. + −
. d*, enter DSD table with d.diff....corr.+
. Enter Hc (tab) from Step 3..............+
. Total is Computed Altitude, Hc..........

Degrees tenths

. Enter Z (tab) from Step 3..............
. Z (diff) from Step 3
  (   ) units (   )dec. corr.(+Inc,
                              − Decr.)
. Total is Z.(Azimuth Angle)

Step 5: Compute Zn. (True Azimuth):

	North Latitude		South Latitude	
	LHA greater than 180°	LHA Less than 180°	LHA greater than 180°	LHA less than 180°
	000°.0	360°.0	180°.0	180°.0
. Enter Z.	+	−	−	+

. Total is Zn.

Step 6: Compute Intercept:

| | Deg | min tenths |

. Enter Ho (#15)......... +
. Enter Hc from Step 4... −
. Difference is Intercept   A T
  (Hc greater, away)

Step 7: Plotting Data:

. Assumed Longitude (Step 1) _____ W E
. Latitude (rounded) (Step 2) _____ N S
. Azimuth (Step 5).......... _____
. Intercept (Step 6)........ _____ A T

Weems & Plath
Education Division
In Association with Navigation Institute

Figure 3-6. H.O. 229 Workform: Stars

where you compare the corrected sextant angle to the angle computed from the H. O. 229 table to obtain the intercept. Step seven organizes the data for plotting on the chart or UPS.

Each section of the form contains helpful hints and suggestions. The next three chapters show you how each part of the form is used to solve celestial navigation problems.

Look at Figure 3-6 and you'll see that you already know how to fill out the first seven items. Item 1 is the name of the star, item 2 is the date, Greenwich of course, item 3 is the watch time while item four is the watch error. Item five is the corrected GMT after you have added or subtracted the watch error. Items six and seven are the DR position for the time of the observation.

4

The Nautical Almanac
(Time: 1 Hour)

The *Nautical Almanac* for each year contains the GP's of all the celestial bodies for that year. The almanac is available from the U. S. Government Printing Office, Washington, D. C. 20402 or from your navigation supply store. Appendix 2 contains reprinted extracts from the 1983 almanac.

You can use Appendix 2 to calculate all the problems in this book. It has been arranged so it looks like a real almanac. In the front and back covers you will find the altitude or refraction tables. These are used to correct your sextant reading due to the fact that light rays coming from the celestial bodies toward the earth are bent as they pass through the earth's atmosphere.

The white, or daily pages, gives you information about the location of the celestial bodies for a given day and whole hour. Seldom in celestial navigation will you observe a body where the GMT is in whole hours. Usually, there are some minutes and seconds in the time. Since celestial bodies keep moving all the time, a two-step process is required to locate their position in the almanac:

First locate the position of the body for the date and whole hour of observation in the daily pages.

Then locate how far the body moved during the minutes and seconds after the whole hour. This information comes from the yellow pages, or increments section, in the back of the almanac. The daily pages and increments are then added together to give the exact location of the celestial body for the time of the sight.

Coordinates of Celestial Bodies

The almanac lists the coordinates of the celestial bodies. The Greenwich Hour Angle (GHA) of a body is the longitude of the GP measured west starting at zero, the Greenwich meridian, through a complete 360° circle. Since GHA goes all the way around the world, there is no need to label it east or west.

The Declination (Dec.) of a body is the latitude of the GP measured north or south of the equator. Declination, like latitude, cannot exceed 90°N or 90°S. It is always labeled N or S in the almanac.

Both the GHA and declination will be given in degrees, minutes, and tenths. When obtaining data from the almanac, use the daily pages data for the whole hour of GMT exactly as shown on the watch or chronometer. This will always be the whole hour prior to the minutes and seconds of observation. For example, if you observed the sun at 14 hours 59 minutes 59 seconds GMT you would use the daily pages almanac data for 14 hours.

Daily Pages of the *Nautical Almanac*

Most of the *Nautical Almanac* consists of the white daily pages. The two pages facing each other, as Figures 4-1 and 4-2 indicate, cover a three day period. The days and times in the almanac are all referenced to GMT.

The days and GMT dates that are covered by the page are noted at the top and along the left-hand margin of each page.

The left-hand pages contain information needed for the stars and the four navigational planets. The right-hand pages contain information for the sun and the moon.

Daily Page Information for Stars and Planets *(Refer to Figure 4-1)*

Along the top of the page are column headings.

Aries

Aries is not a celestial body, but a reference point used for determining the GHA of the stars. Aries, in a sense, represents the variable part of the GP of a star. To obtain the GHA of a star you add the

GHA of Aries to the star's own longitude which is represented by the SHA or Sidereal Hour Angle. The GHA of Aries is given for each whole hour of the three-day period covered by each page.

Venus, Mars, Jupiter, and Saturn

The GHA and declination of each of the four navigational planets is given for each hour of the three-day period. At the bottom of each planet column, d and v values are listed. These values are used in combination with a table found in the yellow pages to make a small adjustment to the GHA and declination. The v value and the table adjust the GHA; the d value and the table adjust the declination. The d and v values are given in tenths or minutes and tenths. The v and d values indicate whether the adjustment from the yellow page table is added or subtracted to the GHA or declination.

If the v value listed in the daily pages is preceded by a minus sign the correction from the yellow page table is subtracted from GHA. If the v value is given in the daily page with no sign, it is considered + and the correction from the yellow page table is added to GHA. For example, the v value for Venus for June 3, 4, or 5 is −0.3′ while the v value for Mars for this time period is a +0.6′. This means the yellow page correction to GHA would be subtracted from the GHA of Venus and added to the GHA of Mars.

The d value—listed at the bottom of the declination column for the planets—is positive if the declination increases during the day the sight was taken. It is negative if the declination decreases during the day the sight was taken. The yellow page correction is added if the d value is + and subtracted if the d value is −. For example, the d value for any Venus sight taken on June 3, 4, or 5 would be

112   1983 JUNE 3, 4, 5 (FRI., SAT., SUN.)

G.M.T.	ARIES G.H.A.	VENUS −3.8 G.H.A.	Dec.	MARS +1.7 G.H.A.	Dec.	JUPITER −2.1 G.H.A.	Dec.	SATURN +0.6 G.H.A.	Dec.	Name	S.H.A.	Dec.
3 00	250 53.0	131 40.3	N23 18.7	180 27.0	N22 39.3	7 21.0	S20 18.3	43 34.0	S 8 24.4	Acamar	315 36.1	S40 22.2
01	265 55.4	146 40.1	18.1	195 27.7	39.5	22 23.8	18.2	58 36.5	24.4	Achernar	335 44.1	S57 19.1
02	280 57.9	161 39.8	17.6	210 28.3	39.8	37 26.6	18.2	73 39.1	24.4	Acrux	173 35.0	S63 00.6
03	296 00.4	176 39.5 ··	17.0	225 28.9 ··	40.1	52 29.4 ··	18.1	88 41.7 ··	24.3	Adhara	255 30.9	S28 57.0
04	311 02.8	191 39.2	16.5	240 29.5	40.3	67 32.2	18.1	103 44.2	24.3	Aldebaran	291 16.1	N16 28.5
05	326 05.3	206 38.9	15.9	255 30.1	40.6	82 35.0	18.0	118 46.8	24.3			
06	341 07.7	221 38.6	N23 15.4	270 30.7	N22 40.8	97 37.8	S20 18.0	133 49.4	S 8 24.2	Alioth	166 40.4	N56 03.3
07	356 10.2	236 38.3	14.8	285 31.3	41.1	112 40.6	17.9	148 52.0	24.2	Alkaid	153 16.5	N49 24.0
08	11 12.7	251 38.1	14.2	300 31.9	41.3	127 43.4	17.9	163 54.5	24.2	Al Na'ir	28 12.3	S47 02.4
F 09	26 15.1	266 37.8 ··	13.7	315 32.5 ··	41.6	142 46.2 ··	17.8	178 57.1 ··	24.2	Alnilam	276 10.0	S 1 12.7
R 10	41 17.6	281 37.5	13.1	330 33.1	41.8	157 49.0	17.8	193 59.7	24.1	Alphard	218 18.8	S 8 35.2
I 11	56 20.1	296 37.2	12.6	345 33.7	42.1	172 51.7	17.7	209 02.2	24.1			
D 12	71 22.5	311 36.9	N23 12.0	0 34.3	N22 42.3	187 54.5	S20 17.7	224 04.8	S 8 24.1	Alphecca	126 30.1	N26 46.3
A 13	86 25.0	326 36.7	11.4	15 34.9	42.6	202 57.3	17.6	239 07.4	24.0	Alpheratz	358 07.5	N28 59.6
Y 14	101 27.5	341 36.4	10.9	30 35.5	42.8	218 00.1	17.6	254 09.9	24.0	Altair	62 30.4	N 8 49.3
15	116 29.9	356 36.1 ··	10.3	45 36.1 ··	43.1	233 02.9 ··	17.5	269 12.5 ··	24.0	Ankaa	353 38.4	S42 23.7
16	131 32.4	11 35.8	09.7	60 36.7	43.3	248 05.7	17.5	284 15.1	23.9	Antares	112 54.1	S26 23.8
17	146 34.9	26 35.5	09.2	75 37.3	43.6	263 08.5	17.4	299 17.7	23.9			
18	161 37.3	41 35.3	N23 08.6	90 37.9	N22 43.8	278 11.3	S20 17.4	314 20.2	S 8 23.9	Arcturus	146 16.4	N19 16.2
19	176 39.8	56 35.0	08.0	105 38.5	44.1	293 14.1	17.3	329 22.8	23.9	Atria	108 16.1	S68 59.9
20	191 42.2	71 34.7	07.5	120 39.1	44.3	308 16.9	17.3	344 25.4	23.8	Avior	234 27.9	S59 27.5
21	206 44.7	86 34.5 ··	06.9	135 39.7 ··	44.6	323 19.7 ··	17.2	359 27.9 ··	23.8	Bellatrix	278 57.0	N 6 20.1
22	221 47.2	101 34.2	06.3	150 40.3	44.8	338 22.5	17.2	14 30.5	23.8	Betelgeuse	271 26.5	N 7 24.3
23	236 49.6	116 33.9	05.8	165 40.9	45.1	353 25.3	17.1	29 33.1	23.7			
4 00	251 52.1	131 33.7	N23 05.2	180 41.5	N22 45.3	8 28.1	S20 17.1	44 35.6	S 8 23.7	Canopus	264 06.9	S52 41.3
01	266 54.6	146 33.4	04.6	195 42.1	45.5	23 30.9	17.0	59 38.2	23.7	Capella	281 08.9	N45 58.9
02	281 57.0	161 33.1	04.0	210 42.7	45.8	38 33.7	17.0	74 40.8	23.6	Deneb	49 46.9	N45 12.9
03	296 59.5	176 32.9 ··	03.5	225 43.3 ··	46.0	53 36.5 ··	16.9	89 43.3 ··	23.6	Denebola	182 57.0	N14 40.0
04	312 02.0	191 32.6	02.9	240 43.9	46.3	68 39.2	16.9	104 45.9	23.6	Diphda	349 19.1	S18 04.7
05	327 04.4	206 32.3	02.3	255 44.5	46.5	83 42.0	16.8	119 48.5	23.6			
06	342 06.9	221 32.1	N23 01.7	270 45.1	N22 46.8	98 44.8	S20 16.8	134 51.1	S 8 23.5	Dubhe	194 19.6	N61 50.8
07	357 ··	236 31.8	01.1	285 45.7	47.0	113 47.6	16.7	149 53.6	23.5	Elnath	278 42.1	N28 35.6
08	12 11.8	251 31.5	00.6	300 46.3	47.3	128 50.4	16.7	164 56.2	23.5	Eltanin	90 56.3	N51 29.3
S 09	27 14.3	266 31.3	23 00.0	315 46.9 ··	47.5	143 53.2 ··	16.6	179 58.8 ··	23.4	Enif	34 09.6	N 9 47.7
A 10	42 16.7	281 31.0	22 59.4	330 47.5	47.7	158 56.0	16.6	195 01.3	23.4	Fomalhaut	15 49.2	S29 42.6
T 11	57 19.2	296 30.8	58.8	345 48.1	48.0	173 58.8	16.5	210 03.9	23.4			
R 12	72 21.7	311 30.5	N22 58.2	0 48.7	N22 48.2	189 01.6	S20 16.5	225 06.5	S 8 23.4	Gacrux	172 26.5	S57 01.4
D 13	87 24.1	326 30.3	57.7	15 49.3	48.5	204 04.4	16.4	240 09.0	23.3	Gienah	176 15.9	S17 27.0
A 14	102 26.6	341 30.0	57.1	30 49.9	48.7	219 07.2	16.4	255 11.6	23.3	Hadar	149 20.2	S60 17.7
Y 15	117 29.1	356 29.8 ··	56.5	45 50.5 ··	48.9	234 10.0 ··	16.3	270 14.2 ··	23.3	Hamal	328 27.0	N23 22.9
16	132 31.5	11 29.5	55.9	60 51.1	49.2	249 12.8	16.3	285 16.7	23.2	Kaus Aust.	84 13.9	S34 23.6
17	147 34.0	26 29.2	55.3	75 51.7	49.4	264 15.6	16.2	300 19.3	23.2			
18	162 36.5	41 29.0	N22 54.7	90 52.3	N22 49.7	279 18.4	S20 16.2	315 21.9	S 8 23.2	Kochab	137 17.8	N74 13.6
19	177 38.9	56 28.7	54.1	105 52.9	49.9	294 21.1	16.1	330 24.4	23.2	Markab	14 01.3	N15 06.7
20	192 41.4	71 28.5	53.5	120 53.5	50.1	309 23.9	16.1	345 27.0	23.1	Menkar	314 39.4	N 4 01.4
21	207 43.9	86 28.3 ··	52.9	135 54.1 ··	50.4	324 26.7 ··	16.0	0 29.6 ··	23.1	Menkent	148 34.5	S36 17.4
22	222 46.3	101 28.0	52.4	150 54.7	50.6	339 29.5	16.0	15 32.1	23.1	Miaplacidus	221 45.1	S69 39.1
23	237 48.8	116 27.8	51.8	165 55.3	50.9	354 32.3	15.9	30 34.7	23.0			
5 00	252 51.2	131 27.5	N22 51.2	180 55.9	N22 51.1	9 35.1	S20 15.9	45 37.3	S 8 23.0	Mirfak	309 13.9	N49 48.0
01	267 53.7	146 27.3	50.6	195 56.5	51.3	24 37.9	15.8	60 39.8	23.0	Nunki	76 26.4	S26 19.1
02	282 56.2	161 27.0	50.0	210 57.1	51.6	39 40.7	15.8	75 42.4	23.0	Peacock	53 54.9	S56 47.2
03	297 58.6	176 26.8 ··	49.4	225 57.7 ··	51.8	54 43.5 ··	15.7	90 44.9 ··	22.9	Pollux	243 56.1	N28 04.2
04	313 01.1	191 26.5	48.8	240 58.3	52.0	69 46.3	15.7	105 47.5	22.9	Procyon	245 24.0	N 5 16.1
05	328 03.6	206 26.3	48.2	255 58.9	52.3	84 49.1	15.6	120 50.1	22.9			
06	343 06.0	221 26.1	N22 47.6	270 59.5	N22 52.5	99 51.9	S20 15.6	135 52.6	S 8 22.8	Rasalhague	96 27.5	N12 34.2
07	358 08.5	236 25.8	47.0	286 00.1	52.8	114 54.6	15.5	150 55.2	22.8	Regulus	208 08.0	N12 03.1
08	13 11.0	251 25.6	46.4	301 00.7	53.0	129 57.4	15.5	165 57.8	22.8	Rigel	281 34.5	S 8 13.3
S 09	28 13.4	266 25.4 ··	45.8	316 01.3 ··	53.2	145 00.2 ··	15.4	181 00.3 ··	22.8	Rigil Kent.	140 22.8	S60 46.1
U 10	43 15.9	281 25.1	45.2	331 01.9	53.5	160 03.0	15.4	196 02.9	22.7	Sabik	102 38.6	S15 42.3
N 11	58 18.3	296 24.9	44.6	346 02.5	53.7	175 05.8	15.3	211 05.5	22.7			
D 12	73 20.8	311 24.7	N22 44.0	1 03.1	N22 53.9	190 08.6	S20 15.3	226 08.0	S 8 22.7	Schedar	350 07.2	N56 26.4
A 13	88 23.3	326 24.4	43.4	16 03.7	54.2	205 11.4	15.2	241 10.6	22.7	Shaula	96 52.7	S37 05.6
Y 14	103 25.7	341 24.2	42.8	31 04.3	54.4	220 14.2	15.2	256 13.2	22.6	Sirius	258 54.3	S16 41.6
15	118 28.2	356 24.0 ··	42.2	46 04.9 ··	54.6	235 17.0 ··	15.1	271 15.7 ··	22.6	Spica	158 55.3	S11 04.5
16	133 30.7	11 23.7	41.6	61 05.5	54.8	250 19.8	15.1	286 18.3	22.6	Suhail	223 09.6	S43 22.1
17	148 33.1	26 23.5	41.0	76 06.1	55.1	265 22.6	15.0	301 20.8	22.5			
18	163 35.6	41 23.3	N22 40.4	91 06.7	N22 55.3	280 25.3	S20 15.0	316 23.4	S 8 22.5	Vega	80 54.1	N38 45.9
19	178 38.1	56 23.1	39.8	106 07.3	55.5	295 28.1	14.9	331 26.0	22.5	Zuben'ubi	137 30.6	S15 58.4
20	193 40.5	71 22.8	39.2	121 07.9	55.8	310 30.9	14.9	346 28.5	22.5			
21	208 43.0	86 22.6 ··	38.6	136 08.5 ··	56.0	325 33.7 ··	14.8	1 31.1 ··	22.4		S.H.A.	Mer. Pass.
22	223 45.5	101 22.4	37.9	151 09.1	56.2	340 36.5	14.8	16 33.7	22.4	Venus	239 41.5	15 14
23	238 47.9	116 22.2	37.3	166 09.7	56.5	355 39.3	14.7	31 36.2	22.4	Mars	288 49.4	11 57
Mer. Pass. 7 11.3		v −0.3 d 0.6		v 0.6 d 0.2		v 2.8 d 0.1		v 2.6 d 0.0		Jupiter	116 36.0	23 22
										Saturn	152 43.5	20 58

Figure 4-1. From the *Nautical Almanac,* 1983, daily pages, June 3, 4, and 5 showing the stars and planets.

1983 JUNE 3, 4, 5 (FRI., SAT., SUN.)

G.M.T.	SUN G.H.A.	SUN Dec.	MOON G.H.A.	v	Dec.	d	H.P.
3 00	180 31.3	N22 12.8	274 57.1	14.3	S15 14.7	9.9	54.4
01	195 31.2	13.2	289 30.4	14.4	15 04.8	9.9	54.4
02	210 31.1	13.5	304 03.8	14.5	14 54.9	10.1	54.4
03	225 31.0	.. 13.8	318 37.3	14.4	14 44.8	10.0	54.4
04	240 30.9	14.1	333 10.7	14.5	14 34.8	10.2	54.4
05	255 30.8	14.4	347 44.2	14.5	14 24.6	10.2	54.5
06	270 30.7	N22 14.8	2 17.7	14.6	S14 14.4	10.3	54.5
07	285 30.6	15.1	16 51.3	14.5	14 04.1	10.3	54.5
08	300 30.5	15.4	31 24.8	14.6	13 53.8	10.4	54.5
F 09	315 30.4	.. 15.7	45 58.4	14.7	13 43.4	10.4	54.5
R 10	330 30.3	16.0	60 32.1	14.6	13 33.0	10.5	54.5
I 11	345 30.2	16.3	75 05.7	14.7	13 22.4	10.5	54.6
D 12	0 30.1	N22 16.6	89 39.4	14.7	S13 11.9	10.7	54.6
A 13	15 30.0	16.9	104 13.1	14.8	13 01.2	10.7	54.6
Y 14	30 29.9	17.3	118 46.9	14.7	12 50.5	10.7	54.6
15	45 29.8	.. 17.6	133 20.6	14.8	12 39.8	10.8	54.6
16	60 29.7	17.9	147 54.4	14.8	12 29.0	10.9	54.6
17	75 29.6	18.2	162 28.2	14.9	12 18.1	10.9	54.6
18	90 29.5	N22 18.5	177 02.1	14.8	S12 07.2	11.0	54.7
19	105 29.4	18.8	191 35.9	14.9	11 56.2	11.0	54.7
20	120 29.3	19.1	206 09.8	14.9	11 45.2	11.1	54.7
21	135 29.2	.. 19.4	220 43.7	14.9	11 34.1	11.1	54.7
22	150 29.1	..	235 17.6	15.0	11 23.0	11.2	54.7
23	165 29.0	20.0	249 51.6	14.9	11 11.8	11.3	54.7
4 00	180 28.9	N22 20.3	264 25.5	15.0	S11 00.5	11.3	54.8
01	195 28.8	20.6	278 59.5	15.0	10 49.2	11.3	54.8
02	210 28.7	20.9	293 33.5	15.0	10 37.9	11.4	54.8
03	225 28.6	.. 21.2	308 07.5	15.0	10 26.5	11.5	54.8
04	240 28.5	21.5	322 41.5	15.0	10 15.0	11.5	54.8
05	255 28.3	21.8	337 15.5	15.1	10 03.5	11.5	54.9
06	270 28.2	N22 22.1	351 49.6	15.0	S 9 52.0	11.6	54.9
07	285 28.1	22.4	6 23.6	15.1	9 40.4	11.6	54.9
S 08	300 28.0	22.7	20 57.7	15.1	9 28.8	11.7	54.9
A 09	315 27.9	.. 23.0	35 31.8	15.0	9 17.1	11.8	54.9
T 10	330 27.8	23.3	50 05.8	15.1	9 05.3	11.8	55.0
U 11	345 27.7	23.6	64 39.9	15.1	8 53.5	11.8	55.0
R 12	0 27.6	N22 23.9	79 14.0	15.2	S 8 41.7	11.9	55.0
D 13	15 27.5	24.2	93 48.2	15.1	8 29.8	11.9	55.0
A 14	30 27.4	24.5	108 22.3	15.1	8 17.9	11.9	55.1
Y 15	45 27.3	.. 24.8	122 56.4	15.1	8 06.0	12.0	55.1
16	60 27.2	25.1	137 30.5	15.1	7 54.0	12.1	55.1
17	75 27.1	25.4	152 04.6	15.2	7 41.9	12.1	55.1
18	90 27.0	N22 25.7	166 38.8	15.1	S 7 29.8	12.1	55.1
19	105 26.9	26.0	181 12.9	15.1	7 17.7	12.2	55.2
20	120 26.8	26.3	195 47.0	15.2	7 05.5	12.2	55.2
21	135 26.7	.. 26.6	210 21.2	15.1	6 53.3	12.2	55.2
22	150 26.6	26.9	224 55.3	15.1	6 41.1	12.3	55.2
23	165 26.4	27.1	239 29.4	15.1	6 28.8	12.3	55.3
5 00	180 26.3	N22 27.4	254 03.5	15.2	S 6 16.5	12.4	55.3
01	195 26.2	27.7	268 37.7	15.1	6 04.1	12.4	55.3
02	210 26.1	28.0	283 11.8	15.1	5 51.7	12.4	55.3
03	225 26.0	.. 28.3	297 45.9	15.1	5 39.3	12.5	55.4
04	240 25.9	28.6	312 20.0	15.1	5 26.8	12.5	55.4
05	255 25.8	28.9	326 54.1	15.1	5 14.3	12.5	55.4
06	270 25.7	N22 29.1	341 28.2	15.0	S 5 01.8	12.6	55.4
07	285 25.6	29.4	356 02.2	15.1	4 49.2	12.6	55.5
08	300 25.5	29.7	10 36.3	15.1	4 36.6	12.6	55.5
S 09	315 25.4	.. 30.0	25 10.4	15.0	4 24.0	12.7	55.5
U 10	330 25.3	30.3	39 44.4	15.0	4 11.3	12.7	55.6
N 11	345 25.2	30.5	54 18.4	15.0	3 58.6	12.7	55.6
D 12	0 25.0	N22 30.8	68 52.4	15.0	S 3 45.9	12.7	55.6
13	15 24.9	31.1	83 26.4	15.0	3 33.2	12.8	55.6
Y 14	30 24.8	31.4	98 00.4	14.9	3 20.4	12.8	55.7
15	45 24.7	.. 31.7	112 34.3	15.0	3 07.6	12.8	55.7
16	60 24.6	31.9	127 08.3	14.9	2 54.8	12.9	55.7
17	75 24.5	32.2	141 42.2	14.9	2 41.9	12.9	55.8
18	90 24.4	N22 32.5	156 16.1	14.9	S 2 29.0	12.9	55.8
19	105 24.3	32.8	170 50.0	14.8	2 16.1	12.9	55.8
20	120 24.2	33.0	185 23.8	14.9	2 03.2	13.0	55.8
21	135 24.1	.. 33.3	199 57.7	14.8	1 50.2	13.0	55.9
22	150 23.9	33.6	214 31.5	14.7	1 37.2	13.0	55.9
23	165 23.8	33.9	229 05.2	14.8	1 24.2	13.0	55.9
	S.D. 15.8	d 0.3	S.D. 14.9		15.0		15.2

Moonrise

Lat.	Twilight Naut.	Civil	Sunrise	3	4	5	6
N 72	□	□	□	03 23	02 48	02 22	02 00
N 70	□	□	□	02 53	02 31	02 14	01 59
68	□	□	□	02 30	02 18	02 07	01 58
66	////	////	01 02	02 12	02 07	02 02	01 57
64	////	////	01 52	01 57	01 57	01 57	01 56
62	////	////	02 23	01 45	01 49	01 53	01 56
60	////	01 19	02 46	01 34	01 42	01 49	01 55
N 58	////	01 56	03 04	01 25	01 36	01 46	01 55
56	////	02 21	03 20	01 17	01 31	01 43	01 54
54	01 12	02 41	03 33	01 10	01 26	01 40	01 54
52	01 46	02 57	03 44	01 03	01 22	01 38	01 53
50	02 10	03 11	03 54	00 57	01 18	01 36	01 53
45	02 51	03 39	04 15	00 45	01 09	01 31	01 52
N 40	03 19	04 00	04 32	00 34	01 02	01 27	01 52
35	03 41	04 17	04 47	00 25	00 55	01 24	01 51
30	03 59	04 32	04 59	00 17	00 50	01 20	01 51
20	04 27	04 55	05 20	00 03	00 40	01 15	01 50
N 10	04 48	05 15	05 38	24 31	00 31	01 10	01 50
0	05 06	05 32	05 55	24 23	00 23	01 06	01 49
S 10	05 22	05 48	06 11	24 15	00 15	01 02	01 48
20	05 38	06 05	06 29	24 07	00 07	00 57	01 48
30	05 53	06 23	06 49	23 57	24 52	00 52	01 47
35	06 01	06 33	07 01	23 51	24 48	00 48	01 47
40	06 10	06 44	07 14	23 45	24 45	00 45	01 46
45	06 20	06 56	07 30	23 37	24 41	00 41	01 46
S 50	06 30	07 12	07 49	23 28	24 36	00 36	01 45
52	06 35	07 18	07 59	23 24	24 34	00 34	01 45
54	06 41	07 26	08 09	23 19	24 31	00 31	01 45
56	06 46	07 34	08 21	23 14	24 28	00 28	01 44
58	06 52	07 44	08 34	23 08	24 25	00 25	01 44
S 60	06 59	07 55	08 50	23 01	24 22	00 22	01 44

Moonset

Lat.	Sunset	Twilight Civil	Naut.	3	4	5	6
N 72	□	□	□	08 37	10 43	12 39	14 34
N 70	□	□	□	09 06	10 58	12 45	14 32
68	□	□	□	09 28	11 10	12 49	14 29
66	22 59	////	////	09 45	11 19	12 53	14 28
64	22 06	////	////	09 58	11 27	12 56	14 26
62	21 35	////	////	10 10	11 34	12 58	14 25
60	21 12	22 40	////	10 19	11 40	13 01	14 24
N 58	20 53	22 02	////	10 28	11 45	13 03	14 22
56	20 38	21 36	////	10 35	11 49	13 05	14 22
54	20 24	21 16	22 47	10 42	11 53	13 06	14 21
52	20 13	21 00	22 12	10 48	11 57	13 08	14 20
50	20 03	20 46	21 48	10 53	12 00	13 09	14 19
45	19 41	20 18	21 06	11 04	12 08	13 12	14 18
N 40	19 24	19 57	20 37	11 14	12 14	13 14	14 17
35	19 10	19 39	20 15	11 22	12 19	13 16	14 15
30	18 58	19 25	19 58	11 29	12 23	13 18	14 14
20	18 37	19 01	19 30	11 41	12 31	13 21	14 13
N 10	18 19	18 41	19 08	11 51	12 38	13 24	14 11
0	18 02	18 24	18 50	12 01	12 44	13 27	14 10
S 10	17 45	18 08	18 34	12 11	12 50	13 29	14 09
20	17 28	17 51	18 19	12 21	12 57	13 32	14 07
30	17 07	17 33	18 05	12 33	13 04	13 35	14 05
35	16 56	17 23	17 55	12 39	13 08	13 36	14 04
40	16 42	17 12	17 46	12 47	13 13	13 38	14 03
45	16 26	17 00	17 36	12 56	13 19	13 40	14 02
S 50	16 07	16 45	17 26	13 07	13 25	13 43	14 00
52	15 58	16 38	17 21	13 11	13 29	13 44	14 00
54	15 47	16 30	17 15	13 17	13 32	13 46	13 59
56	15 35	16 22	17 10	13 23	13 36	13 47	13 58
58	15 22	16 12	17 04	13 29	13 40	13 49	13 57
S 60	15 06	16 01	16 57	13 37	13 44	13 50	13 56

	SUN			MOON			
Day	Eqn. of Time 00h	12h	Mer. Pass.	Mer. Pass. Upper	Lower	Age	Phase
	m s	m s	h m	h m	h m	d	
3	02 05	02 01	11 58	05 51	18 12	22	
4	01 56	01 51	11 58	06 34	18 55	23	◑
5	01 46	01 40	11 58	07 16	19 38	24	

Figure 4-2. From the *Nautical Almanac,* 1983, daily pages, June 3, 4, and 5 showing the sun and the moon.

−0.6′ while the d value for a sight of Mars taken during the same time would be +0.2′. The yellow page correction to declination would be subtracted from a Venus sight but added to a Mars sight.

When you record the declination of the planets, make sure you pick up the N or S designations and the whole degrees since these are given intermittently down the columns. For example, the declination of Venus for 04 hours, Friday, June 3, 1983 is N23°16.5′.

Stars

Along the right-hand column there is an alphabetical list of 57 stars. These have been selected by the editors of the almanac because they are the stars bright enough to be seen during twilight. The list gives the name of the star together with its Sidereal Hour Angle

(SHA) and declination. Stars have no v or d corrections. The SHA and declinations are given once for each star and are accurate for all three days covered by the page.

The SHA from the list of stars is combined with the GHA of Aries for the GMT of the sight to obtain the GHA of the star. When adding the SHA to the GHA of Aries, remember you may obtain a total greater than 360°. Since the GHA of a body cannot be more than 360° west of Greenwich, you simply subtract 360° from the total to obtain the GHA.

Recording Information on the Workform *(Refer to Figures 4-1 and 4-3)*

There is a section in the workform to record the information from both the daily pages and the yellow pages of the

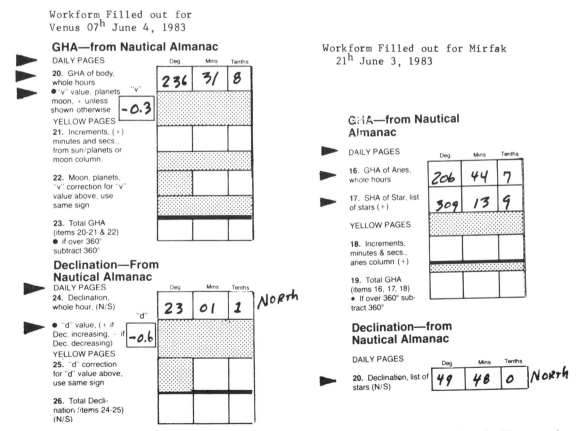

Figure 4-3. Daily page information from the *Nautical Almanac* recorded in workform for Venus and Mirfak.

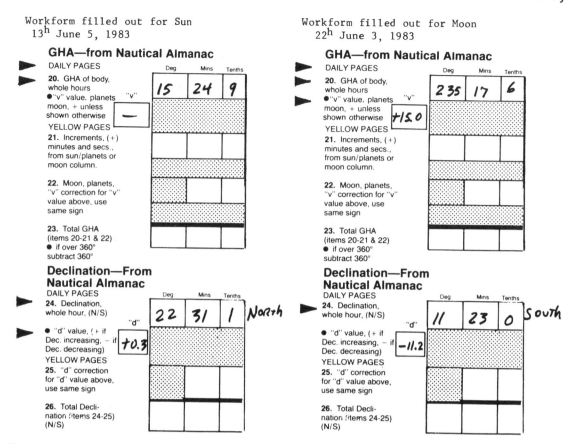

Figure 4-4. Daily page information from the *Nautical Almanac* recorded in workform for the sun and the moon.

almanac. Daily page information for the planets is recorded at items 20 and 24. In item 20, the GHA for the whole hour is recorded. The v value at the bottom of the GHA column is entered, with its sign, in the v box outside the main column. The reason: the v correction from the yellow page table, not the v value from the daily page is applied to the GHA.

The declination for the whole hour is entered in item 24 along with a notation whether the declination is north or south. The d value at the bottom of the declination column is entered in the box outside the main column. As the form suggests, the sign of the d value is + if the declination is increasing and − if the declination is decreasing. Figure 4-3 shows how to record the daily page information for a sight of Venus taken at 07 hours 10 minutes 43 seconds GMT on June 4, 1983. It

also shows how to record the daily page information for a sight of Mirfak taken at 21 hours 10 minutes 08 seconds on June 3, 1983. Figure 4-1 is marked to indicate where the information was obtained from the daily pages of the almanac.

Daily Page Information for the Sun and Moon

Along the top of the right-hand pages of the almanac you will find the sun and moon columns.

Sun

The GHA and declination of the sun is given for every hour of the three day period. At the bottom of the declination column for the sun, a d value is given which covers the three days for that page. The d value for the sun is used with the table in the yellow pages to obtain a correction to the declination. The d value for the sun is handled the same way as the planets: if the sun's declination is increasing the d value and tabular correction are added to the declination, if the sun's declination is decreasing the d value and correction are subtracted from the declination. There is no v value for the sun.

Moon

All the information needed for the moon is contained on a single line reading from left to right. The GHA is given first, followed by the v value, the declination, the d value and the HP or horizontal parallax. This last number is not part of the GHA or declination of the moon. It is used to enter a table to obtain a correction to the sextant reading.

At the bottom of the sun and moon columns are SD values. These are semidiameters of the sun and moon. Because the sun and moon are large bodies, navigator's measure the angle between the horizon and their rims, not their centers. The SD numbers are related to the correction necessary to adjust the sextant reading for this factor. Since the sun and moon altitude tables in the front and back covers of the almanac already take the semi-diameter into account, we can disregard them.

Notice how the whole degrees of declination are given intermittently in the sun column, while only the N or S designation for the declination is given intermittently in the moon column.

Filling out the Workform for Sun and Moon *(Refer to Figures 4-2 and 4-4)*

Data from the daily pages for the sun are entered in the workform exactly the same as for the planets except the v value is left blank. Figure 4-4 shows how to record the daily page information for a sight of the sun at 13 hours 11 minutes 20 seconds GMT, June 5, 1983. Figure 4-2 is marked to indicate where the data was found in the daily pages.

Information about the moon is entered in the form following the same format described for the sun and planets. Figure 4-4 shows how to record daily page information for a moon sight taken at 22 hours 11 minutes 07 seconds GMT on June 3, 1983. Figure 4-2 is marked to indicate where the data was located in the daily pages of the almanac.

Information from the Yellow or Increments Pages *(Refer to Figure 4-5)*

The yellow pages of the almanac—called the increments pages—are used for adjusting the location of celestial bodies for the minutes and seconds of GMT beyond the whole hour. Each increment page contains two separate tables, one table for each minute on the page. Each of these tables is divided into two separate tables. The first, or left-hand table for each minute, is called the increment table. It contains three columns:

The first is used with either sun or planet sights.
The second, Aries, is used with star sights.
The third is used only for the moon.

The second table, to the right of the increment table, is called the corrections table. It is used to obtain the v or d correction that corresponds to the v or d value from the daily page.

The increments and corrections section of the almanac is entered by first locating the tables that correspond to the correct minute of GMT. The minutes are

10ᵐ	SUN PLANETS	ARIES	MOON	v or d	Corrⁿ	v or d	Corrⁿ	v or d	Corrⁿ
s	° ′	° ′	° ′	′	′	′	′	′	′
00	2 30.0	2 30.4	2 23.2	0.0	0.0	6.0	1.1	12.0	2.1
01	2 30.3	2 30.7	2 23.4	0.1	0.0	6.1	1.1	12.1	2.1
02	2 30.5	2 30.9	2 23.6	0.2	0.0	6.2	1.1	12.2	2.1
03	2 30.8	2 31.2	2 23.9	0.3	0.1	6.3	1.1	12.3	2.2
04	2 31.0	2 31.4	2 24.1	0.4	0.1	6.4	1.1	12.4	2.2
05	2 31.3	2 31.7	2 24.4	0.5	0.1	6.5	1.1	12.5	2.2
06	2 31.5	2 31.9	2 24.6	0.6	0.1	6.6	1.2	12.6	2.2
07	2 31.8	2 32.2	2 24.8	0.7	0.1	6.7	1.2	12.7	2.2
08	2 32.0	2 32.4	2 25.1	0.8	0.1	6.8	1.2	12.8	2.2
09	2 32.3	2 32.7	2 25.3	0.9	0.2	6.9	1.2	12.9	2.3
10	2 32.5	2 32.9	2 25.6	1.0	0.2	7.0	1.2	13.0	2.3
11	2 32.8	2 33.2	2 25.8	1.1	0.2	7.1	1.2	13.1	2.3
12	2 33.0	2 33.4	2 26.0	1.2	0.2	7.2	1.3	13.2	2.3
13	2 33.3	2 33.7	2 26.3	1.3	0.2	7.3	1.3	13.3	2.3
14	2 33.5	2 33.9	2 26.5	1.4	0.2	7.4	1.3	13.4	2.3
15	2 33.8	2 34.2	2 26.7	1.5	0.3	7.5	1.3	13.5	2.4
16	2 34.0	2 34.4	2 27.0	1.6	0.3	7.6	1.3	13.6	2.4
17	2 34.3	2 34.7	2 27.2	1.7	0.3	7.7	1.3	13.7	2.4
18	2 34.5	2 34.9	2 27.5	1.8	0.3	7.8	1.4	13.8	2.4
19	2 34.8	2 35.2	2 27.7	1.9	0.3	7.9	1.4	13.9	2.4
20	2 35.0	2 35.4	2 27.9	2.0	0.4	8.0	1.4	14.0	2.4
21	2 35.3	2 35.7	2 28.2	2.1	0.4	8.1	1.4	14.1	2.5
22	2 35.5	2 35.9	2 28.4	2.2	0.4	8.2	1.4	14.2	2.5
23	2 35.8	2 36.2	2 28.7	2.3	0.4	8.3	1.5	14.3	2.5
24	2 36.0	2 36.4	2 28.9	2.4	0.4	8.4	1.5	14.4	2.5
25	2 36.3	2 36.7	2 29.1	2.5	0.4	8.5	1.5	14.5	2.5
26	2 36.5	2 36.9	2 29.4	2.6	0.5	8.6	1.5	14.6	2.6
27	2 36.8	2 37.2	2 29.6	2.7	0.5	8.7	1.5	14.7	2.6
28	2 37.0	2 37.4	2 29.8	2.8	0.5	8.8	1.5	14.8	2.6
29	2 37.3	2 37.7	2 30.1	2.9	0.5	8.9	1.6	14.9	2.6
30	2 37.5	2 37.9	2 30.3	3.0	0.5	9.0	1.6	15.0	2.6
31	2 37.8	2 38.2	2 30.6	3.1	0.5	9.1	1.6	15.1	2.6
32	2 38.0	2 38.4	2 30.8	3.2	0.6	9.2	1.6	15.2	2.7
33	2 38.3	2 38.7	2 31.0	3.3	0.6	9.3	1.6	15.3	2.7
34	2 38.5	2 38.9	2 31.3	3.4	0.6	9.4	1.6	15.4	2.7
35	2 38.8	2 39.2	2 31.5	3.5	0.6	9.5	1.7	15.5	2.7
36	2 39.0	2 39.4	2 31.8	3.6	0.6	9.6	1.7	15.6	2.7
37	2 39.3	2 39.7	2 32.0	3.7	0.6	9.7	1.7	15.7	2.7
38	2 39.5	2 39.9	2 32.2	3.8	0.7	9.8	1.7	15.8	2.8
39	2 39.8	2 40.2	2 32.5	3.9	0.7	9.9	1.7	15.9	2.8
40	2 40.0	2 40.4	2 32.7	4.0	0.7	10.0	1.8	16.0	2.8
41	2 40.3	2 40.7	2 32.9	4.1	0.7	10.1	1.8	16.1	2.8
42	2 40.5	2 40.9	2 33.2	4.2	0.7	10.2	1.8	16.2	2.8
43	2 40.8	2 41.2	2 33.4	4.3	0.8	10.3	1.8	16.3	2.9
44	2 41.0	2 41.4	2 33.7	4.4	0.8	10.4	1.8	16.4	2.9
45	2 41.3	2 41.7	2 33.9	4.5	0.8	10.5	1.8	16.5	2.9
46	2 41.5	2 41.9	2 34.1	4.6	0.8	10.6	1.9	16.6	2.9
47	2 41.8	2 42.2	2 34.4	4.7	0.8	10.7	1.9	16.7	2.9
48	2 42.0	2 42.4	2 34.6	4.8	0.8	10.8	1.9	16.8	2.9
49	2 42.3	2 42.7	2 34.9	4.9	0.9	10.9	1.9	16.9	3.0
50	2 42.5	2 42.9	2 35.1	5.0	0.9	11.0	1.9	17.0	3.0
51	2 42.8	2 43.2	2 35.3	5.1	0.9	11.1	1.9	17.1	3.0
52	2 43.0	2 43.4	2 35.6	5.2	0.9	11.2	2.0	17.2	3.0
53	2 43.3	2 43.7	2 35.8	5.3	0.9	11.3	2.0	17.3	3.0
54	2 43.5	2 43.9	2 36.1	5.4	0.9	11.4	2.0	17.4	3.0
55	2 43.8	2 44.2	2 36.3	5.5	1.0	11.5	2.0	17.5	3.1
56	2 44.0	2 44.4	2 36.5	5.6	1.0	11.6	2.0	17.6	3.1
57	2 44.3	2 44.7	2 36.8	5.7	1.0	11.7	2.0	17.7	3.1
58	2 44.5	2 45.0	2 37.0	5.8	1.0	11.8	2.1	17.8	3.1
59	2 44.8	2 45.2	2 37.2	5.9	1.0	11.9	2.1	17.9	3.1
60	2 45.0	2 45.5	2 37.5	6.0	1.1	12.0	2.1	18.0	3.2

11ᵐ	SUN PLANETS	ARIES	MOON	v or d	Corrⁿ	v or d	Corrⁿ	v or d	Corrⁿ
s	° ′	° ′	° ′	′	′	′	′	′	′
00	2 45.0	2 45.5	2 37.5	0.0	0.0	6.0	1.2	12.0	2.3
01	2 45.3	2 45.7	2 37.7	0.1	0.0	6.1	1.2	12.1	2.3
02	2 45.5	2 46.0	2 38.0	0.2	0.0	6.2	1.2	12.2	2.3
03	2 45.8	2 46.2	2 38.2	0.3	0.1	6.3	1.2	12.3	2.4
04	2 46.0	2 46.5	2 38.4	0.4	0.1	6.4	1.2	12.4	2.4
05	2 46.3	2 46.7	2 38.7	0.5	0.1	6.5	1.2	12.5	2.4
06	2 46.5	2 47.0	2 38.9	0.6	0.1	6.6	1.3	12.6	2.4
07	2 46.8	2 47.2	2 39.2	0.7	0.1	6.7	1.3	12.7	2.4
08	2 47.0	2 47.5	2 39.4	0.8	0.2	6.8	1.3	12.8	2.5
09	2 47.3	2 47.7	2 39.6	0.9	0.2	6.9	1.3	12.9	2.5
10	2 47.5	2 48.0	2 39.9	1.0	0.2	7.0	1.3	13.0	2.5
11	2 47.8	2 48.2	2 40.1	1.1	0.2	7.1	1.4	13.1	2.5
12	2 48.0	2 48.5	2 40.3	1.2	0.2	7.2	1.4	13.2	2.5
13	2 48.3	2 48.7	2 40.6	1.3	0.2	7.3	1.4	13.3	2.5
14	2 48.5	2 49.0	2 40.8	1.4	0.3	7.4	1.4	13.4	2.6
15	2 48.8	2 49.2	2 41.1	1.5	0.3	7.5	1.4	13.5	2.6
16	2 49.0	2 49.5	2 41.3	1.6	0.3	7.6	1.5	13.6	2.6
17	2 49.3	2 49.7	2 41.5	1.7	0.3	7.7	1.5	13.7	2.6
18	2 49.5	2 50.0	2 41.8	1.8	0.3	7.8	1.5	13.8	2.6
19	2 49.8	2 50.2	2 42.0	1.9	0.4	7.9	1.5	13.9	2.7
20	2 50.0	2 50.5	2 42.3	2.0	0.4	8.0	1.5	14.0	2.7
21	2 50.3	2 50.7	2 42.5	2.1	0.4	8.1	1.6	14.1	2.7
22	2 50.5	2 51.0	2 42.7	2.2	0.4	8.2	1.6	14.2	2.7
23	2 50.8	2 51.2	2 43.0	2.3	0.4	8.3	1.6	14.3	2.7
24	2 51.0	2 51.5	2 43.2	2.4	0.5	8.4	1.6	14.4	2.8
25	2 51.3	2 51.7	2 43.4	2.5	0.5	8.5	1.6	14.5	2.8
26	2 51.5	2 52.0	2 43.7	2.6	0.5	8.6	1.6	14.6	2.8
27	2 51.8	2 52.2	2 43.9	2.7	0.5	8.7	1.7	14.7	2.8
28	2 52.0	2 52.5	2 44.2	2.8	0.5	8.8	1.7	14.8	2.8
29	2 52.3	2 52.7	2 44.4	2.9	0.6	8.9	1.7	14.9	2.9
30	2 52.5	2 53.0	2 44.6	3.0	0.6	9.0	1.7	15.0	2.9
31	2 52.8	2 53.2	2 44.9	3.1	0.6	9.1	1.7	15.1	2.9
32	2 53.0	2 53.5	2 45.1	3.2	0.6	9.2	1.8	15.2	2.9
33	2 53.3	2 53.7	2 45.4	3.3	0.6	9.3	1.8	15.3	2.9
34	2 53.5	2 54.0	2 45.6	3.4	0.7	9.4	1.8	15.4	3.0
35	2 53.8	2 54.2	2 45.8	3.5	0.7	9.5	1.8	15.5	3.0
36	2 54.0	2 54.5	2 46.1	3.6	0.7	9.6	1.8	15.6	3.0
37	2 54.3	2 54.7	2 46.3	3.7	0.7	9.7	1.9	15.7	3.0
38	2 54.5	2 55.0	2 46.6	3.8	0.7	9.8	1.9	15.8	3.0
39	2 54.8	2 55.2	2 46.8	3.9	0.7	9.9	1.9	15.9	3.0
40	2 55.0	2 55.5	2 47.0	4.0	0.8	10.0	1.9	16.0	3.1
41	2 55.3	2 55.7	2 47.3	4.1	0.8	10.1	1.9	16.1	3.1
42	2 55.5	2 56.0	2 47.5	4.2	0.8	10.2	2.0	16.2	3.1
43	2 55.8	2 56.2	2 47.7	4.3	0.8	10.3	2.0	16.3	3.1
44	2 56.0	2 56.5	2 48.0	4.4	0.8	10.4	2.0	16.4	3.1
45	2 56.3	2 56.7	2 48.2	4.5	0.9	10.5	2.0	16.5	3.2
46	2 56.5	2 57.0	2 48.5	4.6	0.9	10.6	2.0	16.6	3.2
47	2 56.8	2 57.2	2 48.7	4.7	0.9	10.7	2.1	16.7	3.2
48	2 57.0	2 57.5	2 48.9	4.8	0.9	10.8	2.1	16.8	3.2
49	2 57.3	2 57.7	2 49.2	4.9	0.9	10.9	2.1	16.9	3.2
50	2 57.5	2 58.0	2 49.4	5.0	1.0	11.0	2.1	17.0	3.3
51	2 57.8	2 58.2	2 49.7	5.1	1.0	11.1	2.1	17.1	3.3
52	2 58.0	2 58.5	2 49.9	5.2	1.0	11.2	2.1	17.2	3.3
53	2 58.3	2 58.7	2 50.1	5.3	1.0	11.3	2.2	17.3	3.3
54	2 58.5	2 59.0	2 50.4	5.4	1.0	11.4	2.2	17.4	3.3
55	2 58.8	2 59.2	2 50.6	5.5	1.1	11.5	2.2	17.5	3.4
56	2 59.0	2 59.5	2 50.8	5.6	1.1	11.6	2.2	17.6	3.4
57	2 59.3	2 59.7	2 51.1	5.7	1.1	11.7	2.2	17.7	3.4
58	2 59.5	3 00.0	2 51.3	5.8	1.1	11.8	2.3	17.8	3.4
59	2 59.8	3 00.2	2 51.6	5.9	1.1	11.9	2.3	17.9	3.4
60	3 00.0	3 00.5	2 51.8	6.0	1.2	12.0	2.3	18.0	3.5

Figure 4-5. Increments and corrections page for 10 minutes and 11 minutes from the *Nautical Almanac,* 1983.

indicated by the bold face type in the corners. The seconds are given by the numbers 00 through 60 that are in columnar order under the minute designations.

Increments Table

The increments are found by going down the correct minute column until you find the line that corresponds to the seconds of GMT. You then take the increment from the correct column—sun/planets, Aries, or moon.

PRACTICE PROBLEMS *(Use Figure 4-5)*

1. What is the increment of the sun for 10 minutes 47 seconds?
2. What is the increment of Venus for 11 minutes 30 seconds?
3. What is the increment of Aries for 10 minutes 14 seconds?
4. What is the increment of the moon for 11 minutes 29 seconds?

ANSWERS

1. 2°41.8′ 2. 2°52.5′ 3. 2°33.9′ 4. 2°44.4′

The increment for the sun, moon, or planets is entered in item 21 of the sun, moon, planet workform. The increment for the stars is entered at item 18 of the star workform. The increment is always added to the GHA and or SHA of the body.

Corrections Table

The corrections table is entered by first locating the v or d number from the daily pages in one of the three v or d columns. The correction is the number just to the right of—and on the same line as—the v or d number. The correction is applied to the GHA or declination using the same sign as the v or d number from the daily pages used to locate it. In other words, if the v or d number is plus the

correction is added. If the v or d number is minus, the correction is subtracted.

Examples: (Refer to Figure 4-5) You are using the 10 minute increment/corrections tables. You require the correction for a daily page v value of +0.6′. The correction is +0.1′.

You are using the 11 minute increment table. You require a correction for a daily page d value of −11.6′. The correction is −2.2′.

PRACTICE PROBLEMS *(Refer to Figure 4-5)*

1. What is the correction for a daily page d value of −0.5′ from the 10 minute table?
2. What is the correction for a daily page v value of +0.9′ from the 11 minute correction table?

ANSWERS

1. −0.1′ 2. +0.2′

Complete GHA and Declination Workforms

Figure 4-5 is marked to indicate where the following increments and corrections information was located in order to complete the Venus, Mirfak, Sun, and Moon problems:

Name of body	Increments of GMT	Daily page v or d values and sign
Venus	10 min. 43 sec.	v − 0.3′; d − 0.6′
Mirfak	10 min. 08 sec.	-- --
Sun	11 min. 20 sec.	d + 0.3′; --
Moon	11 min. 07 sec.	v +15.0′; d −11.2′

Figures 4-6 and 4-7 are marked to indicate how the increments and corrections data were recorded on the workform and combined with the daily page information to obtain the GHA and declination of the four bodies.

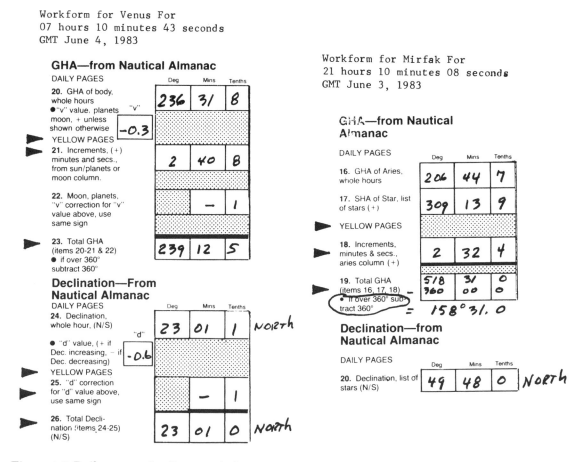

Figure 4-6. Daily page and yellow page information recorded for Venus and Mirfak.

Nautical Almanac Practice Problems (Refer to Appendix 2, for information needed to work problems)

DAILY PAGE INFORMATION

1. For 14 hours on June 7, 1983 what is the GHA, declination, and d value of the sun?

2. For 06 hours on June 6, 1983 what is the GHA of Aries and the SHA and declination of Kochab?

3. For 13 hours on June 8, 1983 what is the GHA, declination, v and d values for Jupiter?

4. For 05 hours on June 3, 1983 what is the GHA, declination, v and d value for the moon?

ANSWERS

1. GHA 30°19.4′; Declination N22°43.9′; d value +0.2′

2. GHA Aries 344°05.2′; SHA 137°17.8′; declination N74°13.7′

3. GHA 208°32.1′; declination S20°11.6′; v +2.8′; d −0.0′

4. GHA 347°44.2′; declination S14°24.6′; v +14.5′; d −10.2′

YELLOW PAGE INFORMATION

1. What is the increment of the sun for 02 minutes 41 seconds? From the 02 minute table, what is the d correction for a daily page d value of +0.2′?

2. What is the increment of Aries for 06 minutes 11 seconds?

3. What is the increment for Jupiter for 10 minutes 19 seconds? What is the v correction for a daily page v value of +2.8′ from the 10 minute increments/corrections table? What is the d correction from this table for a daily page d value of −0.0′?

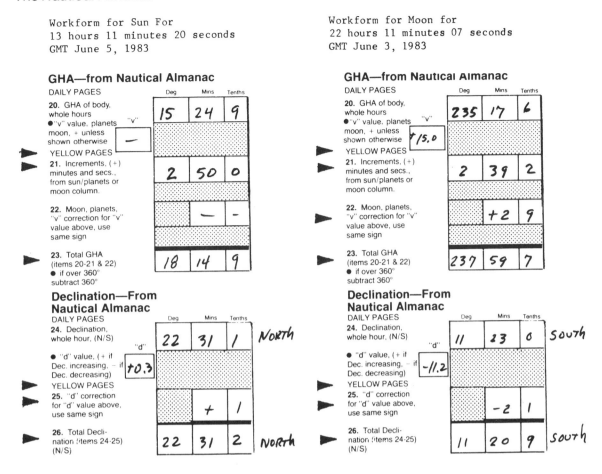

Figure 4-7. Daily page and yellow page information recorded for the sun and the moon.

4. What is the increment for the moon for 05 minutes 51 seconds? What is the v correction from the 05 minute increments/corrections table for a daily page v value of +14.5'? What is the d correction from this table for a daily page d value of −10.2'?

ANSWERS

1. Increment is 0°40.3'; d correction is 0.0'

2. Increment is 1°33.0'

3. Increment is 2°34.8'; v correction +0.5'; d correction 0.0'

4. Increment is 1°23.8'; v correction +1.3'; d correction −0.9'

COMPLETE GHA AND DECLINATION

1. What is the GHA and declination of the sun for June 4, 1983 at 18 hours 10 minutes 44 seconds GMT?

2. What is the GHA and declination of Alphard (a star) for June 6, 1983 at 09 hours 09 minutes 11 seconds?

3. What is the GHA and declination of Mars for June 5, 1983 at 07 hours 08 minutes 15 seconds GMT?

4. What is the GHA and declination of the moon for June 3, 1983 at 07 hours 10 minutes 04 seconds?

ANSWERS

1. GHA 93°08.0; declination N22°25.8'

2. GHA 249°49.5'; declination S8°35.2'

3. GHA 288°04.0'; declination N22°52.8'

4. GHA 19°17.9'; declination S14°02.3'

5

The Marine Sextant
(Time: 1 Hour)

The sextant is a device for measuring angles. As Figure 5-1 shows, the sextant is used by navigators to measure the angle between the horizon and a celestial body. This chapter will show you how to use a sextant, adjust the mirrors, and make the corrections to your sextant reading. This alone, however, will not make you a good observer—it takes practice. Your first sights may be off by ten to fifteen nautical miles. With a few hours of practice you should be able to come within three to five miles of a known position. It's a good idea to practice taking sights near buoys or lighthouses so you can tell how close your lines of position are to a known position.

Figure 5-2 shows the parts of a marine sextant. The main frame gives the instrument its size, shape, and strength. The eyepiece and scope magnify the image of the celestial body and improve the accuracy of observations. A 4 power scope is recommended for pleasure boaters. Finding a star with a sextant is a difficult task therefore, look for a sextant with good optics and large size mirrors. The release clamp frees the index arm to

Figure 5-1. The sextant measures the angle, or altitude, of the celestial body above the horizon. Here the sextant measures a star with an altitude of 60°.

move along the main arc. The sunshades protect your eyes when looking at the sun. The main arc measures degrees, the micrometer drum measures minutes, and the vernier scale measures tenths of minutes. Each degree on a sextant is divided into 60 minutes and each minute is divided into ten tenths.

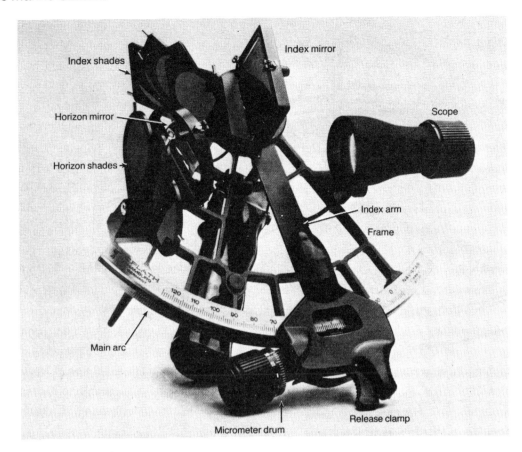

Figure 5-2. The parts of a sextant.

The sextant angle represents the distance in nautical miles the observer is from the GP of a celestial body. The sextant angle is compared with the computed angle from H. O. 229 to obtain the intercept. The intercept represents the distance between the observed circle of position and the computed circle of position. The reason the intercept can be plotted as nautical miles is because one minute of arc on a sextant is equal to one minute of latitude on the earth and one minute of latitude equals one nautical mile.

How to Take Care of Your Sextant

With care, a sextant should last a lifetime. To protect this precision instrument you should follow these guidelines:

1. Pick up your sextant only by the main frame or handle. Never pick it up by the scope, mirrors, or sunshades.
2. Store the sextant aboard ship in a safe place and secure it so it will not come loose in rough weather.
3. Keep your sextant free of salt. If seawater or salt spray coats the mirrors or the instrument, rinse the sextant, but not the scope, with fresh water. Wipe clean with lens tissue and coat the moving parts and frame with light machine oil.
4. When you clean the lenses and mirrors of your sextant, use the same caution you would observe with a fine camera. Wipe away any particles of dirt with a camel's hair brush and clean the lenses and mirrors with lens cleaner and tissue.

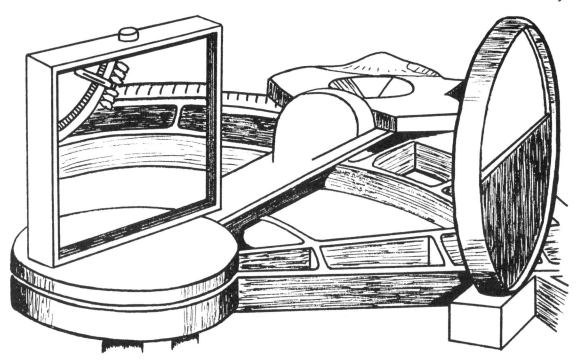

Figure 5-3. The sextant should be laid down on its side to check for index error.

How to Adjust Your Sextant

When you buy a sextant, or before you take one on a voyage, you should test it to make sure it is properly adjusted. However, you should not adjust your sextant any more than necessary, since overadjustment tends to cause wear on the adjusting screws and can cause the sextant to lose its ability to remain in adjustment. The following procedure is used to adjust a sextant:

Step 1. Set the sextant down on a level surface with the index mirror closest to you and the micrometer drum and index arm facing away. As Figure 5-3 indicates, at eye level you can look in the index mirror and see both the reflected image of the main arc and the main arc itself. The reflected image of the arc should appear to join the actual arc if the sextant is properly adjusted. In Figure 5-3 the reflected image appears a little higher so an ad-

justment is necessary. Use the adjusting wrench supplied with your sextant to turn the adjusting screw on the back of the index mirror until the reflected and actual arc appear as one continuous line.

Step 2. To remove index error, set the sextant to 0°. This means both the main arc and micrometer drum are at zero. Then use a distant horizon to sight through the eyepiece. On the left of Figure 5-4 the horizon is even so no index adjustment is necessary. On the right, the horizon is broken or uneven so index error is present and an adjustment is necessary. Figure 5-5 shows where to find the index adjustment and perpendicular adjustment screws on most sextants. With the sextant lying down on a table and the bottom of the horizon mirror facing you, you should see two adjusting screws. The index adjustment screw is the one closest to the main frame of the sextant. While looking through

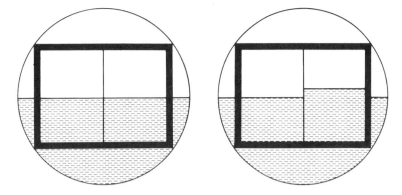

Figure 5-4. If the horizon is even, there is no index error; if horizon is uneven, index error is present.

the sextant at the horizon, turn this screw until the horizon forms a straight line.

Step 3. The final adjustment insures that the horizon mirror is perpendicular to the main frame of the sextant. There are two ways to tell if a perpendicular adjustment is necessary:

(a) If you find that there are two stars appearing side by side instead of just one when you take your sights the mirrors are out of alignment.

(b) Set the sextant to zero degrees. Look at a natural horizon and turn the micrometer drum, if necessary, until the horizon forms a continuous, unbroken line. Look through the eyepiece at the horizon and rotate the sextant from left to right with a rocking motion. Figure 5-6 shows the two possibilities. If the horizon remains unbroken as you rock the sextant, no adjustment is necessary. If the horizon becomes uneven, then a perpendicular adjustment is required. The perpendicular adjustment screw is the screw on the back of the horizon mirror which is furthest away from the main frame of the sextant.

As you adjust your sextant, you may find it necessary to repeat the steps several times before everything is in order because as you adjust one component, it may affect the other.

Reading the Sextant

Because there is a direct relationship between the sextant and the distance represented by the intercept, it is very important to learn to read the instrument correctly. For example, if you misread the degrees from the main arc by only one degree, your line of position will be thrown off by 60 minutes or 60 nautical miles. If you misread the minutes from the micrometer drum by one minute, your line of position will be off by one nautical mile.

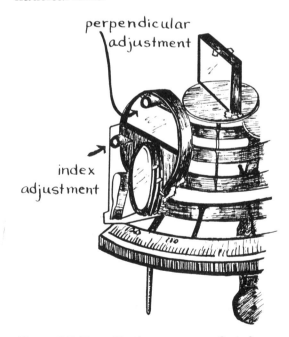

Figure 5-5. Two adjusting screws, one for index adjustments and one for perpendicular adjustments, are located on the back of the horizon mirror on most sextants.

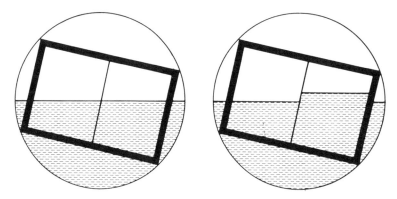

Figure 5-6. If the horizon becomes uneven as the sextant is tilted or rocked from left to right, a perpendicular adjustment is needed.

The sextant is read in three steps: (Refer to Figure 5-7)

1. Read the whole degrees from the main arc by noting the position of the mark on the index arm. Most sextants have the whole degrees etched on the arc every ten degrees with little "ticks" for the degrees in between. Since the degree reading is critical you must use extra caution in reading the main arc. Figure 5-7 shows 39° on the main arc.
2. The minutes are read directly from the micrometer drum by noting where the drum lines up with the zero mark. In this case we have 51 minutes on the micrometer drum.
3. On many sextants, you can read them to the nearest 0.2' or two tenths of a minute. On these, the tenths are read

from the vernier scale by noting which mark on the scale lines up with any one of the minute marks etched on the micrometer drum. On a vernier scale, each tick usually equals 0.2'. Since the minute lines on the drum and the lines on the vernier scale appear to "join" at the 0.2' mark, this vernier scale is read as 0.2'. The correct reading for Figure 5-7 is 39°51.2'.

If there are any zeroes in your minutes/tenths reading, for example 45°01.4', make sure you write them down. A reading with no zeroes but some tenths would be recorded as 45°00.6'. Later on, when you add or subtract corrections to the sextant reading, the missing zeroes become important.

Most of the time, the whole degree indicator will lie between two numbers on the main arc. When reading a sextant, always use the smaller of the two numbers. In Figure 5-7 the degree indicator is between 39° and 40°. Since there are 51' on the micrometer drum, the degree indicator is actually closer to the 40 degree mark than the 39 degree mark. Therefore, you might be tempted to record 40°. You must be careful here. The sextant is not at 40° yet. It is at 39°51' and you must follow the rule: when the whole degree indicator falls between two degree marks, always use the smaller number

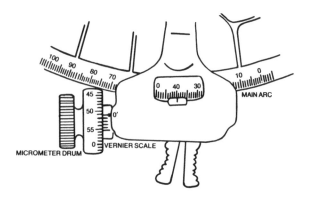

Figure 5-7. Sextant reading 39°51.2'

even if the indicator is closer to the larger number.

Sometimes you can't tell what degree mark you should use just by looking at the main arc alone. For example, let's assume that you can't tell by looking at it whether the sextant is at the end of the 49° area or just slightly into the 50° area of the arc. You can determine this by looking at the micrometer drum. If the drum reads 58' or 59' then you are obviously at the end of the 49° area. If the drum reads 01' or 02' then you know you have just passed the 49° area of the arc and are now into the start of the 50° sector.

Figure 5-8. Navigator holding the sextant properly. Instrument is held with the right hand while the left hand adjusts the micrometer drum.

Using the Sextant

Figure 5-8 shows how to hold a sextant. Notice how the navigator holds the sextant with one hand while releasing the index arm clamp with the other. He's looking at the horizon in the direction of the celestial body while moving the index arm back and forth. Once the body appears in the sextant, he will release the clamp and move his free hand to the micrometer drum. Then he will turn the drum until the body is brought down to the horizon. He will rock the sextant gently back and forth to make sure that the body touches the horizon when the sextant is perpendicular to the earth. Finally, he'll note the exact GMT and record the sextant reading.

Checking for Index Error

As you use a sextant, the index mirror can get slightly out of alignment due to shock, vibration, or bumping. Therefore everytime you use the sextant, you should check first for index error. If the error is tolerable, say +/− 2 or 3 minutes do not adjust the sextant. Simply determine the amount of the error and whether you add or subtract it from the sextant reading. The reason you do not adjust minor errors is because constant turning of the adjusting screws will wear them out.

If the index error is above zero it poses no problem. For example, if the micrometer reads 2.2' when the horizon is an even line the sextant is "shooting above zero" by 2.2' and you know you'll have to subtract 2.2' from any reading to correct for the error.

However, when the reading is below zero you have to look carefully at the micrometer drum and vernier scale to see how many minutes and tenths you have to add to bring the instrument back to zero. Assume you had a sextant where the index error was a −1.4'. In this case, the micrometer drum and vernier scale would read 60' minus 1.4' or 58.6'. The sextant, however, is not 58.6' out of adjustment. To get the sextant back to zero you have only to turn the drum 1.4'. Since the sextant is shooting low, you must add 1.4′ to bring it to zero. The index correction that you would add to all your sextant readings is a +1.4′.

Upper and Lower Limbs

Since the sun and the moon are large bodies, navigators can measure the angle between the horizon and the lower or upper rim. When the angle is measured between the horizon and the upper rim it is called an upper limb sight. When the angle is measured between the horizon and the lower rim it is called a lower limb sight. Figure 5-9 shows the difference between an upper and lower limb sight of the sun. Since stars and planets are tiny dots of light, they have no upper or lower limbs.

Techniques on Taking Sights

Try to position yourself in the center of the boat. Brace yourself against the mast to minimize motion. If there is a running sea, try to take your sights at the top of the crests. Observations taken from the trough of a wave will be somewhat in error.

Motion and spray can sometimes be reduced by a course change during the few minutes when sights are being taken.

You can avoid loss of your sextant by attaching a cord to the main frame, and putting it around your neck.

If someone is available to help you, let them record the GMT's and sextant readings.

Avoid low altitude sights (below 10°) since they are usually less reliable and require additional steps to correct the sextant reading.

When observing celestial bodies, try for good angular distribution of your sights. In piloting, you don't get good results with bearings taken on two buoys

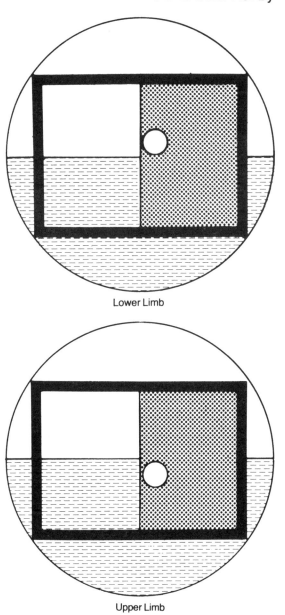

Figure 5-9. *Top*, if the bottom edge of the sun or moon is brought down to the horizon, the sight was a lower limb; *bottom*, if the top edge of the sun or moon is brought down to the horizon, the sight was an upper limb.

side by side. The same is true for celestial. If you are working on a 2-star fix, try for stars separated by about 90°. If you are working on a 3-star fix, find stars separated by about 60°.

Try to take at least two shots of each body. That way if you make a mistake on the first sight, you can still work out the second one.

If you're having trouble with star or planet sights, use a technique called inverting the sextant. To do this, set the arc and drum to zero, turn the sextant upside down and look at the star or planet, not the horizon. In this position, the handle will be in your left hand and the release clamp in your right hand. Release the clamp and slowly and smoothly follow the star or planet as it appears to "fall" toward the horizon. Once you see the horizon coming up to meet the star or planet, release the clamp, return the sextant to its normal position, and sweep the horizon until you find the body. Make the final adjustment with the micrometer drum, obtain the sextant angle, and record the GMT.

Corrections to the Sextant Reading

Once you obtain a sextant shot, you have to correct the reading for four factors:

1. Index error
2. Instrument error
3. Height of eye or dip
4. Refraction or altitude

The sextant correction portion of the workform is used to apply the corrections. You have already dealt with one of the corrections called index error.

Figure 5-10. An example of an instrument certificate for a sextant.

Instrument Error

Instrument error is the fixed or unadjustable error built into a sextant. Metal sextant manufacturers usually furnish a certificate indicating the instrument error for various readings. The best sextants have instrument errors that are so slight that the instruments are certified free of error for practical use. The inspection certificates are usually mounted inside the lid of the sextant case. Figure 5-10 is a copy of an instrument error certificate. As Figure 5-10 indicates, instrument errors are recorded on the certificate for various readings throughout the arc. The error can vary from one reading to another and the errors can be plus or minus.

The certificate shows that all readings between 15° and 30° will be in error by −0.2'. At 45° there is no error but at 60° the error becomes +0.2'. At 75° the error is +0.3' and at 90° the error is 0.5'. (There is not much use in looking at errors beyond 90° since at this angle the celestial body is directly over your head.)

The signs of the instrument errors as listed on the certificate must be reversed as you apply them. If the certificate shows an error of +0.1' between 20° and 30° that means the sextant is reading "high" by one-tenth of a minute for any sight taken at those angles. To remove the error you have to subtract one tenth. The rules, then, for applying instrument errors are the same that you use to apply index errors.

PRACTICE PROBLEMS

Use Figure 5-10 to identify the instrument error and the instrument correction for the following sights:

Sextant reading	Instrument error	Instrument correction
1. 77°01.4'	_____	_____
2. 48°34.2'	_____	_____
3. 33°55.8'	_____	_____

ANSWERS

1. Error +0.3'; correction −0.3'
2. Zero error; zero correction
3. Error −0.2'; correction +0.2'

Correction for Height of Eye (dip)

The higher the observer's eye from the water, the greater the sextant angle. The reason: as you go higher, the horizon appears to drop or "dip" down.

To determine your height of eye from a yacht, use the lead line to measure the distance in feet from the edge of the water to the height of your eye. The measurement should be taken from the place on the boat where you usually observe celestial bodies. You need do this only once, because the dip correction for the boat will always remain the same. The sextant correction for the height of eye is given from the "dip" table in the almanac which you'll find in two places:

Inside the front cover on page A-2.
Inside the back cover, to the right of the 0-35° moon altitude tables.

These tables have been reprinted as part of Appendix 2. Figure 5-11, taken from the almanac, shows how to locate a height of eye of 10 feet and take out the dip correction. Note that the dip table gives the height of eye both in meters and feet. In the altitude tables (and some H. O. 229 tables as well) you have to find the numbers in the table that bracket or include a given number. This means you need one number in the table that is higher and one that is lower than the given number. In our example, the 10 feet height of eye lies between 9.8 and 10.5 feet in the feet column. The correction, −3.1 minutes, is found in the correction column to the left. (This −3.1' correction would also be used for any height of eye between 3.0 and 3.2 meters.) All dip corrections have minus signs and are therefore subtracted from the sextant reading.

Sextant Correction Symbols

Before going any further, let's take a look at the shorthand symbols for the various sextant corrections and the place on the workforms where the data is entered.

The uncorrected sextant reading from the instrument itself is called the Sextant Reading or Hs.

The sextant reading corrected for index error, instrument error, and dip is called the Apparent Altitude or Ha.

The fully corrected sextant reading is called the Observed Altitude or Ho.

The computed angle from the H. O. 229 table is called the Hc.

(Hs stands for height, sextant; Ha stands for height, apparent; Ho stands for height, observed; and Hc stands for height, computed.)

There are two steps in the process of correcting the sextant. In step 1, you apply index error, instrument error, and dip to obtain the partially corrected sextant reading called the apparent altitude (Ha). The apparent altitude is then used in step 2, for entering the Altitude Correction Tables to find and apply the corrections necessary to offset the fact that light rays from celestial bodies are bent or "refracted" as they come through the earth's atmosphere. The altitude corrections are applied to the apparent altitude (Ha) to obtain the fully corrected sextant reading (Ho). From now on we will use the shorthand symbols for the various angles.

Sextant Correction Workforms

There is space on the sun, moon, planets, and star workforms to record the sex-

ALTITUDE CORRECTION TABLES 10°-90°—SUN, STARS, PLANETS

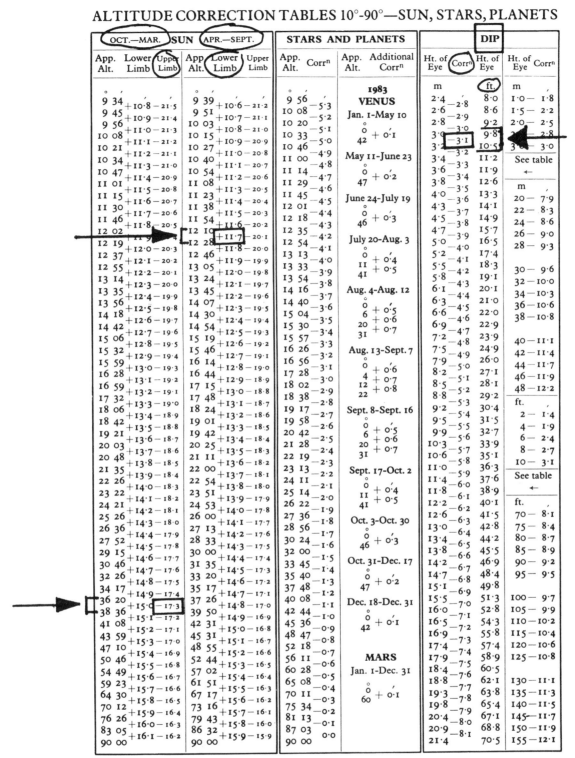

App. Alt. = Apparent altitude = Sextant altitude corrected for index error and dip.
For daylight observations of Venus, see pages 259 and 260.

Figure 5-11. Altitude tables for the sun, stars, and planets (10°-90°) with information marked for lower and upper limb sun sights. Note dip or height of eye table at the right. From the *Nautical Almanac*, 1983.

tant reading and all the corrections. The workforms also have handy reminders printed on them to help correct the sextant reading properly. The table, below, shows where to enter the data on the two workforms.

Data entry	Sun, Moon, Planet form, item	Star form, item
Sextant reading (Hs)	9	8
Instrument correction	10	9
Index correction	11	10
Dip correction	12	11
Apparent altitude (Ha)	13	12
Altitude corrections	14-18	13-14
Observed altitude (Ho)	19	15

PRACTICE PROBLEMS

The following problems will give you some practice applying the index correction, instrument correction, and dip correction to the sextant reading (Hs) to obtain the apparent altitude (Ha).

1. Hs 43°18.1'; index correction +3.0'; instrument correction −0.1'; height of eye 13.5 feet. Ha = _____

2. Hs 37°01.3'; index correction −2.6'; instrument correction +0.2'; height of eye 21.5 feet. Ha = _____

3. Hs 22°12.1'; index correction −1.1'; instrument correction +0.1'; height of eye 11 feet. Ha = _____

4. Hs 30°59.7'; index correction +2.4'; no instrument error; height of eye 17.5 feet. Ha = _____

5. Hs 44°22.0'; no index error; no instrument error; height of eye 26 feet. Ha = _____

ANSWERS

1. Ha 43°17.4'	2. Ha 36°54.4'
3. Ha 22°07.9'	4. Ha 30°58.0'
5. Ha 44°17.1'	

Altitude Correction Tables

The altitude correction tables, as noted earlier, correct the sextant reading for the bending of light rays as they pass through the earth's atmosphere. There are three separate tables: one for the sun; one for the stars and planets; and one for the moon. The sun, and star/planet tables are found on the inside front cover of the *Nautical Almanac* while the moon table is found on two pages inside the back cover. These tables have been reprinted in Appendix 2 of the book.

Altitude Corrections for the Sun

The altitude correction tables for the sun are found on the inside covers of the *Nautical Almanac*. The left table—for sights taken between 10° and 90°—is the table you will use almost everytime. If you were ever forced to take a low altitude sight where the sun is below 10°, use the table on the inside right cover of the almanac. In the 10° to 90° table, you use the left half for all sights taken between October and March and the right half for sights taken between April and September.

To enter the table, find the two apparent altitudes that bracket your apparent altitude. Just to the right of the apparent altitude column are two corrections: one for lower limb sights and one for upper limb sights. The correction for lower limb sights is added to the apparent altitude while the correction for upper limb sights is subtracted from the apparent altitude.

Examples: 1. You observed the lower limb of the sun on June 8, 1983 and obtained a sextant reading of 12°13.0'. Height of eye was 10.0 feet, index correction +2.1'; instrument error, zero. What is the observed altitude (Ho)?

2. You observed the upper limb of the sun on November 10, 1983 and obtained a sextant reading of 37°41.3'. Height of eye was 10.0 feet, index correction +1.7', in-

Sextant Corrections *Lower Limb*
—general

	Deg	Mins	Tenths
9. Sextant Reading (Hs)	12	13	0
10. Instrument Corr. (+ or −)		--	--
11. Index Correction (+ or −)		+2	1
12. Dip Correction for _10_ feet −)		−3	1
13. Total (Items 9-12) is Apparent Altitude (Ha). **Sextant corrections from inside front/ back covers of Almanac**	12	12	0
14. Altitude Correction (+ or −)		+11	7
15. Venus, Mars only, add'l correction (+ or −)		—	—
16. Moon only, Corr. for daily page HP: _____ (+)		—	—
17. Moon only, if *upper* limb −30′		—	—
18. Non-Standard conditions only, add'l Corr.		—	—
19. Total (Items 13-18) is Observed Altitude (Ho)	12	23	7

Sextant Corrections *Upper Limb*
—general

	Deg	Mins	Tenths
9. Sextant Reading (Hs)	37	41	3
10. Instrument Corr. (+ or −)		--	-
11. Index Correction (+ or −)		+1	7
12. Dip Correction for _10_ feet −)		−3	1
13. Total (Items 9-12) is Apparent Altitude (Ha). **Sextant corrections from inside front/ back covers of Almanac**	37	39	9
14. Altitude Correction (+ or −)		−17	3
15. Venus, Mars only, add'l correction (+ or −)		−	−
16. Moon only, Corr. for daily page HP: _____ (+)		—	—
17. Moon only, if *upper* limb −30′		−	−
18. Non-Standard conditions only, add'l Corr.		−	−
19. Total (Items 13-18) is Observed Altitude (Ho)	37	22	6

Figure 5-12. Sextant correction portion of workform filled out for sights of the lower and upper limb of the sun.

strument error zero. What is the observed altitude (Ho)?

Figure 5-11 is marked to show where the information was found in the altitude correction table. Figure 5-12 shows how the workforms were filled out.

Altitude Corrections for Stars and Planets

The altitude correction table for stars and planets is located just to the right of the sun table. Since stars and planets have no upper or lower limbs, this table is easy to use.

First, locate where the star or planet's apparent altitude fits between two apparent altitudes in the table. Then take the correction from the column to the right. Star and planet altitude corrections are subtracted from the apparent altitude.

The right side of the star/planet table provides an additional correction for observations of either Venus or Mars. To find this correction, locate the dates that include the date of observation, and then find the apparent altitudes that bracket the apparent altitude of the body. The corrections are given to the right of the apparent altitudes. Notice that the apparent altitudes here are very widely spaced, the corrections quite small, and that for some apparent altitudes there is no additional correction required.

Examples: 1. You observed Kochab (a star) on June 8, 1983. The sextant reading was 14°10.0′; index correction −3.1′; no instrument error, and height of eye 10 feet. What is the observed altitude (Ho)?

2. You observed Venus on June 4, 1983. The sextant reading was 44°28.9′. Height of eye was 10 feet, index correction −2.0′; no instrument error. What is the observed altitude (Ho)?

3. You observed Mars on June 3, 1983. The sextant reading was 28°35.6′.

ALTITUDE CORRECTION TABLES 10°-90°—SUN, STARS, PLANETS

SUN

OCT.—MAR. App. Alt.	Lower Limb	Upper Limb	APR.—SEPT. App. Alt.	Lower Limb	Upper Limb
° ′	′	′	° ′	′	′
9 34	+10·8	−21·5	9 39	+10·6	−21·2
9 45	+10·9	−21·4	9 51	+10·7	−21·1
9 56	+11·0	−21·3	10 03	+10·8	−21·0
10 08	+11·1	−21·2	10 15	+10·9	−20·9
10 21	+11·2	−21·1	10 27	+11·0	−20·8
10 34	+11·3	−21·0	10 40	+11·1	−20·7
10 47	+11·4	−20·9	10 54	+11·2	−20·6
11 01	+11·5	−20·8	11 08	+11·3	−20·5
11 15	+11·6	−20·7	11 23	+11·4	−20·4
11 30	+11·7	−20·6	11 38	+11·5	−20·3
11 46	+11·8	−20·5	11 54	+11·6	−20·2
12 02	+11·9	−20·4	12 10	+11·7	−20·1
12 19	+12·0	−20·3	12 28	+11·8	−20·0
12 37	+12·1	−20·2	12 46	+11·9	−19·9
12 55	+12·2	−20·1	13 05	+12·0	−19·8
13 14	+12·3	−20·0	13 24	[illegible]	[illegible]
13 35	+12·4	−19·9	13 45	+12·2	−19·6
13 56	+12·5	−19·8	14 07	+12·3	−19·5
14 18	+12·6	−19·7	14 30	+12·4	−19·4
14 42	+12·7	−19·6	14 54	+12·5	−19·3
15 06	+12·8	−19·5	15 19	+12·6	−19·2
15 32	+12·9	−19·4	15 46	+12·7	−19·1
15 59	+13·0	−19·3	16 14	+12·8	−19·0
16 28	+13·1	−19·2	16 44	+12·9	−18·9
16 59	+13·2	−19·1	17 15	+13·0	−18·8
17 32	+13·3	−19·0	17 48	+13·1	−18·7
18 06	+13·4	−18·9	18 24	+13·2	−18·6
18 42	+13·5	−18·8	19 01	+13·3	−18·5
19 21	+13·6	−18·7	19 42	+13·4	−18·4
20 03	+13·7	−18·6	20 25	+13·5	−18·3
20 48	+13·8	−18·5	21 11	+13·6	−18·2
21 35	+13·9	−18·4	22 00	+13·7	−18·1
22 26	+14·0	−18·3	22 54	+13·8	−18·0
23 22	+14·1	−18·2	23 51	+13·9	−17·9
24 21	+14·2	−18·1	24 53	+14·0	−17·8
25 26	+14·3	−18·0	26 00	+14·1	[illegible]
26 36	+14·4	−17·9	27 13	+14·2	−17·6
27 52	+14·5	−17·8	28 33	+14·3	−17·5
29 15	+14·6	−17·7	30 00	+14·4	−17·4
30 46	+14·7	−17·6	31 35	+14·5	−17·3
32 26	+14·8	−17·5	33 20	+14·6	−17·2
34 17	+14·9	−17·4	35 17	+14·7	−17·1
36 20	+15·0	−17·3	37 26	+14·8	−17·0
38 36	+15·1	−17·2	39 50	+14·9	[illegible]
41 08	+15·2	−17·1	42 31	+15·0	−16·8
43 59	+15·3	−17·0	45 31	+15·1	−16·7
47 10	+15·4	−16·9	48 55	+15·2	−16·6
50 46	+15·5	−16·8	52 44	+15·3	−16·5
54 49	+15·6	−16·7	57 02	+15·4	−16·4
59 23	+15·7	−16·6	61 51	+15·5	−16·3
64 30	+15·8	−16·5	67 17	+15·6	−16·2
70 12	+15·9	−16·4	73 16	+15·7	−16·1
76 26	+16·0	−16·3	79 43	+15·8	−16·0
83 05	+16·1	−16·2	86 32	+15·9	−15·9
90 00			90 00		

STARS AND PLANETS

App. Alt.	Corrⁿ
° ′	′
9 56	−5·3
10 08	−5·2
10 20	−5·1
10 33	−5·0
10 46	−4·9
11 00	−4·8
11 14	[illegible]
11 29	−4·6
11 45	−4·5
12 01	−4·4
12 18	−4·3
12 35	−4·2
12 54	−4·1
13 13	−4·0
13 33	−3·9
13 54	−3·8
14 16	−3·7
14 40	−3·6
15 04	−3·5
15 30	−3·4
15 57	−3·3
16 26	−3·2
16 56	−3·1
17 28	−3·0
18 02	−2·9
18 38	−2·8
19 17	−2·7
19 58	−2·6
20 42	−2·5
21 28	−2·4
22 19	−2·3
23 13	−2·2
24 11	−2·1
25 14	−2·0
26 22	−1·9
27 36	−1·8
28 56	−1·7
30 24	−1·6
32 00	−1·5
33 45	−1·4
35 40	−1·3
37 48	−1·2
40 08	−1·1
42 44	−1·0
45 36	−0·9
48 47	−0·8
52 18	−0·7
56 11	−0·6
60 28	−0·5
65 08	[illegible]
[illegible]	[illegible]
75 34	−0·2
81 13	−0·1
87 03	0·0
90 00	

App. Alt. — Additional Corrⁿ

1983 VENUS

Period	App. Alt.	Additional Corrⁿ
Jan. 1-May 10	0°–42	+ 0·1′
May 11-June 23	0°–47	+ 0·2
June 24-July 19	0°–46	+ 0·3′
July 20-Aug. 3	0°–11	+ 0·4′
	11–41	+ 0·5
Aug. 4-Aug. 12	0°–6	+ 0·5′
	6–20	+ 0·6
	20–31	+ 0·7
Aug. 13-Sept. 7	0°–4	+ 0·6′
	4–12	+ 0·7
	12–22	+ 0·8
Sept. 8-Sept. 16	0°–6	+ 0·5′
	6–20	+ 0·6
	20–31	+ 0·7
Sept. 17-Oct. 2	0°–11	+ 0·4′
	11–41	+ 0·5
Oct. 3-Oct. 30	0°–46	+ 0·3′
Oct. 31-Dec. 17	0°–47	+ 0·2′
Dec. 18-Dec. 31	0°–42	+ 0·1′

MARS

Period	App. Alt.	Additional Corrⁿ
Jan. 1-Dec. 31	0°–60	+ 0·1

DIP

Ht. of Eye (m)	Corrⁿ (′)	Ht. of Eye (ft.)
2·4	−2·8	8·0
2·6	−2·9	8·6
2·8	−3·0	9·2
3·0	−3·1	9·8
3·2	−3·2	10·5
3·4	−3·3	11·2
3·6	−3·4	11·9
3·8	−3·5	12·6
4·0	−3·6	13·3
4·3	−3·7	14·1
4·5	−3·8	14·9
4·7	−3·9	15·7
5·0	−4·0	16·5
5·2	−4·1	17·4
5·5	−4·2	18·3
5·8	−4·3	19·1
6·1	−4·4	20·1
6·3	−4·5	21·0
6·6	−4·6	22·0
6·9	−4·7	22·9
7·2	−4·8	23·9
7·5	−4·9	24·9
7·9	−5·0	26·0
8·2	−5·1	27·1
8·5	−5·2	28·1
8·8	−5·3	29·2
9·2	−5·4	30·4
9·5	−5·5	31·5
9·9	−5·6	32·7
10·3	−5·7	33·9
10·6	−5·8	35·1
11·0	−5·9	36·3
11·4	−6·0	37·6
11·8	−6·1	38·9
12·2	−6·2	40·1
12·6	−6·3	41·5
13·0	−6·4	42·8
13·4	−6·5	44·2
13·8	−6·6	45·5
14·2	−6·7	46·9
14·7	−6·8	48·4
15·1	−6·9	49·8
15·5	−7·0	51·3
16·0	−7·1	52·8
16·5	−7·2	54·3
16·9	−7·3	55·8
17·4	−7·4	57·4
17·9	−7·5	58·9
18·4	−7·6	60·5
18·8	−7·7	62·1
19·3	−7·8	63·8
19·8	−7·9	65·4
20·4	−8·0	67·1
20·9	−8·1	68·8
21·4		70·5

Ht. of Eye	Corrⁿ
m	′
1·0	− 1·8
1·5	− 2·2
2·0	− 2·5
2·5	− 2·8
3·0	− 3·0
See table ←	
m	′
20	− 7·9
22	− 8·3
24	− 8·6
26	− 9·0
28	− 9·3
30	− 9·6
32	− 10·0
34	− 10·3
36	− 10·6
38	− 10·8
40	− 11·1
42	− 11·4
44	− 11·7
46	− 11·9
48	− 12·2
ft.	′
2	− 1·4
4	− 1·9
6	− 2·4
8	− 2·7
10	− 3·1
See table ←	
ft.	′
70	− 8·1
75	− 8·4
80	− 8·7
85	− 8·9
90	− 9·2
95	− 9·5
100	− 9·7
105	− 9·9
110	− 10·2
115	− 10·4
120	− 10·6
125	− 10·8
130	− 11·1
135	− 11·3
140	− 11·5
145	− 11·7
150	− 11·9
155	− 12·1

App. Alt. = Apparent altitude = Sextant altitude corrected for index error and dip.
For daylight observations of Venus, see pages 259 and 260.

Figure 5-13. Altitude tables for the sun, stars, and planets (10°-90°) with information marked for star, and Venus and Mars sights. Note additional corrections for Venus and Mars. From the *Nautical Almanac*, 1983.

Sextant Corrections VENUS

—general

	Deg	Mins	Tenths
9. Sextant Reading (Hs)	44	28	9
10. Instrument Corr. (+ or −)		−	−
11. Index Correction (+ or −)		−2	0
12. Dip Correction for __10__ feet −)		−3	1
13. Total (Items 9-12) is Apparent Altitude (Ha).	44	23	8

Sextant corrections from inside front/ back covers of Almanac

	Deg	Mins	Tenths
14. Altitude Correction (+ or −)		−1	0
15. (Venus) Mars only, add'l correction (+ or −)		+0	2
16. Moon only, Corr. for daily page HP: ____ (+)		—	
17. Moon only, if upper limb −30′		—	
18. Non-Standard conditions only, add'l Corr.		—	
19. Total (Items 13-18) is Observed Altitude (Ho)	44	23	0

Sextant Corrections MARS

—general

	Deg	Mins	Tenths
9. Sextant Reading (Hs)	28	35	6
10. Instrument Corr. (+ or −)		−0	2
11. Index Correction (+ or −)		+1	2
12. Dip Correction for __10__ feet −)		−3	1
13. Total (Items 9-12) is Apparent Altitude (Ha).	28	33	5

Sextant corrections from inside front/ back covers of Almanac

	Deg	Mins	Tenths
14. Altitude Correction (+ or −)		−1	8
15. Venus, Mars only, add'l correction (+ or −)		+0	1
16. Moon only, Corr. for daily page HP: ____ (+)		—	
17. Moon only, if upper limb −30′		—	
18. Non-Standard conditions only, add'l Corr.		—	
19. Total (Items 13-18) is Observed Altitude (Ho)	28	31	8

KOCHAB

Sextant Corrections—general

	Deg	Min	Tenths
8. Sextant Reading (Hs)	14	10	0
9. Instrument Corr. (+ or −)		−	−
10. Index Correction (+ or −)		−3	1
11. Dip Correction for __10__ feet (−)		−3	1
12. Total (Items 8-11) is Apparent Altitude (Ha).	14	03	8

Sextant corrections from inside front cover of Almanac

	Deg	Min	Tenths
13. Altitude Correction (+ or −)		−3	8
14. Additional Correction for Non-Standard Conditions		−	−
15. Total (Items 12-14) is Observed Altitude (Ho)	14	00	0

Figure 5-14. Sextant correction workform filled out for sights of Kochab, Venus, and Mars.

Height of eye was 10 feet, index correction +1.2′; instrument correction −0.2′. What is the observed altitude (Ho)?

Figure 5-13 is marked to show where the information was found in the altitude correction table. Figure 5-14 shows how the sextant correction part of the workforms was filled out.

Altitude Corrections for the Moon

The altitude corrections for the moon are found on two pages inside the back cover of the *Nautical Almanac*. Since there are always at least two altitude corrections for the moon, and because these tables are laid out differently than the others, take a close look at them.

On the left-hand page there are tables to use for sights between 0° and 35° and on the right-hand page there are tables to use for sights between 35° and 90°. Each page contains two separate tables. The top table gives you corrections for various apparent altitudes while the bottom table provides a correction for the horizontal parallax or HP value found in the daily pages. In the top table there are columns of corrections for every 5° of apparent altitude.

First, find the column headings in the top table that contain the whole degree of your apparent altitude. For example, if your apparent altitude was 17°24.0′ you would look in the 0°-35° table and use the column headed 15°-19°. Then go down the column until you reach the 17° portion. Under the 17° section, there are six altitude corrections—one for every 10′ of apparent altitude. By glancing at the side margins of the table, you find the minutes of apparent altitude that is closest to your apparent altitude. In this case, the 24.0 minutes of apparent altitude is closest to 20′. Therefore, you would use

62.6 as the first altitude correction. All corrections from the moon table are added to the apparent altitude.

Assume that your example sight was a lower limb observation taken at 12 hours 11 minutes 05 seconds on June 4, 1983. To find the correction from the lower table, you first obtain the HP of the moon from the moon column of the daily pages for 12 hours on June 4, 1983. The HP of the moon for that time is 55.0′. This is recorded on the line outside the box on the workform at item 16. In the second half of the table, you go down the 15°-19° column until you line up with the closest daily page HP value on the left or right side. The L column has corrections for lower limb sights and the U column has corrections for upper limb sights. In this case, the closest HP value to 55.0′ is 54.9′, and the sight is a lower limb, so you use the correction in the 15°-19° column from the lower portion of the table across from the HP of 54.9′. The correction, 1.6′, is also added to the apparent altitude.

Unless the sight was an upper limb, you are finished with the altitude corrections for the sight. As the workform and written instructions in the *Nautical Almanac* indicate, if you observed the upper limb you would subtract 30′ from the apparent altitude. This last correction is applied in addition to the other corrections.

Examples: 1. You observed the lower limb of the moon on June 4, 1983 at 23 hours 06 minutes 10 seconds GMT. There was no instrument error, the index correction was +2.0′, and your height of eye was 10 feet. The sextant reading was 31°55.6′. Locate the daily page HP value, and apply the altitude corrections to obtain the observed altitude (Ho). Figures 5-15 and 5-16 are marked to show where the information was found in the moon altitude table and how the workform was filled out.

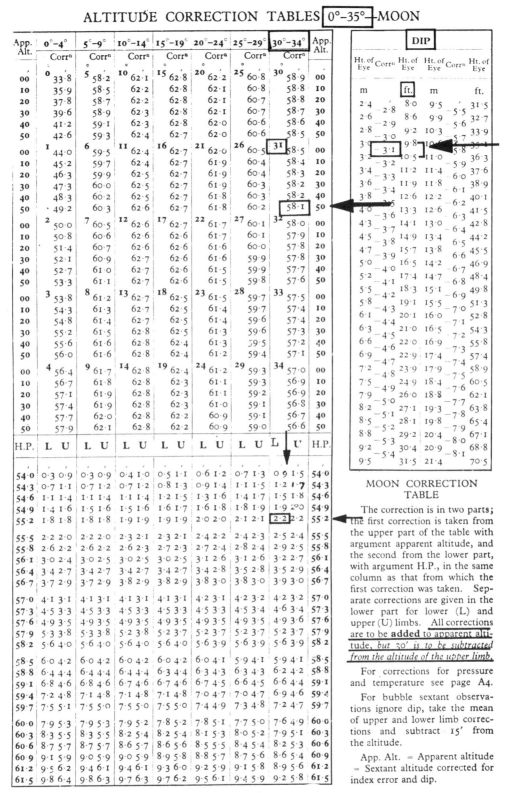

Figure 5-15. Altitude tables 0°-35° for the moon marked to show where information for a lower limb sight is found. From the *Nautical Almanac*, 1983.

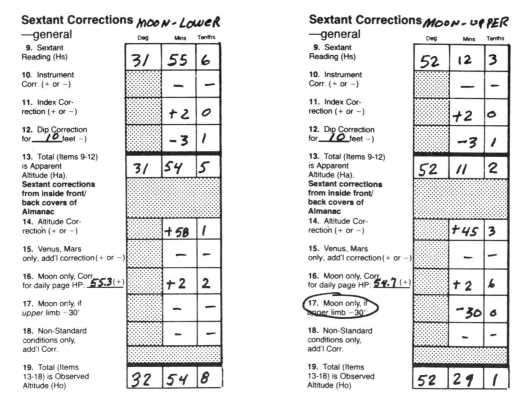

Figure 5-16. Sextant correction portion of the workform filled out for a lower limb and an upper limb sight of the moon.

2. You observed the upper limb of the moon on June 3, 1983 at 22 hours 43 minutes 10 seconds GMT. There was no instrument error, the index correction was +2.0′, and your height of eye was 10 feet. The sextant reading was 52°12.3′. Locate the daily page HP value and apply the altitude corrections to obtain the observed altitude (Ho). Figures 5-17 and 5-16 are marked to show where the information was found in the moon altitude table and how the workform was filled out.

Non-standard Conditions

The standard altitude correction tables for the sun, stars, planets, and the moon take into account the effect of normal temperatures and barometric pressures on the sextant reading.

On the rarest of occasions, you may take a sight where there are extremely high or low temperatures, or extremely high or low barometric pressures. You will find a special altitude correction table for these conditions—and instructions for using it—on page A-4 of the *Nautical Almanac*. The correction for non-standard conditions is entered on item 18 of the sun, moon, planet workform and item 14 of the star workform.

PRACTICE PROBLEMS *(Refer to Appendix 2)*

Given the following information, find the observed altitude (Ho) for these sights:

1. Sun, upper limb. April 12, 1983. Hs 37°12.0′; index correction −2.3′; instrument correction +0.2′; height of eye 11 feet.

2. Sun, lower limb. April 4, 1983. Hs 32°11.6′; index correction +2.0′; no instrument error; height of eye 27.6 feet.

3. Jupiter, May 5, 1983. Hs 33°36.7′; index correction −3.0′; no instrument error; height of eye 30.5 feet.

ALTITUDE CORRECTION TABLES 35°–90°—MOON

App. Alt.	35°–39°	40°–44°	45°–49°	50°–54°	55°–59°	60°–64°	65°–69°	70°–74°	75°–79°	80°–84°	85°–89°	App. Alt.
	Corrⁿ	Corrⁿ	Corrⁿ	Corrⁿ	Corrⁿ	Corrⁿ	Corrⁿ	Corrⁿ	Corrⁿ	Corrⁿ	Corrⁿ	
00	35 56.5	40 53.7	45 50.5	50 46.9	55 43.1	60 38.9	65 34.6	70 30.1	75 25.3	80 20.5	85 15.6	00
10	56.4	53.6	50.4	46.8	42.9	38.8	34.4	29.9	25.2	20.4	15.5	10
20	56.3	53.5	50.2	46.7	42.8	38.7	34.3	29.7	25.0	20.2	15.3	20
30	56.2	53.4	50.1	46.5	42.7	38.5	34.1	29.6	24.9	20.0	15.1	30
40	56.2	53.3	50.0	46.4	42.5	38.4	34.0	29.4	24.7	19.9	15.0	40
50	56.1	53.2	49.9	46.3	42.4	38.2	33.8	29.3	24.5	19.7	14.8	50
00	36 56.0	41 53.1	46 49.8	51 46.2	56 42.3	61 38.1	66 33.7	71 29.1	76 24.4	81 19.6	86 14.6	00
10	55.9	53.0	49.7	46.0	42.1	37.9	33.5	29.0	24.2	19.4	14.5	10
20	55.8	52.8	49.5	45.9	42.0	37.8	33.4	28.8	24.1	19.2	14.3	20
30	55.7	52.7	49.4	45.8	41.8	37.7	33.2	28.7	23.9	19.1	14.1	30
40	55.6	52.6	49.3	45.7	41.7	37.5	33.1	28.5	23.8	18.9	14.0	40
50	55.5	52.5	49.2	45.5	41.6	37.4	32.9	28.3	23.6	18.7	13.8	50
00	37 55.4	42 52.4	47 49.1	52 45.4	57 41.4	62 37.2	67 32.8	72 28.2	77 23.4	82 18.6	87 13.7	00
10	55.3	52.3	49.0	45.3	41.3	37.1	32.6	28.0	23.3	18.4	13.5	10
20	55.2	52.2	48.8	45.2	41.2	36.9	32.5	27.9	23.1	18.2	13.3	20
30	55.1	52.1	48.7	45.0	41.0	36.8	32.3	27.7	22.9	18.1	13.2	30
40	55.0	52.0	48.6	44.9	40.9	36.6	32.2	27.6	22.8	17.9	13.0	40
50	55.0	51.9	48.5	44.8	40.8	36.5	32.0	27.4	22.6	17.8	12.8	50
00	38 54.9	43 51.8	48 48.4	53 44.6	58 40.6	63 36.4	68 31.9	73 27.2	78 22.5	83 17.6	88 12.7	00
10	54.8	51.7	48.2	44.5	40.5	36.2	31.7	27.1	22.3	17.4	12.5	10
20	54.7	51.6	48.1	44.4	40.3	36.1	31.6	26.9	22.1	17.3	12.3	20
30	54.6	51.5	48.0	44.2	40.2	35.9	31.4	26.8	22.0	17.1	12.2	30
40	54.5	51.4	47.9	44.1	40.1	35.8	31.3	26.6	21.8	16.9	12.0	40
50	54.4	51.2	47.8	44.0	39.9	35.6	31.1	26.5	21.7	16.8	11.8	50
00	39 54.3	44 51.1	49 47.6	54 43.9	59 39.8	64 35.5	69 31.0	74 26.3	79 21.5	84 16.6	89 11.7	00
10	54.2	51.0	47.5	43.7	39.6	35.3	30.8	26.1	21.3	16.5	11.5	10
20	54.1	50.9	47.4	43.6	39.5	35.2	30.7	26.0	21.2	16.3	11.4	20
30	54.0	50.8	47.3	43.5	39.4	35.0	30.5	25.8	21.0	16.1	11.2	30
40	53.9	50.7	47.2	43.3	39.2	34.9	30.4	25.7	20.9	16.0	11.0	40
50	53.8	50.6	47.0	43.2	39.1	34.7	30.2	25.5	20.7	15.8	10.9	50

H.P.	L U	L U	L U	L U	L U	L U	L U	L U	L U	L U	L U	H.P.
54.0	1.1 1.7	1.3 1.9	1.5 2.1	1.7 2.4	2.0 2.6	2.3 2.9	2.6 3.2	2.9 3.5	3.2 3.8	3.5 4.1	3.8 4.5	54.0
54.3	1.4 1.8	1.6 2.0	1.8 2.2	2.0 2.5	2.3 2.7	2.5 3.0	2.8 3.2	3.0 3.5	3.3 3.8	3.6 4.1	3.9 4.4	54.3
54.6	1.7 2.0	1.9 2.2	2.1 2.4	2.3 2.6	2.5 2.8	2.7 3.0	3.0 3.3	3.2 3.5	3.5 3.8	3.7 4.1	4.0 4.3	54.6
54.9	2.0 2.2	2.2 2.3	2.3 2.5	2.5 2.7	2.7 2.9	2.9 3.1	3.2 3.3	3.4 3.5	3.6 3.8	3.9 4.0	4.1 4.3	54.9
55.2	2.3 2.3	2.5 2.4	2.6 2.6	2.8 2.8	3.0 2.9	3.2 3.1	3.4 3.3	3.6 3.5	3.8 3.7	4.0 4.0	4.2 4.2	55.2
55.5	2.7 2.5	2.8 2.6	2.9 2.7	3.1 2.9	3.2 3.0	3.4 3.2	3.6 3.4	3.7 3.5	3.9 3.7	4.1 3.9	4.3 4.1	55.5
55.8	3.0 2.6	3.1 2.7	3.2 2.8	3.3 3.0	3.5 3.1	3.6 3.3	3.8 3.4	3.9 3.6	4.1 3.7	4.2 3.9	4.4 4.0	55.8
56.1	3.3 2.8	3.4 2.9	3.5 3.0	3.6 3.1	3.7 3.2	3.8 3.3	4.0 3.4	4.1 3.6	4.2 3.7	4.3 3.8	4.5 4.0	56.1
56.4	3.6 2.9	3.7 3.0	3.8 3.1	3.9 3.2	3.9 3.3	4.0 3.4	4.1 3.5	4.3 3.6	4.4 3.7	4.5 3.8	4.6 3.9	56.4
56.7	3.9 3.1	4.0 3.1	4.1 3.2	4.1 3.3	4.2 3.3	4.3 3.4	4.3 3.5	4.4 3.6	4.5 3.7	4.6 3.8	4.7 3.8	56.7
57.0	4.3 3.2	4.3 3.3	4.3 3.3	4.4 3.4	4.4 3.4	4.5 3.5	4.5 3.5	4.6 3.6	4.7 3.6	4.7 3.7	4.8 3.8	57.0
57.3	4.6 3.4	4.6 3.4	4.6 3.4	4.6 3.5	4.7 3.5	4.7 3.5	4.7 3.6	4.8 3.6	4.8 3.7	4.8 3.7	4.9 3.7	57.3
57.6	4.9 3.6	4.9 3.6	4.9 3.6	4.9 3.6	4.9 3.6	4.9 3.6	4.9 3.6	5.0 3.6	5.0 3.6	5.0 3.6	5.0 3.6	57.6
57.9	5.2 3.7	5.2 3.7	5.2 3.7	5.2 3.7	5.2 3.7	5.1 3.6	5.1 3.6	5.1 3.6	5.1 3.6	5.1 3.6	5.1 3.6	57.9
58.2	5.5 3.9	5.5 3.8	5.5 3.8	5.4 3.8	5.4 3.7	5.4 3.7	5.3 3.7	5.3 3.6	5.2 3.6	5.2 3.5	5.2 3.5	58.2
58.5	5.9 4.0	5.8 4.0	5.8 3.9	5.7 3.9	5.6 3.8	5.6 3.8	5.5 3.7	5.5 3.6	5.4 3.6	5.3 3.5	5.3 3.4	58.5
58.8	6.2 4.2	6.1 4.1	6.0 4.1	6.0 4.0	5.9 3.9	5.8 3.8	5.7 3.7	5.6 3.6	5.5 3.5	5.4 3.5	5.3 3.4	58.8
59.1	6.5 4.3	6.4 4.3	6.3 4.2	6.2 4.1	6.1 4.0	6.0 3.9	5.9 3.8	5.8 3.6	5.7 3.5	5.6 3.4	5.4 3.3	59.1
59.4	6.8 4.5	6.7 4.4	6.5 4.2	6.4 4.1	6.2 3.9	6.1 3.8	6.0 3.7	5.8 3.5	5.7 3.4	5.5 3.2	5.4 3.2	59.4
59.7	7.1 4.6	7.0 4.5	6.9 4.4	6.8 4.3	6.6 4.1	6.5 4.0	6.3 3.8	6.2 3.7	6.0 3.5	5.8 3.3	5.6 3.2	59.7
60.0	7.5 4.8	7.3 4.7	7.2 4.5	7.0 4.4	6.9 4.2	6.7 4.0	6.5 3.9	6.3 3.7	6.1 3.5	5.9 3.3	5.7 3.1	60.0
60.3	7.8 5.0	7.6 4.8	7.5 4.7	7.3 4.5	7.1 4.3	6.9 4.1	6.7 3.9	6.5 3.7	6.3 3.5	6.0 3.2	5.8 3.0	60.3
60.6	8.1 5.1	7.9 5.0	7.7 4.8	7.6 4.6	7.3 4.4	7.1 4.2	6.9 3.9	6.7 3.7	6.4 3.4	6.2 3.2	5.9 2.9	60.6
60.9	8.4 5.3	8.2 5.1	8.0 4.9	7.8 4.7	7.6 4.5	7.3 4.2	7.1 4.0	6.8 3.7	6.6 3.4	6.3 3.2	6.0 2.9	60.9
61.2	8.7 5.4	8.5 5.2	8.3 5.0	8.1 4.8	7.8 4.5	7.6 4.3	7.3 4.0	7.0 3.7	6.7 3.4	6.4 3.1	6.1 2.8	61.2
61.5	9.1 5.6	8.8 5.4	8.6 5.1	8.3 4.9	8.1 4.6	7.8 4.3	7.5 4.0	7.2 3.7	6.9 3.4	6.5 3.1	6.2 2.7	61.5

xxxv

Figure 5-17. Altitude tables 35°-90° for the moon marked to show where information for an upper limb sight is found. In addition to the other corrections, 30 minutes is subtracted from the altitude of the moon for upper limb sights.

4. Venus, July 20, 1983. Hs 44°12.9'; index correction +2.7'; no instrument error; height of eye 41 feet.

5. Mars, November 24, 1983. Hs 40°03.2'; index correction −1.1'; instrument correction −0.2'; height of eye 9.3 feet.

6. Moon, upper limb. Hs 31°20.7'; index correction −3.1'; no instrument error; height of eye 14 feet. Date: June 4, 1983. GMT 06 hours 31 minutes 10 seconds.

7. Moon, lower limb. Hs 29°38.5'; index correction, +2.2'; instrument correction −0.3';

height of eye 8 feet. Date: June 4, 1983. GMT 07 hours 13 minutes 12 seconds.

8. Kochab (a star), April 18, 1983. Hs 46°28.4'; index correction −1.6'; instrument correction +0.1'; height of eye 12 feet.

ANSWERS

1. 36°49.6'   2. 32°23.0'   3. 33°26.8'
4. 44°08.4'   5. 39°57.8'   6. 31°44.4'
7. 30°38.5'   8. 46°22.6'

6

Using H. O. 229
(Time: 2 Hours)

The H. O. 229 table, published by the U.S. government and available from nautical supply stores, is the most useful and most accurate table in existence for solving celestial navigation problems. Six volumes cover the world:

Volume I covers latitudes 0°-15°
Volume II covers latitudes 15°-30°
Volume III covers latitudes 30°-45°
Volume IV covers latitudes 45°-60°
Volume V covers latitudes 60°-75°
Volume VI covers latitudes 75°-90°

All problems in this book can be solved using the almanac reprints in Appendix 2 and Volume III of H. O. 229 covering latitudes 30°-45°. Since all volumes follow the same format, once Volume III of H. O. 229 is mastered, you can work with any other volume.

Each volume covers the given latitudes both north and south of the equator. Thus Volume III could be used to solve problems for latitudes 30°-45° north or south. The H. O. 229 tables contain precomputed solutions to celestial problems. There is a solution for every whole degree of latitude and every 30' of longi-

tude in the table. What you must do is find the solution from the table that is closest to your DR position. You do this by rounding off the DR latitude to the nearest whole degree and assuming a longitude within + or − 30' of the DR longitude which permits you to conveniently enter the table.

In this part of the book, you will learn how to use the information from the left-hand column of the workform to enter the H. O. 229 tables and solve complete celestial problems.

As the workform indicates, there are seven steps required:

Step 1 involves adjusting the DR longitude and combining it with the GHA of the body in such a way that a local hour angle (LHA), which is a whole degree, is obtained. To do this you must learn what the LHA is, and how to select the correct assumed longitude.

Step 2 organizes the data for entering the H. O. 229 tables. Here, you must learn how the tables are laid out and how to enter the table with

LHA diagram, west longitude
LHA = 135°

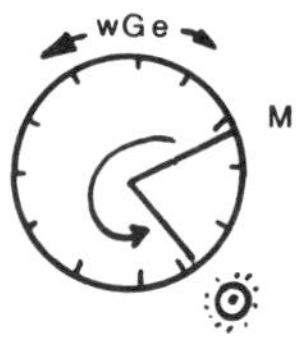

LHA diagram, east longitude
LHA = 285°

Figure 6-1. LHA diagrams are used to visualize the relationship between your DR longitude and the GHA of the body. *Top*, shows west longitude (LHA = 135°); and *bottom*, east longitude (LHA = 285°).

the LHA, whole degrees of declination, and the DR latitude rounded to the nearest whole degree.

Step 3 involves obtaining the data you need from the main body of the table.

Step 4 requires you to learn how to adjust the data from the main body of the table using the "interpolation" tables in the front and back covers of H. O. 229.

Step 5 is used to compute the true direction of the GP of the celestial body from the assumed position, which is simply the DR position adjusted to enter the table.

Step 6 compares the computed angle from the H. O. 229 table with the corrected sextant angle to obtain the intercept.

Step 7 simply organizes all the data you need to construct the celestial line of position on the chart including the assumed position, intercept, and azimuth.

The left-hand side of the H. O. 229 workform organizes all the information

you need to work a sight including the DR position, sextant corrections, and almanac data. The right-hand side of the workform guides you through the seven-step process of using the H. O. 229 table. Whenever you need information from the left-hand side of the form, the instructions on the right-hand side will contain an item reference number. For example, if the right-hand side instructions asked you to: enter DR latitude (number 7), you would enter the DR latitude from item seven on the left-hand side of the form. If the information you need is already in the right-hand column, a step reference number will help you find it.

Step 1, Local Hour Angle and Assumed Longitude

The main body of the H. O. 229 tables are entered using three numbers, two of which you already know:

> DR latitude, rounded to the nearest whole degree
> Declination, whole degrees (not rounded)

The third number you need to enter the table is a combination of two numbers you already know:

> GHA of the body, and,
> Your DR longitude

The "combining" of GHA and your DR longitude gives you the Local Hour Angle or LHA. The LHA is the number of degrees between the observer's longitude, measured west, to the celestial body.

The rule for obtaining LHA from GHA and longitude is:

West longitude: Subtract the DR longitude from the GHA of the body. (If your DR longitude exceeds the GHA, place a minus sign before the difference and algebraically add 360° to the result.)

East longitude: Add your DR longitude to the GHA of the body. (If your total is over 360° subtract 360°.)

LHA diagram: The LHA diagram at the top right-hand side of the workform is used to visually work out your approximate LHA. This diagram is similar to the time diagrams you are already familiar with. The capital G at the top represents Greenwich; the dotted line down the center separates east and west longitudes. The arrows W and E represent westerly and easterly directions. To construct an LHA diagram first locate your own DR longitude using the symbol M; then locate the GHA of the body. Remember, GHA is measured west from Greenwich through a complete 360° circle. The LHA represents the angle, and the distance in degrees, from your DR longitude (M) measured westward to the body. The LHA diagram is constructed using rounded (whole degree) numbers. It is a visual aid useful in checking your precise LHA calculations for gross error.

Examples: 1. LHA diagram, west longitude. Your DR longitude is 75°05.1′W and the GHA of the body is 210°27.1′. Construct the LHA diagram.

2. LHA diagram, east longitude. Your DR longitude is 75°05.1′E and the GHA of the body is 210°27.1′. Construct the LHA diagram. Figure 6-1 shows how the LHA diagrams should look. The LHA for west longitude is approximately 135°; the LHA for east longitude is approximately 285°.

PRACTICE PROBLEMS

Using the information below, construct an LHA diagram and obtain the approximate LHA for the following:

1. DR longitude 76°41′W; GHA 310°21.4′
2. DR longitude 110°W; GHA 30°08.7′
3. DR longitude 154°W; GHA 191°19.4′
4. DR longitude 81°12.3′E; GHA 43°13.2′
5. DR longitude 32°15.4′E; GHA 274°11.4′

6. DR longitude 121°12′E; GHA 312°17.1′

ANSWERS

1. 233° 2. 280° 3. 37°
4. 124° 5. 306° 6. 73°

LHA Workform

The right-hand side of the H. O. 229 workform, step 1, is laid out according to the rules for combining the GHA and DR longitude to produce the LHA. In step 1, you first enter the GHA in the east or west longitude block. However, in order to obtain an LHA in whole degrees which is also within + or − 30′ of your DR longitude, you must "assume" a longitude. In order to obtain an LHA in whole degrees, when combined with the GHA, the assumed longitude must cancel out or eliminate the minutes and tenths of GHA. This is done solely for the convenience of entering the H. O. 229 tables, since the tables can only be entered with a whole degree of LHA. By following the workform, and the step-by-step instructions that follow, you will assume the correct longitude and obtain the solution from H. O. 229 that is closest to your DR position.

To determine the assumed longitude, you start with the DR longitude then subtract 30′. When you have this number, add 1° to the result. As the workform indicates, you now have two longitude numbers that form a range. One number is 30′ higher than your DR longitude and one number is 30′ lower than your DR longitude. Now look at the minutes and tenths of GHA and select an assumed longitude that (a) lies within the range, and (b) combines with GHA in such a way as to cancel out the minutes and tenths to produce an LHA in whole degrees.

At first, this may seem like a complex task. However, when you break it down into steps, it is very easy.

Example for west longitude: Your DR longitude is 75°05.1'W and the GHA is 210°27.1'. What is the assumed longitude and LHA?

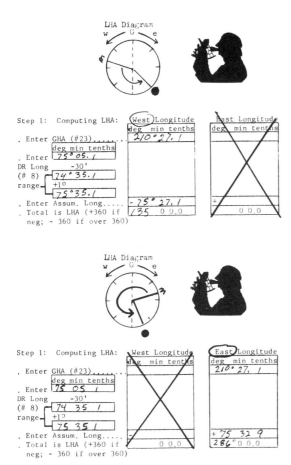

Figure 6-2. LHA diagrams and LHA portion of workform filled out for west and east longitudes.

Figure 6-2 shows how the range was calculated and how the GHA was entered in the west section of the form. Since the rule requires you to subtract the assumed longitude from GHA if you are in west longitude, the only way to "eliminate" or cancel out the 27.1' minutes and tenths of GHA is to subtract 27.1'. Therefore, the minutes and tenths of assumed longitude must be 27.1'. Then look at the range to determine which whole degree, 75° or 74°, you can use with the 27.1' and still stay within the range.

You cannot use 74°27.1' because it is too low. The assumed longitude cannot be lower than 74°35.1' or higher than 75°35.1'. You can, however, use 75°27.1' because it "fits" within the boundaries of the range of acceptable assumed longitudes. As Figure 6-2 indicates, the LHA is 135°.

In west longitude, you must be careful if the assumed longitude is greater than the GHA. For example, suppose you had a GHA of 31°21.0' and an assumed longitude of 71°21.0'W. The difference would be a −40°. Since you cannot have a negative LHA, you must add 360° to the negative 40° to obtain the LHA of 320°.

Example for east longitude: Your DR longitude is 75°05.1'E; and the GHA is 210°27.1°. What is the assumed longitude and LHA?

Figure 6-2 shows how the range was calculated and how the GHA was entered in the east section of the workform. In east longitude the rule requires you to add the assumed longitude to the GHA in order to cancel out or "eliminate" the minutes and tenths of GHA. To do this, use a number that when added to the GHA minutes and tenths totals 60 minutes. That way, the 60' in the minutes, tenths column can be "eliminated" by simply adding 1° to the degrees column. To find out what number you have to add to the GHA minutes and tenths you subtract the GHA minutes and tenths from 60'. In our example, we need to get rid of 27.1'. By subtracting 27.1' from 60' we obtain 32.9'. We now know that the minutes and tenths of assumed longitude which—when added to the GHA minutes, tenths—will total 60' is 32.9°. By looking at the whole degrees of longitude from the range we find that we cannot use 74° because 74°32.9' is below 74°35.1' and outside the range. You can however, use 75° as the whole degrees of assumed longitude because 75°32.9' "fits" within the parameters of the range of acceptable assumed longitudes. As Figure 6-2 indicates, the LHA is 286°. (Remember, add 1° to the degrees column because the minutes column totals 60′.)

PRACTICE PROBLEMS

Use the following information to compute the assumed longitude and LHA:

1. DR longitude 74°59.1′W; GHA 271°15.8′
2. DR longitude 76°18.0′W; GHA 29°18.4′
3. DR longitude 129°14.2′W; GHA 318°49.3′
4. DR longitude 110°14.1′E; GHA 44°18.6′
5. DR longitude 171°15.0′E; GHA 321°41.2′
6. DR longitude 140°31.4′E; GHA 268°12.4′

ANSWERS

1. Assumed longitude 75°15.8′W; LHA 196°
2. Assumed longitude 76°18.4′W; LHA 313°
3. Assumed longitude 128°49.3′W; LHA 190°
4. Assumed longitude 110°41.4′E; LHA 155°
5. Assumed longitude 171°18.8′E; LHA 133°
6. Assumed longitude 140°47.6′E; LHA 49°

Step 2, Data for Entering the H. O. 229 Table

The H. O. 229 table is entered with three numbers, all of which are in whole degrees.

The Local Hour Angle (LHA)
The DR latitude, rounded to the nearest whole degree
The declination, whole degrees, as given in the almanac

Remember, when rounding the DR latitude, there are 60′ in a degree. Therefore, if there are 30′ or more in the DR latitude, round up to the next whole degree. The declination is not rounded to enter H. O. 229. You should use the whole

degrees from the workform exactly as they came from the *Nautical Almanac*. In step 2, circle the appropriate N or S to the right of the latitude and declination entries to indicate whether they are north or south. If both the latitude and declination are north, or both south, circle the word same. If one is north, and the other south, circle the word contrary.

Figure 6-3 shows two workforms correctly filled out: one where declination and latitude are same and one where declination and latitude are contrary.

Figure 6-3. Data for entering H.O. 229 recorded on workform, for example, where latitude and declination are same, and contrary.

Step 3, Obtaining Data from H. O. 229 *(Refer to Vol. III, H. O. 229)*

Each volume of H. O. 229 is really two separate volumes bound in one. Part one of Volume III, pages 1-183, gives solutions for latitudes 30° to 37° inclusive. Part two, pages 184-365, gives solutions for latitudes 38° to 45° inclusive. Appendix 3 shows the layout of the H. O. 229 tables with the main body in the middle and the interpolation tables inside the front and back covers. Appendix 3 was extracted from H. O. 229, Volume III.

The first step in using H. O. 229 is to locate the half of the table that contains the whole degrees of latitude you are working with. For example, assume your

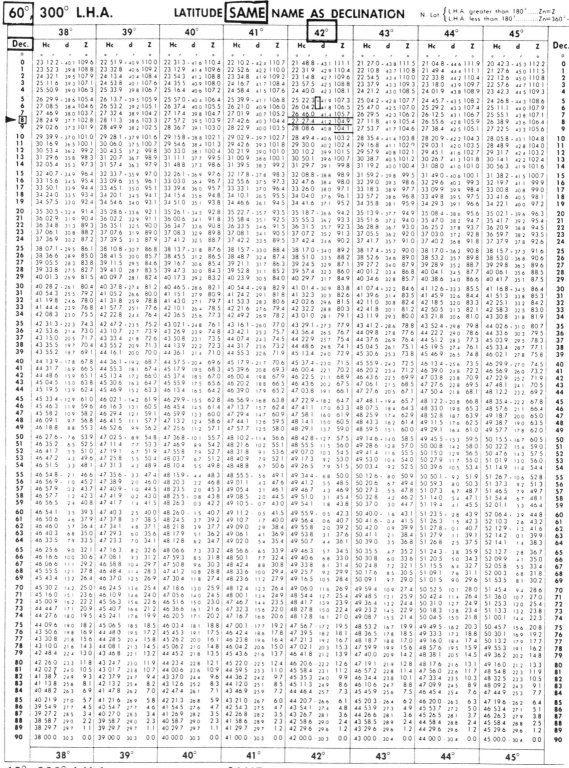

Figure 6-4. Extracted from H.O. 229, Volume III. LHA 60° and 300°; SAME, for latitudes 38°-45°.

latitude is 42°N. This means you will be working with part 2 of Volume III pages 184-365 with solutions for latitudes 38° to 45°.

The next step is to locate the page that corresponds to the LHA. Assume your LHA is 300°. In H. O. 229 LHA's are listed in pairs in bold type at the top and bottom of each page. Figure 6-4 shows a typical left-hand page listing solutions for two LHA's, in this case 60° and 300°, where the latitude is the same name as declination. Figure 6-5 shows a typical right-hand page which also contains solutions for LHA's of 60° and 300° but where latitude is contrary to declination. Partway down the right-hand page, you'll find some ruled lines. This is the contrary/same line. Solutions below the line are for the two LHA's at the bottom of the right-hand page, in this case LHA's 120° and 240°. As this section is labelled with the bold face type notation SAME these solutions are also for situations where the latitude and declination have the same name.

PRACTICE PROBLEMS

Use the information below to locate the correct page of H. O. 229 Volume III. If left-hand page, record page number. If right-hand page, indicate page number and right top (contrary) or right bottom (same).

1. LHA 76°; latitude 36°N; declination 29°N.
2. LHA 76°; latitude 36°S; declination 1°N.
3. LHA 256°; latitude 36°N; declination 29°N.
4. LHA 357°; latitude 31°S; declination 18°N.
5. LHA 55°; latitude 37°N; declination 14°S.
6. LHA 171°; latitude 42°N; declination 54°N.

ANSWERS

1. 154   2. 155, right top
3. 155, right bottom   4. 9, right top
5. 113, right top   6. 203, right bottom

Recording Data from the Table

Assume you need the data from the table for:

LHA 300°; latitude 42°N; declination 8°N. (Latitude & Declination Same)

Figure 6-4 is marked to show where the data was found in the table. Then the information is recorded in step 3 of the workform. In this case, you entered the table from the top with the whole degrees of latitude, and from the side with the whole degrees of declination.

The following information was recorded from the table:

The computed altitude (Hc). Here Hc was 27°27.4'.

The d number with its sign. The sign is given intermittently throughout the table. If there is no sign beside the d number, take the sign immediately above it. In about 1 out of 100 sights, the d number in the table is followed by an asterisk (*). When this happens, record the d numbers above and below the d from the table. Obtain the difference between the d above and below the tabulated d. Here d was +41.2'.

The Z number or Z. In addition to the tabulated Z record the Z immediately below the Z in the table. Obtain the difference and write it on the Z difference line. If the Z is increasing as you go down the table circle the increasing as a reminder; if the Z is decreasing as you go down the table circle the decreasing as a reminder. Here, Z was 104.9°; Z below 104.1°; and the Z difference was .8° decreasing.

Explanation of the Data from the Table

The Hc or computed altitude from the main body of the table will be adjusted for the minutes and tenths of declination to give you the total computed altitude from the H. O. 229 table. This altitude will be compared with the corrected sextant reading to obtain the intercept.

The d number represents the difference in the computed altitude between

LATITUDE CONTRARY NAME TO DECLINATION L.H.A. 60°, 300°

Dec.	38°			39°			40°			41°			42°			43°			44°			45°			Dec.
	Hc	d	Z	Hc	d	Z	Hc	d	Z	Hc	d	Z	Hc	d	Z	Hc	d	Z	Hc	d	Z	Hc	d	Z	
°	° ′	′	°	° ′	′	°	° ′	′	°	° ′	′	°	° ′	′	°	° ′	′	°	° ′	′	°	° ′	′	°	°
0	23 12.2	-40.3	109.6	22 51.9	-41.1	110.0	22 31.3	-41.9	110.4	22 10.2	-42.6	110.7	21 48.8	-43.4	111.1	21 27.0	-44.1	111.5	21 04.8	-44.8	111.9	20 42.3	-45.5	112.2	0
1	22 31.9	40.5	110.4	22 10.8	41.3	110.8	21 49.4	42.1	111.1	21 27.6	42.8	111.5	21 05.4	43.5	111.9	20 42.9	44.2	112.2	20 20.0	44.9	112.6	19 56.8	45.6	112.9	1
2	21 51.4	40.8	111.2	21 29.5	41.5	111.5	21 07.3	42.3	111.9	20 44.8	43.0	112.3	20 21.9	43.7	112.6	19 58.7	44.5	112.9	19 35.1	45.1	113.3	19 11.2	45.7	113.6	2
3	21 10.6	41.0	112.0	20 48.0	41.8	112.3	20 25.0	42.4	112.7	20 01.8	43.2	113.0	19 38.2	43.9	113.3	19 14.2	44.5	113.7	18 50.0	45.2	114.0	18 25.5	45.9	114.3	3
4	20 29.6	41.2	112.7	20 06.2	41.9	113.1	19 42.6	42.7	113.4	19 18.6	43.4	113.7	18 54.3	44.1	114.1	18 29.7	44.8	114.4	18 04.8	45.4	114.7	17 39.6	46.0	115.0	4
5	19 48.4	-41.4	113.5	19 24.3	-42.1	113.8	18 59.9	-42.8	114.2	18 35.2	-43.5	114.5	18 10.2	-44.2	114.8	17 44.9	-44.9	115.1	17 19.4	-45.6	115.3	16 53.6	-46.2	115.6	5
6	19 07.0	41.6	114.3	18 42.2	42.3	114.6	18 17.1	43.0	114.9	17 51.7	43.7	115.2	17 26.0	44.4	115.5	17 00.0	45.0	115.8	16 33.8	45.6	116.0	16 07.4	46.3	116.3	6
7	18 25.4	41.8	115.0	17 59.9	42.5	115.3	17 34.1	43.2	115.6	17 08.0	43.9	115.9	16 41.6	44.5	116.2	16 15.0	45.1	116.4	15 48.2	45.8	116.7	15 21.1	46.4	117.0	7
8	17 43.6	41.9	115.8	17 17.4	42.6	116.1	16 50.9	43.3	116.4	16 24.1	44.0	116.6	15 57.1	44.6	116.9	15 29.9	45.3	117.1	15 02.4	45.9	117.4	14 34.7	46.5	117.6	8
9	17 01.7	42.1	116.5	16 34.8	42.8	116.8	16 07.6	43.5	117.1	15 40.1	44.1	117.3	15 12.5	44.8	117.6	14 44.6	45.4	117.8	14 16.5	46.0	118.0	13 48.2	46.6	118.3	9
10	16 19.6	-42.3	117.3	15 52.0	-43.0	117.5	15 24.1	-43.6	117.8	14 56.0	-44.2	118.0	14 27.7	-44.9	118.3	13 59.2	-45.5	118.5	13 30.5	-46.1	118.7	13 01.6	-46.7	118.9	10
11	15 37.3	42.4	118.0	15 09.0	43.1	118.3	14 40.5	43.7	118.5	14 11.8	44.4	118.7	13 42.8	45.0	118.9	13 13.7	45.6	119.2	12 44.4	46.3	119.4	12 14.9	46.9	119.6	11
12	14 54.9	42.5	118.8	14 25.9	43.2	119.0	13 56.8	43.9	119.2	13 27.4	44.5	119.4	12 57.8	45.1	119.6	12 28.1	45.7	119.8	11 58.1	46.3	120.0	11 28.0	46.8	120.2	12
13	14 12.4	42.7	119.5	13 42.7	43.3	119.7	13 12.9	44.0	119.9	12 42.9	44.6	120.1	12 12.7	45.2	120.3	11 42.4	45.8	120.5	11 11.8	46.4	120.7	10 41.2	47.0	120.8	13
14	13 29.7	42.8	120.2	12 59.4	43.4	120.4	12 28.9	44.0	120.6	11 58.3	44.7	120.8	11 27.5	45.3	121.0	10 56.6	45.9	121.1	10 25.4	46.4	121.3	9 54.2	47.0	121.5	14
15	12 46.9	-42.9	120.9	12 16.0	-43.6	121.1	11 44.9	-44.2	121.3	11 13.6	-44.8	121.5	10 42.2	-45.4	121.6	10 10.7	-46.0	121.8	9 39.0	-46.6	121.9	9 07.2	-47.1	122.1	15
16	12 04.0	43.1	121.6	11 32.4	43.6	121.8	11 00.7	44.3	122.0	10 28.8	44.8	122.2	9 56.8	45.4	122.3	9 24.7	46.0	122.5	8 52.4	46.6	122.6	8 20.1	47.2	122.7	16
17	11 20.9	43.1	122.4	10 48.8	43.8	122.5	10 16.4	44.3	122.7	9 44.0	45.0	122.8	9 11.4	45.6	123.0	8 38.7	46.1	123.1	8 05.8	46.6	123.2	7 32.9	47.2	123.3	17
18	10 37.8	43.2	123.1	10 05.0	43.8	123.2	9 32.1	44.5	123.4	8 59.0	45.0	123.5	8 25.8	45.6	123.6	7 52.6	46.2	123.7	7 19.2	46.7	123.9	6 45.7	47.3	124.0	18
19	9 54.6	43.3	123.8	9 21.2	43.9	123.9	8 47.6	44.5	124.0	8 14.0	45.1	124.2	7 40.2	45.6	124.3	7 06.4	46.2	124.4	6 32.5	46.8	124.5	5 58.4	47.2	124.6	19
20	9 11.3	-43.4	124.5	8 37.3	-44.0	124.6	8 03.1	-44.5	124.7	7 28.9	-45.1	124.8	6 54.6	-45.7	124.9	6 20.2	-46.3	125.0	5 45.7	-46.8	125.1	5 11.2	-47.4	125.2	20
21	8 27.9	43.5	125.2	7 53.3	44.1	125.3	7 18.6	44.7	125.4	6 43.8	45.2	125.5	6 08.9	45.8	125.6	5 33.9	46.3	125.7	4 58.9	46.8	125.8	4 23.8	47.3	125.8	21
22	7 44.4	43.5	125.9	7 09.2	44.1	126.0	6 33.9	44.7	126.1	5 58.6	45.3	126.2	5 23.1	45.8	126.2	4 47.6	46.3	126.3	4 12.1	46.9	126.4	3 36.5	47.4	126.4	22
23	7 00.9	43.6	126.6	6 25.1	44.2	126.7	5 49.2	44.7	126.7	5 13.3	45.3	126.8	4 37.3	45.8	126.9	4 01.3	46.4	127.0	3 25.2	46.9	127.0	2 49.1	47.4	127.0	23
24	6 17.3	43.7	127.3	5 40.9	44.2	127.3	5 04.5	44.8	127.4	4 28.0	45.3	127.5	3 51.5	45.9	127.5	3 14.9	46.4	127.6	2 38.3	46.9	127.6	2 01.7	47.5	127.7	24
25	5 33.6	-43.7	127.9	4 56.7	-44.2	128.0	4 19.7	-44.8	128.1	3 42.7	-45.3	128.1	3 05.6	-45.9	128.2	2 28.5	-46.4	128.2	1 51.4	-46.9	128.3	1 14.2	-47.4	128.3	25
26	4 49.9	43.7	128.6	4 12.5	44.3	128.7	3 34.9	44.8	128.7	2 57.4	45.4	128.8	2 19.7	45.9	128.8	1 42.1	46.4	128.9	1 04.5	47.0	128.9	0 26.8	-47.4	128.9	26
27	4 06.2	43.8	129.3	3 28.2	44.4	129.4	2 50.1	44.9	129.4	2 12.0	45.4	129.4	1 33.8	45.9	129.5	0 55.7	46.4	129.5	0 17.5	-46.9	129.5	0 20.6	+47.5	50.5	27
28	3 22.4	43.8	130.0	2 43.8	44.3	130.0	2 05.2	44.9	130.1	1 26.6	45.4	130.1	0 47.9	45.9	130.1	0 09.3	-46.5	130.1	0 29.4	+46.9	49.9	1 08.1	47.4	49.9	28
29	2 38.6	43.8	130.7	1 59.5	44.4	130.7	1 20.3	44.8	130.7	0 41.2	-45.4	130.8	0 02.0	-45.9	130.8	0 37.2	+46.4	49.2	1 16.3	47.0	49.3	1 55.5	47.4	49.3	29
30	1 54.8	-43.8	131.4	1 15.1	-44.3	131.4	0 35.5	-44.9	131.4	0 04.2	+45.4	48.6	0 43.9	+45.9	48.6	1 23.6	+46.4	48.6	2 03.3	+46.9	48.6	2 42.9	+47.4	48.7	30
31	1 11.0	43.9	132.1	0 30.8	-44.4	132.1	0 09.4	+44.9	47.9	0 49.6	45.4	47.9	1 29.8	45.9	48.0	2 10.0	46.4	48.0	2 50.2	46.9	48.0	3 30.3	47.4	48.0	31
32	0 27.1	-43.9	132.7	0 13.6	+44.4	47.3	0 54.3	44.9	47.3	1 35.0	45.4	47.3	2 15.7	45.9	47.3	2 56.4	46.4	47.3	3 37.1	46.8	47.4	4 17.7	47.3	47.4	32
33	0 16.8	+43.8	46.6	0 58.0	44.4	46.6	1 39.2	44.9	46.6	2 20.4	45.4	46.6	3 01.6	45.9	46.7	3 42.8	46.3	46.7	4 23.9	46.8	46.8	5 05.0	47.3	46.8	33
34	1 00.6	43.8	45.9	1 42.4	44.3	45.9	2 24.1	44.8	45.9	3 05.8	45.4	46.0	3 47.5	45.8	46.0	4 29.1	46.4	46.1	5 10.7	46.8	46.1	5 52.3	47.3	46.2	34
35	1 44.4	+43.9	45.2	2 26.7	+44.3	45.2	3 08.9	+44.9	45.3	3 51.2	+45.3	45.3	4 33.3	+45.8	45.4	5 15.5	+46.2	45.4	5 57.5	+46.8	45.5	6 39.6	+47.2	45.6	35
36	2 28.3	43.8	44.5	3 11.0	44.3	44.6	3 53.8	44.8	44.6	4 36.5	45.3	44.7	5 19.1	45.8	44.7	6 01.7	46.3	44.8	6 44.3	46.7	44.9	7 26.8	47.1	45.0	36
37	3 12.1	43.8	43.8	3 55.3	44.3	43.9	4 38.6	44.7	43.9	5 21.8	45.2	44.0	6 04.9	45.7	44.1	6 48.0	46.1	44.1	7 31.0	46.6	44.2	8 13.9	47.1	44.3	37
38	3 55.9	43.7	43.2	4 39.6	44.3	43.2	5 23.3	44.7	43.3	6 07.0	45.2	43.3	6 50.6	45.7	43.4	7 34.1	46.2	43.5	8 17.6	46.6	43.6	9 01.0	47.1	43.7	38
39	4 39.6	43.7	42.5	5 23.9	44.1	42.5	6 08.0	44.7	42.6	6 52.2	45.1	42.7	7 36.3	45.6	42.8	8 20.3	46.0	42.9	9 04.2	46.5	43.0	9 48.1	47.0	43.1	39
40	5 23.3	+43.7	41.8	6 08.0	+44.2	41.9	6 52.7	+44.6	41.9	7 37.3	+45.1	42.0	8 21.9	+45.5	42.1	9 06.3	+46.0	42.2	9 50.7	+46.5	42.3	10 35.1	+46.9	42.4	40
41	6 07.0	43.6	41.1	6 52.2	44.1	41.2	7 37.3	44.6	41.3	8 22.4	45.0	41.3	9 07.4	45.5	41.5	9 52.3	46.0	41.6	10 37.2	46.4	41.7	11 22.0	46.8	41.8	41
42	6 50.6	43.5	40.4	7 36.3	44.0	40.5	8 21.9	44.4	40.6	9 07.4	44.9	40.7	9 52.9	45.4	40.8	10 38.3	45.8	40.9	11 23.6	46.2	41.0	12 08.8	46.7	41.2	42
43	7 34.1	43.5	39.7	8 20.3	43.9	39.8	9 06.3	44.4	39.9	9 52.3	44.9	40.0	10 38.3	45.3	40.1	11 24.1	45.7	40.2	12 09.8	46.2	40.4	12 55.5	46.6	40.5	43
44	8 17.6	43.4	39.0	9 04.2	43.9	39.1	9 50.7	44.4	39.2	10 37.2	44.8	39.3	11 23.6	45.2	39.5	12 09.8	45.7	39.6	12 56.0	46.1	39.7	13 42.1	46.6	39.9	44
45	9 01.0	+43.4	38.3	9 48.1	+43.8	38.4	10 35.1	+44.2	38.5	11 22.0	+44.6	38.7	12 08.8	+45.1	38.8	12 55.5	+45.5	38.9	13 42.1	+46.0	39.1	14 28.7	+46.4	39.2	45
46	9 44.4	43.2	37.6	10 31.9	43.7	37.7	11 19.3	44.1	37.8	12 06.6	44.6	38.0	12 53.9	45.0	38.1	13 41.0	45.5	38.3	14 28.1	45.9	38.4	15 15.1	46.3	38.6	46
47	10 27.6	43.2	36.9	11 15.6	43.6	37.0	12 03.4	44.0	37.2	12 51.2	44.5	37.3	13 38.9	44.9	37.4	14 26.5	45.3	37.6	15 14.0	45.7	37.7	16 01.4	46.2	37.9	47
48	11 10.8	43.0	36.2	11 59.2	43.4	36.3	12 47.4	44.0	36.5	13 35.7	44.3	36.6	14 23.8	44.8	36.7	15 11.8	45.2	36.9	15 59.7	45.7	37.1	16 47.6	46.0	37.3	48
49	11 53.8	43.0	35.5	12 42.6	43.4	35.6	13 31.4	43.8	35.8	14 20.0	44.2	35.9	15 08.6	44.6	36.1	15 57.0	45.1	36.2	16 45.4	45.5	36.4	17 33.6	45.9	36.6	49
50	12 36.8	+42.8	34.8	13 26.0	+43.3	34.9	14 15.2	+43.7	35.1	15 04.2	+44.1	35.2	15 53.2	+44.5	35.4	16 42.1	+44.9	35.5	17 30.9	+45.3	35.7	18 19.5	+45.8	35.9	50
51	13 19.6	42.7	34.1	14 09.3	43.1	34.2	14 58.9	43.5	34.3	15 48.3	44.0	34.5	16 37.7	44.4	34.7	17 27.0	44.8	34.8	18 16.2	45.2	35.0	19 05.3	45.6	35.2	51
52	14 02.3	42.6	33.3	14 52.4	43.0	33.5	15 42.4	43.4	33.6	16 32.3	43.8	33.8	17 22.1	44.3	34.0	18 11.8	44.7	34.1	19 01.4	45.1	34.3	19 50.9	45.5	34.5	52
53	14 44.9	42.4	32.6	15 35.4	42.8	32.8	16 25.8	43.3	32.9	17 16.1	43.7	33.1	18 06.4	44.0	33.3	18 56.5	44.5	33.4	19 46.5	44.9	33.6	20 36.4	45.3	33.8	53
54	15 27.3	42.3	31.9	16 18.2	42.7	32.0	17 09.1	43.1	32.2	17 59.8	43.5	32.4	18 50.4	43.9	32.5	19 41.0	44.3	32.7	20 31.4	44.7	32.9	21 21.7	45.1	33.1	54
55	16 09.6	+42.2	31.1	17 00.9	+42.6	31.3	17 52.2	+42.9	31.5	18 43.3	+43.3	31.6	19 34.3	+43.8	31.8	20 25.3	+44.1	32.0	21 16.1	+44.5	32.2	22 06.8	+44.9	32.4	55
56	16 51.8	42.0	30.4	17 43.5	42.4	30.6	18 35.1	42.8	30.7	19 26.6	43.2	30.9	20 18.1	43.5	31.1	21 09.4	43.9	31.3	22 00.6	44.4	31.5	22 51.7	44.8	31.7	56
57	17 33.8	41.8	29.7	18 25.9	42.2	29.8	19 17.9	42.6	30.0	20 09.8	43.0	30.2	21 01.6	43.4	30.4	21 53.3	43.8	30.6	22 45.0	44.1	30.8	23 36.5	44.5	31.0	57
58	18 15.6	41.6	28.9	19 08.1	42.0	29.1	20 00.5	42.3	29.2	20 52.8	42.7	29.4	21 45.0	43.1	29.6	22 37.1	43.5	29.8	23 29.1	43.9	30.0	24 21.0	44.3	30.2	58
59	18 57.2	41.4	28.1	19 50.1	41.8	28.3	20 42.8	42.2	28.5	21 35.5	42.6	28.7	22 28.1	43.0	28.9	23 20.6	43.4	29.1	24 13.0	43.7	29.3	25 05.3	44.1	29.5	59
60	19 38.6	+41.3	27.4	20 31.9	+41.6	27.5	21 25.0	+42.0	27.7	22 18.1	+42.4	27.9	23 11.1	+42.7	28.1	24 04.0	+43.1	28.3	24 56.7	+43.5	28.5	25 49.4	+43.8	28.8	60
61	20 19.9	41.0	26.6	21 13.5	41.4	26.8	22 07.0	41.8	26.9	23 00.5	42.1	27.1	23 53.8	42.5	27.3	24 47.1	42.8	27.5	25 40.2	43.3	27.8	26 33.2	43.7	28.0	61
62	21 00.9	40.9	25.8	21 54.9	41.2	26.0	22 48.8	41.5	26.2	23 42.6	41.9	26.4	24 36.3	42.3	26.6	25 29.9	42.7	26.8	26 23.5	42.9	27.0	27 16.9	43.3	27.2	62
63	21 41.8	40.6	25.0	22 36.1	40.9	25.2	23 30.3	41.3	25.4	24 24.5	41.7	25.6	25 18.6	42.0	25.8	26 12.6	42.3	26.0	27 06.4	42.8	26.2	28 00.2	43.1	26.4	63
64	22 22.4	40.3	24.2	23 17.0	40.8	24.4	24 11.6	41.1	24.6	25 06.2	41.4	24.8	26 00.6	41.7	25.0	26 54.9	42.1	25.2	27 49.2	42.4	25.4	28 43.3	42.8	25.7	64
65	23 02.7	+40.2	23.4	23 57.8	+40.4	23.6	24 52.7	+40.8	23.8	25 47.6	+41.1	24.0	26 42.3	+41.5	24.2	27 37.0	+41.8	24.4	28 31.6	+42.2	24.6	29 26.1	+42.5	24.9	65
66	23 42.9	39.8	22.6	24 38.2	40.2	22.8	25 33.5	40.5	23.0	26 28.7	40.8	23.2	27 23.8	41.2	23.4	28 18.8	41.6	23.6	29 13.8	41.8	23.8	30 08.6	42.2	24.0	66
67	24 22.7	39.6	21.8	25 18.4	39.9	22.0	26 14.0	40.3	22.2	27 09.5	40.6	22.4	28 05.0	40.9	22.6	29 00.4	41.2	22.8	29 55.6	41.6	23.0	30 50.8	41.9	23.2	67
68	25 02.3	39.4	21.0	25 58.3	39.7	21.2	26 54.3	39.9	21.3	27 50.1	40.3	21.5	28 45.9	40.6	21.7	29 41.6	40.9	21.9	30 37.2	41.2	22.1	31 32.7	41.6	22.4	68
69	25 41.7	39.0	20.1	26 38.0	39.3	20.3	27 34.2	39.6	20.5	28 30.4	39.9	20.7	29 26.5	40.2	20.9	30 22.5	40.6	21.1	31 18.4	40.9	21.3	32 14.3	41.2	21.5	69
70	26 20.7	+38.7	19.3	27 17.3	+39.0	19.5	28 13.8	+39.4	19.6	29 10.3	+39.6	19.8	30 06.7	+39.9	20.0	31 03.1	+40.2	20.2	31 59.3	+40.6	20.4	32 55.5	+40.9	20.7	70
71	26 59.4	38.5	18.4	27 56.3	38.7	18.6	28 53.2	38.9	18.8	29 49.9	39.3	19.0	30 46.6	39.6	19.2	31 43.3	39.9	19.4	32 39.9	40.1	19.6	33 36.4	40.4	19.8	71
72	27 37.9	38.1	17.6	28 35.0	38.4	17.7	29 32.1	38.7	17.9	30 29.2	38.9	18.1	31 26.2	39.2	18.3	32 23.2	39.4	18.5	33 20.0	39.8	18.7	34 16.8	40.1	18.9	72
73	28 16.0	37.7	16.7	29 13.4	38.0	16.9	30 10.8	38.3	17.0	31 08.1	38.6	17.2	32 05.4	38.8	17.4	33 02.6	39.2	17.6	33 59.8	39.4	17.8	34 56.9	39.7	18.0	73
74	28 53.7	37.4	15.8	29 51.4	37.7	16.0	30 49.1	37.9	16.1	31 46.7	38.2	16.3	32 44.2	38.5	16.5	33 41.8	38.7	16.7	34 39.2	39.0	16.9	35 36.6	39.2	17.1	74
75	29 31.1	+37.1	14.9	30 29.1	+37.3	15.1	31 27.0	+37.5	15.2	32 24.9	+37.7	15.4	33 22.7	+38.0	15.6	34 20.5	+38.2	15.8	35 18.2	+38.5	15.9	36 15.8	+38.8	16.1	75
76	30 08.2	36.6	14.0	31 06.4	36.9	14.2	32 04.5	37.1	14.3	33 02.6	37.4	14.5	34 00.7	37.6	14.6	34 58.7	37.9	14.8	35 56.7	38.1	15.0	36 54.6	38.4	15.2	76
77	30 44.8	36.3	13.1	31 43.3	36.4	13.2	32 41.6	36.7	13.4	33 40.0	36.9	13.5	34 38.3	37.2	13.7	35 36.6	37.4	13.9	36 34.8	37.6	14.0	37 33.0	37.9	14.2	77
78	31 21.1	35.9	12.2	32 19.7	36.1	12.3	33 18.3	36.3	12.4	34 16.9	36.5	12.6	35 15.5	36.7	12.7	36 14.0	36.9	12.9	37 12.4	37.2	13.1	38 10.9	37.3	13.2	78
79	31 57.0	35.4	11.2	32 55.8	35.6	11.4	33 54.6	35.8	11.5	34 53.4	36.0	11.6	35 52.2	36.2	11.8	36 50.9	36.4	11.9	37 49.6	36.6	12.1	38 48.2	36.9	12.2	79
80	32 32.4	+35.0	10.3	33 31.4	+35.2	10.4	34 30.4	+35.4	10.5	35 29.4	+35.6	10.6	36 28.4	+35.7	10.8	37 27.3	+35.9	10.9	38 26.2	+36.1	11.1	39 25.1	+36.3	11.2	80
81	33 07.4	34.6	9.3	34 06.6	34.7	9.4	35 05.8	34.9	9.5	36 05.0	35.0	9.7	37 04.1	35.2	9.8	38 03.2	35.4	9.9	39 02.3	35.6	10.0	40 01.4	35.7	10.2	81
82	33 42.0	34.0	8.3	34 41.3	34.2	8.4	35 40.7	34.3	8.5	36 40.0	34.5	8.6	37 39.3	34.7	8.8	38 38.6	34.8	8.9	39 37.9	35.0	9.0	40 37.1	35.2	9.1	82
83	34 16.0	33.6	7.3	35 15.5	33.8	7.4	36 15.0	33.9	7.5	37 14.5	34.0	7.6	38 14.0	34.1	7.7	39 13.4	34.3	7.8	40 12.9	34.4	7.9	41 12.3	34.5	8.1	83
84	34 49.6	33.1	6.3	35 49.3	33.2	6.4	36 48.9	33.3	6.5	37 48.5	33.4	6.6	38 48.1	33.5	6.7	39 47.7	33.6	6.8	40 47.3	33.7	6.9	41 46.8	33.9	7.0	84
85	35 22.7	+32.6	5.3	36 22.5	+32.6	5.4	37 22.2	+32.8	5.4	38 21.9	+32.9	5.5	39 21.6	+33.0	5.6	40 21.3	+33.1	5.7	41 21.0	+33.2	5.8	42 20.7	+33.3	5.9	85
86	35 55.3	32.0	4.3	36 55.1	32.1	4.3	37 55.0	32.1	4.4	38 54.8	32.2	4.5	39 54.6	32.3	4.5	40 54.4	32.4	4.6	41 54.2	32.5	4.7	42 54.0	32.6	4.7	86
87	36 27.3	31.5	3.2	37 27.2	31.6	3.3	38 27.1	31.6	3.3	39 27.0	31.7	3.4	40 26.9	31.7	3.4	41 26.8	31.8	3.5	42 26.7	31.8	3.5	43 26.6	31.9	3.6	87
88	36 58.8	30.9	2.2	37 58.8	30.9	2.2	38 58.7	31.0	2.2	39 58.7	31.0	2.3	40 58.6	31.1	2.3	41 58.6	31.0	2.3	42 58.5	31.1	2.4	43 58.5	31.1	2.4	88
89	37 29.7	30.3	1.1	38 29.7	30.3	1.1	39 29.7	30.3	1.1	40 29.7	30.3	1.1	41 29.7	30.3	1.2	42 29.6	30.4	1.2	43 29.6	30.4	1.2	44 29.6	30.4	1.2	89
90	38 00.0	+29.7	0.0	39 00.0	+29.7	0.0	40 00.0	+29.7	0.0	41 00.0	+29.7	0.0	42 00.0	+29.6	0.0	43 00.0	+29.6	0.0	44 00.0	+29.6	0.0	45 00.0	+29.6	0.0	90
	38°			39°			40°			41°			42°			43°			44°			45°			

S. Lat. { L.H.A. greater than 180°......Zn=180°−Z; L.H.A. less than 180°............Zn=180°+Z

LATITUDE SAME NAME AS DECLINATION L.H.A. 120°, 240°

Figure 6-5. Extracted from H.O. 229, Volume III. LHA 60° and 300°; CONTRARY for latitudes 38°-45°. Also note, below contrary/same line additional SAME solutions for LHA 120°-240°, latitudes 38°-45°.

the tabulated Hc and the next whole degree of declination. The d number will be used later to obtain a correction to the computed altitude.

The Z number (or azimuth angle) from the table is related to the direction of the GP of the celestial body as computed from the assumed position. The tabular Z represents the direction as it would be computed using trigonometric tables. This number will later be converted to a navigationally more useful true direction depending on whether you are in north or south latitude, or whether LHA is greater or less than 180°.

PRACTICE PROBLEMS *(Refer to Volume III, H. O. 229)*

Use the following information to obtain the Hc, d (with sign), Z, Z diff., and if applicable d, diff. from the H. O. 229 table:

1. LHA 346°; DR latitude 30°S; declination 20°S
2. LHA 10°; DR latitude 43°N; declination 25°S
3. LHA 124°; DR latitude 45°N; declination 46°N

ANSWERS

1. Hc 73°52.2'; d +38.3; d diff. 4.4; Z 125.1; Z diff. 2.8, dec.
2. Hc 21°22.7'; d −59.4; Z 170.3; Z diff. 0.1, inc.
3. Hc 13°31.9'; d +47.8; Z 36.3; Z diff. 0.6, dec.

Step 4, Corrections from the Interpolation Table

The computed altitude (Hc) and azimuth angle (Z) from the main body of the table are based on computations assuming a whole degree of declination. To give you additional precision, the Hc and Z must be adjusted to take into account the minutes and tenths or increments of declination. The minutes and tenths of declination, the d number, d difference, and Z difference will be used to enter special tables in the front and back covers of H. O. 229 to obtain corrections which are applied to the Hc and Z. These tables are called the interpolation tables.

Learning how to use the interpolation tables is the most complex part of the H. O. 229 system. However, if you use the workforms and follow the instructions, you should get accurate results.

There are four pages of interpolation tables. The two pages inside the front cover are used to adjust the Hc and Z for increments of declinations from 0.0' to 31.9'. The two pages inside the back cover are used to adjust the main table data for increments of declination from 28.0' to 59.9'. (There is a small overlap between the tables.)

Layout of the Tables

As Figure 6-6 shows, the interpolation tables are really a series of smaller tables. To illustrate this, a part of one page has been broken down into its component tables. Table 1 would be used for declination increments or minutes and tenths of declination consisting of 16.0' through 16.9' inclusive. Table 2 would be used for declination increments between 17.0' through 17.9' while table 3 would be used for declination increments of 18.0' through 18.9' and so on.

The Tens Table

Within each table there are three separate tables. The tens table is entered from the left with the minutes and tenths of declination and from the top with the number of tens in the d tab number from the main body of the table. The correction, found at the intersection of the numbers is added to the computed altitude if the d was plus and subtracted if the d was minus.

Units/Decimals Table

The units/decimals table, just to the right of the tens table, is entered using the second and third digits of the d number. (Since the d number has three digits, the first number is tens, the second units, and the third decimals.) The first number

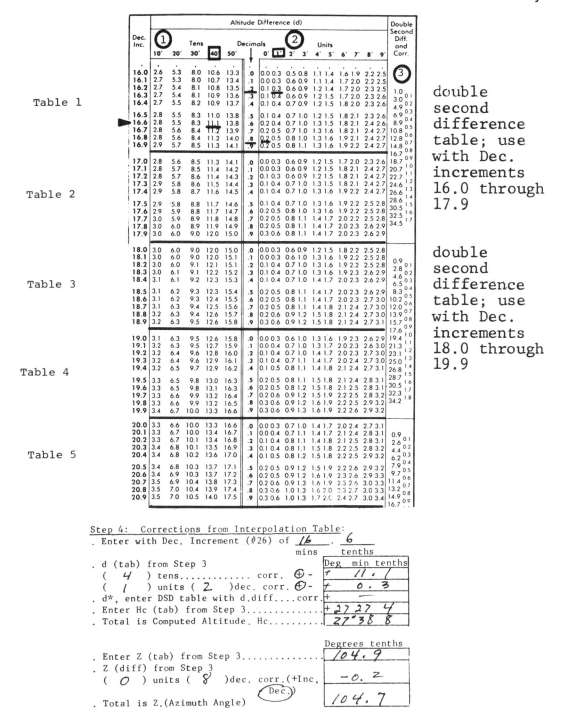

Figure 6-6. Extract from H.O. 229, Interpolation Tables, and workform filled out.

in the d (tab) from the main table is used to enter the tens table. The second digit in the d tab—the units—is used to enter the top of the units/decimals table while the third digit—the decimals—is used to enter the left side of the table. The correc-

tion is found at the intersection of the two numbers. The units/decimals correction is added to the computed altitude if the d is plus and subtracted if the d is minus. When using the units/decimals table, you must remember to use the table adjacent to, and just to the right of, the declination increment/tens table for that particular sight.

Double Second Difference Table

The double second difference (DSD) table, to the far right, is used only for those sights where the d in the main table was followed by an asterisk or dot. The left column of the DSD table is entered with the d difference and the correction taken from the right column. You must remember to use the DSD table adjacent to, and to the right of, the table where you found the correction for the declination increment and the units/decimals. The double second difference correction is always added to the computed altitude.

Z Correction

The units/decimals table is also used to make a correction to the Z. The Z difference, a one or two digit number, is broken down into units and decimals and used to obtain a correction. The correction—which must be obtained from the same units/decimals table used earlier—is added to Z if the Z was increasing and subtracted from Z if the Z was decreasing.

Example: The declination increment is 16.6'; the d tab is +41.2, there is no d diff.; Z diff. is 0.8 decreasing. Hc is 27°27.4' and Z from the table is 104.9°. What is the Hc and Z? Figure 6-6 shows where the information was found in the interpolation tables and how the workform was filled out. The Hc is 27°38.8' and the Z is 104.7°. The tens correction is +11.1'; units/dec. correction +0.3. The Z diff. correction is −0.2'.

PRACTICE PROBLEMS

1. The Hc (tab) was 36°18.2'; Z (tab) 29.6°; dec. increment 51.4'; d (tab) +26.4; and Z diff.

1.3 decreasing. Use the interpolation tables to compute the Hc and Z.

2. The Hc (tab) was 53°09.1'; Z (tab) 141.4°; dec. increment 11.3'; d (tab) +11.1; and Z diff. 0.9 increasing. Use the interpolation tables to compute the Hc and Z.

3. The Hc (tab) was 70°03.8'; Z (tab) 240.1°; dec. increment 22.9'; d (tab) −31.4; double second difference is needed for d diff. of 27; and Z diff. 1.4 decreasing. Use the interpolation tables to compute the Hc and Z.

ANSWERS

1. Hc 36°40.8'; Z 28.5°
2. Hc 53°11.2'; Z 141.6°
3. Hc 69°53.4'; Z 239.6°

Step 5, Computing the True Azimuth

In this step the Z from the table—which is a trigonometric table angle—is converted to the true azimuth or true direction. This is the direction of the GP of the body from the assumed position you used to figure the sight. The rules for converting the Z from the table to the Zn or true direction are given at the top right-hand side of the "same" pages, and the bottom left side of the "contrary" pages of the H. O. 229 table. The rules are:

> In south latitude, if LHA is greater than 180°, azimuth = 180 − Z from the table.
> In south latitude, if LHA is smaller than 180°, azimuth = 180 + Z from the table.
> In north latitude, if LHA is greater than 180°, azimuth = Z from the table. (They are the same.)
> In north latitude, if LHA is smaller than 180°, azimuth = 360° − Z from the table.

These rules are graphically represented by the boxes in step 5 which make it easy for you to remember and complete the conversion from Z to Zn. First, decide which blocks apply, north or south latitude, then, depending on the LHA, enter the Z from step four in the appropriate block.

Example: A navigator in north latitude has an LHA greater than 180° and a Z of 104.7°. What is the Zn or true azimuth? Figure 6-7 is marked to show how the answer of 104.7° was obtained. Remember, when working with Z numbers, you are adding and subtracting angles expressed in degrees and decimal degrees not the degrees, minutes, and tenths we usually work with in navigation. The only difference here is that if you have to borrow a degree, you borrow 10-tenths rather than 60 minutes. If you have over 10-tenths in the tenths column, add one degree to the degree column. Of course, if the total exceeds 360° subtract 360.

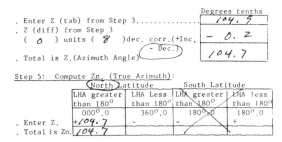

Figure 6-7. Azimuth portion of workform filled out showing how Z correction was applied to Z from the table and how Z is converted to Zn or true azimuth.

PRACTICE PROBLEMS

Use the information below to compute the true azimuth:

1. You are in north latitude with LHA less than 180°. Z is 234.6°.

2. You are in south latitude with LHA greater than 180°. Z is 27.7°.

3. You are in north latitude with LHA greater than 180°. Z is 331.4°.

4. You are in south latitude with LHA less than 180°. Z is 110.6°.

ANSWERS

1. 125.4° 2. 152.3° 3. 331.4° 4. 290.6°

Step 6, Computing the Intercept

In this step the observed altitude (Ho) is compared with the computed altitude (Hc). The difference between the angles, as you know, is the intercept. The intercept represents the distance from the position you assumed to enter the H. O. 229 table to the line of position. The line of position is really one small segment of the large circle of position given by the sextant. This step is easy, but very important.

In the workform, Ho is entered as a plus and Hc as a minus. First, obtain the difference between the two numbers by subtracting the smaller from the larger.

  If Ho is larger than Hc the difference will be plus and you circle the T to remind you that the intercept is drawn toward the azimuth.

  If Hc is larger than Ho the difference will be minus and you circle the A to remind you that the intercept is drawn away from the azimuth.

Usually the intercept will be in minutes and tenths. However, if there are any whole degrees in the intercept, multiply them by 60′ and add the result to the minutes and tenths.

Step 7, Plotting Data

This final step organizes the information you need to plot the celestial line of position including:

The assumed longitude from step 1.
The rounded latitude from step 2.
The azimuth from step 5.
The intercept from step 6.

Make sure you record the *assumed* longitude and *rounded* latitude, *not* the DR longitude and latitude. The sight, remember, was worked out from the assumed position not the DR position. The azimuth is rounded to the nearest whole degree. If there are 5 or more tenths of azimuth round up to the next degree. This is done because you cannot plot lines of position to tenths of a degree of azimuth.

PRACTICE PROBLEMS

Use the information below to compute the intercept and label it toward or away:
  1. Ho 72°31.9'; Hc 72°11.4'.
  2. Ho 24°11.8'; Hc 24°31.4'.
  3. Ho 60°09.4'; Hc 59°57.4'.
  4. Ho 33°27.6'; Hc 33°39.8'.
  5. Ho 46°11.3'; Hc 45°09.2'.

ANSWERS

  1. +20.5 toward
  2. −19.6 away
  3. +12.0 toward
  4. −12.2 away
  5. +62.1 toward

Example: (Refer to Appendix 2, and Figures 6-4 and 6-6) Your DR position was 42°18'N; 71°36'W when you observed the lower limb of the sun on June 3, 1983 at 20 hours 43 minutes 59 seconds GMT. The sextant reading was 36°49.6', no instrument error, index correction −1.4', height of eye 10 feet. What is the assumed longitude, rounded latitude, azimuth, and intercept? *Solution:* The assumed longitude is 71°29.1'W; rounded latitude 42°N; azimuth 268°; intercept +16.8 toward. Figure 6-8 gives the complete solution.

PRACTICE PROBLEMS *(Refer to Appendix 2, and Vol. III of H. O. 229)*

There are four practice problems. The first two can be worked out and plotted as a two-star fix. The second two can be worked out and plotted as a running fix on the sun. In solving problems with H. O. 229 you should be able to come within a few tenths of a mile of intercept and the nearest whole degree of azimuth. If you are off a tenth or two, you may be making small "technical" errors which are not navigationally significant. If you are several miles off on intercept or off by a degree of azimuth, you are making navigationally significant mistakes. The fixes, if worked out on a Universal Plotting Sheet, should be correct to within + or − 2' (two minutes) of latitude and longitude.

Problems 1 and 2. (Two-star fix) You are in DR 39°15'N; 79°05'W on June 6, 1983 when you obtain observations on two stars. There is no index error, no instrument error, and height of eye is 10 feet. Star 1, Dubhe, was observed at 10 hours 07 minutes 09 seconds GMT with a sextant reading of 11°31.4'. Star 2, Hamal, was observed at 10 hours 09 minutes 05 seconds GMT with a sextant reading of 34°35.7'. What is the intercept and azimuth of each star? What is the latitude and longitude of the fix?

Answer (For solution see Figures 6-9 and 6-10)

Dubhe: azimuth, 351°; intercept −37.3 away

Hamal: azimuth, 86°; intercept +17.7 toward

Fix: 38°28.5'N; 78°32.8'W.

Problems 3 and 4. (Running sun fix) You are in DR 42°05'N; 77°25'W on 5 June 1983 when you obtain a sight on the lower limb of the sun at 13 hours 01 minutes 01 seconds GMT. The sextant reading is 34°47.9'. There is no index error, no instrument error, and height of eye is 10 feet. What is the azimuth and intercept?

Later that same day (5 June 1983) you obtain another sight taken on the lower limb of the sun at 17 hours 35 minutes 04 seconds GMT. The boat has traveled a distance of 25.2 nautical miles on a course of 301° (true) since the first sun sight. (Instructions for plotting a running fix are found in Chapter 2, pages 35-40.) You now are in DR 42°18'N; 77°54'W. The sextant reading is 69°58.0',

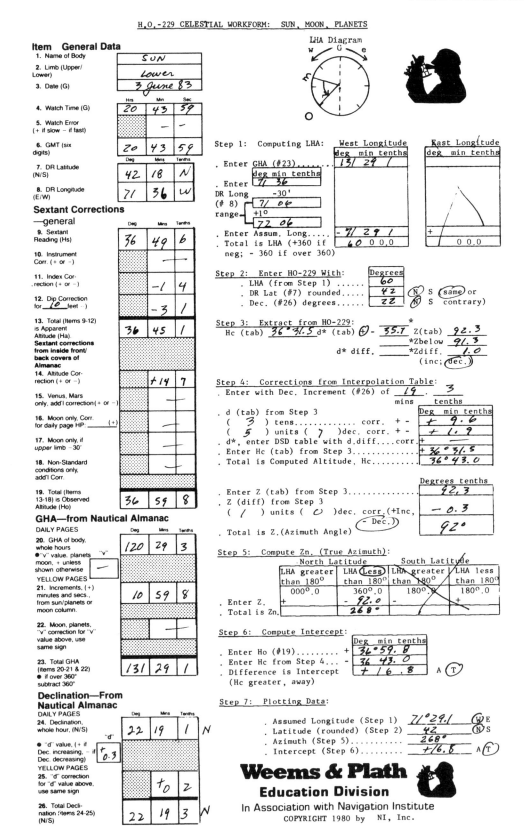

Figure 6-8. Solution to example problem.

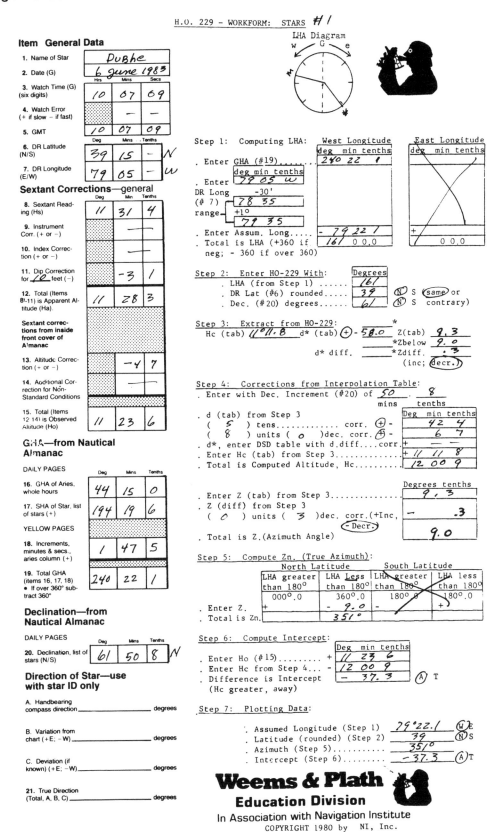

H.O. 229 - WORKFORM: STARS #1

Item General Data

1. Name of Star — *Dubhe*
2. Date (G) — *6 June 1983*

	Hrs	Mins	Secs
3. Watch Time (G) (six digits)	10	07	69
4. Watch Error (+ if slow – if fast)		—	—
5. GMT	10	07	09

	Deg	Mins	Tenths	
6. DR Latitude (N/S)	39	15	—	N
7. DR Longitude (E/W)	79	05	—	W

Sextant Corrections—general

	Deg	Min	Tenths
8. Sextant Reading (Hs)	11	31	4
9. Instrument Corr. (+ or –)			—
10. Index Correction (+ or –)			—
11. Dip Correction for __10__ feet (–)		-3	1
12. Total (Items 8-11) is Apparent Altitude (Ha).	11	28	3

Sextant corrections from inside front cover of Almanac

		Deg	Min	Tenths
13. Altitude Correction (+ or –)			-4	7
14. Additional Correction for Non-Standard Conditions			—	
15. Total (Items 12-14) is Observed Altitude (Ho)		11	23	6

GHA—from Nautical Almanac

DAILY PAGES

	Deg	Mins	Tenths
16. GHA of Aries, whole hours	44	15	0
17. SHA of Star, list of stars (+)	194	19	6

YELLOW PAGES

18. Increments, minutes & secs., aries column (+)	1	47	5
19. Total GHA (items 16, 17, 18) • If over 360° subtract 360°	240	22	1

Declination—from Nautical Almanac

DAILY PAGES

	Deg	Min	Tenths	
20. Declination, list of stars (N/S)	61	50	8	N

Direction of Star—use with star ID only

A. Handbearing compass direction _____ degrees

B. Variation from chart (+E; –W) _____ degrees

C. Deviation (if known) (+E; –W) _____ degrees

21. True Direction (Total, A, B, C) _____ degrees

Step 1: Computing LHA:

. Enter GHA (#19)........

	deg	min	tenths
West Longitude	240	22	1

. Enter

deg	min	tenths
79 05 W		

DR Long -30'
(# 7) | 78 | 35 |
range— +1° | 79 | 35 |

. Enter Assum. Long..... – 79 22 1
. Total is LHA (+360 if neg; – 360 if over 360) 161 | 00.0

East Longitude +   0 0.0

Step 2: Enter HO-229 With: Degrees
. LHA (from Step 1)   161
. DR Lat (#6) rounded.....   39   N S (same or
. Dec. (#20) degrees......   61   N S contrary)

Step 3: Extract from HO-229:   *
Hc (tab) 11°11.8 d* (tab) (+) – 58.0 Z(tab) 9.3
                           d* diff.   *Zbelow 9.0
                                           *Zdiff.   .3
                                           (inc; decr.)

Step 4: Corrections from Interpolation Table:
. Enter with Dec. Increment (#20) of 50   8
                                       mins tenths

	Deg	min	tenths
. d (tab) from Step 3			
(5) tens.......... corr. (+) –		42	4
(8) units (0)dec. corr.(+) –		6	7
. d*, enter DSD table with d.diff....corr. +			
. Enter Hc (tab) from Step 3.......... +	11	11	8
. Total is Computed Altitude, Hc.........	12	00	9

                                           Degrees tenths
. Enter Z (tab) from Step 3.............   9.3
. Z (diff) from Step 3
  (0) units (3)dec. corr.(+Inc,   –   .3
                               – Decr.)
. Total is Z.(Azimuth Angle)   9.0

Step 5: Compute Zn. (True Azimuth):

	North Latitude		South Latitude	
	LHA greater than 180°	LHA Less than 180°	LHA greater than 180°	LHA less than 180°
	000°.0	360°.0	180°.0	180°.0
. Enter Z.	+	– 9.0	–	+
. Total is Zn.		351°		

Step 6: Compute Intercept:

	Deg	min	tenths
. Enter Ho (#15)........ +	11	23	6
. Enter Hc from Step 4... –	12	00	9
. Difference is Intercept	–	37.	3	(A) T
(Hc greater, away)			

Step 7: Plotting Data:

. Assumed Longitude (Step 1) 79°22.1 W E
. Latitude (rounded) (Step 2) 39   N S
. Azimuth (Step 5)........... 351°
. Intercept (Step 6)........ –37.3   (A) T

Figure 6-9. Solution to Dubhe.

H.O. 229 - WORKFORM: STARS

Item   General Data

1. Name of Star — HAMAL

2. Date (G) — 6 JUNE 1983

3. Watch Time (G) (six digits)

Hrs	Mins	Secs
10	09	05

4. Watch Error (+ if slow — if fast) — —

5. GMT

10	09	05

6. DR Latitude (N/S)

Deg	Mins	. Tenths
39	15	N

7. DR Longitude (E/W)

79	05	W

Sextant Corrections—general

	Deg	Min	Tenths
8. Sextant Reading (Hs)	34	35	7
9. Instrument Corr. (+ or −)		—	
10. Index Correction (+ or −)		—	
11. Dip Correction for __10__ feet (−)		−3	1
12. Total (Items 8½-11) is Apparent Altitude (Ha).	34	32	6
Sextant corrections from inside front cover of Almanac			
13. Altitude Correction (+ or −)		−1	4
14. Additional Correction for Non-Standard Conditions		—	
15. Total (Items 12-14) is Observed Altitude (Ho)	34	31	2

GHA—from Nautical Almanac

DAILY PAGES

	Deg	Mins	Tenths
16. GHA of Aries, whole hours	44	15	0
17. SHA of Star, list of stars (+)	328	27	0
YELLOW PAGES			
18. Increments, minutes & secs., aries column (+)	2	16	6
19. Total GHA (items 16, 17, 18) • If over 360° subtract 360°	14	58	6

Declination—from Nautical Almanac

DAILY PAGES

	Deg	Mins	Tenths	
20. Declination, list of stars (N/S)	23	22	9	North

Direction of Star—use with star ID only

A. Handbearing compass direction _____ degrees

B. Variation from chart (+E; −W) _____ degrees

C. Deviation (if known) (+E; −W) _____ degrees

21. True Direction (Total, A, B, C) _____ degrees

LHA Diagram

Step 1:   Computing LHA:

. Enter GHA (#19) ....

	West Longitude		East Longitude		
	deg	min	tenths	deg	min	tenths
	14	58	6			

. Enter DR Long (# 7)

deg	min	tenths
79	05.0	

−30′

78	35.0

range +1°

79	35.0

. Enter Assum. Long..... −78° 58 6

. Total is LHA (+360 if neg; − 360 if over 360) 296 00.0   00.0

Step 2:   Enter HO-229 With:

	Degrees
. LHA (from Step 1)	296
. DR Lat (#6) rounded.....	39
. Dec. (#20) degrees......	23

N S (same or N S contrary)

Step 3:   Extract from HO-229:

Hc (tab) 34 01.2   d* (tab) ⊕ − 32.1   Z(tab) 86.6
                                         *Zbelow 85.5
d* diff.   *Zdiff. 1.1
                                         (inc; decr.)

Step 4:   Corrections from Interpolation Table:

. Enter with Dec. Increment (#20) of 22 9

	mins	tenths
	Deg	min	tenths

. d (tab) from Step 3
  (3) tens............ corr. ⊕ −   11.5
  (2) units (/)dec. corr. ⊕ −   .8
. d*, enter DSD table with d.diff....corr.+
. Enter Hc (tab) from Step 3.............+ 34 01.2
. Total is Computed Altitude, Hc........ 34 13.5

	Degrees	tenths
. Enter Z (tab) from Step 3............... 86.6
. Z (diff) from Step 3
  (/) units (/)dec. corr.(+Inc,   − .4
                        − Decr.)
. Total is Z.(Azimuth Angle)   86.2

Step 5:   Compute Zn. (True Azimuth):

	North Latitude		South Latitude	
	LHA greater than 180	LHA Less than 180	LHA greater than 180	LHA less than 180
	000°.0	360°.0	180°.0	180°.0
. Enter Z.	+ 86.2	−	−	+
. Total is Zn.	86.2			

Step 6:   Compute Intercept:

	Deg	min	tenths
. Enter Ho (#15)......... +	34	31	2
. Enter Hc from Step 4...	34	13	5
. Difference is Intercept	+	17	7

(Hc greater, away)   A T

Step 7:   Plotting Data:

. Assumed Longitude (Step 1) 78° 58.6 W E
. Latitude (rounded) (Step 2) 39 N S
. Azimuth (Step 5).......... 86
. Intercept (Step 6)........ 17.7 A T

Weems & Plath

EDUCATION DIVISION

In Association with Navigation Institute
COPYRIGHT 1980 by NI, Inc.

Figure 6-10. Solution to Hamal.

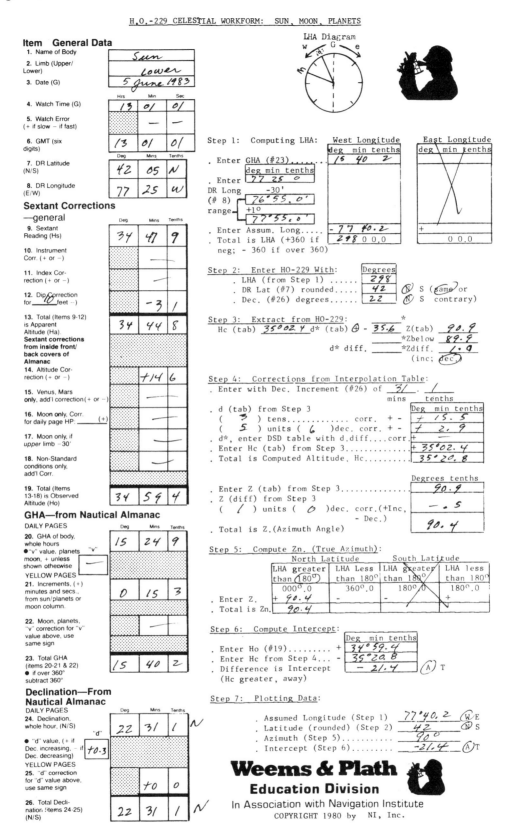

Figure 6-11. Solution to first sun sight, 13 hours 01 minute 01 second.

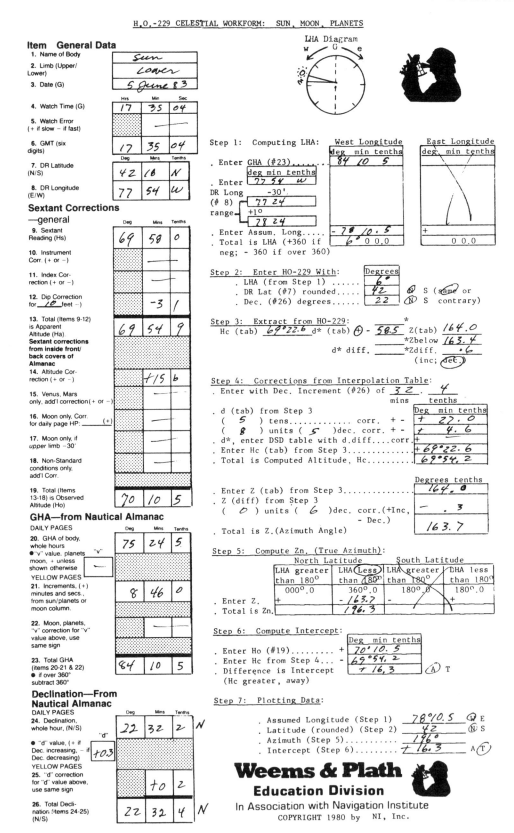

Figure 6-12. Solution to second sun sight, 17 hours 35 minutes 04 seconds.

there is no index error, no instrument error, and height of eye 10 feet. What is the azimuth and intercept? What is the latitude and longitude of the running fix?

Answer (For solution see Figures 6-11 and 6-12)

First sun sight: azimuth 90°; intercept −21.4′ away.

Second sun sight: azimuth 196°; intercept +16.3 toward.

Running fix: 41°49.0′N; 78°39.0′W.

7

Identifying Stars and Planets
(Time: 1 Hour)

On a clear night, there are over 3 million stars visible to the naked eye. With so many stars around, it's no wonder many navigators become intimidated about "shooting the stars." The biggest single reason more people don't use stars and planets in their navigation is because they are not confident they can identify them. Star and planet identification is really quite easy once you learn the concepts.

To begin with you don't have to become an astronomer or memorize dozens of constellations to use stars and planets. Star and planet sights are not taken at night, but at twilight. This means only those bodies that are bright enough to see when there is enough light for a visible horizon should concern you.

The *Nautical Almanac* lists 57 navigation stars, selected because of their location above the horizon and their relative brightness. The almanac also lists the 4 navigational planets. While it is *possible* to observe stars not on the daily page list, it is extremely *unlikely*. In over 15,000 miles of offshore sailing, I only observed *one* star that was not on the list!

Further, not all the 57 stars or 4 planets listed will be visible on any given morning or evening. For example, the list of stars includes both northern and southern hemisphere stars. Some of the stars and planets listed are below the horizon and are not visible; others may be obscured by a cloud. Sometimes visibility is reduced and only a few really bright stars or planets are available for sights. Even with good visibility, you may only have a choice of 6 to 8 bodies. The issue is not which of 3 million stars did you see, or even which of the 57 stars did you see, but which of the 6 or 8 stars or planets available did you see.

There are three different methods for sorting out the stars and planets:

First, use of the almanac and H. O. 229 to identify stars and planets after you have observed them with the sextant.

Second, use of these same tools to predict in advance the approximate sextant reading and handbearing compass direction of the 4 navigational planets.

Finally, use of the starfinder to identify stars.

Using the *Nautical Almanac* and H. O. 229 to Identify Stars and Planets

The almanac and H. O. 229 can be used to identify stars and planets *after* you have observed them with the sextant. With this system, at twilight, using your sextant shoot the brightest most prominent bodies you can see. As you observe the bodies with the sextant, record the sextant angle, GMT, and the handbearing compass direction of the body. Then use the almanac and H. O. 229 table to complete the steps listed in the star and planet identification workform, Figure 7-1.

The workform shows you how to convert the handbearing compass direction to the approximate true direction (or azimuth) of the star or planet. The other steps in the workform show you how to enter the H. O. 229 table to compute the approximate declination and approximate SHA of the star or planet you observed. Then use the approximate SHA and declination of the unknown body to consult the daily page list of stars and planets to find the tabulated SHA and declination which is the closest "match."

The almanac lists the tabulated SHA and declinations for the 57 stars in the right-hand side of the daily pages. The SHA of the planets is also given at the bottom of the star column while the declination of the planets is given in the planet column just to the right of the GHA.

Remember, the values for SHA and declination from the star and planet identification process are not precise. Therefore the match between the computed values and the tabulated values of SHA and declination will seldom be exact. They should be close enough, however, to permit you to identify the body. Once the body is identified then use the tabulated SHA and declination (for stars) or the tabulated GHA and declination (for planets) to complete the sight reduction problem.

Star and Planet Identification Workform

As Figure 7-1 indicates, the star and planet identification process involves four steps. The form also shows you how to convert the handbearing compass direction of the body to the true direction.

Step 1, data for entering H. O. 229. As the form indicates, you enter the "same" portion of H. O. 229 (left-hand pages or bottom right-hand page) using these three numbers:

1. The direction of the body (true) as LHA. If latitude is north you simply use that number. If latitude is south, you must perform one of two operations, whichever is mathematically possible. If the true direction of the body exceeds 180° you subtract 180°; if the true direction is less than 180° you subtract the true direction from 180°.
2. The DR latitude rounded to the nearest whole degree. Circle N or S on the workform to remind you if latitude is north or south.
3. The sextant reading (Hs) as declination. The sextant reading, uncorrected, is rounded to the nearest whole degree and used as the declination to enter H. O. 229.

Step 2, obtaining data from H. O. 229. First, record the Hc from the table as the approximate declination of the star or planet. The declination is contrary to latitude only if Hc was found on the right-hand page, above the contrary/same line.

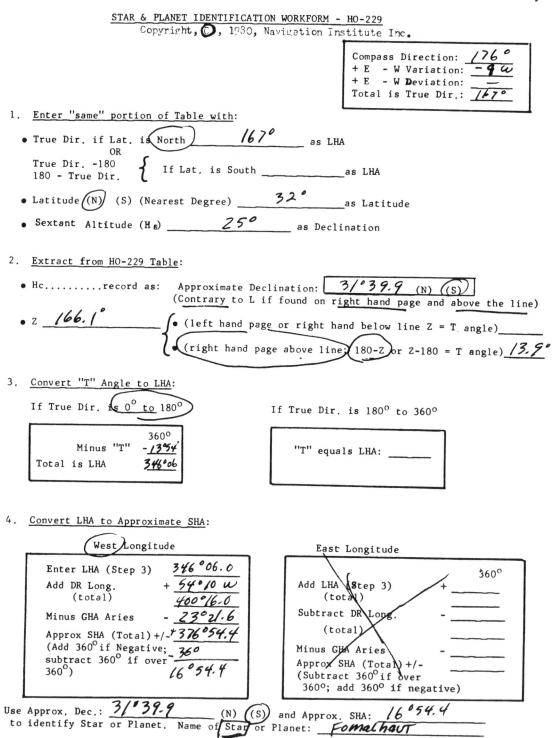

Figure 7-1. This workform shows how to use H.O. 229 to identify stars and planets.

Otherwise, it is the same as latitude. Declination has the same name as latitude if Hc is found on the left-hand pages, or on the right-hand page below the contrary/same line.

Then take the Z from the table and follow the workform instructions for converting Z to a number called the T angle. The T angle is similar to LHA except that it represents the smallest angle, measured east or west from the observer's longitude to the GHA of the body.

The instructions in step 1 and 2 tell you to enter the "same" portion of the H. O. 229 table. They also tell you how to label and handle information from the right-hand page both above and below the contrary/same line. Since information from the right-hand page above the line is from the "contrary" part of H. O. 229 this, at first, may seem inconsistent. When working star and planet identifications problems with this workform, you *always* enter H. O. 229 through the "same" portion of the table. To find the answer, however, you may have to move up past the contrary/same line.

Example: Enter H. O. 229 "same" portion of table with true direction of 187° as LHA; latitude of 43°N as latitude and sextant reading (Hs) of 35° as declination. Even though you entered the "same" portion of the table, to find the answer you had to cross the contrary/same line. In this case the Hc of 11°44.3′ is the approximate declination. It is south because it was found on the right-hand page above the line.

Step 3, converting the T angle to LHA. The T angle is converted to a Local Hour Angle by following the instructions printed on the workform. If the true direction of the body is between 0° and 180°, subtract the T angle from 360° to obtain the LHA.

Step 4, converting LHA to approximate SHA. In this final step, the LHA is converted to an approximate SHA for the star or planet. Be sure to use the correct west or east longitude and remember to obtain the total GHA of Aries. This means the GHA of Aries for the whole hour, plus any increments. While the GHA of Aries is not used with the sight reduction for planets, it is used to identify the planets. Once you obtain the approximate declination and SHA you can then use the daily page listings for stars and planets to identify the body.

PRACTICE PROBLEM

You observed an unknown star or planet on June 6, 1983 at 08 hours 36 minutes 40 seconds GMT in DR 32°15′N; 54°10′W. There was no watch error. Your sextant reading was 25°13.3′, and the handbearing compass direction of the body was 176°. Charted variation 9° west, deviation unknown. What is the approximate declination and SHA of the body? What is the approximate declination and SHA of this star or planet?

ANSWER

Figure 7-1 gives the solution to this problem. The approximate declination is 31°39.9′S; and the approximate SHA is 16°54.4′. If you look at the index of stars, and the data for planets for June 6, 1983 in Appendix 2, you will see that the star Fomalhaut with a tabulated declination of S29°42.6′ and a tabulated SHA of 15°49.2′ is the closest match.

(Technical Note: The Z numbers from the table are in degrees and tenths of degrees, not degrees, minutes, and tenths. Almost all the numbers you worked with in navigation—including those from other parts of H. O. 229, the almanac, the sextant, and the chart—are in degrees, minutes, and tenths. If you find it more convenient, you can convert the tenths in the Z number to minutes. To do this you multiply the tenths of degrees times 60 minutes. Example: Convert 174.6° to degrees and minutes. Solution: Multiply 60 minutes times .6 to give you 36 minutes. Add the 36 minutes to the degrees for a total of 174°36′. When working star and planet identification problems the conversion is useful (but for purposes of accuracy not required) because you have to combine the Z number, and its derivatives, with numbers containing degrees and minutes. In the sight reduction problems, this is not required because you are adding and subtracting de-

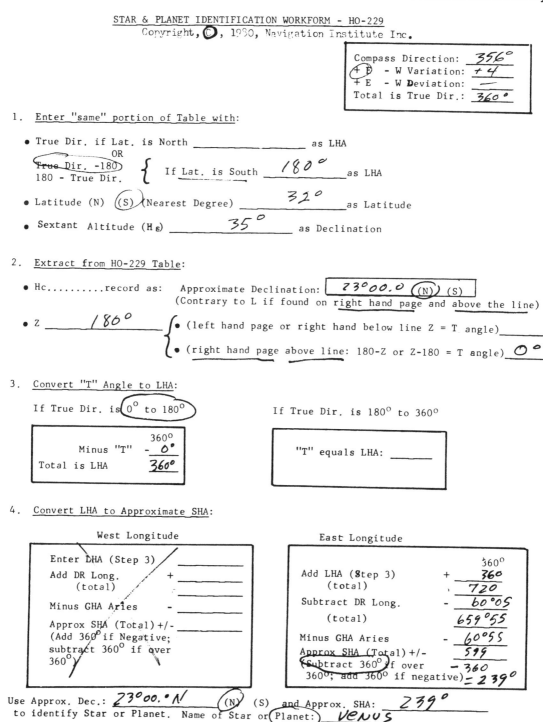

Figure 7-2. When using the form, be sure to check the SHA and declination of the four planets.

grees and decimals of degrees. If you ignore this conversion, your approximate SHA's will differ a little from the answers in the book. However, your answers will still be close enough to identify the star or planet.)

PRACTICE PROBLEM

On June 4, 1983 you are in 32°01′S; 60°05′E when you observe an unknown star or planet at 11 hours 14 minutes 21 seconds GMT. There is no watch error, and your sextant reading is 35°07.3′. The handbearing compass direction of the body was 356° and the charted variation 4°E. Deviation, unknown. Use the star and planet identification program to calculate the approximate declination and SHA of the star or planet. Also refer to Appendix 2, and Volume III of H. O. 229.

ANSWER

Figure 7-2 gives the solution to this problem. The approximate declination is 23°N; the approximate SHA 239°. A check of the almanac pages for June 4, 1983 (including the lower right-hand corner for planet SHA's) shows that the planet Venus with a tabulated daily page declination of 22°58.8'N and a tabulated SHA of 239°41.5' is the closest match.

How to Use H. O. 229 to Predict the Location of the Planets

If you look at the evening or morning sky, you will find that planets look different than stars. A star twinkles. It appears as a tiny dim dot of icy blue light. Planets appear closer, brighter, and larger than stars. Often, they glow with a white or white-yellow light.

If you are unfamiliar with the location of Venus, Mars, Jupiter, and Saturn you can shoot them first and identify them later. You can also identify them first and shoot them later. If you do this, you will know in advance which planets are available and where you can look to find them.

The system for predicting the location of the four navigational planets involves a variation of the method used to identify stars and planets after you observed them:

First, you estimate the GMT of morning or evening twilight.

Then you use the *Nautical Almanac* to find the GHA of each of the four planets for the GMT of twilight.

The GHA of the planet is combined with the DR longitude (advanced to the place where you expect to be at twilight) to obtain the LHA of the planet.

The LHA, DR latitude (advanced to the place you expect to be at twilight), and declination of the planet are used to enter H. O. 229 to determine if the planet is above the horizon and if so what is its approximate sextant angle and true direction. The planet location workform, Figure 7-3, organizes your work.

Example: You expect to be in DR 35°16'N; 69°08'W on June 3, 1983. You expect evening twilight to occur around 20 hours 10 minutes GMT. The charted variation is 5°W. Will Venus be above the horizon and if so what is its approximate altitude (Hs) and true direction (Zn)? What is the handbearing compass direction? *Solution:* The problem is solved using the workform, the almanac reprints in the book, and H. O. 229, Volume III. On slow moving boats, such as cruising sailboats, the GMT of today's A.M. or P.M. twilight can be estimated with sufficient precision by using the time of the desired event for the day before. The DR position, of course, should be advanced to the position where you expect to be at the time of twilight.

Step 1: The LHA of the planet is computed by combining the GHA of the body with your DR longitude according to the rules explained in the workform. The rule here is the same one you follow for sight reduction: in west longitude, subtract longitude from GHA; in east longitude, add longitude to GHA. If you get a negative answer, add 360; if the answer is over 360 subtract 360.

Step 2: Enter H. O. 229 with the LHA, rounded to the nearest whole degree, the DR latitude, rounded, and the whole degrees of declination. At this point, however, you must check to see if the LHA lies between the values 90°-270° and lati-

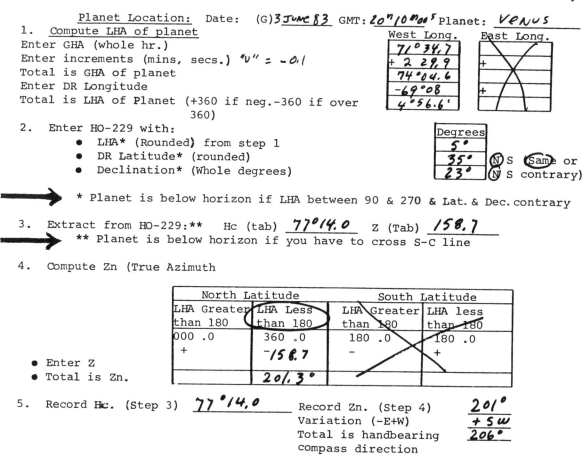

Figure 7-3. This form is used to predict, in advance, the location of the planets. In some cases, the planet is below the horizon and not available.

tude and declination are contrary. If both of these conditions are met, go no further. The planet is below the horizon and will not be visible.

If this is not the case, enter H. O. 229 and take out the Hc and the Z from the table. However, if you had to cross the contrary/same line to obtain Hc and Z, go no further. The planet is below your horizon. Remember, you can cross the contrary/same line by entering the H. O. 229 table from the top working down, or by entering from the bottom and working up. Either way, if you have to cross the line to obtain a planet prediction answer, stop.

As Figure 7-3 indicates, the planet Venus in the example problem was above the horizon. The Hc of 77°14.0′ from H. O. 229 is the approximate sextant angle of

the planet at twilight. The Z from the table, 158.9°, is converted to the true azimuth following the same rules you learned for sight reduction. Here the azimuth is 201° (rounded). The true direction of 201° is converted to a handbearing compass direction of 206° by applying the 5° westerly variation to the true direction. Now you know that during evening twilight, you can preset the sextant for 74°14′ and look for Venus in the handbearing compass direction of 206°. These numbers, however, are estimates. The precise altitude and direction of the planet will vary a bit depending on the accuracy of the time and DR estimates.

When working with the planets, remember that if a planet is below the horizon in the morning it could be visible during evening twilight or vice versa.

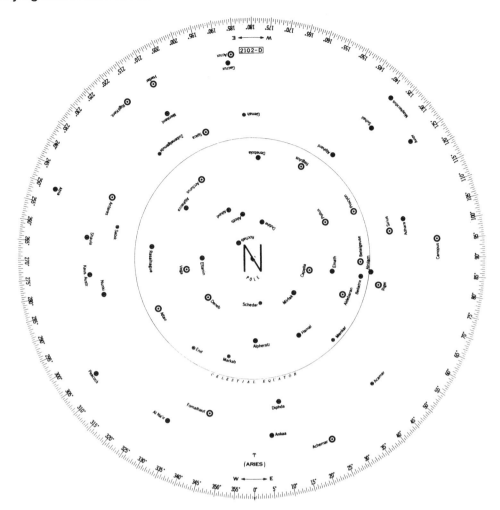

Figure 7-4. The base plate of the starfinder lists the 57 navigation stars.

The planet location procedure gives you the approximate location of the planets. As an added bonus, the data you obtain for a planet will be useful (at sailing boat speeds) for several days, perhaps as much as a week beyond the time of the initial calculation.

PRACTICE PROBLEMS

You expect to be in DR 34°09′N; 67°10′W on the morning of June 6, 1983. You expect A.M. twilight to occur at 11 hours 31 minutes GMT. The variation from the chart shows 5° west. For (1) Jupiter and (2) Mars determine if the planet is above or below the horizon. If it is above the horizon determine the approximate altitude and true direction. Finally, apply the variation to obtain the handbearing compass direction of the planet.

ANSWERS

1. Jupiter is below the horizon. (LHA lies between 90°-270° and latitude and declination are contrary.

2. Mars is above the horizon. The approximate altitude is 25°44.1′; the true direction 80°; handbearing compass direction 85°.

Using the 2102-D Starfinder to Identify Stars

The starfinder is used in conjunction with the *Nautical Almanac* for each year so the starfinder itself does not go out of

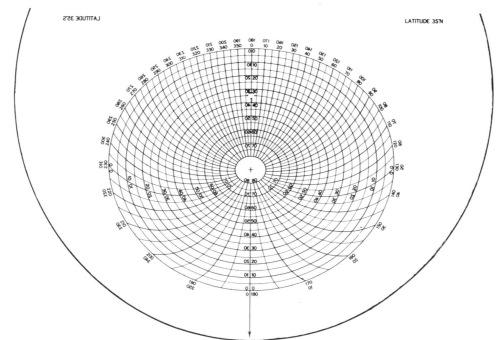

Figure 7-5. The altitude circles and azimuth lines are used to locate the stars. These circles and lines are found on the blue discs that come with the starfinder.

date. The two parts of the starfinder you will work with here are the base plate and the star altitude/azimuth discs.

The base plate is a stiff white plastic disc which has the location and name of the navigation stars printed on it. One side of the disc is for the northern hemisphere and one side is for the southern hemisphere. Around the edge of the base plate there is a 0° to 360° ring, much like a true compass rose. These numbers, however, are not used for direction, but represent the LHA of Aries. Figure 7-4 shows the base plate for the Northern Hemisphere. The starfinder kit contains nine transparent star altitude/azimuth discs printed with blue ink on clear plastic. These discs start at 5° latitude and increase in 10° increments to 85°. (There is also a red template which is used to locate bodies other than the 57 navigational stars on the base plate.)

The base plate refers to the stars by the same names listed in the daily page list in the almanac. The magnitude, or brightness, of each star is indicated by

the size of its symbol on the base plate. First magnitude stars are represented by a large heavy ring; second magnitude stars by a smaller ring, and the third magnitude stars by a thin small ring. The first magnitude stars are the brightest and the ones you will see most often.

The altitude/azimuth discs are reversible so they can be used with either the northern or southern hemisphere base plate. On the outside of the blue discs, are a series of numbers 0° to 360°. These represent the azimuth of the stars. They correspond to the curved lines that start at the center of the blue disc and spread out like the spokes of a wheel. The azimuth of any star found along the line is indicated by the number at the end of the line.

In addition to the curved spokes, the blue discs contain a series of elliptically-shaped circles starting with a small circle in the center and growing larger like the growth rings of a tree. These circles correspond to the various sextant altitudes that are marked on them. The blue

Star Identification (Copyright, 1981, Navigation Institute, Inc.)

Sextant Reading: *31° 02.3* Handbearing Compass Direction: *88*
Date: (G) *5 June 83* GMT: *09ʰ05ᵐ19ˢ* Variation (+E; -W) *-8 w*
DR: Lat: *39 45 N* Long: *66°04 W* True Direction of Star *80°*

1. Compute LHA of Aries

	West Long.		East Long.	
Enter GHA Aries (whole hr.)	28° 13.4			
Enter Increments Aries (mins. secs.)	+ 1 20.0		+	
Total is GHA Aries	29 33.4			
Enter DR Longitude	-66 04. W		+	
Total is LHA Aries (+360 if neg. -360 if over 360)	323° 29.4			

2. Use "N" star base if DR Lat. is North; use "S" if DR Lat. is South

3. Use blue disc nearest DR latitude. Mount on star base. *(35°N BASE)*

4. Rotate blue disc until arrow points to LHA of Aries (whole degrees.) *323°*

5. Locate star closest to sextant reading and true direction of star.
   Name of Star: *HAMAL*

Figure 7-6. This workform is used to help you set up the starfinder. It shows how to calculate the LHA of Aries for the time you observed the stars.

discs also have one long straight arrow printed on them that extends out to the edge of the disc. Figure 7-5 shows the blue disc for 35° with the north latitude side reading up.

To use the starfinder follow these steps:

Select the correct star base for the hemisphere where you are sailing.

Select the blue disc nearest your DR latitude and mount it (correct side reading up) on the base plate.

Use the *Nautical Almanac* to calculate the GHA of Aries (whole hours plus increments) for the GMT you observed the star. Remember, the GHA of Aries is used with all stars and you do not need to know the name of a star to obtain the GHA and increments of Aries.

Calculate the LHA of Aries by subtracting west longitude from the GHA of Aries or adding east longitude to the GHA of Aries. Of course, if you obtain a negative value, add 360° and if the value is over 360° subtract 360°.

Rotate the blue disc until the blue arrow points to the LHA of Aries on the base plate.

Finally, use the sextant reading rounded to the nearest whole degree and the true direction of the star you observed to locate the name of the star on the starfinder. The true direction is obtained by applying the charted variation to the handbearing compass direction of the star. To find a star, locate the sextant reading that corresponds closest to one of the concentric circles, and follow the circle around the disc until it intersects with the spoke or line corresponding to the azimuth or true direction of the star. Your star should be close to the intersection of the altitude circle and azimuth line. Figure 7-6 is a workform that organizes all the information you need to set up the starfinder.

Example: On June 5, 1983 you observed an unknown star at 09 hours 05 minutes 19 seconds GMT while in DR

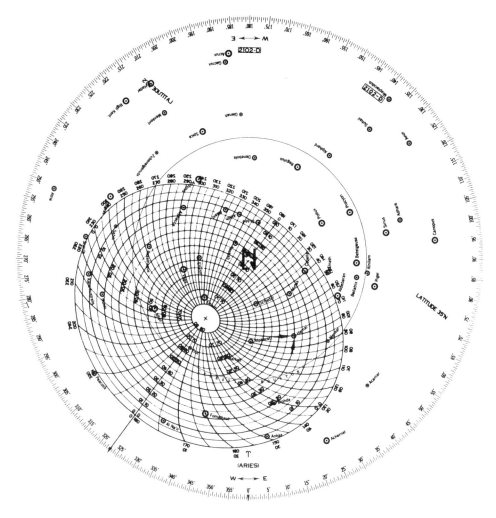

Figure 7-7. The 35° disc is mounted on the N base plate with the pointer oriented to the LHA of Aries for time of observation which was 323°. Hamal, the desired star, was found by finding the intersection of the 30° altitude ring and the 80° azimuth line.

39°15′N; 66°04′W. The handbearing compass direction of the star was 88° and the charted variation 8°W. Use the starfinder to identify the star. The sextant reading for the star was 31°02.3′. *Solution:* Figure 7-6 is marked to indicate how the GHA of Aries and the LHA of Aries were calculated. The form also shows how the handbearing compass direction was converted to a true direction. In this case the LHA of Aries was 323°29.4′ and the true direction 80°. Figure 7-7 shows how the latitude 35°N disc was mounted on the north base plate with the arrow pointing to the LHA (rounded) of 323°. The star you are looking for, Hamal, is

located at the intersection of the 30° altitude ring and the 80° azimuth line.

Now that you know the name of the star, you can look up the SHA and declination of the star in the daily pages and proceed with solving the sight reduction part of the problem. Remember, the starfinder gives you the *approximate* altitude and azimuth of the stars. Use the starfinder to find the star which is close, but not necessarily, an exact match.

The starfinder can be used to identify stars after you observed them, or to predict in advance their approximate sextant angles and directions. To do the latter, advance your DR position to the area you expect to be during A.M. or P.M. twilight. Most of the time you can use the GMT for the day's previous A.M. or P.M. sights for the next day's estimated GMT of twilight.

Then set up the starfinder for the LHA of Aries for this time and use the altitude rings and azimuth lines to make a list of the approximate sextant altitudes and azimuths of the first magnitude stars. When compiling the list, avoid stars that are under 10° or over 80° of altitude since these will be difficult to observe. Before you use the handbearing compass to look for the stars, convert the starfinder directions from true to compass by applying the charted variation, and deviation, if known. When going from true to compass, subtract easterly errors and add westerly errors.

PRACTICE PROBLEMS

On June 4, 1983, around 07 hours 11 minutes GMT, you observed four unknown stars.

Your DR position is 44°10′N; 67°33′W and the charted variation is 6°W. Use the starfinder and almanac reprints in Appendix 2 to compute the LHA of Aries and identify the following stars:

Star Number	Sextant Reading	Hand-bearing Compass Direction	True Direction	Name of Star
1.	54°11.3′	181°	_____	_____
2.	46°18.2′	136°	_____	_____
3.	25°03.4′	341°	_____	_____
4.	20°13.8′	281°	_____	_____

ANSWERS

(LHA of Aries, rounded, is 292°)

1. 175°; Altair
2. 130°; Enif

3. 335°; Dubhe
4. 275°; Arcturus

8

Fixes at Noon; Long Distance Sailing; Cruise Preparation
(Time: 45 Minutes)

The Noon Sight

You have known since school days that the sun rises in the east and sets in the west. On its westerly travels around the world, the sun also crosses each meridian of longitude. As Figure 8-1 indicates, when the sun crosses a meridian of longitude it appears to be at its highest altitude to an observer standing on that meridian.

The observation of the sun at its highest altitude as it crosses your longitude is called the meridian passage of the sun or more commonly the noon sight. The noon sight has some advantages. First, you can work out both your latitude and longitude with just the *Nautical Almanac* and pencil and paper, there are no sight reduction tables involved. Second, you can work out a fairly reliable latitude line even if you do not have precise time available. You do this by estimating the time of meridian passage—to the nearest hour—and obtaining the declination of the sun for the estimated time. Since the sun's declination does not change much (less than 1 minute per hour) you can use the declination for an approximate time and still obtain an adequate estimate of

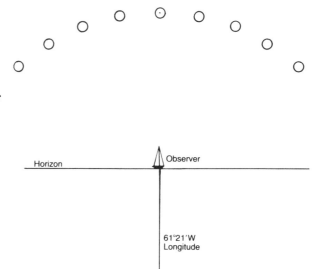

Figure 8-1. When the sun crosses the observer's longitude, it appears to be at its highest altitude.

your latitude. Later, you will see how the declination is used to help compute your latitude.

The noon sight also has some disadvantages. First, you need a fairly accurate estimate of the time meridian passage occurs at your longitude. Otherwise, you could end up spending a lot of time on deck taking sights. Secondly, meridian passage occurs only one time, and for one instant, during each day. Finally, the latitude portion of the noon sight is very reliable (particularly if you have an accurate timpiece) but the longitude portion should be viewed with some caution because longitude depends on observing the sun at the exact GMT when it reached its highest point.

Predicting the GMT of Meridian Passage

To determine when meridian passage will occur at your longitude, use the daily pages of the almanac to find the time of meridian passage for the sun at Greenwich, England. For example, if you wanted the time of meridian passage for the sun at Greenwich for June 3, 1983, look in the lower right-hand corner of the almanac page for the sun and moon. Figure 8-2 is marked to show where the data is found. On June 3, 1983 meridian passage at Greenwich occurred at 11 hours 58 minutes. Now that you know the time meridian passage occurred at Greenwich, the zero meridian of longitude, you must add or subtract some time to account for your own longitude. If you wanted the time of meridian passage at 39°13′N; 61°21′W, you can obtain the time adjustment for your longitude by looking at the "Conversion of Arc to Time" table in the *Nautical Almanac*. This table, reprinted in Appendix 2, is found right before the increments-corrections tables in the back of the almanac.

To use the table, first determine how much time must be applied to Greenwich for the whole degrees of longitude. The first six columns are used to convert whole degrees into their hour and minute time equivalents. The seventh column is used to convert the minutes of longitude into minutes and seconds of time. (The

eighth through tenth columns are used for converting fractions of minutes of longitude into time, but you will not use them because this kind of precision is not needed here.) Figure 8-3 is marked to show where data for 61°21′ was found. In this case, the time adjustment for 61° is 4 hours 04 minutes. The adjustment for 21′ of longitude is 1 minute 24 seconds. Combining the two gives you 4 hours 05 minutes 24 seconds. Since you are in west longitude, this time is added to the time of meridian passage at Greenwich to obtain the estimated time of meridian passage at your longitude:

> 11 hours 58 minutes
>   (meridian passage at Greenwich)
> + 4 hours 05 minutes 24 seconds
> ―――――――――――――――――――――――――
> 16 hours 03 minutes 24 seconds

If you were in east longitude, the longitude-time equivalent would be subtracted from the time of meridian passage at Greenwich.

Taking the Noon Sight

You should always go on deck about five to ten minutes before the predicted time of meridian passage, just in case your estimated longitude is in error. Take a series of timed observations of the sun beginning before meridian passage and continuing for several minutes after. If your chronometer is working, record both the GMT and the sextant reading for the observations. As the sun crosses your meridian, it appears to stay at one angle for a minute or two. During this time you will obtain several sights that have almost the same altitude. The sun will then begin to start down again, and you will obtain altitudes that decrease.

Then carefully look at your worksheet to determine which observation to use as the noon sight. You will have to

G.M.T.	SUN G.H.A.	Dec.	MOON G.H.A.	v	Dec.	d	H.P.
	° '	° '	° '	'	° '	'	'
3 00	180 31.3	N22 12.8	274 57.1	14.3	S15 14.7	9.9	54.4
01	195 31.2	13.2	289 30.4	14.4	15 04.8	9.9	54.4
02	210 31.1	13.5	304 03.8	14.5	14 54.9	10.1	54.4
03	225 31.0 ··	13.8	318 37.3	14.4	14 44.8	10.0	54.4
04	240 30.9	14.1	333 10.7	14.5	14 34.8	10.2	54.5
05	255 30.8	14.4	347 44.2	14.5	14 24.6	10.2	54.5
06	270 30.7	N22 14.8	2 17.7	14.6	S14 14.4	10.3	54.5
07	285 30.6	15.1	16 51.3	14.5	14 04.1	10.3	54.5
08	300 30.5	15.4	31 24.8	14.6	13 53.8	10.4	54.5
F 09	315 30.4 ··	15.7	45 58.4	14.7	13 43.4	10.4	54.5
R 10	330 30.3	16.0	60 32.1	14.6	13 33.0	10.6	54.5
I 11	345 30.2	16.3	75 05.7	14.7	13 22.4	10.5	54.6
D 12	0 30.1	N22 16.6	89 39.4	14.7	S13 11.9	10.7	54.6
A 13	15 30.0	16.9	104 13.1	14.8	13 01.2	10.7	54.6
Y 14	30 29.9	17.3	118 46.9	14.7	12 50.5	10.7	54.6
15	45 29.8 ··	17.6	133 20.6	14.8	12 39.8	10.8	54.6
16	60 29.7	17.9	147 54.4	14.8	12 29.0	10.9	54.6
17	75 29.6	18.2	162 28.2	14.9	12 18.1	10.9	54.6
18	90 29.5	N22 18.5	177 02.1	14.8	S12 07.2	11.0	54.7
19	105 29.4	18.8	191 35.9	14.9	11 56.2	11.0	54.7
20	120 29.3	19.1	206 09.8	14.9	11 45.2	11.1	54.7
21	135 29.2 ··	19.4	220 43.7	14.9	11 34.1	11.1	54.7
22	150 29.1	19.7	235 17.6	15.0	11 23.0	11.2	54.7
23	165 29.0	20.0	249 51.6	14.9	11 11.8	11.3	54.7
4 00	180 28.9	N22 20.3	264 25.5	15.0	S11 00.5	11.3	54.8
01	195 28.8	20.6	278 59.5	15.0	10 49.2	11.3	54.8
02	210 28.7	20.9	293 33.5	15.0	10 37.9	11.4	54.8
03	225 28.6 ··	21.2	308 07.5	15.0	10 26.5	11.5	54.8
04	240 28.5	21.5	322 41.5	15.0	10 15.0	11.5	54.8
05	255 28.3	21.8	337 15.5	15.1	10 03.5	11.5	54.9
06	270 28.2	N22 22.1	351 49.6	15.0	S 9 52.0	11.6	54.9
07	285 28.1	22.4	6 23.6	15.1	9 40.4	11.6	54.9
S 08	300 28.0	22.7	20 57.7	15.1	9 28.8	11.7	54.9
A 09	315 27.9 ··	23.0	35 31.8	15.0	9 17.1	11.8	54.9
T 10	330 27.8	23.3	50 05.8	15.1	9 05.3	11.8	55.0
U 11	345 27.7	23.6	64 39.9	15.1	8 53.5	11.8	55.0
R 12	0 27.6	N22 23.9	79 14.0	15.2	S 8 41.7	11.9	55.0
D 13	15 27.5	24.2	93 48.2	15.1	8 29.8	11.9	55.0
A 14	30 27.4	24.5	108 22.3	15.1	8 17.9	11.9	55.1
Y 15	45 27.3 ··	24.8	122 56.4	15.1	8 06.0	12.0	55.1
16	60 27.2	25.1	137 30.5	15.1	7 54.0	12.1	55.1
17	75 27.1	25.4	152 04.6	15.2	7 41.9	12.1	55.1
18	90 27.0	N22 25.7	166 38.8	15.1	S 7 29.8	12.1	55.1
19	105 26.9	26.0	181 12.9	15.1	7 17.7	12.2	55.2
20	120 26.8	26.3	195 47.0	15.2	7 05.5	12.2	55.2
21	135 26.7 ··	26.6	210 21.2	15.1	6 53.3	12.2	55.2
22	150 26.6	26.9	224 55.3	15.1	6 41.1	12.3	55.2
23	165 26.4	27.1	239 29.4	15.1	6 28.8	12.3	55.3
5 00	180 26.3	N22 27.4	254 03.5	15.2	S 6 16.5	12.4	55.3
01	195 26.2	27.7	268 37.7	15.1	6 04.1	12.4	55.3
02	210 26.1	28.0	283 11.8	15.1	5 51.7	12.4	55.3
03	225 26.0 ··	28.3	297 45.9	15.1	5 39.3	12.5	55.4
04	240 25.9	28.6	312 20.0	15.1	5 26.8	12.5	55.4
05	255 25.8	28.9	326 54.1	15.1	5 14.3	12.5	55.4
06	270 25.7	N22 29.1	341 28.2	15.0	S 5 01.8	12.6	55.4
07	285 25.6	29.4	356 02.2	15.1	4 49.2	12.6	55.5
08	300 25.5	29.7	10 36.3	15.1	4 36.6	12.6	55.5
S 09	315 25.4 ··	30.0	25 10.4	15.0	4 24.0	12.7	55.5
U 10	330 25.3	30.3	39 44.4	15.0	4 11.3	12.7	55.6
N 11	345 25.2	30.5	54 18.4	15.0	3 58.6	12.7	55.6
D 12	0 25.0	N22 30.8	68 52.4	15.0	S 3 45.9	12.7	55.6
A 13	15 24.9	31.1	83 26.4	15.0	3 33.2	12.8	55.6
Y 14	30 24.8	31.4	98 00.4	14.9	3 20.4	12.8	55.7
15	45 24.7 ··	31.7	112 34.3	15.0	3 07.6	12.8	55.7
16	60 24.6	31.9	127 08.3	14.9	2 54.8	12.9	55.7
17	75 24.5	32.2	141 42.2	14.9	2 41.9	12.9	55.8
18	90 24.4	N22 32.5	156 16.1	14.9	S 2 29.0	12.9	55.8
19	105 24.3	32.8	170 50.0	14.8	2 16.1	12.9	55.8
20	120 24.2	33.0	185 23.8	14.9	2 03.2	13.0	55.8
21	135 24.1 ··	33.3	199 57.7	14.8	1 50.2	13.0	55.9
22	150 23.9	33.6	214 31.5	14.7	1 37.2	13.0	55.9
23	165 23.8	33.9	229 05.2	14.8	1 24.2	13.0	55.9
	S.D. 15.8	d 0.3	S.D. 14.9		15.0		15.2

Lat.	Twilight Naut.	Civil	Sunrise	Moonrise 3	4	5	6
°	h m	h m	h m	h m	h m	h m	h m
N 72	☐	☐	☐	03 23	02 48	02 22	02 00
N 70	☐	☐	☐	02 53	02 31	02 14	01 59
68	☐	☐	01 02	02 30	02 18	02 07	01 58
66	////	////	01 52	02 12	02 07	02 02	01 57
64	////	////	01 52	01 57	01 57	01 57	01 56
62	////	////	02 23	01 45	01 49	01 53	01 56
60	////	01 19	02 46	01 34	01 42	01 49	01 55
N 58	////	01 56	03 04	01 25	01 36	01 46	01 55
56	////	02 21	03 20	01 17	01 31	01 43	01 54
54	01 12	02 41	03 33	01 10	01 26	01 40	01 54
52	01 46	02 57	03 44	01 03	01 22	01 38	01 53
50	02 10	03 11	03 54	00 57	01 18	01 36	01 53
45	02 51	03 39	04 15	00 45	01 09	01 31	01 52
N 40	03 19	04 00	04 32	00 34	01 02	01 27	01 52
35	03 41	04 17	04 47	00 25	00 55	01 24	01 51
30	03 59	04 32	04 59	00 17	00 50	01 20	01 51
20	04 27	04 55	05 20	00 03	00 40	01 15	01 50
N 10	04 48	05 15	05 38	24 31	00 31	01 10	01 50
0	05 06	05 32	05 55	24 23	00 23	01 06	01 49
S 10	05 22	05 48	06 11	24 15	00 15	01 02	01 48
20	05 38	06 05	06 29	24 07	00 07	00 57	01 48
30	05 53	06 23	06 49	23 57	24 52	00 52	01 47
35	06 01	06 33	07 01	23 51	24 48	00 48	01 47
40	06 10	06 44	07 14	23 45	24 45	00 45	01 46
45	06 20	06 56	07 30	23 37	24 41	00 41	01 46
S 50	06 30	07 12	07 49	23 28	24 36	00 36	01 45
52	06 35	07 18	07 59	23 24	24 34	00 34	01 45
54	06 41	07 26	08 09	23 19	24 31	00 31	01 45
56	06 46	07 34	08 21	23 14	24 28	00 28	01 44
58	06 52	07 44	08 34	23 08	24 25	00 25	01 44
S 60	06 59	07 55	08 50	23 01	24 22	00 22	01 44

Lat.	Sunset	Twilight Civil	Naut.	Moonset 3	4	5	6
°	h m	h m	h m	h m	h m	h m	h m
N 72	☐	☐	☐	08 37	10 43	12 39	14 34
N 70	☐	☐	☐	09 06	10 58	12 45	14 32
68	☐	☐	☐	09 28	11 10	12 49	14 29
66	22 59	////	////	09 45	11 19	12 53	14 28
64	22 06	////	////	09 58	11 27	12 56	14 26
62	21 35	////	////	10 10	11 34	12 58	14 25
60	21 12	22 40	////	10 19	11 40	13 01	14 24
N 58	20 53	22 02	////	10 28	11 45	13 03	14 22
56	20 38	21 36	////	10 35	11 49	13 05	14 22
54	20 24	21 16	22 47	10 42	11 53	13 06	14 21
52	20 13	21 00	22 12	10 48	11 57	13 08	14 20
50	20 03	20 46	21 48	10 53	12 00	13 09	14 19
45	19 41	20 18	21 06	11 04	12 08	13 12	14 18
N 40	19 24	19 57	20 37	11 14	12 14	13 14	14 17
35	19 10	19 39	20 15	11 22	12 19	13 16	14 15
30	18 58	19 25	19 58	11 29	12 23	13 18	14 14
20	18 37	19 01	19 30	11 41	12 31	13 21	14 13
N 10	18 19	18 41	19 08	11 51	12 38	13 24	14 11
0	18 02	18 24	18 50	12 01	12 44	13 27	14 10
S 10	17 45	18 08	18 34	12 11	12 50	13 29	14 09
20	17 28	17 51	18 19	12 21	12 57	13 32	14 07
30	17 07	17 33	18 03	12 33	13 04	13 35	14 05
35	16 56	17 23	17 55	12 39	13 08	13 36	14 04
40	16 42	17 12	17 46	12 47	13 13	13 38	14 03
45	16 26	17 00	17 36	12 56	13 19	13 40	14 02
S 50	16 07	16 45	17 26	13 07	13 25	13 43	14 00
52	15 58	16 38	17 21	13 11	13 29	13 44	14 00
54	15 47	16 30	17 15	13 17	13 32	13 46	13 59
56	15 35	16 22	17 10	13 23	13 36	13 47	13 58
58	15 22	16 12	17 04	13 29	13 40	13 49	13 57
S 60	15 06	16 01	16 57	13 37	13 44	13 50	13 56

	SUN			MOON			
Day	Eqn. of Time 00ʰ	12ʰ	Mer. Pass.	Mer. Pass. Upper	Lower	Age	Phase
	m s	m s	h m	h m	h m	d	
3	02 05	02 01	11 58	05 51	18 12	22	
4	01 56	01 51	11 58	06 34	18 55	23	
5	01 46	01 40	11 58	07 16	19 38	24	

Figure 8-2. From the *Nautical Almanac,* 1983, showing meridian passage for the sun on June 3, 1983.

CONVERSION OF ARC TO TIME

0°–59°		60°–119°		120°–179°		180°–239°		240°–299°		300°–359°			0′·00	0′·25	0′·50	0′·75
°	h m	°	h m	°	h m	°	h m	°	h m	°	h m	′	m s	m s	m s	m s
0	0 00	60	4 00	120	8 00	180	12 00	240	16 00	300	20 00	0	0 00	0 01	0 02	0 03
1	0 04	61	4 04	121	8 04	181	12 04	241	16 04	301	20 04	1	0 04	0 05	0 06	0 07
2	0 08	62	4 08	122	8 08	182	12 08	242	16 08	302	20 08	2	0 08	0 09	0 10	0 11
3	0 12	63	4 12	123	8 12	183	12 12	243	16 12	303	20 12	3	0 12	0 13	0 14	0 15
4	0 16	64	4 16	124	8 16	184	12 16	244	16 16	304	20 16	4	0 16	0 17	0 18	0 19
5	0 20	65	4 20	125	8 20	185	12 20	245	16 20	305	20 20	5	0 20	0 21	0 22	0 23
6	0 24	66	4 24	126	8 24	186	12 24	246	16 24	306	20 24	6	0 24	0 25	0 26	0 27
7	0 28	67	4 28	127	8 28	187	12 28	247	16 28	307	20 28	7	0 28	0 29	0 30	0 31
8	0 32	68	4 32	128	8 32	188	12 32	248	16 32	308	20 32	8	0 32	0 33	0 34	0 35
9	0 36	69	4 36	129	8 36	189	12 36	249	16 36	309	20 36	9	0 36	0 37	0 38	0 39
10	0 40	70	4 40	130	8 40	190	12 40	250	16 40	310	20 40	10	0 40	0 41	0 42	0 43
11	0 44	71	4 44	131	8 44	191	12 44	251	16 44	311	20 44	11	0 44	0 45	0 46	0 47
12	0 48	72	4 48	132	8 48	192	12 48	252	16 48	312	20 48	12	0 48	0 49	0 50	0 51
13	0 52	73	4 52	133	8 52	193	12 52	253	16 52	313	20 52	13	0 52	0 53	0 54	0 55
14	0 56	74	4 56	134	8 56	194	12 56	254	16 56	314	20 56	14	0 56	0 57	0 58	0 59
15	1 00	75	5 00	135	9 00	195	13 00	255	17 00	315	21 00	15	1 00	1 01	1 02	1 03
16	1 04	76	5 04	136	9 04	196	13 04	256	17 04	316	21 04	16	1 04	1 05	1 06	1 07
17	1 08	77	5 08	137	9 08	197	13 08	257	17 08	317	21 08	17	1 08	1 09	1 10	1 11
18	1 12	78	5 12	138	9 12	198	13 12	258	17 12	318	21 12	18	1 12	1 13	1 14	1 15
19	1 16	79	5 16	139	9 16	199	13 16	259	17 16	319	21 16	19	1 16	1 17	1 18	1 19
20	1 20	80	5 20	140	9 20	200	13 20	260	17 20	320	21 20	20	1 20	1 21	1 22	1 23
21	1 24	81	5 24	141	9 24	201	13 24	261	17 24	321	21 24	21	1 24	1 25	1 26	1 27
22	1 28	82	5 28	142	9 28	202	13 28	262	17 28	322	21 28	22	1 28	1 29	1 30	1 31
23	1 32	83	5 32	143	9 32	203	13 32	263	17 32	323	21 32	23	1 32	1 33	1 34	1 35
24	1 36	84	5 36	144	9 36	204	13 36	264	17 36	324	21 36	24	1 36	1 37	1 38	1 39
25	1 40	85	5 40	145	9 40	205	13 40	265	17 40	325	21 40	25	1 40	1 41	1 42	1 43
26	1 44	86	5 44	146	9 44	206	13 44	266	17 44	326	21 44	26	1 44	1 45	1 46	1 47
27	1 48	87	5 48	147	9 48	207	13 48	267	17 48	327	21 48	27	1 48	1 49	1 50	1 51
28	1 52	88	5 52	148	9 52	208	13 52	268	17 52	328	21 52	28	1 52	1 53	1 54	1 55
29	1 56	89	5 56	149	9 56	209	13 56	269	17 56	329	21 56	29	1 56	1 57	1 58	1 59
30	2 00	90	6 00	150	10 00	210	14 00	270	18 00	330	22 00	30	2 00	2 01	2 02	2 03
31	2 04	91	6 04	151	10 04	211	14 04	271	18 04	331	22 04	31	2 04	2 05	2 06	2 07
32	2 08	92	6 08	152	10 08	212	14 08	272	18 08	332	22 08	32	2 08	2 09	2 10	2 11
33	2 12	93	6 12	153	10 12	213	14 12	273	18 12	333	22 12	33	2 12	2 13	2 14	2 15
34	2 16	94	6 16	154	10 16	214	14 16	274	18 16	334	22 16	34	2 16	2 17	2 18	2 19
35	2 20	95	6 20	155	10 20	215	14 20	275	18 20	335	22 20	35	2 20	2 21	2 22	2 23
36	2 24	96	6 24	156	10 24	216	14 24	276	18 24	336	22 24	36	2 24	2 25	2 26	2 27
37	2 28	97	6 28	157	10 28	217	14 28	277	18 28	337	22 28	37	2 28	2 29	2 30	2 31
38	2 32	98	6 32	158	10 32	218	14 32	278	18 32	338	22 32	38	2 32	2 33	2 34	2 35
39	2 36	99	6 36	159	10 36	219	14 36	279	18 36	339	22 36	39	2 36	2 37	2 38	2 39
40	2 40	100	6 40	160	10 40	220	14 40	280	18 40	340	22 40	40	2 40	2 41	2 42	2 43
41	2 44	101	6 44	161	10 44	221	14 44	281	18 44	341	22 44	41	2 44	2 45	2 46	2 47
42	2 48	102	6 48	162	10 48	222	14 48	282	18 48	342	22 48	42	2 48	2 49	2 50	2 51
43	2 52	103	6 52	163	10 52	223	14 52	283	18 52	343	22 52	43	2 52	2 53	2 54	2 55
44	2 56	104	6 56	164	10 56	224	14 56	284	18 56	344	22 56	44	2 56	2 57	2 58	2 59
45	3 00	105	7 00	165	11 00	225	15 00	285	19 00	345	23 00	45	3 00	3 01	3 02	3 03
46	3 04	106	7 04	166	11 04	226	15 04	286	19 04	346	23 04	46	3 04	3 05	3 06	3 07
47	3 08	107	7 08	167	11 08	227	15 08	287	19 08	347	23 08	47	3 08	3 09	3 10	3 11
48	3 12	108	7 12	168	11 12	228	15 12	288	19 12	348	23 12	48	3 12	3 13	3 14	3 15
49	3 16	109	7 16	169	11 16	229	15 16	289	19 16	349	23 16	49	3 16	3 17	3 18	3 19
50	3 20	110	7 20	170	11 20	230	15 20	290	19 20	350	23 20	50	3 20	3 21	3 22	3 23
51	3 24	111	7 24	171	11 24	231	15 24	291	19 24	351	23 24	51	3 24	3 25	3 26	3 27
52	3 28	112	7 28	172	11 28	232	15 28	292	19 28	352	23 28	52	3 28	3 29	3 30	3 31
53	3 32	113	7 32	173	11 32	233	15 32	293	19 32	353	23 32	53	3 32	3 33	3 34	3 35
54	3 36	114	7 36	174	11 36	234	15 36	294	19 36	354	23 36	54	3 36	3 37	3 38	3 39
55	3 40	115	7 40	175	11 40	235	15 40	295	19 40	355	23 40	55	3 40	3 41	3 42	3 43
56	3 44	116	7 44	176	11 44	236	15 44	296	19 44	356	23 44	56	3 44	3 45	3 46	3 47
57	3 48	117	7 48	177	11 48	237	15 48	297	19 48	357	23 48	57	3 48	3 49	3 50	3 51
58	3 52	118	7 52	178	11 52	238	15 52	298	19 52	358	23 52	58	3 52	3 53	3 54	3 55
59	3 56	119	7 56	179	11 56	239	15 56	299	19 56	359	23 56	59	3 56	3 57	3 58	3 59

The above table is for converting expressions in arc to their equivalent in time ; its main use in this Almanac is for the conversion of longitude for application to L.M.T. (*added* if *west*, *subtracted* if *east*) to give G.M.T. or vice versa, particularly in the case of sunrise, sunset, etc.

Figure 8-3. From the *Nautical Almanac, 1983,* showing conversion of 61°21′ W longitude into time equivalent.

develop the judgment to eliminate those sights where the times and sextant readings appear inconsistent with the others. As noted earlier, the latitude portion of the noon sight is not nearly so dependent on accurate time as the longitude portion. With longitude, four seconds of error in time translates to one minute of error in longitude. Since the sun appears to hover at the highest altitude for several minutes, determining the exact GMT of meridian passage is not easy.

One technique for determining the GMT of meridian passage is to take sights of equal altitude before and after meridian passage and average the time of the two sights. The average time is then used as the time of meridian passage in conjunction with the highest sextant reading during the time of passage.

For example, assume your worksheet for a series of noon sights looked like this:

GMT:	hours	minutes	seconds	sextant readings
	15	00	55	61°31.1'
→	15	02	20	61°31.7'
	15	02	38	61°31.8'
	15	04	30	61°32.2'
	15	05	25	61°32.3'
	15	06	15	61°32.3'
	15	07	05	61°32.3'
	15	07	56	61°32.0'
→	15	08	30	61°31.7'
	15	09	11	61°30.9'

From the information on the worksheet, it is obvious that meridian passage occurred sometime between 15 hours 05 minutes 25 seconds and 15 hours 07 minutes 05 seconds when the maximum altitude of 61°32.3' was reached. The question is, what time do you use?

The arrows on the worksheet show that the sun reached an altitude of 61°31.7' on the way up, and again on the way down. Since the sun moves at a constant rate, related to time, you can obtain

the time for the two equal altitude sights—one taken before meridian passage, and one taken after meridian passage—and average them to obtain the time of meridian passage:

15 hours 02 minutes 20 seconds
+ 15 hours 08 minutes 30 seconds

30 hours 10 minutes 50 seconds
divided by 2 =
15 hours 05 minutes 25 seconds.

The average time, 15 hours 05 minutes 25 seconds is used with the sextant reading of 61°32.3' to calculate the latitude and longitude. To insure that sights of equal altitude are obtained, you can make a mental note of a convenient altitude as the sun is going up, then preset the sextant to this altitude and observe the sun after meridian passage until the preset altitude is reached.

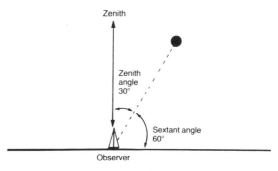

Figure 8-4. The zenith angle is equal to a 90° angle minus the corrected sextant reading. Therefore, 90° minus sextant reading of 60° = 30° zenith angle.

Latitude by Noon Sight

The calculations for latitude by the noon sight are so simple you can work them out on the back of an envelope. Latitude at noon is found by first subtracting the corrected sextant angle (Ho) from 90° and then adding or subtracting the declination of the sun for the GMT of observation.

The angle that you obtain when you subtract Ho from 90° is called the zenith angle. As Figure 8-4 shows, if the sun were directly over your head the sextant angle would be 90°. The sextant angle of the sun, in this case, is 60°, the zenith angle which represents the distance the sun must travel to be directly overhead, is 30°. The zenith represents how far the GP of the sun is from the observer.

The declination of the sun represents the sun's distance, north or south, of the equator. When you think about it, there are only three possible ways in which the zenith angle and the declination can relate to each other:

1. The sun lies between the observer and the equator.
2. The observer is between the equator and the sun.
3. The equator lies between the observer and the sun.

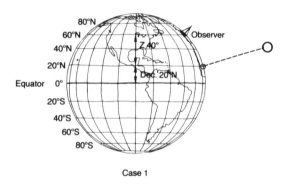

Figure 8-5. Case 1. Declination less than latitude and both north or south. Declination of 20° + Z of 40° = 60°N latitude of observer. Latitude is north because declination and latitude were both north.

CASE 1

Figure 8-5 illustrates case 1. Since the sun is between the observer and the equator, the sun's declination will be less than the observer's latitude. Since both are on the same side of the equator, the declination and latitude will have the same name, e.g. both are north or both south. Therefore, the rule for case 1, where declination is less than latitude and they have the same name is:

latitude = declination + zenith angle

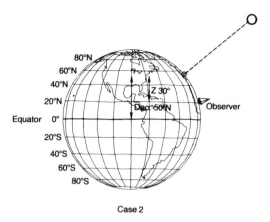

Figure 8-6. Case 2. Declination greater than latitude and both north or south. Declination of 50° − Z of 30° = 20°N latitude of observer. Latitude is north because declination and latitude were both north.

CASE 2

Figure 8-6 illustrates case 2. Here the sun's declination is greater than your latitude so the observer is between the GP of the sun and the equator. Both, however, are on the same side of the equator. The rule for case 2 where declination is greater than latitude and both have the same name is:

latitude = declination − zenith angle

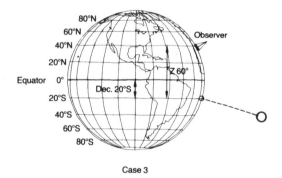

Figure 8-7. Case 3. Declination and latitude are contrary, one north, the other south. Z of 60° − latitude of 20° = 40° latitude of observer. Latitude is north.

CASE 3

Figure 8-7 illustrates case 3. In this instance, the declination of the sun lies in one hemisphere and the latitude of the observer lies in the other. Declination

Item   General Data

1. Name of Body — `SUN - NOON`

2. Limb (Upper/Lower) — `LOWER`

3. Date (G) — `6 JUNE 83`

	Hrs	Min	Sec
4. Watch Time (G)	16	15	31
5. Watch Error (+ if slow – if fast)		—	
6. GMT (six digits)	16	15	31

	Deg	Mins	Tenths
7. DR Latitude (N/S)	39	13	N
8. DR Longitude (E/W)	64	18	W

Sextant Corrections
—general

	Deg	Mins	Tenths
9. Sextant Reading (Hs)	73	12	8
10. Instrument Corr. (+ or –)		—	
11. Index Correction (+ or –)		—	
12. Dip Correction for __10__ feet –)		–3	1
13. Total (Items 9-12) is Apparent Altitude (Ha).	73	09	7

Sextant corrections from inside front/back covers of Almanac

14. Altitude Correction (+ or –)		+15	6
15. Venus, Mars only, add'l correction (+ or –)		—	
16. Moon only, Corr. for daily page HP: ____ (+)		—	
17. Moon only, if *upper* limb –30'		—	
18. Non-Standard conditions only, add'l Corr.		—	
19. Total (Items 13-18) is Observed Altitude (Ho)	73	25	3

GHA—from Nautical Almanac

DAILY PAGES

	Deg	Mins	Tenths
20. GHA of body, whole hours ● "v" value, planets moon, + unless shown otherwise "v" [—]	60	21	9

YELLOW PAGES

21. Increments, (+) minutes and secs., from sun/planets or moon column.	3	52	8
22. Moon, planets, "v" correction for "v" value above, use same sign		—	
23. Total GHA (items 20-21 & 22) ● if over 360° subtract 360°	64	14	7

Declination—From Nautical Almanac

DAILY PAGES

	Deg	Mins	Tenths	
24. Declination, whole hour, (N/S)	22	38	4	N

● "d" value, (+ if Dec. increasing, – if Dec. decreasing) "d" [+0.2]

YELLOW PAGES

25. "d" correction for "d" value above, use same sign		+	1	
26. Total Declination (Items 24-25) (N/S)	22	38	5	N

---

1. Calculate Zenith Angle
   Enter Ho (item 19)
   Total is Zenith Angle

	Deg.	Min.	Tenths
	89°	59'	10
	–73	25	3
	16	34	7

o (Dec. less than Lat.) (both N) or both S

   Enter Dec. (Item 26)
   Enter Zenith Angle
   Total is Latitude
   (N if both N; S if both S)

	Deg.	Min.	Tenths	
	22	38	5	NORTH
	+16	34	7	
	39°	13.2		North

o Dec. greater than Lat, both N or both S

   Enter Dec. (Item 26)
   Enter Zenith Angle
   Total is Latitude
   (N if both N; S if both S)

	Deg	Min	Tenths
	–		

o Dec. and Latitude are contrary, one N, One S

   Enter Zenith Angle
   Enter Dec. (Item 26)
   Total is Latitude

	Deg.	Min.	Tenths
	–		

(West Longitude)

   GHA of Sun from Item 23 = Longitude

   `64° 14.7' WEST`

East Longitude

   Enter GHA (Item 23)
   Total is Longitude

	Deg.	Min.	Tenths
	359	59	10
	–		

GMT and Sextant Readings (Hs)

GMT			Hs.		
Hours	Minutes	Seconds	Deg.	Min.	Tenths

Copyright, C, 1983, Navigation Institute, Inc.

Figure 8-8. Solution to noon sight problem.

and latitude are contrary since one is north, the other south. The rule is:

latitude = zenith angle − declination

Where the DR latitude and declination have the same name, the computed latitude, obviously, will take that name. If declination and latitude are contrary most of the time there is no problem. Most sailors know if they are in the northern or southern hemisphere but around the equator there may be some ambiguity. If this becomes a problem, regular sun sights should be taken instead of noon sights.

Noon Sight Workform

Figure 8-8 is a noon sight workform which contains all the information to help you calculate the zenith angle, and combine the zenith angle with the declination to obtain your latitude. There is also space on the form to record up to 22 sights.

Longitude by Noon Sight

Obtaining a sight at the exact time of meridian passage is rather difficult. For this reason, the longitude portion of the noon sight should not be considered as precise as the latitude portion. Once you have the sight, however, figuring the longitude is remarkably easy. As the workform indicates, in west longitude the GHA of the sun (daily pages plus increments) for the GMT of the noon sight is your longitude. In east longitude, you simply subtract the GHA from 360° to obtain the longitude.

PRACTICE PROBLEMS (Refer to Appendix 2)

You are in DR 39°13′N; 64°18′W and want to take a noon sight of the sun. The date is 6 June, 1983. What is the estimated GMT of meridian passage for your longitude? You ob-

tained the noon sight on the lower limb of the sun at 16 hours 15 minutes 31 seconds GMT. The sextant reading was 73°12.8′; no index error, no instrument error, and the height of eye was 10 feet. What is your zenith angle? What is your latitude and longitude?

ANSWERS (For complete solution, see Figure 8-8)

The estimated time of meridian passage is 16 hours 16 minutes GMT. The zenith angle is: 16°34.7′. Latitude is 39°13.2′N; longitude is 64°14.7′W.

Great Circle Sailing

In piloting, a rhumb line is a straight line between two points on a chart. Where short distances are involved, up to 500-600 miles, a rhumb line is also the shortest distance between any two points. When sailing rhumb line courses, the direction does not change. However, when you start sailing long distances, like crossing an ocean, you can save a lot of distance by following the great circle course. For example, on a Pacific Ocean passage the distance saved could represent hundreds of miles. A great circle is the shortest distance between two points on a globe. It is a line on the surface of the earth, which if drawn all the way around the world, would cut the earth in two equal parts. A great circle course differs from a rhumb line course in that it continuously changes direction.

You should use a great circle course when you want to take advantage of the shorter distance. Great circle sailing is particularly useful in the higher latitudes and on east-west passages.

The easiest way to figure the great circle course is to use a special chart called a gnomonic chart. These charts—often referred to as great circle charts—are published by the Defense Mapping Agency, Hydrographic Center (DMAHC) and are available from navigation supply stores. The top of Figure 8-9 shows how a

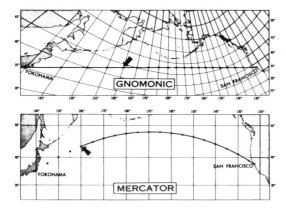

Figure 8-9. A straight line between two points is drawn on the Gnomonic Chart. The coordinates are then transferred to a standard, or mercator, chart.

navigator used a gnomonic chart to draw a straight line between the point of departure, San Francisco, to the destination, Yokohama, Japan. The bottom of Figure 8-9 shows how the gnomonic chart was used to make a list of convenient points along the great circle track which were transferred to a standard nautical chart. In this case, the navigator plotted the coordinates of the great circle course for every five degrees of longitude along the route. Finally, a series of straight lines is drawn between the dots. On this voyage, the skipper will sail this series of rhumb line courses which will approximate the great circle course.

If you find there is a land mass, such as an island, directly in the path of the great circle course, sail to a safe latitude below the obstruction, leave the great circle course and sail along this latitude until you are clear of the obstruction. Then you can resume great circle sailing again.

Planning a Cruise

One of the most useful tools for planning a cruise is a pilot chart. Pilot charts, published by DMAHC, contain information about the weather, wind patterns, wave heights, tropical storms, currents, fog, and ice for a given area. Monthly pilot charts are available for the North Atlantic and North Pacific oceans. Yearly pilot charts are available for the South Atlantic, South Pacific, and Indian oceans.

The information on the pilot charts is gathered over many years and averaged before being printed on the chart. You should use pilot charts to determine the most favorable conditions for a voyage. Figure 8-10 is an extract from the April, 1982 Pilot Chart of the North Atlantic.

Sailors should pay particular attention to the wind roses on pilot charts. The "feathers" sticking out from the wind roses indicate the direction, frequency, and intensity of the prevailing winds in that area. Wind conditions are given for the eight major points of the compass. The arrows indicate the direction from which the wind is blowing. The length of the shaft indicates the percent of the time the wind blows from that direction. The number of feathers shows the average force of the wind on the Beaufort scale. For example, five feathers indicates force five which is 17 to 21 knots. In those cases where the wind blows mainly from one direction (say over thirty percent) the shaft would be too long so it is broken and a number representing the percentage is listed along the shaft. The number in the center of the wind rose circle indicates the percentage of calms reported in that area.

Publications and References

In addition to great circle and pilot charts, anyone planning a voyage should refer to a number of other references including government and privately published sources including:

Light Lists: Published by DMAHC for foreign waters and by the Coast Guard

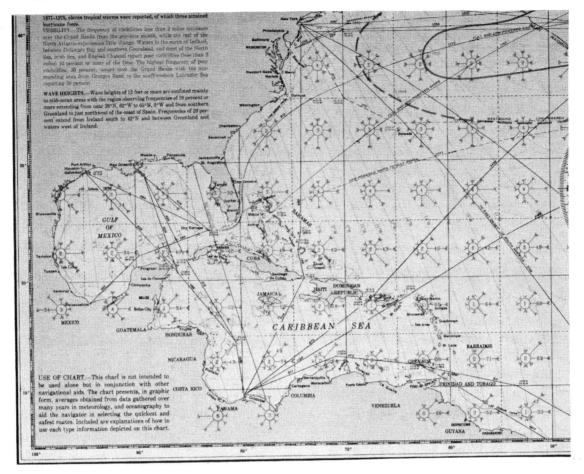

Figure 8-10. Extract from the April, 1982 pilot chart of the North Atlantic.

for U.S. waters, these books give the position and characteristics of major lights and aids to navigation.

Tide Tables: Published by the U.S. government, these books give the predicted times of high and low tides for major points called reference stations.

Coast Pilot: A nine-volume series published by the U.S. government, these provide information with respect to the U.S. coastal waters. While primarily designed for military and merchant vessels, they are of some use to yachtsmen.

Radio Aids to Navigation: Published by the U.S. government, these list the location and signals of all major radio beacons and broadcasts of use to the mariner.

Sailing Directions: Published by the U.S. government, these contain information about overseas coasts, islands, harbors and navigation aids. Since they come in a loose-leaf format, you would be wise to order the optional ring binders for them. They are of limited use to small boat sailors. (These government publications can be purchased from nautical supply stores.)

Ocean Passages For The World: This is a unique book published in Great Britain (but available from navigation supply stores in the United States) which contains special charts, sailing directions, and information of use to sail-powered vessels.

Bowditch, Volume I: This 1,300-page government volume is a compendium of information, facts, tables, and explanations covering virtually every aspect of navigation.

Charts: You should have complete coverages, in the appropriate scales, for the area in which you are cruising. Along the U.S. East Coast you can save considerable space and money by purchasing ring-bound folios containing reproductions of the latest government charts from private publishers.

The U.S. intra-coastal waterway is covered in a series of excellent cruising guides available from Waterway Guide, 6151 Powers Ferry Road, N.W., Atlanta, Georgia 30339.

Anyone heading for the Eastern Caribbean would do well to consider stocking a set of the Imray-Iolare charts which include a great deal of information, such as close-inshore detail, useful ranges, harbor insets, and recent changes not found on government charts of the region. These charts are based on the personal surveys of noted cruising sailor and author Donald M. Street. In the United States they are available from Weems & Plath, 214 Eastern Avenue, Annapolis, Maryland 21403.

Appendix 1.
Sample Workforms (Blank)

H.O.-229 CELESTIAL WORKFORM: SUN, MOON, PLANETS

Item General Data

1. Name of Body

2. Limb (Upper/Lower)

3. Date (G)

	Hrs	Min	Sec
4. Watch Time (G)			
5. Watch Error (+ if slow − if fast)			
6. GMT (six digits)			

	Deg	Mins	Tenths
7. DR Latitude (N/S)			
8. DR Longitude (E/W)			

Sextant Corrections
—general

	Deg	Mins	Tenths
9. Sextant Reading (Hs)			
10. Instrument Corr. (+ or −)			
11. Index Correction (+ or −)			
12. Dip Correction for ___ feet −)			
13. Total (Items 9-12) is Apparent Altitude (Ha).			

Sextant corrections from inside front/back covers of Almanac

	Deg	Mins	Tenths
14. Altitude Correction (+ or −)			
15. Venus, Mars only, add'l correction (+ or −)			
16. Moon only, Corr. for daily page HP: ___ (+)			
17. Moon only, if *upper limb* −30'			
18. Non-Standard conditions only, add'l Corr.			
19. Total (Items 13-18) is Observed Altitude (Ho)			

GHA—from Nautical Almanac
DAILY PAGES

	Deg	Mins	Tenths
20. GHA of body, whole hours ● "v" value, planets "v" moon, + unless shown otherwise			
YELLOW PAGES **21.** Increments. (+) minutes and secs., from sun/planets or moon column.			
22. Moon, planets, "v" correction for "v" value above, use same sign			
23. Total GHA (items 20-21 & 22) ● if over 360° subtract 360°			

Declination—From Nautical Almanac
DAILY PAGES

	Deg	Mins	Tenths
24. Declination, whole hour, (N/S)			
● "d" value, (+ if Dec. increasing, − if Dec. decreasing) "d"			
YELLOW PAGES **25.** "d" correction for "d" value above, use same sign			
26. Total Declination items 24-25) (N/S)			

LHA Diagram

W — G — e

Step 1: Computing LHA:

West Longitude — deg min tenths

East Longitude — deg min tenths

. Enter GHA (#23)....... deg min tenths

. Enter DR Long (# 8)   −30'

range= +1°

. Enter Assum. Long.....   −   0 0.0   +   0 0.0

. Total is LHA (+360 if neg; − 360 if over 360)

Step 2: Enter HO-229 With: Degrees

. LHA (from Step 1) ......

. DR Lat (#7) rounded.....   N S (same or

. Dec. (#26) degrees......   N S contrary)

Step 3: Extract from HO-229: _____ *

Hc (tab) _____ d* (tab) + − _____ Z(tab) _____

     _____ *Zbelow _____

d* diff. _____ *Zdiff.

(inc; dec.)

Step 4: Corrections from Interpolation Table:

. Enter with Dec. Increment (#26) of _____ . _____

   mins   tenths   Deg min tenths

. d (tab) from Step 3

( ) tens............ corr. + −

( ) units ( )dec. corr. + −

. d*, enter DSD table with d.diff....corr. +

. Enter Hc (tab) from Step 3............. +

. Total is Computed Altitude, Hc.........

   Degrees tenths

. Enter Z (tab) from Step 3.............

. Z (diff) from Step 3

( ) units ( )dec. corr.(+Inc, − Dec.)

. Total is Z.(Azimuth Angle)

Step 5: Compute Zn. (True Azimuth):

	North Latitude		South Latitude	
	LHA greater than 180°	LHA Less than 180°	LHA greater than 180°	LHA less than 180°
	000°.0	360°.0	180°.0	180°.0
. Enter Z.	+	−	−	+

. Total is Zn.

Step 6: Compute Intercept:

   Deg min tenths

. Enter Ho (#19)........ +

. Enter Hc from Step 4... −

. Difference is Intercept   A   T

(Hc greater, away)

Step 7: Plotting Data:

. Assumed Longitude (Step 1) _____ W E

. Latitude (rounded) (Step 2) _____ N S

. Azimuth (Step 5).......... _____

. Intercept (Step 6)........ _____ A T

H.O. 229 - WORKFORM: STARS

Item General Data

1. Name of Star

2. Date (G)

3. Watch Time (G) (six digits) — Hrs | Mins | Secs

4. Watch Error. (+ if slow − if fast)

5. GMT

6. DR Latitude (N/S) — Deg | Mins | .Tenths

7. DR Longitude (E/W)

Sextant Corrections—general

Deg | Min | Tenths

8. Sextant Reading (Hs)

9. Instrument Corr. (+ or −)

10. Index Correction (+ or −)

11. Dip Correction for _____ feet (−)

12. Total (Items 8-11) is Apparent Altitude (Ha).

Sextant corrections from inside front cover of Almanac

13. Altitude Correction (+ or −)

14. Additional Correction for Non-Standard Conditions

15. Total (Items 12-14) is Observed Altitude (Ho)

GHA—from Nautical Almanac

DAILY PAGES — Deg | Mins | Tenths

16. GHA of Aries, whole hours

17. SHA of Star, list of stars (+)

YELLOW PAGES

18. Increments, minutes & secs., aries column (+)

19. Total GHA (items 16, 17, 18) ● If over 360° subtract 360°

Declination—from Nautical Almanac

DAILY PAGES — Deg | Mins | Tenths

20. Declination, list of stars (N/S)

Direction of Star—use with star ID only

A. Handbearing compass direction _____ degrees

B. Variation from chart (+E; −W) _____ degrees

C. Deviation (if known) (+E; −W) _____ degrees

21. True Direction (Total, A, B, C) _____ degrees

LHA Diagram
w — G — e

Step 1: Computing LHA:

West Longitude — deg min tenths

East Longitude — deg min tenths

. Enter GHA (#19)..........

deg min tenths

. Enter DR Long (#7) range — −30'   +1°

. Enter Assum. Long.....

. Total is LHA (+360 if neg; − 360 if over 360)

West Longitude: −   0 0.0

East Longitude: +   0 0.0

Step 2: Enter HO-229 With: Degrees

. LHA (from Step 1) ......

. DR Lat (#6) rounded.....   N S (same or

. Dec. (#20) degrees......   N S contrary)

Step 3: Extract from HO-229:

Hc (tab) _____ d* (tab) + − _____ *

_____ Z(tab)

*Zbelow _____

d* diff. _____ *Zdiff. _____

(inc; decr.)

Step 4: Corrections from Interpolation Table:

. Enter with Dec. Increment (#20) of _____ .

mins | tenths   Deg | min | tenths

. d (tab) from Step 3
(   ) tens............ corr. + −
(   ) units (   )dec. corr. + −
. d*, enter DSD table with d.diff....corr.+
. Enter Hc (tab) from Step 3.............+
. Total is Computed Altitude, Hc........

Degrees | tenths

. Enter Z (tab) from Step 3..............
. Z (diff) from Step 3
(   ) units (   )dec. corr.(+Inc,
                            −Decr.)
. Total is Z.(Azimuth Angle)

Step 5: Compute Zn. (True Azimuth):

	North Latitude		South Latitude	
	LHA greater than 180°	LHA Less than 180°	LHA greater than 180°	LHA less than 180°
	000°.0	360°.0	180°.0	180°.0
. Enter Z.	+	−	−	+

. Total is Zn.

Step 6: Compute Intercept:

Deg | min | tenths

. Enter Ho (#15)......... +
. Enter Hc from Step 4... −
. Difference is Intercept   A T
(Hc greater, away)

Step 7: Plotting Data:

. Assumed Longitude (Step 1) _____ W E
. Latitude (rounded) (Step 2) _____ N S
. Azimuth (Step 5).......... _____
. Intercept (Step 6).......: _____ A T

Weems & Plath
Education Division
In Association with Navigation Institute
COPYRIGHT 1980 by NI, Inc.

STAR & PLANET IDENTIFICATION WORKFORM - HO-229
Copyright, Ⓒ, 1980, Navigation Institute Inc.

```
┌─────────────────────────────────┐
│ Compass Direction: _____      │
│ + E  - W Variation: _____      │
│ + E  - W Deviation: _____      │
│ Total is True Dir.: _____      │
└─────────────────────────────────┘
```

1. Enter "same" portion of Table with:

    • True Dir. if Lat. is North _____ as LHA
            OR
      True Dir. -180 {
      180 - True Dir.   If Lat. is South _____ as LHA

    • Latitude (N) (S) (Nearest Degree) _____ as Latitude

    • Sextant Altitude (H $_s$) _____ as Declination

2. Extract from HO-229 Table:

    • Hc.........record as: Approximate Declination: [(N) (S)]
                              (Contrary to L if found on right hand page and above the line)

    • Z _____ { • (left hand page or right hand below line Z = T angle)_____
                           { • (right hand page above line: 180-Z or Z-180 = T angle)_____

3. Convert "T" Angle to LHA:

    If True Dir. is 0° to 180°   If True Dir. is 180° to 360°

    ┌─────────────────────────┐   ┌─────────────────────────┐
    │   360°   │   │   │
    │   Minus "T" - _____   │   │   "T" equals LHA: _____ │
    │ Total is LHA   _____   │   │   │
    └─────────────────────────┘   └─────────────────────────┘

4. Convert LHA to Approximate SHA:

              West Longitude   East Longitude

    ┌──────────────────────────────┐   ┌──────────────────────────────┐
    │ Enter LHA (Step 3) _____ │   │   360°   │
    │ Add DR Long.   + _____   │   │ Add LHA (Step 3)   + _____ │
    │   (total)   + _____   │   │   (total)   _____ │
    │ Minus GHA Aries - _____   │   │ Subtract DR Long. - _____ │
    │ Approx SHA (Total)+/- _____ │   │   (total)   _____ │
    │ (Add 360° if Negative;   │   │ Minus GHA Aries   - _____ │
    │ subtract 360° if over   │   │ Approx SHA (Total)+/- _____ │
    │ 360°)   │   │ (Subtract 360° if over   │
    │   │   │ 360°; add 360° if negative)   │
    └──────────────────────────────┘   └──────────────────────────────┘

Use Approx. Dec.: _____ (N) (S) and Approx. SHA: _____
   to identify Star or Planet. Name of Star or Planet: _____

Star Identification (Copyright, 1981, Navigation Institute, Inc.)

Sextant Reading: _____   Handbearing Compass Direction: _____
Date: (G) _____ GMT: _____   Variation (+E; -W)   _____
DR: Lat: _____ Long: _____   True Direction of Star   _____
1. Compute LHA of Aries   West Long.   East Long.
Enter GHA Aries (whole hr.)
Enter Increments Aries (mins. secs.)   [+   ]   [+   ]
Total is GHA Aries
Enter DR Longitude   [-   ]   [+   ]
Total is LHA Aries (+360 if neg. -360 if over 360)

2. Use "N" star base if DR Lat. is North; use "S" if DR Lat. is South

3. Use blue disc nearest DR latitude. Mount on star base.

4. Rotate blue disc until arrow points to LHA of Aries (whole degrees.)

5. Locate star closest to sextant reading and true direction of star.
                    Name of Star: _____

Planet Location: Date: (G) _____ GMT: _____ Planet: _____
1. Compute LHA of planet   West Long.   East Long.
Enter GHA (whole hr.)
Enter increments (mins, secs.)   [+   ]   [+   ]
Total is GHA of planet
Enter DR Longitude   [-   ]   [+   ]
Total is LHA of Planet (+360 if neg.-360 if over
                    360)
2. Enter HO-229 with: [Degrees]
    ● LHA* (Rounded) from step 1   [   ]
    ● DR Latitude* (rounded)   [   ] N S (Same or
    ● Declination* (Whole degrees)   N S contrary)

➤ * Planet is below horizon if LHA between 90 & 270 & Lat. & Dec. contrary

3. Extract from HO-229:**   Hc (tab) _____ Z (Tab) _____
➤ ** Planet is below horizon if you have to cross S-C line

4. Compute Zn (True Azimuth

	North Latitude		South Latitude	
	LHA Greater than 180	LHA Less than 180	LHA Greater than 180	LHA less than 180
	000 .0 +	360 .0 -	180 .0 -	180 .0 +

    ● Enter Z
    ● Total is Zn.

5. Record Hc. (Step 3) _____   Record Zn. (Step 4) _____
                                           Variation (-E+W)   _____
                                           Total is handbearing _____
                                           compass direction

Latitude, Longitude From Meridian Passage of the Sun

Item   General Data

1. Name of Body

2. Limb (Upper/Lower)

3. Date (G)

	Hrs	Min	Sec
4. Watch Time (G)			
5. Watch Error (+ if slow — if fast)			
6. GMT (six digits)			

	Deg	Mins	Tenths
7. DR Latitude (N/S)			
8. DR Longitude (E/W)			

Sextant Corrections —general

	Deg	Mins	Tenths
9. Sextant Reading (Hs)			
10. Instrument Corr. (+ or −)			
11. Index Correction (+ or −)			
12. Dip Correction for _____ feet −)			
13. Total (Items 9-12) is Apparent Altitude (Ha).			

Sextant corrections from inside front/back covers of Almanac

	Deg	Mins	Tenths
14. Altitude Correction (+ or −)			
15. Venus, Mars only, add'l correction (+ or −)			
16. Moon only, Corr. for daily page HP: _____ (+)			
17. Moon only, if upper limb −30'			
18. Non-Standard conditions only, add'l Corr.			
19. Total (Items 13-18) is Observed Altitude (Ho)			

GHA—from Nautical Almanac
DAILY PAGES

	Deg	Mins	Tenths
20. GHA of body, whole hours ● "v" value, planets moon, + unless shown otherwise "v" [box]			

YELLOW PAGES

21. Increments, (+) minutes and secs., from sun/planets or moon column.			
22. Moon, planets, "v" correction for "v" value above, use same sign			
23. Total GHA (items 20-21 & 22) ● if over 360° subtract 360°			

Declination—From Nautical Almanac
DAILY PAGES

	Deg	Mins	Tenths
24. Declination, whole hour, (N/S)			
● "d" value, (+ if Dec. increasing, − if Dec. decreasing) "d" [box]			

YELLOW PAGES

25. "d" correction for "d" value above, use same sign			
26. Total Declination (items 24-25) (N/S)			

Latitude

1. Calculate Zenith Angle
   Enter Ho (item 19)
   Total is Zenith Angle

	Deg.	Min.	Tenths
	89°	59'	10
−			

o **Dec. less than Lat, both N or both S**

Enter Dec. (Item 26)
Enter Zenith Angle
Total is Latitude
(N if both N; S if both S)

	Deg.	Min.	Tenths
+			

o **Dec. greater than Lat, both N or both S**

Enter Dec. (Item 26)
Enter Zenith Angle
Total is Latitude
(N if both N; S if both S)

	Deg	Min	Tenths
−			

o **Dec. and Latitude are contrary, one N, One S**

Enter Zenith Angle
Enter Dec. (Item 26)
Total is Latitude

	Deg.	Min.	Tenths
−			

Longitude

West Longitude

GHA of Sun from Item 23 = Longitude

East Longitude

Enter GHA (Item 23)
Total is Longitude

	Deg.	Min.	Tenths
	359	59	10
−			

GMT and Sextant Readings (Hs)

GMT			Hs.		
Hours	Minutes	Seconds	Deg.	Min.	Tenths

Copyright, C, 1983, Navigation Institute, Inc.

Appendix 2.
Extracts from the 1983 *Nautical Almanac*

THE

NAUTICAL ALMANAC

FOR THE YEAR
1983

<table>
<tr><td>WASHINGTON:</td><td>LONDON:</td></tr>
<tr><td>Issued by the
Nautical Almanac Office
United States
Naval Observatory
under the
authority of the
Secretary of the Navy</td><td>Issued by
Her Majesty's
Nautical Almanac Office
by order
of the
Secretary of State
for Defence</td></tr>
</table>

U.S. GOVERNMENT PRINTING OFFICE

WASHINGTON : 1981

For sale by the Superintendent of Documents, U.S. Government Printing Office
Washington, D.C. 20402

ALTITUDE CORRECTION TABLES 10°-90°—SUN, STARS, PLANETS

SUN

OCT.—MAR. App. Alt.	Lower Limb	Upper Limb	APR.—SEPT. App. Alt.	Lower Limb	Upper Limb
9 34	+10.8	−21.5	9 39	+10.6	−21.2
9 45	+10.9	−21.4	9 51	+10.7	−21.1
9 56	+11.0	−21.3	10 03	+10.8	−21.0
10 08	+11.1	−21.2	10 15	+10.9	−20.9
10 21	+11.2	−21.1	10 27	+11.0	−20.8
10 34	+11.3	−21.0	10 40	+11.1	−20.7
10 47	+11.4	−20.9	10 54	+11.2	−20.6
11 01	+11.5	−20.8	11 08	+11.3	−20.5
11 15	+11.6	−20.7	11 23	+11.4	−20.4
11 30	+11.7	−20.6	11 38	+11.5	−20.3
11 46	+11.8	−20.5	11 54	+11.6	−20.2
12 02	+11.9	−20.4	12 10	+11.7	−20.1
12 19	+12.0	−20.3	12 28	+11.8	−20.0
12 37	+12.1	−20.2	12 46	+11.9	−19.9
12 55	+12.2	−20.1	13 05	+12.0	−19.8
13 14	+12.3	−20.0	13 24	+12.1	−19.7
13 35	+12.4	−19.9	13 45	+12.2	−19.6
13 56	+12.5	−19.8	14 07	+12.3	−19.5
14 18	+12.6	−19.7	14 30	+12.4	−19.4
14 42	+12.7	−19.6	14 54	+12.5	−19.3
15 06	+12.8	−19.5	15 19	+12.6	−19.2
15 32	+12.9	−19.4	15 46	+12.7	−19.1
15 59	+13.0	−19.3	16 14	+12.8	−19.0
16 28	+13.1	−19.2	16 44	+12.9	−18.9
16 59	+13.2	−19.1	17 15	+13.0	−18.8
17 32	+13.3	−19.0	17 48	+13.1	−18.7
18 06	+13.4	−18.9	18 24	+13.2	−18.6
18 42	+13.5	−18.8	19 01	+13.3	−18.5
19 21	+13.6	−18.7	19 42	+13.4	−18.4
20 03	+13.7	−18.6	20 25	+13.5	−18.3
20 48	+13.8	−18.5	21 11	+13.6	−18.2
21 35	+13.9	−18.4	22 00	+13.7	−18.1
22 26	+14.0	−18.3	22 54	+13.8	−18.0
23 22	+14.1	−18.2	23 51	+13.9	−17.9
24 21	+14.2	−18.1	24 53	+14.0	−17.8
25 26	+14.3	−18.0	26 00	+14.1	−17.7
26 36	+14.4	−17.9	27 13	+14.2	−17.6
27 52	+14.5	−17.8	28 33	+14.3	−17.5
29 15	+14.6	−17.7	30 00	+14.4	−17.4
30 46	+14.7	−17.6	31 35	+14.5	−17.3
32 26	+14.8	−17.5	33 20	+14.6	−17.2
34 17	+14.9	−17.4	35 17	+14.7	−17.1
36 20	+15.0	−17.3	37 26	+14.8	−17.0
38 36	+15.1	−17.2	39 50	+14.9	−16.9
41 08	+15.2	−17.1	42 31	+15.0	−16.8
43 59	+15.3	−17.0	45 31	+15.1	−16.7
47 10	+15.4	−16.9	48 55	+15.2	−16.6
50 46	+15.5	−16.8	52 44	+15.3	−16.5
54 49	+15.6	−16.7	57 02	+15.4	−16.4
59 23	+15.7	−16.6	61 51	+15.5	−16.3
64 30	+15.8	−16.5	67 17	+15.6	−16.2
70 12	+15.9	−16.4	73 16	+15.7	−16.1
76 26	+16.0	−16.3	79 43	+15.8	−16.0
83 05	+16.1	−16.2	86 32	+15.9	−15.9
90 00			90 00		

STARS AND PLANETS

App. Alt.	Corrn
9 56	−5.3
10 08	−5.2
10 20	−5.1
10 33	−5.0
10 46	−4.9
11 00	−4.8
11 14	−4.7
11 29	−4.6
11 45	−4.5
12 01	−4.4
12 18	−4.3
12 35	−4.2
12 54	−4.1
13 13	−4.0
13 33	−3.9
13 54	−3.8
14 16	−3.7
14 40	−3.6
15 04	−3.5
15 30	−3.4
15 57	−3.3
16 26	−3.2
16 56	−3.1
17 28	−3.0
18 02	−2.9
18 38	−2.8
19 17	−2.7
19 58	−2.6
20 42	−2.5
21 28	−2.4
22 19	−2.3
23 13	−2.2
24 11	−2.1
25 14	−2.0
26 22	−1.9
27 36	−1.8
28 56	−1.7
30 24	−1.6
32 00	−1.5
33 45	−1.4
35 40	−1.3
37 48	−1.2
40 08	−1.1
42 44	−1.0
45 36	−0.9
48 47	−0.8
52 18	−0.7
56 11	−0.6
60 28	−0.5
65 08	−0.4
70 11	−0.3
75 34	−0.2
81 13	−0.1
87 03	0.0
90 00	

Additional Corrn

1983

VENUS

Jan. 1-May 10
App. Alt.	Additional Corrn
42	+0.1

May 11-June 23
| 47 | +0.2 |

June 24-July 19
| 46 | +0.3 |

July 20-Aug. 3
| 11 | +0.4 |
| 41 | +0.5 |

Aug. 4-Aug. 12
6	+0.5
20	+0.6
31	+0.7

Aug. 13-Sept. 7
4	+0.6
12	+0.7
22	+0.8

Sept. 8-Sept. 16
6	+0.5
20	+0.6
31	+0.7

Sept. 17-Oct. 2
| 11 | +0.4 |
| 41 | +0.5 |

Oct. 3-Oct. 30
| 46 | +0.3 |

Oct. 31-Dec. 17
| 47 | +0.2 |

Dec. 18-Dec. 31
| 42 | +0.1 |

MARS

Jan. 1-Dec. 31
| 60 | +0.1 |

DIP

Ht. of Eye (m)	Corrn	Ht. of Eye (ft.)	Ht. of Eye (m)	Corrn
2.4	−2.8	8.0	1.0	−1.8
2.6	−2.9	8.6	1.5	−2.2
2.8	−3.0	9.2	2.0	−2.5
3.0	−3.1	9.8	2.5	−2.8
3.2	−3.2	10.5	3.0	−3.0
3.4	−3.3	11.2	See table ←	
3.6	−3.4	11.9		
3.8	−3.5	12.6	(m)	
4.0	−3.6	13.3	20	−7.9
4.3	−3.7	14.1	22	−8.3
4.5	−3.8	14.9	24	−8.6
4.7	−3.9	15.7	26	−9.0
5.0	−4.0	16.5	28	−9.3
5.2	−4.1	17.4		
5.5	−4.2	18.3	30	−9.6
5.8	−4.3	19.1	32	−10.0
6.1	−4.4	20.1	34	−10.3
6.3	−4.5	21.0	36	−10.6
6.6	−4.6	22.0	38	−10.8
6.9	−4.7	22.9		
7.2	−4.8	23.9	40	−11.1
7.5	−4.9	24.9	42	−11.4
7.9	−5.0	26.0	44	−11.7
8.2	−5.1	27.1	46	−11.9
8.5	−5.2	28.1	48	−12.2
8.8	−5.3	29.2		
9.2	−5.4	30.4	(ft.)	
9.5	−5.5	31.5	2	−1.4
9.9	−5.6	32.7	4	−1.9
10.3	−5.7	33.9	6	−2.4
10.6	−5.8	35.1	8	−2.7
11.0	−5.9	36.3	10	−3.1
11.4	−6.0	37.6	See table ←	
11.8	−6.1	38.9		
12.2	−6.2	40.1	(ft.)	
12.6	−6.3	41.5	70	−8.1
13.0	−6.4	42.8	75	−8.4
13.4	−6.5	44.2	80	−8.7
13.8	−6.6	45.5	85	−8.9
14.2	−6.7	46.9	90	−9.2
14.7	−6.8	48.4	95	−9.5
15.1	−6.9	49.8		
15.5	−7.0	51.3	100	−9.7
16.0	−7.1	52.8	105	−9.9
16.5	−7.2	54.3	110	−10.2
16.9	−7.3	55.8	115	−10.4
17.4	−7.4	57.4	120	−10.6
17.9	−7.5	58.9	125	−10.8
18.4	−7.6	60.5		
18.8	−7.7	62.1	130	−11.1
19.3	−7.8	63.8	135	−11.3
19.8	−7.9	65.4	140	−11.5
20.4	−8.0	67.1	145	−11.7
20.9	−8.1	68.8	150	−11.9
21.4		70.5	155	−12.1

App. Alt. = Apparent altitude = Sextant altitude corrected for index error and dip.
For daylight observations of Venus, see pages 259 and 260.

ALTITUDE CORRECTION TABLES 0°–10°—SUN, STARS, PLANETS A3

App. Alt.	OCT.–MAR. SUN Lower Limb	Upper Limb	APR.–SEPT. SUN Lower Limb	Upper Limb	STARS PLANETS
° ′	′	′	′	′	′
0 00	−18·2	−50·5	−18·4	−50·2	−34·5
03	17·5	49·8	17·8	49·6	33·8
06	16·9	49·2	17·1	48·9	33·2
09	16·3	48·6	16·5	48·3	32·6
12	15·7	48·0	15·9	47·7	32·0
15	15·1	47·4	15·3	47·1	31·4
0 18	−14·5	−46·8	−14·8	−46·6	−30·8
21	14·0	46·3	14·2	46·0	30·3
24	13·5	45·8	13·7	45·5	29·8
27	12·9	45·2	13·2	45·0	29·2
30	12·4	44·7	12·7	44·5	28·7
33	11·9	44·2	12·2	44·0	28·2
0 36	−11·5	−43·8	−11·7	−43·5	−27·8
39	11·0	43·3	11·2	43·0	27·3
42	10·5	42·8	10·8	42·6	26·8
45	10·1	42·4	10·3	42·1	26·4
48	9·6	41·9	9·9	41·7	25·9
51	9·2	41·5	9·5	41·3	25·5
0 54	−8·8	−41·1	−9·1	−40·9	−25·1
0 57	8·4	40·7	8·7	40·5	24·7
1 00	8·0	40·3	8·3	40·1	24·3
03	7·7	40·0	7·9	39·7	24·0
06	7·3	39·6	7·5	39·3	23·6
09	6·9	39·2	7·2	39·0	23·2
1 12	−6·6	−38·9	−6·8	−38·6	−22·9
15	6·2	38·5	6·5	38·3	22·5
18	5·9	38·2	6·2	38·0	22·2
21	5·6	37·9	5·8	37·6	21·9
24	5·3	37·6	5·5	37·3	21·6
27	4·9	37·2	5·2	37·0	21·2
1 30	−4·6	−36·9	−4·9	−36·7	−20·9
35	4·2	36·5	4·4	36·2	20·5
40	3·7	36·0	4·0	35·8	20·0
45	3·2	35·5	3·5	35·3	19·5
50	2·8	35·1	3·1	34·9	19·1
1 55	2·4	34·7	2·6	34·4	18·7
2 00	−2·0	−34·3	−2·2	−34·0	−18·3
05	1·6	33·9	1·8	33·6	17·9
10	1·2	33·5	1·5	33·3	17·5
15	0·9	33·2	1·1	32·9	17·2
20	0·5	32·8	0·8	32·6	16·8
25	−0·2	32·5	0·4	32·2	16·5
2 30	+0·2	−32·1	−0·1	−31·9	−16·1
35	0·5	31·8	+0·2	31·6	15·8
40	0·8	31·5	0·5	31·3	15·5
45	1·1	31·2	0·8	31·0	15·2
50	1·4	30·9	1·1	30·7	14·9
2 55	1·6	30·7	1·4	30·4	14·7
3 00	+1·9	−30·4	+1·7	−30·1	−14·4
05	2·2	30·1	1·9	29·9	14·1
10	2·4	29·9	2·1	29·7	13·9
15	2·6	29·7	2·4	29·4	13·7
20	2·9	29·4	2·6	29·2	13·4
25	3·1	29·2	2·9	28·9	13·2
3 30	+3·3	−29·0	+3·1	−28·7	−13·0

App. Alt.	OCT.–MAR. SUN Lower Limb	Upper Limb	APR.–SEPT. SUN Lower Limb	Upper Limb	STARS PLANETS
° ′	′	′	′	′	′
3 30	+3·3	−29·0	+3·1	−28·7	−13·0
35	3·6	28·7	3·3	28·5	12·7
40	3·8	28·5	3·5	28·3	12·5
45	4·0	28·3	3·7	28·1	12·3
50	4·2	28·1	3·9	27·9	12·1
3 55	4·4	27·9	4·1	27·7	11·9
4 00	+4·5	−27·8	+4·3	−27·5	−11·8
05	4·7	27·6	4·5	27·3	11·6
10	4·9	27·4	4·6	27·2	11·4
15	5·1	27·2	4·8	27·0	11·2
20	5·2	27·1	5·0	26·8	11·1
25	5·4	26·9	5·1	26·7	10·9
4 30	+5·6	−26·7	+5·3	−26·5	−10·7
35	5·7	26·6	5·5	26·3	10·6
40	5·9	26·4	5·6	26·2	10·4
45	6·0	26·3	5·8	26·0	10·3
50	6·2	26·1	5·9	25·9	10·1
4 55	6·3	26·0	6·0	25·8	10·0
5 00	+6·4	−25·9	+6·2	−25·6	−9·9
05	6·6	25·7	6·3	25·5	9·7
10	6·7	25·6	6·4	25·4	9·6
15	6·8	25·5	6·6	25·2	9·5
20	6·9	25·4	6·7	25·1	9·4
25	7·1	25·2	6·8	25·0	9·2
5 30	+7·2	−25·1	+6·9	−24·9	−9·1
35	7·3	25·0	7·0	24·8	9·0
40	7·4	24·9	7·2	24·6	8·9
45	7·5	24·8	7·3	24·5	8·8
50	7·6	24·7	7·4	24·4	8·7
5 55	7·7	24·6	7·5	24·3	8·6
6 00	+7·8	−24·5	+7·6	−24·2	−8·5
10	8·0	24·3	7·8	24·0	8·3
20	8·2	24·1	8·0	23·8	8·1
30	8·4	23·9	8·1	23·7	7·9
40	8·6	23·7	8·3	23·5	7·7
6 50	8·7	23·6	8·5	23·3	7·6
7 00	+8·9	−23·4	+8·6	−23·2	−7·4
10	9·1	23·2	8·8	23·0	7·2
20	9·2	23·1	9·0	22·8	7·1
30	9·3	23·0	9·1	22·7	7·0
40	9·5	22·8	9·2	22·6	6·8
7 50	9·6	22·7	9·4	22·4	6·7
8 00	+9·7	−22·6	+9·5	−22·3	−6·6
10	9·9	22·4	9·6	22·2	6·4
20	10·0	22·3	9·7	22·1	6·3
30	10·1	22·2	9·8	22·0	6·2
40	10·2	22·1	10·0	21·8	6·1
8 50	10·3	22·0	10·1	21·7	6·0
9 00	+10·4	−21·9	+10·2	−21·6	−5·9
10	10·5	21·8	10·3	21·5	5·8
20	10·6	21·7	10·4	21·4	5·7
30	10·7	21·6	10·5	21·3	5·6
40	10·8	21·5	10·6	21·2	5·5
9 50	10·9	21·4	10·6	21·2	5·4
10 00	+11·0	−21·3	+10·7	−21·1	−5·3

Additional corrections for temperature and pressure are given on the following page.

For bubble sextant observations ignore dip and use the star corrections for Sun, planets, and stars.

A4 ALTITUDE CORRECTION TABLES—ADDITIONAL CORRECTIONS

ADDITIONAL REFRACTION CORRECTIONS FOR NON-STANDARD CONDITIONS

Temperature

−20°F.   −10°   0°   +10°   20°   30°   40°   50°   60°   70°   80°   90°   100°F.

−30°C.   −20   −10°   0°   +10°   20°   30°   40°C.

Pressure in millibars / Pressure in inches

Zones: A B C D E F G H J K L M N

App. Alt.	A	B	C	D	E	F	G	H	J	K	L	M	N	App. Alt.
0 00	−6.9	−5.7	−4.6	−3.4	−2.3	−1.1	0.0	+1.1	+2.3	+3.4	+4.6	+5.7	+6.9	0 00
0 30	5.2	4.4	3.5	2.6	1.7	0.9	0.0	0.9	1.7	2.6	3.5	4.4	5.2	0 30
1 00	4.3	3.5	2.8	2.1	1.4	0.7	0.0	0.7	1.4	2.1	2.8	3.5	4.3	1 00
1 30	3.5	2.9	2.4	1.8	1.2	0.6	0.0	0.6	1.2	1.8	2.4	2.9	3.5	1 30
2 00	3.0	2.5	2.0	1.5	1.0	0.5	0.0	0.5	1.0	1.5	2.0	2.5	3.0	2 00
2 30	−2.5	−2.1	−1.6	−1.2	−0.8	−0.4	0.0	+0.4	+0.8	+1.2	+1.6	+2.1	+2.5	2 30
3 00	2.2	1.8	1.5	1.1	0.7	0.4	0.0	0.4	0.7	1.1	1.5	1.8	2.2	3 00
3 30	2.0	1.6	1.3	1.0	0.7	0.3	0.0	0.3	0.7	1.0	1.3	1.6	2.0	3 30
4 00	1.8	1.5	1.2	0.9	0.6	0.3	0.0	0.3	0.6	0.9	1.2	1.5	1.8	4 00
4 30	1.6	1.4	1.1	0.8	0.5	0.3	0.0	0.3	0.5	0.8	1.1	1.4	1.6	4 30
5 00	−1.5	−1.3	−1.0	−0.8	−0.5	−0.2	0.0	+0.2	+0.5	+0.8	+1.0	+1.3	+1.5	5 00
6	1.3	1.1	0.9	0.6	0.4	0.2	0.0	0.2	0.4	0.6	0.9	1.1	1.3	6
7	1.1	0.9	0.7	0.6	0.4	0.2	0.0	0.2	0.4	0.6	0.7	0.9	1.1	7
8	1.0	0.8	0.7	0.5	0.3	0.2	0.0	0.2	0.3	0.5	0.7	0.8	1.0	8
9	0.9	0.7	0.6	0.4	0.3	0.1	0.0	0.1	0.3	0.4	0.6	0.7	0.9	9
10 00	−0.8	−0.7	−0.5	−0.4	−0.3	−0.1	0.0	+0.1	+0.3	+0.4	+0.5	+0.7	+0.8	10 00
12	0.7	0.6	0.5	0.3	0.2	0.1	0.0	0.1	0.2	0.3	0.5	0.6	0.7	12
14	0.6	0.5	0.4	0.3	0.2	0.1	0.0	0.1	0.2	0.3	0.4	0.5	0.6	14
16	0.5	0.4	0.3	0.3	0.2	0.1	0.0	0.1	0.2	0.3	0.3	0.4	0.5	16
18	0.4	0.4	0.3	0.2	0.2	0.1	0.0	0.1	0.2	0.2	0.3	0.4	0.4	18
20 00	−0.4	−0.3	−0.3	−0.2	−0.1	−0.1	0.0	+0.1	+0.1	+0.2	+0.3	+0.3	+0.4	20 00
25	0.3	0.3	0.2	0.2	0.1	−0.1	0.0	+0.1	0.1	0.2	0.2	0.3	0.3	25
30	0.3	0.2	0.2	0.1	0.1	0.0	0.0	0.0	0.1	0.1	0.2	0.2	0.3	30
35	0.2	0.2	0.1	0.1	0.1	0.0	0.0	0.0	0.1	0.1	0.1	0.2	0.2	35
40	0.2	0.1	0.1	0.1	−0.1	0.0	0.0	0.0	+0.1	0.1	0.1	0.1	0.2	40
50 00	−0.1	−0.1	−0.1	−0.1	0.0	0.0	0.0	0.0	0.0	+0.1	+0.1	+0.1	+0.1	50 00

The graph is entered with arguments temperature and pressure to find a zone letter; using as arguments this zone letter and apparent altitude (sextant altitude corrected for dip), a correction is taken from the table. This correction is to be applied to the sextant altitude in addition to the corrections for standard conditions (for the Sun, stars and planets from page A2 and for the Moon from pages xxxiv and xxxv).

112   **1983 JUNE 3, 4, 5 (FRI., SAT., SUN.)**

G.M.T. (d h)	ARIES G.H.A.	VENUS −3.8 G.H.A.	Dec.	MARS +1.7 G.H.A.	Dec.	JUPITER −2.1 G.H.A.	Dec.	SATURN +0.6 G.H.A.	Dec.	STARS Name	S.H.A.	Dec.
3 00	250 53.0	131 40.3 N23	18.7	180 27.0 N22	39.3	7 21.0 S20	18.3	43 34.0 S 8	24.4	Acamar	315 36.1	S40 22.2
01	265 55.4	146 40.1	18.1	195 27.7	39.5	22 23.8	18.2	58 36.5	24.4	Achernar	335 44.1	S57 19.1
02	280 57.9	161 39.8	17.6	210 28.3	39.8	37 26.6	18.2	73 39.1	24.4	Acrux	173 35.0	S63 00.6
03	296 00.4	176 39.5 ··	17.0	225 28.9 ··	40.1	52 29.4 ··	18.1	88 41.7 ··	24.3	Adhara	255 30.9	S28 57.0
04	311 02.8	191 39.2	16.5	240 29.5	40.3	67 32.2	18.1	103 44.2	24.3	Aldebaran	291 16.1	N16 28.5
05	326 05.3	206 38.9	15.9	255 30.1	40.6	82 35.0	18.0	118 46.8	24.3			
06	341 07.7	221 38.6 N23	15.4	270 30.7 N22	40.8	97 37.8 S20	18.0	133 49.4 S 8	24.2	Alioth	166 40.4	N56 03.3
07	356 10.2	236 38.3	14.8	285 31.3	41.1	112 40.6	17.9	148 52.0	24.2	Alkaid	153 16.5	N49 24.0
08	11 12.7	251 38.1	14.2	300 31.9	41.3	127 43.4	17.9	163 54.5	24.2	Al Na'ir	28 12.3	S47 02.4
F 09	26 15.1	266 37.8 ··	13.7	315 32.5 ··	41.6	142 46.2 ··	17.8	178 57.1 ··	24.2	Alnilam	276 10.0	S 1 12.7
R 10	41 17.6	281 37.5	13.1	330 33.1	41.8	157 49.0	17.8	193 59.7	24.1	Alphard	218 18.8	S 8 35.2
I 11	56 20.1	296 37.2	12.6	345 33.7	42.1	172 51.7	17.7	209 02.2	24.1			
D 12	71 22.5	311 36.9 N23	12.0	0 34.3 N22	42.3	187 54.5 S20	17.7	224 04.8 S 8	24.1	Alphecca	126 30.1	N26 46.3
A 13	86 25.0	326 36.7	11.4	15 34.9	42.6	202 57.3	17.6	239 07.4	24.0	Alpheratz	358 07.5	N28 59.6
Y 14	101 27.5	341 36.4	10.9	30 35.5	42.8	218 00.1	17.6	254 09.9	24.0	Altair	62 30.4	N 8 49.3
15	116 29.9	356 36.1 ··	10.3	45 36.1 ··	43.1	233 02.9 ··	17.5	269 12.5 ··	24.0	Ankaa	353 38.4	S42 23.7
16	131 32.4	11 35.8	09.7	60 36.7	43.3	248 05.7	17.5	284 15.1	23.9	Antares	112 54.1	S26 23.8
17	146 34.9	26 35.5	09.2	75 37.3	43.6	263 08.5	17.4	299 17.7	23.9			
18	161 37.3	41 35.3 N23	08.6	90 37.9 N22	43.8	278 11.3 S20	17.4	314 20.2 S 8	23.9	Arcturus	146 16.4	N19 16.2
19	176 39.8	56 35.0	08.0	105 38.5	44.1	293 14.1	17.3	329 22.8	23.9	Atria	108 16.1	S68 59.9
20	191 42.2	71 34.7	07.5	120 39.1	44.3	308 16.9	17.3	344 25.4	23.8	Avior	234 27.9	S59 27.5
21	206 44.7	86 34.5 ··	06.9	135 39.7 ··	44.6	323 19.7 ··	17.2	359 27.9 ··	23.8	Bellatrix	278 57.0	N 6 20.1
22	221 47.2	101 34.2	06.3	150 40.3	44.8	338 22.5	17.2	14 30.5	23.8	Betelgeuse	271 26.5	N 7 24.3
23	236 49.6	116 33.9	05.8	165 40.9	45.1	353 25.3	17.1	29 33.1	23.7			
4 00	251 52.1	131 33.7 N23	05.2	180 41.5 N22	45.3	8 28.1 S20	17.1	44 35.6 S 8	23.7	Canopus	264 06.9	S52 41.3
01	266 54.6	146 33.4	04.6	195 42.1	45.5	23 30.9	17.0	59 38.2	23.7	Capella	281 08.9	N45 58.9
02	281 57.0	161 33.1	04.0	210 42.7	45.8	38 33.7	17.0	74 40.8	23.6	Deneb	49 46.9	N45 12.9
03	296 59.5	176 32.9 ··	03.5	225 43.3 ··	46.0	53 36.5 ··	16.9	89 43.3 ··	23.6	Denebola	182 57.0	N14 40.0
04	312 02.0	191 32.6	02.9	240 43.9	46.3	68 39.2	16.9	104 45.9	23.6	Diphda	349 19.1	S18 04.7
05	327 04.4	206 32.3	02.3	255 44.5	46.5	83 42.0	16.8	119 48.5	23.6			
06	342 06.9	221 32.1 N23	01.7	270 45.1 N22	46.8	98 44.8 S20	16.8	134 51.1 S 8	23.5	Dubhe	194 19.6	N61 50.8
07	357 09.4	236 31.8	01.1	285 45.7	47.0	113 47.6	16.7	149 53.6	23.5	Elnath	278 42.1	N28 35.6
S 08	12 11.8	251 31.5	00.6	300 46.3	47.3	128 50.4	16.7	164 56.2	23.5	Eltanin	90 56.3	N51 29.3
A 09	27 14.3	266 31.3 23	00.0	315 46.9 ··	47.5	143 53.2 ··	16.6	179 58.8 ··	23.4	Enif	34 09.6	N 9 47.7
T 10	42 16.7	281 31.0 22	59.4	330 47.5	47.7	158 56.0	16.6	195 01.3	23.4	Fomalhaut	15 49.2	S29 42.6
U 11	57 19.2	296 30.8	58.8	345 48.1	48.0	173 58.8	16.5	210 03.9	23.4			
R 12	72 21.7	311 30.5 N22	58.2	0 48.7 N22	48.2	189 01.6 S20	16.5	225 06.5 S 8	23.4	Gacrux	172 26.5	S57 01.4
D 13	87 24.1	326 30.3	57.7	15 49.3	48.5	204 04.4	16.4	240 09.0	23.3	Gienah	176 15.9	S17 27.0
A 14	102 26.6	341 30.0	57.1	30 49.9	48.7	219 07.2	16.4	255 11.6	23.3	Hadar	149 20.2	S60 17.7
Y 15	117 29.1	356 29.8 ··	56.5	45 50.5 ··	48.9	234 10.0 ··	16.3	270 14.2 ··	23.3	Hamal	328 27.0	N23 22.9
16	132 31.5	11 29.5	55.9	60 51.1	49.2	249 12.8	16.3	285 16.7	23.2	Kaus Aust.	84 13.9	S34 23.6
17	147 34.0	26 29.2	55.3	75 51.7	49.4	264 15.6	16.2	300 19.3	23.2			
18	162 36.5	41 29.0 N22	54.7	90 52.3 N22	49.7	279 18.4 S20	16.2	315 21.9 S 8	23.2	Kochab	137 17.8	N74 13.6
19	177 38.9	56 28.7	54.1	105 52.9	49.9	294 21.1	16.1	330 24.4	23.2	Markab	14 01.3	N15 06.7
20	192 41.4	71 28.5	53.5	120 53.5	50.1	309 23.9	16.1	345 27.0	23.1	Menkar	314 39.4	N 4 01.4
21	207 43.9	86 28.3 ··	53.0	135 54.1 ··	50.4	324 26.7 ··	16.0	0 29.6 ··	23.1	Menkent	148 34.5	S36 17.4
22	222 46.3	101 28.0	52.4	150 54.7	50.6	339 29.5	16.0	15 32.1	23.1	Miaplacidus	221 45.1	S69 39.1
23	237 48.8	116 27.8	51.8	165 55.3	50.9	354 32.3	15.9	30 34.7	23.0			
5 00	252 51.2	131 27.5 N22	51.2	180 55.9 N22	51.1	9 35.1 S20	15.9	45 37.3 S 8	23.0	Mirfak	309 13.9	N49 48.0
01	267 53.7	146 27.3	50.6	195 56.5	51.3	24 37.9	15.8	60 39.8	23.0	Nunki	76 26.4	S26 19.1
02	282 56.2	161 27.0	50.0	210 57.1	51.6	39 40.7	15.8	75 42.4	23.0	Peacock	53 54.9	S56 47.2
03	297 58.6	176 26.8 ··	49.4	225 57.7 ··	51.8	54 43.5 ··	15.7	90 44.9 ··	22.9	Pollux	243 56.1	N28 04.2
04	313 01.1	191 26.5	48.8	240 58.3	52.0	69 46.3	15.7	105 47.5	22.9	Procyon	245 24.0	N 5 16.1
05	328 03.6	206 26.3	48.2	255 58.9	52.3	84 49.1	15.6	120 50.1	22.9			
06	343 06.0	221 26.1 N22	47.6	270 59.5 N22	52.5	99 51.9 S20	15.6	135 52.6 S 8	22.8	Rasalhague	96 27.5	N12 34.2
07	358 08.5	236 25.8	47.0	286 00.1	52.8	114 54.6	15.5	150 55.2	22.8	Regulus	208 08.0	N12 03.1
08	13 11.0	251 25.6	46.4	301 00.7	53.0	129 57.4	15.5	165 57.8	22.8	Rigel	281 34.5	S 8 13.3
S 09	28 13.4	266 25.4 ··	45.8	316 01.3 ··	53.2	145 00.2 ··	15.4	181 00.3 ··	22.8	Rigil Kent.	140 22.8	S60 46.1
U 10	43 15.9	281 25.1	45.2	331 01.9	53.5	160 03.0	15.4	196 02.9	22.7	Sabik	102 38.6	S15 42.3
N 11	58 18.3	296 24.9	44.6	346 02.5	53.7	175 05.8	15.3	211 05.5	22.7			
D 12	73 20.8	311 24.7 N22	44.0	1 03.1 N22	53.9	190 08.6 S20	15.3	226 08.0 S 8	22.7	Schedar	350 07.2	N56 26.4
A 13	88 23.3	326 24.4	43.4	16 03.7	54.2	205 11.4	15.2	241 10.6	22.7	Shaula	96 52.7	S37 05.6
Y 14	103 25.7	341 24.2	42.8	31 04.3	54.4	220 14.2	15.2	256 13.2	22.6	Sirius	258 54.3	S16 41.6
15	118 28.2	356 24.0 ··	42.2	46 04.9 ··	54.6	235 17.0 ··	15.1	271 15.7 ··	22.6	Spica	158 55.3	S11 04.5
16	133 30.7	11 23.7	41.6	61 05.5	54.8	250 19.8	15.1	286 18.3	22.6	Suhail	223 09.6	S43 22.1
17	148 33.1	26 23.5	41.0	76 06.1	55.1	265 22.6	15.0	301 20.8	22.5			
18	163 35.6	41 23.3 N22	40.4	91 06.7 N22	55.3	280 25.3 S20	15.0	316 23.4 S 8	22.5	Vega	80 54.1	N38 45.9
19	178 38.1	56 23.1	39.8	106 07.3	55.5	295 28.1	14.9	331 26.0	22.5	Zuben'ubi	137 30.6	S15 58.4
20	193 40.5	71 22.8	39.2	121 07.9	55.8	310 30.9	14.9	346 28.5	22.5			
21	208 43.0	86 22.6 ··	38.6	136 08.5 ··	56.0	325 33.7 ··	14.8	1 31.1 ··	22.4			
22	223 45.5	101 22.4	37.9	151 09.1	56.2	340 36.5	14.8	16 33.7	22.4			
23	238 47.9	116 22.2	37.3	166 09.7	56.5	355 39.3	14.7	31 36.2	22.4			

	S.H.A.	Mer. Pass.
Venus	239 41.5	15 14
Mars	288 49.4	11 57
Jupiter	116 36.0	23 22
Saturn	152 43.5	20 58

Mer. Pass.	7h 11.3m	v −0.3 d 0.6	v 0.6 d 0.2	v 2.8 d 0.1	v 2.6 d 0.0

1983 JUNE 3, 4, 5 (FRI., SAT., SUN.)   113

SUN and MOON

G.M.T.	SUN G.H.A.	Dec.	MOON G.H.A.	v	Dec.	d	H.P.
3 00	180 31.3	N22 12.8	274 57.1	14.3	S15 14.7	9.9	54.4
01	195 31.2	13.2	289 30.4	14.4	15 04.8	9.9	54.4
02	210 31.1	13.5	304 03.8	14.5	14 54.9	10.1	54.4
03	225 31.0 ··	13.8	318 37.3	14.4	14 44.8	10.0	54.4
04	240 30.9	14.1	333 10.7	14.5	14 34.8	10.2	54.5
05	255 30.8	14.4	347 44.2	14.5	14 24.6	10.2	54.5
06	270 30.7	N22 14.8	2 17.7	14.6	S14 14.4	10.3	54.5
07	285 30.6	15.1	16 51.3	14.5	14 04.1	10.3	54.5
F 08	300 30.5	15.4	31 24.8	14.6	13 53.8	10.4	54.5
R 09	315 30.4 ··	15.7	45 58.4	14.7	13 43.4	10.4	54.5
I 10	330 30.3	16.0	60 32.1	14.6	13 33.0	10.6	54.5
D 11	345 30.2	16.3	75 05.7	14.7	13 22.4	10.5	54.6
A 12	0 30.1	N22 16.6	89 39.4	14.7	S13 11.9	10.7	54.6
Y 13	15 30.0	16.9	104 13.1	14.8	13 01.2	10.7	54.6
14	30 29.9	17.3	118 46.9	14.7	12 50.5	10.7	54.6
15	45 29.8 ··	17.6	133 20.6	14.8	12 39.8	10.8	54.6
16	60 29.7	17.9	147 54.4	14.8	12 29.0	10.9	54.6
17	75 29.6	18.2	162 28.2	14.9	12 18.1	10.9	54.6
18	90 29.5	N22 18.5	177 02.1	14.8	S12 07.2	11.0	54.7
19	105 29.4	18.8	191 35.9	14.9	11 56.2	11.0	54.7
20	120 29.3	19.1	206 09.8	14.9	11 45.2	11.1	54.7
21	135 29.2 ··	19.4	220 43.7	14.9	11 34.1	11.1	54.7
22	150 29.1	19.7	235 17.6	15.0	11 23.0	11.2	54.7
23	165 29.0	20.0	249 51.6	14.9	11 11.8	11.3	54.7
4 00	180 28.9	N22 20.3	264 25.5	15.0	S11 00.5	11.3	54.8
01	195 28.8	20.6	278 59.5	15.0	10 49.2	11.3	54.8
02	210 28.7	20.9	293 33.5	15.0	10 37.9	11.4	54.8
03	225 28.6 ··	21.2	308 07.5	15.0	10 26.5	11.5	54.8
04	240 28.5	21.5	322 41.5	15.0	10 15.0	11.5	54.8
05	255 28.3	21.8	337 15.5	15.1	10 03.5	11.5	54.9
06	270 28.2	N22 22.1	351 49.6	15.0	S 9 52.0	11.6	54.9
07	285 28.1	22.4	6 23.6	15.1	9 40.4	11.6	54.9
S 08	300 28.0	22.7	20 57.7	15.1	9 28.8	11.7	54.9
A 09	315 27.9 ··	23.0	35 31.8	15.0	9 17.1	11.8	54.9
T 10	330 27.8	23.3	50 05.8	15.1	9 05.3	11.8	55.0
U 11	345 27.7	23.6	64 39.9	15.1	8 53.5	11.8	55.0
R 12	0 27.6	N22 23.9	79 14.0	15.2	S 8 41.7	11.9	55.0
D 13	15 27.5	24.2	93 48.2	15.1	8 29.8	11.9	55.0
A 14	30 27.4	24.5	108 22.3	15.1	8 17.9	11.9	55.1
Y 15	45 27.3 ··	24.8	122 56.4	15.1	8 06.0	12.0	55.1
16	60 27.2	25.1	137 30.5	15.1	7 54.0	12.1	55.1
17	75 27.1	25.4	152 04.6	15.2	7 41.9	12.1	55.1
18	90 27.0	N22 25.7	166 38.8	15.1	S 7 29.8	12.1	55.1
19	105 26.9	26.0	181 12.9	15.1	7 17.7	12.2	55.2
20	120 26.8	26.3	195 47.0	15.2	7 05.5	12.2	55.2
21	135 26.7 ··	26.6	210 21.2	15.1	6 53.3	12.2	55.2
22	150 26.6	26.9	224 55.3	15.1	6 41.1	12.3	55.2
23	165 26.4	27.1	239 29.4	15.1	6 28.8	12.3	55.3
5 00	180 26.3	N22 27.4	254 03.5	15.2	S 6 16.5	12.4	55.3
01	195 26.2	27.7	268 37.7	15.1	6 04.1	12.4	55.3
02	210 26.1	28.0	283 11.8	15.1	5 51.7	12.4	55.3
03	225 26.0 ··	28.3	297 45.9	15.1	5 39.3	12.5	55.4
04	240 25.9	28.6	312 20.0	15.1	5 26.8	12.5	55.4
05	255 25.8	28.9	326 54.1	15.1	5 14.3	12.5	55.4
06	270 25.7	N22 29.1	341 28.2	15.0	S 5 01.8	12.6	55.4
07	285 25.6	29.4	356 02.2	15.1	4 49.2	12.6	55.5
08	300 25.5	29.7	10 36.3	15.1	4 36.6	12.6	55.5
S 09	315 25.4 ··	30.0	25 10.4	15.0	4 24.0	12.7	55.5
U 10	330 25.3	30.3	39 44.4	15.0	4 11.3	12.7	55.6
N 11	345 25.2	30.5	54 18.4	15.0	3 58.6	12.7	55.6
D 12	0 25.0	N22 30.8	68 52.4	15.0	S 3 45.9	12.7	55.6
A 13	15 24.9	31.1	83 26.4	15.0	3 33.2	12.8	55.6
Y 14	30 24.8	31.4	98 00.4	14.9	3 20.4	12.8	55.7
15	45 24.7 ··	31.7	112 34.3	15.0	3 07.6	12.8	55.7
16	60 24.6	31.9	127 08.3	14.9	2 54.8	12.9	55.7
17	75 24.5	32.2	141 42.2	14.9	2 41.9	12.9	55.7
18	90 24.4	N22 32.5	156 16.1	14.9	S 2 29.0	12.9	55.8
19	105 24.3	32.8	170 50.0	14.8	2 16.1	12.9	55.8
20	120 24.2	33.0	185 23.8	14.9	2 03.2	13.0	55.8
21	135 24.1 ··	33.3	199 57.7	14.8	1 50.2	13.0	55.9
22	150 23.9	33.6	214 31.5	14.7	1 37.2	13.0	55.9
23	165 23.8	33.9	229 05.2	14.8	1 24.2	13.0	55.9
	S.D. 15.8	d 0.3	S.D. 14.9		15.0		15.2

Twilight, Sunrise, Moonrise

Lat.	Naut.	Civil	Sunrise	3	4	5	6
N 72	□	□	□	03 23	02 48	02 22	02 00
N 70	□	□	□	02 53	02 31	02 14	01 59
68	□	□	□	02 30	02 18	02 07	01 58
66	////	////	01 02	02 12	02 07	02 02	01 57
64	////	////	01 52	01 57	01 57	01 57	01 56
62	////	////	02 23	01 45	01 49	01 53	01 56
60	////	01 19	02 46	01 34	01 42	01 49	01 55
N 58	////	01 56	03 04	01 25	01 36	01 46	01 55
56	////	02 21	03 20	01 17	01 31	01 43	01 54
54	01 12	02 41	03 33	01 10	01 26	01 40	01 54
52	01 46	02 57	03 44	01 03	01 22	01 38	01 53
50	02 10	03 11	03 54	00 57	01 18	01 36	01 53
45	02 51	03 39	04 15	00 45	01 09	01 31	01 52
N 40	03 19	04 00	04 32	00 34	01 02	01 27	01 52
35	03 41	04 17	04 47	00 25	00 55	01 24	01 51
30	03 59	04 32	04 59	00 17	00 50	01 20	01 51
20	04 27	04 55	05 20	00 03	00 40	01 15	01 50
N 10	04 48	05 15	05 38	24 51	00 31	01 10	01 50
0	05 06	05 32	05 55	24 23	00 23	01 06	01 49
S 10	05 22	05 48	06 11	24 15	00 15	01 02	01 48
20	05 38	06 05	06 29	24 07	00 07	00 57	01 48
30	05 53	06 23	06 49	23 57	24 52	00 52	01 47
35	06 01	06 33	07 01	23 51	24 48	00 48	01 47
40	06 10	06 44	07 14	23 45	24 45	00 45	01 46
45	06 20	06 56	07 30	23 37	24 41	00 41	01 46
S 50	06 30	07 12	07 49	23 28	24 36	00 36	01 45
52	06 35	07 18	07 59	23 24	24 34	00 34	01 45
54	06 41	07 26	08 09	23 19	24 31	00 31	01 45
56	06 46	07 34	08 21	23 14	24 28	00 28	01 44
58	06 52	07 44	08 34	23 08	24 25	00 25	01 44
S 60	06 59	07 55	08 50	23 01	24 22	00 22	01 44

Sunset, Twilight, Moonset

Lat.	Sunset	Civil	Naut.	3	4	5	6
N 72	□	□	□	08 37	10 43	12 39	14 34
N 70	□	□	□	09 06	10 58	12 45	14 32
68	□	□	□	09 28	11 10	12 49	14 29
66	22 59	////	////	09 45	11 19	12 53	14 28
64	22 06	////	////	09 58	11 27	12 56	14 26
62	21 35	////	////	10 10	11 34	12 58	14 25
60	21 12	22 40	////	10 19	11 40	13 01	14 24
N 58	20 53	22 02	////	10 28	11 45	13 03	14 22
56	20 38	21 36	////	10 35	11 49	13 05	14 22
54	20 24	21 16	22 47	10 42	11 53	13 06	14 21
52	20 13	21 00	22 12	10 48	11 57	13 08	14 20
50	20 03	20 46	21 48	10 53	12 00	13 09	14 19
45	19 41	20 18	21 06	11 04	12 08	13 12	14 18
N 40	19 24	19 57	20 37	11 14	12 14	13 14	14 17
35	19 10	19 39	20 15	11 22	12 19	13 16	14 15
30	18 58	19 25	19 58	11 29	12 23	13 18	14 14
20	18 37	19 01	19 30	11 41	12 31	13 21	14 13
N 10	18 19	18 41	19 08	11 51	12 38	13 24	14 11
0	18 02	18 24	18 50	12 01	12 44	13 27	14 10
S 10	17 45	18 08	18 34	12 11	12 50	13 29	14 09
20	17 28	17 51	18 19	12 21	12 57	13 32	14 07
30	17 07	17 33	18 03	12 33	13 04	13 35	14 05
35	16 56	17 23	17 55	12 39	13 08	13 36	14 04
40	16 42	17 12	17 48	12 47	13 13	13 38	14 03
45	16 26	17 00	17 36	12 56	13 19	13 40	14 02
S 50	16 07	16 45	17 26	13 07	13 25	13 43	14 00
52	15 58	16 38	17 21	13 11	13 29	13 44	14 00
54	15 47	16 30	17 15	13 17	13 32	13 46	13 59
56	15 35	16 22	17 10	13 23	13 36	13 47	13 58
58	15 22	16 12	17 04	13 29	13 40	13 49	13 57
S 60	15 06	16 01	16 57	13 37	13 44	13 50	13 56

SUN and MOON — Meridian Passage

Day	SUN Eqn. of Time 00h	12h	Mer. Pass.	MOON Mer. Pass. Upper	Lower	Age	Phase
3	02 05	02 01	11 58	05 51	18 12	22	
4	01 56	01 51	11 58	06 34	18 55	23	
5	01 46	01 40	11 58	07 16	19 38	24	◑

114

1983 JUNE 6, 7, 8 (MON., TUES., WED.)

G.M.T.	ARIES G.H.A.	VENUS −3.9 G.H.A. Dec.	MARS +1.7 G.H.A. Dec.	JUPITER −2.1 G.H.A. Dec.	SATURN +0.7 G.H.A. Dec.	STARS Name	S.H.A.	Dec.
6 00	253 50.4	131 22.0 N22 36.7	181 10.3 N22 56.7	10 42.1 S20 14.7	46 38.8 S 8 22.4	Acamar	315 36.1	S40 22.2
01	268 52.8	146 21.7 36.1	196 10.9 56.9	25 44.9 14.6	61 41.3 22.3	Achernar	335 44.1	S57 19.1
02	283 55.3	161 21.5 35.5	211 11.5 57.1	40 47.7 14.6	76 43.9 22.3	Acrux	173 35.0	S63 00.6
03	298 57.8	176 21.3 .. 34.9	226 12.1 .. 57.4	55 50.5 .. 14.5	91 46.5 .. 22.3	Adhara	255 30.9	S28 57.0
04	314 00.2	191 21.1 34.3	241 12.7 57.6	70 53.3 14.5	106 49.0 22.2	Aldebaran	291 16.1	N16 28.5
05	329 02.7	206 20.9 33.6	256 13.3 57.8	85 56.0 14.4	121 51.6 22.2			
06	344 05.2	221 20.7 N22 33.0	271 13.9 N22 58.0	100 58.8 S20 14.4	136 54.1 S 8 22.2	Alioth	166 40.4	N56 03.3
07	359 07.6	236 20.4 32.4	286 14.5 58.3	116 01.6 14.3	151 56.7 22.2	Alkaid	153 16.6	N49 24.0
08	14 10.1	251 20.2 31.8	301 15.1 58.5	131 04.4 14.3	166 59.3 22.1	Al Na'ir	28 12.3	S47 02.4
M 09	29 12.6	266 20.0 .. 31.2	316 15.7 .. 58.7	146 07.2 .. 14.2	182 01.8 .. 22.1	Alnilam	276 10.0	S 1 12.7
O 10	44 15.0	281 19.8 30.6	331 16.3 58.9	161 10.0 14.2	197 04.4 22.1	Alphard	218 18.8	S 8 35.2
N 11	59 17.5	296 19.6 29.9	346 16.9 59.2	176 12.8 14.1	212 07.0 22.1			
D 12	74 20.0	311 19.4 N22 29.3	1 17.5 N22 59.4	191 15.6 S20 14.1	227 09.5 S 8 22.0	Alphecca	126 30.1	N26 46.3
A 13	89 22.4	326 19.2 28.7	16 18.1 59.6	206 18.4 14.0	242 12.1 22.0	Alpheratz	358 07.5	N28 59.6
Y 14	104 24.9	341 19.0 28.1	31 18.7 59.8	221 21.1 14.0	257 14.6 22.0	Altair	62 30.4	N 8 49.3
15	119 27.3	356 18.8 .. 27.4	46 19.3 23 00.1	236 23.9 .. 13.9	272 17.2 .. 22.0	Ankaa	353 38.4	S42 23.7
16	134 29.8	11 18.6 26.8	61 19.9 00.3	251 26.7 13.9	287 19.8 21.9	Antares	112 54.1	S26 23.8
17	149 32.3	26 18.4 26.2	76 20.5 00.5	266 29.5 13.8	302 22.3 21.9			
18	164 34.7	41 18.2 N22 25.6	91 21.1 N23 00.7	281 32.3 S20 13.8	317 24.9 S 8 21.9	Arcturus	146 16.4	N19 16.2
19	179 37.2	56 18.0 24.9	106 21.7 01.0	296 35.1 13.7	332 27.4 21.9	Atria	108 16.1	S68 59.9
20	194 39.7	71 17.8 24.3	121 22.3 01.2	311 37.9 13.7	347 30.0 21.8	Avior	234 27.9	S59 27.5
21	209 42.1	86 17.6 .. 23.7	136 22.9 .. 01.4	326 40.7 .. 13.6	2 32.6 .. 21.8	Bellatrix	278 57.0	N 6 20.1
22	224 44.6	101 17.4 23.1	151 23.5 01.6	341 43.5 13.6	17 35.1 21.8	Betelgeuse	271 26.5	N 7 24.3
23	239 47.1	116 17.2 22.4	166 24.1 01.8	356 46.2 13.5	32 37.7 21.8			
7 00	254 49.5	131 17.0 N22 21.8	181 24.7 N23 02.1	11 49.0 S20 13.5	47 40.2 S 8 21.7	Canopus	264 06.9	S52 41.3
01	269 52.0	146 16.8 21.2	196 25.3 02.3	26 51.8 13.4	62 42.8 21.7	Capella	281 08.9	N45 58.9
02	284 54.4	161 16.6 20.5	211 25.9 02.5	41 54.6 13.4	77 45.3 21.7	Deneb	49 46.9	N45 12.9
03	299 56.9	176 16.4 .. 19.9	226 26.5 .. 02.7	56 57.4 .. 13.3	92 47.9 .. 21.6	Denebola	182 57.0	N14 40.1
04	314 59.4	191 16.2 19.3	241 27.1 02.9	72 00.2 13.3	107 50.5 21.6	Diphda	349 19.0	S18 04.7
05	330 01.8	206 16.0 18.6	256 27.7 03.2	87 03.0 13.2	122 53.0 21.6			
06	345 04.3	221 15.8 N22 18.0	271 28.3 N23 03.4	102 05.8 S20 13.2	137 55.6 S 8 21.6	Dubhe	194 19.6	N61 50.8
07	0 06.8	236 15.6 17.4	286 28.9 03.6	117 08.5 13.1	152 58.1 21.5	Elnath	278 42.1	N28 35.6
08	15 09.2	251 15.5 16.7	301 29.5 03.8	132 11.3 13.1	168 00.7 21.5	Eltanin	90 56.3	N51 29.3
T 09	30 11.7	266 15.3 .. 16.1	316 30.1 .. 04.0	147 14.1 .. 13.0	183 03.3 .. 21.5	Enif	34 09.6	N 9 47.7
U 10	45 14.2	281 15.1 15.4	331 30.7 04.2	162 16.9 13.0	198 05.8 21.5	Fomalhaut	15 49.2	S29 42.6
E 11	60 16.6	296 14.9 14.8	346 31.3 04.4	177 19.7 12.9	213 08.4 21.4			
S 12	75 19.1	311 14.7 N22 14.2	1 31.9 N23 04.7	192 22.5 S20 12.9	228 10.9 S 8 21.4	Gacrux	172 26.5	S57 01.4
D 13	90 21.6	326 14.5 13.5	16 32.5 04.9	207 25.3 12.8	243 13.5 21.4	Gienah	176 15.9	S17 27.0
A 14	105 24.0	341 14.3 12.9	31 33.1 05.1	222 28.1 12.8	258 16.0 21.4	Hadar	149 20.3	S60 17.7
Y 15	120 26.5	356 14.2 .. 12.2	46 33.7 .. 05.3	237 30.8 .. 12.7	273 18.6 .. 21.3	Hamal	328 27.0	N23 22.9
16	135 28.9	11 14.0 11.6	61 34.3 05.5	252 33.6 12.7	288 21.2 21.3	Kaus Aust.	84 13.9	S34 23.6
17	150 31.4	26 13.8 11.0	76 34.9 05.7	267 36.4 12.6	303 23.7 21.3			
18	165 33.9	41 13.6 N22 10.3	91 35.5 N23 05.9	282 39.2 S20 12.6	318 26.3 S 8 21.3	Kochab	137 17.8	N74 13.7
19	180 36.3	56 13.5 09.7	106 36.1 06.2	297 42.0 12.5	333 28.8 21.3	Markab	14 01.3	N15 06.7
20	195 38.8	71 13.3 09.0	121 36.7 06.4	312 44.8 12.5	348 31.4 21.2	Menkar	314 39.4	N 4 01.4
21	210 41.3	86 13.1 .. 08.4	136 37.3 .. 06.6	327 47.6 .. 12.4	3 33.9 .. 21.2	Menkent	148 34.5	S36 17.4
22	225 43.7	101 12.9 07.7	151 37.9 06.8	342 50.3 12.4	18 36.5 21.2	Miaplacidus	221 45.2	S69 39.1
23	240 46.2	116 12.8 07.1	166 38.5 07.0	357 53.1 12.3	33 39.0 21.2			
8 00	255 48.7	131 12.6 N22 06.4	181 39.1 N23 07.2	12 55.9 S20 12.3	48 41.6 S 8 21.1	Mirfak	309 13.9	N49 48.0
01	270 51.1	146 12.4 05.8	196 39.7 07.4	27 58.7 12.2	63 44.2 21.1	Nunki	76 26.4	S26 19.1
02	285 53.6	161 12.3 05.1	211 40.3 07.6	43 01.5 12.2	78 46.7 21.1	Peacock	53 54.9	S56 47.2
03	300 56.1	176 12.1 .. 04.5	226 40.9 .. 07.8	58 04.3 .. 12.1	93 49.3 .. 21.1	Pollux	243 56.1	N28 04.2
04	315 58.5	191 11.9 03.8	241 41.5 08.1	73 07.1 12.1	108 51.8 21.0	Procyon	245 24.0	N 5 16.1
05	331 01.0	206 11.8 03.2	256 42.1 08.3	88 09.8 12.0	123 54.4 21.0			
06	346 03.4	221 11.6 N22 02.5	271 42.7 N23 08.5	103 12.6 S20 12.0	138 56.9 S 8 21.0	Rasalhague	96 27.4	N12 34.2
W 07	1 05.9	236 11.4 01.9	286 43.3 08.7	118 15.4 11.9	153 59.5 21.0	Regulus	208 08.0	N12 03.1
E 08	16 08.4	251 11.3 01.2	301 43.9 08.9	133 18.2 11.9	169 02.0 20.9	Rigel	281 34.5	S 8 13.3
D 09	31 10.8	266 11.1 22 00.5	316 44.5 .. 09.1	148 21.0 .. 11.8	184 04.6 .. 20.9	Rigil Kent.	140 22.8	S60 46.1
N 10	46 13.3	281 11.0 21 59.9	331 45.1 09.3	163 23.8 11.8	199 07.1 20.9	Sabik	102 38.6	S15 42.3
E 11	61 15.8	296 10.8 59.2	346 45.7 09.5	178 26.5 11.7	214 09.7 20.9			
S 12	76 18.2	311 10.6 N21 58.6	1 46.3 N23 09.7	193 29.3 S20 11.7	229 12.3 S 8 20.8	Schedar	350 07.2	N56 26.4
D 13	91 20.7	326 10.5 57.9	16 46.9 09.9	208 32.1 11.6	244 14.8 20.8	Shaula	96 52.7	S37 05.6
A 14	106 23.2	341 10.3 57.3	31 47.5 10.1	223 34.9 11.6	259 17.4 20.8	Sirius	258 54.3	S16 41.6
Y 15	121 25.6	356 10.2 .. 56.6	46 48.1 .. 10.3	238 37.7 .. 11.5	274 19.9 .. 20.8	Spica	158 55.3	S11 04.5
16	136 28.1	11 10.0 55.9	61 48.7 10.5	253 40.5 11.5	289 22.5 20.8	Suhail	223 09.7	S43 22.0
17	151 30.5	26 09.9 55.3	76 49.3 10.7	268 43.3 11.4	304 25.0 20.7			
18	166 33.0	41 09.7 N21 54.6	91 49.9 N23 10.9	283 46.0 S20 11.4	319 27.6 S 8 20.7	Vega	80 54.1	N38 45.9
19	181 35.5	56 09.6 53.9	106 50.5 11.2	298 48.8 11.3	334 30.1 20.7	Zuben'ubi	137 30.6	S15 58.4
20	196 37.9	71 09.4 53.3	121 51.1 11.4	313 51.6 11.3	349 32.7 20.7		S.H.A.	Mer. Pass.
21	211 40.4	86 09.3 .. 52.6	136 51.7 .. 11.6	328 54.4 .. 11.2	4 35.2 .. 20.6			
22	226 42.9	101 09.1 52.0	151 52.3 11.8	343 57.2 11.2	19 37.8 20.6	Venus	236 27.5	15 15
23	241 45.3	116 09.0 51.3	166 52.9 12.0	359 00.0 11.1	34 40.3 20.6	Mars	286 35.2	11 54
Mer. Pass.	6 59.5	v −0.2 d 0.6	v 0.6 d 0.2	v 2.8 d 0.0	v 2.6 d 0.0	Jupiter	116 59.5	23 08
						Saturn	152 50.7	20 46

1983 JUNE 6, 7, 8 (MON., TUES., WED.)

SUN and MOON — G.H.A. / Dec.

G.M.T.	SUN G.H.A.	SUN Dec.	MOON G.H.A.	v	MOON Dec.	d	H.P.
6 00	180 23.7	N22 34.1	243 39.0	14.7	S 1 11.2	13.0	56.0
01	195 23.6	34.4	258 12.7	14.7	0 58.2	13.1	56.0
02	210 23.5	34.7	272 46.4	14.6	0 45.1	13.1	56.0
03	225 23.4 ··	34.9	287 20.0	14.7	0 32.0	13.1	56.1
04	240 23.3	35.2	301 53.7	14.6	0 18.9	13.1	56.1
05	255 23.2	35.5	316 27.3	14.5	S 0 05.8	13.1	56.1
06	270 23.1	N22 35.7	331 00.8	14.5	N 0 07.3	13.1	56.1
07	285 22.9	36.0	345 34.3	14.5	0 20.4	13.2	56.2
08	300 22.8	36.3	0 07.8	14.5	0 33.6	13.2	56.2
M 09	315 22.7 ··	36.5	14 41.3	14.4	0 46.8	13.2	56.2
O 10	330 22.6	36.8	29 14.7	14.4	1 00.0	13.2	56.3
N 11	345 22.5	37.1	43 48.1	14.3	1 13.2	13.2	56.3
D 12	0 22.4	N22 37.3	58 21.4	14.3	N 1 26.4	13.2	56.3
A 13	15 22.3	37.6	72 54.7	14.3	1 39.6	13.2	56.4
Y 14	30 22.2	37.9	87 28.0	14.2	1 52.8	13.2	56.4
15	45 22.0 ··	38.1	102 01.2	14.1	2 06.0	13.3	56.4
16	60 21.9	38.4	116 34.3	14.1	2 19.3	13.2	56.5
17	75 21.8	38.6	131 07.4	14.1	2 32.5	13.3	56.5
18	90 21.7	N22 38.9	145 40.5	14.0	N 2 45.8	13.3	56.5
19	105 21.6	39.2	160 13.5	14.0	2 59.1	13.2	56.6
20	120 21.5	39.4	174 46.5	13.9	3 12.3	13.3	56.6
21	135 21.4 ··	39.7	189 19.4	13.9	3 25.6	13.2	56.6
22	150 21.2	39.9	203 52.3	13.8	3 38.8	13.3	56.7
23	165 21.1	40.2	218 25.1	13.8	3 52.1	13.3	56.7
7 00	180 21.0	N22 40.4	232 57.9	13.7	N 4 05.4	13.2	56.7
01	195 20.9	40.7	247 30.6	13.6	4 18.6	13.3	56.8
02	210 20.8	41.0	262 03.2	13.6	4 31.9	13.3	56.8
03	225 20.7 ··	41.2	276 35.8	13.6	4 45.2	13.3	56.8
04	240 20.6	41.5	291 08.4	13.4	4 58.4	13.3	56.9
05	255 20.4	41.7	305 40.8	13.5	5 11.7	13.2	56.9
06	270 20.3	N22 42.0	320 13.3	13.3	N 5 24.9	13.3	57.0
07	285 20.2	42.2	334 45.6	13.3	5 38.2	13.2	57.0
08	300 20.1	42.5	349 17.9	13.3	5 51.4	13.2	57.0
T 09	315 20.0 ··	42.7	3 50.2	13.1	6 04.6	13.2	57.1
U 10	330 19.9	43.0	18 22.3	13.1	6 17.8	13.2	57.1
E 11	345 19.8	43.2	32 54.4	13.1	6 31.0	13.2	57.1
S 12	0 19.6	N22 43.4	47 26.5	12.9	N 6 44.2	13.2	57.2
D 13	15 19.5	43.7	61 58.4	12.9	6 57.4	13.1	57.2
A 14	30 19.4	43.9	76 30.3	12.9	7 10.5	13.2	57.2
Y 15	45 19.3 ··	44.2	91 02.2	12.7	7 23.7	13.1	57.3
16	60 19.2	44.4	105 33.9	12.7	7 36.8	13.1	57.3
17	75 19.1	44.7	120 05.6	12.6	7 49.9	13.1	57.3
18	90 18.9	N22 44.9	134 37.2	12.6	N 8 03.0	13.0	57.4
19	105 18.8	45.2	149 08.8	12.4	8 16.0	13.1	57.4
20	120 18.7	45.4	163 40.2	12.4	8 29.1	13.0	57.4
21	135 18.6 ··	45.6	178 11.6	12.3	8 42.1	13.0	57.5
22	150 18.5	45.9	192 42.9	12.3	8 55.1	13.0	57.5
23	165 18.4	46.1	207 14.2	12.1	9 08.1	12.9	57.6
8 00	180 18.2	N22 46.4	221 45.3	12.1	N 9 21.0	12.9	57.6
01	195 18.1	46.6	236 16.4	12.0	9 33.9	12.9	57.6
02	210 18.0	46.8	250 47.4	11.9	9 46.8	12.8	57.7
03	225 17.9 ··	47.1	265 18.3	11.8	9 59.6	12.8	57.7
04	240 17.8	47.3	279 49.1	11.8	10 12.4	12.8	57.7
05	255 17.6	47.5	294 19.9	11.6	10 25.2	12.8	57.8
06	270 17.5	N22 47.8	308 50.5	11.6	N10 38.0	12.7	57.8
W 07	285 17.4	48.0	323 21.1	11.5	10 50.7	12.6	57.8
E 08	300 17.3	48.2	337 51.6	11.4	11 03.3	12.7	57.9
D 09	315 17.2 ··	48.5	352 22.0	11.3	11 16.0	12.6	57.9
N 10	330 17.1	48.7	6 52.3	11.2	11 28.6	12.5	58.0
E 11	345 16.9	48.9	21 22.5	11.1	11 41.1	12.5	58.0
S 12	0 16.8	N22 49.2	35 52.6	11.0	N11 53.6	12.5	58.0
D 13	15 16.7	49.4	50 22.6	11.0	12 06.1	12.4	58.1
A 14	30 16.6	49.6	64 52.6	10.8	12 18.5	12.4	58.1
Y 15	45 16.5 ··	49.8	79 22.4	10.8	12 30.9	12.3	58.1
16	60 16.3	50.1	93 52.2	10.7	12 43.2	12.2	58.2
17	75 16.2	50.3	108 21.9	10.5	12 55.4	12.2	58.2
18	90 16.1	N22 50.5	122 51.4	10.5	N13 07.6	12.2	58.2
19	105 16.0	50.8	137 20.9	10.4	13 19.8	12.1	58.3
20	120 15.9	51.0	151 50.3	10.2	13 31.9	12.0	58.3
21	135 15.7 ··	51.2	166 19.5	10.2	13 43.9	12.0	58.3
22	150 15.6	51.4	180 48.7	10.1	13 55.9	12.0	58.4
23	165 15.5	51.6	195 17.8	10.0	14 07.9	11.8	58.4
	S.D. 15.8	d 0.2	S.D. 15.4		15.6		15.8

Twilight / Sunrise / Moonrise

Lat.	Naut.	Civil	Sunrise	Moonrise 6	7	8	9
N 72	□	□	□	02 00	01 37	01 12	00 35
N 70	□	□	□	01 59	01 43	01 26	01 04
68	□	□	□	01 58	01 48	01 38	01 25
66	////	////	00 48	01 57	01 52	01 47	01 42
64	////	////	01 46	01 56	01 56	01 55	01 56
62	////	////	02 18	01 56	01 59	02 02	02 08
60	////	01 11	02 42	01 55	02 01	02 09	02 18
N 58	////	01 51	03 01	01 55	02 04	02 14	02 27
56	////	02 17	03 17	01 54	02 06	02 19	02 35
54	01 05	02 38	03 30	01 54	02 08	02 23	02 42
52	01 41	02 55	03 42	01 53	02 09	02 27	02 48
50	02 06	03 09	03 53	01 53	02 11	02 31	02 54
45	02 49	03 37	04 14	01 52	02 15	02 39	03 06
N 40	03 18	03 59	04 31	01 52	02 17	02 45	03 17
35	03 40	04 16	04 46	01 51	02 20	02 51	03 26
30	03 58	04 31	04 58	01 51	02 22	02 56	03 33
20	04 26	04 55	05 20	01 50	02 26	03 05	03 47
N 10	04 48	05 15	05 38	01 50	02 30	03 13	03 59
0	05 07	05 33	05 55	01 49	02 33	03 20	04 10
S 10	05 23	05 49	06 12	01 48	02 37	03 27	04 22
20	05 39	06 06	06 30	01 48	02 40	03 35	04 34
30	05 54	06 24	06 50	01 47	02 45	03 45	04 48
35	06 03	06 34	07 02	01 47	02 47	03 50	04 56
40	06 12	06 46	07 16	01 46	02 50	03 56	05 05
45	06 22	06 58	07 32	01 46	02 53	04 03	05 17
S 50	06 33	07 14	07 52	01 45	02 57	04 12	05 30
52	06 38	07 21	08 01	01 45	02 59	04 16	05 36
54	06 43	07 29	08 12	01 45	03 01	04 20	05 43
56	06 49	07 37	08 24	01 44	03 03	04 25	05 51
58	06 55	07 47	08 38	01 44	03 05	04 31	06 00
S 60	07 02	07 58	08 54	01 44	03 08	04 37	06 10

Sunset / Twilight / Moonset

Lat.	Sunset	Civil	Naut.	Moonset 6	7	8	9
N 72	□	□	□	14 34	16 36	18 55	□
N 70	□	□	□	14 32	16 24	18 28	21 00
68	□	□	□	14 29	16 15	18 08	20 17
66	23 15	////	////	14 28	16 07	17 53	19 48
64	22 14	////	////	14 26	16 00	17 40	19 27
62	21 40	////	////	14 25	15 55	17 29	19 10
60	21 16	22 49	////	14 24	15 50	17 20	18 55
N 58	20 57	22 08	////	14 22	15 45	17 12	18 43
56	20 41	21 41	////	14 22	15 42	17 05	18 33
54	20 27	21 20	22 55	14 21	15 38	16 59	18 24
52	20 16	21 03	22 17	14 20	15 35	16 54	18 15
50	20 05	20 49	21 52	14 19	15 32	16 49	18 08
45	19 44	20 20	21 09	14 18	15 26	16 38	17 52
N 40	19 26	19 59	20 40	14 17	15 21	16 29	17 40
35	19 12	19 41	20 17	14 15	15 17	16 21	17 29
30	18 59	19 26	19 59	14 14	15 13	16 14	17 19
20	18 38	19 02	19 31	14 13	15 06	16 03	17 03
N 10	18 19	18 42	19 09	14 11	15 01	15 53	16 49
0	18 02	18 25	18 51	14 10	14 55	15 43	16 36
S 10	17 45	18 08	18 34	14 09	14 50	15 34	16 22
20	17 28	17 51	18 19	14 07	14 44	15 24	16 08
30	17 07	17 33	18 03	14 05	14 38	15 13	15 52
35	16 55	17 23	17 55	14 04	14 34	15 06	15 43
40	16 41	17 12	17 46	14 03	14 30	14 59	15 33
45	16 25	16 59	17 36	14 02	14 25	14 50	15 20
S 50	16 05	16 43	17 24	14 00	14 19	14 40	15 05
52	15 56	16 36	17 19	14 00	14 16	14 35	14 59
54	15 45	16 28	17 14	13 59	14 13	14 30	14 51
56	15 33	16 20	17 08	13 58	14 10	14 24	14 42
58	15 19	16 10	17 02	13 57	14 07	14 18	14 33
S 60	15 03	15 59	16 55	13 56	14 03	14 11	14 22

SUN / MOON

Day	SUN Eqn. of Time 00h	SUN Eqn. of Time 12h	Mer. Pass.	MOON Mer. Pass. Upper	Lower	Age	Phase
	m s	m s	h m	h m	h m	d	
6	01 35	01 30	11 59	07 59	20 22	25	
7	01 24	01 19	11 59	08 44	21 07	26	
8	01 13	01 07	11 59	09 32	21 57	27	◗

CONVERSION OF ARC TO TIME

0°–59°	h m	60°–119°	h m	120°–179°	h m	180°–239°	h m	240°–299°	h m	300°–359°	h m	′	0′·00 m s	0′·25 m s	0′·50 m s	0′·75 m s
0	0 00	60	4 00	120	8 00	180	12 00	240	16 00	300	20 00	0	0 00	0 01	0 02	0 03
1	0 04	61	4 04	121	8 04	181	12 04	241	16 04	301	20 04	1	0 04	0 05	0 06	0 07
2	0 08	62	4 08	122	8 08	182	12 08	242	16 08	302	20 08	2	0 08	0 09	0 10	0 11
3	0 12	63	4 12	123	8 12	183	12 12	243	16 12	303	20 12	3	0 12	0 13	0 14	0 15
4	0 16	64	4 16	124	8 16	184	12 16	244	16 16	304	20 16	4	0 16	0 17	0 18	0 19
5	0 20	65	4 20	125	8 20	185	12 20	245	16 20	305	20 20	5	0 20	0 21	0 22	0 23
6	0 24	66	4 24	126	8 24	186	12 24	246	16 24	306	20 24	6	0 24	0 25	0 26	0 27
7	0 28	67	4 28	127	8 28	187	12 28	247	16 28	307	20 28	7	0 28	0 29	0 30	0 31
8	0 32	68	4 32	128	8 32	188	12 32	248	16 32	308	20 32	8	0 32	0 33	0 34	0 35
9	0 36	69	4 36	129	8 36	189	12 36	249	16 36	309	20 36	9	0 36	0 37	0 38	0 39
10	0 40	70	4 40	130	8 40	190	12 40	250	16 40	310	20 40	10	0 40	0 41	0 42	0 43
11	0 44	71	4 44	131	8 44	191	12 44	251	16 44	311	20 44	11	0 44	0 45	0 46	0 47
12	0 48	72	4 48	132	8 48	192	12 48	252	16 48	312	20 48	12	0 48	0 49	0 50	0 51
13	0 52	73	4 52	133	8 52	193	12 52	253	16 52	313	20 52	13	0 52	0 53	0 54	0 55
14	0 56	74	4 56	134	8 56	194	12 56	254	16 56	314	20 56	14	0 56	0 57	0 58	0 59
15	1 00	75	5 00	135	9 00	195	13 00	255	17 00	315	21 00	15	1 00	1 01	1 02	1 03
16	1 04	76	5 04	136	9 04	196	13 04	256	17 04	316	21 04	16	1 04	1 05	1 06	1 07
17	1 08	77	5 08	137	9 08	197	13 08	257	17 08	317	21 08	17	1 08	1 09	1 10	1 11
18	1 12	78	5 12	138	9 12	198	13 12	258	17 12	318	21 12	18	1 12	1 13	1 14	1 15
19	1 16	79	5 16	139	9 16	199	13 16	259	17 16	319	21 16	19	1 16	1 17	1 18	1 19
20	1 20	80	5 20	140	9 20	200	13 20	260	17 20	320	21 20	20	1 20	1 21	1 22	1 23
21	1 24	81	5 24	141	9 24	201	13 24	261	17 24	321	21 24	21	1 24	1 25	1 26	1 27
22	1 28	82	5 28	142	9 28	202	13 28	262	17 28	322	21 28	22	1 28	1 29	1 30	1 31
23	1 32	83	5 32	143	9 32	203	13 32	263	17 32	323	21 32	23	1 32	1 33	1 34	1 35
24	1 36	84	5 36	144	9 36	204	13 36	264	17 36	324	21 36	24	1 36	1 37	1 38	1 39
25	1 40	85	5 40	145	9 40	205	13 40	265	17 40	325	21 40	25	1 40	1 41	1 42	1 43
26	1 44	86	5 44	146	9 44	206	13 44	266	17 44	326	21 44	26	1 44	1 45	1 46	1 47
27	1 48	87	5 48	147	9 48	207	13 48	267	17 48	327	21 48	27	1 48	1 49	1 50	1 51
28	1 52	88	5 52	148	9 52	208	13 52	268	17 52	328	21 52	28	1 52	1 53	1 54	1 55
29	1 56	89	5 56	149	9 56	209	13 56	269	17 56	329	21 56	29	1 56	1 57	1 58	1 59
30	2 00	90	6 00	150	10 00	210	14 00	270	18 00	330	22 00	30	2 00	2 01	2 02	2 03
31	2 04	91	6 04	151	10 04	211	14 04	271	18 04	331	22 04	31	2 04	2 05	2 06	2 07
32	2 08	92	6 08	152	10 08	212	14 08	272	18 08	332	22 08	32	2 08	2 09	2 10	2 11
33	2 12	93	6 12	153	10 12	213	14 12	273	18 12	333	22 12	33	2 12	2 13	2 14	2 15
34	2 16	94	6 16	154	10 16	214	14 16	274	18 16	334	22 16	34	2 16	2 17	2 18	2 19
35	2 20	95	6 20	155	10 20	215	14 20	275	18 20	335	22 20	35	2 20	2 21	2 22	2 23
36	2 24	96	6 24	156	10 24	216	14 24	276	18 24	336	22 24	36	2 24	2 25	2 26	2 27
37	2 28	97	6 28	157	10 28	217	14 28	277	18 28	337	22 28	37	2 28	2 29	2 30	2 31
38	2 32	98	6 32	158	10 32	218	14 32	278	18 32	338	22 32	38	2 32	2 33	2 34	2 35
39	2 36	99	6 36	159	10 36	219	14 36	279	18 36	339	22 36	39	2 36	2 37	2 38	2 39
40	2 40	100	6 40	160	10 40	220	14 40	280	18 40	340	22 40	40	2 40	2 41	2 42	2 43
41	2 44	101	6 44	161	10 44	221	14 44	281	18 44	341	22 44	41	2 44	2 45	2 46	2 47
42	2 48	102	6 48	162	10 48	222	14 48	282	18 48	342	22 48	42	2 48	2 49	2 50	2 51
43	2 52	103	6 52	163	10 52	223	14 52	283	18 52	343	22 52	43	2 52	2 53	2 54	2 55
44	2 56	104	6 56	164	10 56	224	14 56	284	18 56	344	22 56	44	2 56	2 57	2 58	2 59
45	3 00	105	7 00	165	11 00	225	15 00	285	19 00	345	23 00	45	3 00	3 01	3 02	3 03
46	3 04	106	7 04	166	11 04	226	15 04	286	19 04	346	23 04	46	3 04	3 05	3 06	3 07
47	3 08	107	7 08	167	11 08	227	15 08	287	19 08	347	23 08	47	3 08	3 09	3 10	3 11
48	3 12	108	7 12	168	11 12	228	15 12	288	19 12	348	23 12	48	3 12	3 13	3 14	3 15
49	3 16	109	7 16	169	11 16	229	15 16	289	19 16	349	23 16	49	3 16	3 17	3 18	3 19
50	3 20	110	7 20	170	11 20	230	15 20	290	19 20	350	23 20	50	3 20	3 21	3 22	3 23
51	3 24	111	7 24	171	11 24	231	15 24	291	19 24	351	23 24	51	3 24	3 25	3 26	3 27
52	3 28	112	7 28	172	11 28	232	15 28	292	19 28	352	23 28	52	3 28	3 29	3 30	3 31
53	3 32	113	7 32	173	11 32	233	15 32	293	19 32	353	23 32	53	3 32	3 33	3 34	3 35
54	3 36	114	7 36	174	11 36	234	15 36	294	19 36	354	23 36	54	3 36	3 37	3 38	3 39
55	3 40	115	7 40	175	11 40	235	15 40	295	19 40	355	23 40	55	3 40	3 41	3 42	3 43
56	3 44	116	7 44	176	11 44	236	15 44	296	19 44	356	23 44	56	3 44	3 45	3 46	3 47
57	3 48	117	7 48	177	11 48	237	15 48	297	19 48	357	23 48	57	3 48	3 49	3 50	3 51
58	3 52	118	7 52	178	11 52	238	15 52	298	19 52	358	23 52	58	3 52	3 53	3 54	3 55
59	3 56	119	7 56	179	11 56	239	15 56	299	19 56	359	23 56	59	3 56	3 57	3 58	3 59

The above table is for converting expressions in arc to their equivalent in time; its main use in this Almanac is for the conversion of longitude for application to L.M.T. (*added if west, subtracted if east*) to give G.M.T. or vice versa, particularly in the case of sunrise, sunset, etc.

INCREMENTS AND CORRECTIONS

0ᵐ ... **1ᵐ**

0 s	SUN PLANETS ° '	ARIES ° '	MOON ° '	v or d	Corrⁿ	v or d	Corrⁿ	v or d	Corrⁿ	1 s	SUN PLANETS ° '	ARIES ° '	MOON ° '	v or d	Corrⁿ	v or d	Corrⁿ	v or d	Corrⁿ
00	0 00·0	0 00·0	0 00·0	0·0	0·0	6·0	0·1	12·0	0·1	00	0 15·0	0 15·0	0 14·3	0·0	0·0	6·0	0·2	12·0	0·3
01	0 00·3	0 00·3	0 00·2	0·1	0·0	6·1	0·1	12·1	0·1	01	0 15·3	0 15·3	0 14·6	0·1	0·0	6·1	0·2	12·1	0·3
02	0 00·5	0 00·5	0 00·5	0·2	0·0	6·2	0·1	12·2	0·1	02	0 15·5	0 15·5	0 14·8	0·2	0·0	6·2	0·2	12·2	0·3
03	0 00·8	0 00·8	0 00·7	0·3	0·0	6·3	0·1	12·3	0·1	03	0 15·8	0 15·8	0 15·0	0·3	0·0	6·3	0·2	12·3	0·3
04	0 01·0	0 01·0	0 01·0	0·4	0·0	6·4	0·1	12·4	0·1	04	0 16·0	0 16·0	0 15·3	0·4	0·0	6·4	0·2	12·4	0·3
05	0 01·3	0 01·3	0 01·2	0·5	0·0	6·5	0·1	12·5	0 1	05	0 16·3	0 16·3	0 15·5	0·5	0·0	6·5	0·2	12·5	0·3
06	0 01·5	0 01·5	0 01·4	0·6	0·0	6·6	0·1	12·6	0·1	06	0 16·5	0 16·5	0 15·7	0·6	0·0	6·6	0·2	12·6	0·3
07	0 01·8	0 01·8	0 01·7	0·7	0·0	6·7	0·1	12·7	0·1	07	0 16·8	0 16·8	0 16·0	0·7	0·0	6·7	0·2	12·7	0·3
08	0 02·0	0 02·0	0 01·9	0·8	0·0	6·8	0·1	12·8	0·1	08	0 17·0	0 17·0	0 16·2	0·8	0·0	6·8	0·2	12·8	0·3
09	0 02·3	0 02·3	0 02·1	0·9	0·0	6·9	0·1	12·9	0·1	09	0 17·3	0 17·3	0 16·5	0·9	0·0	6·9	0·2	12·9	0·3
10	0 02·5	0 02·5	0 02·4	1·0	0·0	7·0	0·1	13·0	0·1	10	0 17·5	0 17·5	0 16·7	1·0	0·0	7·0	0·2	13·0	0·3
11	0 02·8	0 02·8	0 02·6	1·1	0·0	7·1	0·1	13·1	0·1	11	0 17·8	0 17·8	0 16·9	1·1	0·0	7·1	0·2	13·1	0·3
12	0 03·0	0 03·0	0 02·9	1·2	0·0	7·2	0·1	13·2	0·1	12	0 18·0	0 18·0	0 17·2	1·2	0·0	7·2	0·2	13·2	0·3
13	0 03·3	0 03·3	0 03·1	1·3	0·0	7·3	0·1	13·3	0·1	13	0 18·3	0 18·3	0 17·4	1·3	0·0	7·3	0·2	13·3	0·3
14	0 03·5	0 03·5	0 03·3	1·4	0·0	7·4	0·1	13·4	0·1	14	0 18·5	0 18·6	0 17·7	1·4	0·0	7·4	0·2	13·4	0·3
15	0 03·8	0 03·8	0 03·6	1·5	0·0	7·5	0·1	13·5	0·1	15	0 18·8	0 18·8	0 17·9	1·5	0·0	7·5	0·2	13·5	0·3
16	0 04·0	0 04·0	0 03·8	1·6	0·0	7·6	0·1	13·6	0·1	16	0 19·0	0 19·1	0 18·1	1·6	0·0	7·6	0·2	13·6	0·3
17	0 04·3	0 04·3	0 04·1	1·7	0·0	7·7	0·1	13·7	0·1	17	0 19·3	0 19·3	0 18·4	1·7	0·0	7·7	0·2	13·7	0·3
18	0 04·5	0 04·5	0 04·3	1·8	0·0	7·8	0·1	13·8	0·1	18	0 19·5	0 19·6	0 18·6	1·8	0·0	7·8	0·2	13·8	0·3
19	0 04·8	0 04·8	0 04·5	1·9	0·0	7·9	0·1	13·9	0·1	19	0 19·8	0 19·8	0 18·9	1·9	0·0	7·9	0·2	13·9	0·3
20	0 05·0	0 05·0	0 04·8	2·0	0·0	8·0	0·1	14·0	0·1	20	0 20·0	0 20·1	0 19·1	2·0	0·1	8·0	0·2	14·0	0·4
21	0 05·3	0 05·3	0 05·0	2·1	0·0	8·1	0·1	14·1	0·1	21	0 20·3	0 20·3	0 19·3	2·1	0·1	8·1	0·2	14·1	0·4
22	0 05·5	0 05·5	0 05·2	2·2	0·0	8·2	0·1	14·2	0·1	22	0 20·5	0 20·6	0 19·6	2·2	0·1	8·2	0·2	14·2	0·4
23	0 05·8	0 05·8	0 05·5	2·3	0·0	8·3	0·1	14·3	0·1	23	0 20·8	0 20·8	0 19·8	2·3	0·1	8·3	0·2	14·3	0·4
24	0 06·0	0 06·0	0 05·7	2·4	0·0	8·4	0·1	14·4	0·1	24	0 21·0	0 21·1	0 20·0	2·4	0·1	8·4	0·2	14·4	0·4
25	0 06·3	0 06·3	0 06·0	2·5	0·0	8·5	0·1	14·5	0·1	25	0 21·3	0 21·3	0 20·3	2·5	0·1	8·5	0·2	14·5	0·4
26	0 06·5	0 06·5	0 06·2	2·6	0·0	8·6	0·1	14·6	0·1	26	0 21·5	0 21·6	0 20·5	2·6	0·1	8·6	0·2	14·6	0·4
27	0 06·8	0 06·8	0 06·4	2·7	0·0	8·7	0·1	14·7	0·1	27	0 21·8	0 21·8	0 20·8	2·7	0·1	8·7	0·2	14·7	0·4
28	0 07·0	0 07·0	0 06·7	2·8	0·0	8·8	0·1	14·8	0·1	28	0 22·0	0 22·1	0 21·0	2·8	0·1	8·8	0·2	14·8	0·4
29	0 07·3	0 07·3	0 06·9	2·9	0·0	8·9	0·1	14·9	0·1	29	0 22·3	0 22·3	0 21·2	2·9	0·1	8·9	0·2	14·9	0·4
30	0 07·5	0 07·5	0 07·2	3·0	0·0	9·0	0·1	15·0	0·1	30	0 22·5	0 22·6	0 21·5	3·0	0·1	9·0	0·2	15·0	0·4
31	0 07·8	0 07·8	0 07·4	3·1	0·0	9·1	0·1	15·1	0·1	31	0 22·8	0 22·8	0 21·7	3·1	0·1	9·1	0·2	15·1	0·4
32	0 08·0	0 08·0	0 07·6	3·2	0·0	9·2	0·1	15·2	0·1	32	0 23·0	0 23·1	0 22·0	3·2	0·1	9·2	0·2	15·2	0·4
33	0 08·3	0 08·3	0 07·9	3·3	0·0	9·3	0·1	15·3	0·1	33	0 23·3	0 23·3	0 22·2	3·3	0·1	9·3	0·2	15·3	0·4
34	0 08·5	0 08·5	0 08·1	3·4	0·0	9·4	0·1	15·4	0·1	34	0 23·5	0 23·6	0 22·4	3·4	0·1	9·4	0·2	15·4	0·4
35	0 08·8	0 08·8	0 08·4	3·5	0·0	9·5	0·1	15·5	0·1	35	0 23·8	0 23·8	0 22·7	3·5	0·1	9·5	0·2	15·5	0·4
36	0 09·0	0 09·0	0 08·6	3·6	0·0	9·6	0·1	15·6	0·1	36	0 24·0	0 24·1	0 22·9	3·6	0·1	9·6	0·2	15·6	0·4
37	0 09·3	0 09·3	0 08·8	3·7	0·0	9·7	0·1	15·7	0·1	37	0 24·3	0 24·3	0 23·1	3·7	0·1	9·7	0·2	15·7	0·4
38	0 09·5	0 09·5	0 09·1	3·8	0·0	9·8	0·1	15·8	0·1	38	0 24·5	0 24·6	0 23·4	3·8	0·1	9·8	0·2	15·8	0·4
39	0 09·8	0 09·8	0 09·3	3·9	0·0	9·9	0·1	15·9	0·1	39	0 24·8	0 24·8	0 23·6	3·9	0·1	9·9	0·2	15·9	0·4
40	0 10·0	0 10·0	0 09·5	4·0	0·0	10·0	0·1	16·0	0·1	40	0 25·0	0 25·1	0 23·9	4·0	0·1	10·0	0·3	16·0	0·4
41	0 10·3	0 10·3	0 09·8	4·1	0·0	10·1	0·1	16·1	0·1	41	0 25·3	0 25·3	0 24·1	4·1	0·1	10·1	0·3	16·1	0·4
42	0 10·5	0 10·5	0 10·0	4·2	0·0	10·2	0·1	16·2	0·1	42	0 25·5	0 25·6	0 24·3	4·2	0·1	10·2	0·3	16·2	0·4
43	0 10·8	0 10·8	0 10·3	4·3	0·0	10·3	0·1	16·3	0·1	43	0 25·8	0 25·8	0 24·6	4·3	0·1	10·3	0·3	16·3	0·4
44	0 11·0	0 11·0	0 10·5	4·4	0·0	10·4	0·1	16·4	0·1	44	0 26·0	0 26·1	0 24·8	4·4	0·1	10·4	0·3	16·4	0·4
45	0 11·3	0 11·3	0 10·7	4·5	0·0	10·5	0·1	16·5	0·1	45	0 26·3	0 26·3	0 25·1	4·5	0·1	10·5	0·3	16·5	0·4
46	0 11·5	0 11·5	0 11·0	4·6	0·0	10·6	0·1	16·6	0·1	46	0 26·5	0 26·6	0 25·3	4·6	0·1	10·6	0·3	16·6	0·4
47	0 11·8	0 11·8	0 11·2	4·7	0·0	10·7	0·1	16·7	0·1	47	0 26·8	0 26·8	0 25·5	4·7	0·1	10·7	0·3	16·7	0·4
48	0 12·0	0 12·0	0 11·5	4·8	0·0	10·8	0·1	16·8	0·1	48	0 27·0	0 27·1	0 25·8	4·8	0·1	10·8	0·3	16·8	0·4
49	0 12·3	0 12·3	0 11·7	4·9	0·0	10·9	0·1	16·9	0·1	49	0 27·3	0 27·3	0 26·0	4·9	0·1	10·9	0·3	16·9	0·4
50	0 12·5	0 12·5	0 11·9	5·0	0·0	11·0	0·1	17·0	0·1	50	0 27·5	0 27·6	0 26·2	5·0	0·1	11·0	0·3	17·0	0·4
51	0 12·8	0 12·8	0 12·2	5·1	0·0	11·1	0·1	17·1	0·1	51	0 27·8	0 27·8	0 26·5	5·1	0·1	11·1	0·3	17·1	0·4
52	0 13·0	0 13·0	0 12·4	5·2	0·0	11·2	0·1	17·2	0·1	52	0 28·0	0 28·1	0 26·7	5·2	0·1	11·2	0·3	17·2	0·4
53	0 13·3	0 13·3	0 12·6	5·3	0·0	11·3	0·1	17·3	0·1	53	0 28·3	0 28·3	0 27·0	5·3	0·1	11·3	0·3	17·3	0·4
54	0 13·5	0 13·5	0 12·9	5·4	0·0	11·4	0·1	17·4	0·1	54	0 28·5	0 28·6	0 27·2	5·4	0·1	11·4	0·3	17·4	0·4
55	0 13·8	0 13·8	0 13·1	5·5	0·0	11·5	0·1	17·5	0·1	55	0 28·8	0 28·8	0 27·4	5·5	0·1	11·5	0·3	17·5	0·4
56	0 14·0	0 14·0	0 13·4	5·6	0·0	11·6	0·1	17·6	0·1	56	0 29·0	0 29·1	0 27·7	5·6	0·1	11·6	0·3	17·6	0·4
57	0 14·3	0 14·3	0 13·6	5·7	0·0	11·7	0·1	17·7	0·1	57	0 29·3	0 29·3	0 27·9	5·7	0·1	11·7	0·3	17·7	0·4
58	0 14·5	0 14·5	0 13·8	5·8	0·0	11·8	0·1	17·8	0·1	58	0 29·5	0 29·6	0 28·2	5·8	0·1	11·8	0·3	17·8	0·4
59	0 14·8	0 14·8	0 14·1	5·9	0·0	11·9	0·1	17·9	0·1	59	0 29·8	0 29·8	0 28·4	5·9	0·1	11·9	0·3	17·9	0·4
60	0 15·0	0 15·0	0 14·3	6·0	0·1	12·0	0·1	18·0	0·2	60	0 30·0	0 30·1	0 28·6	6·0	0·2	12·0	0·3	18·0	0·5

INCREMENTS AND CORRECTIONS

2^m **3^m**

2 s	SUN PLANETS ° ′	ARIES ° ′	MOON ° ′	v or Corrn d ′ ′	v or Corrn d ′ ′	v or Corrn d ′ ′	3 s	SUN PLANETS ° ′	ARIES ° ′	MOON ° ′	v or Corrn d ′ ′	v or Corrn d ′ ′	v or Corrn d ′ ′
00	0 30.0	0 30.1	0 28.6	0.0 0.0	6.0 0.3	12.0 0.5	00	0 45.0	0 45.1	0 43.0	0.0 0.0	6.0 0.4	12.0 0.7
01	0 30.3	0 30.3	0 28.9	0.1 0.0	6.1 0.3	12.1 0.5	01	0 45.3	0 45.4	0 43.2	0.1 0.0	6.1 0.4	12.1 0.7
02	0 30.5	0 30.6	0 29.1	0.2 0.0	6.2 0.3	12.2 0.5	02	0 45.5	0 45.6	0 43.4	0.2 0.0	6.2 0.4	12.2 0.7
03	0 30.8	0 30.8	0 29.3	0.3 0.0	6.3 0.3	12.3 0.5	03	0 45.8	0 45.9	0 43.7	0.3 0.0	6.3 0.4	12.3 0.7
04	0 31.0	0 31.1	0 29.6	0.4 0.0	6.4 0.3	12.4 0.5	04	0 46.0	0 46.1	0 43.9	0.4 0.0	6.4 0.4	12.4 0.7
05	0 31.3	0 31.3	0 29.8	0.5 0.0	6.5 0.3	12.5 0.5	05	0 46.3	0 46.4	0 44.1	0.5 0.0	6.5 0.4	12.5 0.7
06	0 31.5	0 31.6	0 30.1	0.6 0.0	6.6 0.3	12.6 0.5	06	0 46.5	0 46.6	0 44.4	0.6 0.0	6.6 0.4	12.6 0.7
07	0 31.8	0 31.8	0 30.3	0.7 0.0	6.7 0.3	12.7 0.5	07	0 46.8	0 46.9	0 44.6	0.7 0.0	6.7 0.4	12.7 0.7
08	0 32.0	0 32.1	0 30.5	0.8 0.0	6.8 0.3	12.8 0.5	08	0 47.0	0 47.1	0 44.9	0.8 0.0	6.8 0.4	12.8 0.7
09	0 32.3	0 32.3	0 30.8	0.9 0.0	6.9 0.3	12.9 0.5	09	0 47.3	0 47.4	0 45.1	0.9 0.1	6.9 0.4	12.9 0.8
10	0 32.5	0 32.6	0 31.0	1.0 0.0	7.0 0.3	13.0 0.5	10	0 47.5	0 47.6	0 45.3	1.0 0.1	7.0 0.4	13.0 0.8
11	0 32.8	0 32.8	0 31.3	1.1 0.0	7.1 0.3	13.1 0.5	11	0 47.8	0 47.9	0 45.6	1.1 0.1	7.1 0.4	13.1 0.8
12	0 33.0	0 33.1	0 31.5	1.2 0.1	7.2 0.3	13.2 0.6	12	0 48.0	0 48.1	0 45.8	1.2 0.1	7.2 0.4	13.2 0.8
13	0 33.3	0 33.3	0 31.7	1.3 0.1	7.3 0.3	13.3 0.6	13	0 48.3	0 48.4	0 46.1	1.3 0.1	7.3 0.4	13.3 0.8
14	0 33.5	0 33.6	0 32.0	1.4 0.1	7.4 0.3	13.4 0.6	14	0 48.5	0 48.6	0 46.3	1.4 0.1	7.4 0.4	13.4 0.8
15	0 33.8	0 33.8	0 32.2	1.5 0.1	7.5 0.3	13.5 0.6	15	0 48.8	0 48.9	0 46.5	1.5 0.1	7.5 0.4	13.5 0.8
16	0 34.0	0 34.1	0 32.5	1.6 0.1	7.6 0.3	13.6 0.6	16	0 49.0	0 49.1	0 46.8	1.6 0.1	7.6 0.4	13.6 0.8
17	0 34.3	0 34.3	0 32.7	1.7 0.1	7.7 0.3	13.7 0.6	17	0 49.3	0 49.4	0 47.0	1.7 0.1	7.7 0.4	13.7 0.8
18	0 34.5	0 34.6	0 32.9	1.8 0.1	7.8 0.3	13.8 0.6	18	0 49.5	0 49.6	0 47.2	1.8 0.1	7.8 0.5	13.8 0.8
19	0 34.8	0 34.8	0 33.2	1.9 0.1	7.9 0.3	13.9 0.6	19	0 49.8	0 49.9	0 47.5	1.9 0.1	7.9 0.5	13.9 0.8
20	0 35.0	0 35.1	0 33.4	2.0 0.1	8.0 0.3	14.0 0.6	20	0 50.0	0 50.1	0 47.7	2.0 0.1	8.0 0.5	14.0 0.8
21	0 35.3	0 35.3	0 33.6	2.1 0.1	8.1 0.3	14.1 0.6	21	0 50.3	0 50.4	0 48.0	2.1 0.1	8.1 0.5	14.1 0.8
22	0 35.5	0 35.6	0 33.9	2.2 0.1	8.2 0.3	14.2 0.6	22	0 50.5	0 50.6	0 48.2	2.2 0.1	8.2 0.5	14.2 0.8
23	0 35.8	0 35.8	0 34.1	2.3 0.1	8.3 0.3	14.3 0.6	23	0 50.8	0 50.9	0 48.4	2.3 0.1	8.3 0.5	14.3 0.8
24	0 36.0	0 36.1	0 34.4	2.4 0.1	8.4 0.4	14.4 0.6	24	0 51.0	0 51.1	0 48.7	2.4 0.1	8.4 0.5	14.4 0.8
25	0 36.3	0 36.3	0 34.6	2.5 0.1	8.5 0.4	14.5 0.6	25	0 51.3	0 51.4	0 48.9	2.5 0.1	8.5 0.5	14.5 0.8
26	0 36.5	0 36.6	0 34.8	2.6 0.1	8.6 0.4	14.6 0.6	26	0 51.5	0 51.6	0 49.2	2.6 0.2	8.6 0.5	14.6 0.9
27	0 36.8	0 36.9	0 35.1	2.7 0.1	8.7 0.4	14.7 0.6	27	0 51.8	0 51.9	0 49.4	2.7 0.2	8.7 0.5	14.7 0.9
28	0 37.0	0 37.1	0 35.3	2.8 0.1	8.8 0.4	14.8 0.6	28	0 52.0	0 52.1	0 49.6	2.8 0.2	8.8 0.5	14.8 0.9
29	0 37.3	0 37.4	0 35.6	2.9 0.1	8.9 0.4	14.9 0.6	29	0 52.3	0 52.4	0 49.9	2.9 0.2	8.9 0.5	14.9 0.9
30	0 37.5	0 37.6	0 35.8	3.0 0.1	9.0 0.4	15.0 0.6	30	0 52.5	0 52.6	0 50.1	3.0 0.2	9.0 0.5	15.0 0.9
31	0 37.8	0 37.9	0 36.0	3.1 0.1	9.1 0.4	15.1 0.6	31	0 52.8	0 52.9	0 50.3	3.1 0.2	9.1 0.5	15.1 0.9
32	0 38.0	0 38.1	0 36.3	3.2 0.1	9.2 0.4	15.2 0.6	32	0 53.0	0 53.1	0 50.6	3.2 0.2	9.2 0.5	15.2 0.9
33	0 38.3	0 38.4	0 36.5	3.3 0.1	9.3 0.4	15.3 0.6	33	0 53.3	0 53.4	0 50.8	3.3 0.2	9.3 0.5	15.3 0.9
34	0 38.5	0 38.6	0 36.7	3.4 0.1	9.4 0.4	15.4 0.6	34	0 53.5	0 53.6	0 51.1	3.4 0.2	9.4 0.5	15.4 0.9
35	0 38.8	0 38.9	0 37.0	3.5 0.1	9.5 0.4	15.5 0.6	35	0 53.8	0 53.9	0 51.3	3.5 0.2	9.5 0.6	15.5 0.9
36	0 39.0	0 39.1	0 37.2	3.6 0.2	9.6 0.4	15.6 0.7	36	0 54.0	0 54.1	0 51.5	3.6 0.2	9.6 0.6	15.6 0.9
37	0 39.3	0 39.4	0 37.5	3.7 0.2	9.7 0.4	15.7 0.7	37	0 54.3	0 54.4	0 51.8	3.7 0.2	9.7 0.6	15.7 0.9
38	0 39.5	0 39.6	0 37.7	3.8 0.2	9.8 0.4	15.8 0.7	38	0 54.5	0 54.6	0 52.0	3.8 0.2	9.8 0.6	15.8 0.9
39	0 39.8	0 39.9	0 37.9	3.9 0.2	9.9 0.4	15.9 0.7	39	0 54.8	0 54.9	0 52.3	3.9 0.2	9.9 0.6	15.9 0.9
40	0 40.0	0 40.1	0 38.2	4.0 0.2	10.0 0.4	16.0 0.7	40	0 55.0	0 55.2	0 52.5	4.0 0.2	10.0 0.6	16.0 0.9
41	0 40.3	0 40.4	0 38.4	4.1 0.2	10.1 0.4	16.1 0.7	41	0 55.3	0 55.4	0 52.7	4.1 0.2	10.1 0.6	16.1 0.9
42	0 40.5	0 40.6	0 38.7	4.2 0.2	10.2 0.4	16.2 0.7	42	0 55.5	0 55.7	0 53.0	4.2 0.2	10.2 0.6	16.2 0.9
43	0 40.8	0 40.9	0 38.9	4.3 0.2	10.3 0.4	16.3 0.7	43	0 55.8	0 55.9	0 53.2	4.3 0.3	10.3 0.6	16.3 1.0
44	0 41.0	0 41.1	0 39.1	4.4 0.2	10.4 0.4	16.4 0.7	44	0 56.0	0 56.2	0 53.4	4.4 0.3	10.4 0.6	16.4 1.0
45	0 41.3	0 41.4	0 39.4	4.5 0.2	10.5 0.4	16.5 0.7	45	0 56.3	0 56.4	0 53.7	4.5 0.3	10.5 0.6	16.5 1.0
46	0 41.5	0 41.6	0 39.6	4.6 0.2	10.6 0.4	16.6 0.7	46	0 56.5	0 56.7	0 53.9	4.6 0.3	10.6 0.6	16.6 1.0
47	0 41.8	0 41.9	0 39.8	4.7 0.2	10.7 0.4	16.7 0.7	47	0 56.8	0 56.9	0 54.2	4.7 0.3	10.7 0.6	16.7 1.0
48	0 42.0	0 42.1	0 40.1	4.8 0.2	10.8 0.5	16.8 0.7	48	0 57.0	0 57.2	0 54.4	4.8 0.3	10.8 0.6	16.8 1.0
49	0 42.3	0 42.4	0 40.3	4.9 0.2	10.9 0.5	16.9 0.7	49	0 57.3	0 57.4	0 54.6	4.9 0.3	10.9 0.6	16.9 1.0
50	0 42.5	0 42.6	0 40.6	5.0 0.2	11.0 0.5	17.0 0.7	50	0 57.5	0 57.7	0 54.9	5.0 0.3	11.0 0.6	17.0 1.0
51	0 42.8	0 42.9	0 40.8	5.1 0.2	11.1 0.5	17.1 0.7	51	0 57.8	0 57.9	0 55.1	5.1 0.3	11.1 0.6	17.1 1.0
52	0 43.0	0 43.1	0 41.0	5.2 0.2	11.2 0.5	17.2 0.7	52	0 58.0	0 58.2	0 55.4	5.2 0.3	11.2 0.7	17.2 1.0
53	0 43.3	0 43.4	0 41.3	5.3 0.2	11.3 0.5	17.3 0.7	53	0 58.3	0 58.4	0 55.6	5.3 0.3	11.3 0.7	17.3 1.0
54	0 43.5	0 43.6	0 41.5	5.4 0.2	11.4 0.5	17.4 0.7	54	0 58.5	0 58.7	0 55.8	5.4 0.3	11.4 0.7	17.4 1.0
55	0 43.8	0 43.9	0 41.8	5.5 0.2	11.5 0.5	17.5 0.7	55	0 58.8	0 58.9	0 56.1	5.5 0.3	11.5 0.7	17.5 1.0
56	0 44.0	0 44.1	0 42.0	5.6 0.2	11.6 0.5	17.6 0.7	56	0 59.0	0 59.2	0 56.3	5.6 0.3	11.6 0.7	17.6 1.0
57	0 44.3	0 44.4	0 42.2	5.7 0.2	11.7 0.5	17.7 0.7	57	0 59.3	0 59.4	0 56.6	5.7 0.3	11.7 0.7	17.7 1.0
58	0 44.5	0 44.6	0 42.5	5.8 0.2	11.8 0.5	17.8 0.7	58	0 59.5	0 59.7	0 56.8	5.8 0.3	11.8 0.7	17.8 1.0
59	0 44.8	0 44.9	0 42.7	5.9 0.2	11.9 0.5	17.9 0.7	59	0 59.8	0 59.9	0 57.0	5.9 0.3	11.9 0.7	17.9 1.0
60	0 45.0	0 45.1	0 43.0	6.0 0.3	12.0 0.5	18.0 0.8	60	1 00.0	1 00.2	0 57.3	6.0 0.4	12.0 0.7	18.0 1.1

4^m   INCREMENTS AND CORRECTIONS   **5^m**

4 s	SUN PLANETS	ARIES	MOON	v or d	Corrn	v or d	Corrn	v or d	Corrn
00	1 00·0	1 00·2	0 57·3	0·0	0·0	6·0	0·5	12·0	0·9
01	1 00·3	1 00·4	0 57·5	0·1	0·0	6·1	0·5	12·1	0·9
02	1 00·5	1 00·7	0 57·7	0·2	0·0	6·2	0·5	12·2	0·9
03	1 00·8	1 00·9	0 58·0	0·3	0·0	6·3	0·5	12·3	0·9
04	1 01·0	1 01·2	0 58·2	0·4	0·0	6·4	0·5	12·4	0·9
05	1 01·3	1 01·4	0 58·5	0·5	0·0	6·5	0·5	12·5	0·9
06	1 01·5	1 01·7	0 58·7	0·6	0·0	6·6	0·5	12·6	0·9
07	1 01·8	1 01·9	0 58·9	0·7	0·1	6·7	0·5	12·7	1·0
08	1 02·0	1 02·2	0 59·2	0·8	0·1	6·8	0·5	12·8	1·0
09	1 02·3	1 02·4	0 59·4	0·9	0·1	6·9	0·5	12·9	1·0
10	1 02·5	1 02·7	0 59·7	1·0	0·1	7·0	0·5	13·0	1·0
11	1 02·8	1 02·9	0 59·9	1·1	0·1	7·1	0·5	13·1	1·0
12	1 03·0	1 03·2	1 00·1	1·2	0·1	7·2	0·5	13·2	1·0
13	1 03·3	1 03·4	1 00·4	1·3	0·1	7·3	0·5	13·3	1·0
14	1 03·5	1 03·7	1 00·6	1·4	0·1	7·4	0·6	13·4	1·0
15	1 03·8	1 03·9	1 00·8	1·5	0·1	7·5	0·6	13·5	1·0
16	1 04·0	1 04·2	1 01·1	1·6	0·1	7·6	0·6	13·6	1·0
17	1 04·3	1 04·4	1 01·3	1·7	0·1	7·7	0·6	13·7	1·0
18	1 04·5	1 04·7	1 01·6	1·8	0·1	7·8	0·6	13·8	1·0
19	1 04·8	1 04·9	1 01·8	1·9	0·1	7·9	0·6	13·9	1·0
20	1 05·0	1 05·2	1 02·0	2·0	0·2	8·0	0·6	14·0	1·1
21	1 05·3	1 05·4	1 02·3	2·1	0·2	8·1	0·6	14·1	1·1
22	1 05·5	1 05·7	1 02·5	2·2	0·2	8·2	0·6	14·2	1·1
23	1 05·8	1 05·9	1 02·8	2·3	0·2	8·3	0·6	14·3	1·1
24	1 06·0	1 06·2	1 03·0	2·4	0·2	8·4	0·6	14·4	1·1
25	1 06·3	1 06·4	1 03·2	2·5	0·2	8·5	0·6	14·5	1·1
26	1 06·5	1 06·7	1 03·5	2·6	0·2	8·6	0·6	14·6	1·1
27	1 06·8	1 06·9	1 03·7	2·7	0·2	8·7	0·7	14·7	1·1
28	1 07·0	1 07·2	1 03·9	2·8	0·2	8·8	0·7	14·8	1·1
29	1 07·3	1 07·4	1 04·2	2·9	0·2	8·9	0·7	14·9	1·1
30	1 07·5	1 07·7	1 04·4	3·0	0·2	9·0	0·7	15·0	1·1
31	1 07·8	1 07·9	1 04·7	3·1	0·2	9·1	0·7	15·1	1·1
32	1 08·0	1 08·2	1 04·9	3·2	0·2	9·2	0·7	15·2	1·1
33	1 08·3	1 08·4	1 05·1	3·3	0·2	9·3	0·7	15·3	1·1
34	1 08·5	1 08·7	1 05·4	3·4	0·3	9·4	0·7	15·4	1·2
35	1 08·8	1 08·9	1 05·6	3·5	0·3	9·5	0·7	15·5	1·2
36	1 09·0	1 09·2	1 05·9	3·6	0·3	9·6	0·7	15·6	1·2
37	1 09·3	1 09·4	1 06·1	3·7	0·3	9·7	0·7	15·7	1·2
38	1 09·5	1 09·7	1 06·3	3·8	0·3	9·8	0·7	15·8	1·2
39	1 09·8	1 09·9	1 06·6	3·9	0·3	9·9	0·7	15·9	1·2
40	1 10·0	1 10·2	1 06·8	4·0	0·3	10·0	0·8	16·0	1·2
41	1 10·3	1 10·4	1 07·0	4·1	0·3	10·1	0·8	16·1	1·2
42	1 10·5	1 10·7	1 07·3	4·2	0·3	10·2	0·8	16·2	1·2
43	1 10·8	1 10·9	1 07·5	4·3	0·3	10·3	0·8	16·3	1·2
44	1 11·0	1 11·2	1 07·8	4·4	0·3	10·4	0·8	16·4	1·2
45	1 11·3	1 11·4	1 08·0	4·5	0·3	10·5	0·8	16·5	1·2
46	1 11·5	1 11·7	1 08·2	4·6	0·3	10·6	0·8	16·6	1·2
47	1 11·8	1 11·9	1 08·5	4·7	0·4	10·7	0·8	16·7	1·3
48	1 12·0	1 12·2	1 08·7	4·8	0·4	10·8	0·8	16·8	1·3
49	1 12·3	1 12·4	1 09·0	4·9	0·4	10·9	0·8	16·9	1·3
50	1 12·5	1 12·7	1 09·2	5·0	0·4	11·0	0·8	17·0	1·3
51	1 12·8	1 12·9	1 09·4	5·1	0·4	11·1	0·8	17·1	1·3
52	1 13·0	1 13·2	1 09·7	5·2	0·4	11·2	0·8	17·2	1·3
53	1 13·3	1 13·5	1 09·9	5·3	0·4	11·3	0·8	17·3	1·3
54	1 13·5	1 13·7	1 10·2	5·4	0·4	11·4	0·9	17·4	1·3
55	1 13·8	1 14·0	1 10·4	5·5	0·4	11·5	0·9	17·5	1·3
56	1 14·0	1 14·2	1 10·6	5·6	0·4	11·6	0·9	17·6	1·3
57	1 14·3	1 14·5	1 10·9	5·7	0·4	11·7	0·9	17·7	1·3
58	1 14·5	1 14·7	1 11·1	5·8	0·4	11·8	0·9	17·8	1·3
59	1 14·8	1 15·0	1 11·3	5·9	0·4	11·9	0·9	17·9	1·3
60	1 15·0	1 15·2	1 11·6	6·0	0·5	12·0	0·9	18·0	1·4

5 s	SUN PLANETS	ARIES	MOON	v or d	Corrn	v or d	Corrn	v or d	Corrn
00	1 15·0	1 15·2	1 11·6	0·0	0·0	6·0	0·6	12·0	1·1
01	1 15·3	1 15·5	1 11·8	0·1	0·0	6·1	0·6	12·1	1·1
02	1 15·5	1 15·7	1 12·1	0·2	0·0	6·2	0·6	12·2	1·1
03	1 15·8	1 16·0	1 12·3	0·3	0·0	6·3	0·6	12·3	1·1
04	1 16·0	1 16·2	1 12·5	0·4	0·0	6·4	0·6	12·4	1·1
05	1 16·3	1 16·5	1 12·8	0·5	0·0	6·5	0·6	12·5	1·1
06	1 16·5	1 16·7	1 13·0	0·6	0·1	6·6	0·6	12·6	1·2
07	1 16·8	1 17·0	1 13·3	0·7	0·1	6·7	0·6	12·7	1·2
08	1 17·0	1 17·2	1 13·5	0·8	0·1	6·8	0·6	12·8	1·2
09	1 17·3	1 17·5	1 13·7	0·9	0·1	6·9	0·6	12·9	1·2
10	1 17·5	1 17·7	1 14·0	1·0	0·1	7·0	0·6	13·0	1·2
11	1 17·8	1 18·0	1 14·2	1·1	0·1	7·1	0·7	13·1	1·2
12	1 18·0	1 18·2	1 14·4	1·2	0·1	7·2	0·7	13·2	1·2
13	1 18·3	1 18·5	1 14·7	1·3	0·1	7·3	0·7	13·3	1·2
14	1 18·5	1 18·7	1 14·9	1·4	0·1	7·4	0·7	13·4	1·2
15	1 18·8	1 19·0	1 15·2	1·5	0·1	7·5	0·7	13·5	1·2
16	1 19·0	1 19·2	1 15·4	1·6	0·1	7·6	0·7	13·6	1·2
17	1 19·3	1 19·5	1 15·6	1·7	0·2	7·7	0·7	13·7	1·3
18	1 19·5	1 19·7	1 15·9	1·8	0·2	7·8	0·7	13·8	1·3
19	1 19·8	1 20·0	1 16·1	1·9	0·2	7·9	0·7	13·9	1·3
20	1 20·0	1 20·2	1 16·4	2·0	0·2	8·0	0·7	14·0	1·3
21	1 20·3	1 20·5	1 16·6	2·1	0·2	8·1	0·7	14·1	1·3
22	1 20·5	1 20·7	1 16·8	2·2	0·2	8·2	0·8	14·2	1·3
23	1 20·8	1 21·0	1 17·1	2·3	0·2	8·3	0·8	14·3	1·3
24	1 21·0	1 21·2	1 17·3	2·4	0·2	8·4	0·8	14·4	1·3
25	1 21·3	1 21·5	1 17·5	2·5	0·2	8·5	0·8	14·5	1·3
26	1 21·5	1 21·7	1 17·8	2·6	0·2	8·6	0·8	14·6	1·3
27	1 21·8	1 22·0	1 18·0	2·7	0·2	8·7	0·8	14·7	1·3
28	1 22·0	1 22·2	1 18·3	2·8	0·3	8·8	0·8	14·8	1·4
29	1 22·3	1 22·5	1 18·5	2·9	0·3	8·9	0·8	14·9	1·4
30	1 22·5	1 22·7	1 18·7	3·0	0·3	9·0	0·8	15·0	1·4
31	1 22·8	1 23·0	1 19·0	3·1	0·3	9·1	0·8	15·1	1·4
32	1 23·0	1 23·2	1 19·2	3·2	0·3	9·2	0·8	15·2	1·4
33	1 23·3	1 23·5	1 19·5	3·3	0·3	9·3	0·9	15·3	1·4
34	1 23·5	1 23·7	1 19·7	3·4	0·3	9·4	0·9	15·4	1·4
35	1 23·8	1 24·0	1 19·9	3·5	0·3	9·5	0·9	15·5	1·4
36	1 24·0	1 24·2	1 20·2	3·6	0·3	9·6	0·9	15·6	1·4
37	1 24·3	1 24·5	1 20·4	3·7	0·3	9·7	0·9	15·7	1·4
38	1 24·5	1 24·7	1 20·7	3·8	0·3	9·8	0·9	15·8	1·4
39	1 24·8	1 25·0	1 20·9	3·9	0·4	9·9	0·9	15·9	1·5
40	1 25·0	1 25·2	1 21·1	4·0	0·4	10·0	0·9	16·0	1·5
41	1 25·3	1 25·5	1 21·4	4·1	0·4	10·1	0·9	16·1	1·5
42	1 25·5	1 25·7	1 21·6	4·2	0·4	10·2	0·9	16·2	1·5
43	1 25·8	1 26·0	1 21·8	4·3	0·4	10·3	0·9	16·3	1·5
44	1 26·0	1 26·2	1 22·1	4·4	0·4	10·4	1·0	16·4	1·5
45	1 26·3	1 26·5	1 22·3	4·5	0·4	10·5	1·0	16·5	1·5
46	1 26·5	1 26·7	1 22·6	4·6	0·4	10·6	1·0	16·6	1·5
47	1 26·8	1 27·0	1 22·8	4·7	0·4	10·7	1·0	16·7	1·5
48	1 27·0	1 27·2	1 23·0	4·8	0·4	10·8	1·0	16·8	1·5
49	1 27·3	1 27·5	1 23·3	4·9	0·4	10·9	1·0	16·9	1·5
50	1 27·5	1 27·7	1 23·5	5·0	0·5	11·0	1·0	17·0	1·6
51	1 27·8	1 28·0	1 23·8	5·1	0·5	11·1	1·0	17·1	1·6
52	1 28·0	1 28·2	1 24·0	5·2	0·5	11·2	1·0	17·2	1·6
53	1 28·3	1 28·5	1 24·2	5·3	0·5	11·3	1·0	17·3	1·6
54	1 28·5	1 28·7	1 24·5	5·4	0·5	11·4	1·0	17·4	1·6
55	1 28·8	1 29·0	1 24·7	5·5	0·5	11·5	1·1	17·5	1·6
56	1 29·0	1 29·2	1 24·9	5·6	0·5	11·6	1·1	17·6	1·6
57	1 29·3	1 29·5	1 25·2	5·7	0·5	11·7	1·1	17·7	1·6
58	1 29·5	1 29·7	1 25·4	5·8	0·5	11·8	1·1	17·8	1·6
59	1 29·8	1 30·0	1 25·7	5·9	0·5	11·9	1·1	17·9	1·6
60	1 30·0	1 30·2	1 25·9	6·0	0·6	12·0	1·1	18·0	1·7

6ᵐ   INCREMENTS AND CORRECTIONS   **7ᵐ**

6	SUN PLANETS	ARIES	MOON	v or d Corrⁿ	v or d Corrⁿ	v or d Corrⁿ	7	SUN PLANETS	ARIES	MOON	v or d Corrⁿ	v or d Corrⁿ	v or d Corrⁿ
00	1 30.0	1 30.2	1 25.9	0.0 0.0	6.0 0.7	12.0 1.3	00	1 45.0	1 45.3	1 40.2	0.0 0.0	6.0 0.8	12.0 1.5
01	1 30.3	1 30.5	1 26.1	0.1 0.0	6.1 0.7	12.1 1.3	01	1 45.3	1 45.5	1 40.5	0.1 0.0	6.1 0.8	12.1 1.5
02	1 30.5	1 30.7	1 26.4	0.2 0.0	6.2 0.7	12.2 1.3	02	1 45.5	1 45.8	1 40.7	0.2 0.0	6.2 0.8	12.2 1.5
03	1 30.8	1 31.0	1 26.6	0.3 0.0	6.3 0.7	12.3 1.3	03	1 45.8	1 46.0	1 40.9	0.3 0.0	6.3 0.8	12.3 1.5
04	1 31.0	1 31.2	1 26.9	0.4 0.0	6.4 0.7	12.4 1.3	04	1 46.0	1 46.3	1 41.2	0.4 0.1	6.4 0.8	12.4 1.6
05	1 31.3	1 31.5	1 27.1	0.5 0.1	6.5 0.7	12.5 1.4	05	1 46.3	1 46.5	1 41.4	0.5 0.1	6.5 0.8	12.5 1.6
06	1 31.5	1 31.8	1 27.3	0.6 0.1	6.6 0.7	12.6 1.4	06	1 46.5	1 46.8	1 41.6	0.6 0.1	6.6 0.8	12.6 1.6
07	1 31.8	1 32.0	1 27.6	0.7 0.1	6.7 0.7	12.7 1.4	07	1 46.8	1 47.0	1 41.9	0.7 0.1	6.7 0.8	12.7 1.6
08	1 32.0	1 32.3	1 27.8	0.8 0.1	6.8 0.7	12.8 1.4	08	1 47.0	1 47.3	1 42.1	0.8 0.1	6.8 0.9	12.8 1.6
09	1 32.3	1 32.5	1 28.0	0.9 0.1	6.9 0.7	12.9 1.4	09	1 47.3	1 47.5	1 42.4	0.9 0.1	6.9 0.9	12.9 1.6
10	1 32.5	1 32.8	1 28.3	1.0 0.1	7.0 0.8	13.0 1.4	10	1 47.5	1 47.8	1 42.6	1.0 0.1	7.0 0.9	13.0 1.6
11	1 32.8	1 33.0	1 28.5	1.1 0.1	7.1 0.8	13.1 1.4	11	1 47.8	1 48.0	1 42.8	1.1 0.1	7.1 0.9	13.1 1.6
12	1 33.0	1 33.3	1 28.8	1.2 0.1	7.2 0.8	13.2 1.4	12	1 48.0	1 48.3	1 43.1	1.2 0.2	7.2 0.9	13.2 1.7
13	1 33.3	1 33.5	1 29.0	1.3 0.1	7.3 0.8	13.3 1.4	13	1 48.3	1 48.5	1 43.3	1.3 0.2	7.3 0.9	13.3 1.7
14	1 33.5	1 33.8	1 29.2	1.4 0.2	7.4 0.8	13.4 1.5	14	1 48.5	1 48.8	1 43.6	1.4 0.2	7.4 0.9	13.4 1.7
15	1 33.8	1 34.0	1 29.5	1.5 0.2	7.5 0.8	13.5 1.5	15	1 48.8	1 49.0	1 43.8	1.5 0.2	7.5 0.9	13.5 1.7
16	1 34.0	1 34.3	1 29.7	1.6 0.2	7.6 0.8	13.6 1.5	16	1 49.0	1 49.3	1 44.0	1.6 0.2	7.6 1.0	13.6 1.7
17	1 34.3	1 34.5	1 30.0	1.7 0.2	7.7 0.8	13.7 1.5	17	1 49.3	1 49.5	1 44.3	1.7 0.2	7.7 1.0	13.7 1.7
18	1 34.5	1 34.8	1 30.2	1.8 0.2	7.8 0.8	13.8 1.5	18	1 49.5	1 49.8	1 44.5	1.8 0.2	7.8 1.0	13.8 1.7
19	1 34.8	1 35.0	1 30.4	1.9 0.2	7.9 0.9	13.9 1.5	19	1 49.8	1 50.1	1 44.8	1.9 0.2	7.9 1.0	13.9 1.7
20	1 35.0	1 35.3	1 30.7	2.0 0.2	8.0 0.9	14.0 1.5	20	1 50.0	1 50.3	1 45.0	2.0 0.3	8.0 1.0	14.0 1.8
21	1 35.3	1 35.5	1 30.9	2.1 0.2	8.1 0.9	14.1 1.5	21	1 50.3	1 50.6	1 45.2	2.1 0.3	8.1 1.0	14.1 1.8
22	1 35.5	1 35.8	1 31.1	2.2 0.2	8.2 0.9	14.2 1.5	22	1 50.5	1 50.8	1 45.5	2.2 0.3	8.2 1.0	14.2 1.8
23	1 35.8	1 36.0	1 31.4	2.3 0.2	8.3 0.9	14.3 1.5	23	1 50.8	1 51.1	1 45.7	2.3 0.3	8.3 1.0	14.3 1.8
24	1 36.0	1 36.3	1 31.6	2.4 0.3	8.4 0.9	14.4 1.6	24	1 51.0	1 51.3	1 45.9	2.4 0.3	8.4 1.1	14.4 1.8
25	1 36.3	1 36.5	1 31.9	2.5 0.3	8.5 0.9	14.5 1.6	25	1 51.3	1 51.6	1 46.2	2.5 0.3	8.5 1.1	14.5 1.8
26	1 36.5	1 36.8	1 32.1	2.6 0.3	8.6 0.9	14.6 1.6	26	1 51.5	1 51.8	1 46.4	2.6 0.3	8.6 1.1	14.6 1.8
27	1 36.8	1 37.0	1 32.3	2.7 0.3	8.7 0.9	14.7 1.6	27	1 51.8	1 52.1	1 46.7	2.7 0.3	8.7 1.1	14.7 1.8
28	1 37.0	1 37.3	1 32.6	2.8 0.3	8.8 1.0	14.8 1.6	28	1 52.0	1 52.3	1 46.9	2.8 0.4	8.8 1.1	14.8 1.9
29	1 37.3	1 37.5	1 32.8	2.9 0.3	8.9 1.0	14.9 1.6	29	1 52.3	1 52.6	1 47.1	2.9 0.4	8.9 1.1	14.9 1.9
30	1 37.5	1 37.8	1 33.1	3.0 0.3	9.0 1.0	15.0 1.6	30	1 52.5	1 52.8	1 47.4	3.0 0.4	9.0 1.1	15.0 1.9
31	1 37.8	1 38.0	1 33.3	3.1 0.3	9.1 1.0	15.1 1.6	31	1 52.8	1 53.1	1 47.6	3.1 0.4	9.1 1.1	15.1 1.9
32	1 38.0	1 38.3	1 33.5	3.2 0.3	9.2 1.0	15.2 1.6	32	1 53.0	1 53.3	1 47.9	3.2 0.4	9.2 1.2	15.2 1.9
33	1 38.3	1 38.5	1 33.8	3.3 0.4	9.3 1.0	15.3 1.7	33	1 53.3	1 53.6	1 48.1	3.3 0.4	9.3 1.2	15.3 1.9
34	1 38.5	1 38.8	1 34.0	3.4 0.4	9.4 1.0	15.4 1.7	34	1 53.5	1 53.8	1 48.3	3.4 0.4	9.4 1.2	15.4 1.9
35	1 38.8	1 39.0	1 34.3	3.5 0.4	9.5 1.0	15.5 1.7	35	1 53.8	1 54.1	1 48.6	3.5 0.4	9.5 1.2	15.5 1.9
36	1 39.0	1 39.3	1 34.5	3.6 0.4	9.6 1.0	15.6 1.7	36	1 54.0	1 54.3	1 48.8	3.6 0.5	9.6 1.2	15.6 2.0
37	1 39.3	1 39.5	1 34.7	3.7 0.4	9.7 1.1	15.7 1.7	37	1 54.3	1 54.6	1 49.0	3.7 0.5	9.7 1.2	15.7 2.0
38	1 39.5	1 39.8	1 35.0	3.8 0.4	9.8 1.1	15.8 1.7	38	1 54.5	1 54.8	1 49.3	3.8 0.5	9.8 1.2	15.8 2.0
39	1 39.8	1 40.0	1 35.2	3.9 0.4	9.9 1.1	15.9 1.7	39	1 54.8	1 55.1	1 49.5	3.9 0.5	9.9 1.2	15.9 2.0
40	1 40.0	1 40.3	1 35.4	4.0 0.4	10.0 1.1	16.0 1.7	40	1 55.0	1 55.3	1 49.8	4.0 0.5	10.0 1.3	16.0 2.0
41	1 40.3	1 40.5	1 35.7	4.1 0.4	10.1 1.1	16.1 1.7	41	1 55.3	1 55.6	1 50.0	4.1 0.5	10.1 1.3	16.1 2.0
42	1 40.5	1 40.8	1 35.9	4.2 0.5	10.2 1.1	16.2 1.8	42	1 55.5	1 55.8	1 50.2	4.2 0.5	10.2 1.3	16.2 2.0
43	1 40.8	1 41.0	1 36.2	4.3 0.5	10.3 1.1	16.3 1.8	43	1 55.8	1 56.1	1 50.5	4.3 0.5	10.3 1.3	16.3 2.0
44	1 41.0	1 41.3	1 36.4	4.4 0.5	10.4 1.1	16.4 1.8	44	1 56.0	1 56.3	1 50.7	4.4 0.6	10.4 1.3	16.4 2.1
45	1 41.3	1 41.5	1 36.6	4.5 0.5	10.5 1.1	16.5 1.8	45	1 56.3	1 56.6	1 51.0	4.5 0.6	10.5 1.3	16.5 2.1
46	1 41.5	1 41.8	1 36.9	4.6 0.5	10.6 1.1	16.6 1.8	46	1 56.5	1 56.8	1 51.2	4.6 0.6	10.6 1.3	16.6 2.1
47	1 41.8	1 42.0	1 37.1	4.7 0.5	10.7 1.2	16.7 1.8	47	1 56.8	1 57.1	1 51.4	4.7 0.6	10.7 1.3	16.7 2.1
48	1 42.0	1 42.3	1 37.4	4.8 0.5	10.8 1.2	16.8 1.8	48	1 57.0	1 57.3	1 51.7	4.8 0.6	10.8 1.4	16.8 2.1
49	1 42.3	1 42.5	1 37.6	4.9 0.5	10.9 1.2	16.9 1.8	49	1 57.3	1 57.6	1 51.9	4.9 0.6	10.9 1.4	16.9 2.1
50	1 42.5	1 42.8	1 37.8	5.0 0.5	11.0 1.2	17.0 1.8	50	1 57.5	1 57.8	1 52.1	5.0 0.6	11.0 1.4	17.0 2.1
51	1 42.8	1 43.0	1 38.1	5.1 0.6	11.1 1.2	17.1 1.9	51	1 57.8	1 58.1	1 52.4	5.1 0.6	11.1 1.4	17.1 2.1
52	1 43.0	1 43.3	1 38.3	5.2 0.6	11.2 1.2	17.2 1.9	52	1 58.0	1 58.3	1 52.6	5.2 0.7	11.2 1.4	17.2 2.2
53	1 43.3	1 43.5	1 38.5	5.3 0.6	11.3 1.2	17.3 1.9	53	1 58.3	1 58.6	1 52.9	5.3 0.7	11.3 1.4	17.3 2.2
54	1 43.5	1 43.8	1 38.8	5.4 0.6	11.4 1.2	17.4 1.9	54	1 58.5	1 58.8	1 53.1	5.4 0.7	11.4 1.4	17.4 2.2
55	1 43.8	1 44.0	1 39.0	5.5 0.6	11.5 1.2	17.5 1.9	55	1 58.8	1 59.1	1 53.3	5.5 0.7	11.5 1.4	17.5 2.2
56	1 44.0	1 44.3	1 39.3	5.6 0.6	11.6 1.3	17.6 1.9	56	1 59.0	1 59.3	1 53.6	5.6 0.7	11.6 1.5	17.6 2.2
57	1 44.3	1 44.5	1 39.5	5.7 0.6	11.7 1.3	17.7 1.9	57	1 59.3	1 59.6	1 53.8	5.7 0.7	11.7 1.5	17.7 2.2
58	1 44.5	1 44.8	1 39.7	5.8 0.6	11.8 1.3	17.8 1.9	58	1 59.5	1 59.8	1 54.1	5.8 0.7	11.8 1.5	17.8 2.2
59	1 44.8	1 45.0	1 40.0	5.9 0.6	11.9 1.3	17.9 1.9	59	1 59.8	2 00.1	1 54.3	5.9 0.7	11.9 1.5	17.9 2.2
60	1 45.0	1 45.3	1 40.2	6.0 0.7	12.0 1.3	18.0 2.0	60	2 00.0	2 00.3	1 54.5	6.0 0.8	12.0 1.5	18.0 2.3

8ᵐ INCREMENTS AND CORRECTIONS 9ᵐ

8 s	SUN PLANETS	ARIES	MOON	v or d	Corrⁿ	v or d	Corrⁿ	v or d	Corrⁿ
00	2 00·0	2 00·3	1 54·5	0·0	0·0	6·0	0·9	12·0	1·7
01	2 00·3	2 00·6	1 54·8	0·1	0·0	6·1	0·9	12·1	1·7
02	2 00·5	2 00·8	1 55·0	0·2	0·0	6·2	0·9	12·2	1·7
03	2 00·8	2 01·1	1 55·2	0·3	0·0	6·3	0·9	12·3	1·7
04	2 01·0	2 01·3	1 55·5	0·4	0·1	6·4	0·9	12·4	1·8
05	2 01·3	2 01·6	1 55·7	0·5	0·1	6·5	0·9	12·5	1·8
06	2 01·5	2 01·8	1 56·0	0·6	0·1	6·6	0·9	12·6	1·8
07	2 01·8	2 02·1	1 56·2	0·7	0·1	6·7	0·9	12·7	1·8
08	2 02·0	2 02·3	1 56·4	0·8	0·1	6·8	1·0	12·8	1·8
09	2 02·3	2 02·6	1 56·7	0·9	0·1	6·9	1·0	12·9	1·8
10	2 02·5	2 02·8	1 56·9	1·0	0·1	7·0	1·0	13·0	1·8
11	2 02·8	2 03·1	1 57·2	1·1	0·2	7·1	1·0	13·1	1·9
12	2 03·0	2 03·3	1 57·4	1·2	0·2	7·2	1·0	13·2	1·9
13	2 03·3	2 03·6	1 57·6	1·3	0·2	7·3	1·0	13·3	1·9
14	2 03·5	2 03·8	1 57·9	1·4	0·2	7·4	1·0	13·4	1·9
15	2 03·8	2 04·1	1 58·1	1·5	0·2	7·5	1·1	13·5	1·9
16	2 04·0	2 04·3	1 58·4	1·6	0·2	7·6	1·1	13·6	1·9
17	2 04·3	2 04·6	1 58·6	1·7	0·2	7·7	1·1	13·7	1·9
18	2 04·5	2 04·8	1 58·8	1·8	0·3	7·8	1·1	13·8	2·0
19	2 04·8	2 05·1	1 59·1	1·9	0·3	7·9	1·1	13·9	2·0
20	2 05·0	2 05·3	1 59·3	2·0	0·3	8·0	1·1	14·0	2·0
21	2 05·3	2 05·6	1 59·5	2·1	0·3	8·1	1·1	14·1	2·0
22	2 05·5	2 05·8	1 59·8	2·2	0·3	8·2	1·2	14·2	2·0
23	2 05·8	2 06·1	2 00·0	2·3	0·3	8·3	1·2	14·3	2·0
24	2 06·0	2 06·3	2 00·3	2·4	0·3	8·4	1·2	14·4	2·0
25	2 06·3	2 06·6	2 00·5	2·5	0·4	8·5	1·2	14·5	2·1
26	2 06·5	2 06·8	2 00·7	2·6	0·4	8·6	1·2	14·6	2·1
27	2 06·8	2 07·1	2 01·0	2·7	0·4	8·7	1·2	14·7	2·1
28	2 07·0	2 07·3	2 01·2	2·8	0·4	8·8	1·2	14·8	2·1
29	2 07·3	2 07·6	2 01·5	2·9	0·4	8·9	1·3	14·9	2·1
30	2 07·5	2 07·8	2 01·7	3·0	0·4	9·0	1·3	15·0	2·1
31	2 07·8	2 08·1	2 01·9	3·1	0·4	9·1	1·3	15·1	2·1
32	2 08·0	2 08·4	2 02·2	3·2	0·5	9·2	1·3	15·2	2·2
33	2 08·3	2 08·6	2 02·4	3·3	0·5	9·3	1·3	15·3	2·2
34	2 08·5	2 08·9	2 02·6	3·4	0·5	9·4	1·3	15·4	2·2
35	2 08·8	2 09·1	2 02·9	3·5	0·5	9·5	1·3	15·5	2·2
36	2 09·0	2 09·4	2 03·1	3·6	0·5	9·6	1·4	15·6	2·2
37	2 09·3	2 09·6	2 03·4	3·7	0·5	9·7	1·4	15·7	2·2
38	2 09·5	2 09·9	2 03·6	3·8	0·5	9·8	1·4	15·8	2·2
39	2 09·8	2 10·1	2 03·8	3·9	0·6	9·9	1·4	15·9	2·3
40	2 10·0	2 10·4	2 04·1	4·0	0·6	10·0	1·4	16·0	2·3
41	2 10·3	2 10·6	2 04·3	4·1	0·6	10·1	1·4	16·1	2·3
42	2 10·5	2 10·9	2 04·6	4·2	0·6	10·2	1·4	16·2	2·3
43	2 10·8	2 11·1	2 04·8	4·3	0·6	10·3	1·5	16·3	2·3
44	2 11·0	2 11·4	2 05·0	4·4	0·6	10·4	1·5	16·4	2·3
45	2 11·3	2 11·6	2 05·3	4·5	0·6	10·5	1·5	16·5	2·3
46	2 11·5	2 11·9	2 05·5	4·6	0·7	10·6	1·5	16·6	2·4
47	2 11·8	2 12·1	2 05·7	4·7	0·7	10·7	1·5	16·7	2·4
48	2 12·0	2 12·4	2 06·0	4·8	0·7	10·8	1·5	16·8	2·4
49	2 12·3	2 12·6	2 06·2	4·9	0·7	10·9	1·5	16·9	2·4
50	2 12·5	2 12·9	2 06·5	5·0	0·7	11·0	1·6	17·0	2·4
51	2 12·8	2 13·1	2 06·7	5·1	0·7	11·1	1·6	17·1	2·4
52	2 13·0	2 13·4	2 06·9	5·2	0·7	11·2	1·6	17·2	2·4
53	2 13·3	2 13·6	2 07·2	5·3	0·8	11·3	1·6	17·3	2·5
54	2 13·5	2 13·9	2 07·4	5·4	0·8	11·4	1·6	17·4	2·5
55	2 13·8	2 14·1	2 07·7	5·5	0·8	11·5	1·6	17·5	2·5
56	2 14·0	2 14·4	2 07·9	5·6	0·8	11·6	1·6	17·6	2·5
57	2 14·3	2 14·6	2 08·1	5·7	0·8	11·7	1·7	17·7	2·5
58	2 14·5	2 14·9	2 08·4	5·8	0·8	11·8	1·7	17·8	2·5
59	2 14·8	2 15·1	2 08·6	5·9	0·8	11·9	1·7	17·9	2·5
60	2 15·0	2 15·4	2 08·9	6·0	0·9	12·0	1·7	18·0	2·6

9 s	SUN PLANETS	ARIES	MOON	v or d	Corrⁿ	v or d	Corrⁿ	v or d	Corrⁿ
00	2 15·0	2 15·4	2 08·9	0·0	0·0	6·0	1·0	12·0	1·9
01	2 15·3	2 15·6	2 09·1	0·1	0·0	6·1	1·0	12·1	1·9
02	2 15·5	2 15·9	2 09·3	0·2	0·0	6·2	1·0	12·2	1·9
03	2 15·8	2 16·1	2 09·6	0·3	0·0	6·3	1·0	12·3	1·9
04	2 16·0	2 16·4	2 09·8	0·4	0·1	6·4	1·0	12·4	2·0
05	2 16·3	2 16·6	2 10·0	0·5	0·1	6·5	1·0	12·5	2·0
06	2 16·5	2 16·9	2 10·3	0·6	0·1	6·6	1·0	12·6	2·0
07	2 16·8	2 17·1	2 10·5	0·7	0·1	6·7	1·1	12·7	2·0
08	2 17·0	2 17·4	2 10·8	0·8	0·1	6·8	1·1	12·8	2·0
09	2 17·3	2 17·6	2 11·0	0·9	0·1	6·9	1·1	12·9	2·0
10	2 17·5	2 17·9	2 11·2	1·0	0·2	7·0	1·1	13·0	2·1
11	2 17·8	2 18·1	2 11·5	1·1	0·2	7·1	1·1	13·1	2·1
12	2 18·0	2 18·4	2 11·7	1·2	0·2	7·2	1·1	13·2	2·1
13	2 18·3	2 18·6	2 12·0	1·3	0·2	7·3	1·2	13·3	2·1
14	2 18·5	2 18·9	2 12·2	1·4	0·2	7·4	1·2	13·4	2·1
15	2 18·8	2 19·1	2 12·4	1·5	0·2	7·5	1·2	13·5	2·1
16	2 19·0	2 19·4	2 12·7	1·6	0·3	7·6	1·2	13·6	2·2
17	2 19·3	2 19·6	2 12·9	1·7	0·3	7·7	1·2	13·7	2·2
18	2 19·5	2 19·9	2 13·1	1·8	0·3	7·8	1·2	13·8	2·2
19	2 19·8	2 20·1	2 13·4	1·9	0·3	7·9	1·3	13·9	2·2
20	2 20·0	2 20·4	2 13·6	2·0	0·3	8·0	1·3	14·0	2·2
21	2 20·3	2 20·6	2 13·9	2·1	0·3	8·1	1·3	14·1	2·2
22	2 20·5	2 20·9	2 14·1	2·2	0·3	8·2	1·3	14·2	2·2
23	2 20·8	2 21·1	2 14·3	2·3	0·4	8·3	1·3	14·3	2·3
24	2 21·0	2 21·4	2 14·6	2·4	0·4	8·4	1·3	14·4	2·3
25	2 21·3	2 21·6	2 14·8	2·5	0·4	8·5	1·3	14·5	2·3
26	2 21·5	2 21·9	2 15·1	2·6	0·4	8·6	1·4	14·6	2·3
27	2 21·8	2 22·1	2 15·3	2·7	0·4	8·7	1·4	14·7	2·3
28	2 22·0	2 22·4	2 15·5	2·8	0·4	8·8	1·4	14·8	2·3
29	2 22·3	2 22·6	2 15·8	2·9	0·5	8·9	1·4	14·9	2·4
30	2 22·5	2 22·9	2 16·0	3·0	0·5	9·0	1·4	15·0	2·4
31	2 22·8	2 23·1	2 16·2	3·1	0·5	9·1	1·4	15·1	2·4
32	2 23·0	2 23·4	2 16·5	3·2	0·5	9·2	1·5	15·2	2·4
33	2 23·3	2 23·6	2 16·7	3·3	0·5	9·3	1·5	15·3	2·4
34	2 23·5	2 23·9	2 17·0	3·4	0·5	9·4	1·5	15·4	2·4
35	2 23·8	2 24·1	2 17·2	3·5	0·6	9·5	1·5	15·5	2·5
36	2 24·0	2 24·4	2 17·4	3·6	0·6	9·6	1·5	15·6	2·5
37	2 24·3	2 24·6	2 17·7	3·7	0·6	9·7	1·5	15·7	2·5
38	2 24·5	2 24·9	2 17·9	3·8	0·6	9·8	1·6	15·8	2·5
39	2 24·8	2 25·1	2 18·2	3·9	0·6	9·9	1·6	15·9	2·5
40	2 25·0	2 25·4	2 18·4	4·0	0·6	10·0	1·6	16·0	2·5
41	2 25·3	2 25·6	2 18·6	4·1	0·6	10·1	1·6	16·1	2·5
42	2 25·5	2 25·9	2 18·9	4·2	0·7	10·2	1·6	16·2	2·6
43	2 25·8	2 26·1	2 19·1	4·3	0·7	10·3	1·6	16·3	2·6
44	2 26·0	2 26·4	2 19·3	4·4	0·7	10·4	1·6	16·4	2·6
45	2 26·3	2 26·7	2 19·6	4·5	0·7	10·5	1·7	16·5	2·6
46	2 26·5	2 26·9	2 19·8	4·6	0·7	10·6	1·7	16·6	2·6
47	2 26·8	2 27·2	2 20·1	4·7	0·7	10·7	1·7	16·7	2·6
48	2 27·0	2 27·4	2 20·3	4·8	0·8	10·8	1·7	16·8	2·7
49	2 27·3	2 27·7	2 20·5	4·9	0·8	10·9	1·7	16·9	2·7
50	2 27·5	2 27·9	2 20·8	5·0	0·8	11·0	1·7	17·0	2·7
51	2 27·8	2 28·2	2 21·0	5·1	0·8	11·1	1·8	17·1	2·7
52	2 28·0	2 28·4	2 21·3	5·2	0·8	11·2	1·8	17·2	2·7
53	2 28·3	2 28·7	2 21·5	5·3	0·8	11·3	1·8	17·3	2·7
54	2 28·5	2 28·9	2 21·7	5·4	0·9	11·4	1·8	17·4	2·8
55	2 28·8	2 29·2	2 22·0	5·5	0·9	11·5	1·8	17·5	2·8
56	2 29·0	2 29·4	2 22·2	5·6	0·9	11·6	1·8	17·6	2·8
57	2 29·3	2 29·7	2 22·5	5·7	0·9	11·7	1·9	17·7	2·8
58	2 29·5	2 29·9	2 22·7	5·8	0·9	11·8	1·9	17·8	2·8
59	2 29·8	2 30·2	2 22·9	5·9	0·9	11·9	1·9	17·9	2·8
60	2 30·0	2 30·4	2 23·2	6·0	1·0	12·0	1·9	18·0	2·9

10ᵐ   INCREMENTS AND CORRECTIONS   11ᵐ

10ᵐ	SUN PLANETS	ARIES	MOON	v or Corrⁿ d	v or Corrⁿ d	v or Corrⁿ d
s	° ′	° ′	° ′	′ ′	′ ′	′ ′
00	2 30·0	2 30·4	2 23·2	0·0 0·0	6·0 1·1	12·0 2·1
01	2 30·3	2 30·7	2 23·4	0·1 0·0	6·1 1·1	12·1 2·1
02	2 30·5	2 30·9	2 23·6	0·2 0·0	6·2 1·1	12·2 2·1
03	2 30·8	2 31·2	2 23·9	0·3 0·1	6·3 1·1	12·3 2·2
04	2 31·0	2 31·4	2 24·1	0·4 0·1	6·4 1·1	12·4 2·2
05	2 31·3	2 31·7	2 24·4	0·5 0·1	6·5 1·1	12·5 2·2
06	2 31·5	2 31·9	2 24·6	0·6 0·1	6·6 1·2	12·6 2·2
07	2 31·8	2 32·2	2 24·8	0·7 0·1	6·7 1·2	12·7 2·2
08	2 32·0	2 32·4	2 25·1	0·8 0·1	6·8 1·2	12·8 2·2
09	2 32·3	2 32·7	2 25·3	0·9 0·2	6·9 1·2	12·9 2·3
10	2 32·5	2 32·9	2 25·6	1·0 0·2	7·0 1·2	13·0 2·3
11	2 32·8	2 33·2	2 25·8	1·1 0·2	7·1 1·2	13·1 2·3
12	2 33·0	2 33·4	2 26·0	1·2 0·2	7·2 1·3	13·2 2·3
13	2 33·3	2 33·7	2 26·3	1·3 0·2	7·3 1·3	13·3 2·3
14	2 33·5	2 33·9	2 26·5	1·4 0·2	7·4 1·3	13·4 2·3
15	2 33·8	2 34·2	2 26·7	1·5 0·3	7·5 1·3	13·5 2·4
16	2 34·0	2 34·4	2 27·0	1·6 0·3	7·6 1·3	13·6 2·4
17	2 34·3	2 34·7	2 27·2	1·7 0·3	7·7 1·3	13·7 2·4
18	2 34·5	2 34·9	2 27·5	1·8 0·3	7·8 1·4	13·8 2·4
19	2 34·8	2 35·2	2 27·7	1·9 0·3	7·9 1·4	13·9 2·4
20	2 35·0	2 35·4	2 27·9	2·0 0·4	8·0 1·4	14·0 2·5
21	2 35·3	2 35·7	2 28·2	2·1 0·4	8·1 1·4	14·1 2·5
22	2 35·5	2 35·9	2 28·4	2·2 0·4	8·2 1·4	14·2 2·5
23	2 35·8	2 36·2	2 28·7	2·3 0·4	8·3 1·5	14·3 2·5
24	2 36·0	2 36·4	2 28·9	2·4 0·4	8·4 1·5	14·4 2·5
25	2 36·3	2 36·7	2 29·1	2·5 0·4	8·5 1·5	14·5 2·5
26	2 36·5	2 36·9	2 29·4	2·6 0·5	8·6 1·5	14·6 2·6
27	2 36·8	2 37·2	2 29·6	2·7 0·5	8·7 1·5	14·7 2·6
28	2 37·0	2 37·4	2 29·8	2·8 0·5	8·8 1·5	14·8 2·6
29	2 37·3	2 37·7	2 30·1	2·9 0·5	8·9 1·6	14·9 2·6
30	2 37·5	2 37·9	2 30·3	3·0 0·5	9·0 1·6	15·0 2·6
31	2 37·8	2 38·2	2 30·6	3·1 0·5	9·1 1·6	15·1 2·6
32	2 38·0	2 38·4	2 30·8	3·2 0·6	9·2 1·6	15·2 2·7
33	2 38·3	2 38·7	2 31·0	3·3 0·6	9·3 1·6	15·3 2·7
34	2 38·5	2 38·9	2 31·3	3·4 0·6	9·4 1·6	15·4 2·7
35	2 38·8	2 39·2	2 31·5	3·5 0·6	9·5 1·7	15·5 2·7
36	2 39·0	2 39·4	2 31·8	3·6 0·6	9·6 1·7	15·6 2·7
37	2 39·3	2 39·7	2 32·0	3·7 0·6	9·7 1·7	15·7 2·7
38	2 39·5	2 39·9	2 32·2	3·8 0·7	9·8 1·7	15·8 2·8
39	2 39·8	2 40·2	2 32·5	3·9 0·7	9·9 1·7	15·9 2·8
40	2 40·0	2 40·4	2 32·7	4·0 0·7	10·0 1·8	16·0 2·8
41	2 40·3	2 40·7	2 32·9	4·1 0·7	10·1 1·8	16·1 2·8
42	2 40·5	2 40·9	2 33·2	4·2 0·7	10·2 1·8	16·2 2·8
43	2 40·8	2 41·2	2 33·4	4·3 0·8	10·3 1·8	16·3 2·9
44	2 41·0	2 41·4	2 33·7	4·4 0·8	10·4 1·8	16·4 2·9
45	2 41·3	2 41·7	2 33·9	4·5 0·8	10·5 1·8	16·5 2·9
46	2 41·5	2 41·9	2 34·1	4·6 0·8	10·6 1·9	16·6 2·9
47	2 41·8	2 42·2	2 34·4	4·7 0·8	10·7 1·9	16·7 2·9
48	2 42·0	2 42·4	2 34·6	4·8 0·8	10·8 1·9	16·8 2·9
49	2 42·3	2 42·7	2 34·9	4·9 0·9	10·9 1·9	16·9 3·0
50	2 42·5	2 42·9	2 35·1	5·0 0·9	11·0 1·9	17·0 3·0
51	2 42·8	2 43·2	2 35·3	5·1 0·9	11·1 1·9	17·1 3·0
52	2 43·0	2 43·4	2 35·6	5·2 0·9	11·2 2·0	17·2 3·0
53	2 43·3	2 43·7	2 35·8	5·3 0·9	11·3 2·0	17·3 3·0
54	2 43·5	2 43·9	2 36·1	5·4 0·9	11·4 2·0	17·4 3·0
55	2 43·8	2 44·2	2 36·3	5·5 1·0	11·5 2·0	17·5 3·1
56	2 44·0	2 44·4	2 36·5	5·6 1·0	11·6 2·0	17·6 3·1
57	2 44·3	2 44·7	2 36·8	5·7 1·0	11·7 2·0	17·7 3·1
58	2 44·5	2 45·0	2 37·0	5·8 1·0	11·8 2·1	17·8 3·1
59	2 44·8	2 45·2	2 37·2	5·9 1·0	11·9 2·1	17·9 3·1
60	2 45·0	2 45·5	2 37·5	6·0 1·1	12·0 2·1	18·0 3·2

11ᵐ	SUN PLANETS	ARIES	MOON	v or Corrⁿ d	v or Corrⁿ d	v or Corrⁿ d
s	° ′	° ′	° ′	′ ′	′ ′	′ ′
00	2 45·0	2 45·5	2 37·5	0·0 0·0	6·0 1·2	12·0 2·3
01	2 45·3	2 45·7	2 37·7	0·1 0·0	6·1 1·2	12·1 2·3
02	2 45·5	2 46·0	2 38·0	0·2 0·0	6·2 1·2	12·2 2·3
03	2 45·8	2 46·2	2 38·2	0·3 0·1	6·3 1·2	12·3 2·4
04	2 46·0	2 46·5	2 38·4	0·4 0·1	6·4 1·2	12·4 2·4
05	2 46·3	2 46·7	2 38·7	0·5 0·1	6·5 1·2	12·5 2·4
06	2 46·5	2 47·0	2 38·9	0·6 0·1	6·6 1·3	12·6 2·4
07	2 46·8	2 47·2	2 39·2	0·7 0·1	6·7 1·3	12·7 2·4
08	2 47·0	2 47·5	2 39·4	0·8 0·2	6·8 1·3	12·8 2·5
09	2 47·3	2 47·7	2 39·6	0·9 0·2	6·9 1·3	12·9 2·5
10	2 47·5	2 48·0	2 39·9	1·0 0·2	7·0 1·3	13·0 2·5
11	2 47·8	2 48·2	2 40·1	1·1 0·2	7·1 1·4	13·1 2·5
12	2 48·0	2 48·5	2 40·3	1·2 0·2	7·2 1·4	13·2 2·5
13	2 48·3	2 48·7	2 40·6	1·3 0·2	7·3 1·4	13·3 2·5
14	2 48·5	2 49·0	2 40·8	1·4 0·3	7·4 1·4	13·4 2·6
15	2 48·8	2 49·2	2 41·1	1·5 0·3	7·5 1·4	13·5 2·6
16	2 49·0	2 49·5	2 41·3	1·6 0·3	7·6 1·5	13·6 2·6
17	2 49·3	2 49·7	2 41·5	1·7 0·3	7·7 1·5	13·7 2·6
18	2 49·5	2 50·0	2 41·8	1·8 0·3	7·8 1·5	13·8 2·6
19	2 49·8	2 50·2	2 42·0	1·9 0·4	7·9 1·5	13·9 2·7
20	2 50·0	2 50·5	2 42·3	2·0 0·4	8·0 1·5	14·0 2·7
21	2 50·3	2 50·7	2 42·5	2·1 0·4	8·1 1·6	14·1 2·7
22	2 50·5	2 51·0	2 42·7	2·2 0·4	8·2 1·6	14·2 2·7
23	2 50·8	2 51·2	2 43·0	2·3 0·4	8·3 1·6	14·3 2·7
24	2 51·0	2 51·5	2 43·2	2·4 0·5	8·4 1·6	14·4 2·8
25	2 51·3	2 51·7	2 43·4	2·5 0·5	8·5 1·6	14·5 2·8
26	2 51·5	2 52·0	2 43·7	2·6 0·5	8·6 1·6	14·6 2·8
27	2 51·8	2 52·2	2 43·9	2·7 0·5	8·7 1·7	14·7 2·8
28	2 52·0	2 52·5	2 44·2	2·8 0·5	8·8 1·7	14·8 2·8
29	2 52·3	2 52·7	2 44·4	2·9 0·6	8·9 1·7	14·9 2·9
30	2 52·5	2 53·0	2 44·6	3·0 0·6	9·0 1·7	15·0 2·9
31	2 52·8	2 53·2	2 44·9	3·1 0·6	9·1 1·7	15·1 2·9
32	2 53·0	2 53·5	2 45·1	3·2 0·6	9·2 1·8	15·2 2·9
33	2 53·3	2 53·7	2 45·4	3·3 0·6	9·3 1·8	15·3 2·9
34	2 53·5	2 54·0	2 45·6	3·4 0·7	9·4 1·8	15·4 3·0
35	2 53·8	2 54·2	2 45·8	3·5 0·7	9·5 1·8	15·5 3·0
36	2 54·0	2 54·5	2 46·1	3·6 0·7	9·6 1·8	15·6 3·0
37	2 54·3	2 54·7	2 46·3	3·7 0·7	9·7 1·9	15·7 3·0
38	2 54·5	2 55·0	2 46·6	3·8 0·7	9·8 1·9	15·8 3·0
39	2 54·8	2 55·2	2 46·8	3·9 0·7	9·9 1·9	15·9 3·0
40	2 55·0	2 55·5	2 47·0	4·0 0·8	10·0 1·9	16·0 3·1
41	2 55·3	2 55·7	2 47·3	4·1 0·8	10·1 1·9	16·1 3·1
42	2 55·5	2 56·0	2 47·5	4·2 0·8	10·2 2·0	16·2 3·1
43	2 55·8	2 56·2	2 47·7	4·3 0·8	10·3 2·0	16·3 3·1
44	2 56·0	2 56·5	2 48·0	4·4 0·8	10·4 2·0	16·4 3·1
45	2 56·3	2 56·7	2 48·2	4·5 0·9	10·5 2·0	16·5 3·2
46	2 56·5	2 57·0	2 48·5	4·6 0·9	10·6 2·0	16·6 3·2
47	2 56·8	2 57·2	2 48·7	4·7 0·9	10·7 2·1	16·7 3·2
48	2 57·0	2 57·5	2 48·9	4·8 0·9	10·8 2·1	16·8 3·2
49	2 57·3	2 57·7	2 49·2	4·9 0·9	10·9 2·1	16·9 3·2
50	2 57·5	2 58·0	2 49·4	5·0 1·0	11·0 2·1	17·0 3·3
51	2 57·8	2 58·2	2 49·7	5·1 1·0	11·1 2·1	17·1 3·3
52	2 58·0	2 58·5	2 49·9	5·2 1·0	11·2 2·1	17·2 3·3
53	2 58·3	2 58·7	2 50·1	5·3 1·0	11·3 2·2	17·3 3·3
54	2 58·5	2 59·0	2 50·4	5·4 1·0	11·4 2·2	17·4 3·3
55	2 58·8	2 59·2	2 50·6	5·5 1·1	11·5 2·2	17·5 3·4
56	2 59·0	2 59·5	2 50·8	5·6 1·1	11·6 2·2	17·6 3·4
57	2 59·3	2 59·7	2 51·1	5·7 1·1	11·7 2·2	17·7 3·4
58	2 59·5	3 00·0	2 51·3	5·8 1·1	11·8 2·3	17·8 3·4
59	2 59·8	3 00·2	2 51·6	5·9 1·1	11·9 2·3	17·9 3·4
60	3 00·0	3 00·5	2 51·8	6·0 1·2	12·0 2·3	18·0 3·5

12ᵐ　　INCREMENTS AND CORRECTIONS　　13ᵐ

12ˢ	SUN PLANETS	ARIES	MOON	v or d Corrⁿ	v or d Corrⁿ	v or d Corrⁿ
00	3 00·0	3 00·5	2 51·8	0·0 0·0	6·0 1·3	12·0 2·5
01	3 00·3	3 00·7	2 52·0	0·1 0·0	6·1 1·3	12·1 2·5
02	3 00·5	3 01·0	2 52·3	0·2 0·0	6·2 1·3	12·2 2·5
03	3 00·8	3 01·2	2 52·5	0·3 0·1	6·3 1·3	12·3 2·6
04	3 01·0	3 01·5	2 52·8	0·4 0·1	6·4 1·3	12·4 2·6
05	3 01·3	3 01·7	2 53·0	0·5 0·1	6·5 1·4	12·5 2·6
06	3 01·5	3 02·0	2 53·2	0·6 0·1	6·6 1·4	12·6 2·6
07	3 01·8	3 02·2	2 53·5	0·7 0·1	6·7 1·4	12·7 2·6
08	3 02·0	3 02·5	2 53·7	0·8 0·2	6·8 1·4	12·8 2·7
09	3 02·3	3 02·7	2 53·9	0·9 0·2	6·9 1·4	12·9 2·7
10	3 02·5	3 03·0	2 54·2	1·0 0·2	7·0 1·5	13·0 2·7
11	3 02·8	3 03·3	2 54·4	1·1 0·2	7·1 1·5	13·1 2·7
12	3 03·0	3 03·5	2 54·7	1·2 0·3	7·2 1·5	13·2 2·8
13	3 03·3	3 03·8	2 54·9	1·3 0·3	7·3 1·5	13·3 2·8
14	3 03·5	3 04·0	2 55·1	1·4 0·3	7·4 1·5	13·4 2·8
15	3 03·8	3 04·3	2 55·4	1·5 0·3	7·5 1·6	13·5 2·8
16	3 04·0	3 04·5	2 55·6	1·6 0·3	7·6 1·6	13·6 2·8
17	3 04·3	3 04·8	2 55·9	1·7 0·4	7·7 1·6	13·7 2·9
18	3 04·5	3 05·0	2 56·1	1·8 0·4	7·8 1·6	13·8 2·9
19	3 04·8	3 05·3	2 56·3	1·9 0·4	7·9 1·6	13·9 2·9
20	3 05·0	3 05·5	2 56·6	2·0 0·4	8·0 1·7	14·0 2·9
21	3 05·3	3 05·8	2 56·8	2·1 0·4	8·1 1·7	14·1 2·9
22	3 05·5	3 06·0	2 57·0	2·2 0·5	8·2 1·7	14·2 3·0
23	3 05·8	3 06·3	2 57·3	2·3 0·5	8·3 1·7	14·3 3·0
24	3 06·0	3 06·5	2 57·5	2·4 0·5	8·4 1·8	14·4 3·0
25	3 06·3	3 06·8	2 57·8	2·5 0·5	8·5 1·8	14·5 3·0
26	3 06·5	3 07·0	2 58·0	2·6 0·5	8·6 1·8	14·6 3·0
27	3 06·8	3 07·3	2 58·2	2·7 0·6	8·7 1·8	14·7 3·1
28	3 07·0	3 07·5	2 58·5	2·8 0·6	8·8 1·8	14·8 3·1
29	3 07·3	3 07·8	2 58·7	2·9 0·6	8·9 1·9	14·9 3·1
30	3 07·5	3 08·0	2 59·0	3·0 0·6	9·0 1·9	15·0 3·1
31	3 07·8	3 08·3	2 59·2	3·1 0·6	9·1 1·9	15·1 3·1
32	3 08·0	3 08·5	2 59·4	3·2 0·7	9·2 1·9	15·2 3·2
33	3 08·3	3 08·8	2 59·7	3·3 0·7	9·3 1·9	15·3 3·2
34	3 08·5	3 09·0	2 59·9	3·4 0·7	9·4 2·0	15·4 3·2
35	3 08·8	3 09·3	3 00·2	3·5 0·7	9·5 2·0	15·5 3·2
36	3 09·0	3 09·5	3 00·4	3·6 0·8	9·6 2·0	15·6 3·3
37	3 09·3	3 09·8	3 00·6	3·7 0·8	9·7 2·0	15·7 3·3
38	3 09·5	3 10·0	3 00·9	3·8 0·8	9·8 2·0	15·8 3·3
39	3 09·8	3 10·3	3 01·1	3·9 0·8	9·9 2·1	15·9 3·3
40	3 10·0	3 10·5	3 01·3	4·0 0·8	10·0 2·1	16·0 3·3
41	3 10·3	3 10·8	3 01·6	4·1 0·9	10·1 2·1	16·1 3·4
42	3 10·5	3 11·0	3 01·8	4·2 0·9	10·2 2·1	16·2 3·4
43	3 10·8	3 11·3	3 02·1	4·3 0·9	10·3 2·1	16·3 3·4
44	3 11·0	3 11·5	3 02·3	4·4 0·9	10·4 2·2	16·4 3·4
45	3 11·3	3 11·8	3 02·5	4·5 0·9	10·5 2·2	16·5 3·4
46	3 11·5	3 12·0	3 02·8	4·6 1·0	10·6 2·2	16·6 3·5
47	3 11·8	3 12·3	3 03·0	4·7 1·0	10·7 2·2	16·7 3·5
48	3 12·0	3 12·5	3 03·3	4·8 1·0	10·8 2·3	16·8 3·5
49	3 12·3	3 12·8	3 03·5	4·9 1·0	10·9 2·3	16·9 3·5
50	3 12·5	3 13·0	3 03·7	5·0 1·0	11·0 2·3	17·0 3·5
51	3 12·8	3 13·3	3 04·0	5·1 1·1	11·1 2·3	17·1 3·6
52	3 13·0	3 13·5	3 04·2	5·2 1·1	11·2 2·3	17·2 3·6
53	3 13·3	3 13·8	3 04·4	5·3 1·1	11·3 2·4	17·3 3·6
54	3 13·5	3 14·0	3 04·7	5·4 1·1	11·4 2·4	17·4 3·6
55	3 13·8	3 14·3	3 04·9	5·5 1·1	11·5 2·4	17·5 3·6
56	3 14·0	3 14·5	3 05·2	5·6 1·2	11·6 2·4	17·6 3·7
57	3 14·3	3 14·8	3 05·4	5·7 1·2	11·7 2·4	17·7 3·7
58	3 14·5	3 15·0	3 05·6	5·8 1·2	11·8 2·5	17·8 3·7
59	3 14·8	3 15·3	3 05·9	5·9 1·2	11·9 2·5	17·9 3·7
60	3 15·0	3 15·5	3 06·1	6·0 1·3	12·0 2·5	18·0 3·8

13ˢ	SUN PLANETS	ARIES	MOON	v or d Corrⁿ	v or d Corrⁿ	v or d Corrⁿ
00	3 15·0	3 15·5	3 06·1	0·0 0·0	6·0 1·4	12·0 2·7
01	3 15·3	3 15·8	3 06·4	0·1 0·0	6·1 1·4	12·1 2·7
02	3 15·5	3 16·0	3 06·6	0·2 0·0	6·2 1·4	12·2 2·7
03	3 15·8	3 16·3	3 06·8	0·3 0·1	6·3 1·4	12·3 2·8
04	3 16·0	3 16·5	3 07·1	0·4 0·1	6·4 1·4	12·4 2·8
05	3 16·3	3 16·8	3 07·3	0·5 0·1	6·5 1·5	12·5 2·8
06	3 16·5	3 17·0	3 07·5	0·6 0·1	6·6 1·5	12·6 2·8
07	3 16·8	3 17·3	3 07·8	0·7 0·2	6·7 1·5	12·7 2·9
08	3 17·0	3 17·5	3 08·0	0·8 0·2	6·8 1·5	12·8 2·9
09	3 17·3	3 17·8	3 08·3	0·9 0·2	6·9 1·6	12·9 2·9
10	3 17·5	3 18·0	3 08·5	1·0 0·2	7·0 1·6	13·0 2·9
11	3 17·8	3 18·3	3 08·7	1·1 0·2	7·1 1·6	13·1 2·9
12	3 18·0	3 18·5	3 09·0	1·2 0·3	7·2 1·6	13·2 3·0
13	3 18·3	3 18·8	3 09·2	1·3 0·3	7·3 1·6	13·3 3·0
14	3 18·5	3 19·0	3 09·5	1·4 0·3	7·4 1·7	13·4 3·0
15	3 18·8	3 19·3	3 09·7	1·5 0·3	7·5 1·7	13·5 3·0
16	3 19·0	3 19·5	3 09·9	1·6 0·4	7·6 1·7	13·6 3·1
17	3 19·3	3 19·8	3 10·2	1·7 0·4	7·7 1·7	13·7 3·1
18	3 19·5	3 20·0	3 10·4	1·8 0·4	7·8 1·8	13·8 3·1
19	3 19·8	3 20·3	3 10·7	1·9 0·4	7·9 1·8	13·9 3·1
20	3 20·0	3 20·5	3 10·9	2·0 0·5	8·0 1·8	14·0 3·2
21	3 20·3	3 20·8	3 11·1	2·1 0·5	8·1 1·8	14·1 3·2
22	3 20·5	3 21·0	3 11·4	2·2 0·5	8·2 1·8	14·2 3·2
23	3 20·8	3 21·3	3 11·6	2·3 0·5	8·3 1·9	14·3 3·2
24	3 21·0	3 21·6	3 11·8	2·4 0·5	8·4 1·9	14·4 3·2
25	3 21·3	3 21·8	3 12·1	2·5 0·6	8·5 1·9	14·5 3·3
26	3 21·5	3 22·1	3 12·3	2·6 0·6	8·6 1·9	14·6 3·3
27	3 21·8	3 22·3	3 12·6	2·7 0·6	8·7 2·0	14·7 3·3
28	3 22·0	3 22·6	3 12·8	2·8 0·6	8·8 2·0	14·8 3·3
29	3 22·3	3 22·8	3 13·0	2·9 0·7	8·9 2·0	14·9 3·4
30	3 22·5	3 23·1	3 13·3	3·0 0·7	9·0 2·0	15·0 3·4
31	3 22·8	3 23·3	3 13·5	3·1 0·7	9·1 2·0	15·1 3·4
32	3 23·0	3 23·6	3 13·8	3·2 0·7	9·2 2·1	15·2 3·4
33	3 23·3	3 23·8	3 14·0	3·3 0·7	9·3 2·1	15·3 3·4
34	3 23·5	3 24·1	3 14·2	3·4 0·8	9·4 2·1	15·4 3·5
35	3 23·8	3 24·3	3 14·5	3·5 0·8	9·5 2·1	15·5 3·5
36	3 24·0	3 24·6	3 14·7	3·6 0·8	9·6 2·2	15·6 3·5
37	3 24·3	3 24·8	3 14·9	3·7 0·8	9·7 2·2	15·7 3·5
38	3 24·5	3 25·1	3 15·2	3·8 0·9	9·8 2·2	15·8 3·6
39	3 24·8	3 25·3	3 15·4	3·9 0·9	9·9 2·2	15·9 3·6
40	3 25·0	3 25·6	3 15·7	4·0 0·9	10·0 2·3	16·0 3·6
41	3 25·3	3 25·8	3 15·9	4·1 0·9	10·1 2·3	16·1 3·6
42	3 25·5	3 26·1	3 16·1	4·2 0·9	10·2 2·3	16·2 3·6
43	3 25·8	3 26·3	3 16·4	4·3 1·0	10·3 2·3	16·3 3·7
44	3 26·0	3 26·6	3 16·6	4·4 1·0	10·4 2·3	16·4 3·7
45	3 26·3	3 26·8	3 16·9	4·5 1·0	10·5 2·4	16·5 3·7
46	3 26·5	3 27·1	3 17·1	4·6 1·0	10·6 2·4	16·6 3·7
47	3 26·8	3 27·3	3 17·3	4·7 1·1	10·7 2·4	16·7 3·8
48	3 27·0	3 27·6	3 17·6	4·8 1·1	10·8 2·4	16·8 3·8
49	3 27·3	3 27·8	3 17·8	4·9 1·1	10·9 2·5	16·9 3·8
50	3 27·5	3 28·1	3 18·0	5·0 1·1	11·0 2·5	17·0 3·8
51	3 27·8	3 28·3	3 18·3	5·1 1·1	11·1 2·5	17·1 3·8
52	3 28·0	3 28·6	3 18·5	5·2 1·2	11·2 2·5	17·2 3·9
53	3 28·3	3 28·8	3 18·8	5·3 1·2	11·3 2·5	17·3 3·9
54	3 28·5	3 29·1	3 19·0	5·4 1·2	11·4 2·6	17·4 3·9
55	3 28·8	3 29·3	3 19·2	5·5 1·2	11·5 2·6	17·5 3·9
56	3 29·0	3 29·6	3 19·5	5·6 1·3	11·6 2·6	17·6 4·0
57	3 29·3	3 29·8	3 19·7	5·7 1·3	11·7 2·6	17·7 4·0
58	3 29·5	3 30·1	3 20·0	5·8 1·3	11·8 2·7	17·8 4·0
59	3 29·8	3 30·3	3 20·2	5·9 1·3	11·9 2·7	17·9 4·0
60	3 30·0	3 30·6	3 20·4	6·0 1·4	12·0 2·7	18·0 4·1

14ᵐ   INCREMENTS AND CORRECTIONS   15ᵐ

14ᵐ s	SUN PLANETS	ARIES	MOON	v or d	Corrn	v or d	Corrn	v or d	Corrn
00	3 30.0	3 30.6	3 20.4	0.0	0.0	6.0	1.5	12.0	2.9
01	3 30.3	3 30.8	3 20.7	0.1	0.0	6.1	1.5	12.1	2.9
02	3 30.5	3 31.1	3 20.9	0.2	0.0	6.2	1.5	12.2	2.9
03	3 30.8	3 31.3	3 21.1	0.3	0.1	6.3	1.5	12.3	3.0
04	3 31.0	3 31.6	3 21.4	0.4	0.1	6.4	1.5	12.4	3.0
05	3 31.3	3 31.8	3 21.6	0.5	0.1	6.5	1.6	12.5	3.0
06	3 31.5	3 32.1	3 21.9	0.6	0.1	6.6	1.6	12.6	3.0
07	3 31.8	3 32.3	3 22.1	0.7	0.2	6.7	1.6	12.7	3.1
08	3 32.0	3 32.6	3 22.3	0.8	0.2	6.8	1.6	12.8	3.1
09	3 32.3	3 32.8	3 22.6	0.9	0.2	6.9	1.7	12.9	3.1
10	3 32.5	3 33.1	3 22.8	1.0	0.2	7.0	1.7	13.0	3.1
11	3 32.8	3 33.3	3 23.1	1.1	0.3	7.1	1.7	13.1	3.2
12	3 33.0	3 33.6	3 23.3	1.2	0.3	7.2	1.7	13.2	3.2
13	3 33.3	3 33.8	3 23.5	1.3	0.3	7.3	1.8	13.3	3.2
14	3 33.5	3 34.1	3 23.8	1.4	0.3	7.4	1.8	13.4	3.2
15	3 33.8	3 34.3	3 24.0	1.5	0.4	7.5	1.8	13.5	3.3
16	3 34.0	3 34.6	3 24.3	1.6	0.4	7.6	1.8	13.6	3.3
17	3 34.3	3 34.8	3 24.5	1.7	0.4	7.7	1.9	13.7	3.3
18	3 34.5	3 35.1	3 24.7	1.8	0.4	7.8	1.9	13.8	3.3
19	3 34.8	3 35.3	3 25.0	1.9	0.5	7.9	1.9	13.9	3.4
20	3 35.0	3 35.6	3 25.2	2.0	0.5	8.0	1.9	14.0	3.4
21	3 35.3	3 35.8	3 25.4	2.1	0.5	8.1	2.0	14.1	3.4
22	3 35.5	3 36.1	3 25.7	2.2	0.5	8.2	2.0	14.2	3.4
23	3 35.8	3 36.3	3 25.9	2.3	0.6	8.3	2.0	14.3	3.5
24	3 36.0	3 36.6	3 26.2	2.4	0.6	8.4	2.0	14.4	3.5
25	3 36.3	3 36.8	3 26.4	2.5	0.6	8.5	2.1	14.5	3.5
26	3 36.5	3 37.1	3 26.6	2.6	0.6	8.6	2.1	14.6	3.5
27	3 36.8	3 37.3	3 26.9	2.7	0.7	8.7	2.1	14.7	3.6
28	3 37.0	3 37.6	3 27.1	2.8	0.7	8.8	2.1	14.8	3.6
29	3 37.3	3 37.8	3 27.4	2.9	0.7	8.9	2.2	14.9	3.6
30	3 37.5	3 38.1	3 27.6	3.0	0.7	9.0	2.2	15.0	3.6
31	3 37.8	3 38.3	3 27.8	3.1	0.7	9.1	2.2	15.1	3.6
32	3 38.0	3 38.6	3 28.1	3.2	0.8	9.2	2.2	15.2	3.7
33	3 38.3	3 38.8	3 28.3	3.3	0.8	9.3	2.2	15.3	3.7
34	3 38.5	3 39.1	3 28.5	3.4	0.8	9.4	2.3	15.4	3.7
35	3 38.8	3 39.3	3 28.8	3.5	0.8	9.5	2.3	15.5	3.7
36	3 39.0	3 39.6	3 29.0	3.6	0.9	9.6	2.3	15.6	3.8
37	3 39.3	3 39.9	3 29.3	3.7	0.9	9.7	2.3	15.7	3.8
38	3 39.5	3 40.1	3 29.5	3.8	0.9	9.8	2.4	15.8	3.8
39	3 39.8	3 40.4	3 29.7	3.9	0.9	9.9	2.4	15.9	3.8
40	3 40.0	3 40.6	3 30.0	4.0	1.0	10.0	2.4	16.0	3.9
41	3 40.3	3 40.9	3 30.2	4.1	1.0	10.1	2.4	16.1	3.9
42	3 40.5	3 41.1	3 30.5	4.2	1.0	10.2	2.5	16.2	3.9
43	3 40.8	3 41.4	3 30.7	4.3	1.0	10.3	2.5	16.3	3.9
44	3 41.0	3 41.6	3 30.9	4.4	1.1	10.4	2.5	16.4	4.0
45	3 41.3	3 41.9	3 31.2	4.5	1.1	10.5	2.5	16.5	4.0
46	3 41.5	3 42.1	3 31.4	4.6	1.1	10.6	2.6	16.6	4.0
47	3 41.8	3 42.4	3 31.6	4.7	1.1	10.7	2.6	16.7	4.0
48	3 42.0	3 42.6	3 31.9	4.8	1.2	10.8	2.6	16.8	4.1
49	3 42.3	3 42.9	3 32.1	4.9	1.2	10.9	2.6	16.9	4.1
50	3 42.5	3 43.1	3 32.4	5.0	1.2	11.0	2.7	17.0	4.1
51	3 42.8	3 43.4	3 32.6	5.1	1.2	11.1	2.7	17.1	4.1
52	3 43.0	3 43.6	3 32.8	5.2	1.3	11.2	2.7	17.2	4.2
53	3 43.3	3 43.9	3 33.1	5.3	1.3	11.3	2.7	17.3	4.2
54	3 43.5	3 44.1	3 33.3	5.4	1.3	11.4	2.8	17.4	4.2
55	3 43.8	3 44.4	3 33.6	5.5	1.3	11.5	2.8	17.5	4.2
56	3 44.0	3 44.6	3 33.8	5.6	1.4	11.6	2.8	17.6	4.3
57	3 44.3	3 44.9	3 34.0	5.7	1.4	11.7	2.8	17.7	4.3
58	3 44.5	3 45.1	3 34.3	5.8	1.4	11.8	2.9	17.8	4.3
59	3 44.8	3 45.4	3 34.5	5.9	1.4	11.9	2.9	17.9	4.3
60	3 45.0	3 45.6	3 34.8	6.0	1.5	12.0	2.9	18.0	4.4

15ᵐ s	SUN PLANETS	ARIES	MOON	v or d	Corrn	v or d	Corrn	v or d	Corrn
00	3 45.0	3 45.6	3 34.8	0.0	0.0	6.0	1.6	12.0	3.1
01	3 45.3	3 45.9	3 35.0	0.1	0.0	6.1	1.6	12.1	3.1
02	3 45.5	3 46.1	3 35.2	0.2	0.1	6.2	1.6	12.2	3.2
03	3 45.8	3 46.4	3 35.5	0.3	0.1	6.3	1.6	12.3	3.2
04	3 46.0	3 46.6	3 35.7	0.4	0.1	6.4	1.7	12.4	3.2
05	3 46.3	3 46.9	3 35.9	0.5	0.1	6.5	1.7	12.5	3.2
06	3 46.5	3 47.1	3 36.2	0.6	0.2	6.6	1.7	12.6	3.3
07	3 46.8	3 47.4	3 36.4	0.7	0.2	6.7	1.7	12.7	3.3
08	3 47.0	3 47.6	3 36.7	0.8	0.2	6.8	1.8	12.8	3.3
09	3 47.3	3 47.9	3 36.9	0.9	0.2	6.9	1.8	12.9	3.3
10	3 47.5	3 48.1	3 37.1	1.0	0.3	7.0	1.8	13.0	3.4
11	3 47.8	3 48.4	3 37.4	1.1	0.3	7.1	1.8	13.1	3.4
12	3 48.0	3 48.6	3 37.6	1.2	0.3	7.2	1.9	13.2	3.4
13	3 48.3	3 48.9	3 37.9	1.3	0.3	7.3	1.9	13.3	3.4
14	3 48.5	3 49.1	3 38.1	1.4	0.4	7.4	1.9	13.4	3.5
15	3 48.8	3 49.4	3 38.3	1.5	0.4	7.5	1.9	13.5	3.5
16	3 49.0	3 49.6	3 38.6	1.6	0.4	7.6	2.0	13.6	3.5
17	3 49.3	3 49.9	3 38.8	1.7	0.4	7.7	2.0	13.7	3.5
18	3 49.5	3 50.1	3 39.0	1.8	0.5	7.8	2.0	13.8	3.6
19	3 49.8	3 50.4	3 39.3	1.9	0.5	7.9	2.0	13.9	3.6
20	3 50.0	3 50.6	3 39.5	2.0	0.5	8.0	2.1	14.0	3.6
21	3 50.3	3 50.9	3 39.8	2.1	0.5	8.1	2.1	14.1	3.6
22	3 50.5	3 51.1	3 40.0	2.2	0.6	8.2	2.1	14.2	3.7
23	3 50.8	3 51.4	3 40.2	2.3	0.6	8.3	2.1	14.3	3.7
24	3 51.0	3 51.6	3 40.5	2.4	0.6	8.4	2.2	14.4	3.7
25	3 51.3	3 51.9	3 40.7	2.5	0.6	8.5	2.2	14.5	3.7
26	3 51.5	3 52.1	3 41.0	2.6	0.7	8.6	2.2	14.6	3.8
27	3 51.8	3 52.4	3 41.2	2.7	0.7	8.7	2.2	14.7	3.8
28	3 52.0	3 52.6	3 41.4	2.8	0.7	8.8	2.3	14.8	3.8
29	3 52.3	3 52.9	3 41.7	2.9	0.7	8.9	2.3	14.9	3.8
30	3 52.5	3 53.1	3 41.9	3.0	0.8	9.0	2.3	15.0	3.9
31	3 52.8	3 53.4	3 42.1	3.1	0.8	9.1	2.4	15.1	3.9
32	3 53.0	3 53.6	3 42.4	3.2	0.8	9.2	2.4	15.2	3.9
33	3 53.3	3 53.9	3 42.6	3.3	0.9	9.3	2.4	15.3	4.0
34	3 53.5	3 54.1	3 42.9	3.4	0.9	9.4	2.4	15.4	4.0
35	3 53.8	3 54.4	3 43.1	3.5	0.9	9.5	2.5	15.5	4.0
36	3 54.0	3 54.6	3 43.3	3.6	0.9	9.6	2.5	15.6	4.0
37	3 54.3	3 54.9	3 43.6	3.7	1.0	9.7	2.5	15.7	4.1
38	3 54.5	3 55.1	3 43.8	3.8	1.0	9.8	2.5	15.8	4.1
39	3 54.8	3 55.4	3 44.1	3.9	1.0	9.9	2.6	15.9	4.1
40	3 55.0	3 55.6	3 44.3	4.0	1.0	10.0	2.6	16.0	4.1
41	3 55.3	3 55.9	3 44.5	4.1	1.1	10.1	2.6	16.1	4.2
42	3 55.5	3 56.1	3 44.8	4.2	1.1	10.2	2.6	16.2	4.2
43	3 55.8	3 56.4	3 45.0	4.3	1.1	10.3	2.7	16.3	4.2
44	3 56.0	3 56.6	3 45.2	4.4	1.1	10.4	2.7	16.4	4.2
45	3 56.3	3 56.9	3 45.5	4.5	1.2	10.5	2.7	16.5	4.3
46	3 56.5	3 57.1	3 45.7	4.6	1.2	10.6	2.7	16.6	4.3
47	3 56.8	3 57.4	3 46.0	4.7	1.2	10.7	2.8	16.7	4.3
48	3 57.0	3 57.6	3 46.2	4.8	1.2	10.8	2.8	16.8	4.3
49	3 57.3	3 57.9	3 46.4	4.9	1.3	10.9	2.8	16.9	4.4
50	3 57.5	3 58.2	3 46.7	5.0	1.3	11.0	2.8	17.0	4.4
51	3 57.8	3 58.4	3 46.9	5.1	1.3	11.1	2.9	17.1	4.4
52	3 58.0	3 58.7	3 47.2	5.2	1.3	11.2	2.9	17.2	4.4
53	3 58.3	3 58.9	3 47.4	5.3	1.4	11.3	2.9	17.3	4.5
54	3 58.5	3 59.2	3 47.6	5.4	1.4	11.4	2.9	17.4	4.5
55	3 58.8	3 59.4	3 47.9	5.5	1.4	11.5	3.0	17.5	4.5
56	3 59.0	3 59.7	3 48.1	5.6	1.4	11.6	3.0	17.6	4.5
57	3 59.3	3 59.9	3 48.4	5.7	1.5	11.7	3.0	17.7	4.6
58	3 59.5	4 00.2	3 48.6	5.8	1.5	11.8	3.0	17.8	4.6
59	3 59.8	4 00.4	3 48.8	5.9	1.5	11.9	3.1	17.9	4.6
60	4 00.0	4 00.7	3 49.1	6.0	1.6	12.0	3.1	18.0	4.7

16ᵐ INCREMENTS AND CORRECTIONS 17ᵐ

16	SUN PLANETS	ARIES	MOON	v or d Corrⁿ	v or d Corrⁿ	v or d Corrⁿ
s	° ′	° ′	° ′	′ ′	′ ′	′ ′
00	4 00·0	4 00·7	3 49·1	0·0 0·0	6·0 1·7	12·0 3·3
01	4 00·3	4 00·9	3 49·3	0·1 0·0	6·1 1·7	12·1 3·3
02	4 00·5	4 01·2	3 49·5	0·2 0·1	6·2 1·7	12·2 3·4
03	4 00·8	4 01·4	3 49·8	0·3 0·1	6·3 1·7	12·3 3·4
04	4 01·0	4 01·7	3 50·0	0·4 0·1	6·4 1·8	12·4 3·4
05	4 01·3	4 01·9	3 50·3	0·5 0·1	6·5 1·8	12·5 3·4
06	4 01·5	4 02·2	3 50·5	0·6 0·2	6·6 1·8	12·6 3·5
07	4 01·8	4 02·4	3 50·7	0·7 0·2	6·7 1·8	12·7 3·5
08	4 02·0	4 02·7	3 51·0	0·8 0·2	6·8 1·9	12·8 3·5
09	4 02·3	4 02·9	3 51·2	0·9 0·2	6·9 1·9	12·9 3·5
10	4 02·5	4 03·2	3 51·5	1·0 0·3	7·0 1·9	13·0 3·6
11	4 02·8	4 03·4	3 51·7	1·1 0·3	7·1 2·0	13·1 3·6
12	4 03·0	4 03·7	3 51·9	1·2 0·3	7·2 2·0	13·2 3·6
13	4 03·3	4 03·9	3 52·2	1·3 0·4	7·3 2·0	13·3 3·7
14	4 03·5	4 04·2	3 52·4	1·4 0·4	7·4 2·0	13·4 3·7
15	4 03·8	4 04·4	3 52·6	1·5 0·4	7·5 2·1	13·5 3·7
16	4 04·0	4 04·7	3 52·9	1·6 0·4	7·6 2·1	13·6 3·7
17	4 04·3	4 04·9	3 53·1	1·7 0·5	7·7 2·1	13·7 3·8
18	4 04·5	4 05·2	3 53·4	1·8 0·5	7·8 2·1	13·8 3·8
19	4 04·8	4 05·4	3 53·6	1·9 0·5	7·9 2·2	13·9 3·8
20	4 05·0	4 05·7	3 53·8	2·0 0·6	8·0 2·2	14·0 3·9
21	4 05·3	4 05·9	3 54·1	2·1 0·6	8·1 2·2	14·1 3·9
22	4 05·5	4 06·2	3 54·3	2·2 0·6	8·2 2·3	14·2 3·9
23	4 05·8	4 06·4	3 54·6	2·3 0·6	8·3 2·3	14·3 3·9
24	4 06·0	4 06·7	3 54·8	2·4 0·7	8·4 2·3	14·4 4·0
25	4 06·3	4 06·9	3 55·0	2·5 0·7	8·5 2·3	14·5 4·0
26	4 06·5	4 07·2	3 55·3	2·6 0·7	8·6 2·4	14·6 4·0
27	4 06·8	4 07·4	3 55·5	2·7 0·7	8·7 2·4	14·7 4·0
28	4 07·0	4 07·7	3 55·7	2·8 0·8	8·8 2·4	14·8 4·1
29	4 07·3	4 07·9	3 56·0	2·9 0·8	8·9 2·4	14·9 4·1
30	4 07·5	4 08·2	3 56·2	3·0 0·8	9·0 2·5	15·0 4·1
31	4 07·8	4 08·4	3 56·5	3·1 0·9	9·1 2·5	15·1 4·2
32	4 08·0	4 08·7	3 56·7	3·2 0·9	9·2 2·5	15·2 4·2
33	4 08·3	4 08·9	3 56·9	3·3 0·9	9·3 2·6	15·3 4·2
34	4 08·5	4 09·2	3 57·2	3·4 0·9	9·4 2·6	15·4 4·2
35	4 08·8	4 09·4	3 57·4	3·5 1·0	9·5 2·6	15·5 4·3
36	4 09·0	4 09·7	3 57·7	3·6 1·0	9·6 2·6	15·6 4·3
37	4 09·3	4 09·9	3 57·9	3·7 1·0	9·7 2·7	15·7 4·3
38	4 09·5	4 10·2	3 58·1	3·8 1·0	9·8 2·7	15·8 4·3
39	4 09·8	4 10·4	3 58·4	3·9 1·1	9·9 2·7	15·9 4·4
40	4 10·0	4 10·7	3 58·6	4·0 1·1	10·0 2·8	16·0 4·4
41	4 10·3	4 10·9	3 58·8	4·1 1·1	10·1 2·8	16·1 4·4
42	4 10·5	4 11·2	3 59·1	4·2 1·2	10·2 2·8	16·2 4·5
43	4 10·8	4 11·4	3 59·3	4·3 1·2	10·3 2·8	16·3 4·5
44	4 11·0	4 11·7	3 59·6	4·4 1·2	10·4 2·9	16·4 4·5
45	4 11·3	4 11·9	3 59·8	4·5 1·2	10·5 2·9	16·5 4·5
46	4 11·5	4 12·2	4 00·0	4·6 1·3	10·6 2·9	16·6 4·6
47	4 11·8	4 12·4	4 00·3	4·7 1·3	10·7 2·9	16·7 4·6
48	4 12·0	4 12·7	4 00·5	4·8 1·3	10·8 3·0	16·8 4·6
49	4 12·3	4 12·9	4 00·8	4·9 1·3	10·9 3·0	16·9 4·6
50	4 12·5	4 13·2	4 01·0	5·0 1·4	11·0 3·0	17·0 4·7
51	4 12·8	4 13·4	4 01·2	5·1 1·4	11·1 3·1	17·1 4·7
52	4 13·0	4 13·7	4 01·5	5·2 1·4	11·2 3·1	17·2 4·7
53	4 13·3	4 13·9	4 01·7	5·3 1·5	11·3 3·1	17·3 4·8
54	4 13·5	4 14·2	4 02·0	5·4 1·5	11·4 3·1	17·4 4·8
55	4 13·8	4 14·4	4 02·2	5·5 1·5	11·5 3·2	17·5 4·8
56	4 14·0	4 14·7	4 02·4	5·6 1·5	11·6 3·2	17·6 4·8
57	4 14·3	4 14·9	4 02·7	5·7 1·6	11·7 3·2	17·7 4·9
58	4 14·5	4 15·2	4 02·9	5·8 1·6	11·8 3·2	17·8 4·9
59	4 14·8	4 15·4	4 03·1	5·9 1·6	11·9 3·3	17·9 4·9
60	4 15·0	4 15·7	4 03·4	6·0 1·7	12·0 3·3	18·0 5·0

17	SUN PLANETS	ARIES	MOON	v or d Corrⁿ	v or d Corrⁿ	v or d Corrⁿ
s	° ′	° ′	° ′	′ ′	′ ′	′ ′
00	4 15·0	4 15·7	4 03·4	0·0 0·0	6·0 1·8	12·0 3·5
01	4 15·3	4 15·9	4 03·6	0·1 0·0	6·1 1·8	12·1 3·5
02	4 15·5	4 16·2	4 03·9	0·2 0·1	6·2 1·8	12·2 3·6
03	4 15·8	4 16·5	4 04·1	0·3 0·1	6·3 1·8	12·3 3·6
04	4 16·0	4 16·7	4 04·3	0·4 0·1	6·4 1·9	12·4 3·6
05	4 16·3	4 17·0	4 04·6	0·5 0·1	6·5 1·9	12·5 3·6
06	4 16·5	4 17·2	4 04·8	0·6 0·2	6·6 1·9	12·6 3·7
07	4 16·8	4 17·5	4 05·1	0·7 0·2	6·7 2·0	12·7 3·7
08	4.17·0	4 17·7	4 05·3	0·8 0·2	6·8 2·0	12·8 3·7
09	4 17·3	4 18·0	4 05·5	0·9 0·3	6·9 2·0	12·9 3·8
10	4 17·5	4 18·2	4 05·8	1·0 0·3	7·0 2·0	13·0 3·8
11	4 17·8	4 18·5	4 06·0	1·1 0·3	7·1 2·1	13·1 3·8
12	4 18·0	4 18·7	4 06·2	1·2 0·4	7·2 2·1	13·2 3·9
13	4 18·3	4 19·0	4 06·5	1·3 0·4	7·3 2·1	13·3 3·9
14	4 18·5	4 19·2	4 06·7	1·4 0·4	7·4 2·2	13·4 3·9
15	4 18·8	4 19·5	4 07·0	1·5 0·4	7·5 2·2	13·5 3·9
16	4 19·0	4 19·7	4 07·2	1·6 0·5	7·6 2·2	13·6 4·0
17	4 19·3	4 20·0	4 07·4	1·7 0·5	7·7 2·2	13·7 4·0
18	4 19·5	4 20·2	4 07·7	1·8 0·5	7·8 2·3	13·8 4·0
19	4 19·8	4 20·5	4 07·9	1·9 0·6	7·9 2·3	13·9 4·1
20	4 20·0	4 20·7	4 08·2	2·0 0·6	8·0 2·3	14·0 4·1
21	4 20·3	4 21·0	4 08·4	2·1 0·6	8·1 2·4	14·1 4·1
22	4 20·5	4 21·2	4 08·6	2·2 0·6	8·2 2·4	14·2 4·1
23	4 20·8	4 21·5	4 08·9	2·3 0·7	8·3 2·4	14·3 4·2
24	4 21·0	4 21·7	4 09·1	2·4 0·7	8·4 2·5	14·4 4·2
25	4 21·3	4 22·0	4 09·3	2·5 0·7	8·5 2·5	14·5 4·2
26	4 21·5	4 22·2	4 09·6	2·6 0·8	8·6 2·5	14·6 4·3
27	4 21·8	4 22·5	4 09·8	2·7 0·8	8·7 2·5	14·7 4·3
28	4 22·0	4 22·7	4 10·1	2·8 0·8	8·8 2·6	14·8 4·3
29	4 22·3	4 23·0	4 10·3	2·9 0·8	8·9 2·6	14·9 4·3
30	4 22·5	4 23·2	4 10·5	3·0 0·9	9·0 2·6	15·0 4·4
31	4 22·8	4 23·5	4 10·8	3·1 0·9	9·1 2·7	15·1 4·4
32	4 23·0	4 23·7	4 11·0	3·2 0·9	9·2 2·7	15·2 4·4
33	4 23·3	4 24·0	4 11·3	3·3 1·0	9·3 2·7	15·3 4·5
34	4 23·5	4 24·2	4 11·5	3·4 1·0	9·4 2·7	15·4 4·5
35	4 23·8	4 24·5	4 11·7	3·5 1·0	9·5 2·8	15·5 4·5
36	4 24·0	4 24·7	4 12·0	3·6 1·1	9·6 2·8	15·6 4·6
37	4 24·3	4 25·0	4 12·2	3·7 1·1	9·7 2·8	15·7 4·6
38	4 24·5	4 25·2	4 12·5	3·8 1·1	9·8 2·9	15·8 4·6
39	4 24·8	4 25·5	4 12·7	3·9 1·1	9·9 2·9	15·9 4·6
40	4 25·0	4 25·7	4 12·9	4·0 1·2	10·0 2·9	16·0 4·7
41	4 25·3	4 26·0	4 13·2	4·1 1·2	10·1 2·9	16·1 4·7
42	4 25·5	4 26·2	4 13·4	4·2 1·2	10·2 3·0	16·2 4·7
43	4 25·8	4 26·5	4 13·6	4·3 1·3	10·3 3·0	16·3 4·8
44	4 26·0	4 26·7	4 13·9	4·4 1·3	10·4 3·0	16·4 4·8
45	4 26·3	4 27·0	4 14·1	4·5 1·3	10·5 3·1	16·5 4·8
46	4 26·5	4 27·2	4 14·4	4·6 1·3	10·6 3·1	16·6 4·8
47	4 26·8	4 27·5	4 14·6	4·7 1·4	10·7 3·1	16·7 4·9
48	4 27·0	4 27·7	4 14·8	4·8 1·4	10·8 3·2	16·8 4·9
49	4 27·3	4 28·0	4 15·1	4·9 1·4	10·9 3·2	16·9 4·9
50	4 27·5	4 28·2	4 15·3	5·0 1·5	11·0 3·2	17·0 5·0
51	4 27·8	4 28·5	4 15·6	5·1 1·5	11·1 3·2	17·1 5·0
52	4 28·0	4 28·7	4 15·8	5·2 1·5	11·2 3·3	17·2 5·0
53	4 28·3	4 29·0	4 16·0	5·3 1·5	11·3 3·3	17·3 5·0
54	4 28·5	4 29·2	4 16·3	5·4 1·6	11·4 3·3	17·4 5·1
55	4 28·8	4 29·5	4 16·5	5·5 1·6	11·5 3·4	17·5 5·1
56	4 29·0	4 29·7	4 16·7	5·6 1·6	11·6 3·4	17·6 5·1
57	4 29·3	4 30·0	4 17·0	5·7 1·7	11·7 3·4	17·7 5·2
58	4 29·5	4 30·2	4 17·2	5·8 1·7	11·8 3·4	17·8 5·2
59	4 29·8	4 30·5	4 17·5	5·9 1·7	11·9 3·5	17·9 5·2
60	4 30·0	4 30·7	4 17·7	6·0 1·8	12·0 3·5	18·0 5·3

x

INCREMENTS AND CORRECTIONS

18ᵐ   **19ᵐ**

18	SUN PLANETS	ARIES	MOON	v or d	Corrⁿ	v or d	Corrⁿ	v or d	Corrⁿ	19	SUN PLANETS	ARIES	MOON	v or d	Corrⁿ	v or d	Corrⁿ	v or d	Corrⁿ
s	° ′	° ′	° ′	′	′	′	′	′	′	s	° ′	° ′	° ′	′	′	′	′	′	′
00	4 30·0	4 30·7	4 17·7	0·0	0·0	6·0	1·9	12·0	3·7	00	4 45·0	4 45·8	4 32·0	0·0	0·0	6·0	2·0	12·0	3·9
01	4 30·3	4 31·0	4 17·9	0·1	0·0	6·1	1·9	12·1	3·7	01	4 45·3	4 46·0	4 32·3	0·1	0·0	6·1	2·0	12·1	3·9
02	4 30·5	4 31·2	4 18·2	0·2	0·1	6·2	1·9	12·2	3·8	02	4 45·5	4 46·3	4 32·5	0·2	0·1	6·2	2·0	12·2	4·0
03	4 30·8	4 31·5	4 18·4	0·3	0·1	6·3	1·9	12·3	3·8	03	4 45·8	4 46·5	4 32·7	0·3	0·1	6·3	2·0	12·3	4·0
04	4 31·0	4 31·7	4 18·7	0·4	0·1	6·4	2·0	12·4	3·8	04	4 46·0	4 46·8	4 33·0	0·4	0·1	6·4	2·1	12·4	4·0
05	4 31·3	4 32·0	4 18·9	0·5	0·2	6·5	2·0	12·5	3·9	05	4 46·3	4 47·0	4 33·2	0·5	0·2	6·5	2·1	12·5	4·1
06	4 31·5	4 32·2	4 19·1	0·6	0·2	6·6	2·0	12·6	3·9	06	4 46·5	4 47·3	4 33·4	0·6	0·2	6·6	2·1	12·6	4·1
07	4 31·8	4 32·5	4 19·4	0·7	0·2	6·7	2·1	12·7	3·9	07	4 46·8	4 47·5	4 33·7	0·7	0·2	6·7	2·2	12·7	4·1
08	4 32·0	4 32·7	4 19·6	0·8	0·2	6·8	2·1	12·8	3·9	08	4 47·0	4 47·8	4 33·9	0·8	0·3	6·8	2·2	12·8	4·2
09	4 32·3	4 33·0	4 19·8	0·9	0·3	6·9	2·1	12·9	4·0	09	4 47·3	4 48·0	4 34·2	0·9	0·3	6·9	2·2	12·9	4·2
10	4 32·5	4 33·2	4 20·1	1·0	0·3	7·0	2·2	13·0	4·0	10	4 47·5	4 48·3	4 34·4	1·0	0·3	7·0	2·3	13·0	4·2
11	4 32·8	4 33·5	4 20·3	1·1	0·3	7·1	2·2	13·1	4·0	11	4 47·8	4 48·5	4 34·6	1·1	0·4	7·1	2·3	13·1	4·3
12	4 33·0	4 33·7	4 20·6	1·2	0·4	7·2	2·2	13·2	4·1	12	4 48·0	4 48·8	4 34·9	1·2	0·4	7·2	2·3	13·2	4·3
13	4 33·3	4 34·0	4 20·8	1·3	0·4	7·3	2·3	13·3	4·1	13	4 48·3	4 49·0	4 35·1	1·3	0·4	7·3	2·4	13·3	4·3
14	4 33·5	4 34·2	4 21·0	1·4	0·4	7·4	2·3	13·4	4·1	14	4 48·5	4 49·3	4 35·4	1·4	0·5	7·4	2·4	13·4	4·4
15	4 33·8	4 34·5	4 21·3	1·5	0·5	7·5	2·3	13·5	4·2	15	4 48·8	4 49·5	4 35·6	1·5	0·5	7·5	2·4	13·5	4·4
16	4 34·0	4 34·8	4 21·5	1·6	0·5	7·6	2·3	13·6	4·2	16	4 49·0	4 49·8	4 35·8	1·6	0·5	7·6	2·5	13·6	4·4
17	4 34·3	4 35·0	4 21·8	1·7	0·5	7·7	2·4	13·7	4·2	17	4 49·3	4 50·0	4 36·1	1·7	0·6	7·7	2·5	13·7	4·5
18	4 34·5	4 35·3	4 22·0	1·8	0·6	7·8	2·4	13·8	4·3	18	4 49·5	4 50·3	4 36·3	1·8	0·6	7·8	2·5	13·8	4·5
19	4 34·8	4 35·5	4 22·2	1·9	0·6	7·9	2·4	13·9	4·3	19	4 49·8	4 50·5	4 36·6	1·9	0·6	7·9	2·6	13·9	4·5
20	4 35·0	4 35·8	4 22·5	2·0	0·6	8·0	2·5	14·0	4·3	20	4 50·0	4 50·8	4 36·8	2·0	0·7	8·0	2·6	14·0	4·6
21	4 35·3	4 36·0	4 22·7	2·1	0·6	8·1	2·5	14·1	4·3	21	4 50·3	4 51·0	4 37·0	2·1	0·7	8·1	2·6	14·1	4·6
22	4 35·5	4 36·3	4 22·9	2·2	0·7	8·2	2·5	14·2	4·4	22	4 50·5	4 51·3	4 37·3	2·2	0·7	8·2	2·7	14·2	4·6
23	4 35·8	4 36·5	4 23·2	2·3	0·7	8·3	2·6	14·3	4·4	23	4 50·8	4 51·5	4 37·5	2·3	0·7	8·3	2·7	14·3	4·6
24	4 36·0	4 36·8	4 23·4	2·4	0·7	8·4	2·6	14·4	4·4	24	4 51·0	4 51·8	4 37·7	2·4	0·8	8·4	2·7	14·4	4·7
25	4 36·3	4 37·0	4 23·7	2·5	0·8	8·5	2·6	14·5	4·5	25	4 51·3	4 52·0	4 38·0	2·5	0·8	8·5	2·8	14·5	4·7
26	4 36·5	4 37·3	4 23·9	2·6	0·8	8·6	2·7	14·6	4·5	26	4 51·5	4 52·3	4 38·2	2·6	0·8	8·6	2·8	14·6	4·7
27	4 36·8	4 37·5	4 24·1	2·7	0·8	8·7	2·7	14·7	4·5	27	4 51·8	4 52·5	4 38·5	2·7	0·9	8·7	2·8	14·7	4·8
28	4 37·0	4 37·8	4 24·4	2·8	0·9	8·8	2·7	14·8	4·6	28	4 52·0	4 52·8	4 38·7	2·8	0·9	8·8	2·9	14·8	4·8
29	4 37·3	4 38·0	4 24·6	2·9	0·9	8·9	2·7	14·9	4·6	29	4 52·3	4 53·1	4 38·9	2·9	0·9	8·9	2·9	14·9	4·8
30	4 37·5	4 38·3	4 24·9	3·0	0·9	9·0	2·8	15·0	4·6	30	4 52·5	4 53·3	4 39·2	3·0	1·0	9·0	2·9	15·0	4·9
31	4 37·8	4 38·5	4 25·1	3·1	1·0	9·1	2·8	15·1	4·7	31	4 52·8	4 53·6	4 39·4	3·1	1·0	9·1	3·0	15·1	4·9
32	4 38·0	4 38·8	4 25·3	3·2	1·0	9·2	2·8	15·2	4·7	32	4 53·0	4 53·8	4 39·7	3·2	1·0	9·2	3·0	15·2	4·9
33	4 38·3	4 39·0	4 25·6	3·3	1·0	9·3	2·9	15·3	4·7	33	4 53·3	4 54·1	4 39·9	3·3	1·1	9·3	3·0	15·3	5·0
34	4 38·5	4 39·3	4 25·8	3·4	1·0	9·4	2·9	15·4	4·7	34	4 53·5	4 54·3	4 40·1	3·4	1·1	9·4	3·1	15·4	5·0
35	4 38·8	4 39·5	4 26·1	3·5	1·1	9·5	2·9	15·5	4·8	35	4 53·8	4 54·6	4 40·4	3·5	1·1	9·5	3·1	15·5	5·0
36	4 39·0	4 39·8	4 26·3	3·6	1·1	9·6	3·0	15·6	4·8	36	4 54·0	4 54·8	4 40·6	3·6	1·2	9·6	3·1	15·6	5·1
37	4 39·3	4 40·0	4 26·5	3·7	1·1	9·7	3·0	15·7	4·8	37	4 54·3	4 55·1	4 40·8	3·7	1·2	9·7	3·2	15·7	5·1
38	4 39·5	4 40·3	4 26·8	3·8	1·2	9·8	3·0	15·8	4·9	38	4 54·5	4 55·3	4 41·1	3·8	1·2	9·8	3·2	15·8	5·1
39	4 39·8	4 40·5	4 27·0	3·9	1·2	9·9	3·1	15·9	4·9	39	4 54·8	4 55·6	4 41·3	3·9	1·3	9·9	3·2	15·9	5·2
40	4 40·0	4 40·8	4 27·2	4·0	1·2	10·0	3·1	16·0	4·9	40	4 55·0	4 55·8	4 41·6	4·0	1·3	10·0	3·3	16·0	5·2
41	4 40·3	4 41·0	4 27·5	4·1	1·3	10·1	3·1	16·1	5·0	41	4 55·3	4 56·1	4 41·8	4·1	1·3	10·1	3·3	16·1	5·2
42	4 40·5	4 41·3	4 27·7	4·2	1·3	10·2	3·1	16·2	5·0	42	4 55·5	4 56·3	4 42·0	4·2	1·4	10·2	3·3	16·2	5·3
43	4 40·8	4 41·5	4 28·0	4·3	1·3	10·3	3·2	16·3	5·0	43	4 55·8	4 56·6	4 42·3	4·3	1·4	10·3	3·3	16·3	5·3
44	4 41·0	4 41·8	4 28·2	4·4	1·4	10·4	3·2	16·4	5·1	44	4 56·0	4 56·8	4 42·5	4·4	1·4	10·4	3·4	16·4	5·3
45	4 41·3	4 42·0	4 28·4	4·5	1·4	10·5	3·2	16·5	5·1	45	4 56·3	4 57·1	4 42·8	4·5	1·5	10·5	3·4	16·5	5·4
46	4 41·5	4 42·3	4 28·7	4·6	1·4	10·6	3·3	16·6	5·1	46	4 56·5	4 57·3	4 43·0	4·6	1·5	10·6	3·4	16·6	5·4
47	4 41·8	4 42·5	4 28·9	4·7	1·4	10·7	3·3	16·7	5·1	47	4 56·8	4 57·6	4 43·2	4·7	1·5	10·7	3·5	16·7	5·4
48	4 42·0	4 42·8	4 29·2	4·8	1·5	10·8	3·3	16·8	5·2	48	4 57·0	4 57·8	4 43·5	4·8	1·6	10·8	3·5	16·8	5·5
49	4 42·3	4 43·0	4 29·4	4·9	1·5	10·9	3·4	16·9	5·2	49	4 57·3	4 58·1	4 43·7	4·9	1·6	10·9	3·5	16·9	5·5
50	4 42·5	4 43·3	4 29·6	5·0	1·5	11·0	3·4	17·0	5·2	50	4 57·5	4 58·3	4 43·9	5·0	1·6	11·0	3·6	17·0	5·5
51	4 42·8	4 43·5	4 29·9	5·1	1·6	11·1	3·4	17·1	5·3	51	4 57·8	4 58·6	4 44·2	5·1	1·7	11·1	3·6	17·1	5·6
52	4 43·0	4 43·8	4 30·1	5·2	1·6	11·2	3·5	17·2	5·3	52	4 58·0	4 58·8	4 44·4	5·2	1·7	11·2	3·6	17·2	5·6
53	4 43·3	4 44·0	4 30·3	5·3	1·6	11·3	3·5	17·3	5·3	53	4 58·3	4 59·1	4 44·7	5·3	1·7	11·3	3·7	17·3	5·6
54	4 43·5	4 44·3	4 30·6	5·4	1·7	11·4	3·5	17·4	5·4	54	4 58·5	4 59·3	4 44·9	5·4	1·8	11·4	3·7	17·4	5·7
55	4 43·8	4 44·5	4 30·8	5·5	1·7	11·5	3·5	17·5	5·4	55	4 58·8	4 59·6	4 45·1	5·5	1·8	11·5	3·7	17·5	5·7
56	4 44·0	4 44·8	4 31·1	5·6	1·7	11·6	3·6	17·6	5·4	56	4 59·0	4 59·8	4 45·4	5·6	1·8	11·6	3·8	17·6	5·7
57	4 44·3	4 45·0	4 31·3	5·7	1·8	11·7	3·6	17·7	5·5	57	4 59·3	5 00·1	4 45·6	5·7	1·9	11·7	3·8	17·7	5·8
58	4 44·5	4 45·3	4 31·5	5·8	1·8	11·8	3·6	17·8	5·5	58	4 59·5	5 00·3	4 45·9	5·8	1·9	11·8	3·8	17·8	5·8
59	4 44·8	4 45·5	4 31·8	5·9	1·8	11·9	3·7	17·9	5·5	59	4 59·8	5 00·6	4 46·1	5·9	1·9	11·9	3·9	17·9	5·8
60	4 45·0	4 45·8	4 32·0	6·0	1·9	12·0	3·7	18·0	5·6	60	5 00·0	5 00·8	4 46·3	6·0	2·0	12·0	3·9	18·0	5·9

20ᵐ INCREMENTS AND CORRECTIONS 21ᵐ

20ᵐ s	SUN PLANETS	ARIES	MOON	v or d Corrⁿ	v or d Corrⁿ	v or d Corrⁿ	21ᵐ s	SUN PLANETS	ARIES	MOON	v or d Corrⁿ	v or d Corrⁿ	v or d Corrⁿ
	° ′	° ′	° ′	′ ′	′ ′	′ ′		° ′	° ′	° ′	′ ′	′ ′	′ ′
00	5 00·0	5 00·8	4 46·3	0·0 0·0	6·0 2·1	12·0 4·1	00	5 15·0	5 15·9	5 00·7	0·0 0·0	6·0 2·2	12·0 4·3
01	5 00·3	5 01·1	4 46·6	0·1 0·0	6·1 2·1	12·1 4·1	01	5 15·3	5 16·1	5 00·9	0·1 0·0	6·1 2·2	12·1 4·3
02	5 00·5	5 01·3	4 46·8	0·2 0·1	6·2 2·1	12·2 4·2	02	5 15·5	5 16·4	5 01·1	0·2 0·1	6·2 2·2	12·2 4·4
03	5 00·8	5 01·6	4 47·0	0·3 0·1	6·3 2·2	12·3 4·2	03	5 15·8	5 16·6	5 01·4	0·3 0·1	6·3 2·3	12·3 4·4
04	5 01·0	5 01·8	4 47·3	0·4 0·1	6·4 2·2	12·4 4·2	04	5 16·0	5 16·9	5 01·6	0·4 0·1	6·4 2·3	12·4 4·4
05	5 01·3	5 02·1	4 47·5	0·5 0·2	6·5 2·2	12·5 4·3	05	5 16·3	5 17·1	5 01·8	0·5 0·2	6·5 2·3	12·5 4·5
06	5 01·5	5 02·3	4 47·8	0·6 0·2	6·6 2·3	12·6 4·3	06	5 16·5	5 17·4	5 02·1	0·6 0·2	6·6 2·4	12·6 4·5
07	5 01·8	5 02·6	4 48·0	0·7 0·2	6·7 2·3	12·7 4·3	07	5 16·8	5 17·6	5 02·3	0·7 0·3	6·7 2·4	12·7 4·6
08	5 02·0	5 02·8	4 48·2	0·8 0·3	6·8 2·3	12·8 4·4	08	5 17·0	5 17·9	5 02·6	0·8 0·3	6·8 2·4	12·8 4·6
09	5 02·3	5 03·1	4 48·5	0·9 0·3	6·9 2·4	12·9 4·4	09	5 17·3	5 18·1	5 02·8	0·9 0·3	6·9 2·5	12·9 4·6
10	5 02·5	5 03·3	4 48·7	1·0 0·3	7·0 2·4	13·0 4·4	10	5 17·5	5 18·4	5 03·0	1·0 0·4	7·0 2·5	13·0 4·7
11	5 02·8	5 03·6	4 49·0	1·1 0·4	7·1 2·4	13·1 4·5	11	5 17·8	5 18·6	5 03·3	1·1 0·4	7·1 2·5	13·1 4·7
12	5 03·0	5 03·8	4 49·2	1·2 0·4	7·2 2·5	13·2 4·5	12	5 18·0	5 18·9	5 03·5	1·2 0·4	7·2 2·6	13·2 4·7
13	5 03·3	5 04·1	4 49·4	1·3 0·4	7·3 2·5	13·3 4·5	13	5 18·3	5 19·1	5 03·8	1·3 0·5	7·3 2·6	13·3 4·8
14	5 03·5	5 04·3	4 49·7	1·4 0·5	7·4 2·5	13·4 4·6	14	5 18·5	5 19·4	5 04·0	1·4 0·5	7·4 2·7	13·4 4·8
15	5 03·8	5 04·6	4 49·9	1·5 0·5	7·5 2·6	13·5 4·6	15	5 18·8	5 19·6	5 04·2	1·5 0·5	7·5 2·7	13·5 4·8
16	5 04·0	5 04·8	4 50·2	1·6 0·5	7·6 2·6	13·6 4·6	16	5 19·0	5 19·9	5 04·5	1·6 0·6	7·6 2·7	13·6 4·9
17	5 04·3	5 05·1	4 50·4	1·7 0·6	7·7 2·6	13·7 4·7	17	5 19·3	5 20·1	5 04·7	1·7 0·6	7·7 2·8	13·7 4·9
18	5 04·5	5 05·3	4 50·6	1·8 0·6	7·8 2·7	13·8 4·7	18	5 19·5	5 20·4	5 04·9	1·8 0·6	7·8 2·8	13·8 4·9
19	5 04·8	5 05·6	4 50·9	1·9 0·6	7·9 2·7	13·9 4·7	19	5 19·8	5 20·6	5 05·2	1·9 0·7	7·9 2·8	13·9 5·0
20	5 05·0	5 05·8	4 51·1	2·0 0·7	8·0 2·7	14·0 4·8	20	5 20·0	5 20·9	5 05·4	2·0 0·7	8·0 2·9	14·0 5·0
21	5 05·3	5 06·1	4 51·3	2·1 0·7	8·1 2·8	14·1 4·8	21	5 20·3	5 21·1	5 05·7	2·1 0·8	8·1 2·9	14·1 5·1
22	5 05·5	5 06·3	4 51·6	2·2 0·8	8·2 2·8	14·2 4·9	22	5 20·5	5 21·4	5 05·9	2·2 0·8	8·2 2·9	14·2 5·1
23	5 05·8	5 06·6	4 51·8	2·3 0·8	8·3 2·8	14·3 4·9	23	5 20·8	5 21·6	5 06·1	2·3 0·8	8·3 3·0	14·3 5·1
24	5 06·0	5 06·8	4 52·1	2·4 0·8	8·4 2·9	14·4 4·9	24	5 21·0	5 21·9	5 06·4	2·4 0·9	8·4 3·0	14·4 5·2
25	5 06·3	5 07·1	4 52·3	2·5 0·9	8·5 2·9	14·5 5·0	25	5 21·3	5 22·1	5 06·6	2·5 0·9	8·5 3·0	14·5 5·2
26	5 06·5	5 07·3	4 52·5	2·6 0·9	8·6 2·9	14·6 5·0	26	5 21·5	5 22·4	5 06·9	2·6 0·9	8·6 3·1	14·6 5·2
27	5 06·8	5 07·6	4 52·8	2·7 0·9	8·7 3·0	14·7 5·0	27	5 21·8	5 22·6	5 07·1	2·7 1·0	8·7 3·1	14·7 5·3
28	5 07·0	5 07·8	4 53·0	2·8 1·0	8·8 3·0	14·8 5·1	28	5 22·0	5 22·9	5 07·3	2·8 1·0	8·8 3·2	14·8 5·3
29	5 07·3	5 08·1	4 53·3	2·9 1·0	8·9 3·0	14·9 5·1	29	5 22·3	5 23·1	5 07·6	2·9 1·0	8·9 3·2	14·9 5·3
30	5 07·5	5 08·3	4 53·5	3·0 1·0	9·0 3·1	15·0 5·1	30	5 22·5	5 23·4	5 07·8	3·0 1·1	9·0 3·2	15·0 5·4
31	5 07·8	5 08·6	4 53·7	3·1 1·1	9·1 3·1	15·1 5·2	31	5 22·8	5 23·6	5 08·0	3·1 1·1	9·1 3·3	15·1 5·4
32	5 08·0	5 08·8	4 54·0	3·2 1·1	9·2 3·1	15·2 5·2	32	5 23·0	5 23·9	5 08·3	3·2 1·1	9·2 3·3	15·2 5·4
33	5 08·3	5 09·1	4 54·2	3·3 1·1	9·3 3·2	15·3 5·2	33	5 23·3	5 24·1	5 08·5	3·3 1·2	9·3 3·3	15·3 5·5
34	5 08·5	5 09·3	4 54·4	3·4 1·2	9·4 3·2	15·4 5·3	34	5 23·5	5 24·4	5 08·8	3·4 1·2	9·4 3·4	15·4 5·5
35	5 08·8	5 09·6	4 54·7	3·5 1·2	9·5 3·2	15·5 5·3	35	5 23·8	5 24·6	5 09·0	3·5 1·3	9·5 3·4	15·5 5·6
36	5 09·0	5 09·8	4 54·9	3·6 1·2	9·6 3·3	15·6 5·3	36	5 24·0	5 24·9	5 09·2	3·6 1·3	9·6 3·4	15·6 5·6
37	5 09·3	5 10·1	4 55·2	3·7 1·3	9·7 3·3	15·7 5·4	37	5 24·3	5 25·1	5 09·5	3·7 1·3	9·7 3·5	15·7 5·6
38	5 09·5	5 10·3	4 55·4	3·8 1·3	9·8 3·3	15·8 5·4	38	5 24·5	5 25·4	5 09·7	3·8 1·4	9·8 3·5	15·8 5·7
39	5 09·8	5 10·6	4 55·6	3·9 1·3	9·9 3·4	15·9 5·4	39	5 24·8	5 25·6	5 10·0	3·9 1·4	9·9 3·5	15·9 5·7
40	5 10·0	5 10·8	4 55·9	4·0 1·4	10·0 3·4	16·0 5·5	40	5 25·0	5 25·9	5 10·2	4·0 1·4	10·0 3·6	16·0 5·7
41	5 10·3	5 11·1	4 56·1	4·1 1·4	10·1 3·5	16·1 5·5	41	5 25·3	5 26·1	5 10·4	4·1 1·5	10·1 3·6	16·1 5·8
42	5 10·5	5 11·4	4 56·4	4·2 1·4	10·2 3·5	16·2 5·5	42	5 25·5	5 26·4	5 10·7	4·2 1·5	10·2 3·7	16·2 5·8
43	5 10·8	5 11·6	4 56·6	4·3 1·5	10·3 3·5	16·3 5·6	43	5 25·8	5 26·6	5 10·9	4·3 1·5	10·3 3·7	16·3 5·8
44	5 11·0	5 11·9	4 56·8	4·4 1·5	10·4 3·6	16·4 5·6	44	5 26·0	5 26·9	5 11·1	4·4 1·6	10·4 3·7	16·4 5·9
45	5 11·3	5 12·1	4 57·1	4·5 1·5	10·5 3·6	16·5 5·6	45	5 26·3	5 27·1	5 11·4	4·5 1·6	10·5 3·8	16·5 5·9
46	5 11·5	5 12·4	4 57·3	4·6 1·6	10·6 3·6	16·6 5·7	46	5 26·5	5 27·4	5 11·6	4·6 1·6	10·6 3·8	16·6 5·9
47	5 11·8	5 12·6	4 57·5	4·7 1·6	10·7 3·7	16·7 5·7	47	5 26·8	5 27·6	5 11·9	4·7 1·7	10·7 3·8	16·7 6·0
48	5 12·0	5 12·9	4 57·8	4·8 1·6	10·8 3·7	16·8 5·7	48	5 27·0	5 27·9	5 12·1	4·8 1·7	10·8 3·9	16·8 6·0
49	5 12·3	5 13·1	4 58·0	4·9 1·7	10·9 3·7	16·9 5·8	49	5 27·3	5 28·1	5 12·3	4·9 1·8	10·9 3·9	16·9 6·1
50	5 12·5	5 13·4	4 58·3	5·0 1·7	11·0 3·8	17·0 5·8	50	5 27·5	5 28·4	5 12·6	5·0 1·8	11·0 3·9	17·0 6·1
51	5 12·8	5 13·6	4 58·5	5·1 1·7	11·1 3·8	17·1 5·8	51	5 27·8	5 28·6	5 12·8	5·1 1·8	11·1 4·0	17·1 6·1
52	5 13·0	5 13·9	4 58·7	5·2 1·8	11·2 3·8	17·2 5·9	52	5 28·0	5 28·9	5 13·1	5·2 1·9	11·2 4·0	17·2 6·2
53	5 13·3	5 14·1	4 59·0	5·3 1·8	11·3 3·9	17·3 5·9	53	5 28·3	5 29·1	5 13·3	5·3 1·9	11·3 4·0	17·3 6·2
54	5 13·5	5 14·4	4 59·2	5·4 1·8	11·4 3·9	17·4 5·9	54	5 28·5	5 29·4	5 13·5	5·4 1·9	11·4 4·1	17·4 6·2
55	5 13·8	5 14·6	4 59·5	5·5 1·9	11·5 3·9	17·5 6·0	55	5 28·8	5 29·7	5 13·8	5·5 2·0	11·5 4·1	17·5 6·3
56	5 14·0	5 14·9	4 59·7	5·6 1·9	11·6 4·0	17·6 6·0	56	5 29·0	5 29·9	5 14·0	5·6 2·0	11·6 4·2	17·6 6·3
57	5 14·3	5 15·1	4 59·9	5·7 1·9	11·7 4·0	17·7 6·0	57	5 29·3	5 30·2	5 14·3	5·7 2·0	11·7 4·2	17·7 6·3
58	5 14·5	5 15·4	5 00·2	5·8 2·0	11·8 4·0	17·8 6·1	58	5 29·5	5 30·4	5 14·5	5·8 2·1	11·8 4·2	17·8 6·4
59	5 14·8	5 15·6	5 00·4	5·9 2·0	11·9 4·1	17·9 6·1	59	5 29·8	5 30·7	5 14·7	5·9 2·1	11·9 4·3	17·9 6·4
60	5 15·0	5 15·9	5 00·7	6·0 2·1	12·0 4·1	18·0 6·2	60	5 30·0	5 30·9	5 15·0	6·0 2·2	12·0 4·3	18·0 6·5

22ᵐ   INCREMENTS AND CORRECTIONS   23ᵐ

22ᵐ s	SUN PLANETS ° ′	ARIES ° ′	MOON ° ′	v or d Corrⁿ ′ ′	v or d Corrⁿ ′ ′	v or d Corrⁿ ′ ′
00	5 30·0	5 30·9	5 15·0	0·0 0·0	6·0 2·3	12·0 4·5
01	5 30·3	5 31·2	5 15·2	0·1 0·0	6·1 2·3	12·1 4·5
02	5 30·5	5 31·4	5 15·4	0·2 0·1	6·2 2·3	12·2 4·6
03	5 30·8	5 31·7	5 15·7	0·3 0·1	6·3 2·4	12·3 4·6
04	5 31·0	5 31·9	5 15·9	0·4 0·2	6·4 2·4	12·4 4·7
05	5 31·3	5 32·2	5 16·2	0·5 0·2	6·5 2·4	12·5 4·7
06	5 31·5	5 32·4	5 16·4	0·6 0·2	6·6 2·5	12·6 4·7
07	5 31·8	5 32·7	5 16·6	0·7 0·3	6·7 2·5	12·7 4·8
08	5 32·0	5 32·9	5 16·9	0·8 0·3	6·8 2·6	12·8 4·8
09	5 32·3	5 33·2	5 17·1	0·9 0·3	6·9 2·6	12·9 4·8
10	5 32·5	5 33·4	5 17·4	1·0 0·4	7·0 2·6	13·0 4·9
11	5 32·8	5 33·7	5 17·6	1·1 0·4	7·1 2·7	13·1 4·9
12	5 33·0	5 33·9	5 17·8	1·2 0·5	7·2 2·7	13·2 5·0
13	5 33·3	5 34·2	5 18·1	1·3 0·5	7·3 2·7	13·3 5·0
14	5 33·5	5 34·4	5 18·3	1·4 0·5	7·4 2·8	13·4 5·0
15	5 33·8	5 34·7	5 18·5	1·5 0·6	7·5 2·8	13·5 5·1
16	5 34·0	5 34·9	5 18·8	1·6 0·6	7·6 2·9	13·6 5·1
17	5 34·3	5 35·2	5 19·0	1·7 0·6	7·7 2·9	13·7 5·1
18	5 34·5	5 35·4	5 19·3	1·8 0·7	7·8 2·9	13·8 5·2
19	5 34·8	5 35·7	5 19·5	1·9 0·7	7·9 3·0	13·9 5·2
20	5 35·0	5 35·9	5 19·7	2·0 0·8	8·0 3·0	14·0 5·3
21	5 35·3	5 36·2	5 20·0	2·1 0·8	8·1 3·0	14·1 5·3
22	5 35·5	5 36·4	5 20·2	2·2 0·8	8·2 3·1	14·2 5·3
23	5 35·8	5 36·7	5 20·5	2·3 0·9	8·3 3·1	14·3 5·4
24	5 36·0	5 36·9	5 20·7	2·4 0·9	8·4 3·2	14·4 5·4
25	5 36·3	5 37·2	5 20·9	2·5 0·9	8·5 3·2	14·5 5·4
26	5 36·5	5 37·4	5 21·2	2·6 1·0	8·6 3·2	14·6 5·5
27	5 36·8	5 37·7	5 21·4	2·7 1·0	8·7 3·3	14·7 5·5
28	5 37·0	5 37·9	5 21·6	2·8 1·1	8·8 3·3	14·8 5·6
29	5 37·3	5 38·2	5 21·9	2·9 1·1	8·9 3·3	14·9 5·6
30	5 37·5	5 38·4	5 22·1	3·0 1·1	9·0 3·4	15·0 5·6
31	5 37·8	5 38·7	5 22·4	3·1 1·2	9·1 3·4	15·1 5·7
32	5 38·0	5 38·9	5 22·6	3·2 1·2	9·2 3·5	15·2 5·7
33	5 38·3	5 39·2	5 22·8	3·3 1·2	9·3 3·5	15·3 5·7
34	5 38·5	5 39·4	5 23·1	3·4 1·3	9·4 3·5	15·4 5·8
35	5 38·8	5 39·7	5 23·3	3·5 1·3	9·5 3·6	15·5 5·8
36	5 39·0	5 39·9	5 23·6	3·6 1·4	9·6 3·6	15·6 5·9
37	5 39·3	5 40·2	5 23·8	3·7 1·4	9·7 3·6	15·7 5·9
38	5 39·5	5 40·4	5 24·0	3·8 1·4	9·8 3·7	15·8 5·9
39	5 39·8	5 40·7	5 24·3	3·9 1·5	9·9 3·7	15·9 6·0
40	5 40·0	5 40·9	5 24·5	4·0 1·5	10·0 3·8	16·0 6·0
41	5 40·3	5 41·2	5 24·7	4·1 1·5	10·1 3·8	16·1 6·0
42	5 40·5	5 41·4	5 25·0	4·2 1·6	10·2 3·8	16·2 6·1
43	5 40·8	5 41·7	5 25·2	4·3 1·6	10·3 3·9	16·3 6·1
44	5 41·0	5 41·9	5 25·5	4·4 1·7	10·4 3·9	16·4 6·2
45	5 41·3	5 42·2	5 25·7	4·5 1·7	10·5 3·9	16·5 6·2
46	5 41·5	5 42·4	5 25·9	4·6 1·7	10·6 4·0	16·6 6·2
47	5 41·8	5 42·7	5 26·2	4·7 1·8	10·7 4·0	16·7 6·3
48	5 42·0	5 42·9	5 26·4	4·8 1·8	10·8 4·1	16·8 6·3
49	5 42·3	5 43·2	5 26·7	4·9 1·8	10·9 4·1	16·9 6·3
50	5 42·5	5 43·4	5 26·9	5·0 1·9	11·0 4·1	17·0 6·4
51	5 42·8	5 43·7	5 27·1	5·1 1·9	11·1 4·2	17·1 6·4
52	5 43·0	5 43·9	5 27·4	5·2 2·0	11·2 4·2	17·2 6·5
53	5 43·3	5 44·2	5 27·6	5·3 2·0	11·3 4·2	17·3 6·5
54	5 43·5	5 44·4	5 27·9	5·4 2·0	11·4 4·3	17·4 6·5
55	5 43·8	5 44·7	5 28·1	5·5 2·1	11·5 4·3	17·5 6·6
56	5 44·0	5 44·9	5 28·3	5·6 2·1	11·6 4·4	17·6 6·6
57	5 44·3	5 45·2	5 28·6	5·7 2·1	11·7 4·4	17·7 6·6
58	5 44·5	5 45·4	5 28·8	5·8 2·2	11·8 4·4	17·8 6·7
59	5 44·8	5 45·7	5 29·0	5·9 2·2	11·9 4·5	17·9 6·7
60	5 45·0	5 45·9	5 29·3	6·0 2·3	12·0 4·5	18·0 6·8

23ᵐ s	SUN PLANETS ° ′	ARIES ° ′	MOON ° ′	v or d Corrⁿ ′ ′	v or d Corrⁿ ′ ′	v or d Corrⁿ ′ ′
00	5 45·0	5 45·9	5 29·3	0·0 0·0	6·0 2·4	12·0 4·7
01	5 45·3	5 46·2	5 29·5	0·1 0·0	6·1 2·4	12·1 4·7
02	5 45·5	5 46·4	5 29·8	0·2 0·1	6·2 2·4	12·2 4·8
03	5 45·8	5 46·7	5 30·0	0·3 0·1	6·3 2·5	12·3 4·8
04	5 46·0	5 46·9	5 30·2	0·4 0·2	6·4 2·5	12·4 4·9
05	5 46·3	5 47·2	5 30·5	0·5 0·2	6·5 2·5	12·5 4·9
06	5 46·5	5 47·4	5 30·7	0·6 0·2	6·6 2·6	12·6 4·9
07	5 46·8	5 47·7	5 31·0	0·7 0·3	6·7 2·6	12·7 5·0
08	5 47·0	5 48·0	5 31·2	0·8 0·3	6·8 2·7	12·8 5·0
09	5 47·3	5 48·2	5 31·4	0·9 0·4	6·9 2·7	12·9 5·1
10	5 47·5	5 48·5	5 31·7	1·0 0·4	7·0 2·7	13·0 5·1
11	5 47·8	5 48·7	5 31·9	1·1 0·4	7·1 2·8	13·1 5·1
12	5 48·0	5 49·0	5 32·1	1·2 0·5	7·2 2·8	13·2 5·2
13	5 48·3	5 49·2	5 32·4	1·3 0·5	7·3 2·9	13·3 5·2
14	5 48·5	5 49·5	5 32·6	1·4 0·5	7·4 2·9	13·4 5·2
15	5 48·8	5 49·7	5 32·9	1·5 0·6	7·5 2·9	13·5 5·3
16	5 49·0	5 50·0	5 33·1	1·6 0·6	7·6 3·0	13·6 5·3
17	5 49·3	5 50·2	5 33·3	1·7 0·7	7·7 3·0	13·7 5·4
18	5 49·5	5 50·5	5 33·6	1·8 0·7	7·8 3·1	13·8 5·4
19	5 49·8	5 50·7	5 33·8	1·9 0·7	7·9 3·1	13·9 5·4
20	5 50·0	5 51·0	5 34·1	2·0 0·8	8·0 3·1	14·0 5·5
21	5 50·3	5 51·2	5 34·3	2·1 0·8	8·1 3·2	14·1 5·5
22	5 50·5	5 51·5	5 34·5	2·2 0·9	8·2 3·2	14·2 5·6
23	5 50·8	5 51·7	5 34·8	2·3 0·9	8·3 3·3	14·3 5·6
24	5 51·0	5 52·0	5 35·0	2·4 0·9	8·4 3·3	14·4 5·6
25	5 51·3	5 52·2	5 35·2	2·5 1·0	8·5 3·3	14·5 5·7
26	5 51·5	5 52·5	5 35·5	2·6 1·0	8·6 3·4	14·6 5·7
27	5 51·8	5 52·7	5 35·7	2·7 1·1	8·7 3·4	14·7 5·8
28	5 52·0	5 53·0	5 36·0	2·8 1·1	8·8 3·4	14·8 5·8
29	5 52·3	5 53·2	5 36·2	2·9 1·1	8·9 3·5	14·9 5·8
30	5 52·5	5 53·5	5 36·4	3·0 1·2	9·0 3·5	15·0 5·9
31	5 52·8	5 53·7	5 36·7	3·1 1·2	9·1 3·6	15·1 5·9
32	5 53·0	5 54·0	5 36·9	3·2 1·3	9·2 3·6	15·2 6·0
33	5 53·3	5 54·2	5 37·2	3·3 1·3	9·3 3·6	15·3 6·0
34	5 53·5	5 54·5	5 37·4	3·4 1·3	9·4 3·7	15·4 6·0
35	5 53·8	5 54·7	5 37·6	3·5 1·4	9·5 3·7	15·5 6·1
36	5 54·0	5 55·0	5 37·9	3·6 1·4	9·6 3·8	15·6 6·1
37	5 54·3	5 55·2	5 38·1	3·7 1·4	9·7 3·8	15·7 6·1
38	5 54·5	5 55·5	5 38·4	3·8 1·5	9·8 3·8	15·8 6·2
39	5 54·8	5 55·7	5 38·6	3·9 1·5	9·9 3·9	15·9 6·2
40	5 55·0	5 56·0	5 38·8	4·0 1·6	10·0 3·9	16·0 6·3
41	5 55·3	5 56·2	5 39·1	4·1 1·6	10·1 4·0	16·1 6·3
42	5 55·5	5 56·5	5 39·3	4·2 1·6	10·2 4·0	16·2 6·3
43	5 55·8	5 56·7	5 39·5	4·3 1·7	10·3 4·0	16·3 6·4
44	5 56·0	5 57·0	5 39·8	4·4 1·7	10·4 4·1	16·4 6·4
45	5 56·3	5 57·2	5 40·0	4·5 1·8	10·5 4·1	16·5 6·5
46	5 56·5	5 57·5	5 40·3	4·6 1·8	10·6 4·2	16·6 6·5
47	5 56·8	5 57·7	5 40·5	4·7 1·8	10·7 4·2	16·7 6·5
48	5 57·0	5 58·0	5 40·7	4·8 1·9	10·8 4·2	16·8 6·6
49	5 57·3	5 58·2	5 41·0	4·9 1·9	10·9 4·3	16·9 6·6
50	5 57·5	5 58·5	5 41·2	5·0 2·0	11·0 4·3	17·0 6·7
51	5 57·8	5 58·7	5 41·5	5·1 2·0	11·1 4·3	17·1 6·7
52	5 58·0	5 59·0	5 41·7	5·2 2·0	11·2 4·4	17·2 6·7
53	5 58·3	5 59·2	5 41·9	5·3 2·1	11·3 4·4	17·3 6·8
54	5 58·5	5 59·5	5 42·2	5·4 2·1	11·4 4·5	17·4 6·8
55	5 58·8	5 59·7	5 42·4	5·5 2·2	11·5 4·5	17·5 6·9
56	5 59·0	6 00·0	5 42·6	5·6 2·2	11·6 4·5	17·6 6·9
57	5 59·3	6 00·2	5 42·9	5·7 2·2	11·7 4·6	17·7 6·9
58	5 59·5	6 00·5	5 43·1	5·8 2·3	11·8 4·6	17·8 7·0
59	5 59·8	6 00·7	5 43·4	5·9 2·3	11·9 4·7	17·9 7·0
60	6 00·0	6 01·0	5 43·6	6·0 2·4	12·0 4·7	18·0 7·1

24^m INCREMENTS AND CORRECTIONS   25^m

24^m s	SUN PLANETS	ARIES	MOON	v or Corrn d	v or Corrn d	v or Corrn d	25^m s	SUN PLANETS	ARIES	MOON	v or Corrn d	v or Corrn d	v or Corrn d
00	6 00·0	6 01·0	5 43·6	0·0 0·0	6·0 2·5	12·0 4·9	00	6 15·0	6 16·0	5 57·9	0·0 0·0	6·0 2·6	12·0 5·1
01	6 00·3	6 01·2	5 43·8	0·1 0·0	6·1 2·5	12·1 4·9	01	6 15·3	6 16·3	5 58·2	0·1 0·0	6·1 2·6	12·1 5·1
02	6 00·5	6 01·5	5 44·1	0·2 0·1	6·2 2·5	12·2 5·0	02	6 15·5	6 16·5	5 58·4	0·2 0·1	6·2 2·6	12·2 5·2
03	6 00·8	6 01·7	5 44·3	0·3 0·1	6·3 2·6	12·3 5·0	03	6 15·8	6 16·8	5 58·6	0·3 0·1	6·3 2·7	12·3 5·2
04	6 01·0	6 02·0	5 44·6	0·4 0·2	6·4 2·6	12·4 5·1	04	6 16·0	6 17·0	5 58·9	0·4 0·2	6·4 2·7	12·4 5·3
05	6 01·3	6 02·2	5 44·8	0·5 0·2	6·5 2·7	12·5 5·1	05	6 16·3	6 17·3	5 59·1	0·5 0·2	6·5 2·8	12·5 5·3
06	6 01·5	6 02·5	5 45·0	0·6 0·2	6·6 2·7	12·6 5·1	06	6 16·5	6 17·5	5 59·3	0·6 0·3	6·6 2·8	12·6 5·4
07	6 01·8	6 02·7	5 45·3	0·7 0·3	6·7 2·7	12·7 5·2	07	6 16·8	6 17·8	5 59·6	0·7 0·3	6·7 2·8	12·7 5·4
08	6 02·0	6 03·0	5 45·5	0·8 0·3	6·8 2·8	12·8 5·2	08	6 17·0	6 18·0	5 59·8	0·8 0·3	6·8 2·9	12·8 5·4
09	6 02·3	6 03·2	5 45·7	0·9 0·4	6·9 2·8	12·9 5·3	09	6 17·3	6 18·3	6 00·1	0·9 0·4	6·9 2·9	12·9 5·5
10	6 02·5	6 03·5	5 46·0	1·0 0·4	7·0 2·9	13·0 5·3	10	6 17·5	6 18·5	6 00·3	1·0 0·4	7·0 3·0	13·0 5·5
11	6 02·8	6 03·7	5 46·2	1·1 0·4	7·1 2·9	13·1 5·3	11	6 17·8	6 18·8	6 00·5	1·1 0·5	7·1 3·0	13·1 5·6
12	6 03·0	6 04·0	5 46·5	1·2 0·5	7·2 2·9	13·2 5·4	12	6 18·0	6 19·0	6 00·8	1·2 0·5	7·2 3·1	13·2 5·6
13	6 03·3	6 04·2	5 46·7	1·3 0·5	7·3 3·0	13·3 5·4	13	6 18·3	6 19·3	6 01·0	1·3 0·6	7·3 3·1	13·3 5·7
14	6 03·5	6 04·5	5 46·9	1·4 0·6	7·4 3·0	13·4 5·5	14	6 18·5	6 19·5	6 01·3	1·4 0·6	7·4 3·1	13·4 5·7
15	6 03·8	6 04·7	5 47·2	1·5 0·6	7·5 3·1	13·5 5·5	15	6 18·8	6 19·8	6 01·5	1·5 0·6	7·5 3·2	13·5 5·7
16	6 04·0	6 05·0	5 47·4	1·6 0·7	7·6 3·1	13·6 5·6	16	6 19·0	6 20·0	6 01·7	1·6 0·7	7·6 3·2	13·6 5·8
17	6 04·3	6 05·2	5 47·7	1·7 0·7	7·7 3·1	13·7 5·6	17	6 19·3	6 20·3	6 02·0	1·7 0·7	7·7 3·3	13·7 5·8
18	6 04·5	6 05·5	5 47·9	1·8 0·7	7·8 3·2	13·8 5·6	18	6 19·5	6 20·5	6 02·2	1·8 0·8	7·8 3·3	13·8 5·9
19	6 04·8	6 05·7	5 48·1	1·9 0·8	7·9 3·2	13·9 5·7	19	6 19·8	6 20·8	6 02·5	1·9 0·8	7·9 3·4	13·9 5·9
20	6 05·0	6 06·0	5 48·4	2·0 0·8	8·0 3·3	14·0 5·7	20	6 20·0	6 21·0	6 02·7	2·0 0·9	8·0 3·4	14·0 6·0
21	6 05·3	6 06·3	5 48·6	2·1 0·9	8·1 3·3	14·1 5·8	21	6 20·3	6 21·3	6 02·9	2·1 0·9	8·1 3·4	14·1 6·0
22	6 05·5	6 06·5	5 48·8	2·2 0·9	8·2 3·3	14·2 5·8	22	6 20·5	6 21·5	6 03·2	2·2 0·9	8·2 3·5	14·2 6·0
23	6 05·8	6 06·8	5 49·1	2·3 0·9	8·3 3·4	14·3 5·8	23	6 20·8	6 21·8	6 03·4	2·3 1·0	8·3 3·5	14·3 6·1
24	6 06·0	6 07·0	5 49·3	2·4 1·0	8·4 3·4	14·4 5·9	24	6 21·0	6 22·0	6 03·6	2·4 1·0	8·4 3·6	14·4 6·1
25	6 06·3	6 07·3	5 49·6	2·5 1·0	8·5 3·5	14·5 5·9	25	6 21·3	6 22·3	6 03·9	2·5 1·1	8·5 3·6	14·5 6·2
26	6 06·5	6 07·5	5 49·8	2·6 1·1	8·6 3·5	14·6 6·0	26	6 21·5	6 22·5	6 04·1	2·6 1·1	8·6 3·7	14·6 6·2
27	6 06·8	6 07·8	5 50·0	2·7 1·1	8·7 3·6	14·7 6·0	27	6 21·8	6 22·8	6 04·4	2·7 1·1	8·7 3·7	14·7 6·2
28	6 07·0	6 08·0	5 50·3	2·8 1·1	8·8 3·6	14·8 6·0	28	6 22·0	6 23·0	6 04·6	2·8 1·2	8·8 3·7	14·8 6·3
29	6 07·3	6 08·3	5 50·5	2·9 1·2	8·9 3·6	14·9 6·1	29	6 22·3	6 23·3	6 04·8	2·9 1·2	8·9 3·8	14·9 6·3
30	6 07·5	6 08·5	5 50·8	3·0 1·2	9·0 3·7	15·0 6·1	30	6 22·5	6 23·5	6 05·1	3·0 1·3	9·0 3·8	15·0 6·4
31	6 07·8	6 08·8	5 51·0	3·1 1·3	9·1 3·7	15·1 6·2	31	6 22·8	6 23·8	6 05·3	3·1 1·3	9·1 3·9	15·1 6·4
32	6 08·0	6 09·0	5 51·2	3·2 1·3	9·2 3·8	15·2 6·2	32	6 23·0	6 24·0	6 05·6	3·2 1·4	9·2 3·9	15·2 6·5
33	6 08·3	6 09·3	5 51·5	3·3 1·3	9·3 3·8	15·3 6·2	33	6 23·3	6 24·3	6 05·8	3·3 1·4	9·3 4·0	15·3 6·5
34	6 08·5	6 09·5	5 51·7	3·4 1·4	9·4 3·8	15·4 6·3	34	6 23·5	6 24·5	6 06·0	3·4 1·4	9·4 4·0	15·4 6·5
35	6 08·8	6 09·8	5 52·0	3·5 1·4	9·5 3·9	15·5 6·3	35	6 23·8	6 24·8	6 06·3	3·5 1·5	9·5 4·0	15·5 6·6
36	6 09·0	6 10·0	5 52·2	3·6 1·5	9·6 3·9	15·6 6·4	36	6 24·0	6 25·1	6 06·5	3·6 1·5	9·6 4·1	15·6 6·6
37	6 09·3	6 10·3	5 52·4	3·7 1·5	9·7 4·0	15·7 6·4	37	6 24·3	6 25·3	6 06·7	3·7 1·6	9·7 4·1	15·7 6·7
38	6 09·5	6 10·5	5 52·7	3·8 1·6	9·8 4·0	15·8 6·5	38	6 24·5	6 25·6	6 07·0	3·8 1·6	9·8 4·2	15·8 6·7
39	6 09·8	6 10·8	5 52·9	3·9 1·6	9·9 4·0	15·9 6·5	39	6 24·8	6 25·8	6 07·2	3·9 1·7	9·9 4·2	15·9 6·8
40	6 10·0	6 11·0	5 53·1	4·0 1·6	10·0 4·1	16·0 6·5	40	6 25·0	6 26·1	6 07·5	4·0 1·7	10·0 4·3	16·0 6·8
41	6 10·3	6 11·3	5 53·4	4·1 1·7	10·1 4·1	16·1 6·6	41	6 25·3	6 26·3	6 07·7	4·1 1·7	10·1 4·3	16·1 6·8
42	6 10·5	6 11·5	5 53·6	4·2 1·7	10·2 4·2	16·2 6·6	42	6 25·5	6 26·6	6 07·9	4·2 1·8	10·2 4·3	16·2 6·9
43	6 10·8	6 11·8	5 53·9	4·3 1·8	10·3 4·2	16·3 6·7	43	6 25·8	6 26·8	6 08·2	4·3 1·8	10·3 4·4	16·3 6·9
44	6 11·0	6 12·0	5 54·1	4·4 1·8	10·4 4·2	16·4 6·7	44	6 26·0	6 27·1	6 08·4	4·4 1·9	10·4 4·4	16·4 7·0
45	6 11·3	6 12·3	5 54·3	4·5 1·8	10·5 4·3	16·5 6·7	45	6 26·3	6 27·3	6 08·7	4·5 1·9	10·5 4·5	16·5 7·0
46	6 11·5	6 12·5	5 54·6	4·6 1·9	10·6 4·3	16·6 6·8	46	6 26·5	6 27·6	6 08·9	4·6 2·0	10·6 4·5	16·6 7·1
47	6 11·8	6 12·8	5 54·8	4·7 1·9	10·7 4·4	16·7 6·8	47	6 26·8	6 27·8	6 09·1	4·7 2·0	10·7 4·5	16·7 7·1
48	6 12·0	6 13·0	5 55·1	4·8 2·0	10·8 4·4	16·8 6·9	48	6 27·0	6 28·1	6 09·4	4·8 2·0	10·8 4·6	16·8 7·1
49	6 12·3	6 13·3	5 55·3	4·9 2·0	10·9 4·5	16·9 6·9	49	6·27·3	6 28·3	6 09·6	4·9 2·1	10·9 4·6	16·9 7·2
50	6 12·5	6 13·5	5 55·5	5·0 2·0	11·0 4·5	17·0 6·9	50	6 27·5	6 28·6	6 09·8	5·0 2·1	11·0 4·7	17·0 7·2
51	6 12·8	6 13·8	5 55·8	5·1 2·1	11·1 4·5	17·1 7·0	51	6 27·8	6 28·8	6 10·1	5·1 2·2	11·1 4·7	17·1 7·3
52	6 13·0	6 14·0	5 56·0	5·2 2·1	11·2 4·6	17·2 7·0	52	6 28·0	6 29·1	6 10·3	5·2 2·2	11·2 4·8	17·2 7·3
53	6 13·3	6 14·3	5 56·2	5·3 2·2	11·3 4·6	17·3 7·1	53	6 28·3	6 29·3	6 10·6	5·3 2·3	11·3 4·8	17·3 7·4
54	6 13·5	6 14·5	5 56·5	5·4 2·2	11·4 4·7	17·4 7·1	54	6 28·5	6 29·6	6 10·8	5·4 2·3	11·4 4·8	17·4 7·4
55	6 13·8	6 14·8	5 56·7	5·5 2·2	11·5 4·7	17·5 7·1	55	6 28·8	6 29·8	6 11·0	5·5 2·3	11·5 4·9	17·5 7·4
56	6 14·0	6 15·0	5 57·0	5·6 2·3	11·6 4·7	17·6 7·2	56	6 29·0	6 30·1	6 11·3	5·6 2·4	11·6 4·9	17·6 7·5
57	6 14·3	6 15·3	5 57·2	5·7 2·3	11·7 4·8	17·7 7·2	57	6 29·3	6 30·3	6 11·5	5·7 2·4	11·7 5·0	17·7 7·5
58	6 14·5	6 15·5	5 57·4	5·8 2·4	11·8 4·8	17·8 7·3	58	6 29·5	6 30·6	6 11·8	5·8 2·5	11·8 5·0	17·8 7·6
59	6 14·8	6 15·8	5 57·7	5·9 2·4	11·9 4·9	17·9 7·3	59	6 29·8	6 30·8	6 12·0	5·9 2·5	11·9 5·1	17·9 7·6
60	6 15·0	6 16·0	5 57·9	6·0 2·5	12·0 4·9	18·0 7·4	60	6 30·0	6 31·1	6 12·2	6·0 2·6	12·0 5·1	18·0 7·7

26ᵐ   INCREMENTS AND CORRECTIONS   27ᵐ

26 m	SUN PLANETS	ARIES	MOON	v or Corrⁿ / d		v or Corrⁿ / d		v or Corrⁿ / d	
s	° ′	° ′	° ′	′	′	′	′	′	′
00	6 30·0	6 31·1	6 12·2	0·0	0·0	6·0	2·7	12·0	5·3
01	6 30·3	6 31·3	6 12·5	0·1	0·0	6·1	2·7	12·1	5·3
02	6 30·5	6 31·6	6 12·7	0·2	0·1	6·2	2·7	12·2	5·4
03	6 30·8	6 31·8	6 12·9	0·3	0·1	6·3	2·8	12·3	5·4
04	6 31·0	6 32·1	6 13·2	0·4	0·2	6·4	2·8	12·4	5·5
05	6 31·3	6 32·3	6 13·4	0·5	0·2	6·5	2·9	12·5	5·5
06	6 31·5	6 32·6	6 13·7	0·6	0·3	6·6	2·9	12·6	5·6
07	6 31·8	6 32·8	6 13·9	0·7	0·3	6·7	3·0	12·7	5·6
08	6 32·0	6 33·1	6 14·1	0·8	0·4	6·8	3·0	12·8	5·7
09	6 32·3	6 33·3	6 14·4	0·9	0·4	6·9	3·0	12·9	5·7
10	6 32·5	6 33·6	6 14·6	1·0	0·4	7·0	3·1	13·0	5·7
11	6 32·8	6 33·8	6 14·9	1·1	0·5	7·1	3·1	13·1	5·8
12	6 33·0	6 34·1	6 15·1	1·2	0·5	7·2	3·2	13·2	5·8
13	6 33·3	6 34·3	6 15·3	1·3	0·6	7·3	3·2	13·3	5·9
14	6 33·5	6 34·6	6 15·6	1·4	0·6	7·4	3·3	13·4	5·9
15	6 33·8	6 34·8	6 15·8	1·5	0·7	7·5	3·3	13·5	6·0
16	6 34·0	6 35·1	6 16·1	1·6	0·7	7·6	3·4	13·6	6·0
17	6 34·3	6 35·3	6 16·3	1·7	0·8	7·7	3·4	13·7	6·1
18	6 34·5	6 35·6	6 16·5	1·8	0·8	7·8	3·4	13·8	6·1
19	6 34·8	6 35·8	6 16·8	1·9	0·8	7·9	3·5	13·9	6·1
20	6 35·0	6 36·1	6 17·0	2·0	0·9	8·0	3·5	14·0	6·2
21	6 35·3	6 36·3	6 17·2	2·1	0·9	8·1	3·6	14·1	6·2
22	6 35·5	6 36·6	6 17·5	2·2	1·0	8·2	3·6	14·2	6·3
23	6 35·8	6 36·8	6 17·7	2·3	1·0	8·3	3·7	14·3	6·3
24	6 36·0	6 37·1	6 18·0	2·4	1·1	8·4	3·7	14·4	6·4
25	6 36·3	6 37·3	6 18·2	2·5	1·1	8·5	3·8	14·5	6·4
26	6 36·5	6 37·6	6 18·4	2·6	1·1	8·6	3·8	14·6	6·4
27	6 36·8	6 37·8	6 18·7	2·7	1·2	8·7	3·8	14·7	6·5
28	6 37·0	6 38·1	6 18·9	2·8	1·2	8·8	3·9	14·8	6·5
29	6 37·3	6 38·3	6 19·2	2·9	1·3	8·9	3·9	14·9	6·6
30	6 37·5	6 38·6	6 19·4	3·0	1·3	9·0	4·0	15·0	6·6
31	6 37·8	6 38·8	6 19·6	3·1	1·4	9·1	4·0	15·1	6·7
32	6 38·0	6 39·1	6 19·9	3·2	1·4	9·2	4·1	15·2	6·7
33	6 38·3	6 39·3	6 20·1	3·3	1·5	9·3	4·1	15·3	6·8
34	6 38·5	6 39·6	6 20·3	3·4	1·5	9·4	4·2	15·4	6·8
35	6 38·8	6 39·8	6 20·6	3·5	1·5	9·5	4·2	15·5	6·8
36	6 39·0	6 40·1	6 20·8	3·6	1·6	9·6	4·2	15·6	6·9
37	6 39·3	6 40·3	6 21·1	3·7	1·6	9·7	4·3	15·7	6·9
38	6 39·5	6 40·6	6 21·3	3·8	1·7	9·8	4·3	15·8	7·0
39	6 39·8	6 40·8	6 21·5	3·9	1·7	9·9	4·4	15·9	7·0
40	6 40·0	6 41·1	6 21·8	4·0	1·8	10·0	4·4	16·0	7·1
41	6 40·3	6 41·3	6 22·0	4·1	1·8	10·1	4·5	16·1	7·1
42	6 40·5	6 41·6	6 22·3	4·2	1·9	10·2	4·5	16·2	7·2
43	6 40·8	6 41·8	6 22·5	4·3	1·9	10·3	4·5	16·3	7·2
44	6 41·0	6 42·1	6 22·7	4·4	1·9	10·4	4·6	16·4	7·2
45	6 41·3	6 42·3	6 23·0	4·5	2·0	10·5	4·6	16·5	7·3
46	6 41·5	6 42·6	6 23·2	4·6	2·0	10·6	4·7	16·6	7·3
47	6 41·8	6 42·8	6 23·4	4·7	2·1	10·7	4·7	16·7	7·4
48	6 42·0	6 43·1	6 23·7	4·8	2·1	10·8	4·8	16·8	7·4
49	6 42·3	6 43·4	6 23·9	4·9	2·2	10·9	4·8	16·9	7·5
50	6 42·5	6 43·6	6 24·2	5·0	2·2	11·0	4·9	17·0	7·5
51	6 42·8	6 43·9	6 24·4	5·1	2·3	11·1	4·9	17·1	7·6
52	6 43·0	6 44·1	6 24·6	5·2	2·3	11·2	4·9	17·2	7·6
53	6 43·3	6 44·4	6 24·9	5·3	2·3	11·3	5·0	17·3	7·6
54	6 43·5	6 44·6	6 25·1	5·4	2·4	11·4	5·0	17·4	7·7
55	6 43·8	6 44·9	6 25·4	5·5	2·4	11·5	5·1	17·5	7·7
56	6 44·0	6 45·1	6 25·6	5·6	2·5	11·6	5·1	17·6	7·8
57	6 44·3	6 45·4	6 25·8	5·7	2·5	11·7	5·2	17·7	7·8
58	6 44·5	6 45·6	6 26·1	5·8	2·6	11·8	5·2	17·8	7·9
59	6 44·8	6 45·9	6 26·3	5·9	2·6	11·9	5·3	17·9	7·9
60	6 45·0	6 46·1	6 26·6	6·0	2·7	12·0	5·3	18·0	8·0

27 m	SUN PLANETS	ARIES	MOON	v or Corrⁿ / d		v or Corrⁿ / d		v or Corrⁿ / d	
s	° ′	° ′	° ′	′	′	′	′	′	′
00	6 45·0	6 46·1	6 26·6	0·0	0·0	6·0	2·8	12·0	5·5
01	6 45·3	6 46·4	6 26·8	0·1	0·0	6·1	2·8	12·1	5·5
02	6 45·5	6 46·6	6 27·0	0·2	0·1	6·2	2·8	12·2	5·6
03	6 45·8	6 46·9	6 27·3	0·3	0·1	6·3	2·9	12·3	5·6
04	6 46·0	6 47·1	6 27·5	0·4	0·2	6·4	2·9	12·4	5·7
05	6 46·3	6 47·4	6 27·7	0·5	0·2	6·5	3·0	12·5	5·7
06	6 46·5	6 47·6	6 28·0	0·6	0·3	6·6	3·0	12·6	5·8
07	6 46·8	6 47·9	6 28·2	0·7	0·3	6·7	3·1	12·7	5·8
08	6 47·0	6 48·1	6 28·5	0·8	0·4	6·8	3·1	12·8	5·9
09	6 47·3	6 48·4	6 28·7	0·9	0·4	6·9	3·2	12·9	5·9
10	6 47·5	6 48·6	6 28·9	1·0	0·5	7·0	3·2	13·0	6·0
11	6 47·8	6 48·9	6 29·2	1·1	0·5	7·1	3·3	13·1	6·0
12	6 48·0	6 49·1	6 29·4	1·2	0·6	7·2	3·3	13·2	6·1
13	6 48·3	6 49·4	6 29·7	1·3	0·6	7·3	3·3	13·3	6·1
14	6 48·5	6 49·6	6 29·9	1·4	0·6	7·4	3·4	13·4	6·1
15	6 48·8	6 49·9	6 30·1	1·5	0·7	7·5	3·4	13·5	6·2
16	6 49·0	6 50·1	6 30·4	1·6	0·7	7·6	3·5	13·6	6·2
17	6 49·3	6 50·4	6 30·6	1·7	0·8	7·7	3·5	13·7	6·3
18	6 49·5	6 50·6	6 30·8	1·8	0·8	7·8	3·6	13·8	6·3
19	6 49·8	6 50·9	6 31·1	1·9	0·9	7·9	3·6	13·9	6·4
20	6 50·0	6 51·1	6 31·3	2·0	0·9	8·0	3·7	14·0	6·4
21	6 50·3	6 51·4	6 31·6	2·1	1·0	8·1	3·7	14·1	6·5
22	6 50·5	6 51·6	6 31·8	2·2	1·0	8·2	3·8	14·2	6·5
23	6 50·8	6 51·9	6 32·0	2·3	1·1	8·3	3·8	14·3	6·6
24	6 51·0	6 52·1	6 32·3	2·4	1·1	8·4	3·9	14·4	6·6
25	6 51·3	6 52·4	6 32·5	2·5	1·1	8·5	3·9	14·5	6·6
26	6 51·5	6 52·6	6 32·8	2·6	1·2	8·6	3·9	14·6	6·7
27	6 51·8	6 52·9	6 33·0	2·7	1·2	8·7	4·0	14·7	6·7
28	6 52·0	6 53·1	6 33·2	2·8	1·3	8·8	4·0	14·8	6·8
29	6 52·3	6 53·4	6 33·5	2·9	1·3	8·9	4·1	14·9	6·8
30	6 52·5	6 53·6	6 33·7	3·0	1·4	9·0	4·1	15·0	6·9
31	6 52·8	6 53·9	6 33·9	3·1	1·4	9·1	4·2	15·1	6·9
32	6 53·0	6 54·1	6 34·2	3·2	1·5	9·2	4·2	15·2	7·0
33	6 53·3	6 54·4	6 34·4	3·3	1·5	9·3	4·3	15·3	7·0
34	6 53·5	6 54·6	6 34·7	3·4	1·6	9·4	4·3	15·4	7·1
35	6 53·8	6 54·9	6 34·9	3·5	1·6	9·5	4·4	15·5	7·1
36	6 54·0	6 55·1	6 35·1	3·6	1·7	9·6	4·4	15·6	7·2
37	6 54·3	6 55·4	6 35·4	3·7	1·7	9·7	4·4	15·7	7·2
38	6 54·5	6 55·6	6 35·6	3·8	1·7	9·8	4·5	15·8	7·2
39	6 54·8	6 55·9	6 35·9	3·9	1·8	9·9	4·5	15·9	7·3
40	6 55·0	6 56·1	6 36·1	4·0	1·8	10·0	4·6	16·0	7·3
41	6 55·3	6 56·4	6 36·3	4·1	1·9	10·1	4·6	16·1	7·4
42	6 55·5	6 56·6	6 36·6	4·2	1·9	10·2	4·7	16·2	7·4
43	6 55·8	6 56·9	6 36·8	4·3	2·0	10·3	4·7	16·3	7·5
44	6 56·0	6 57·1	6 37·0	4·4	2·0	10·4	4·8	16·4	7·5
45	6 56·3	6 57·4	6 37·3	4·5	2·1	10·5	4·8	16·5	7·6
46	6 56·5	6 57·6	6 37·5	4·6	2·1	10·6	4·9	16·6	7·6
47	6 56·8	6 57·9	6 37·8	4·7	2·2	10·7	4·9	16·7	7·7
48	6 57·0	6 58·1	6 38·0	4·8	2·2	10·8	5·0	16·8	7·7
49	6 57·3	6 58·4	6 38·2	4·9	2·2	10·9	5·0	16·9	7·7
50	6 57·5	6 58·6	6 38·5	5·0	2·3	11·0	5·0	17·0	7·8
51	6 57·8	6 58·9	6 38·7	5·1	2·3	11·1	5·1	17·1	7·8
52	6 58·0	6 59·1	6 39·0	5·2	2·4	11·2	5·1	17·2	7·9
53	6 58·3	6 59·4	6 39·2	5·3	2·4	11·3	5·2	17·3	7·9
54	6 58·5	6 59·6	6 39·4	5·4	2·5	11·4	5·2	17·4	8·0
55	6 58·8	6 59·9	6 39·7	5·5	2·5	11·5	5·3	17·5	8·0
56	6 59·0	7 00·1	6 39·9	5·6	2·6	11·6	5·3	17·6	8·1
57	6 59·3	7 00·4	6 40·2	5·7	2·6	11·7	5·4	17·7	8·1
58	6 59·5	7 00·6	6 40·4	5·8	2·7	11·8	5·4	17·8	8·2
59	6 59·8	7 00·9	6 40·6	5·9	2·7	11·9	5·5	17·9	8·2
60	7 00·0	7 01·1	6 40·9	6·0	2·8	12·0	5·5	18·0	8·3

28ᵐ INCREMENTS AND CORRECTIONS **29ᵐ**

28ᵐ s	SUN PLANETS ° ′	ARIES ° ′	MOON ° ′	v or d ′	Corrⁿ ′	v or d ′	Corrⁿ ′	v or d ′	Corrⁿ ′
00	7 00·0	7 01·1	6 40·9	0·0	0·0	6·0	2·9	12·0	5·7
01	7 00·3	7 01·4	6 41·1	0·1	0·0	6·1	2·9	12·1	5·7
02	7 00·5	7 01·7	6 41·3	0·2	0·1	6·2	2·9	12·2	5·8
03	7 00·8	7 01·9	6 41·6	0·3	0·1	6·3	3·0	12·3	5·8
04	7 01·0	7 02·2	6 41·8	0·4	0·2	6·4	3·0	12·4	5·9
05	7 01·3	7 02·4	6 42·1	0·5	0·2	6·5	3·1	12·5	5·9
06	7 01·5	7 02·7	6 42·3	0·6	0·3	6·6	3·1	12·6	6·0
07	7 01·8	7 02·9	6 42·5	0·7	0·3	6·7	3·2	12·7	6·0
08	7 02·0	7 03·2	6 42·8	0·8	0·4	6·8	3·2	12·8	6·1
09	7 02·3	7 03·4	6 43·0	0·9	0·4	6·9	3·3	12·9	6·1
10	7 02·5	7 03·7	6 43·3	1·0	0·5	7·0	3·3	13·0	6·2
11	7 02·8	7 03·9	6 43·5	1·1	0·5	7·1	3·4	13·1	6·2
12	7 03·0	7 04·2	6 43·7	1·2	0·6	7·2	3·4	13·2	6·3
13	7 03·3	7 04·4	6 44·0	1·3	0·6	7·3	3·5	13·3	6·3
14	7 03·5	7 04·7	6 44·2	1·4	0·7	7·4	3·5	13·4	6·4
15	7 03·8	7 04·9	6 44·4	1·5	0·7	7·5	3·6	13·5	6·4
16	7 04·0	7 05·2	6 44·7	1·6	0·8	7·6	3·6	13·6	6·5
17	7 04·3	7 05·4	6 44·9	1·7	0·8	7·7	3·7	13·7	6·5
18	7 04·5	7 05·7	6 45·2	1·8	0·9	7·8	3·7	13·8	6·6
19	7 04·8	7 05·9	6 45·4	1·9	0·9	7·9	3·8	13·9	6·6
20	7 05·0	7 06·2	6 45·6	2·0	1·0	8·0	3·8	14·0	6·7
21	7 05·3	7 06·4	6 45·9	2·1	1·0	8·1	3·8	14·1	6·7
22	7 05·5	7 06·7	6 46·1	2·2	1·0	8·2	3·9	14·2	6·7
23	7 05·8	7 06·9	6 46·4	2·3	1·1	8·3	3·9	14·3	6·8
24	7 06·0	7 07·2	6 46·6	2·4	1·1	8·4	4·0	14·4	6·8
25	7 06·3	7 07·4	6 46·8	2·5	1·2	8·5	4·0	14·5	6·9
26	7 06·5	7 07·7	6 47·1	2·6	1·2	8·6	4·1	14·6	6·9
27	7 06·8	7 07·9	6 47·3	2·7	1·3	8·7	4·1	14·7	7·0
28	7 07·0	7 08·2	6 47·5	2·8	1·3	8·8	4·2	14·8	7·0
29	7 07·3	7 08·4	6 47·8	2·9	1·4	8·9	4·2	14·9	7·1
30	7 07·5	7 08·7	6 48·0	3·0	1·4	9·0	4·3	15·0	7·1
31	7 07·8	7 08·9	6 48·3	3·1	1·5	9·1	4·3	15·1	7·2
32	7 08·0	7 09·2	6 48·5	3·2	1·5	9·2	4·4	15·2	7·2
33	7 08·3	7 09·4	6 48·7	3·3	1·6	9·3	4·4	15·3	7·3
34	7 08·5	7 09·7	6 49·0	3·4	1·6	9·4	4·5	15·4	7·3
35	7 08·8	7 09·9	6 49·2	3·5	1·7	9·5	4·5	15·5	7·4
36	7 09·0	7 10·2	6 49·5	3·6	1·7	9·6	4·6	15·6	7·4
37	7 09·3	7 10·4	6 49·7	3·7	1·8	9·7	4·6	15·7	7·5
38	7 09·5	7 10·7	6 49·9	3·8	1·8	9·8	4·7	15·8	7·5
39	7 09·8	7 10·9	6 50·2	3·9	1·9	9·9	4·7	15·9	7·6
40	7 10·0	7 11·2	6 50·4	4·0	1·9	10·0	4·8	16·0	7·6
41	7 10·3	7 11·4	6 50·6	4·1	1·9	10·1	4·8	16·1	7·6
42	7 10·5	7 11·7	6 50·9	4·2	2·0	10·2	4·8	16·2	7·7
43	7 10·8	7 11·9	6 51·1	4·3	2·0	10·3	4·9	16·3	7·7
44	7 11·0	7 12·2	6 51·4	4·4	2·1	10·4	4·9	16·4	7·8
45	7 11·3	7 12·4	6 51·6	4·5	2·1	10·5	5·0	16·5	7·8
46	7 11·5	7 12·7	6 51·8	4·6	2·2	10·6	5·0	16·6	7·9
47	7 11·8	7 12·9	6 52·1	4·7	2·2	10·7	5·1	16·7	7·9
48	7 12·0	7 13·2	6 52·3	4·8	2·3	10·8	5·1	16·8	8·0
49	7 12·3	7 13·4	6 52·6	4·9	2·3	10·9	5·2	16·9	8·0
50	7 12·5	7 13·7	6 52·8	5·0	2·4	11·0	5·2	17·0	8·1
51	7 12·8	7 13·9	6 53·0	5·1	2·4	11·1	5·3	17·1	8·1
52	7 13·0	7 14·2	6 53·3	5·2	2·5	11·2	5·3	17·2	8·2
53	7 13·3	7 14·4	6 53·5	5·3	2·5	11·3	5·4	17·3	8·2
54	7 13·5	7 14·7	6 53·8	5·4	2·6	11·4	5·4	17·4	8·3
55	7 13·8	7 14·9	6 54·0	5·5	2·6	11·5	5·5	17·5	8·3
56	7 14·0	7 15·2	6 54·2	5·6	2·7	11·6	5·5	17·6	8·4
57	7 14·3	7 15·4	6 54·5	5·7	2·7	11·7	5·6	17·7	8·4
58	7 14·5	7 15·7	6 54·7	5·8	2·8	11·8	5·6	17·8	8·5
59	7 14·8	7 15·9	6 54·9	5·9	2·8	11·9	5·7	17·9	8·5
60	7 15·0	7 16·2	6 55·2	6·0	2·9	12·0	5·7	18·0	8·6

29ᵐ s	SUN PLANETS ° ′	ARIES ° ′	MOON ° ′	v or d ′	Corrⁿ ′	v or d ′	Corrⁿ ′	v or d ′	Corrⁿ ′
00	7 15·0	7 16·2	6 55·2	0·0	0·0	6·0	3·0	12·0	5·9
01	7 15·3	7 16·4	6 55·4	0·1	0·0	6·1	3·0	12·1	5·9
02	7 15·5	7 16·7	6 55·7	0·2	0·1	6·2	3·0	12·2	6·0
03	7 15·8	7 16·9	6 55·9	0·3	0·1	6·3	3·1	12·3	6·0
04	7 16·0	7 17·2	6 56·1	0·4	0·2	6·4	3·1	12·4	6·1
05	7 16·3	7 17·4	6 56·4	0·5	0·2	6·5	3·2	12·5	6·1
06	7 16·5	7 17·7	6 56·6	0·6	0·3	6·6	3·2	12·6	6·2
07	7 16·8	7 17·9	6 56·9	0·7	0·3	6·7	3·3	12·7	6·2
08	7 17·0	7 18·2	6 57·1	0·8	0·4	6·8	3·3	12·8	6·3
09	7 17·3	7 18·4	6 57·3	0·9	0·4	6·9	3·4	12·9	6·3
10	7 17·5	7 18·7	6 57·6	1·0	0·5	7·0	3·4	13·0	6·4
11	7 17·8	7 18·9	6 57·8	1·1	0·5	7·1	3·5	13·1	6·4
12	7 18·0	7 19·2	6 58·0	1·2	0·6	7·2	3·5	13·2	6·5
13	7 18·3	7 19·4	6 58·3	1·3	0·6	7·3	3·6	13·3	6·5
14	7 18·5	7 19·7	6 58·5	1·4	0·7	7·4	3·6	13·4	6·6
15	7 18·8	7 20·0	6 58·8	1·5	0·7	7·5	3·7	13·5	6·6
16	7 19·0	7 20·2	6 59·0	1·6	0·8	7·6	3·7	13·6	6·7
17	7 19·3	7 20·5	6 59·2	1·7	0·8	7·7	3·8	13·7	6·7
18	7 19·5	7 20·7	6 59·5	1·8	0·9	7·8	3·8	13·8	6·8
19	7 19·8	7 21·0	6 59·7	1·9	0·9	7·9	3·9	13·9	6·8
20	7 20·0	7 21·2	7 00·0	2·0	1·0	8·0	3·9	14·0	6·9
21	7 20·3	7 21·5	7 00·2	2·1	1·0	8·1	4·0	14·1	6·9
22	7 20·5	7 21·7	7 00·4	2·2	1·1	8·2	4·0	14·2	7·0
23	7 20·8	7 22·0	7 00·7	2·3	1·1	8·3	4·1	14·3	7·0
24	7 21·0	7 22·2	7 00·9	2·4	1·2	8·4	4·1	14·4	7·1
25	7 21·3	7 22·5	7 01·1	2·5	1·2	8·5	4·2	14·5	7·1
26	7 21·5	7 22·7	7 01·4	2·6	1·3	8·6	4·2	14·6	7·2
27	7 21·8	7 23·0	7 01·6	2·7	1·3	8·7	4·3	14·7	7·2
28	7 22·0	7 23·2	7 01·9	2·8	1·4	8·8	4·3	14·8	7·3
29	7 22·3	7 23·5	7 02·1	2·9	1·4	8·9	4·4	14·9	7·3
30	7 22·5	7 23·7	7 02·3	3·0	1·5	9·0	4·4	15·0	7·4
31	7 22·8	7 24·0	7 02·6	3·1	1·5	9·1	4·5	15·1	7·4
32	7 23·0	7 24·2	7 02·8	3·2	1·6	9·2	4·5	15·2	7·5
33	7 23·3	7 24·5	7 03·1	3·3	1·6	9·3	4·6	15·3	7·5
34	7 23·5	7 24·7	7 03·3	3·4	1·7	9·4	4·6	15·4	7·6
35	7 23·8	7 25·0	7 03·5	3·5	1·7	9·5	4·7	15·5	7·6
36	7 24·0	7 25·2	7 03·8	3·6	1·8	9·6	4·7	15·6	7·7
37	7 24·3	7 25·5	7 04·0	3·7	1·8	9·7	4·8	15·7	7·7
38	7 24·5	7 25·7	7 04·3	3·8	1·9	9·8	4·8	15·8	7·8
39	7 24·8	7 26·0	7 04·5	3·9	1·9	9·9	4·9	15·9	7·8
40	7 25·0	7 26·2	7 04·7	4·0	2·0	10·0	4·9	16·0	7·9
41	7 25·3	7 26·5	7 05·0	4·1	2·0	10·1	5·0	16·1	7·9
42	7 25·5	7 26·7	7 05·2	4·2	2·1	10·2	5·0	16·2	8·0
43	7 25·8	7 27·0	7 05·4	4·3	2·1	10·3	5·1	16·3	8·0
44	7 26·0	7 27·2	7 05·7	4·4	2·2	10·4	5·1	16·4	8·1
45	7 26·3	7 27·5	7 05·9	4·5	2·2	10·5	5·2	16·5	8·1
46	7 26·5	7 27·7	7 06·2	4·6	2·3	10·6	5·2	16·6	8·2
47	7 26·8	7 28·0	7 06·4	4·7	2·3	10·7	5·3	16·7	8·2
48	7 27·0	7 28·2	7 06·6	4·8	2·4	10·8	5·3	16·8	8·3
49	7 27·3	7 28·5	7 06·9	4·9	2·4	10·9	5·4	16·9	8·3
50	7 27·5	7 28·7	7 07·1	5·0	2·5	11·0	5·4	17·0	8·4
51	7 27·8	7 29·0	7 07·4	5·1	2·5	11·1	5·5	17·1	8·4
52	7 28·0	7 29·2	7 07·6	5·2	2·6	11·2	5·5	17·2	8·5
53	7 28·3	7 29·5	7 07·8	5·3	2·6	11·3	5·6	17·3	8·5
54	7 28·5	7 29·7	7 08·1	5·4	2·7	11·4	5·6	17·4	8·6
55	7 28·8	7 30·0	7 08·3	5·5	2·7	11·5	5·7	17·5	8·6
56	7 29·0	7 30·2	7 08·5	5·6	2·8	11·6	5·7	17·6	8·7
57	7 29·3	7 30·5	7 08·8	5·7	2·8	11·7	5·8	17·7	8·7
58	7 29·5	7 30·7	7 09·0	5·8	2·9	11·8	5·8	17·8	8·8
59	7 29·8	7 31·0	7 09·3	5·9	2·9	11·9	5·9	17·9	8·8
60	7 30·0	7 31·2	7 09·5	6·0	3·0	12·0	5·9	18·0	8·9

INCREMENTS AND CORRECTIONS

30ᵐ   **31ᵐ**

30ᵐ s	SUN PLANETS	ARIES	MOON	v or d	Corrⁿ	v or d	Corrⁿ	v or d	Corrⁿ
00	7 30.0	7 31.2	7 09.5	0.0	0.0	6.0	3.1	12.0	6.1
01	7 30.3	7 31.5	7 09.7	0.1	0.1	6.1	3.1	12.1	6.2
02	7 30.5	7 31.7	7 10.0	0.2	0.1	6.2	3.2	12.2	6.2
03	•7 30.8	7 32.0	7 10.2	0.3	0.2	6.3	3.2	12.3	6.3
04	7 31.0	7 32.2	7 10.5	0.4	0.2	6.4	3.3	12.4	6.3
05	7 31.3	7 32.5	7 10.7	0.5	0.3	6.5	3.3	12.5	6.4
06	7 31.5	7 32.7	7 10.9	0.6	0.3	6.6	3.4	12.6	6.4
07	7 31.8	7 33.0	7 11.2	0.7	0.4	6.7	3.4	12.7	6.5
08	7 32.0	7 33.2	7 11.4	0.8	0.4	6.8	3.5	12.8	6.5
09	7 32.3	7 33.5	7 11.6	0.9	0.5	6.9	3.5	12.9	6.6
10	7 32.5	7 33.7	7 11.9	1.0	0.5	7.0	3.6	13.0	6.6
11	7 32.8	7 34.0	7 12.1	1.1	0.6	7.1	3.6	13.1	6.7
12	7 33.0	7 34.2	7 12.4	1.2	0.6	7.2	3.7	13.2	6.7
13	7 33.3	7 34.5	7 12.6	1.3	0.7	7.3	3.7	13.3	6.8
14	7 33.5	7 34.7	7 12.8	1.4	0.7	7.4	3.8	13.4	6.8
15	7 33.8	7 35.0	7 13.1	1.5	0.8	7.5	3.8	13.5	6.9
16	7 34.0	7 35.2	7 13.3	1.6	0.8	7.6	3.9	13.6	6.9
17	7 34.3	7 35.5	7 13.6	1.7	0.9	7.7	3.9	13.7	7.0
18	7 34.5	7 35.7	7 13.8	1.8	0.9	7.8	4.0	13.8	7.0
19	7 34.8	7 36.0	7 14.0	1.9	1.0	7.9	4.0	13.9	7.1
20	7 35.0	7 36.2	7 14.3	2.0	1.0	8.0	4.1	14.0	7.1
21	7 35.3	7 36.5	7 14.5	2.1	1.1	8.1	4.1	14.1	7.2
22	7 35.5	7 36.7	7 14.7	2.2	1.1	8.2	4.2	14.2	7.2
23	7 35.8	7 37.0	7 15.0	2.3	1.2	8.3	4.2	14.3	7.3
24	7 36.0	7 37.2	7 15.2	2.4	1.2	8.4	4.3	14.4	7.3
25	7 36.3	7 37.5	7 15.5	2.5	1.3	8.5	4.3	14.5	7.4
26	7 36.5	7 37.7	7 15.7	2.6	1.3	8.6	4.4	14.6	7.4
27	7 36.8	7 38.0	7 15.9	2.7	1.4	8.7	4.4	14.7	7.5
28	7 37.0	7 38.3	7 16.2	2.8	1.4	8.8	4.5	14.8	7.5
29	7 37.3	7 38.5	7 16.4	2.9	1.5	8.9	4.5	14.9	7.6
30	7 37.5	7 38.8	7 16.7	3.0	1.5	9.0	4.6	15.0	7.6
31	7 37.8	7 39.0	7 16.9	3.1	1.6	9.1	4.6	15.1	7.7
32	7 38.0	7 39.3	7 17.1	3.2	1.6	9.2	4.7	15.2	7.7
33	7 38.3	7 39.5	7 17.4	3.3	1.7	9.3	4.7	15.3	7.8
34	7 38.5	7 39.8	7 17.6	3.4	1.7	9.4	4.8	15.4	7.8
35	7 38.8	7 40.0	7 17.9	3.5	1.8	9.5	4.8	15.5	7.9
36	7 39.0	7 40.3	7 18.1	3.6	1.8	9.6	4.9	15.6	7.9
37	7 39.3	7 40.5	7 18.3	3.7	1.9	9.7	4.9	15.7	8.0
38	7 39.5	7 40.8	7 18.6	3.8	1.9	9.8	5.0	15.8	8.0
39	7 39.8	7 41.0	7 18.8	3.9	2.0	9.9	5.0	15.9	8.1
40	7 40.0	7 41.3	7 19.0	4.0	2.0	10.0	5.1	16.0	8.1
41	7 40.3	7 41.5	7 19.3	4.1	2.1	10.1	5.1	16.1	8.2
42	7 40.5	7 41.8	7 19.5	4.2	2.1	10.2	5.2	16.2	8.2
43	7 40.8	7 42.0	7 19.8	4.3	2.2	10.3	5.2	16.3	8.3
44	7 41.0	7 42.3	7 20.0	4.4	2.2	10.4	5.3	16.4	8.3
45	7 41.3	7 42.5	7 20.2	4.5	2.3	10.5	5.3	16.5	8.4
46	7 41.5	7 42.8	7 20.5	4.6	2.3	10.6	5.4	16.6	8.4
47	7 41.8	7 43.0	7 20.7	4.7	2.4	10.7	5.4	16.7	8.5
48	7 42.0	7 43.3	7 21.0	4.8	2.4	10.8	5.5	16.8	8.5
49	7 42.3	7 43.5	7 21.2	4.9	2.5	10.9	5.5	16.9	8.6
50	7 42.5	7 43.8	7 21.4	5.0	2.5	11.0	5.6	17.0	8.6
51	7 42.8	7 44.0	7 21.7	5.1	2.6	11.1	5.6	17.1	8.7
52	7 43.0	7 44.3	7 21.9	5.2	2.6	11.2	5.7	17.2	8.7
53	7 43.3	7 44.5	7 22.1	5.3	2.7	11.3	5.7	17.3	8.8
54	7 43.5	7 44.8	7 22.4	5.4	2.7	11.4	5.8	17.4	8.8
55	7 43.8	7 45.0	7 22.6	5.5	2.8	11.5	5.8	17.5	8.9
56	7 44.0	7 45.3	7 22.9	5.6	2.8	11.6	5.9	17.6	8.9
57	7 44.3	7 45.5	7 23.1	5.7	2.9	11.7	5.9	17.7	9.0
58	7 44.5	7 45.8	7 23.3	5.8	2.9	11.8	6.0	17.8	9.0
59	7 44.8	7 46.0	7 23.6	5.9	3.0	11.9	6.0	17.9	9.1
60	7 45.0	7 46.3	7 23.8	6.0	3.1	12.0	6.1	18.0	9.2

31ᵐ s	SUN PLANETS	ARIES	MOON	v or d	Corrⁿ	v or d	Corrⁿ	v or d	Corrⁿ
00	7 45.0	7 46.3	7 23.8	0.0	0.0	6.0	3.2	12.0	6.3
01	7 45.3	7 46.5	7 24.1	0.1	0.1	6.1	3.2	12.1	6.4
02	7 45.5	7 46.8	7 24.3	0.2	0.1	6.2	3.3	12.2	6.4
03	7 45.8	7 47.0	7 24.5	0.3	0.2	6.3	3.3	12.3	6.5
04	7 46.0	7 47.3	7 24.8	0.4	0.2	6.4	3.4	12.4	6.5
05	7 46.3	7 47.5	7 25.0	0.5	0.3	6.5	3.4	12.5	6.6
06	7 46.5	7 47.8	7 25.2	0.6	0.3	6.6	3.5	12.6	6.6
07	7 46.8	7 48.0	7 25.5	0.7	0.4	6.7	3.5	12.7	6.7
08	7 47.0	7 48.3	7 25.7	0.8	0.4	6.8	3.6	12.8	6.7
09	7 47.3	7 48.5	7 26.0	0.9	0.5	6.9	3.6	12.9	6.8
10	7 47.5	7 48.8	7 26.2	1.0	0.5	7.0	3.7	13.0	6.8
11	7 47.8	7 49.0	7 26.4	1.1	0.6	7.1	3.7	13.1	6.9
12	7 48.0	7 49.3	7 26.7	1.2	0.6	7.2	3.8	13.2	6.9
13	7 48.3	7 49.5	7 26.9	1.3	0.7	7.3	3.8	13.3	7.0
14	7 48.5	7 49.8	7 27.2	1.4	0.7	7.4	3.9	13.4	7.0
15	7 48.8	7 50.0	7 27.4	1.5	0.8	7.5	3.9	13.5	7.1
16	7 49.0	7 50.3	7 27.6	1.6	0.8	7.6	4.0	13.6	7.1
17	7 49.3	7 50.5	7 27.9	1.7	0.9	7.7	4.0	13.7	7.2
18	7 49.5	7 50.8	7 28.1	1.8	0.9	7.8	4.1	13.8	7.2
19	7 49.8	7 51.0	7 28.4	1.9	1.0	7.9	4.1	13.9	7.3
20	7 50.0	7 51.3	7 28.6	2.0	1.1	8.0	4.2	14.0	7.4
21	7 50.3	7 51.5	7 28.8	2.1	1.1	8.1	4.3	14.1	7.4
22	7 50.5	7 51.8	7 29.1	2.2	1.2	8.2	4.3	14.2	7.5
23	7 50.8	7 52.0	7 29.3	2.3	1.2	8.3	4.4	14.3	7.5
24	7 51.0	7 52.3	7 29.5	2.4	1.3	8.4	4.4	14.4	7.6
25	7 51.3	7 52.5	7 29.8	2.5	1.3	8.5	4.5	14.5	7.6
26	7 51.5	7 52.8	7 30.0	2.6	1.4	8.6	4.5	14.6	7.7
27	7 51.8	7 53.0	7 30.3	2.7	1.4	8.7	4.6	14.7	7.7
28	7 52.0	7 53.3	7 30.5	2.8	1.5	8.8	4.6	14.8	7.8
29	7 52.3	7 53.5	7 30.7	2.9	1.5	8.9	4.7	14.9	7.8
30	7 52.5	7 53.8	7 31.0	3.0	1.6	9.0	4.7	15.0	7.9
31	7 52.8	7 54.0	7 31.2	3.1	1.6	9.1	4.8	15.1	7.9
32	7 53.0	7 54.3	7 31.5	3.2	1.7	9.2	4.8	15.2	8.0
33	7 53.3	7 54.5	7 31.7	3.3	1.7	9.3	4.9	15.3	8.0
34	7 53.5	7 54.8	7 31.9	3.4	1.8	9.4	4.9	15.4	8.1
35	7 53.8	7 55.0	7 32.2	3.5	1.8	9.5	5.0	15.5	8.1
36	7 54.0	7 55.3	7 32.4	3.6	1.9	9.6	5.0	15.6	8.2
37	7 54.3	7 55.5	7 32.6	3.7	1.9	9.7	5.1	15.7	8.2
38	7 54.5	7 55.8	7 32.9	3.8	2.0	9.8	5.1	15.8	8.3
39	7 54.8	7 56.0	7 33.1	3.9	2.0	9.9	5.2	15.9	8.3
40	7 55.0	7 56.3	7 33.4	4.0	2.1	10.0	5.3	16.0	8.4
41	7 55.3	7 56.6	7 33.6	4.1	2.2	10.1	5.3	16.1	8.5
42	7 55.5	7 56.8	7 33.8	4.2	2.2	10.2	5.4	16.2	8.5
43	7 55.8	7 57.1	7 34.1	4.3	2.3	10.3	5.4	16.3	8.6
44	7 56.0	7 57.3	7 34.3	4.4	2.3	10.4	5.5	16.4	8.6
45	7 56.3	7 57.6	7 34.6	4.5	2.4	10.5	5.5	16.5	8.7
46	7 56.5	7 57.8	7 34.8	4.6	2.4	10.6	5.6	16.6	8.7
47	7 56.8	7 58.1	7 35.0	4.7	2.5	10.7	5.6	16.7	8.8
48	7 57.0	7 58.3	7 35.3	4.8	2.5	10.8	5.7	16.8	8.8
49	7 57.3	7 58.6	7 35.5	4.9	2.6	10.9	5.7	16.9	8.9
50	7 57.5	7 58.8	7 35.7	5.0	2.6	11.0	5.8	17.0	8.9
51	7 57.8	7 59.1	7 36.0	5.1	2.7	11.1	5.8	17.1	9.0
52	7 58.0	7 59.3	7 36.2	5.2	2.7	11.2	5.9	17.2	9.0
53	7 58.3	7 59.6	7 36.5	5.3	2.8	11.3	5.9	17.3	9.1
54	7 58.5	7 59.8	7 36.7	5.4	2.8	11.4	6.0	17.4	9.1
55	7 58.8	8 00.1	7 36.9	5.5	2.9	11.5	6.0	17.5	9.2
56	7 59.0	8 00.3	7 37.2	5.6	2.9	11.6	6.1	17.6	9.2
57	7 59.3	8 00.6	7 37.4	5.7	3.0	11.7	6.1	17.7	9.3
58	7 59.5	8 00.8	7 37.7	5.8	3.0	11.8	6.2	17.8	9.3
59	7 59.8	8 01.1	7 37.9	5.9	3.1	11.9	6.2	17.9	9.4
60	8 00.0	8 01.3	7 38.1	6.0	3.2	12.0	6.3	18.0	9.5

32ᵐ   INCREMENTS AND CORRECTIONS   33ᵐ

32ᵐ s	SUN PLANETS	ARIES	MOON	v or Corrⁿ d	v or Corrⁿ d	v or Corrⁿ d	33ᵐ s	SUN PLANETS	ARIES	MOON	v or Corrⁿ d	v or Corrⁿ d	v or Corrⁿ d
00	8 00·0	8 01·3	7 38·1	0·0 0·0	6·0 3·3	12·0 6·5	00	8 15·0	8 16·4	7 52·5	0·0 0·0	6·0 3·4	12·0 6·7
01	8 00·3	8 01·6	7 38·4	0·1 0·1	6·1 3·3	12·1 6·6	01	8 15·3	8 16·6	7 52·7	0·1 0·1	6·1 3·4	12·1 6·8
02	8 00·5	8 01·8	7 38·6	0·2 0·1	6·2 3·4	12·2 6·6	02	8 15·5	8 16·9	7 52·9	0·2 0·1	6·2 3·5	12·2 6·8
03	8 00·8	8 02·1	7 38·8	0·3 0·2	6·3 3·4	12·3 6·7	03	8 15·8	8 17·1	7 53·2	0·3 0·2	6·3 3·5	12·3 6·9
04	8 01·0	8 02·3	7 39·1	0·4 0·2	6·4 3·5	12·4 6·7	04	8 16·0	8 17·4	7 53·4	0·4 0·2	6·4 3·6	12·4 6·9
05	8 01·3	8 02·6	7 39·3	0·5 0·3	6·5 3·5	12·5 6·8	05	8 16·3	8 17·6	7 53·6	0·5 0·3	6·5 3·6	12·5 7·0
06	8 01·5	8 02·8	7 39·6	0·6 0·3	6·6 3·6	12·6 6·8	06	8 16·5	8 17·9	7 53·9	0·6 0·3	6·6 3·7	12·6 7·0
07	8 01·8	8 03·1	7 39·8	0·7 0·4	6·7 3·6	12·7 6·9	07	8 16·8	8 18·1	7 54·1	0·7 0·4	6·7 3·7	12·7 7·1
08	8 02·0	8 03·3	7 40·0	0·8 0·4	6·8 3·7	12·8 6·9	08	8 17·0	8 18·4	7 54·4	0·8 0·4	6·8 3·8	12·8 7·1
09	8 02·3	8 03·6	7 40·3	0·9 0·5	6·9 3·7	12·9 7·0	09	8 17·3	8 18·6	7 54·6	0·9 0·5	6·9 3·9	12·9 7·2
10	8 02·5	8 03·8	7 40·5	1·0 0·5	7·0 3·8	13·0 7·0	10	8 17·5	8 18·9	7 54·8	1·0 0·6	7·0 3·9	13·0 7·3
11	8 02·8	8 04·1	7 40·8	1·1 0·6	7·1 3·8	13·1 7·1	11	8 17·8	8 19·1	7 55·1	1·1 0·6	7·1 4·0	13·1 7·3
12	8 03·0	8 04·3	7 41·0	1·2 0·7	7·2 3·9	13·2 7·2	12	8 18·0	8 19·4	7 55·3	1·2 0·7	7·2 4·0	13·2 7·4
13	8 03·3	8 04·6	7 41·2	1·3 0·7	7·3 4·0	13·3 7·2	13	8 18·3	8 19·6	7 55·6	1·3 0·7	7·3 4·1	13·3 7·4
14	8 03·5	8 04·8	7 41·5	1·4 0·8	7·4 4·0	13·4 7·3	14	8 18·5	8 19·9	7 55·8	1·4 0·8	7·4 4·1	13·4 7·5
15	8 03·8	8 05·1	7 41·7	1·5 0·8	7·5 4·1	13·5 7·3	15	8 18·8	8 20·1	7 56·0	1·5 0·8	7·5 4·2	13·5 7·5
16	8 04·0	8 05·3	7 42·0	1·6 0·9	7·6 4·1	13·6 7·4	16	8 19·0	8 20·4	7 56·3	1·6 0·9	7·6 4·2	13·6 7·6
17	8 04·3	8 05·6	7 42·2	1·7 0·9	7·7 4·2	13·7 7·4	17	8 19·3	8 20·6	7 56·5	1·7 0·9	7·7 4·3	13·7 7·6
18	8 04·5	8 05·8	7 42·4	1·8 1·0	7·8 4·2	13·8 7·5	18	8 19·5	8 20·9	7 56·7	1·8 1·0	7·8 4·4	13·8 7·7
19	8 04·8	8 06·1	7 42·7	1·9 1·0	7·9 4·3	13·9 7·5	19	8 19·8	8 21·1	7 57·0	1·9 1·1	7·9 4·4	13·9 7·8
20	8 05·0	8 06·3	7 42·9	2·0 1·1	8·0 4·3	14·0 7·6	20	8 20·0	8 21·4	7 57·2	2·0 1·1	8·0 4·5	14·0 7·8
21	8 05·3	8 06·6	7 43·1	2·1 1·1	8·1 4·4	14·1 7·6	21	8 20·3	8 21·6	7 57·5	2·1 1·2	8·1 4·5	14·1 7·9
22	8 05·5	8 06·8	7 43·4	2·2 1·2	8·2 4·4	14·2 7·7	22	8 20·5	8 21·9	7 57·7	2·2 1·2	8·2 4·6	14·2 7·9
23	8 05·8	8 07·1	7 43·6	2·3 1·2	8·3 4·5	14·3 7·7	23	8 20·8	8 22·1	7 57·9	2·3 1·3	8·3 4·6	14·3 8·0
24	8 06·0	8 07·3	7 43·9	2·4 1·3	8·4 4·6	14·4 7·8	24	8 21·0	8 22·4	7 58·2	2·4 1·3	8·4 4·7	14·4 8·0
25	8 06·3	8 07·6	7 44·1	2·5 1·4	8·5 4·6	14·5 7·9	25	8 21·3	8 22·6	7 58·4	2·5 1·4	8·5 4·7	14·5 8·1
26	8 06·5	8 07·8	7 44·3	2·6 1·4	8·6 4·7	14·6 7·9	26	8 21·5	8 22·9	7 58·7	2·6 1·5	8·6 4·8	14·6 8·2
27	8 06·8	8 08·1	7 44·6	2·7 1·5	8·7 4·7	14·7 8·0	27	8 21·8	8 23·1	7 58·9	2·7 1·5	8·7 4·9	14·7 8·2
28	8 07·0	8 08·3	7 44·8	2·8 1·5	8·8 4·8	14·8 8·0	28	8 22·0	8 23·4	7 59·1	2·8 1·6	8·8 4·9	14·8 8·3
29	8 07·3	8 08·6	7 45·1	2·9 1·6	8·9 4·8	14·9 8·1	29	8 22·3	8 23·6	7 59·4	2·9 1·6	8·9 5·0	14·9 8·3
30	8 07·5	8 08·8	7 45·3	3·0 1·6	9·0 4·9	15·0 8·1	30	8 22·5	8 23·9	7 59·6	3·0 1·7	9·0 5·0	15·0 8·4
31	8 07·8	8 09·1	7 45·5	3·1 1·7	9·1 4·9	15·1 8·2	31	8 22·8	8 24·1	7 59·8	3·1 1·7	9·1 5·1	15·1 8·4
32	8 08·0	8 09·3	7 45·8	3·2 1·7	9·2 5·0	15·2 8·2	32	8 23·0	8 24·4	8 00·1	3·2 1·8	9·2 5·1	15·2 8·5
33	8 08·3	8 09·6	7 46·0	3·3 1·8	9·3 5·0	15·3 8·3	33	8 23·3	8 24·6	8 00·3	3·3 1·8	9·3 5·2	15·3 8·5
34	8 08·5	8 09·8	7 46·2	3·4 1·8	9·4 5·1	15·4 8·3	34	8 23·5	8 24·9	8 00·6	3·4 1·9	9·4 5·2	15·4 8·6
35	8 08·8	8 10·1	7 46·5	3·5 1·9	9·5 5·1	15·5 8·4	35	8 23·8	8 25·1	8 00·8	3·5 2·0	9·5 5·3	15·5 8·7
36	8 09·0	8 10·3	7 46·7	3·6 2·0	9·6 5·2	15·6 8·5	36	8 24·0	8 25·4	8 01·0	3·6 2·0	9·6 5·4	15·6 8·7
37	8 09·3	8 10·6	7 47·0	3·7 2·0	9·7 5·3	15·7 8·5	37	8 24·3	8 25·6	8 01·3	3·7 2·1	9·7 5·4	15·7 8·8
38	8 09·5	8 10·8	7 47·2	3·8 2·1	9·8 5·3	15·8 8·6	38	8 24·5	8 25·9	8 01·5	3·8 2·1	9·8 5·5	15·8 8·8
39	8 09·8	8 11·1	7 47·4	3·9 2·1	9·9 5·4	15·9 8·6	39	8 24·8	8 26·1	8 01·8	3·9 2·2	9·9 5·5	15·9 8·9
40	8 10·0	8 11·3	7 47·7	4·0 2·2	10·0 5·4	16·0 8·7	40	8 25·0	8 26·4	8 02·0	4·0 2·2	10·0 5·6	16·0 8·9
41	8 10·3	8 11·6	7 47·9	4·1 2·2	10·1 5·5	16·1 8·7	41	8 25·3	8 26·6	8 02·2	4·1 2·3	10·1 5·6	16·1 9·0
42	8 10·5	8 11·8	7 48·2	4·2 2·3	10·2 5·5	16·2 8·8	42	8 25·5	8 26·9	8 02·5	4·2 2·3	10·2 5·7	16·2 9·0
43	8 10·8	8 12·1	7 48·4	4·3 2·3	10·3 5·6	16·3 8·8	43	8 25·8	8 27·1	8 02·7	4·3 2·4	10·3 5·8	16·3 9·1
44	8 11·0	8 12·3	7 48·6	4·4 2·4	10·4 5·6	16·4 8·9	44	8 26·0	8 27·4	8 02·9	4·4 2·5	10·4 5·8	16·4 9·2
45	8 11·3	8 12·6	7 48·9	4·5 2·4	10·5 5·7	16·5 8·9	45	8 26·3	8 27·6	8 03·2	4·5 2·5	10·5 5·9	16·5 9·2
46	8 11·5	8 12·8	7 49·1	4·6 2·5	10·6 5·7	16·6 9·0	46	8 26·5	8 27·9	8 03·4	4·6 2·6	10·6 5·9	16·6 9·3
47	8 11·8	8 13·1	7 49·3	4·7 2·5	10·7 5·8	16·7 9·0	47	8 26·8	8 28·1	8 03·7	4·7 2·6	10·7 6·0	16·7 9·3
48	8 12·0	8 13·3	7 49·6	4·8 2·6	10·8 5·9	16·8 9·1	48	8 27·0	8 28·4	8 03·9	4·8 2·7	10·8 6·0	16·8 9·4
49	8 12·3	8 13·6	7 49·8	4·9 2·7	10·9 5·9	16·9 9·2	49	8 27·3	8 28·6	8 04·1	4·9 2·7	10·9 6·1	16·9 9·4
50	8 12·5	8 13·8	7 50·1	5·0 2·7	11·0 6·0	17·0 9·2	50	8 27·5	8 28·9	8 04·4	5·0 2·8	11·0 6·1	17·0 9·5
51	8 12·8	8 14·1	7 50·3	5·1 2·8	11·1 6·0	17·1 9·3	51	8 27·8	8 29·1	8 04·6	5·1 2·8	11·1 6·2	17·1 9·5
52	8 13·0	8 14·3	7 50·5	5·2 2·8	11·2 6·1	17·2 9·3	52	8 28·0	8 29·4	8 04·9	5·2 2·9	11·2 6·3	17·2 9·6
53	8 13·3	8 14·6	7 50·8	5·3 2·9	11·3 6·1	17·3 9·4	53	8 28·3	8 29·6	8 05·1	5·3 3·0	11·3 6·3	17·3 9·7
54	8 13·5	8 14·9	7 51·0	5·4 2·9	11·4 6·2	17·4 9·4	54	8 28·5	8 29·9	8 05·3	5·4 3·0	11·4 6·4	17·4 9·7
55	8 13·8	8 15·1	7 51·3	5·5 3·0	11·5 6·2	17·5 9·5	55	8 28·8	8 30·1	8 05·6	5·5 3·1	11·5 6·4	17·5 9·8
56	8 14·0	8 15·4	7 51·5	5·6 3·0	11·6 6·3	17·6 9·5	56	8 29·0	8 30·4	8 05·8	5·6 3·1	11·6 6·5	17·6 9·8
57	8 14·3	8 15·6	7 51·7	5·7 3·1	11·7 6·3	17·7 9·6	57	8 29·3	8 30·6	8 06·1	5·7 3·2	11·7 6·5	17·7 9·9
58	8 14·5	8 15·9	7 52·0	5·8 3·1	11·8 6·4	17·8 9·6	58	8 29·5	8 30·9	8 06·3	5·8 3·2	11·8 6·6	17·8 9·9
59	8 14·8	8 16·1	7 52·2	5·9 3·2	11·9 6·4	17·9 9·7	59	8 29·8	8 31·1	8 06·5	5·9 3·3	11·9 6·6	17·9 10·0
60	8 15·0	8 16·4	7 52·5	6·0 3·3	12·0 6·5	18·0 9·8	60	8 30·0	8 31·4	8 06·8	6·0 3·4	12·0 6·7	18·0 10·1

34ᵐ   INCREMENTS AND CORRECTIONS   35ᵐ

34ᵐ	SUN PLANETS	ARIES	MOON	v or d	Corrⁿ	v or d	Corrⁿ	v or d	Corrⁿ
s	° ′	° ′	° ′	′	′	′	′	′	′
00	8 30·0	8 31·4	8 06·8	0·0	0·0	6·0	3·5	12·0	6·9
01	8 30·3	8 31·6	8 07·0	0·1	0·1	6·1	3·5	12·1	7·0
02	8 30·5	8 31·9	8 07·2	0·2	0·1	6·2	3·6	12·2	7·0
03	8 30·8	8 32·1	8 07·5	0·3	0·2	6·3	3·6	12·3	7·1
04	8 31·0	8 32·4	8 07·7	0·4	0·2	6·4	3·7	12·4	7·1
05	8 31·3	8 32·6	8 08·0	0·5	0·3	6·5	3·7	12·5	7·2
06	8 31·5	8 32·9	8 08·2	0·6	0·3	6·6	3·8	12·6	7·2
07	8 31·8	8 33·2	8 08·4	0·7	0·4	6·7	3·9	12·7	7·3
08	8 32·0	8 33·4	8 08·7	0·8	0·5	6·8	3·9	12·8	7·4
09	8 32·3	8 33·7	8 08·9	0·9	0·5	6·9	4·0	12·9	7·4
10	8 32·5	8 33·9	8 09·2	1·0	0·6	7·0	4·0	13·0	7·5
11	8 32·8	8 34·2	8 09·4	1·1	0·6	7·1	4·1	13·1	7·5
12	8 33·0	8 34·4	8 09·6	1·2	0·7	7·2	4·1	13·2	7·6
13	8 33·3	8 34·7	8 09·9	1·3	0·7	7·3	4·2	13·3	7·6
14	8 33·5	8 34·9	8 10·1	1·4	0·8	7·4	4·3	13·4	7·7
15	8 33·8	8 35·2	8 10·3	1·5	0·9	7·5	4·3	13·5	7·8
16	8 34·0	8 35·4	8 10·6	1·6	0·9	7·6	4·4	13·6	7·8
17	8 34·3	8 35·7	8 10·8	1·7	1·0	7·7	4·4	13·7	7·9
18	8 34·5	8 35·9	8 11·1	1·8	1·0	7·8	4·5	13·8	7·9
19	8 34·8	8 36·2	8 11·3	1·9	1·1	7·9	4·5	13·9	8·0
20	8 35·0	8 36·4	8 11·5	2·0	1·2	8·0	4·6	14·0	8·1
21	8 35·3	8 36·7	8 11·8	2·1	1·2	8·1	4·7	14·1	8·1
22	8 35·5	8 36·9	8 12·0	2·2	1·3	8·2	4·7	14·2	8·2
23	8 35·8	8 37·2	8 12·3	2·3	1·3	8·3	4·8	14·3	8·2
24	8 36·0	8 37·4	8 12·5	2·4	1·4	8·4	4·8	14·4	8·3
25	8 36·3	8 37·7	8 12·7	2·5	1·4	8·5	4·9	14·5	8·3
26	8 36·5	8 37·9	8 13·0	2·6	1·5	8·6	4·9	14·6	8·4
27	8 36·8	8 38·2	8 13·2	2·7	1·6	8·7	5·0	14·7	8·5
28	8 37·0	8 38·4	8 13·4	2·8	1·6	8·8	5·1	14·8	8·5
29	8 37·3	8 38·7	8 13·7	2·9	1·7	8·9	5·1	14·9	8·6
30	8 37·5	8 38·9	8 13·9	3·0	1·7	9·0	5·2	15·0	8·6
31	8 37·8	8 39·2	8 14·2	3·1	1·8	9·1	5·2	15·1	8·7
32	8 38·0	8 39·4	8 14·4	3·2	1·8	9·2	5·3	15·2	8·7
33	8 38·3	8 39·7	8 14·6	3·3	1·9	9·3	5·3	15·3	8·8
34	8 38·5	8 39·9	8 14·9	3·4	2·0	9·4	5·4	15·4	8·9
35	8 38·8	8 40·2	8 15·1	3·5	2·0	9·5	5·5	15·5	8·9
36	8 39·0	8 40·4	8 15·4	3·6	2·1	9·6	5·5	15·6	9·0
37	8 39·3	8 40·7	8 15·6	3·7	2·1	9·7	5·6	15·7	9·0
38	8 39·5	8 40·9	8 15·8	3·8	2·2	9·8	5·6	15·8	9·1
39	8 39·8	8 41·2	8 16·1	3·9	2·2	9·9	5·7	15·9	9·1
40	8 40·0	8 41·4	8 16·3	4·0	2·3	10·0	5·8	16·0	9·2
41	8 40·3	8 41·7	8 16·5	4·1	2·4	10·1	5·8	16·1	9·3
42	8 40·5	8 41·9	8 16·8	4·2	2·4	10·2	5·9	16·2	9·3
43	8 40·8	8 42·2	8 17·0	4·3	2·5	10·3	5·9	16·3	9·4
44	8 41·0	8 42·4	8 17·3	4·4	2·5	10·4	6·0	16·4	9·4
45	8 41·3	8 42·7	8 17·5	4·5	2·6	10·5	6·0	16·5	9·5
46	8 41·5	8 42·9	8 17·7	4·6	2·6	10·6	6·1	16·6	9·5
47	8 41·8	8 43·2	8 18·0	4·7	2·7	10·7	6·2	16·7	9·6
48	8 42·0	8 43·4	8 18·2	4·8	2·8	10·8	6·2	16·8	9·7
49	8 42·3	8 43·7	8 18·5	4·9	2·8	10·9	6·3	16·9	9·7
50	8 42·5	8 43·9	8 18·7	5·0	2·9	11·0	6·3	17·0	9·8
51	8 42·8	8 44·2	8 18·9	5·1	2·9	11·1	6·4	17·1	9·8
52	8 43·0	8 44·4	8 19·2	5·2	3·0	11·2	6·4	17·2	9·9
53	8 43·3	8 44·7	8 19·4	5·3	3·0	11·3	6·5	17·3	9·9
54	8 43·5	8 44·9	8 19·7	5·4	3·1	11·4	6·6	17·4	10·0
55	8 43·8	8 45·2	8 19·9	5·5	3·2	11·5	6·6	17·5	10·1
56	8 44·0	8 45·4	8 20·1	5·6	3·2	11·6	6·7	17·6	10·1
57	8 44·3	8 45·7	8 20·4	5·7	3·3	11·7	6·7	17·7	10·2
58	8 44·5	8 45·9	8 20·6	5·8	3·3	11·8	6·8	17·8	10·2
59	8 44·8	8 46·2	8 20·8	5·9	3·4	11·9	6·8	17·9	10·3
60	8 45·0	8 46·4	8 21·1	6·0	3·5	12·0	6·9	18·0	10·4

35ᵐ	SUN PLANETS	ARIES	MOON	v or d	Corrⁿ	v or d	Corrⁿ	v or d	Corrⁿ
s	° ′	° ′	° ′	′	′	′	′	′	′
00	8 45·0	8 46·4	8 21·1	0·0	0·0	6·0	3·6	12·0	7·1
01	8 45·3	8 46·7	8 21·3	0·1	0·1	6·1	3·6	12·1	7·2
02	8 45·5	8 46·9	8 21·6	0·2	0·1	6·2	3·7	12·2	7·2
03	8 45·8	8 47·2	8 21·8	0·3	0·2	6·3	3·7	12·3	7·3
04	8 46·0	8 47·4	8 22·0	0·4	0·2	6·4	3·8	12·4	7·3
05	8 46·3	8 47·7	8 22·3	0·5	0·3	6·5	3·8	12·5	7·4
06	8 46·5	8 47·9	8 22·5	0·6	0·4	6·6	3·9	.12·6	7·5
07	8 46·8	8 48·2	8 22·8	0·7	0·4	6·7	4·0	12·7	7·5
08	8 47·0	8 48·4	8 23·0	0·8	0·5	6·8	4·0	12·8	7·6
09	8 47·3	8 48·7	8 23·2	0·9	0·5	6·9	4·1	12·9	7·6
10	8 47·5	8 48·9	8 23·5	1·0	0·6	7·0	4·1	13·0	7·7
11	8 47·8	8 49·2	8 23·7	1·1	0·7	7·1	4·2	13·1	7·8
12	8 48·0	8 49·4	8 23·9	1·2	0·7	7·2	4·3	13·2	7·8
13	8 48·3	8 49·7	8 24·2	1·3	0·8	7·3	4·3	13·3	7·9
14	8 48·5	8 49·9	8 24·4	1·4	0·8	7·4	4·4	13·4	7·9
15	8 48·8	8 50·2	8 24·7	1·5	0·9	7·5	4·4	13·5	8·0
16	8 49·0	8 50·4	8 24·9	1·6	0·9	7·6	4·5	13·6	8·0
17	8 49·3	8 50·7	8 25·1	1·7	1·0	7·7	4·6	13·7	8·1
18	8 49·5	8 50·9	8 25·4	1·8	1·1	7·8	4·6	13·8	8·2
19	8 49·8	8 51·2	8 25·6	1·9	1·1	7·9	4·7	13·9	8·2
20	8 50·0	8 51·5	8 25·9	2·0	1·2	8·0	4·7	14·0	8·3
21	8 50·3	8 51·7	8 26·1	2·1	1·2	8·1	4·8	14·1	8·3
22	8 50·5	8 52·0	8 26·3	2·2	1·3	8·2	4·9	14·2	8·4
23	8 50·8	8 52·2	8 26·6	2·3	1·4	8·3	4·9	14·3	8·5
24	8 51·0	8 52·5	8 26·8	2·4	1·4	8·4	5·0	14·4	8·5
25	8 51·3	8 52·7	8 27·0	2·5	1·5	.8·5	5·0	14·5	8·6
26	8 51·5	8 53·0	8 27·3	2·6	1·5	8·6	5·1	14·6	8·6
27	8 51·8	8 53·2	8 27·5	2·7	1·6	8·7	5·1	14·7	8·7
28	8 52·0	8 53·5	8 27·8	2·8	1·7	8·8	5·2	14·8	8·8
29	8 52·3	8 53·7	8 28·0	2·9	1·7	8·9	5·3	14·9	8·8
30	8 52·5	8 54·0	8 28·2	3·0	1·8	9·0	5·3	15·0	8·9
31	8 52·8	8 54·2	8 28·5	3·1	1·8	9·1	5·4	15·1	8·9
32	8 53·0	8 54·5	8 28·7	3·2	1·9	9·2	5·4	15·2	9·0
33	8 53·3	8 54·7	8 29·0	3·3	2·0	9·3	5·5	15·3	9·1
34	8 53·5	8 55·0	8 29·2	3·4	2·0	9·4	5·6	15·4	9·1
35	8 53·8	8 55·2	8 29·4	3·5	2·1	9·5	5·6	15·5	9·2
36	8 54·0	8 55·5	8 29·7	3·6	2·1	9·6	5·7	15·6	9·2
37	8 54·3	8 55·7	8 29·9	3·7	2·2	9·7	5·7	15·7	9·3
38	8 54·5	8 56·0	8 30·2	3·8	2·2	9·8	5·8	15·8	9·3
39	8 54·8	8 56·2	8 30·4	3·9	2·3	9·9	5·9	15·9	9·4
40	8 55·0	8 56·5	8 30·6	4·0	2·4	10·0	5·9	16·0	9·5
41	8 55·3	8 56·7	8 30·9	4·1	2·4	10·1	6·0	16·1	9·5
42	8 55·5	8 57·0	8 31·1	4·2	2·5	10·2	6·0	16·2	9·6
43	8 55·8	8 57·2	8 31·3	4·3	2·5	10·3	6·1	16·3	9·6
44	8 56·0	8 57·5	8 31·6	4·4	2·6	10·4	6·2	16·4	9·7
45	8 56·3	8 57·7	8 31·8	4·5	2·7	10·5	6·2	16·5	9·8
46	8 56·5	8 58·0	8 32·1	4·6	2·7	10·6	6·3	16·6	9·8
47	8 56·8	8 58·2	8 32·3	4·7	2·8	10·7	6·3	16·7	9·9
48	8 57·0	8 58·5	8 32·5	4·8	2·8	10·8	6·4	16·8	9·9
49	8 57·3	8 58·7	8 32·8	4·9	2·9	10·9	6·4	16·9	10·0
50	8 57·5	8 59·0	8 33·0	5·0	3·0	11·0	6·5	17·0	10·1
51	8 57·8	8 59·2	8 33·3	5·1	3·0	11·1	6·6	17·1	10·1
52	8 58·0	8 59·5	8 33·5	5·2	3·1	11·2	6·6	17·2	10·2
53	8 58·3	8 59·7	8 33·7	5·3	3·1	11·3	6·7	17·3	10·2
54	8 58·5	9 00·0	8 34·0	5·4	3·2	11·4	6·7	17·4	10·3
55	8 58·8	9 00·2	8 34·2	5·5	3·3	11·5	6·8	17·5	10·4
56	8 59·0	9 00·5	8 34·4	5·6	3·3	11·6	6·9	17·6	10·4
57	8 59·3	9 00·7	8 34·7	5·7	3·4	11·7	6·9	17·7	10·5
58	8 59·5	9 01·0	8 34·9	5·8	3·4	11·8	7·0	17·8	10·5
59	8 59·8	9 01·2	8 35·2	5·9	3·5	11·9	7·0	17·9	10·6
60	9 00·0	9 01·5	8 35·4	6·0	3·6	12·0	7·1	18·0	10·7

36ᵐ   INCREMENTS AND CORRECTIONS   37ᵐ

36ᵐ	SUN PLANETS	ARIES	MOON	v or Corrⁿ d		v or Corrⁿ d		v or Corrⁿ d		37ᵐ	SUN PLANETS	ARIES	MOON	v or Corrⁿ d		v or Corrⁿ d		v or Corrⁿ d	
s	° ′	° ′	° ′	′	′	′	′	′	′	s	° ′	° ′	° ′	′	′	′	′	′	′
00	9 00·0	9 01·5	8 35·4	0·0	0·0	6·0	3·7	12·0	7·3	00	9 15·0	9 16·5	8 49·7	0·0	0·0	6·0	3·8	12·0	7·5
01	9 00·3	9 01·7	8 35·6	0·1	0·1	6·1	3·7	12·1	7·4	01	9 15·3	9 16·8	8 50·0	0·1	0·1	6·1	3·8	12·1	7·6
02	9 00·5	9 02·0	8 35·9	0·2	0·1	6·2	3·8	12·2	7·4	02	9 15·5	9 17·0	8 50·2	0·2	0·1	6·2	3·9	12·2	7·6
03	9 00·8	9 02·2	8 36·1	0·3	0·2	6·3	3·8	12·3	7·5	03	9 15·8	9 17·3	8 50·4	0·3	0·2	6·3	3·9	12·3	7·7
04	9 01·0	9 02·5	8 36·4	0·4	0·2	6·4	3·9	12·4	7·5	04	9 16·0	9 17·5	8 50·7	0·4	0·3	6·4	4·0	12·4	7·8
05	9 01·3	9 02·7	8 36·6	0·5	0·3	6·5	4·0	12·5	7·6	05	9 16·3	9 17·8	8 50·9	0·5	0·3	6·5	4·1	12·5	7·8
06	9 01·5	9 03·0	8 36·8	0·6	0·4	6·6	4·0	12·6	7·7	06	9 16·5	9 18·0	8 51·1	0·6	0·4	6·6	4·1	12·6	7·9
07	9 01·8	9 03·2	8 37·1	0·7	0·4	6·7	4·1	12·7	7·7	07	9 16·8	9 18·3	8 51·4	0·7	0·4	6·7	4·2	12·7	7·9
08	9 02·0	9 03·5	8 37·3	0·8	0·5	6·8	4·1	12·8	7·8	08	9 17·0	9 18·5	8 51·6	0·8	0·5	6·8	4·3	12·8	8·0
09	9 02·3	9 03·7	8 37·5	0·9	0·5	6·9	4·2	12·9	7·8	09	9 17·3	9 18·8	8 51·9	0·9	0·6	6·9	4·3	12·9	8·1
10	9 02·5	9 04·0	8 37·8	1·0	0·6	7·0	4·3	13·0	7·9	10	9 17·5	9 19·0	8 52·1	1·0	0·6	7·0	4·4	13·0	8·1
11	9 02·8	9 04·2	8 38·0	1·1	0·7	7·1	4·3	13·1	8·0	11	9 17·8	9 19·3	8 52·3	1·1	0·7	7·1	4·4	13·1	8·2
12	9 03·0	9 04·5	8 38·3	1·2	0·7	7·2	4·4	13·2	8·0	12	9 18·0	9 19·5	8 52·6	1·2	0·8	7·2	4·5	13·2	8·3
13	9 03·3	9 04·7	8 38·5	1·3	0·8	7·3	4·4	13·3	8·1	13	9 18·3	9 19·8	8 52·8	1·3	0·8	7·3	4·6	13·3	8·3
14	9 03·5	9 05·0	8 38·7	1·4	0·9	7·4	4·5	13·4	8·2	14	9 18·5	9 20·0	8 53·1	1·4	0·9	7·4	4·6	13·4	8·4
15	9 03·8	9 05·2	8 39·0	1·5	0·9	7·5	4·6	13·5	8·2	15	9 18·8	9 20·3	8 53·3	1·5	0·9	7·5	4·7	13·5	8·4
16	9 04·0	9 05·5	8 39·2	1·6	1·0	7·6	4·6	13·6	8·3	16	9 19·0	9 20·5	8 53·5	1·6	1·0	7·6	4·8	13·6	8·5
17	9 04·3	9 05·7	8 39·5	1·7	1·0	7·7	4·7	13·7	8·3	17	9 19·3	9 20·8	8 53·8	1·7	1·1	7·7	4·8	13·7	8·6
18	9 04·5	9 06·0	8 39·7	1·8	1·1	7·8	4·7	13·8	8·4	18	9 19·5	9 21·0	8 54·0	1·8	1·1	7·8	4·9	13·8	8·6
19	9 04·8	9 06·2	8 39·9	1·9	1·2	7·9	4·8	13·9	8·5	19	9 19·8	9 21·3	8 54·3	1·9	1·2	7·9	4·9	13·9	8·7
20	9 05·0	9 06·5	8 40·2	2·0	1·2	8·0	4·9	14·0	8·5	20	9 20·0	9 21·5	8 54·5	2·0	1·3	8·0	5·0	14·0	8·8
21	9 05·3	9 06·7	8 40·4	2·1	1·3	8·1	4·9	14·1	8·6	21	9 20·3	9 21·8	8 54·7	2·1	1·3	8·1	5·1	14·1	8·8
22	9 05·5	9 07·0	8 40·6	2·2	1·3	8·2	5·0	14·2	8·6	22	9 20·5	9 22·0	8 55·0	2·2	1·4	8·2	5·1	14·2	8·9
23	9 05·8	9 07·2	8 40·9	2·3	1·4	8·3	5·0	14·3	8·7	23	9 20·8	9 22·3	8 55·2	2·3	1·4	8·3	5·2	14·3	8·9
24	9 06·0	9 07·5	8 41·1	2·4	1·5	8·4	5·1	14·4	8·8	24	9 21·0	9 22·5	8 55·4	2·4	1·5	8·4	5·3	14·4	9·0
25	9 06·3	9 07·7	8 41·4	2·5	1·5	8·5	5·2	14·5	8·8	25	9 21·3	9 22·8	8 55·7	2·5	1·6	8·5	5·3	14·5	9·1
26	9 06·5	9 08·0	8 41·6	2·6	1·6	8·6	5·2	14·6	8·9	26	9 21·5	9 23·0	8 55·9	2·6	1·6	8·6	5·4	14·6	9·1
27	9 06·8	9 08·2	8 41·8	2·7	1·6	8·7	5·3	14·7	8·9	27	9 21·8	9 23·3	8 56·2	2·7	1·7	8·7	5·4	14·7	9·2
28	9 07·0	9 08·5	8 42·1	2·8	1·7	8·8	5·4	14·8	9·0	28	9 22·0	9 23·5	8 56·4	2·8	1·8	8·8	5·5	14·8	9·3
29	9 07·3	9 08·7	8 42·3	2·9	1·8	8·9	5·4	14·9	9·1	29	9 22·3	9 23·8	8 56·6	2·9	1·8	8·9	5·6	14·9	9·3
30	9 07·5	9 09·0	8 42·6	3·0	1·8	9·0	5·5	15·0	9·1	30	9 22·5	9 24·0	8 56·9	3·0	1·9	9·0	5·6	15·0	9·4
31	9 07·8	9 09·2	8 42·8	3·1	1·9	9·1	5·5	15·1	9·2	31	9 22·8	9 24·3	8 57·1	3·1	1·9	9·1	5·7	15·1	9·4
32	9 08·0	9 09·5	8 43·0	3·2	1·9	9·2	5·6	15·2	9·2	32	9 23·0	9 24·5	8 57·4	3·2	2·0	9·2	5·8	15·2	9·5
33	9 08·3	9 09·8	8 43·3	3·3	2·0	9·3	5·7	15·3	9·3	33	9 23·3	9 24·8	8 57·6	3·3	2·1	9·3	5·8	15·3	9·6
34	9 08·5	9 10·0	8 43·5	3·4	2·1	9·4	5·7	15·4	9·4	34	9 23·5	9 25·0	8 57·8	3·4	2·1	9·4	5·9	15·4	9·6
35	9 08·8	9 10·3	8 43·8	3·5	2·1	9·5	5·8	15·5	9·4	35	9 23·8	9 25·3	8 58·1	3·5	2·2	9·5	5·9	15·5	9·7
36	9 09·0	9 10·5	8 44·0	3·6	2·2	9·6	5·8	15·6	9·5	36	9 24·0	9 25·5	8 58·3	3·6	2·3	9·6	6·0	15·6	9·8
37	9 09·3	9 10·8	8 44·2	3·7	2·3	9·7	5·9	15·7	9·6	37	9 24·3	9 25·8	8 58·5	3·7	2·3	9·7	6·1	15·7	9·8
38	9 09·5	9 11·0	8 44·5	3·8	2·3	9·8	6·0	15·8	9·6	38	9 24·5	9 26·0	8 58·8	3·8	2·4	9·8	6·1	15·8	9·9
39	9 09·8	9 11·3	8 44·7	3·9	2·4	9·9	6·0	15·9	9·7	39	9 24·8	9 26·3	8 59·0	3·9	2·4	9·9	6·2	15·9	9·9
40	9 10·0	9 11·5	8 44·9	4·0	2·4	10·0	6·1	16·0	9·7	40	9 25·0	9 26·5	8 59·3	4·0	2·5	10·0	6·3	16·0	10·0
41	9 10·3	9 11·8	8 45·2	4·1	2·5	10·1	6·1	16·1	9·8	41	9 25·3	9 26·8	8 59·5	4·1	2·6	10·1	6·3	16·1	10·1
42	9 10·5	9 12·0	8 45·4	4·2	2·6	10·2	6·2	16·2	9·9	42	9 25·5	9 27·0	8 59·7	4·2	2·6	10·2	6·4	16·2	10·1
43	9 10·8	9 12·3	8 45·7	4·3	2·6	10·3	6·3	16·3	9·9	43	9 25·8	9 27·3	9 00·0	4·3	2·7	10·3	6·4	16·3	10·2
44	9 11·0	9 12·5	8 45·9	4·4	2·7	10·4	6·3	16·4	10·0	44	9 26·0	9 27·5	9 00·2	4·4	2·8	10·4	6·5	16·4	10·3
45	9 11·3	9 12·8	8 46·1	4·5	2·7	10·5	6·4	16·5	10·0	45	9 26·3	9 27·8	9 00·5	4·5	2·8	10·5	6·6	16·5	10·3
46	9 11·5	9 13·0	8 46·4	4·6	2·8	10·6	6·4	16·6	10·1	46	9 26·5	9 28·1	9 00·7	4·6	2·9	10·6	6·6	16·6	10·4
47	9 11·8	9 13·3	8 46·6	4·7	2·9	10·7	6·5	16·7	10·2	47	9 26·8	9 28·3	9 00·9	4·7	2·9	10·7	6·7	16·7	10·4
48	9 12·0	9 13·5	8 46·9	4·8	2·9	10·8	6·6	16·8	10·2	48	9 27·0	9 28·6	9 01·2	4·8	3·0	10·8	6·8	16·8	10·5
49	9 12·3	9 13·8	8 47·1	4·9	3·0	10·9	6·6	16·9	10·3	49	9 27·3	9 28·8	9 01·4	4·9	3·1	10·9	6·8	16·9	10·6
50	9 12·5	9 14·0	8 47·3	5·0	3·0	11·0	6·7	17·0	10·3	50	9 27·5	9 29·1	9 01·6	5·0	3·1	11·0	6·9	17·0	10·6
51	9 12·8	9 14·3	8 47·6	5·1	3·1	11·1	6·8	17·1	10·4	51	9 27·8	9 29·3	9 01·9	5·1	3·2	11·1	6·9	17·1	10·7
52	9 13·0	9 14·5	8 47·8	5·2	3·2	11·2	6·8	17·2	10·5	52	9 28·0	9 29·6	9 02·1	5·2	3·3	11·2	7·0	17·2	10·8
53	9 13·3	9 14·8	8 48·0	5·3	3·2	11·3	6·9	17·3	10·5	53	9 28·3	9 29·8	9 02·4	5·3	3·3	11·3	7·1	17·3	10·8
54	9 13·5	9 15·0	8 48·3	5·4	3·3	11·4	6·9	17·4	10·6	54	9 28·5	9 30·1	9 02·6	5·4	3·4	11·4	7·1	17·4	10·9
55	9 13·8	9 15·3	8 48·5	5·5	3·3	11·5	7·0	17·5	10·6	55	9 28·8	9 30·3	9 02·8	5·5	3·4	11·5	7·2	17·5	10·9
56	9 14·0	9 15·5	8 48·8	5·6	3·4	11·6	7·1	17·6	10·7	56	9 29·0	9 30·6	9 03·1	5·6	3·5	11·6	7·3	17·6	11·0
57	9 14·3	9 15·8	8 49·0	5·7	3·5	11·7	7·1	17·7	10·8	57	9 29·3	9 30·8	9 03·3	5·7	3·6	11·7	7·3	17·7	11·1
58	9 14·5	9 16·0	8 49·2	5·8	3·5	11·8	7·2	17·8	10·8	58	9 29·5	9 31·1	9 03·6	5·8	3·6	11·8	7·4	17·8	11·1
59	9 14·8	9 16·3	8 49·5	5·9	3·6	11·9	7·2	17·9	10·9	59	9 29·8	9 31·3	9 03·8	5·9	3·7	11·9	7·4	17·9	11·2
60	9 15·0	9 16·5	8 49·7	6·0	3·7	12·0	7·3	18·0	11·0	60	9 30·0	9 31·6	9 04·0	6·0	3·8	12·0	7·5	18·0	11·3

INCREMENTS AND CORRECTIONS

38ᵐ   **39ᵐ**

38ᵐ	SUN PLANETS	ARIES	MOON	v or Corrⁿ d	v or Corrⁿ d	v or Corrⁿ d
s	° ′	° ′	° ′	′ ′	′ ′	′ ′
00	9 30·0	9 31·6	9 04·0	0·0 0·0	6·0 3·9	12·0 7·7
01	9 30·3	9 31·8	9 04·3	0·1 0·1	6·1 3·9	12·1 7·8
02	9 30·5	9 32·1	9 04·5	0·2 0·1	6·2 4·0	12·2 7·8
03	9 30·8	9 32·3	9 04·7	0·3 0·2	6·3 4·0	12·3 7·9
04	9 31·0	9 32·6	9 05·0	0·4 0·3	6·4 4·1	12·4 8·0
05	9 31·3	9 32·8	9 05·2	0·5 0·3	6·5 4·2	12·5 8·0
06	9 31·5	9 33·1	9 05·5	0·6 0·4	6·6 4·2	12·6 8·1
07	9 31·8	9 33·3	9 05·7	0·7 0·4	6·7 4·3	12·7 8·1
08	9 32·0	9 33·6	9 05·9	0·8 0·5	6·8 4·4	12·8 8·2
09	9 32·3	9 33·8	9 06·2	0·9 0·6	6·9 4·4	12·9 8·3
10	9 32·5	9 34·1	9 06·4	1·0 0·6	7·0 4·5	13·0 8·3
11	9 32·8	9 34·3	9 06·7	1·1 0·7	7·1 4·6	13·1 8·4
12	9 33·0	9 34·6	9 06·9	1·2 0·8	7·2 4·6	13·2 8·5
13	9 33·3	9 34·8	9 07·1	1·3 0·8	7·3 4·7	13·3 8·5
14	9 33·5	9 35·1	9 07·4	1·4 0·9	7·4 4·7	13·4 8·6
15	9 33·8	9 35·3	9 07·6	1·5 1·0	7·5 4·8	13·5 8·7
16	9 34·0	9 35·6	9 07·9	1·6 1·0	7·6 4·9	13·6 8·7
17	9 34·3	9 35·8	9 08·1	1·7 1·1	7·7 4·9	13·7 8·8
18	9 34·5	9 36·1	9 08·3	1·8 1·2	7·8 5·0	13·8 8·9
19	9 34·8	9 36·3	9 08·6	1·9 1·2	7·9 5·1	13·9 8·9
20	9 35·0	9 36·6	9 08·8	2·0 1·3	8·0 5·1	14·0 9·0
21	9 35·3	9 36·8	9 09·0	2·1 1·3	8·1 5·2	14·1 9·0
22	9 35·5	9 37·1	9 09·3	2·2 1·4	8·2 5·3	14·2 9·1
23	9 35·8	9 37·3	9 09·5	2·3 1·5	8·3 5·3	14·3 9·2
24	9 36·0	9 37·6	9 09·8	2·4 1·5	8·4 5·4	14·4 9·2
25	9 36·3	9 37·8	9 10·0	2·5 1·6	8·5 5·5	14·5 9·3
26	9 36·5	9 38·1	9 10·2	2·6 1·7	8·6 5·5	14·6 9·4
27	9 36·8	9 38·3	9 10·5	2·7 1·7	8·7 5·6	14·7 9·4
28	9 37·0	9 38·6	9 10·7	2·8 1·8	8·8 5·6	14·8 9·5
29	9 37·3	9 38·8	9 11·0	2·9 1·9	8·9 5·7	14·9 9·6
30	9 37·5	9 39·1	9 11·2	3·0 1·9	9·0 5·8	15·0 9·6
31	9 37·8	9 39·3	9 11·4	3·1 2·0	9·1 5·8	15·1 9·7
32	9 38·0	9 39·6	9 11·7	3·2 2·1	9·2 5·9	15·2 9·8
33	9 38·3	9 39·8	9 11·9	3·3 2·1	9·3 6·0	15·3 9·8
34	9 38·5	9 40·1	9 12·1	3·4 2·2	9·4 6·0	15·4 9·9
35	9 38·8	9 40·3	9 12·4	3·5 2·2	9·5 6·1	15·5 9·9
36	9 39·0	9 40·6	9 12·6	3·6 2·3	9·6 6·2	15·6 10·0
37	9 39·3	9 40·8	9 12·9	3·7 2·4	9·7 6·2	15·7 10·1
38	9 39·5	9 41·1	9 13·1	3·8 2·4	9·8 6·3	15·8 10·1
39	9 39·8	9 41·3	9 13·3	3·9 2·5	9·9 6·4	15·9 10·2
40	9 40·0	9 41·6	9 13·6	4·0 2·6	10·0 6·4	16·0 10·3
41	9 40·3	9 41·8	9 13·8	4·1 2·6	10·1 6·5	16·1 10·3
42	9 40·5	9 42·1	9 14·1	4·2 2·7	10·2 6·5	16·2 10·4
43	9 40·8	9 42·3	9 14·3	4·3 2·8	10·3 6·6	16·3 10·5
44	9 41·0	9 42·6	9 14·5	4·4 2·8	10·4 6·7	16·4 10·5
45	9 41·3	9 42·8	9 14·8	4·5 2·9	10·5 6·7	16·5 10·6
46	9 41·5	9 43·1	9 15·0	4·6 3·0	10·6 6·8	16·6 10·7
47	9 41·8	9 43·3	9 15·2	4·7 3·0	10·7 6·9	16·7 10·7
48	9 42·0	9 43·6	9 15·5	4·8 3·1	10·8 6·9	16·8 10·8
49	9 42·3	9 43·8	9 15·7	4·9 3·1	10·9 7·0	16·9 10·8
50	9 42·5	9 44·1	9 16·0	5·0 3·2	11·0 7·1	17·0 10·9
51	9 42·8	9 44·3	9 16·2	5·1 3·3	11·1 7·1	17·1 11·0
52	9 43·0	9 44·6	9 16·4	5·2 3·3	11·2 7·2	17·2 11·0
53	9 43·3	9 44·8	9 16·7	5·3 3·4	11·3 7·3	17·3 11·1
54	9 43·5	9 45·1	9 16·9	5·4 3·5	11·4 7·3	17·4 11·2
55	9 43·8	9 45·3	9 17·2	5·5 3·5	11·5 7·4	17·5 11·2
56	9 44·0	9 45·6	9 17·4	5·6 3·6	11·6 7·4	17·6 11·3
57	9 44·3	9 45·8	9 17·6	5·7 3·7	11·7 7·5	17·7 11·4
58	9 44·5	9 46·1	9 17·9	5·8 3·7	11·8 7·6	17·8 11·4
59	9 44·8	9 46·4	9 18·1	5·9 3·8	11·9 7·6	17·9 11·5
60	9 45·0	9 46·6	9 18·4	6·0 3·9	12·0 7·7	18·0 11·6

39ᵐ	SUN PLANETS	ARIES	MOON	v or Corrⁿ d	v or Corrⁿ d	v or Corrⁿ d
s	° ′	° ′	° ′	′ ′	′ ′	′ ′
00	9 45·0	9 46·6	9 18·4	0·0 0·0	6·0 4·0	12·0 7·9
01	9 45·3	9 46·9	9 18·6	0·1 0·1	6·1 4·0	12·1 8·0
02	9 45·5	9 47·1	9 18·8	0·2 0·1	6·2 4·1	12·2 8·0
03	9 45·8	9 47·4	9 19·1	0·3 0·2	6·3 4·1	12·3 8·1
04	9 46·0	9 47·6	9 19·3	0·4 0·3	6·4 4·2	12·4 8·2
05	9 46·3	9 47·9	9 19·5	0·5 0·3	6·5 4·3	12·5 8·2
06	9 46·5	9 48·1	9 19·8	0·6 0·4	6·6 4·3	12·6 8·3
07	9 46·8	9 48·4	9 20·0	0·7 0·5	6·7 4·4	12·7 8·4
08	9 47·0	9 48·6	9 20·3	0·8 0·5	6·8 4·5	12·8 8·4
09	9 47·3	9 48·9	9 20·5	0·9 0·6	6·9 4·5	12·9 8·5
10	9 47·5	9 49·1	9 20·7	1·0 0·7	7·0 4·6	13·0 8·6
11	9 47·8	9 49·4	9 21·0	1·1 0·7	7·1 4·7	13·1 8·6
12	9 48·0	9 49·6	9 21·2	1·2 0·8	7·2 4·7	13·2 8·7
13	9 48·3	9 49·9	9 21·5	1·3 0·9	7·3 4·8	13·3 8·8
14	9 48·5	9 50·1	9 21·7	1·4 0·9	7·4 4·9	13·4 8·8
15	9 48·8	9 50·4	9 21·9	1·5 1·0	7·5 4·9	13·5 8·9
16	9 49·0	9 50·6	9 22·2	1·6 1·1	7·6 5·0	13·6 9·0
17	9 49·3	9 50·9	9 22·4	1·7 1·1	7·7 5·1	13·7 9·0
18	9 49·5	9 51·1	9 22·6	1·8 1·2	7·8 5·1	13·8 9·1
19	9 49·8	9 51·4	9 22·9	1·9 1·3	7·9 5·2	13·9 9·2
20	9 50·0	9 51·6	9 23·1	2·0 1·3	8·0 5·3	14·0 9·2
21	9 50·3	9 51·9	9 23·4	2·1 1·4	8·1 5·3	14·1 9·3
22	9 50·5	9 52·1	9 23·6	2·2 1·4	8·2 5·4	14·2 9·3
23	9 50·8	9 52·4	9 23·8	2·3 1·5	8·3 5·5	14·3 9·4
24	9 51·0	9 52·6	9 24·1	2·4 1·6	8·4 5·5	14·4 9·5
25	9 51·3	9 52·9	9 24·3	2·5 1·6	8·5 5·6	14·5 9·5
26	9 51·5	9 53·1	9 24·6	2·6 1·7	8·6 5·7	14·6 9·6
27	9 51·8	9 53·4	9 24·8	2·7 1·8	8·7 5·7	14·7 9·7
28	9 52·0	9 53·6	9 25·0	2·8 1·8	8·8 5·8	14·8 9·7
29	9 52·3	9 53·9	9 25·3	2·9 1·9	8·9 5·9	14·9 9·8
30	9 52·5	9 54·1	9 25·5	3·0 2·0	9·0 5·9	15·0 9·9
31	9 52·8	9 54·4	9 25·7	3·1 2·0	9·1 6·0	15·1 9·9
32	9 53·0	9 54·6	9 26·0	3·2 2·1	9·2 6·1	15·2 10·0
33	9 53·3	9 54·9	9 26·2	3·3 2·2	9·3 6·1	15·3 10·1
34	9 53·5	9 55·1	9 26·5	3·4 2·2	9·4 6·2	15·4 10·1
35	9 53·8	9 55·4	9 26·7	3·5 2·3	9·5 6·3	15·5 10·2
36	9 54·0	9 55·6	9 26·9	3·6 2·4	9·6 6·3	15·6 10·3
37	9 54·3	9 55·9	9 27·2	3·7 2·4	9·7 6·4	15·7 10·3
38	9 54·5	9 56·1	9 27·4	3·8 2·5	9·8 6·5	15·8 10·4
39	9 54·8	9 56·4	9 27·7	3·9 2·6	9·9 6·5	15·9 10·5
40	9 55·0	9 56·6	9 27·9	4·0 2·6	10·0 6·6	16·0 10·5
41	9 55·3	9 56·9	9 28·1	4·1 2·7	10·1 6·6	16·1 10·6
42	9 55·5	9 57·1	9 28·4	4·2 2·8	10·2 6·7	16·2 10·7
43	9 55·8	9 57·4	9 28·6	4·3 2·8	10·3 6·8	16·3 10·7
44	9 56·0	9 57·6	9 28·8	4·4 2·9	10·4 6·8	16·4 10·8
45	9 56·3	9 57·9	9 29·1	4·5 3·0	10·5 6·9	16·5 10·9
46	9 56·5	9 58·1	9 29·3	4·6 3·0	10·6 7·0	16·6 10·9
47	9 56·8	9 58·4	9 29·6	4·7 3·1	10·7 7·0	16·7 11·0
48	9 57·0	9 58·6	9 29·8	4·8 3·2	10·8 7·1	16·8 11·1
49	9 57·3	9 58·9	9 30·0	4·9 3·2	10·9 7·2	16·9 11·1
50	9 57·5	9 59·1	9 30·3	5·0 3·3	11·0 7·2	17·0 11·2
51	9 57·8	9 59·4	9 30·5	5·1 3·4	11·1 7·3	17·1 11·3
52	9 58·0	9 59·6	9 30·8	5·2 3·4	11·2 7·4	17·2 11·3
53	9 58·3	9 59·9	9 31·0	5·3 3·5	11·3 7·4	17·3 11·4
54	9 58·5	10 00·1	9 31·2	5·4 3·6	11·4 7·5	17·4 11·5
55	9 58·8	10 00·4	9 31·5	5·5 3·6	11·5 7·6	17·5 11·5
56	9 59·0	10 00·6	9 31·7	5·6 3·7	11·6 7·6	17·6 11·6
57	9 59·3	10 00·9	9 32·0	5·7 3·8	11·7 7·7	17·7 11·7
58	9 59·5	10 01·1	9 32·2	5·8 3·8	11·8 7·8	17·8 11·7
59	9 59·8	10 01·4	9 32·4	5·9 3·9	11·9 7·8	17·9 11·8
60	10 00·0	10 01·6	9 32·7	6·0 4·0	12·0 7·9	18·0 11·9

40ᵐ   INCREMENTS AND CORRECTIONS   41ᵐ

40	SUN PLANETS	ARIES	MOON	v or d	Corrⁿ	v or d	Corrⁿ	v or d	Corrⁿ
s	° ′	° ′	° ′	′	′	′	′	′	′
00	10 00·0	10 01·6	9 32·7	0·0	0·0	6·0	4·1	12·0	8·1
01	10 00·3	10 01·9	9 32·9	0·1	0·1	6·1	4·1	12·1	8·2
02	10 00·5	10 02·1	9 33·1	0·2	0·1	6·2	4·2	12·2	8·2
03	10 00·8	10 02·4	9 33·4	0·3	0·2	6·3	4·3	12·3	8·3
04	10 01·0	10 02·6	9 33·6	0·4	0·3	6·4	4·3	12·4	8·4
05	10 01·3	10 02·9	9 33·9	0·5	0·3	6·5	4·4	12·5	8·4
06	10 01·5	10 03·1	9 34·1	0·6	0·4	6·6	4·5	12·6	8·5
07	10 01·8	10 03·4	9 34·3	0·7	0·5	6·7	4·5	12·7	8·6
08	10 02·0	10 03·6	9 34·6	0·8	0·5	6·8	4·6	12·8	8·6
09	10 02·3	10 03·9	9 34·8	0·9	0·6	6·9	4·7	12·9	8·7
10	10 02·5	10 04·1	9 35·1	1·0	0·7	7·0	4·7	13·0	8·8
11	10 02·8	10 04·4	9 35·3	1·1	0·7	7·1	4·8	13·1	8·8
12	10 03·0	10 04·7	9 35·5	1·2	0·8	7·2	4·9	13·2	8·9
13	10 03·3	10 04·9	9 35·8	1·3	0·9	7·3	4·9	13·3	9·0
14	10 03·5	10 05·2	9 36·0	1·4	0·9	7·4	5·0	13·4	9·0
15	10 03·8	10 05·4	9 36·2	1·5	1·0	7·5	5·1	13·5	9·1
16	10 04·0	10 05·7	9 36·5	1·6	1·1	7·6	5·1	13·6	9·2
17	10 04·3	10 05·9	9 36·7	1·7	1·1	7·7	5·2	13·7	9·2
18	10 04·5	10 06·2	9 37·0	1·8	1·2	7·8	5·3	13·8	9·3
19	10 04·8	10 06·4	9 37·2	1·9	1·3	7·9	5·3	13·9	9·4
20	10 05·0	10 06·7	9 37·4	2·0	1·4	8·0	5·4	14·0	9·5
21	10 05·3	10 06·9	9 37·7	2·1	1·4	8·1	5·5	14·1	9·5
22	10 05·5	10 07·2	9 37·9	2·2	1·5	8·2	5·5	14·2	9·6
23	10 05·8	10 07·4	9 38·2	2·3	1·6	8·3	5·6	14·3	9·7
24	10 06·0	10 07·7	9 38·4	2·4	1·6	8·4	5·7	14·4	9·7
25	10 06·3	10 07·9	9 38·6	2·5	1·7	8·5	5·7	14·5	9·8
26	10 06·5	10 08·2	9 38·9	2·6	1·8	8·6	5·8	14·6	9·9
27	10 06·8	10 08·4	9 39·1	2·7	1·8	8·7	5·9	14·7	9·9
28	10 07·0	10 08·7	9 39·3	2·8	1·9	8·8	5·9	14·8	10·0
29	10 07·3	10 08·9	9 39·6	2·9	2·0	8·9	6·0	14·9	10·1
30	10 07·5	10 09·2	9 39·8	3·0	2·0	9·0	6·1	15·0	10·1
31	10 07·8	10 09·4	9 40·1	3·1	2·1	9·1	6·1	15·1	10·2
32	10 08·0	10 09·7	9 40·3	3·2	2·2	9·2	6·2	15·2	10·3
33	10 08·3	10 09·9	9 40·5	3·3	2·2	9·3	6·3	15·3	10·3
34	10 08·5	10 10·2	9 40·8	3·4	2·3	9·4	6·3	15·4	10·4
35	10 08·8	10 10·4	9 41·0	3·5	2·4	9·5	6·4	15·5	10·5
36	10 09·0	10 10·7	9 41·3	3·6	2·4	9·6	6·5	15·6	10·5
37	10 09·3	10 10·9	9 41·5	3·7	2·5	9·7	6·5	15·7	10·6
38	10 09·5	10 11·2	9 41·7	3·8	2·6	9·8	6·6	15·8	10·7
39	10 09·8	10 11·4	9 42·0	3·9	2·6	9·9	6·7	15·9	10·7
40	10 10·0	10 11·7	9 42·2	4·0	2·7	10·0	6·8	16·0	10·8
41	10 10·3	10 11·9	9 42·4	4·1	2·8	10·1	6·8	16·1	10·9
42	10 10·5	10 12·2	9 42·7	4·2	2·8	10·2	6·9	16·2	10·9
43	10 10·8	10 12·4	9 42·9	4·3	2·9	10·3	7·0	16·3	11·0
44	10 11·0	10 12·7	9 43·2	4·4	3·0	10·4	7·0	16·4	11·1
45	10 11·3	10 12·9	9 43·4	4·5	3·0	10·5	7·1	16·5	11·1
46	10 11·5	10 13·2	9 43·6	4·6	3·1	10·6	7·2	16·6	11·2
47	10 11·8	10 13·4	9 43·9	4·7	3·2	10·7	7·2	16·7	11·3
48	10 12·0	10 13·7	9 44·1	4·8	3·2	10·8	7·3	16·8	11·3
49	10 12·3	10 13·9	9 44·4	4·9	3·3	10·9	7·4	16·9	11·4
50	10 12·5	10 14·2	9 44·6	5·0	3·4	11·0	7·4	17·0	11·5
51	10 12·8	10 14·4	9 44·8	5·1	3·4	11·1	7·5	17·1	11·5
52	10 13·0	10 14·7	9 45·1	5·2	3·5	11·2	7·6	17·2	11·6
53	10 13·3	10 14·9	9 45·3	5·3	3·6	11·3	7·6	17·3	11·7
54	10 13·5	10 15·2	9 45·6	5·4	3·6	11·4	7·7	17·4	11·7
55	10 13·8	10 15·4	9 45·8	5·5	3·7	11·5	7·8	17·5	11·8
56	10 14·0	10 15·7	9 46·0	5·6	3·8	11·6	7·8	17·6	11·9
57	10 14·3	10 15·9	9 46·3	5·7	3·8	11·7	7·9	17·7	11·9
58	10 14·5	10 16·2	9 46·5	5·8	3·9	11·8	8·0	17·8	12·0
59	10 14·8	10 16·4	9 46·7	5·9	4·0	11·9	8·0	17·9	12·1
60	10 15·0	10 16·7	9 47·0	6·0	4·1	12·0	8·1	18·0	12·2

41	SUN PLANETS	ARIES	MOON	v or d	Corrⁿ	v or d	Corrⁿ	v or d	Corrⁿ
s	° ′	° ′	° ′	′	′	′	′	′	′
00	10 15·0	10 16·7	9 47·0	0·0	0·0	6·0	4·2	12·0	8·3
01	10 15·3	10 16·9	9 47·2	0·1	0·1	6·1	4·2	12·1	8·4
02	10 15·5	10 17·2	9 47·5	0·2	0·1	6·2	4·3	12·2	8·4
03	10 15·8	10 17·4	9 47·7	0·3	0·2	6·3	4·4	12·3	8·5
04	10 16·0	10 17·7	9 47·9	0·4	0·3	6·4	4·4	12·4	8·6
05	10 16·3	10 17·9	9 48·2	0·5	0·3	6·5	4·5	12·5	8·6
06	10 16·5	10 18·2	9 48·4	0·6	0·4	6·6	4·6	12·6	8·7
07	10 16·8	10 18·4	9 48·7	0·7	0·5	6·7	4·6	12·7	8·8
08	10 17·0	10 18·7	9 48·9	0·8	0·6	6·8	4·7	12·8	8·9
09	10 17·3	10 18·9	9 49·1	0·9	0·6	6·9	4·8	12·9	8·9
10	10 17·5	10 19·2	9 49·4	1·0	0·7	7·0	4·8	13·0	9·0
11	10 17·8	10 19·4	9 49·6	1·1	0·8	7·1	4·9	13·1	9·1
12	10 18·0	10 19·7	9 49·8	1·2	0·8	7·2	5·0	13·2	9·1
13	10 18·3	10 19·9	9 50·1	1·3	0·9	7·3	5·0	13·3	9·2
14	10 18·5	10 20·2	9 50·3	1·4	1·0	7·4	5·1	13·4	9·3
15	10 18·8	10 20·4	9 50·6	1·5	1·0	7·5	5·2	13·5	9·3
16	10 19·0	10 20·7	9 50·8	1·6	1·1	7·6	5·3	13·6	9·4
17	10 19·3	10 20·9	9 51·0	1·7	1·2	7·7	5·3	13·7	9·5
18	10 19·5	10 21·2	9 51·3	1·8	1·2	7·8	5·4	13·8	9·5
19	10 19·8	10 21·4	9 51·5	1·9	1·3	7·9	5·5	13·9	9·6
20	10 20·0	10 21·7	9 51·8	2·0	1·4	8·0	5·5	14·0	9·7
21	10 20·3	10 21·9	9 52·0	2·1	1·5	8·1	5·6	14·1	9·8
22	10 20·5	10 22·2	9 52·2	2·2	1·5	8·2	5·7	14·2	9·8
23	10 20·8	10 22·4	9 52·5	2·3	1·6	8·3	5·7	14·3	9·9
24	10 21·0	10 22·7	9 52·7	2·4	1·7	8·4	5·8	14·4	10·0
25	10 21·3	10 23·0	9 52·9	2·5	1·7	8·5	5·9	14·5	10·0
26	10 21·5	10 23·2	9 53·2	2·6	1·8	8·6	5·9	14·6	10·1
27	10 21·8	10 23·5	9 53·4	2·7	1·9	8·7	6·0	14·7	10·2
28	10 22·0	10 23·7	9 53·7	2·8	1·9	8·8	6·1	14·8	10·2
29	10 22·3	10 24·0	9 53·9	2·9	2·0	8·9	6·2	14·9	10·3
30	10 22·5	10 24·2	9 54·1	3·0	2·1	9·0	6·2	15·0	10·4
31	10 22·8	10 24·5	9 54·4	3·1	2·1	9·1	6·3	15·1	10·4
32	10 23·0	10 24·7	9 54·6	3·2	2·2	9·2	6·4	15·2	10·5
33	10 23·3	10 25·0	9 54·9	3·3	2·3	9·3	6·4	15·3	10·6
34	10 23·5	10 25·2	9 55·1	3·4	2·4	9·4	6·5	15·4	10·7
35	10 23·8	10 25·5	9 55·3	3·5	2·4	9·5	6·6	15·5	10·7
36	10 24·0	10 25·7	9 55·6	3·6	2·5	9·6	6·6	15·6	10·8
37	10 24·3	10 26·0	9 55·8	3·7	2·6	9·7	6·7	15·7	10·9
38	10 24·5	10 26·2	9 56·1	3·8	2·6	9·8	6·8	15·8	10·9
39	10 24·8	10 26·5	9 56·3	3·9	2·7	9·9	6·8	15·9	11·0
40	10 25·0	10 26·7	9 56·5	4·0	2·8	10·0	6·9	16·0	11·1
41	10 25·3	10 27·0	9 56·8	4·1	2·8	10·1	7·0	16·1	11·1
42	10 25·5	10 27·2	9 57·0	4·2	2·9	10·2	7·1	16·2	11·2
43	10 25·8	10 27·5	9 57·2	4·3	3·0	10·3	7·1	16·3	11·3
44	10 26·0	10 27·7	9 57·5	4·4	3·0	10·4	7·2	16·4	11·3
45	10 26·3	10 28·0	9 57·7	4·5	3·1	10·5	7·3	16·5	11·4
46	10 26·5	10 28·2	9 58·0	4·6	3·2	10·6	7·3	16·6	11·5
47	10 26·8	10 28·5	9 58·2	4·7	3·3	10·7	7·4	16·7	11·6
48	10 27·0	10 28·7	9 58·4	4·8	3·3	10·8	7·5	16·8	11·6
49	10 27·3	10 29·0	9 58·7	4·9	3·4	10·9	7·5	16·9	11·7
50	10 27·5	10 29·2	9 58·9	5·0	3·5	11·0	7·6	17·0	11·8
51	10 27·8	10 29·5	9 59·2	5·1	3·5	11·1	7·7	17·1	11·8
52	10 28·0	10 29·7	9 59·4	5·2	3·6	11·2	7·7	17·2	11·9
53	10 28·3	10 30·0	9 59·6	5·3	3·7	11·3	7·8	17·3	12·0
54	10 28·5	10 30·2	9 59·9	5·4	3·7	11·4	7·9	17·4	12·0
55	10 28·8	10 30·5	10 00·1	5·5	3·8	11·5	8·0	17·5	12·1
56	10 29·0	10 30·7	10 00·3	5·6	3·9	11·6	8·0	17·6	12·2
57	10 29·3	10 31·0	10 00·6	5·7	3·9	11·7	8·1	17·7	12·2
58	10 29·5	10 31·2	10 00·8	5·8	4·0	11·8	8·2	17·8	12·3
59	10 29·8	10 31·5	10 01·1	5·9	4·1	11·9	8·2	17·9	12·4
60	10 30·0	10 31·7	10 01·3	6·0	4·2	12·0	8·3	18·0	12·5

INCREMENTS AND CORRECTIONS

42ᵐ   **43ᵐ**

42 s	SUN PLANETS ° ′	ARIES ° ′	MOON ° ′	v or d ′	Corrⁿ ′	v or d ′	Corrⁿ ′	v or d ′	Corrⁿ ′
00	10 30·0	10 31·7	10 01·3	0·0	0·0	6·0	4·3	12·0	8·5
01	10 30·3	10 32·0	10 01·5	0·1	0·1	6·1	4·3	12·1	8·6
02	10 30·5	10 32·2	10 01·8	0·2	0·1	6·2	4·4	12·2	8·6
03	10 30·8	10 32·5	10 02·0	0·3	0·2	6·3	4·5	12·3	8·7
04	10 31·0	10 32·7	10 02·3	0·4	0·3	6·4	4·5	12·4	8·8
05	10 31·3	10 33·0	10 02·5	0·5	0·4	6·5	4·6	12·5	8·9
06	10 31·5	10 33·2	10 02·7	0·6	0·4	6·6	4·7	12·6	8·9
07	10 31·8	10 33·5	10 03·0	0·7	0·5	6·7	4·7	12·7	9·0
08	10 32·0	10 33·7	10 03·2	0·8	0·6	6·8	4·8	12·8	9·1
09	10 32·3	10 34·0	10 03·4	0·9	0·6	6·9	4·9	12·9	9·1
10	10 32·5	10 34·2	10 03·7	1·0	0·7	7·0	5·0	13·0	9·2
11	10 32·8	10 34·5	10 03·9	1·1	0·8	7·1	5·0	13·1	9·3
12	10 33·0	10 34·7	10 04·2	1·2	0·9	7·2	5·1	13·2	9·4
13	10 33·3	10 35·0	10 04·4	1·3	0·9	7·3	5·2	13·3	9·4
14	10 33·5	10 35·2	10 04·6	1·4	1·0	7·4	5·2	13·4	9·5
15	10 33·8	10 35·5	10 04·9	1·5	1·1	7·5	5·3	13·5	9·6
16	10 34·0	10 35·7	10 05·1	1·6	1·1	7·6	5·4	13·6	9·6
17	10 34·3	10 36·0	10 05·4	1·7	1·2	7·7	5·5	13·7	9·7
18	10 34·5	10 36·2	10 05·6	1·8	1·3	7·8	5·5	13·8	9·8
19	10 34·8	10 36·5	10 05·8	1·9	1·3	7·9	5·6	13·9	9·8
20	10 35·0	10 36·7	10 06·1	2·0	1·4	8·0	5·7	14·0	9·9
21	10 35·3	10 37·0	10 06·3	2·1	1·5	8·1	5·7	14·1	10·0
22	10 35·5	10 37·2	10 06·5	2·2	1·6	8·2	5·8	14·2	10·1
23	10 35·8	10 37·5	10 06·8	2·3	1·6	8·3	5·9	14·3	10·1
24	10 36·0	10 37·7	10 07·0	2·4	1·7	8·4	6·0	14·4	10·2
25	10 36·3	10 38·0	10 07·3	2·5	1·8	8·5	6·0	14·5	10·3
26	10 36·5	10 38·2	10 07·5	2·6	1·8	8·6	6·1	14·6	10·3
27	10 36·8	10 38·5	10 07·7	2·7	1·9	8·7	6·2	14·7	10·4
28	10 37·0	10 38·7	10 08·0	2·8	2·0	8·8	6·2	14·8	10·5
29	10 37·3	10 39·0	10 08·2	2·9	2·1	8·9	6·3	14·9	10·6
30	10 37·5	10 39·2	10 08·5	3·0	2·1	9·0	6·4	15·0	10·6
31	10 37·8	10 39·5	10 08·7	3·1	2·2	9·1	6·4	15·1	10·7
32	10 38·0	10 39·7	10 08·9	3·2	2·3	9·2	6·5	15·2	10·8
33	10 38·3	10 40·0	10 09·2	3·3	2·3	9·3	6·6	15·3	10·8
34	10 38·5	10 40·2	10 09·4	3·4	2·4	9·4	6·7	15·4	10·9
35	10 38·8	10 40·5	10 09·7	3·5	2·5	9·5	6·7	15·5	11·0
36	10 39·0	10 40·7	10 09·9	3·6	2·6	9·6	6·8	15·6	11·1
37	10 39·3	10 41·0	10 10·1	3·7	2·6	9·7	6·9	15·7	11·1
38	10 39·5	10 41·3	10 10·4	3·8	2·7	9·8	6·9	15·8	11·2
39	10 39·8	10 41·5	10 10·6	3·9	2·8	9·9	7·0	15·9	11·3
40	10 40·0	10 41·8	10 10·8	4·0	2·8	10·0	7·1	16·0	11·3
41	10 40·3	10 42·0	10 11·1	4·1	2·9	10·1	7·2	16·1	11·4
42	10 40·5	10 42·3	10 11·3	4·2	3·0	10·2	7·2	16·2	11·5
43	10 40·8	10 42·5	10 11·6	4·3	3·0	10·3	7·3	16·3	11·5
44	10 41·0	10 42·8	10 11·8	4·4	3·1	10·4	7·4	16·4	11·6
45	10 41·3	10 43·0	10 12·0	4·5	3·2	10·5	7·4	16·5	11·7
46	10 41·5	10 43·3	10 12·3	4·6	3·3	10·6	7·5	16·6	11·8
47	10 41·8	10 43·5	10 12·5	4·7	3·3	10·7	7·6	16·7	11·8
48	10 42·0	10 43·8	10 12·8	4·8	3·4	10·8	7·7	16·8	11·9
49	10 42·3	10 44·0	10 13·0	4·9	3·5	10·9	7·7	16·9	12·0
50	10 42·5	10 44·3	10 13·2	5·0	3·5	11·0	7·8	17·0	12·0
51	10 42·8	10 44·5	10 13·5	5·1	3·6	11·1	7·9	17·1	12·1
52	10 43·0	10 44·8	10 13·7	5·2	3·7	11·2	7·9	17·2	12·2
53	10 43·3	10 45·0	10 13·9	5·3	3·8	11·3	8·0	17·3	12·3
54	10 43·5	10 45·3	10 14·2	5·4	3·8	11·4	8·1	17·4	12·3
55	10 43·8	10 45·5	10 14·4	5·5	3·9	11·5	8·1	17·5	12·4
56	10 44·0	10.45·8	10 14·7	5·6	4·0	11·6	8·2	17·6	12·5
57	10 44·3	10 46·0	10 14·9	5·7	4·0	11·7	8·3	17·7	12·5
58	10 44·5	10 46·3	10 15·1	5·8	4·1	11·8	8·4	17·8	12·6
59	10 44·8	10 46·5	10 15·4	5·9	4·2	11·9	8·4	17·9	12·7
60	10 45·0	10 46·8	10 15·6	6·0	4·3	12·0	8·5	18·0	12·8

43 s	SUN PLANETS ° ′	ARIES ° ′	MOON ° ′	v or d ′	Corrⁿ ′	v or d ′	Corrⁿ ′	v or d ′	Corrⁿ ′
00	10 45·0	10 46·8	10 15·6	0·0	0·0	6·0	4·4	12·0	8·7
01	10 45·3	10 47·0	10 15·9	0·1	0·1	6·1	4·4	12·1	8·8
02	10 45·5	10 47·3	10 16·1	0·2	0·1	6·2	4·5	12·2	8·8
03	10 45·8	10 47·5	10 16·3	0·3	0·2	6·3	4·6	12·3	8·9
04	10 46·0	10 47·8	10 16·6	0·4	0·3	6·4	4·6	12·4	9·0
05	10 46·3	10 48·0	10 16·8	0·5	0·4	6·5	4·7	12·5	9·1
06	10 46·5	10 48·3	10 17·0	0·6	0·4	6·6	4·8	12·6	9·1
07	10 46·8	10 48·5	10 17·3	0·7	0·5	6·7	4·9	12·7	9·2
08	10 47·0	10 48·8	10 17·5	0·8	0·6	6·8	4·9	12·8	9·3
09	10 47·3	10 49·0	10 17·8	0·9	0·7	6·9	5·0	12·9	9·4
10	10 47·5	10 49·3	10 18·0	1·0	0·7	7·0	5·1	13·0	9·4
11	10 47·8	10 49·5	10 18·2	1·1	0·8	7·1	5·1	13·1	9·5
12	10 48·0	10 49·8	10 18·5	1·2	0·9	7·2	5·2	13·2	9·6
13	10 48·3	10 50·0	10 18·7	1·3	0·9	7·3	5·3	13·3	9·6
14	10 48·5	10 50·3	10 19·0	1·4	1·0	7·4	5·4	13·4	9·7
15	10 48·8	10 50·5	10 19·2	1·5	1·1	7·5	5·4	13·5	9·8
16	10 49·0	10 50·8	10 19·4	1·6	1·2	7·6	5·5	13·6	9·9
17	10 49·3	10 51·0	10 19·7	1·7	1·2	7·7	5·6	13·7	9·9
18	10 49·5	10 51·3	10 19·9	1·8	1·3	7·8	5·7	13·8	10·0
19	10 49·8	10 51·5	10 20·2	1·9	1·4	7·9	5·7	13·9	10·1
20	10 50·0	10 51·8	10 20·4	2·0	1·5	8·0	5·8	14·0	10·2
21	10 50·3	10 52·0	10 20·6	2·1	1·5	8·1	5·9	14·1	10·2
22	10 50·5	10 52·3	10 20·9	2·2	1·6	8·2	5·9	14·2	10·3
23	10 50·8	10 52·5	10 21·1	2·3	1·7	8·3	6·0	14·3	10·4
24	10 51·0	10 52·8	10 21·3	2·4	1·7	8·4	6·1	14·4	10·4
25	10 51·3	10 53·0	10 21·6	2·5	1·8	8·5	6·2	14·5	10·5
26	10 51·5	10 53·3	10 21·8	2·6	1·9	8·6	6·2	14·6	10·6
27	10 51·8	10 53·5	10 22·1	2·7	2·0	8·7	6·3	14·7	10·7
28	10 52·0	10 53·8	10 22·3	2·8	2·0	8·8	6·4	14·8	10·7
29	10 52·3	10 54·0	10 22·5	2·9	2·1	8·9	6·5	14·9	10·8
30	10 52·5	10 54·3	10 22·8	3·0	2·2	9·0	6·5	15·0	10·9
31	10 52·8	10 54·5	10 23·0	3·1	2·2	9·1	6·6	15·1	10·9
32	10 53·0	10 54·8	10 23·3	3·2	2·3	9·2	6·7	15·2	11·0
33	10 53·3	10 55·0	10 23·5	3·3	2·4	9·3	6·7	15·3	11·1
34	10 53·5	10 55·3	10 23·7	3·4	2·5	9·4	6·8	15·4	11·2
35	10 53·8	10 55·5	10 24·0	3·5	2·5	9·5	6·9	15·5	11·2
36	10 54·0	10 55·8	10 24·2	3·6	2·6	9·6	7·0	15·6	11·3
37	10 54·3	10 56·0	10 24·4	3·7	2·7	9·7	7·0	15·7	11·4
38	10 54·5	10 56·3	10 24·7	3·8	2·8	9·8	7·1	15·8	11·5
39	10 54·8	10 56·5	10 24·9	3·9	2·8	9·9	7·2	15·9	11·5
40	10 55·0	10 56·8	10 25·2	4·0	2·9	10·0	7·3	16·0	11·6
41	10 55·3	10 57·0	10 25·4	4·1	3·0	10·1	7·3	16·1	11·7
42	10 55·5	10 57·3	10 25·6	4·2	3·0	10·2	7·4	16·2	11·7
43	10 55·8	10 57·5	10 25·9	4·3	3·1	10·3	7·5	16·3	11·8
44	10 56·0	10 57·8	10 26·1	4·4	3·2	10·4	7·5	16·4	11·9
45	10 56·3	10 58·0	10 26·4	4·5	3·3	10·5	7·6	16·5	12·0
46	10 56·5	10 58·3	10 26·6	4·6	3·3	10·6	7·7	16·6	12·0
47	10 56·8	10 58·5	10 26·8	4·7	3·4	10·7	7·8	16·7	12·1
48	10 57·0	10 58·8	10 27·1	4·8	3·5	10·8	7·8	16·8	12·2
49	10 57·3	10 59·0	10 27·3	4·9	3·6	10·9	7·9	16·9	12·3
50	10 57·5	10 59·3	10 27·5	5·0	3·6	11·0	8·0	17·0	12·3
51	10 57·8	10 59·6	10 27·8	5·1	3·7	11·1	8·0	17·1	12·4
52	10 58·0	10 59·8	10 28·0	5·2	3·8	11·2	8·1	17·2	12·5
53	10 58·3	11 00·1	10 28·3	5·3	3·8	11·3	8·2	17·3	12·5
54	10 58·5	11 00·3	10 28·5	5·4	3·9	11·4	8·3	17·4	12·6
55	10 58·8	11 00·6	10 28·7	5·5	4·0	11·5	8·3	17·5	12·7
56	10 59·0	11 00·8	10 29·0	5·6	4·1	11·6	8·4	17·6	12·8
57	10 59·3	11 01·1	10 29·2	5·7	4·1	11·7	8·5	17·7	12·8
58	10 59·5	11 01·3	10 29·5	5·8	4·2	11·8	8·6	17·8	12·9
59	10 59·8	11 01·6	10 29·7	5·9	4·3	11·9	8·6	17·9	13·0
60	11 00·0	11 01·8	10 29·9	6·0	4·4	12·0	8·7	18·0	13·1

44ᵐ INCREMENTS AND CORRECTIONS 45ᵐ

44 s	SUN PLANETS ° ′	ARIES ° ′	MOON ° ′	v or d ′	Corrⁿ ′	v or d ′	Corrⁿ ′	v or d ′	Corrⁿ ′
00	11 00·0	11 01·8	10 29·9	0·0	0·0	6·0	4·5	12·0	8·9
01	11 00·3	11 02·1	10 30·2	0·1	0·1	6·1	4·5	12·1	9·0
02	11 00·5	11 02·3	10 30·4	0·2	0·1	6·2	4·6	12·2	9·0
03	11 00·8	11 02·6	10 30·6	0·3	0·2	6·3	4·7	12·3	9·1
04	11 01·0	11 02·8	10 30·9	0·4	0·3	6·4	4·7	12·4	9·2
05	11 01·3	11 03·1	10 31·1	0·5	0·4	6·5	4·8	12·5	9·3
06	11 01·5	11 03·3	10 31·4	0·6	0·4	6·6	4·9	12·6	9·3
07	11 01·8	11 03·6	10 31·6	0·7	0·5	6·7	5·0	12·7	9·4
08	11 02·0	11 03·8	10 31·8	0·8	0·6	6·8	5·0	12·8	9·5
09	11 02·3	11 04·1	10 32·1	0·9	0·7	6·9	5·1	12·9	9·6
10	11 02·5	11 04·3	10 32·3	1·0	0·7	7·0	5·2	13·0	9·6
11	11 02·8	11 04·6	10 32·6	1·1	0·8	7·1	5·3	13·1	9·7
12	11 03·0	11 04·8	10 32·8	1·2	0·9	7·2	5·3	13·2	9·8
13	11 03·3	11 05·1	10 33·0	1·3	1·0	7·3	5·4	13·3	9·9
14	11 03·5	11 05·3	10 33·3	1·4	1·0	7·4	5·5	13·4	9·9
15	11 03·8	11 05·6	10 33·5	1·5	1·1	7·5	5·6	13·5	10·0
16	11 04·0	11 05·8	10 33·8	1·6	1·2	7·6	5·6	13·6	10·1
17	11 04·3	11 06·1	10 34·0	1·7	1·3	7·7	5·7	13·7	10·2
18	11 04·5	11 06·3	10 34·2	1·8	1·3	7·8	5·8	13·8	10·2
19	11 04·8	11 06·6	10 34·5	1·9	1·4	7·9	5·9	13·9	10·3
20	11 05·0	11 06·8	10 34·7	2·0	1·5	8·0	5·9	14·0	10·4
21	11 05·3	11 07·1	10 34·9	2·1	1·6	8·1	6·0	14·1	10·5
22	11 05·5	11 07·3	10 35·2	2·2	1·6	8·2	6·1	14·2	10·5
23	11 05·8	11 07·6	10 35·4	2·3	1·7	8·3	6·2	14·3	10·6
24	11 06·0	11 07·8	10 35·7	2·4	1·8	8·4	6·2	14·4	10·7
25	11 06·3	11 08·1	10 35·9	2·5	1·9	8·5	6·3	14·5	10·8
26	11 06·5	11 08·3	10 36·1	2·6	1·9	8·6	6·4	14·6	10·8
27	11 06·8	11 08·6	10 36·4	2·7	2·0	8·7	6·5	14·7	10·9
28	11 07·0	11 08·8	10 36·6	2·8	2·1	8·8	6·5	14·8	11·0
29	11 07·3	11 09·1	10 36·9	2·9	2·2	8·9	6·6	14·9	11·1
30	11 07·5	11 09·3	10 37·1	3·0	2·2	9·0	6·7	15·0	11·1
31	11 07·8	11 09·6	10 37·3	3·1	2·3	9·1	6·7	15·1	11·2
32	11 08·0	11 09·8	10 37·6	3·2	2·4	9·2	6·8	15·2	11·3
33	11 08·3	11 10·1	10 37·8	3·3	2·4	9·3	6·9	15·3	11·3
34	11 08·5	11 10·3	10 38·0	3·4	2·5	9·4	7·0	15·4	11·4
35	11 08·8	11 10·6	10 38·3	3·5	2·6	9·5	7·0	15·5	11·5
36	11 09·0	11 10·8	10 38·5	3·6	2·7	9·6	7·1	15·6	11·6
37	11 09·3	11 11·1	10 38·8	3·7	2·7	9·7	7·2	15·7	11·6
38	11 09·5	11 11·3	10 39·0	3·8	2·8	9·8	7·3	15·8	11·7
39	11 09·8	11 11·6	10 39·2	3·9	2·9	9·9	7·3	15·9	11·8
40	11 10·0	11 11·8	10 39·5	4·0	3·0	10·0	7·4	16·0	11·9
41	11 10·3	11 12·1	10 39·7	4·1	3·0	10·1	7·5	16·1	11·9
42	11 10·5	11 12·3	10 40·0	4·2	3·1	10·2	7·6	16·2	12·0
43	11 10·8	11 12·6	10 40·2	4·3	3·2	10·3	7·6	16·3	12·1
44	11 11·0	11 12·8	10 40·4	4·4	3·3	10·4	7·7	16·4	12·2
45	11 11·3	11 13·1	10 40·7	4·5	3·3	10·5	7·8	16·5	12·2
46	11 11·5	11 13·3	10 40·9	4·6	3·4	10·6	7·9	16·6	12·3
47	11 11·8	11 13·6	10 41·1	4·7	3·5	10·7	7·9	16·7	12·4
48	11 12·0	11 13·8	10 41·4	4·8	3·6	10·8	8·0	16·8	12·5
49	11 12·3	11 14·1	10 41·6	4·9	3·6	10·9	8·1	16·9	12·5
50	11 12·5	11 14·3	10 41·9	5·0	3·7	11·0	8·2	17·0	12·6
51	11 12·8	11 14·6	10 42·1	5·1	3·8	11·1	8·2	17·1	12·7
52	11 13·0	11 14·8	10 42·3	5·2	3·9	11·2	8·3	17·2	12·8
53	11 13·3	11 15·1	10 42·6	5·3	3·9	11·3	8·4	17·3	12·8
54	11 13·5	11 15·3	10 42·8	5·4	4·0	11·4	8·5	17·4	12·9
55	11 13·8	11 15·6	10 43·1	5·5	4·1	11·5	8·5	17·5	13·0
56	11 14·0	11 15·8	10 43·3	5·6	4·2	11·6	8·6	17·6	13·1
57	11 14·3	11 16·1	10 43·5	5·7	4·2	11·7	8·7	17·7	13·1
58	11 14·5	11 16·3	10 43·8	5·8	4·3	11·8	8·8	17·8	13·2
59	11 14·8	11 16·6	10 44·0	5·9	4·4	11·9	8·8	17·9	13·3
60	11 15·0	11 16·8	10 44·3	6·0	4·5	12·0	8·9	18·0	13·4

45 s	SUN PLANETS ° ′	ARIES ° ′	MOON ° ′	v or d ′	Corrⁿ ′	v or d ′	Corrⁿ ′	v or d ′	Corrⁿ ′
00	11 15·0	11 16·8	10 44·3	0·0	0·0	6·0	4·6	12·0	9·1
01	11 15·3	11 17·1	10 44·5	0·1	0·1	6·1	4·6	12·1	9·2
02	11 15·5	11 17·3	10 44·7	0·2	0·2	6·2	4·7	12·2	9·3
03	11 15·8	11 17·6	10 45·0	0·3	0·2	6·3	4·8	12·3	9·3
04	11 16·0	11 17·9	10 45·2	0·4	0·3	6·4	4·9	12·4	9·4
05	11 16·3	11 18·1	10 45·4	0·5	0·4	6·5	4·9	12·5	9·5
06	11 16·5	11 18·4	10 45·7	0·6	0·5	6·6	5·0	12·6	9·6
07	11 16·8	11 18·6	10 45·9	0·7	0·5	6·7	5·1	12·7	9·6
08	11 17·0	11 18·9	10 46·2	0·8	0·6	6·8	5·2	12·8	9·7
09	11 17·3	11 19·1	10 46·4	0·9	0·7	6·9	5·2	12·9	9·8
10	11 17·5	11 19·4	10 46·6	1·0	0·8	7·0	5·3	13·0	9·9
11	11 17·8	11 19·6	10 46·9	1·1	0·8	7·1	5·4	13·1	9·9
12	11 18·0	11 19·9	10 47·1	1·2	0·9	7·2	5·5	13·2	10·0
13	11 18·3	11 20·1	10 47·4	1·3	1·0	7·3	5·5	13·3	10·1
14	11 18·5	11 20·4	10 47·6	1·4	1·1	7·4	5·6	13·4	10·2
15	11 18·8	11 20·6	10 47·8	1·5	1·1	7·5	5·7	13·5	10·2
16	11 19·0	11 20·9	10 48·1	1·6	1·2	7·6	5·8	13·6	10·3
17	11 19·3	11 21·1	10 48·3	1·7	1·3	7·7	5·8	13·7	10·4
18	11 19·5	11 21·4	10 48·5	1·8	1·4	7·8	5·9	13·8	10·5
19	11 19·8	11 21·6	10 48·8	1·9	1·4	7·9	6·0	13·9	10·5
20	11 20·0	11 21·9	10 49·0	2·0	1·5	8·0	6·1	14·0	10·6
21	11 20·3	11 22·1	10 49·3	2·1	1·6	8·1	6·1	14·1	10·7
22	11 20·5	11 22·4	10 49·5	2·2	1·7	8·2	6·2	14·2	10·8
23	11 20·8	11 22·6	10 49·7	2·3	1·7	8·3	6·3	14·3	10·8
24	11 21·0	11 22·9	10 50·0	2·4	1·8	8·4	6·4	14·4	10·9
25	11 21·3	11 23·1	10 50·2	2·5	1·9	8·5	6·4	14·5	11·0
26	11 21·5	11 23·4	10 50·5	2·6	2·0	8·6	6·5	14·6	11·1
27	11 21·8	11 23·6	10 50·7	2·7	2·0	8·7	6·6	14·7	11·1
28	11 22·0	11 23·9	10 50·9	2·8	2·1	8·8	6·7	14·8	11·2
29	11 22·3	11 24·1	10 51·2	2·9	2·2	8·9	6·7	14·9	11·3
30	11 22·5	11 24·4	10 51·4	3·0	2·3	9·0	6·8	15·0	11·4
31	11 22·8	11 24·6	10 51·6	3·1	2·4	9·1	6·9	15·1	11·5
32	11 23·0	11 24·9	10 51·9	3·2	2·4	9·2	7·0	15·2	11·5
33	11 23·3	11 25·1	10 52·1	3·3	2·5	9·3	7·1	15·3	11·6
34	11 23·5	11 25·4	10 52·4	3·4	2·6	9·4	7·1	15·4	11·7
35	11 23·8	11 25·6	10 52·6	3·5	2·7	9·5	7·2	15·5	11·8
36	11 24·0	11 25·9	10 52·8	3·6	2·7	9·6	7·3	15·6	11·8
37	11 24·3	11 26·1	10 53·1	3·7	2·8	9·7	7·4	15·7	11·9
38	11 24·5	11 26·4	10 53·3	3·8	2·9	9·8	7·4	15·8	12·0
39	11 24·8	11 26·6	10 53·6	3·9	3·0	9·9	7·5	15·9	12·1
40	11 25·0	11 26·9	10 53·8	4·0	3·0	10·0	7·6	16·0	12·1
41	11 25·3	11 27·1	10 54·0	4·1	3·1	10·1	7·7	16·1	12·2
42	11 25·5	11 27·4	10 54·3	4·2	3·2	10·2	7·7	16·2	12·3
43	11 25·8	11 27·6	10 54·5	4·3	3·3	10·3	7·8	16·3	12·4
44	11 26·0	11 27·9	10 54·7	4·4	3·3	10·4	7·9	16·4	12·4
45	11 26·3	11 28·1	10 55·0	4·5	3·4	10·5	8·0	16·5	12·5
46	11 26·5	11 28·4	10 55·2	4·6	3·5	10·6	8·0	16·6	12·6
47	11 26·8	11 28·6	10 55·5	4·7	3·6	10·7	8·1	16·7	12·7
48	11 27·0	11 28·9	10 55·7	4·8	3·6	10·8	8·2	16·8	12·7
49	11 27·3	11 29·1	10 55·9	4·9	3·7	10·9	8·3	16·9	12·8
50	11 27·5	11 29·4	10 56·2	5·0	3·8	11·0	8·3	17·0	12·9
51	11 27·8	11 29·6	10 56·4	5·1	3·9	11·1	8·4	17·1	13·0
52	11 28·0	11 29·9	10 56·7	5·2	3·9	11·2	8·5	17·2	13·0
53	11 28·3	11 30·1	10 56·9	5·3	4·0	11·3	8·6	17·3	13·1
54	11 28·5	11 30·4	10 57·1	5·4	4·1	11·4	8·6	17·4	13·2
55	11 28·8	11 30·6	10 57·4	5·5	4·2	11·5	8·7	17·5	13·3
56	11 29·0	11 30·9	10 57·6	5·6	4·2	11·6	8·8	17·6	13·3
57	11 29·3	11 31·1	10 57·9	5·7	4·3	11·7	8·9	17·7	13·4
58	11 29·5	11 31·4	10 58·1	5·8	4·4	11·8	8·9	17·8	13·5
59	11 29·8	11 31·6	10 58·3	5·9	4·5	11·9	9·0	17·9	13·6
60	11 30·0	11 31·9	10 58·6	6·0	4·6	12·0	9·1	18·0	13·7

46	SUN PLANETS	ARIES	MOON	v or d Corrⁿ	v or d Corrⁿ	v or d Corrⁿ
s	° ′	° ′	° ′	′ ′	′ ′	′ ′
00	11 30·0	11 31·9	10 58·6	0·0 0·0	6·0 4·7	12·0 9·3
01	11 30·3	11 32·1	10 58·8	0·1 0·1	6·1 4·7	12·1 9·4
02	11 30·5	11 32·4	10 59·0	0·2 0·2	6·2 4·8	12·2 9·5
03	11 30·8	11 32·6	10 59·3	0·3 0·2	6·3 4·9	12·3 9·5
04	11 31·0	11 32·9	10 59·5	0·4 0·3	6·4 5·0	12·4 9·6
05	11 31·3	11 33·1	10 59·8	0·5 0·4	6·5 5·0	12·5 9·7
06	11 31·5	11 33·4	11 00·0	0·6 0·5	6·6 5·1	12·6 9·8
07	11 31·8	11 33·6	11 00·2	0·7 0·5	6·7 5·2	12·7 9·8
08	11 32·0	11 33·9	11 00·5	0·8 0·6	6·8 5·3	12·8 9·9
09	11 32·3	11 34·1	11 00·7	0·9 0·7	6·9 5·3	12·9 10·0
10	11 32·5	11 34·4	11 01·0	1·0 0·8	7·0 5·4	13·0 10·1
11	11 32·8	11 34·6	11 01·2	1·1 0·9	7·1 5·5	13·1 10·2
12	11 33·0	11 34·9	11 01·4	1·2 0·9	7·2 5·6	13·2 10·2
13	11 33·3	11 35·1	11 01·7	1·3 1·0	7·3 5·7	13·3 10·3
14	11 33·5	11 35·4	11 01·9	1·4 1·1	7·4 5·7	13·4 10·4
15	11 33·8	11 35·6	11 02·1	1·5 1·2	7·5 5·8	13·5 10·5
16	11 34·0	11 35·9	11 02·4	1·6 1·2	7·6 5·9	13·6 10·5
17	11 34·3	11 36·2	11 02·6	1·7 1·3	7·7 6·0	13·7 10·6
18	11 34·5	11 36·4	11 02·9	1·8 1·4	7·8 6·0	13·8 10·7
19	11 34·8	11 36·7	11 03·1	1·9 1·5	7·9 6·1	13·9 10·8
20	11 35·0	11 36·9	11 03·3	2·0 1·6	8·0 6·2	14·0 10·9
21	11 35·3	11 37·2	11 03·6	2·1 1·6	8·1 6·3	14·1 10·9
22	11 35·5	11 37·4	11 03·8	2·2 1·7	8·2 6·4	14·2 11·0
23	11 35·8	11 37·7	11 04·1	2·3 1·8	8·3 6·4	14·3 11·1
24	11 36·0	11 37·9	11 04·3	2·4 1·9	8·4 6·5	14·4 11·2
25	11 36·3	11 38·2	11 04·5	2·5 1·9	8·5 6·6	14·5 11·2
26	11 36·5	11 38·4	11 04·8	2·6 2·0	8·6 6·7	14·6 11·3
27	11 36·8	11 38·7	11 05·0	2·7 2·1	8·7 6·7	14·7 11·4
28	11 37·0	11 38·9	11 05·2	2·8 2·2	8·8 6·8	14·8 11·5
29	11 37·3	11 39·2	11 05·5	2·9 2·2	8·9 6·9	14·9 11·5
30	11 37·5	11 39·4	11 05·7	3·0 2·3	9·0 7·0	15·0 11·6
31	11 37·8	11 39·7	11 06·0	3·1 2·4	9·1 7·1	15·1 11·7
32	11 38·0	11 39·9	11 06·2	3·2 2·5	9·2 7·1	15·2 11·8
33	11 38·3	11 40·2	11 06·4	3·3 2·6	9·3 7·2	15·3 11·9
34	11 38·5	11 40·4	11 06·7	3·4 2·6	9·4 7·3	15·4 11·9
35	11 38·8	11 40·7	11 06·9	3·5 2·7	9·5 7·4	15·5 12·0
36	11 39·0	11 40·9	11 07·2	3·6 2·8	9·6 7·4	15·6 12·1
37	11 39·3	11 41·2	11 07·4	3·7 2·9	9·7 7·5	15·7 12·2
38	11 39·5	11 41·4	11 07·6	3·8 2·9	9·8 7·6	15·8 12·2
39	11 39·8	11 41·7	11 07·9	3·9 3·0	9·9 7·7	15·9 12·3
40	11 40·0	11 41·9	11 08·1	4·0 3·1	10·0 7·8	16·0 12·4
41	11 40·3	11 42·2	11 08·3	4·1 3·2	10·1 7·8	16·1 12·5
42	11 40·5	11 42·4	11 08·6	4·2 3·3	10·2 7·9	16·2 12·6
43	11 40·8	11 42·7	11 08·8	4·3 3·3	10·3 8·0	16·3 12·6
44	11 41·0	11 42·9	11 09·1	4·4 3·4	10·4 8·1	16·4 12·7
45	11 41·3	11 43·2	11 09·3	4·5 3·5	10·5 8·1	16·5 12·8
46	11 41·5	11 43·4	11 09·5	4·6 3·6	10·6 8·2	16·6 12·9
47	11 41·8	11 43·7	11 09·8	4·7 3·6	10·7 8·3	16·7 12·9
48	11 42·0	11 43·9	11 10·0	4·8 3·7	10·8 8·4	16·8 13·0
49	11 42·3	11 44·2	11 10·3	4·9 3·8	10·9 8·4	16·9 13·1
50	11 42·5	11 44·4	11 10·5	5·0 3·9	11·0 8·5	17·0 13·2
51	11 42·8	11 44·7	11 10·7	5·1 4·0	11·1 8·6	17·1 13·3
52	11 43·0	11 44·9	11 11·0	5·2 4·0	11·2 8·7	17·2 13·3
53	11 43·3	11 45·2	11 11·2	5·3 4·1	11·3 8·8	17·3 13·4
54	11 43·5	11 45·4	11 11·5	5·4 4·2	11·4 8·8	17·4 13·5
55	11 43·8	11 45·7	11 11·7	5·5 4·3	11·5 8·9	17·5 13·6
56	11 44·0	11 45·9	11 11·9	5·6 4·3	11·6 9·0	17·6 13·6
57	11 44·3	11 46·2	11 12·2	5·7 4·4	11·7 9·1	17·7 13·7
58	11 44·5	11 46·4	11 12·4	5·8 4·5	11·8 9·1	17·8 13·8
59	11 44·8	11 46·7	11 12·6	5·9 4·6	11·9 9·2	17·9 13·9
60	11 45·0	11 46·9	11 12·9	6·0 4·7	12·0 9·3	18·0 14·0

47	SUN PLANETS	ARIES	MOON	v or d Corrⁿ	v or d Corrⁿ	v or d Corrⁿ
s	° ′	° ′	° ′	′ ′	′ ′	′ ′
00	11 45·0	11 46·9	11 12·9	0·0 0·0	6·0 4·8	12·0 9·5
01	11 45·3	11 47·2	11 13·1	0·1 0·1	6·1 4·8	12·1 9·6
02	11 45·5	11 47·4	11 13·4	0·2 0·2	6·2 4·9	12·2 9·7
03	11 45·8	11 47·7	11 13·6	0·3 0·2	6·3 5·0	12·3 9·7
04	11 46·0	11 47·9	11 13·8	0·4 0·3	6·4 5·1	12·4 9·8
05	11 46·3	11 48·2	11 14·1	0·5 0·4	6·5 5·1	12·5 9·9
06	11 46·5	11 48·4	11 14·3	0·6 0·5	6·6 5·2	12·6 10·0
07	11 46·8	11 48·7	11 14·6	0·7 0·6	6·7 5·3	12·7 10·1
08	11 47·0	11 48·9	11 14·8	0·8 0·6	6·8 5·4	12·8 10·1
09	11 47·3	11 49·2	11 15·0	0·9 0·7	6·9 5·5	12·9 10·2
10	11 47·5	11 49·4	11 15·3	1·0 0·8	7·0 5·5	13·0 10·3
11	11 47·8	11 49·7	11 15·5	1·1 0·9	7·1 5·6	13·1 10·4
12	11 48·0	11 49·9	11 15·7	1·2 1·0	7·2 5·7	13·2 10·5
13	11 48·3	11 50·2	11 16·0	1·3 1·0	7·3 5·8	13·3 10·5
14	11 48·5	11 50·4	11 16·2	1·4 1·1	7·4 5·9	13·4 10·6
15	11 48·8	11 50·7	11 16·5	1·5 1·2	7·5 5·9	13·5 10·7
16	11 49·0	11 50·9	11 16·7	1·6 1·3	7·6 6·0	13·6 10·8
17	11 49·3	11 51·2	11 16·9	1·7 1·3	7·7 6·1	13·7 10·8
18	11 49·5	11 51·4	11 17·2	1·8 1·4	7·8 6·2	13·8 10·9
19	11 49·8	11 51·7	11 17·4	1·9 1·5	7·9 6·3	13·9 11·0
20	11 50·0	11 51·9	11 17·7	2·0 1·6	8·0 6·3	14·0 11·1
21	11 50·3	11 52·2	11 17·9	2·1 1·7	8·1 6·4	14·1 11·2
22	11 50·5	11 52·4	11 18·1	2·2 1·7	8·2 6·5	14·2 11·2
23	11 50·8	11 52·7	11 18·4	2·3 1·8	8·3 6·6	14·3 11·3
24	11 51·0	11 52·9	11 18·6	2·4 1·9	8·4 6·7	14·4 11·4
25	11 51·3	11 53·2	11 18·8	2·5 2·0	8·5 6·7	14·5 11·5
26	11 51·5	11 53·4	11 19·1	2·6 2·1	8·6 6·8	14·6 11·6
27	11 51·8	11 53·7	11 19·3	2·7 2·1	8·7 6·9	14·7 11·6
28	11 52·0	11 53·9	11 19·6	2·8 2·2	8·8 7·0	14·8 11·7
29	11 52·3	11 54·2	11 19·8	2·9 2·3	8·9 7·0	14·9 11·8
30	11 52·5	11 54·5	11 20·0	3·0 2·4	9·0 7·1	15·0 11·9
31	11 52·8	11 54·7	11 20·3	3·1 2·5	9·1 7·2	15·1 12·0
32	11 53·0	11 55·0	11 20·5	3·2 2·5	9·2 7·3	15·2 12·0
33	11 53·3	11 55·2	11 20·8	3·3 2·6	9·3 7·4	15·3 12·1
34	11 53·5	11 55·5	11 21·0	3·4 2·7	9·4 7·4	15·4 12·2
35	11 53·8	11 55·7	11 21·2	3·5 2·8	9·5 7·5	15·5 12·3
36	11 54·0	11 56·0	11 21·5	3·6 2·9	9·6 7·6	15·6 12·4
37	11 54·3	11 56·2	11 21·7	3·7 2·9	9·7 7·7	15·7 12·4
38	11 54·5	11 56·5	11 22·0	3·8 3·0	9·8 7·8	15·8 12·5
39	11 54·8	11 56·7	11 22·2	3·9 3·1	9·9 7·8	15·9 12·6
40	11 55·0	11 57·0	11 22·4	4·0 3·2	10·0 7·9	16·0 12·7
41	11 55·3	11 57·2	11 22·7	4·1 3·2	10·1 8·0	16·1 12·7
42	11 55·5	11 57·5	11 22·9	4·2 3·3	10·2 8·1	16·2 12·8
43	11 55·8	11 57·7	11 23·1	4·3 3·4	10·3 8·2	16·3 12·9
44	11 56·0	11 58·0	11 23·4	4·4 3·5	10·4 8·2	16·4 13·0
45	11 56·3	11 58·2	11 23·6	4·5 3·6	10·5 8·3	16·5 13·1
46	11 56·5	11 58·5	11 23·9	4·6 3·6	10·6 8·4	16·6 13·1
47	11 56·8	11 58·7	11 24·1	4·7 3·7	10·7 8·5	16·7 13·2
48	11 57·0	11 59·0	11 24·3	4·8 3·8	10·8 8·6	16·8 13·3
49	11 57·3	11 59·2	11 24·6	4·9 3·9	10·9 8·6	16·9 13·4
50	11 57·5	11 59·5	11 24·8	5·0 4·0	11·0 8·7	17·0 13·5
51	11 57·8	11 59·7	11 25·1	5·1 4·0	11·1 8·8	17·1 13·5
52	11 58·0	12 00·0	11 25·3	5·2 4·1	11·2 8·9	17·2 13·6
53	11 58·3	12 00·2	11 25·5	5·3 4·2	11·3 8·9	17·3 13·7
54	11 58·5	12 00·5	11 25·8	5·4 4·3	11·4 9·0	17·4 13·8
55	11 58·8	12 00·7	11 26·0	5·5 4·4	11·5 9·1	17·5 13·9
56	11 59·0	12 01·0	11 26·2	5·6 4·4	11·6 9·2	17·6 13·9
57	11 59·3	12 01·2	11 26·5	5·7 4·5	11·7 9·3	17·7 14·0
58	11 59·5	12 01·5	11 26·7	5·8 4·6	11·8 9·3	17·8 14·1
59	11 59·8	12 01·7	11 27·0	5·9 4·7	11·9 9·4	17·9 14·2
60	12 00·0	12 02·0	11 27·2	6·0 4·8	12·0 9·5	18·0 14·3

48ᵐ · INCREMENTS AND CORRECTIONS · 49ᵐ

48ᵐ	SUN PLANETS	ARIES	MOON	v or Corrⁿ d	v or Corrⁿ d	v or Corrⁿ d
s	° ′	° ′	° ′	′ ′	′ ′	′ ′
00	12 00·0	12 02·0	11 27·2	0·0 0·0	6·0 4·9	12·0 9·7
01	12 00·3	12 02·2	11 27·4	0·1 0·1	6·1 4·9	12·1 9·8
02	12 00·5	12 02·5	11 27·7	0·2 0·2	6·2 5·0	12·2 9·9
03	12 00·8	12 02·7	11 27·9	0·3 0·2	6·3 5·1	12·3 9·9
04	12 01·0	12 03·0	11 28·2	0·4 0·3	6·4 5·2	12·4 10·0
05	12 01·3	12 03·2	11 28·4	0·5 0·4	6·5 5·3	12·5 10·1
06	12 01·5	12 03·5	11 28·6	0·6 0·5	6·6 5·3	12·6 10·2
07	12 01·8	12 03·7	11 28·9	0·7 0·6	6·7 5·4	12·7 10·3
08	12 02·0	12 04·0	11 29·1	0·8 0·6	6·8 5·5	12·8 10·3
09	12 02·3	12 04·2	11 29·3	0·9 0·7	6·9 5·6	12·9 10·4
10	12 02·5	12 04·5	11 29·6	1·0 0·8	7·0 5·7	13·0 10·5
11	12 02·8	12 04·7	11 29·8	1·1 0·9	7·1 5·7	13·1 10·6
12	12 03·0	12 05·0	11 30·1	1·2 1·0	7·2 5·8	13·2 10·7
13	12 03·3	12 05·2	11 30·3	1·3 1·1	7·3 5·9	13·3 10·8
14	12 03·5	12 05·5	11 30·5	1·4 1·1	7·4 6·0	13·4 10·8
15	12 03·8	12 05·7	11 30·8	1·5 1·2	7·5 6·1	13·5 10·9
16	12 04·0	12 06·0	11 31·0	1·6 1·3	7·6 6·1	13·6 11·0
17	12 04·3	12 06·2	11 31·3	1·7 1·4	7·7 6·2	13·7 11·1
18	12 04·5	12 06·5	11 31·5	1·8 1·5	7·8 6·3	13·8 11·2
19	12 04·8	12 06·7	11 31·7	1·9 1·5	7·9 6·4	13·9 11·2
20	12 05·0	12 07·0	11 32·0	2·0 1·6	8·0 6·5	14·0 11·3
21	12 05·3	12 07·2	11 32·2	2·1 1·7	8·1 6·5	14·1 11·4
22	12 05·5	12 07·5	11 32·4	2·2 1·8	8·2 6·6	14·2 11·5
23	12 05·8	12 07·7	11 32·7	2·3 1·9	8·3 6·7	14·3 11·6
24	12 06·0	12 08·0	11 32·9	2·4 1·9	8·4 6·8	14·4 11·6
25	12 06·3	12 08·2	11 33·2	2·5 2·0	8·5 6·9	14·5 11·7
26	12 06·5	12 08·5	11 33·4	2·6 2·1	8·6 7·0	14·6 11·8
27	12 06·8	12 08·7	11 33·6	2·7 2·2	8·7 7·0	14·7 11·9
28	12 07·0	12 09·0	11 33·9	2·8 2·3	8·8 7·1	14·8 12·0
29	12 07·3	12 09·2	11 34·1	2·9 2·3	8·9 7·2	14·9 12·0
30	12 07·5	12 09·5	11 34·4	3·0 2·4	9·0 7·3	15·0 12·1
31	12 07·8	12 09·7	11 34·6	3·1 2·5	9·1 7·4	15·1 12·2
32	12 08·0	12 10·0	11 34·8	3·2 2·6	9·2 7·4	15·2 12·3
33	12 08·3	12 10·2	11 35·1	3·3 2·7	9·3 7·5	15·3 12·4
34	12 08·5	12 10·5	11 35·3	3·4 2·7	9·4 7·6	15·4 12·4
35	12 08·8	12 10·7	11 35·6	3·5 2·8	9·5 7·7	15·5 12·5
36	12 09·0	12 11·0	11 35·8	3·6 2·9	9·6 7·8	15·6 12·6
37	12 09·3	12 11·2	11 36·0	3·7 3·0	9·7 7·8	15·7 12·7
38	12 09·5	12 11·5	11 36·3	3·8 3·1	9·8 7·9	15·8 12·8
39	12 09·8	12 11·7	11 36·5	3·9 3·2	9·9 8·0	15·9 12·9
40	12 10·0	12 12·0	11 36·7	4·0 3·2	10·0 8·1	16·0 12·9
41	12 10·3	12 12·2	11 37·0	4·1 3·3	10·1 8·2	16·1 13·0
42	12 10·5	12 12·5	11 37·2	4·2 3·4	10·2 8·2	16·2 13·1
43	12 10·8	12 12·8	11 37·5	4·3 3·5	10·3 8·3	16·3 13·2
44	12 11·0	12 13·0	11 37·7	4·4 3·6	10·4 8·4	16·4 13·3
45	12 11·3	12 13·3	11 37·9	4·5 3·6	10·5 8·5	16·5 13·3
46	12 11·5	12 13·5	11 38·2	4·6 3·7	10·6 8·6	16·6 13·4
47	12 11·8	12 13·8	11 38·4	4·7 3·8	10·7 8·6	16·7 13·5
48	12 12·0	12 14·0	11 38·7	4·8 3·9	10·8 8·7	16·8 13·6
49	12 12·3	12 14·3	11 38·9	4·9 4·0	10·9 8·8	16·9 13·7
50	12 12·5	12 14·5	11 39·1	5·0 4·0	11·0 8·9	17·0 13·7
51	12 12·8	12 14·8	11 39·4	5·1 4·1	11·1 9·0	17·1 13·8
52	12 13·0	12 15·0	11 39·6	5·2 4·2	11·2 9·1	17·2 13·9
53	12 13·3	12 15·3	11 39·8	5·3 4·3	11·3 9·1	17·3 14·0
54	12 13·5	12 15·5	11 40·1	5·4 4·4	11·4 9·2	17·4 14·1
55	12 13·8	12 15·8	11 40·3	5·5 4·4	11·5 9·3	17·5 14·1
56	12 14·0	12 16·0	11 40·6	5·6 4·5	11·6 9·4	17·6 14·2
57	12 14·3	12 16·3	11 40·8	5·7 4·6	11·7 9·5	17·7 14·3
58	12 14·5	12 16·5	11 41·0	5·8 4·7	11·8 9·5	17·8 14·4
59	12 14·8	12 16·8	11 41·3	5·9 4·8	11·9 9·6	17·9 14·5
60	12 15·0	12 17·0	11 41·5	6·0 4·9	12·0 9·7	18·0 14·6

49ᵐ	SUN PLANETS	ARIES	MOON	v or Corrⁿ d	v or Corrⁿ d	v or Corrⁿ d
s	° ′	° ′	° ′	′ ′	′ ′	′ ′
00	12 15·0	12 17·0	11 41·5	0·0 0·0	6·0 5·0	12·0 9·9
01	12 15·3	12 17·3	11 41·8	0·1 0·1	6·1 5·0	12·1 10·0
02	12 15·5	12 17·5	11 42·0	0·2 0·2	6·2 5·1	12·2 10·1
03	12 15·8	12 17·8	11 42·2	0·3 0·2	6·3 5·2	12·3 10·1
04	12 16·0	12 18·0	11 42·5	0·4 0·3	6·4 5·3	12·4 10·2
05	12 16·3	12 18·3	11 42·7	0·5 0·4	6·5 5·4	12·5 10·3
06	12 16·5	12 18·5	11 42·9	0·6 0·5	6·6 5·4	12·6 10·4
07	12 16·8	12 18·8	11 43·2	0·7 0·6	6·7 5·5	12·7 10·5
08	12 17·0	12 19·0	11 43·4	0·8 0·7	6·8 5·6	12·8 10·6
09	12 17·3	12 19·3	11 43·7	0·9 0·7	6·9 5·7	12·9 10·6
10	12 17·5	12 19·5	11 43·9	1·0 0·8	7·0 5·8	13·0 10·7
11	12 17·8	12 19·8	11 44·1	1·1 0·9	7·1 5·9	13·1 10·8
12	12 18·0	12 20·0	11 44·4	1·2 1·0	7·2 5·9	13·2 10·9
13	12 18·3	12 20·3	11 44·6	1·3 1·1	7·3 6·0	13·3 11·0
14	12 18·5	12 20·5	11 44·9	1·4 1·2	7·4 6·1	13·4 11·1
15	12 18·8	12 20·8	11 45·1	1·5 1·2	7·5 6·2	13·5 11·1
16	12 19·0	12 21·0	11 45·3	1·6 1·3	7·6 6·3	13·6 11·2
17	12 19·3	12 21·3	11 45·6	1·7 1·4	7·7 6·4	13·7 11·3
18	12 19·5	12 21·5	11 45·8	1·8 1·5	7·8 6·4	13·8 11·4
19	12 19·8	12 21·8	11 46·1	1·9 1·6	7·9 6·5	13·9 11·5
20	12 20·0	12 22·0	11 46·3	2·0 1·7	8·0 6·6	14·0 11·6
21	12 20·3	12 22·3	11 46·5	2·1 1·7	8·1 6·7	14·1 11·6
22	12 20·5	12 22·5	11 46·8	2·2 1·8	8·2 6·8	14·2 11·7
23	12 20·8	12 22·8	11 47·0	2·3 1·9	8·3 6·8	14·3 11·8
24	12 21·0	12 23·0	11 47·2	2·4 2·0	8·4 6·9	14·4 11·9
25	12 21·3	12 23·3	11 47·5	2·5 2·1	8·5 7·0	14·5 12·0
26	12 21·5	12 23·5	11 47·7	2·6 2·1	8·6 7·1	14·6 12·0
27	12 21·8	12 23·8	11 48·0	2·7 2·2	8·7 7·2	14·7 12·1
28	12 22·0	12 24·0	11 48·2	2·8 2·3	8·8 7·3	14·8 12·2
29	12 22·3	12 24·3	11 48·4	2·9 2·4	8·9 7·3	14·9 12·3
30	12 22·5	12 24·5	11 48·7	3·0 2·5	9·0 7·4	15·0 12·4
31	12 22·8	12 24·8	11 48·9	3·1 2·6	9·1 7·5	15·1 12·5
32	12 23·0	12 25·0	11 49·2	3·2 2·6	9·2 7·6	15·2 12·5
33	12 23·3	12 25·3	11 49·4	3·3 2·7	9·3 7·7	15·3 12·6
34	12 23·5	12 25·5	11 49·6	3·4 2·8	9·4 7·8	15·4 12·7
35	12 23·8	12 25·8	11 49·9	3·5 2·9	9·5 7·8	15·5 12·8
36	12 24·0	12 26·0	11 50·1	3·6 3·0	9·6 7·9	15·6 12·9
37	12 24·3	12 26·3	11 50·3	3·7 3·1	9·7 8·0	15·7 13·0
38	12 24·5	12 26·5	11 50·6	3·8 3·1	9·8 8·1	15·8 13·0
39	12 24·8	12 26·8	11 50·8	3·9 3·2	9·9 8·2	15·9 13·1
40	12 25·0	12 27·0	11 51·1	4·0 3·3	10·0 8·3	16·0 13·2
41	12 25·3	12 27·3	11 51·3	4·1 3·4	10·1 8·3	16·1 13·3
42	12 25·5	12 27·5	11 51·5	4·2 3·5	10·2 8·4	16·2 13·4
43	12 25·8	12 27·8	11 51·8	4·3 3·5	10·3 8·5	16·3 13·4
44	12 26·0	12 28·0	11 52·0	4·4 3·6	10·4 8·6	16·4 13·5
45	12 26·3	12 28·3	11 52·3	4·5 3·7	10·5 8·7	16·5 13·6
46	12 26·5	12 28·5	11 52·5	4·6 3·8	10·6 8·7	16·6 13·7
47	12 26·8	12 28·8	11 52·7	4·7 3·9	10·7 8·8	16·7 13·8
48	12 27·0	12 29·0	11 53·0	4·8 4·0	10·8 8·9	16·8 13·9
49	12 27·3	12 29·3	11 53·2	4·9 4·0	10·9 9·0	16·9 13·9
50	12 27·5	12 29·5	11 53·4	5·0 4·1	11·0 9·1	17·0 14·0
51	12 27·8	12 29·8	11 53·7	5·1 4·2	11·1 9·2	17·1 14·1
52	12 28·0	12 30·0	11 53·9	5·2 4·3	11·2 9·2	17·2 14·2
53	12 28·3	12 30·3	11 54·2	5·3 4·4	11·3 9·3	17·3 14·3
54	12 28·5	12 30·5	11 54·4	5·4 4·5	11·4 9·4	17·4 14·4
55	12 28·8	12 30·8	11 54·6	5·5 4·5	11·5 9·5	17·5 14·4
56	12 29·0	12 31·1	11 54·9	5·6 4·6	11·6 9·6	17·6 14·5
57	12 29·3	12 31·3	11 55·1	5·7 4·7	11·7 9·7	17·7 14·6
58	12 29·5	12 31·6	11 55·4	5·8 4·8	11·8 9·7	17·8 14·7
59	12 29·8	12 31·8	11 55·6	5·9 4·9	11·9 9·8	17·9 14·8
60	12 30·0	12 32·1	11 55·8	6·0 5·0	12·0 9·9	18·0 14·9

50ᵐ   INCREMENTS AND CORRECTIONS   51ᵐ

50ᵐ	SUN PLANETS	ARIES	MOON	v or Corrⁿ d	v or Corrⁿ d	v or Corrⁿ d		51ᵐ	SUN PLANETS	ARIES	MOON	v or Corrⁿ d	v or Corrⁿ d	v or Corrⁿ d
s	° ′	° ′	° ′	′ ′	′ ′	′ ′		s	° ′	° ′	° ′	′ ′	′ ′	′ ′
00	12 30·0	12 32·1	11 55·8	0·0 0·0	6·0 5·1	12·0 10·1		00	12 45·0	12 47·1	12 10·2	0·0 0·0	6·0 5·2	12·0 10·3
01	12 30·3	12 32·3	11 56·1	0·1 0·1	6·1 5·1	12·1 10·2		01	12 45·3	12 47·3	12 10·4	0·1 0·1	6·1 5·2	12·1 10·4
02	12 30·5	12 32·6	11 56·3	0·2 0·2	6·2 5·2	12·2 10·3		02	12 45·5	12 47·6	12 10·6	0·2 0·2	6·2 5·3	12·2 10·5
03	12 30·8	12 32·8	11 56·5	0·3 0·3	6·3 5·3	12·3 10·4		03	12 45·8	12 47·8	12 10·9	0·3 0·3	6·3 5·4	12·3 10·6
04	12 31·0	12 33·1	11 56·8	0·4 0·3	6·4 5·4	12·4 10·4		04	12 46·0	12 48·1	12 11·1	0·4 0·3	6·4 5·5	12·4 10·6
05	12 31·3	12 33·3	11 57·0	0·5 0·4	6·5 5·5	12·5 10·5		05	12 46·3	12 48·3	12 11·3	0·5 0·4	6·5 5·6	12·5 10·7
06	12 31·5	12 33·6	11 57·3	0·6 0·5	6·6 5·6	12·6 10·6		06	12 46·5	12 48·6	12 11·6	0·6 0·5	6·6 5·7	12·6 10·8
07	12 31·8	12 33·8	11 57·5	0·7 0·6	6·7 5·6	12·7 10·7		07	12 46·8	12 48·8	12 11·8	0·7 0·6	6·7 5·8	12·7 10·9
08	12 32·0	12 34·1	11 57·7	0·8 0·7	6·8 5·7	12·8 10·8		08	12 47·0	12 49·1	12 12·1	0·8 0·7	6·8 5·8	12·8 11·0
09	12 32·3	12 34·3	11 58·0	0·9 0·8	6·9 5·8	12·9 10·9		09	12 47·3	12 49·4	12 12·3	0·9 0·8	6·9 5·9	12·9 11·1
10	12 32·5	12 34·6	11 58·2	1·0 0·8	7·0 5·9	13·0 10·9		10	12 47·5	12 49·6	12 12·5	1·0 0·9	7·0 6·0	13·0 11·2
11	12 32·8	12 34·8	11 58·5	1·1 0·9	7·1 6·0	13·1 11·0		11	12 47·8	12 49·9	12 12·8	1·1 0·9	7·1 6·1	13·1 11·2
12	12 33·0	12 35·1	11 58·7	1·2 1·0	7·2 6·1	13·2 11·1		12	12 48·0	12 50·1	12 13·0	1·2 1·0	7·2 6·2	13·2 11·3
13	12 33·3	12 35·3	11 58·9	1·3 1·1	7·3 6·1	13·3 11·2		13	12 48·3	12 50·4	12 13·3	1·3 1·1	7·3 6·3	13·3 11·4
14	12 33·5	12 35·6	11 59·2	1·4 1·2	7·4 6·2	13·4 11·3		14	12 48·5	12 50·6	12 13·5	1·4 1·2	7·4 6·4	13·4 11·5
15	12 33·8	12 35·8	11 59·4	1·5 1·3	7·5 6·3	13·5 11·4		15	12 48·8	12 50·9	12 13·7	1·5 1·3	7·5 6·4	13·5 11·6
16	12 34·0	12 36·1	11 59·7	1·6 1·3	7·6 6·4	13·6 11·4		16	12 49·0	12 51·1	12 14·0	1·6 1·4	7·6 6·5	13·6 11·7
17	12 34·3	12 36·3	11 59·9	1·7 1·4	7·7 6·5	13·7 11·5		17	12 49·3	12 51·4	12 14·2	1·7 1·5	7·7 6·6	13·7 11·8
18	12 34·5	12 36·6	12 00·1	1·8 1·5	7·8 6·6	13·8 11·6		18	12 49·5	12 51·6	12 14·4	1·8 1·5	7·8 6·7	13·8 11·8
19	12 34·8	12 36·8	12 00·4	1·9 1·6	7·9 6·6	13·9 11·7		19	12 49·8	12 51·9	12 14·7	1·9 1·6	7·9 6·8	13·9 11·9
20	12 35·0	12 37·1	12 00·6	2·0 1·7	8·0 6·7	14·0 11·8		20	12 50·0	12 52·1	12 14·9	2·0 1·7	8·0 6·9	14·0 12·0
21	12 35·3	12 37·3	12 00·8	2·1 1·8	8·1 6·8	14·1 11·9		21	12 50·3	12 52·4	12 15·2	2·1 1·8	8·1 7·0	14·1 12·1
22	12 35·5	12 37·6	12 01·1	2·2 1·9	8·2 6·9	14·2 12·0		22	12 50·5	12 52·6	12 15·4	2·2 1·9	8·2 7·0	14·2 12·2
23	12 35·8	12 37·8	12 01·3	2·3 1·9	8·3 7·0	14·3 12·0		23	12 50·8	12 52·9	12 15·6	2·3 2·0	8·3 7·1	14·3 12·3
24	12 36·0	12 38·1	12 01·6	2·4 2·0	8·4 7·1	14·4 12·1		24	12 51·0	12 53·1	12 15·9	2·4 2·1	8·4 7·2	14·4 12·4
25	12 36·3	12 38·3	12 01·8	2·5 2·1	8·5 7·2	14·5 12·2		25	12 51·3	12 53·4	12 16·1	2·5 2·1	8·5 7·3	14·5 12·4
26	12 36·5	12 38·6	12 02·0	2·6 2·2	8·6 7·2	14·6 12·3		26	12 51·5	12 53·6	12 16·4	2·6 2·2	8·6 7·4	14·6 12·5
27	12 36·8	12 38·8	12 02·3	2·7 2·3	8·7 7·3	14·7 12·4		27	12 51·8	12 53·9	12 16·6	2·7 2·3	8·7 7·5	14·7 12·6
28	12 37·0	12 39·1	12 02·5	2·8 2·4	8·8 7·4	14·8 12·5		28	12 52·0	12 54·1	12 16·8	2·8 2·4	8·8 7·6	14·8 12·7
29	12 37·3	12 39·3	12 02·8	2·9 2·4	8·9 7·5	14·9 12·5		29	12 52·3	12 54·4	12 17·1	2·9 2·5	8·9 7·6	14·9 12·8
30	12 37·5	12 39·6	12 03·0	3·0 2·5	9·0 7·6	15·0 12·6		30	12 52·5	12 54·6	12 17·3	3·0 2·6	9·0 7·7	15·0 12·9
31	12 37·8	12 39·8	12 03·2	3·1 2·6	9·1 7·7	15·1 12·7		31	12 52·8	12 54·9	12 17·5	3·1 2·7	9·1 7·8	15·1 13·0
32	12 38·0	12 40·1	12 03·5	3·2 2·7	9·2 7·7	15·2 12·8		32	12 53·0	12 55·1	12 17·8	3·2 2·7	9·2 7·9	15·2 13·0
33	12 38·3	12 40·3	12 03·7	3·3 2·8	9·3 7·8	15·3 12·9		33	12 53·3	12 55·4	12 18·0	3·3 2·8	9·3 8·0	15·3 13·1
34	12 38·5	12 40·6	12 03·9	3·4 2·9	9·4 7·9	15·4 13·0		34	12 53·5	12 55·6	12 18·3	3·4 2·9	9·4 8·1	15·4 13·2
35	12 38·8	12 40·8	12 04·2	3·5 2·9	9·5 8·0	15·5 13·0		35	12 53·8	12 55·9	12 18·5	3·5 3·0	9·5 8·2	15·5 13·3
36	12 39·0	12 41·1	12 04·4	3·6 3·0	9·6 8·1	15·6 13·1		36	12 54·0	12 56·1	12 18·7	3·6 3·1	9·6 8·2	15·6 13·4
37	12 39·3	12 41·3	12 04·7	3·7 3·1	9·7 8·2	15·7 13·2		37	12 54·3	12 56·4	12 19·0	3·7 3·2	9·7 8·3	15·7 13·5
38	12 39·5	12 41·6	12 04·9	3·8 3·2	9·8 8·2	15·8 13·3		38	12 54·5	12 56·6	12 19·2	3·8 3·3	9·8 8·4	15·8 13·6
39	12 39·8	12 41·8	12 05·1	3·9 3·3	9·9 8·3	15·9 13·4		39	12 54·8	12 56·9	12 19·5	3·9 3·3	9·9 8·5	15·9 13·6
40	12 40·0	12 42·1	12 05·4	4·0 3·4	10·0 8·4	16·0 13·5		40	12 55·0	12 57·1	12 19·7	4·0 3·4	10·0 8·6	16·0 13·7
41	12 40·3	12 42·3	12 05·6	4·1 3·5	10·1 8·5	16·1 13·6		41	12 55·3	12 57·4	12 19·9	4·1 3·5	10·1 8·7	16·1 13·8
42	12 40·5	12 42·6	12 05·9	4·2 3·5	10·2 8·6	16·2 13·6		42	12 55·5	12 57·6	12 20·2	4·2 3·6	10·2 8·8	16·2 13·9
43	12 40·8	12 42·8	12 06·1	4·3 3·6	10·3 8·7	16·3 13·7		43	12 55·8	12 57·9	12 20·4	4·3 3·7	10·3 8·8	16·3 14·0
44	12 41·0	12 43·1	12 06·3	4·4 3·7	10·4 8·8	16·4 13·8		44	12 56·0	12 58·1	12 20·6	4·4 3·8	10·4 8·9	16·4 14·1
45	12 41·3	12 43·3	12 06·6	4·5 3·8	10·5 8·8	16·5 13·9		45	12 56·3	12 58·4	12 20·9	4·5 3·9	10·5 9·0	16·5 14·2
46	12 41·5	12 43·6	12 06·8	4·6 3·9	10·6 8·9	16·6 14·0		46	12 56·5	12 58·6	12 21·1	4·6 3·9	10·6 9·1	16·6 14·2
47	12 41·8	12 43·8	12 07·0	4·7 4·0	10·7 9·0	16·7 14·1		47	12 56·8	12 58·9	12 21·4	4·7 4·0	10·7 9·2	16·7 14·3
48	12 42·0	12 44·1	12 07·3	4·8 4·0	10·8 9·1	16·8 14·1		48	12 57·0	12 59·1	12 21·6	4·8 4·1	10·8 9·3	16·8 14·4
49	12 42·3	12 44·3	12 07·5	4·9 4·1	10·9 9·2	16·9 14·2		49	12 57·3	12 59·4	12 21·8	4·9 4·2	10·9 9·4	16·9 14·5
50	12 42·5	12 44·6	12 07·8	5·0 4·2	11·0 9·3	17·0 14·3		50	12 57·5	12 59·6	12 22·1	5·0 4·3	11·0 9·4	17·0 14·6
51	12 42·8	12 44·8	12 08·0	5·1 4·3	11·1 9·3	17·1 14·4		51	12 57·8	12 59·9	12 22·3	5·1 4·4	11·1 9·5	17·1 14·7
52	12 43·0	12 45·1	12 08·2	5·2 4·4	11·2 9·4	17·2 14·5		52	12 58·0	13 00·1	12 22·6	5·2 4·5	11·2 9·6	17·2 14·8
53	12 43·3	12 45·3	12 08·5	5·3 4·5	11·3 9·5	17·3 14·6		53	12 58·3	13 00·4	12 22·8	5·3 4·5	11·3 9·7	17·3 14·8
54	12 43·5	12 45·6	12 08·7	5·4 4·5	11·4 9·6	17·4 14·6		54	12 58·5	13 00·6	12 23·0	5·4 4·6	11·4 9·8	17·4 14·9
55	12 43·8	12 45·8	12 09·0	5·5 4·6	11·5 9·7	17·5 14·7		55	12 58·8	13 00·9	12 23·3	5·5 4·7	11·5 9·9	17·5 15·0
56	12 44·0	12 46·1	12 09·2	5·6 4·7	11·6 9·8	17·6 14·8		56	12 59·0	13 01·1	12 23·5	5·6 4·8	11·6 10·0	17·6 15·1
57	12 44·3	12 46·3	12 09·4	5·7 4·8	11·7 9·8	17·7 14·9		57	12 59·3	13 01·4	12 23·8	5·7 4·9	11·7 10·0	17·7 15·2
58	12 44·5	12 46·6	12 09·7	5·8 4·9	11·8 9·9	17·8 15·0		58	12 59·5	13 01·6	12 24·0	5·8 5·0	11·8 10·1	17·8 15·3
59	12 44·8	12 46·8	12 09·9	5·9 5·0	11·9 10·0	17·9 15·1		59	12 59·8	13 01·9	12 24·2	5·9 5·1	11·9 10·2	17·9 15·4
60	12 45·0	12 47·1	12 10·2	6·0 5·1	12·0 10·1	18·0 15·2		60	13 00·0	13 02·1	12 24·5	6·0 5·2	12·0 10·3	18·0 15·5

52ᵐ INCREMENTS AND CORRECTIONS 53ᵐ

52ᵐ s	SUN PLANETS ° ′	ARIES ° ′	MOON ° ′	v or Corrⁿ d ′ ′	v or Corrⁿ d ′ ′	v or Corrⁿ d ′ ′
00	13 00.0	13 02.1	12 24.5	0.0 0.0	6.0 5.3	12.0 10.5
01	13 00.3	13 02.4	12 24.7	0.1 0.1	6.1 5.3	12.1 10.6
02	13 00.5	13 02.6	12 24.9	0.2 0.2	6.2 5.4	12.2 10.7
03	13 00.8	13 02.9	12 25.2	0.3 0.3	6.3 5.5	12.3 10.8
04	13 01.0	13 03.1	12 25.4	0.4 0.4	6.4 5.6	12.4 10.9
05	13 01.3	13 03.4	12 25.7	0.5 0.4	6.5 5.7	12.5 10.9
06	13 01.5	13 03.6	12 25.9	0.6 0.5	6.6 5.8	12.6 11.0
07	13 01.8	13 03.9	12 26.1	0.7 0.6	6.7 5.9	12.7 11.1
08	13 02.0	13 04.1	12 26.4	0.8 0.7	6.8 6.0	12.8 11.2
09	13 02.3	13 04.4	12 26.6	0.9 0.8	6.9 6.0	12.9 11.3
10	13 02.5	13 04.6	12 26.9	1.0 0.9	7.0 6.1	13.0 11.4
11	13 02.8	13 04.9	12 27.1	1.1 1.0	7.1 6.2	13.1 11.5
12	13 03.0	13 05.1	12 27.3	1.2 1.1	7.2 6.3	13.2 11.6
13	13 03.3	13 05.4	12 27.6	1.3 1.1	7.3 6.4	13.3 11.6
14	13 03.5	13 05.6	12 27.8	1.4 1.2	7.4 6.5	13.4 11.7
15	13 03.8	13 05.9	12 28.0	1.5 1.3	7.5 6.6	13.5 11.8
16	13 04.0	13 06.1	12 28.3	1.6 1.4	7.6 6.7	13.6 11.9
17	13 04.3	13 06.4	12 28.5	1.7 1.5	7.7 6.7	13.7 12.0
18	13 04.5	13 06.6	12 28.8	1.8 1.6	7.8 6.8	13.8 12.1
19	13 04.8	13 06.9	12 29.0	1.9 1.7	7.9 6.9	13.9 12.2
20	13 05.0	13 07.1	12 29.2	2.0 1.8	8.0 7.0	14.0 12.3
21	13 05.3	13 07.4	12 29.5	2.1 1.8	8.1 7.1	14.1 12.3
22	13 05.5	13 07.7	12 29.7	2.2 1.9	8.2 7.2	14.2 12.4
23	13 05.8	13 07.9	12 30.0	2.3 2.0	8.3 7.3	14.3 12.5
24	13 06.0	13 08.2	12 30.2	2.4 2.1	8.4 7.4	14.4 12.6
25	13 06.3	13 08.4	12 30.4	2.5 2.2	8.5 7.4	14.5 12.7
26	13 06.5	13 08.7	12 30.7	2.6 2.3	8.6 7.5	14.6 12.8
27	13 06.8	13 08.9	12 30.9	2.7 2.4	8.7 7.6	14.7 12.9
28	13 07.0	13 09.2	12 31.1	2.8 2.5	8.8 7.7	14.8 13.0
29	13 07.3	13 09.4	12 31.4	2.9 2.5	8.9 7.8	14.9 13.0
30	13 07.5	13 09.7	12 31.6	3.0 2.6	9.0 7.9	15.0 13.1
31	13 07.8	13 09.9	12 31.9	3.1 2.7	9.1 8.0	15.1 13.2
32	13 08.0	13 10.2	12 32.1	3.2 2.8	9.2 8.1	15.2 13.3
33	13 08.3	13 10.4	12 32.3	3.3 2.9	9.3 8.1	15.3 13.4
34	13 08.5	13 10.7	12 32.6	3.4 3.0	9.4 8.2	15.4 13.5
35	13 08.8	13 10.9	12 32.8	3.5 3.1	9.5 8.3	15.5 13.6
36	13 09.0	13 11.2	12 33.1	3.6 3.2	9.6 8.4	15.6 13.7
37	13 09.3	13 11.4	12 33.3	3.7 3.2	9.7 8.5	15.7 13.7
38	13 09.5	13 11.7	12 33.5	3.8 3.3	9.8 8.6	15.8 13.8
39	13 09.8	13 11.9	12 33.8	3.9 3.4	9.9 8.7	15.9 13.9
40	13 10.0	13 12.2	12 34.0	4.0 3.5	10.0 8.8	16.0 14.0
41	13 10.3	13 12.4	12 34.2	4.1 3.6	10.1 8.8	16.1 14.1
42	13 10.5	13 12.7	12 34.5	4.2 3.7	10.2 8.9	16.2 14.2
43	13 10.8	13 12.9	12 34.7	4.3 3.8	10.3 9.0	16.3 14.3
44	13 11.0	13 13.2	12 35.0	4.4 3.9	10.4 9.1	16.4 14.4
45	13 11.3	13 13.4	12 35.2	4.5 3.9	10.5 9.2	16.5 14.4
46	13 11.5	13 13.7	12 35.4	4.6 4.0	10.6 9.3	16.6 14.5
47	13 11.8	13 13.9	12 35.7	4.7 4.1	10.7 9.4	16.7 14.6
48	13 12.0	13 14.2	12 35.9	4.8 4.2	10.8 9.5	16.8 14.7
49	13 12.3	13 14.4	12 36.2	4.9 4.3	10.9 9.5	16.9 14.8
50	13 12.5	13 14.7	12 36.4	5.0 4.4	11.0 9.6	17.0 14.9
51	13 12.8	13 14.9	12 36.6	5.1 4.5	11.1 9.7	17.1 15.0
52	13 13.0	13 15.2	12 36.9	5.2 4.6	11.2 9.8	17.2 15.1
53	13 13.3	13 15.4	12 37.1	5.3 4.6	11.3 9.9	17.3 15.1
54	13 13.5	13 15.7	12 37.4	5.4 4.7	11.4 10.0	17.4 15.2
55	13 13.8	13 15.9	12 37.6	5.5 4.8	11.5 10.1	17.5 15.3
56	13 14.0	13 16.2	12 37.8	5.6 4.9	11.6 10.2	17.6 15.4
57	13 14.3	13 16.4	12 38.1	5.7 5.0	11.7 10.2	17.7 15.5
58	13 14.5	13 16.7	12 38.3	5.8 5.1	11.8 10.3	17.8 15.6
59	13 14.8	13 16.9	12 38.5	5.9 5.2	11.9 10.4	17.9 15.7
60	13 15.0	13 17.2	12 38.8	6.0 5.3	12.0 10.5	18.0 15.8

53ᵐ s	SUN PLANETS ° ′	ARIES ° ′	MOON ° ′	v or Corrⁿ d ′ ′	v or Corrⁿ d ′ ′	v or Corrⁿ d ′ ′
00	13 15.0	13 17.2	12 38.8	0.0 0.0	6.0 5.4	12.0 10.7
01	13 15.3	13 17.4	12 39.0	0.1 0.1	6.1 5.4	12.1 10.8
02	13 15.5	13 17.7	12 39.3	0.2 0.2	6.2 5.5	12.2 10.9
03	13 15.8	13 17.9	12 39.5	0.3 0.3	6.3 5.6	12.3 11.0
04	13 16.0	13 18.2	12 39.7	0.4 0.4	6.4 5.7	12.4 11.1
05	13 16.3	13 18.4	12 40.0	0.5 0.4	6.5 5.8	12.5 11.1
06	13 16.5	13 18.7	12 40.2	0.6 0.5	6.6 5.9	12.6 11.2
07	13 16.8	13 18.9	12 40.5	0.7 0.6	6.7 6.0	12.7 11.3
08	13 17.0	13 19.2	12 40.7	0.8 0.7	6.8 6.1	12.8 11.4
09	13 17.3	13 19.4	12 40.9	0.9 0.8	6.9 6.2	12.9 11.5
10	13 17.5	13 19.7	12 41.2	1.0 0.9	7.0 6.2	13.0 11.6
11	13 17.8	13 19.9	12 41.4	1.1 1.0	7.1 6.3	13.1 11.7
12	13 18.0	13 20.2	12 41.6	1.2 1.1	7.2 6.4	13.2 11.8
13	13 18.3	13 20.4	12 41.9	1.3 1.2	7.3 6.5	13.3 11.9
14	13 18.5	13 20.7	12 42.1	1.4 1.2	7.4 6.6	13.4 11.9
15	13 18.8	13 20.9	12 42.4	1.5 1.3	7.5 6.7	13.5 12.0
16	13 19.0	13 21.2	12 42.6	1.6 1.4	7.6 6.8	13.6 12.1
17	13 19.3	13 21.4	12 42.8	1.7 1.5	7.7 6.9	13.7 12.2
18	13 19.5	13 21.7	12 43.1	1.8 1.6	7.8 7.0	13.8 12.3
19	13 19.8	13 21.9	12 43.3	1.9 1.7	7.9 7.0	13.9 12.4
20	13 20.0	13 22.2	12 43.6	2.0 1.8	8.0 7.1	14.0 12.5
21	13 20.3	13 22.4	12 43.8	2.1 1.9	8.1 7.2	14.1 12.6
22	13 20.5	13 22.7	12 44.0	2.2 2.0	8.2 7.3	14.2 12.7
23	13 20.8	13 22.9	12 44.3	2.3 2.1	8.3 7.4	14.3 12.8
24	13 21.0	13 23.2	12 44.5	2.4 2.1	8.4 7.5	14.4 12.8
25	13 21.3	13 23.4	12 44.7	2.5 2.2	8.5 7.6	14.5 12.9
26	13 21.5	13 23.7	12 45.0	2.6 2.3	8.6 7.7	14.6 13.0
27	13 21.8	13 23.9	12 45.2	2.7 2.4	8.7 7.8	14.7 13.1
28	13 22.0	13 24.2	12 45.5	2.8 2.5	8.8 7.8	14.8 13.2
29	13 22.3	13 24.4	12 45.7	2.9 2.6	8.9 7.9	14.9 13.3
30	13 22.5	13 24.7	12 45.9	3.0 2.7	9.0 8.0	15.0 13.4
31	13 22.8	13 24.9	12 46.2	3.1 2.8	9.1 8.1	15.1 13.5
32	13 23.0	13 25.2	12 46.4	3.2 2.9	9.2 8.2	15.2 13.6
33	13 23.3	13 25.4	12 46.7	3.3 2.9	9.3 8.3	15.3 13.6
34	13 23.5	13 25.7	12 46.9	3.4 3.0	9.4 8.4	15.4 13.7
35	13 23.8	13 26.0	12 47.1	3.5 3.1	9.5 8.5	15.5 13.8
36	13 24.0	13 26.2	12 47.4	3.6 3.2	9.6 8.6	15.6 13.9
37	13 24.3	13 26.5	12 47.6	3.7 3.3	9.7 8.6	15.7 14.0
38	13 24.5	13 26.7	12 47.9	3.8 3.4	9.8 8.7	15.8 14.1
39	13 24.8	13 27.0	12 48.1	3.9 3.5	9.9 8.8	15.9 14.2
40	13 25.0	13 27.2	12 48.3	4.0 3.6	10.0 8.9	16.0 14.3
41	13 25.3	13 27.5	12 48.6	4.1 3.7	10.1 9.0	16.1 14.4
42	13 25.5	13 27.7	12 48.8	4.2 3.7	10.2 9.1	16.2 14.4
43	13 25.8	13 28.0	12 49.0	4.3 3.8	10.3 9.2	16.3 14.5
44	13 26.0	13 28.2	12 49.3	4.4 3.9	10.4 9.3	16.4 14.6
45	13 26.3	13 28.5	12 49.5	4.5 4.0	10.5 9.4	16.5 14.7
46	13 26.5	13 28.7	12 49.8	4.6 4.1	10.6 9.5	16.6 14.8
47	13 26.8	13 29.0	12 50.0	4.7 4.2	10.7 9.5	16.7 14.9
48	13 27.0	13 29.2	12 50.2	4.8 4.3	10.8 9.6	16.8 15.0
49	13 27.3	13 29.5	12 50.5	4.9 4.4	10.9 9.7	16.9 15.1
50	13 27.5	13 29.7	12 50.7	5.0 4.5	11.0 9.8	17.0 15.2
51	13 27.8	13 30.0	12 51.0	5.1 4.5	11.1 9.9	17.1 15.2
52	13 28.0	13 30.2	12 51.2	5.2 4.6	11.2 10.0	17.2 15.3
53	13 28.3	13 30.5	12 51.4	5.3 4.7	11.3 10.1	17.3 15.4
54	13 28.5	13 30.7	12 51.7	5.4 4.8	11.4 10.2	17.4 15.5
55	13 28.8	13 31.0	12 51.9	5.5 4.9	11.5 10.3	17.5 15.6
56	13 29.0	13 31.2	12 52.1	5.6 5.0	11.6 10.3	17.6 15.7
57	13 29.3	13 31.5	12 52.4	5.7 5.1	11.7 10.4	17.7 15.8
58	13 29.5	13 31.7	12 52.6	5.8 5.2	11.8 10.5	17.8 15.9
59	13 29.8	13 32.0	12 52.9	5.9 5.3	11.9 10.6	17.9 16.0
60	13 30.0	13 32.2	12 53.1	6.0 5.4	12.0 10.7	18.0 16.1

54ᵐ INCREMENTS AND CORRECTIONS 55ᵐ

54	SUN PLANETS	ARIES	MOON	v or d Corrⁿ	v or d Corrⁿ	v or d Corrⁿ	55	SUN PLANETS	ARIES	MOON	v or d Corrⁿ	v or d Corrⁿ	v or d Corrⁿ
s	° ′	° ′	° ′	′ ′	′ ′	′ ′	s	° ′	° ′	° ′	′ ′	′ ′	′ ′
00	13 30·0	13 32·2	12 53·1	0·0 0·0	6·0 5·5	12·0 10·9	00	13 45·0	13 47·3	13 07·4	0·0 0·0	6·0 5·6	12·0 11·1
01	13 30·3	13 32·5	12 53·3	0·1 0·1	6·1 5·5	12·1 11·0	01	13 45·3	13 47·5	13 07·7	0·1 0·1	6·1 5·6	12·1 11·2
02	13 30·5	13 32·7	12 53·6	0·2 0·2	6·2 5·6	12·2 11·1	02	13 45·5	13 47·8	13 07·9	0·2 0·2	6·2 5·7	12·2 11·3
03	13 30·8	13 33·0	12 53·8	0·3 0·3	6·3 5·7	12·3 11·2	03	13 45·8	13 48·0	13 08·1	0·3 0·3	6·3 5·8	12·3 11·4
04	13 31·0	13 33·2	12 54·1	0·4 0·4	6·4 5·8	12·4 11·3	04	13 46·0	13 48·3	13 08·4	0·4 0·4	6·4 5·9	12·4 11·5
05	13 31·3	13 33·5	12 54·3	0·5 0·5	6·5 5·9	12·5 11·4	05	13 46·3	13 48·5	13 08·6	0·5 0·5	6·5 6·0	12·5 11·6
06	13 31·5	13 33·7	12 54·5	0·6 0·5	6·6 6·0	12·6 11·4	06	13 46·5	13 48·8	13 08·8	0·6 0·6	6·6 6·1	12·6 11·7
07	13 31·8	13 34·0	12 54·8	0·7 0·6	6·7 6·1	12·7 11·5	07	13 46·8	13 49·0	13 09·1	0·7 0·6	6·7 6·2	12·7 11·7
08	13 32·0	13 34·2	12 55·0	0·8 0·7	6·8 6·2	12·8 11·6	08	13 47·0	13 49·3	13 09·3	0·8 0·7	6·8 6·3	12·8 11·8
09	13 32·3	13 34·5	12 55·2	0·9 0·8	6·9 6·3	12·9 11·7	09	13 47·3	13 49·5	13 09·6	0·9 0·8	6·9 6·4	12·9 11·9
10	13 32·5	13 34·7	12 55·5	1·0 0·9	7·0 6·4	13·0 11·8	10	13 47·5	13 49·8	13 09·8	1·0 0·9	7·0 6·5	13·0 12·0
11	13 32·8	13 35·0	12 55·7	1·1 1·0	7·1 6·4	13·1 11·9	11	13 47·8	13 50·0	13 10·0	1·1 1·0	7·1 6·6	13·1 12·1
12	13 33·0	13 35·2	12 56·0	1·2 1·1	7·2 6·5	13·2 12·0	12	13 48·0	13 50·3	13 10·3	1·2 1·1	7·2 6·7	13·2 12·2
13	13 33·3	13 35·5	12 56·2	1·3 1·2	7·3 6·6	13·3 12·1	13	13 48·3	13 50·5	13 10·5	1·3 1·2	7·3 6·8	13·3 12·3
14	13 33·5	13 35·7	12 56·4	1·4 1·3	7·4 6·7	13·4 12·2	14	13 48·5	13 50·8	13 10·8	1·4 1·3	7·4 6·8	13·4 12·4
15	13 33·8	13 36·0	12 56·7	1·5 1·4	7·5 6·8	13·5 12·3	15	13 48·8	13 51·0	13 11·0	1·5 1·4	7·5 6·9	13·5 12·5
16	13 34·0	13 36·2	12 56·9	1·6 1·5	7·6 6·9	13·6 12·4	16	13 49·0	13 51·3	13 11·2	1·6 1·5	7·6 7·0	13·6 12·6
17	13 34·3	13 36·5	12 57·2	1·7 1·5	7·7 7·0	13·7 12·4	17	13 49·3	13 51·5	13 11·5	1·7 1·6	7·7 7·1	13·7 12·7
18	13 34·5	13 36·7	12 57·4	1·8 1·6	7·8 7·1	13·8 12·5	18	13 49·5	13 51·8	13 11·7	1·8 1·7	7·8 7·2	13·8 12·8
19	13 34·8	13 37·0	12 57·6	1·9 1·7	7·9 7·2	13·9 12·6	19	13 49·8	13 52·0	13 12·0	1·9 1·8	7·9 7·3	13·9 12·9
20	13 35·0	13 37·2	12 57·9	2·0 1·8	8·0 7·3	14·0 12·7	20	13 50·0	13 52·3	13 12·2	2·0 1·9	8·0 7·4	14·0 13·0
21	13 35·3	13 37·5	12 58·1	2·1 1·9	8·1 7·4	14·1 12·8	21	13 50·3	13 52·5	13 12·4	2·1 1·9	8·1 7·5	14·1 13·0
22	13 35·5	13 37·7	12 58·3	2·2 2·0	8·2 7·4	14·2 12·9	22	13 50·5	13 52·8	13 12·7	2·2 2·0	8·2 7·6	14·2 13·1
23	13 35·8	13 38·0	12 58·6	2·3 2·1	8·3 7·5	14·3 13·0	23	13 50·8	13 53·0	13 12·9	2·3 2·1	8·3 7·7	14·3 13·2
24	13 36·0	13 38·2	12 58·8	2·4 2·2	8·4 7·6	14·4 13·1	24	13 51·0	13 53·3	13 13·1	2·4 2·2	8·4 7·8	14·4 13·3
25	13 36·3	13 38·5	12 59·1	2·5 2·3	8·5 7·7	14·5 13·2	25	13 51·3	13 53·5	13 13·4	2·5 2·3	8·5 7·9	14·5 13·4
26	13 36·5	13 38·7	12 59·3	2·6 2·4	8·6 7·8	14·6 13·3	26	13 51·5	13 53·8	13 13·6	2·6 2·4	8·6 8·0	14·6 13·5
27	13 36·8	13 39·0	12 59·5	2·7 2·5	8·7 7·9	14·7 13·4	27	13 51·8	13 54·0	13 13·9	2·7 2·5	8·7 8·0	14·7 13·6
28	13 37·0	13 39·2	12 59·8	2·8 2·5	8·8 8·0	14·8 13·4	28	13 52·0	13 54·3	13 14·1	2·8 2·6	8·8 8·1	14·8 13·7
29	13 37·3	13 39·5	13 00·0	2·9 2·6	8·9 8·1	14·9 13·5	29	13 52·3	13 54·5	13 14·3	2·9 2·7	8·9 8·2	14·9 13·8
30	13 37·5	13 39·7	13 00·3	3·0 2·7	9·0 8·2	15·0 13·6	30	13 52·5	13 54·8	13 14·6	3·0 2·8	9·0 8·3	15·0 13·9
31	13 37·8	13 40·0	13 00·5	3·1 2·8	9·1 8·3	15·1 13·7	31	13 52·8	13 55·0	13 14·8	3·1 2·9	9·1 8·4	15·1 14·0
32	13 38·0	13 40·2	13 00·7	3·2 2·9	9·2 8·4	15·2 13·8	32	13 53·0	13 55·3	13 15·1	3·2 3·0	9·2 8·5	15·2 14·1
33	13 38·3	13 40·5	13 01·0	3·3 3·0	9·3 8·4	15·3 13·9	33	13 53·3	13 55·5	13 15·3	3·3 3·1	9·3 8·6	15·3 14·2
34	13 38·5	13 40·7	13 01·2	3·4 3·1	9·4 8·5	15·4 14·0	34	13 53·5	13 55·8	13 15·5	3·4 3·1	9·4 8·7	15·4 14·2
35	13 38·8	13 41·0	13 01·5	3·5 3·2	9·5 8·6	15·5 14·1	35	13 53·8	13 56·0	13 15·8	3·5 3·2	9·5 8·8	15·5 14·3
36	13 39·0	13 41·2	13 01·7	3·6 3·3	9·6 8·7	15·6 14·2	36	13 54·0	13 56·3	13 16·0	3·6 3·3	9·6 8·9	15·6 14·4
37	13 39·3	13 41·5	13 01·9	3·7 3·4	9·7 8·8	15·7 14·3	37	13 54·3	13 56·5	13 16·2	3·7 3·4	9·7 9·0	15·7 14·5
38	13 39·5	13 41·7	13 02·2	3·8 3·5	9·8 8·9	15·8 14·4	38	13 54·5	13 56·8	13 16·5	3·8 3·5	9·8 9·1	15·8 14·6
39	13 39·8	13 42·0	13 02·4	3·9 3·5	9·9 9·0	15·9 14·4	39	13 54·8	13 57·0	13 16·7	3·9 3·6	9·9 9·2	15·9 14·7
40	13 40·0	13 42·2	13 02·6	4·0 3·6	10·0 9·1	16·0 14·5	40	13 55·0	13 57·3	13 17·0	4·0 3·7	10·0 9·3	16·0 14·8
41	13 40·3	13 42·5	13 02·9	4·1 3·7	10·1 9·2	16·1 14·6	41	13 55·3	13 57·5	13 17·2	4·1 3·8	10·1 9·3	16·1 14·9
42	13 40·5	13 42·7	13 03·1	4·2 3·8	10·2 9·3	16·2 14·7	42	13 55·5	13 57·8	13 17·4	4·2 3·9	10·2 9·4	16·2 15·0
43	13 40·8	13 43·0	13 03·4	4·3 3·9	10·3 9·4	16·3 14·8	43	13 55·8	13 58·0	13 17·7	4·3 4·0	10·3 9·5	16·3 15·1
44	13 41·0	13 43·2	13 03·6	4·4 4·0	10·4 9·4	16·4 14·9	44	13 56·0	13 58·3	13 17·9	4·4 4·1	10·4 9·6	16·4 15·2
45	13 41·3	13 43·5	13 03·8	4·5 4·1	10·5 9·5	16·5 15·0	45	13 56·3	13 58·5	13 18·2	4·5 4·2	10·5 9·7	16·5 15·3
46	13 41·5	13 43·7	13 04·1	4·6 4·2	10·6 9·6	16·6 15·1	46	13 56·5	13 58·8	13 18·4	4·6 4·3	10·6 9·8	16·6 15·4
47	13 41·8	13 44·0	13 04·3	4·7 4·3	10·7 9·7	16·7 15·2	47	13 56·8	13 59·0	13 18·6	4·7 4·3	10·7 9·9	16·7 15·4
48	13 42·0	13 44·3	13 04·6	4·8 4·4	10·8 9·8	16·8 15·3	48	13 57·0	13 59·3	13 18·9	4·8 4·4	10·8 10·0	16·8 15·5
49	13 42·3	13 44·5	13 04·8	4·9 4·5	10·9 9·9	16·9 15·4	49	13 57·3	13 59·5	13 19·1	4·9 4·5	10·9 10·1	16·9 15·6
50	13 42·5	13 44·8	13 05·0	5·0 4·5	11·0 10·0	17·0 15·4	50	13 57·5	13 59·8	13 19·3	5·0 4·6	11·0 10·2	17·0 15·7
51	13 42·8	13 45·0	13 05·3	5·1 4·6	11·1 10·1	17·1 15·5	51	13 57·8	14 00·0	13 19·6	5·1 4·7	11·1 10·3	17·1 15·8
52	13 43·0	13 45·3	13 05·5	5·2 4·7	11·2 10·2	17·2 15·6	52	13 58·0	14 00·3	13 19·8	5·2 4·8	11·2 10·4	17·2 15·9
53	13 43·3	13 45·5	13 05·7	5·3 4·8	11·3 10·3	17·3 15·7	53	13 58·3	14 00·5	13 20·1	5·3 4·9	11·3 10·5	17·3 16·0
54	13 43·5	13 45·8	13 06·0	5·4 4·9	11·4 10·4	17·4 15·8	54	13 58·5	14 00·8	13 20·3	5·4 5·0	11·4 10·5	17·4 16·1
55	13 43·8	13 46·0	13 06·2	5·5 5·0	11·5 10·4	17·5 15·9	55	13 58·8	14 01·0	13 20·5	5·5 5·1	11·5 10·6	17·5 16·2
56	13 44·0	13 46·3	13 06·5	5·6 5·1	11·6 10·5	17·6 16·0	56	13 59·0	14 01·3	13 20·8	5·6 5·2	11·6 10·7	17·6 16·3
57	13 44·3	13 46·5	13 06·7	5·7 5·2	11·7 10·6	17·7 16·1	57	13 59·3	14 01·5	13 21·0	5·7 5·3	11·7 10·8	17·7 16·4
58	13 44·5	13 46·8	13 06·9	5·8 5·3	11·8 10·7	17·8 16·2	58	13 59·5	14 01·8	13 21·3	5·8 5·4	11·8 10·9	17·8 16·5
59	13 44·8	13 47·0	13 07·2	5·9 5·4	11·9 10·8	17·9 16·3	59	13 59·8	14 02·0	13 21·5	5·9 5·5	11·9 11·0	17·9 16·6
60	13 45·0	13 47·3	13 07·4	6·0 5·5	12·0 10·9	18·0 16·4	60	14 00·0	14 02·3	13 21·7	6·0 5·6	12·0 11·1	18·0 16·7

56ᵐ INCREMENTS AND CORRECTIONS 57ᵐ

56ᵐ s	SUN PLANETS	ARIES	MOON	v or Corrⁿ d	v or Corrⁿ d	v or Corrⁿ d
00	14 00·0	14 02·3	13 21·7	0·0 0·0	6·0 5·7	12·0 11·3
01	14 00·3	14 02·6	13 22·0	0·1 0·1	6·1 5·7	12·1 11·4
02	14 00·5	14 02·8	13 22·2	0·2 0·2	6·2 5·8	12·2 11·5
03	14 00·8	14 03·1	13 22·4	0·3 0·3	6·3 5·9	12·3 11·6
04	14 01·0	14 03·3	13 22·7	0·4 0·4	6·4 6·0	12·4 11·7
05	14 01·3	14 03·6	13 22·9	0·5 0·5	6·5 6·1	12·5 11·8
06	14 01·5	14 03·8	13 23·2	0·6 0·6	6·6 6·2	12·6 11·9
07	14 01·8	14 04·1	13 23·4	0·7 0·7	6·7 6·3	12·7 12·0
08	14 02·0	14 04·3	13 23·6	0·8 0·8	6·8 6·4	12·8 12·1
09	14 02·3	14 04·6	13 23·9	0·9 0·8	6·9 6·5	12·9 12·1
10	14 02·5	14 04·8	13 24·1	1·0 0·9	7·0 6·6	13·0 12·2
11	14 02·8	14 05·1	13 24·4	1·1 1·0	7·1 6·7	13·1 12·3
12	14 03·0	14 05·3	13 24·6	1·2 1·1	7·2 6·8	13·2 12·4
13	14 03·3	14 05·6	13 24·8	1·3 1·2	7·3 6·9	13·3 12·5
14	14 03·5	14 05·8	13 25·1	1·4 1·3	7·4 7·0	13·4 12·6
15	14 03·8	14 06·1	13 25·3	1·5 1·4	7·5 7·1	13·5 12·7
16	14 04·0	14 06·3	13 25·6	1·6 1·5	7·6 7·2	13·6 12·8
17	14 04·3	14 06·6	13 25·8	1·7 1·6	7·7 7·3	13·7 12·9
18	14 04·5	14 06·8	13 26·0	1·8 1·7	7·8 7·3	13·8 13·0
19	14 04·8	14 07·1	13 26·3	1·9 1·8	7·9 7·4	13·9 13·1
20	14 05·0	14 07·3	13 26·5	2·0 1·9	8·0 7·5	14·0 13·2
21	14 05·3	14 07·6	13 26·7	2·1 2·0	8·1 7·6	14·1 13·3
22	14 05·5	14 07·8	13 27·0	2·2 2·1	8·2 7·7	14·2 13·4
23	14 05·8	14 08·1	13 27·2	2·3 2·2	8·3 7·8	14·3 13·5
24	14 06·0	14 08·3	13 27·5	2·4 2·3	8·4 7·9	14·4 13·6
25	14 06·3	14 08·6	13 27·7	2·5 2·4	8·5 8·0	14·5 13·7
26	14 06·5	14 08·8	13 27·9	2·6 2·4	8·6 8·1	14·6 13·7
27	14 06·8	14 09·1	13 28·2	2·7 2·5	8·7 8·2	14·7 13·8
28	14 07·0	14 09·3	13 28·4	2·8 2·6	8·8 8·3	14·8 13·9
29	14 07·3	14 09·6	13 28·7	2·9 2·7	8·9 8·4	14·9 14·0
30	14 07·5	14 09·8	13 28·9	3·0 2·8	9·0 8·5	15·0 14·1
31	14 07·8	14 10·1	13 29·1	3·1 2·9	9·1 8·6	15·1 14·2
32	14 08·0	14 10·3	13 29·4	3·2 3·0	9·2 8·7	15·2 14·3
33	14 08·3	14 10·6	13 29·6	3·3 3·1	9·3 8·8	15·3 14·4
34	14 08·5	14 10·8	13 29·8	3·4 3·2	9·4 8·9	15·4 14·5
35	14 08·8	14 11·1	13 30·1	3·5 3·3	9·5 8·9	15·5 14·6
36	14 09·0	14 11·3	13 30·3	3·6 3·4	9·6 9·0	15·6 14·7
37	14 09·3	14 11·6	13 30·6	3·7 3·5	9·7 9·1	15·7 14·8
38	14 09·5	14 11·8	13 30·8	3·8 3·6	9·8 9·2	15·8 14·9
39	14 09·8	14 12·1	13 31·0	3·9 3·7	9·9 9·3	15·9 15·0
40	14 10·0	14 12·3	13 31·3	4·0 3·8	10·0 9·4	16·0 15·1
41	14 10·3	14 12·6	13 31·5	4·1 3·9	10·1 9·5	16·1 15·2
42	14 10·5	14 12·8	13 31·8	4·2 4·0	10·2 9·6	16·2 15·3
43	14 10·8	14 13·1	13 32·0	4·3 4·0	10·3 9·7	16·3 15·3
44	14 11·0	14 13·3	13 32·2	4·4 4·1	10·4 9·8	16·4 15·4
45	14 11·3	14 13·6	13 32·5	4·5 4·2	10·5 9·9	16·5 15·5
46	14 11·5	14 13·8	13 32·7	4·6 4·3	10·6 10·0	16·6 15·6
47	14 11·8	14 14·1	13 32·9	4·7 4·4	10·7 10·1	16·7 15·7
48	14 12·0	14 14·3	13 33·2	4·8 4·5	10·8 10·2	16·8 15·8
49	14 12·3	14 14·6	13 33·4	4·9 4·6	10·9 10·3	16·9 15·9
50	14 12·5	14 14·8	13 33·7	5·0 4·7	11·0 10·4	17·0 16·0
51	14 12·8	14 15·1	13 33·9	5·1 4·8	11·1 10·5	17·1 16·1
52	14 13·0	14 15·3	13 34·1	5·2 4·9	11·2 10·5	17·2 16·2
53	14 13·3	14 15·6	13 34·4	5·3 5·0	11·3 10·6	17·3 16·3
54	14 13·5	14 15·8	13 34·6	5·4 5·1	11·4 10·7	17·4 16·4
55	14 13·8	14 16·1	13 34·9	5·5 5·2	11·5 10·8	17·5 16·5
56	14 14·0	14 16·3	13 35·1	5·6 5·3	11·6 10·9	17·6 16·6
57	14 14·3	14 16·6	13 35·3	5·7 5·4	11·7 11·0	17·7 16·7
58	14 14·5	14 16·8	13 35·6	5·8 5·5	11·8 11·1	17·8 16·8
59	14 14·8	14 17·1	13 35·8	5·9 5·6	11·9 11·2	17·9 16·9
60	14 15·0	14 17·3	13 36·1	6·0 5·7	12·0 11·3	18·0 17·0

57ᵐ s	SUN PLANETS	ARIES	MOON	v or Corrⁿ d	v or Corrⁿ d	v or Corrⁿ d
00	14 15·0	14 17·3	13 36·1	0·0 0·0	6·0 5·8	12·0 11·5
01	14 15·3	14 17·6	13 36·3	0·1 0·1	6·1 5·8	12·1 11·6
02	14 15·5	14 17·8	13 36·5	0·2 0·2	6·2 5·9	12·2 11·7
03	14 15·8	14 18·1	13 36·8	0·3 0·3	6·3 6·0	12·3 11·8
04	14 16·0	14 18·3	13 37·0	0·4 0·4	6·4 6·1	12·4 11·9
05	14 16·3	14 18·6	13 37·2	0·5 0·5	6·5 6·2	12·5 12·0
06	14 16·5	14 18·8	13 37·5	0·6 0·6	6·6 6·3	12·6 12·1
07	14 16·8	14 19·1	13 37·7	0·7 0·7	6·7 6·4	12·7 12·2
08	14 17·0	14 19·3	13 38·0	0·8 0·8	6·8 6·5	12·8 12·3
09	14 17·3	14 19·6	13 38·2	0·9 0·9	6·9 6·6	12·9 12·4
10	14 17·5	14 19·8	13 38·4	1·0 1·0	7·0 6·7	13·0 12·5
11	14 17·8	14 20·1	13 38·7	1·1 1·1	7·1 6·8	13·1 12·6
12	14 18·0	14 20·3	13 38·9	1·2 1·2	7·2 6·9	13·2 12·7
13	14 18·3	14 20·6	13 39·2	1·3 1·2	7·3 7·0	13·3 12·7
14	14 18·5	14 20·9	13 39·4	1·4 1·3	7·4 7·1	13·4 12·8
15	14 18·8	14 21·1	13 39·6	1·5 1·4	7·5 7·2	13·5 12·9
16	14 19·0	14 21·4	13 39·9	1·6 1·5	7·6 7·3	13·6 13·0
17	14 19·3	14 21·6	13 40·1	1·7 1·6	7·7 7·4	13·7 13·1
18	14 19·5	14 21·9	13 40·3	1·8 1·7	7·8 7·5	13·8 13·2
19	14 19·8	14 22·1	13 40·6	1·9 1·8	7·9 7·6	13·9 13·3
20	14 20·0	14 22·4	13 40·8	2·0 1·9	8·0 7·7	14·0 13·4
21	14 20·3	14 22·6	13 41·1	2·1 2·0	8·1 7·8	14·1 13·5
22	14 20·5	14 22·9	13 41·3	2·2 2·1	8·2 7·9	14·2 13·6
23	14 20·8	14 23·1	13 41·5	2·3 2·2	8·3 8·0	14·3 13·7
24	14 21·0	14 23·4	13 41·8	2·4 2·3	8·4 8·1	14·4 13·8
25	14 21·3	14 23·6	13 42·0	2·5 2·4	8·5 8·1	14·5 13·9
26	14 21·5	14 23·9	13 42·3	2·6 2·5	8·6 8·2	14·6 14·0
27	14 21·8	14 24·1	13 42·5	2·7 2·6	8·7 8·3	14·7 14·1
28	14 22·0	14 24·4	13 42·7	2·8 2·7	8·8 8·4	14·8 14·2
29	14 22·3	14 24·6	13 43·0	2·9 2·8	8·9 8·5	14·9 14·3
30	14 22·5	14 24·9	13 43·2	3·0 2·9	9·0 8·6	15·0 14·4
31	14 22·8	14 25·1	13 43·4	3·1 3·0	9·1 8·7	15·1 14·5
32	14 23·0	14 25·4	13 43·7	3·2 3·1	9·2 8·8	15·2 14·6
33	14 23·3	14 25·6	13 43·9	3·3 3·2	9·3 8·9	15·3 14·7
34	14 23·5	14 25·9	13 44·2	3·4 3·3	9·4 9·0	15·4 14·8
35	14 23·8	14 26·1	13 44·4	3·5 3·4	9·5 9·1	15·5 14·9
36	14 24·0	14 26·4	13 44·6	3·6 3·5	9·6 9·2	15·6 15·0
37	14 24·3	14 26·6	13 44·9	3·7 3·5	9·7 9·3	15·7 15·0
38	14 24·5	14 26·9	13 45·1	3·8 3·6	9·8 9·4	15·8 15·1
39	14 24·8	14 27·1	13 45·4	3·9 3·7	9·9 9·5	15·9 15·2
40	14 25·0	14 27·4	13 45·6	4·0 3·8	10·0 9·6	16·0 15·3
41	14 25·3	14 27·6	13 45·8	4·1 3·9	10·1 9·7	16·1 15·4
42	14 25·5	14 27·9	13 46·1	4·2 4·0	10·2 9·8	16·2 15·5
43	14 25·8	14 28·1	13 46·3	4·3 4·1	10·3 9·9	16·3 15·6
44	14 26·0	14 28·4	13 46·5	4·4 4·2	10·4 10·0	16·4 15·7
45	14 26·3	14 28·6	13 46·8	4·5 4·3	10·5 10·1	16·5 15·8
46	14 26·5	14 28·9	13 47·0	4·6 4·4	10·6 10·2	16·6 15·9
47	14 26·8	14 29·1	13 47·3	4·7 4·5	10·7 10·3	16·7 16·0
48	14 27·0	14 29·4	13 47·5	4·8 4·6	10·8 10·4	16·8 16·1
49	14 27·3	14 29·6	13 47·7	4·9 4·7	10·9 10·4	16·9 16·2
50	14 27·5	14 29·9	13 48·0	5·0 4·8	11·0 10·5	17·0 16·3
51	14 27·8	14 30·1	13 48·2	5·1 4·9	11·1 10·6	17·1 16·4
52	14 28·0	14 30·4	13 48·5	5·2 5·0	11·2 10·7	17·2 16·5
53	14 28·3	14 30·6	13 48·7	5·3 5·1	11·3 10·8	17·3 16·6
54	14 28·5	14 30·9	13 48·9	5·4 5·2	11·4 10·9	17·4 16·7
55	14 28·8	14 31·1	13 49·2	5·5 5·3	11·5 11·0	17·5 16·8
56	14 29·0	14 31·4	13 49·4	5·6 5·4	11·6 11·1	17·6 16·9
57	14 29·3	14 31·6	13 49·7	5·7 5·5	11·7 11·2	17·7 17·0
58	14 29·5	14 31·9	13 49·9	5·8 5·6	11·8 11·3	17·8 17·1
59	14 29·8	14 32·1	13 50·1	5·9 5·7	11·9 11·4	17·9 17·2
60	14 30·0	14 32·4	13 50·4	6·0 5·8	12·0 11·5	18·0 17·3

58ᵐ　　INCREMENTS AND CORRECTIONS　　59ᵐ

58ᵐ	SUN PLANETS	ARIES	MOON	v or d Corrⁿ	v or d Corrⁿ	v or d Corrⁿ
s	° ′	° ′	° ′	′ ′	′ ′	′ ′
00	14 30·0	14 32·4	13 50·4	0·0 0·0	6·0 5·9	12·0 11·7
01	14 30·3	14 32·6	13 50·6	0·1 0·1	6·1 5·9	12·1 11·8
02	14 30·5	14 32·9	13 50·8	0·2 0·2	6·2 6·0	12·2 11·9
03	14 30·8	14 33·1	13 51·1	0·3 0·3	6·3 6·1	12·3 12·0
04	14 31·0	14 33·4	13 51·3	0·4 0·4	6·4 6·2	12·4 12·1
05	14 31·3	14 33·6	13 51·6	0·5 0·5	6·5 6·3	12·5 12·2
06	14 31·5	14 33·9	13 51·8	0·6 0·6	6·6 6·4	12·6 12·3
07	14 31·8	14 34·1	13 52·0	0·7 0·7	6·7 6·5	12·7 12·4
08	14 32·0	14 34·4	13 52·3	0·8 0·8	6·8 6·6	12·8 12·5
09	14 32·3	14 34·6	13 52·5	0·9 0·9	6·9 6·7	12·9 12·6
10	14 32·5	14 34·9	13 52·8	1·0 1·0	7·0 6·8	13·0 12·7
11	14 32·8	14 35·1	13 53·0	1·1 1·1	7·1 6·9	13·1 12·8
12	14 33·0	14 35·4	13 53·2	1·2 1·2	7·2 7·0	13·2 12·9
13	14 33·3	14 35·6	13 53·5	1·3 1·3	7·3 7·1	13·3 13·0
14	14 33·5	14 35·9	13 53·7	1·4 1·4	7·4 7·2	13·4 13·1
15	14 33·8	14 36·1	13 53·9	1·5 1·5	7·5 7·3	13·5 13·2
16	14 34·0	14 36·4	13 54·2	1·6 1·6	7·6 7·4	13·6 13·3
17	14 34·3	14 36·6	13 54·4	1·7 1·7	7·7 7·5	13·7 13·4
18	14 34·5	14 36·9	13 54·7	1·8 1·8	7·8 7·6	13·8 13·5
19	14 34·8	14 37·1	13 54·9	1·9 1·9	7·9 7·7	13·9 13·6
20	14 35·0	14 37·4	13 55·1	2·0 2·0	8·0 7·8	14·0 13·7
21	14 35·3	14 37·6	13 55·4	2·1 2·0	8·1 7·9	14·1 13·7
22	14 35·5	14 37·9	13 55·6	2·2 2·1	8·2 8·0	14·2 13·8
23	14 35·8	14 38·1	13 55·9	2·3 2·2	8·3 8·1	14·3 13·9
24	14 36·0	14 38·4	13 56·1	2·4 2·3	8·4 8·2	14·4 14·0
25	14 36·3	14 38·6	13 56·3	2·5 2·4	8·5 8·3	14·5 14·1
26	14 36·5	14 38·9	13 56·6	2·6 2·5	8·6 8·4	14·6 14·2
27	14 36·8	14 39·2	13 56·8	2·7 2·6	8·7 8·5	14·7 14·3
28	14 37·0	14 39·4	13 57·0	2·8 2·7	8·8 8·6	14·8 14·4
29	14 37·3	14 39·7	13 57·3	2·9 2·8	8·9 8·7	14·9 14·5
30	14 37·5	14 39·9	13 57·5	3·0 2·9	9·0 8·8	15·0 14·6
31	14 37·8	14 40·2	13 57·8	3·1 3·0	9·1 8·9	15·1 14·7
32	14 38·0	14 40·4	13 58·0	3·2 3·1	9·2 9·0	15·2 14·8
33	14 38·3	14 40·7	13 58·2	3·3 3·2	9·3 9·1	15·3 14·9
34	14 38·5	14 40·9	13 58·5	3·4 3·3	9·4 9·2	15·4 15·0
35	14 38·8	14 41·2	13 58·7	3·5 3·4	9·5 9·3	15·5 15·1
36	14 39·0	14 41·4	13 59·0	3·6 3·5	9·6 9·4	15·6 15·2
37	14 39·3	14 41·7	13 59·2	3·7 3·6	9·7 9·5	15·7 15·3
38	14 39·5	14 41·9	13 59·4	3·8 3·7	9·8 9·6	15·8 15·4
39	14 39·8	14 42·2	13 59·7	3·9 3·8	9·9 9·7	15·9 15·5
40	14 40·0	14 42·4	13 59·9	4·0 3·9	10·0 9·8	16·0 15·6
41	14 40·3	14 42·7	14 00·1	4·1 4·0	10·1 9·8	16·1 15·7
42	14 40·5	14 42·9	14 00·4	4·2 4·1	10·2 9·9	16·2 15·8
43	14 40·8	14 43·2	14 00·6	4·3 4·2	10·3 10·0	16·3 15·9
44	14 41·0	14 43·4	14 00·9	4·4 4·3	10·4 10·1	16·4 16·0
45	14 41·3	14 43·7	14 01·1	4·5 4·4	10·5 10·2	16·5 16·1
46	14 41·5	14 43·9	14 01·3	4·6 4·5	10·6 10·3	16·6 16·2
47	14 41·8	14 44·2	14 01·6	4·7 4·6	10·7 10·4	16·7 16·3
48	14 42·0	14 44·4	14 01·8	4·8 4·7	10·8 10·5	16·8 16·4
49	14 42·3	14 44·7	14 02·1	4·9 4·8	10·9 10·6	16·9 16·5
50	14 42·5	14 44·9	14 02·3	5·0 4·9	11·0 10·7	17·0 16·6
51	14 42·8	14 45·2	14 02·5	5·1 5·0	11·1 10·8	17·1 16·7
52	14 43·0	14 45·4	14 02·8	5·2 5·1	11·2 10·9	17·2 16·8
53	14 43·3	14 45·7	14 03·0	5·3 5·2	11·3 11·0	17·3 16·9
54	14 43·5	14 45·9	14 03·3	5·4 5·3	11·4 11·1	17·4 17·0
55	14 43·8	14 46·2	14 03·5	5·5 5·4	11·5 11·2	17·5 17·1
56	14 44·0	14 46·4	14 03·7	5·6 5·5	11·6 11·3	17·6 17·2
57	14 44·3	14 46·7	14 04·0	5·7 5·6	11·7 11·4	17·7 17·3
58	14 44·5	14 46·9	14 04·2	5·8 5·7	11·8 11·5	17·8 17·4
59	14 44·8	14 47·2	14 04·4	5·9 5·8	11·9 11·6	17·9 17·5
60	14 45·0	14 47·4	14 04·7	6·0 5·9	12·0 11·7	18·0 17·6

59ᵐ	SUN PLANETS	ARIES	MOON	v or d Corrⁿ	v or d Corrⁿ	v or d Corrⁿ
s	° ′	° ′	° ′	′ ′	′ ′	′ ′
00	14 45·0	14 47·4	14 04·7	0·0 0·0	6·0 6·0	12·0 11·9
01	14 45·3	14 47·7	14 04·9	0·1 0·1	6·1 6·0	12·1 12·0
02	14 45·5	14 47·9	14 05·2	0·2 0·2	6·2 6·1	12·2 12·1
03	14 45·8	14 48·2	14 05·4	0·3 0·3	6·3 6·2	12·3 12·2
04	14 46·0	14 48·4	14 05·6	0·4 0·4	6·4 6·3	12·4 12·3
05	14 46·3	14 48·7	14 05·9	0·5 0·5	6·5 6·4	12·5 12·4
06	14 46·5	14 48·9	14 06·1	0·6 0·6	6·6 6·5	12·6 12·5
07	14 46·8	14 49·2	14 06·4	0·7 0·7	6·7 6·6	12·7 12·6
08	14 47·0	14 49·4	14 06·6	0·8 0·8	6·8 6·7	12·8 12·7
09	14 47·3	14 49·7	14 06·8	0·9 0·9	6·9 6·8	12·9 12·8
10	14 47·5	14 49·9	14 07·1	1·0 1·0	7·0 6·9	13·0 12·9
11	14 47·8	14 50·2	14 07·3	1·1 1·1	7·1 7·0	13·1 13·0
12	14 48·0	14 50·4	14 07·5	1·2 1·2	7·2 7·1	13·2 13·1
13	14 48·3	14 50·7	14 07·8	1·3 1·3	7·3 7·2	13·3 13·2
14	14 48·5	14 50·9	14 08·0	1·4 1·4	7·4 7·3	13·4 13·3
15	14 48·8	14 51·2	14 08·3	1·5 1·5	7·5 7·4	13·5 13·4
16	14 49·0	14 51·4	14 08·5	1·6 1·6	7·6 7·5	13·6 13·5
17	14 49·3	14 51·7	14 08·7	1·7 1·7	7·7 7·6	13·7 13·6
18	14 49·5	14 51·9	14 09·0	1·8 1·8	7·8 7·7	13·8 13·7
19	14 49·8	14 52·2	14 09·2	1·9 1·9	7·9 7·8	13·9 13·8
20	14 50·0	14 52·4	14 09·5	2·0 2·0	8·0 7·9	14·0 13·9
21	14 50·3	14 52·7	14 09·7	2·1 2·1	8·1 8·0	14·1 14·0
22	14 50·5	14 52·9	14 09·9	2·2 2·2	8·2 8·1	14·2 14·1
23	14 50·8	14 53·2	14 10·2	2·3 2·3	8·3 8·2	14·3 14·2
24	14 51·0	14 53·4	14 10·4	2·4 2·4	8·4 8·3	14·4 14·3
25	14 51·3	14 53·7	14 10·6	2·5 2·5	8·5 8·4	14·5 14·4
26	14 51·5	14 53·9	14 10·9	2·6 2·6	8·6 8·5	14·6 14·5
27	14 51·8	14 54·2	14 11·1	2·7 2·7	8·7 8·6	14·7 14·6
28	14 52·0	14 54·4	14 11·4	2·8 2·8	8·8 8·7	14·8 14·7
29	14 52·3	14 54·7	14 11·6	2·9 2·9	8·9 8·8	14·9 14·8
30	14 52·5	14 54·9	14 11·8	3·0 3·0	9·0 8·9	15·0 14·9
31	14 52·8	14 55·2	14 12·1	3·1 3·1	9·1 9·0	15·1 15·0
32	14 53·0	14 55·4	14 12·3	3·2 3·2	9·2 9·1	15·2 15·1
33	14 53·3	14 55·7	14 12·6	3·3 3·3	9·3 9·2	15·3 15·2
34	14 53·5	14 55·9	14 12·8	3·4 3·4	9·4 9·3	15·4 15·3
35	14 53·8	14 56·2	14 13·0	3·5 3·5	9·5 9·4	15·5 15·4
36	14 54·0	14 56·4	14 13·3	3·6 3·6	9·6 9·5	15·6 15·5
37	14 54·3	14 56·7	14 13·5	3·7 3·7	9·7 9·6	15·7 15·6
38	14 54·5	14 56·9	14 13·8	3·8 3·8	9·8 9·7	15·8 15·7
39	14 54·8	14 57·2	14 14·0	3·9 3·9	9·9 9·8	15·9 15·8
40	14 55·0	14 57·5	14 14·2	4·0 4·0	10·0 9·9	16·0 15·9
41	14 55·3	14 57·7	14 14·5	4·1 4·1	10·1 10·0	16·1 16·0
42	14 55·5	14 58·0	14 14·7	4·2 4·2	10·2 10·1	16·2 16·1
43	14 55·8	14 58·2	14 14·9	4·3 4·3	10·3 10·2	16·3 16·2
44	14 56·0	14 58·5	14 15·2	4·4 4·4	10·4 10·3	16·4 16·3
45	14 56·3	14 58·7	14 15·4	4·5 4·5	10·5 10·4	16·5 16·4
46	14 56·5	14 59·0	14 15·7	4·6 4·6	10·6 10·5	16·6 16·5
47	14 56·8	14 59·2	14 15·9	4·7 4·7	10·7 10·6	16·7 16·6
48	14 57·0	14 59·5	14 16·1	4·8 4·8	10·8 10·7	16·8 16·7
49	14 57·3	14 59·7	14 16·4	4·9 4·9	10·9 10·8	16·9 16·8
50	14 57·5	15 00·0	14 16·6	5·0 5·0	11·0 10·9	17·0 16·9
51	14 57·8	15 00·2	14 16·9	5·1 5·1	11·1 11·0	17·1 17·0
52	14 58·0	15 00·5	14 17·1	5·2 5·2	11·2 11·1	17·2 17·1
53	14 58·3	15 00·7	14 17·3	5·3 5·3	11·3 11·2	17·3 17·2
54	14 58·5	15 01·0	14 17·6	5·4 5·4	11·4 11·3	17·4 17·3
55	14 58·8	15 01·2	14 17·8	5·5 5·5	11·5 11·4	17·5 17·4
56	14 59·0	15 01·5	14 18·0	5·6 5·6	11·6 11·5	17·6 17·5
57	14 59·3	15 01·7	14 18·3	5·7 5·7	11·7 11·6	17·7 17·6
58	14 59·5	15 02·0	14 18·5	5·8 5·8	11·8 11·7	17·8 17·7
59	14 59·8	15 02·2	14 18·8	5·9 5·9	11·9 11·8	17·9 17·8
60	15 00·0	15 02·5	14 19·0	6·0 6·0	12·0 11·9	18·0 17·9

ALTITUDE CORRECTION TABLES 0°–35°—MOON

App. Alt.	0°–4° Corrⁿ	5°–9° Corrⁿ	10°–14° Corrⁿ	15°–19° Corrⁿ	20°–24° Corrⁿ	25°–29° Corrⁿ	30°–34° Corrⁿ	App. Alt.
00	0 33·8	5 58·2	10 62·1	15 62·8	20 62·2	25 60·8	30 58·9	00
10	35·9	58·5	62·2	62·8	62·1	60·8	58·8	10
20	37·8	58·7	62·2	62·8	62·1	60·7	58·8	20
30	39·6	58·9	62·3	62·8	62·1	60·7	58·7	30
40	41·2	59·1	62·3	62·8	62·0	60·6	58·6	40
50	42·6	59·3	62·4	62·7	62·0	60·6	58·5	50
00	1 44·0	6 59·5	11 62·4	16 62·7	21 62·0	26 60·5	31 58·5	00
10	45·2	59·7	62·4	62·7	61·9	60·4	58·4	10
20	46·3	59·9	62·5	62·7	61·9	60·4	58·3	20
30	47·3	60·0	62·5	62·7	61·9	60·3	58·2	30
40	48·3	60·2	62·5	62·7	61·8	60·3	58·2	40
50	49·2	60·3	62·6	62·7	61·8	60·2	58·1	50
00	2 50·0	7 60·5	12 62·6	17 62·7	22 61·7	27 60·1	32 58·0	00
10	50·8	60·6	62·6	62·6	61·7	60·1	57·9	10
20	51·4	60·7	62·6	62·6	61·6	60·0	57·8	20
30	52·1	60·9	62·7	62·6	61·6	59·9	57·8	30
40	52·7	61·0	62·7	62·6	61·5	59·9	57·7	40
50	53·3	61·1	62·7	62·6	61·5	59·8	57·6	50
00	3 53·8	8 61·2	13 62·7	18 62·5	23 61·5	28 59·7	33 57·5	00
10	54·3	61·3	62·7	62·5	61·4	59·7	57·4	10
20	54·8	61·4	62·7	62·5	61·4	59·6	57·4	20
30	55·2	61·5	62·8	62·5	61·3	59·6	57·3	30
40	55·6	61·6	62·8	62·4	61·3	59·5	57·2	40
50	56·0	61·6	62·8	62·4	61·2	59·4	57·1	50
00	4 56·4	9 61·7	14 62·8	19 62·4	24 61·2	29 59·3	34 57·0	00
10	56·7	61·8	62·8	62·3	61·1	59·3	56·9	10
20	57·1	61·9	62·8	62·3	61·1	59·2	56·9	20
30	57·4	61·9	62·8	62·3	61·0	59·1	56·8	30
40	57·7	62·0	62·8	62·2	60·9	59·1	56·7	40
50	57·9	62·1	62·8	62·2	60·9	59·0	56·6	50

H.P.	L	U	L	U	L	U	L	U	L	U	L	U	L	U	H.P.
54·0	0·3	0·9	0·3	0·9	0·4	1·0	0·5	1·1	0·6	1·2	0·7	1·3	0·9	1·5	54·0
54·3	0·7	1·1	0·7	1·2	0·7	1·2	0·8	1·3	0·9	1·4	1·1	1·5	1·2	1·7	54·3
54·6	1·1	1·4	1·1	1·4	1·1	1·4	1·2	1·5	1·3	1·6	1·4	1·7	1·5	1·8	54·6
54·9	1·4	1·6	1·5	1·6	1·5	1·6	1·6	1·7	1·6	1·8	1·8	1·9	1·9	2·0	54·9
55·2	1·8	1·8	1·8	1·8	1·9	1·9	1·9	1·9	2·0	2·0	2·1	2·1	2·2	2·2	55·2
55·5	2·2	2·0	2·2	2·0	2·3	2·1	2·3	2·1	2·4	2·2	2·4	2·3	2·5	2·4	55·5
55·8	2·6	2·2	2·6	2·2	2·6	2·3	2·7	2·3	2·7	2·4	2·8	2·4	2·9	2·5	55·8
56·1	3·0	2·4	3·0	2·5	3·0	2·5	3·0	2·5	3·1	2·6	3·1	2·6	3·2	2·7	56·1
56·4	3·4	2·7	3·4	2·7	3·4	2·7	3·4	2·7	3·4	2·8	3·5	2·8	3·5	2·9	56·4
56·7	3·7	2·9	3·7	2·9	3·8	2·9	3·8	2·9	3·8	3·0	3·8	3·0	3·9	3·0	56·7
57·0	4·1	3·1	4·1	3·1	4·1	3·1	4·1	3·1	4·2	3·1	4·2	3·2	4·2	3·2	57·0
57·3	4·5	3·3	4·5	3·3	4·5	3·3	4·5	3·3	4·5	3·3	4·5	3·4	4·6	3·4	57·3
57·6	4·9	3·5	4·9	3·5	4·9	3·5	4·9	3·5	4·9	3·5	4·9	3·5	4·9	3·6	57·6
57·9	5·3	3·8	5·3	3·8	5·2	3·8	5·2	3·7	5·2	3·7	5·2	3·7	5·2	3·7	57·9
58·2	5·6	4·0	5·6	4·0	5·6	4·0	5·6	4·0	5·6	3·9	5·6	3·9	5·6	3·9	58·2
58·5	6·0	4·2	6·0	4·2	6·0	4·2	6·0	4·2	6·0	4·1	5·9	4·1	5·9	4·1	58·5
58·8	6·4	4·4	6·4	4·4	6·4	4·4	6·3	4·4	6·3	4·3	6·3	4·3	6·2	4·2	58·8
59·1	6·8	4·6	6·8	4·6	6·7	4·6	6·7	4·6	6·7	4·5	6·6	4·5	6·6	4·4	59·1
59·4	7·2	4·8	7·1	4·8	7·1	4·8	7·1	4·8	7·0	4·7	7·0	4·7	6·9	4·6	59·4
59·7	7·5	5·1	7·5	5·0	7·5	5·0	7·5	5·0	7·4	4·9	7·3	4·8	7·2	4·7	59·7
60·0	7·9	5·3	7·9	5·3	7·9	5·2	7·8	5·2	7·8	5·1	7·7	5·0	7·6	4·9	60·0
60·3	8·3	5·5	8·3	5·5	8·2	5·4	8·2	5·4	8·1	5·3	8·0	5·2	7·9	5·1	60·3
60·6	8·7	5·7	8·7	5·7	8·6	5·6	8·6	5·6	8·5	5·5	8·4	5·4	8·2	5·3	60·6
60·9	9·1	5·9	9·0	5·9	9·0	5·9	8·9	5·8	8·8	5·7	8·7	5·6	8·6	5·4	60·9
61·2	9·5	6·2	9·4	6·1	9·4	6·1	9·3	6·0	9·2	5·9	9·1	5·8	8·9	5·6	61·2
61·5	9·8	6·4	9·8	6·3	9·7	6·3	9·7	6·2	9·5	6·1	9·4	5·9	9·2	5·8	61·5

DIP

Ht. of Eye (m)	Corrⁿ	Ht. of Eye (ft)	Ht. of Eye (m)	Corrⁿ	Ht. of Eye (ft)
2·4	−2·8	8·0	9·5	−5·5	31·5
2·6	−2·9	8·6	9·9	−5·6	32·7
2·8	−3·0	9·2	10·3	−5·7	33·9
3·0	−3·1	9·8	10·6	−5·8	35·1
3·2	−3·2	10·5	11·0	−5·9	36·3
3·4	−3·3	11·2	11·4	−6·0	37·6
3·6	−3·4	11·9	11·8	−6·1	38·9
3·8	−3·5	12·6	12·2	−6·2	40·1
4·0	−3·6	13·3	12·6	−6·3	41·5
4·3	−3·7	14·1	13·0	−6·4	42·8
4·5	−3·8	14·9	13·4	−6·5	44·2
4·7	−3·9	15·7	13·8	−6·6	45·5
5·0	−4·0	16·5	14·2	−6·7	46·9
5·2	−4·1	17·4	14·7	−6·8	48·4
5·5	−4·2	18·3	15·1	−6·9	49·8
5·8	−4·3	19·1	15·5	−7·0	51·3
6·1	−4·4	20·1	16·0	−7·1	52·8
6·3	−4·5	21·0	16·5	−7·2	54·3
6·6	−4·6	22·0	16·9	−7·3	55·8
6·9	−4·7	22·9	17·4	−7·4	57·4
7·2	−4·8	23·9	17·9	−7·5	58·9
7·5	−4·9	24·9	18·4	−7·6	60·5
7·9	−5·0	26·0	18·8	−7·7	62·1
8·2	−5·1	27·1	19·3	−7·8	63·8
8·5	−5·2	28·1	19·8	−7·9	65·4
8·8	−5·3	29·2	20·4	−8·0	67·1
9·2	−5·4	30·4	20·9	−8·1	68·8
9·5		31·5	21·4		70·5

MOON CORRECTION TABLE

The correction is in two parts; the first correction is taken from the upper part of the table with argument apparent altitude, and the second from the lower part, with argument H.P., in the same column as that from which the first correction was taken. Separate corrections are given in the lower part for lower (L) and upper (U) limbs. All corrections are to be **added** to apparent altitude, *but 30′ is to be subtracted from the altitude of the upper limb.*

For corrections for pressure and temperature see page A4.

For bubble sextant observations ignore dip, take the mean of upper and lower limb corrections and subtract 15′ from the altitude.

App. Alt. = Apparent altitude = Sextant altitude corrected for index error and dip.

ALTITUDE CORRECTION TABLES 35°–90°—MOON

App. Alt.	35°–39° Corrn	40°–44° Corrn	45°–49° Corrn	50°–54° Corrn	55°–59° Corrn	60°–64° Corrn	65°–69° Corrn	70°–74° Corrn	75°–79° Corrn	80°–84° Corrn	85°–89° Corrn	App. Alt.
00	35 56.5	40 53.7	45 50.5	50 46.9	55 43.1	60 38.9	65 34.6	70 30.1	75 25.3	80 20.5	85 15.6	00
10	56.4	53.6	50.4	46.8	42.9	38.8	34.4	29.9	25.2	20.4	15.5	10
20	56.3	53.5	50.2	46.7	42.8	38.7	34.3	29.7	25.0	20.2	15.3	20
30	56.2	53.4	50.1	46.5	42.7	38.5	34.1	29.6	24.9	20.0	15.1	30
40	56.2	53.3	50.0	46.4	42.5	38.4	34.0	29.4	24.7	19.9	15.0	40
50	56.1	53.2	49.9	46.3	42.4	38.2	33.8	29.3	24.5	19.7	14.8	50
00	36 56.0	41 53.1	46 49.8	51 46.2	56 42.3	61 38.1	66 33.7	71 29.1	76 24.4	81 19.6	86 14.6	00
10	55.9	53.0	49.7	46.0	42.1	37.9	33.5	29.0	24.2	19.4	14.5	10
20	55.8	52.8	49.5	45.9	42.0	37.8	33.4	28.8	24.1	19.2	14.3	20
30	55.7	52.7	49.4	45.8	41.8	37.7	33.2	28.7	23.9	19.1	14.1	30
40	55.6	52.6	49.3	45.7	41.7	37.5	33.1	28.5	23.8	18.9	14.0	40
50	55.5	52.5	49.2	45.5	41.6	37.4	32.9	28.3	23.6	18.7	13.8	50
00	37 55.4	42 52.4	47 49.1	52 45.4	57 41.4	62 37.2	67 32.8	72 28.2	77 23.4	82 18.6	87 13.7	00
10	55.3	52.3	49.0	45.3	41.3	37.1	32.6	28.0	23.3	18.4	13.5	10
20	55.2	52.2	48.8	45.2	41.2	36.9	32.5	27.9	23.1	18.2	13.3	20
30	55.1	52.1	48.7	45.0	41.0	36.8	32.3	27.7	22.9	18.1	13.2	30
40	55.0	52.0	48.6	44.9	40.9	36.6	32.2	27.6	22.8	17.9	13.0	40
50	55.0	51.9	48.5	44.8	40.8	36.5	32.0	27.4	22.6	17.8	12.8	50
00	38 54.9	43 51.8	48 48.4	53 44.6	58 40.6	63 36.4	68 31.9	73 27.2	78 22.5	83 17.6	88 12.7	00
10	54.8	51.7	48.2	44.5	40.5	36.2	31.7	27.1	22.3	17.4	12.5	10
20	54.7	51.6	48.1	44.4	40.3	36.1	31.6	26.9	22.1	17.3	12.3	20
30	54.6	51.5	48.0	44.2	40.2	35.9	31.4	26.8	22.0	17.1	12.2	30
40	54.5	51.4	47.9	44.1	40.1	35.8	31.3	26.6	21.8	16.9	12.0	40
50	54.4	51.2	47.8	44.0	39.9	35.6	31.1	26.5	21.7	16.8	11.8	50
00	39 54.3	44 51.1	49 47.6	54 43.9	59 39.8	64 35.5	69 31.0	74 26.3	79 21.5	84 16.6	89 11.7	00
10	54.2	51.0	47.5	43.7	39.6	35.3	30.8	26.1	21.3	16.5	11.5	10
20	54.1	50.9	47.4	43.6	39.5	35.2	30.7	26.0	21.2	16.3	11.4	20
30	54.0	50.8	47.3	43.5	39.4	35.0	30.5	25.8	21.0	16.1	11.2	30
40	53.9	50.7	47.2	43.3	39.2	34.9	30.4	25.7	20.9	16.0	11.0	40
50	53.8	50.6	47.0	43.2	39.1	34.7	30.2	25.5	20.7	15.8	10.9	50

H.P.	L U	L U	L U	L U	L U	L U	L U	L U	L U	L U	L U	H.P.
54.0	1.1 1.7	1.3 1.9	1.5 2.1	1.7 2.4	2.0 2.6	2.3 2.9	2.6 3.2	2.9 3.5	3.2 3.8	3.5 4.1	3.8 4.5	54.0
54.3	1.4 1.8	1.6 2.0	1.8 2.2	2.0 2.5	2.3 2.7	2.5 3.0	2.8 3.2	3.0 3.5	3.3 3.8	3.6 4.1	3.9 4.4	54.3
54.6	1.7 2.0	1.9 2.2	2.1 2.4	2.3 2.6	2.5 2.8	2.7 3.0	3.0 3.3	3.2 3.5	3.5 3.8	3.7 4.1	4.0 4.3	54.6
54.9	2.0 2.2	2.2 2.3	2.3 2.5	2.5 2.7	2.7 2.9	2.9 3.1	3.2 3.3	3.4 3.5	3.6 3.8	3.9 4.0	4.1 4.3	54.9
55.2	2.3 2.3	2.5 2.4	2.6 2.6	2.8 2.8	3.0 2.9	3.2 3.1	3.4 3.3	3.6 3.5	3.8 3.7	4.0 4.0	4.2 4.2	55.2
55.5	2.7 2.5	2.8 2.6	2.9 2.7	3.1 2.9	3.2 3.0	3.4 3.2	3.6 3.4	3.7 3.5	3.9 3.7	4.1 3.9	4.3 4.1	55.5
55.8	3.0 2.6	3.1 2.7	3.2 2.8	3.3 3.0	3.5 3.1	3.6 3.3	3.8 3.4	3.9 3.6	4.1 3.7	4.2 3.9	4.4 4.0	55.8
56.1	3.3 2.8	3.4 2.9	3.5 3.0	3.6 3.1	3.7 3.2	3.8 3.3	4.0 3.4	4.1 3.6	4.2 3.7	4.4 3.8	4.5 4.0	56.1
56.4	3.6 2.9	3.7 3.0	3.8 3.1	3.9 3.2	3.9 3.3	4.0 3.4	4.1 3.5	4.3 3.6	4.4 3.7	4.5 3.8	4.6 3.9	56.4
56.7	3.9 3.1	4.0 3.1	4.1 3.2	4.1 3.3	4.2 3.3	4.3 3.4	4.3 3.5	4.4 3.6	4.5 3.7	4.6 3.8	4.7 3.8	56.7
57.0	4.3 3.2	4.3 3.3	4.3 3.3	4.4 3.4	4.4 3.4	4.5 3.5	4.5 3.5	4.6 3.6	4.7 3.6	4.7 3.7	4.8 3.8	57.0
57.3	4.6 3.4	4.6 3.4	4.6 3.4	4.6 3.5	4.7 3.5	4.7 3.5	4.7 3.6	4.8 3.6	4.8 3.6	4.8 3.7	4.9 3.7	57.3
57.6	4.9 3.6	4.9 3.6	4.9 3.6	4.9 3.6	4.9 3.6	4.9 3.6	4.9 3.6	4.9 3.6	5.0 3.6	5.0 3.6	5.0 3.6	57.6
57.9	5.2 3.7	5.2 3.7	5.2 3.7	5.2 3.7	5.2 3.7	5.1 3.6	5.1 3.6	5.1 3.6	5.1 3.6	5.1 3.6	5.1 3.6	57.9
58.2	5.5 3.9	5.5 3.8	5.5 3.8	5.4 3.8	5.4 3.7	5.4 3.7	5.3 3.7	5.3 3.6	5.2 3.6	5.2 3.5	5.2 3.5	58.2
58.5	5.9 4.0	5.8 4.0	5.8 3.9	5.7 3.9	5.6 3.8	5.6 3.8	5.5 3.7	5.5 3.6	5.4 3.6	5.3 3.5	5.3 3.4	58.5
58.8	6.2 4.2	6.1 4.1	6.0 4.1	6.0 4.0	5.9 3.9	5.8 3.8	5.7 3.7	5.6 3.6	5.5 3.5	5.4 3.5	5.3 3.4	58.8
59.1	6.5 4.3	6.4 4.3	6.3 4.2	6.2 4.1	6.1 4.0	6.0 3.9	5.9 3.8	5.8 3.6	5.7 3.5	5.6 3.4	5.4 3.3	59.1
59.4	6.8 4.5	6.7 4.4	6.6 4.3	6.5 4.2	6.4 4.1	6.2 3.9	6.1 3.8	6.0 3.7	5.8 3.5	5.7 3.4	5.5 3.2	59.4
59.7	7.1 4.6	7.0 4.5	6.9 4.4	6.8 4.3	6.6 4.1	6.5 4.0	6.3 3.8	6.2 3.7	6.0 3.5	5.8 3.3	5.6 3.2	59.7
60.0	7.5 4.8	7.3 4.7	7.2 4.5	7.0 4.4	6.9 4.2	6.7 4.0	6.5 3.9	6.3 3.7	6.1 3.5	5.9 3.3	5.7 3.1	60.0
60.3	7.8 5.0	7.6 4.8	7.5 4.7	7.3 4.5	7.1 4.3	6.9 4.1	6.7 3.9	6.5 3.7	6.3 3.5	6.0 3.2	5.8 3.0	60.3
60.6	8.1 5.1	7.9 5.0	7.7 4.8	7.6 4.6	7.3 4.4	7.1 4.2	6.9 3.9	6.7 3.7	6.4 3.4	6.2 3.2	5.9 2.9	60.6
60.9	8.4 5.3	8.2 5.1	8.0 4.9	7.8 4.7	7.6 4.5	7.3 4.2	7.1 4.0	6.8 3.7	6.6 3.4	6.3 3.2	6.0 2.9	60.9
61.2	8.7 5.4	8.5 5.2	8.3 5.0	8.1 4.8	7.8 4.5	7.6 4.3	7.3 4.0	7.0 3.7	6.7 3.4	6.4 3.1	6.1 2.8	61.2
61.5	9.1 5.6	8.8 5.4	8.6 5.1	8.3 4.9	8.1 4.6	7.8 4.3	7.5 4.0	7.2 3.7	6.9 3.4	6.5 3.1	6.2 2.7	61.5

Appendix 3.
Extracts from H. O. 229

PUB. NO. 229

VOL. 3

SIGHT REDUCTION TABLES

FOR

MARINE NAVIGATION

LATITUDES 30°–45°, Inclusive

PUBLISHED BY THE

DEFENSE MAPPING AGENCY HYDROGRAPHIC CENTER

U.S. GOVERNMENT PRINTING OFFICE

WASHINGTON : 1974

INTERPOLATION TABLE

Dec. Inc.	Altitude Difference (d) Tens 10′	20′	30′	40′	50′	Decimals	Units 0′	1′	2′	3′	4′	5′	6′	7′	8′	9′	Double Second Diff. and Corr.
′	′	′	′	′	′	′	′	′	′	′	′	′	′	′	′	′	′ ′
0.0	0.0	0.0	0.0	0.0	0.0	.0	0.0	0.0	0.0	0.0	0.0	0.0	0.0	0.1	0.1	0.1	0.0 (0.0) 48.2
0.1	0.0	0.0	0.0	0.0	0.1	.1	0.0	0.0	0.0	0.0	0.0	0.0	0.1	0.1	0.1	0.1	
0.2	0.0	0.0	0.1	0.1	0.1	.2	0.0	0.0	0.0	0.0	0.0	0.0	0.1	0.1	0.1	0.1	
0.3	0.0	0.1	0.1	0.2	0.2	.3	0.0	0.0	0.0	0.0	0.0	0.0	0.1	0.1	0.1	0.1	
0.4	0.1	0.1	0.2	0.3	0.3	.4	0.0	0.0	0.0	0.0	0.0	0.0	0.1	0.1	0.1	0.1	
0.5	0.1	0.2	0.3	0.3	0.4	.5	0.0	0.0	0.0	0.0	0.0	0.0	0.1	0.1	0.1	0.1	16.2 (0.1) 48.6
0.6	0.1	0.2	0.3	0.4	0.5	.6	0.0	0.0	0.0	0.0	0.0	0.0	0.1	0.1	0.1	0.1	
0.7	0.1	0.3	0.4	0.5	0.6	.7	0.0	0.0	0.0	0.0	0.0	0.0	0.1	0.1	0.1	0.1	
0.8	0.2	0.3	0.4	0.6	0.7	.8	0.0	0.0	0.0	0.0	0.0	0.0	0.1	0.1	0.1	0.1	
0.9	0.2	0.3	0.5	0.6	0.8	.9	0.0	0.0	0.0	0.0	0.0	0.0	0.1	0.1	0.1	0.1	
1.0	0.1	0.3	0.5	0.6	0.8	.0	0.0	0.0	0.0	0.1	0.1	0.1	0.1	0.2	0.2	0.2	8.2 (0.1) 24.6 (0.2) 41.0
1.1	0.2	0.3	0.5	0.7	0.9	.1	0.0	0.0	0.1	0.1	0.1	0.1	0.2	0.2	0.2	0.2	
1.2	0.2	0.4	0.6	0.8	1.0	.2	0.0	0.0	0.1	0.1	0.1	0.1	0.2	0.2	0.2	0.2	
1.3	0.2	0.4	0.6	0.9	1.1	.3	0.0	0.0	0.1	0.1	0.1	0.1	0.2	0.2	0.2	0.2	
1.4	0.2	0.5	0.7	0.9	1.2	.4	0.0	0.0	0.1	0.1	0.1	0.1	0.2	0.2	0.2	0.2	
1.5	0.3	0.5	0.8	1.0	1.3	.5	0.0	0.0	0.1	0.1	0.1	0.1	0.2	0.2	0.2	0.2	
1.6	0.3	0.5	0.8	1.1	1.3	.6	0.0	0.0	0.1	0.1	0.1	0.1	0.2	0.2	0.2	0.2	
1.7	0.3	0.6	0.9	1.2	1.4	.7	0.0	0.0	0.1	0.1	0.1	0.1	0.2	0.2	0.2	0.2	
1.8	0.3	0.6	0.9	1.2	1.5	.8	0.0	0.0	0.1	0.1	0.1	0.1	0.2	0.2	0.2	0.2	
1.9	0.4	0.7	1.0	1.3	1.6	.9	0.0	0.0	0.1	0.1	0.1	0.1	0.2	0.2	0.2	0.2	
2.0	0.3	0.6	1.0	1.3	1.6	.0	0.0	0.0	0.1	0.1	0.2	0.2	0.2	0.3	0.3	0.4	5.0 (0.1) 15.0 (0.2) 25.0 (0.3) 35.1
2.1	0.3	0.7	1.0	1.4	1.7	.1	0.0	0.0	0.1	0.1	0.2	0.2	0.3	0.3	0.3	0.4	
2.2	0.3	0.7	1.1	1.4	1.8	.2	0.0	0.0	0.1	0.1	0.2	0.2	0.3	0.3	0.3	0.4	
2.3	0.4	0.8	1.1	1.5	1.9	.3	0.0	0.1	0.1	0.1	0.2	0.2	0.3	0.3	0.3	0.4	
2.4	0.4	0.8	1.2	1.6	2.0	.4	0.0	0.1	0.1	0.1	0.2	0.2	0.3	0.3	0.3	0.4	
2.5	0.4	0.8	1.3	1.7	2.1	.5	0.0	0.1	0.1	0.1	0.2	0.2	0.3	0.3	0.4	0.4	
2.6	0.4	0.9	1.3	1.7	2.2	.6	0.0	0.1	0.1	0.1	0.2	0.2	0.3	0.3	0.4	0.4	
2.7	0.5	0.9	1.4	1.8	2.3	.7	0.0	0.1	0.1	0.2	0.2	0.2	0.3	0.3	0.4	0.4	
2.8	0.5	1.0	1.4	1.9	2.4	.8	0.0	0.1	0.1	0.2	0.2	0.2	0.3	0.3	0.4	0.4	
2.9	0.5	1.0	1.5	2.0	2.5	.9	0.0	0.1	0.1	0.2	0.2	0.2	0.3	0.3	0.4	0.4	
3.0	0.5	1.0	1.5	2.0	2.5	.0	0.0	0.1	0.1	0.2	0.2	0.3	0.3	0.4	0.5	0.5	3.6 (0.1) 10.9 (0.2) 18.2 (0.3) 25.5 (0.4) 32.8 (0.5) 40.1
3.1	0.5	1.0	1.5	2.0	2.6	.1	0.0	0.1	0.1	0.2	0.2	0.3	0.4	0.4	0.5	0.5	
3.2	0.5	1.0	1.6	2.1	2.6	.2	0.0	0.1	0.1	0.2	0.2	0.3	0.4	0.4	0.5	0.5	
3.3	0.5	1.1	1.6	2.2	2.7	.3	0.0	0.1	0.1	0.2	0.3	0.3	0.4	0.4	0.5	0.5	
3.4	0.6	1.1	1.7	2.3	2.8	.4	0.0	0.1	0.1	0.2	0.3	0.3	0.4	0.4	0.5	0.5	
3.5	0.6	1.2	1.8	2.3	2.9	.5	0.0	0.1	0.1	0.2	0.3	0.3	0.4	0.4	0.5	0.6	
3.6	0.6	1.2	1.8	2.4	3.0	.6	0.0	0.1	0.2	0.2	0.3	0.3	0.4	0.4	0.5	0.6	
3.7	0.6	1.3	1.9	2.5	3.1	.7	0.0	0.1	0.2	0.2	0.3	0.3	0.4	0.4	0.5	0.6	
3.8	0.7	1.3	1.9	2.6	3.2	.8	0.0	0.1	0.2	0.2	0.3	0.3	0.4	0.5	0.5	0.6	
3.9	0.7	1.3	2.0	2.6	3.3	.9	0.1	0.1	0.2	0.2	0.3	0.3	0.4	0.5	0.5	0.6	
4.0	0.6	1.3	2.0	2.6	3.3	.0	0.0	0.1	0.1	0.2	0.3	0.4	0.4	0.5	0.6	0.7	2.9 (0.1) 8.6 (0.2) 14.4 (0.3) 20.2 (0.4) 25.9 (0.5) 31.7 (0.6) 37.5
4.1	0.7	1.3	2.0	2.7	3.4	.1	0.0	0.1	0.2	0.2	0.3	0.4	0.5	0.5	0.6	0.7	
4.2	0.7	1.4	2.1	2.8	3.5	.2	0.0	0.1	0.2	0.2	0.3	0.4	0.5	0.5	0.6	0.7	
4.3	0.7	1.4	2.1	2.9	3.6	.3	0.0	0.1	0.2	0.2	0.3	0.4	0.5	0.5	0.6	0.7	
4.4	0.7	1.5	2.2	2.9	3.7	.4	0.0	0.1	0.2	0.3	0.3	0.4	0.5	0.6	0.6	0.7	
4.5	0.8	1.5	2.3	3.0	3.8	.5	0.0	0.1	0.2	0.3	0.3	0.4	0.5	0.6	0.6	0.7	
4.6	0.8	1.5	2.3	3.1	3.8	.6	0.0	0.1	0.2	0.3	0.3	0.4	0.5	0.6	0.6	0.7	
4.7	0.8	1.6	2.4	3.2	3.9	.7	0.1	0.1	0.2	0.3	0.4	0.4	0.5	0.6	0.7	0.7	
4.8	0.8	1.6	2.4	3.2	4.0	.8	0.1	0.1	0.2	0.3	0.4	0.4	0.5	0.6	0.7	0.7	
4.9	0.9	1.7	2.5	3.3	4.1	.9	0.1	0.1	0.2	0.3	0.4	0.4	0.5	0.6	0.7	0.7	
5.0	0.8	1.6	2.5	3.3	4.1	.0	0.0	0.1	0.2	0.3	0.4	0.5	0.5	0.6	0.7	0.8	2.4 (0.1) 7.2 (0.2) 12.0 (0.3) 16.8 (0.4) 21.6 (0.5) 26.4 (0.6) 31.2 (0.7) 36.0
5.1	0.8	1.7	2.5	3.4	4.2	.1	0.0	0.1	0.2	0.3	0.4	0.5	0.6	0.7	0.7	0.8	
5.2	0.8	1.7	2.6	3.4	4.3	.2	0.0	0.1	0.2	0.3	0.4	0.5	0.6	0.7	0.8	0.8	
5.3	0.9	1.8	2.6	3.5	4.4	.3	0.0	0.1	0.2	0.3	0.4	0.5	0.6	0.7	0.8	0.9	
5.4	0.9	1.8	2.7	3.6	4.5	.4	0.0	0.1	0.2	0.3	0.4	0.5	0.6	0.7	0.8	0.9	
5.5	0.9	1.8	2.8	3.7	4.6	.5	0.0	0.1	0.2	0.3	0.4	0.5	0.6	0.7	0.8	0.9	
5.6	0.9	1.9	2.8	3.7	4.7	.6	0.1	0.1	0.2	0.3	0.4	0.5	0.6	0.7	0.8	0.9	
5.7	1.0	1.9	2.9	3.8	4.8	.7	0.1	0.2	0.2	0.3	0.4	0.5	0.6	0.7	0.8	0.9	
5.8	1.0	2.0	2.9	3.9	4.9	.8	0.1	0.2	0.3	0.3	0.4	0.5	0.6	0.7	0.8	0.9	
5.9	1.0	2.0	3.0	4.0	5.0	.9	0.1	0.2	0.3	0.4	0.4	0.5	0.6	0.7	0.8	0.9	
6.0	1.0	2.0	3.0	4.0	5.0	.0	0.0	0.1	0.2	0.3	0.4	0.5	0.6	0.8	0.9	1.0	2.1 (0.1) 6.2 (0.2) 10.4 (0.3) 14.5 (0.4) 18.6 (0.5) 22.8 (0.6) 26.9 (0.7) 31.1 (0.8) 35.2
6.1	1.0	2.0	3.0	4.0	5.1	.1	0.0	0.1	0.2	0.3	0.4	0.6	0.7	0.8	0.9	1.0	
6.2	1.0	2.0	3.1	4.1	5.1	.2	0.0	0.1	0.2	0.3	0.5	0.6	0.7	0.8	0.9	1.0	
6.3	1.0	2.1	3.1	4.2	5.2	.3	0.0	0.1	0.2	0.4	0.5	0.6	0.7	0.8	0.9	1.0	
6.4	1.1	2.1	3.2	4.3	5.3	.4	0.0	0.2	0.3	0.4	0.5	0.6	0.7	0.8	0.9	1.0	
6.5	1.1	2.2	3.3	4.3	5.4	.5	0.1	0.2	0.3	0.4	0.5	0.6	0.7	0.8	0.9	1.0	
6.6	1.1	2.2	3.3	4.4	5.5	.6	0.1	0.2	0.3	0.4	0.5	0.6	0.7	0.8	0.9	1.0	
6.7	1.1	2.3	3.4	4.5	5.6	.7	0.1	0.2	0.3	0.4	0.5	0.6	0.7	0.8	0.9	1.1	
6.8	1.2	2.3	3.4	4.6	5.7	.8	0.1	0.2	0.3	0.4	0.5	0.6	0.7	0.8	1.0	1.1	
6.9	1.2	2.3	3.5	4.6	5.8	.9	0.1	0.2	0.3	0.4	0.5	0.6	0.7	0.9	1.0	1.1	
7.0	1.1	2.3	3.5	4.6	5.8	.0	0.0	0.1	0.2	0.4	0.5	0.6	0.7	0.9	1.0	1.1	1.8 (0.1) 5.5 (0.2) 9.1 (0.3) 12.8 (0.4) 16.5 (0.5) 20.1 (0.6) 23.8 (0.7) 27.4 (0.8) 31.1 (0.9) 34.7
7.1	1.2	2.3	3.5	4.7	5.9	.1	0.0	0.1	0.3	0.4	0.5	0.6	0.8	0.9	1.0	1.1	
7.2	1.2	2.4	3.6	4.8	6.0	.2	0.0	0.1	0.3	0.4	0.5	0.6	0.8	0.9	1.0	1.1	
7.3	1.2	2.4	3.6	4.9	6.1	.3	0.0	0.2	0.3	0.4	0.5	0.7	0.8	0.9	1.0	1.2	
7.4	1.2	2.5	3.7	4.9	6.2	.4	0.0	0.2	0.3	0.4	0.5	0.7	0.8	0.9	1.0	1.2	
7.5	1.3	2.5	3.8	5.0	6.3	.5	0.1	0.2	0.3	0.4	0.6	0.7	0.8	0.9	1.1	1.2	
7.6	1.3	2.5	3.8	5.1	6.3	.6	0.1	0.2	0.3	0.4	0.6	0.7	0.8	0.9	1.1	1.2	
7.7	1.3	2.6	3.9	5.2	6.4	.7	0.1	0.2	0.3	0.5	0.6	0.7	0.8	1.0	1.1	1.2	
7.8	1.3	2.6	3.9	5.2	6.5	.8	0.1	0.2	0.3	0.5	0.6	0.7	0.8	1.0	1.1	1.2	
7.9	1.4	2.7	4.0	5.3	6.6	.9	0.1	0.2	0.4	0.5	0.6	0.7	0.9	1.0	1.1	1.2	
	10′	20′	30′	40′	50′		0′	1′	2′	3′	4′	5′	6′	7′	8′	9′	

Dec. Inc.	Altitude Difference (d) Tens 10′	20′	30′	40′	50′	Decimals	Units 0′	1′	2′	3′	4′	5′	6′	7′	8′	9′	Double Second Diff. and Corr.
′	′	′	′	′	′	′	′	′	′	′	′	′	′	′	′	′	′ ′
8.0	1.3	2.6	4.0	5.3	6.6	.0	0.0	0.1	0.3	0.4	0.6	0.7	0.8	1.0	1.1	1.3	1.6 (0.1) 4.8 (0.2) 8.0 (0.3) 11.2 (0.4) 14.5 (0.5) 17.7 (0.6) 20.9 (0.7) 24.1 (0.8) 27.3 (0.9) 30.5 (1.0) 33.7 (1.1) 36.9
8.1	1.3	2.7	4.0	5.4	6.7	.1	0.0	0.2	0.3	0.4	0.6	0.7	0.9	1.0	1.1	1.3	
8.2	1.3	2.7	4.1	5.4	6.8	.2	0.0	0.2	0.3	0.5	0.6	0.7	0.9	1.0	1.2	1.3	
8.3	1.4	2.8	4.1	5.5	6.9	.3	0.0	0.2	0.3	0.5	0.6	0.8	0.9	1.0	1.2	1.3	
8.4	1.4	2.8	4.2	5.6	7.0	.4	0.1	0.2	0.3	0.5	0.6	0.8	0.9	1.0	1.2	1.3	
8.5	1.4	2.8	4.3	5.7	7.1	.5	0.1	0.2	0.4	0.5	0.6	0.8	0.9	1.1	1.2	1.3	
8.6	1.4	2.9	4.3	5.7	7.2	.6	0.1	0.2	0.4	0.5	0.7	0.8	0.9	1.1	1.2	1.4	
8.7	1.5	2.9	4.4	5.8	7.3	.7	0.1	0.2	0.4	0.5	0.7	0.8	0.9	1.1	1.2	1.4	
8.8	1.5	3.0	4.4	5.9	7.4	.8	0.1	0.3	0.4	0.5	0.7	0.8	1.0	1.1	1.2	1.4	
8.9	1.5	3.0	4.5	6.0	7.5	.9	0.1	0.3	0.4	0.6	0.7	0.8	1.0	1.1	1.3	1.4	
9.0	1.5	3.0	4.5	6.0	7.5	.0	0.0	0.2	0.3	0.5	0.6	0.8	0.9	1.1	1.3	1.4	
9.1	1.5	3.0	4.5	6.0	7.6	.1	0.0	0.2	0.3	0.5	0.6	0.8	1.0	1.1	1.3	1.4	
9.2	1.5	3.0	4.6	6.1	7.6	.2	0.0	0.2	0.3	0.5	0.7	0.8	1.0	1.1	1.3	1.5	
9.3	1.5	3.1	4.6	6.2	7.7	.3	0.0	0.2	0.4	0.5	0.7	0.8	1.0	1.2	1.3	1.5	
9.4	1.6	3.1	4.7	6.3	7.8	.4	0.1	0.2	0.4	0.5	0.7	0.9	1.0	1.2	1.3	1.5	
9.5	1.6	3.2	4.8	6.3	7.9	.5	0.1	0.2	0.4	0.6	0.7	0.9	1.0	1.2	1.3	1.5	1.4 (0.1) 4.2 (0.2) 7.1 (0.3) 9.9 (0.4) 12.7 (0.5) 15.5 (0.6) 18.4 (0.7) 21.2 (0.8) 24.0 (0.9) 26.8 (1.0) 29.7 (1.1) 32.5 (1.2) 35.3
9.6	1.6	3.2	4.8	6.4	8.0	.6	0.1	0.3	0.4	0.6	0.7	0.9	1.0	1.2	1.4	1.5	
9.7	1.6	3.3	4.9	6.5	8.1	.7	0.1	0.3	0.4	0.6	0.7	0.9	1.1	1.2	1.4	1.5	
9.8	1.7	3.3	4.9	6.6	8.2	.8	0.1	0.3	0.4	0.6	0.8	0.9	1.1	1.2	1.4	1.6	
9.9	1.7	3.3	5.0	6.6	8.3	.9	0.1	0.3	0.5	0.6	0.8	0.9	1.1	1.3	1.4	1.6	
10.0	1.6	3.3	5.0	6.6	8.3	.0	0.0	0.2	0.3	0.5	0.7	0.9	1.0	1.2	1.4	1.6	
10.1	1.7	3.3	5.0	6.7	8.4	.1	0.0	0.2	0.4	0.5	0.7	0.9	1.1	1.2	1.4	1.6	
10.2	1.7	3.4	5.1	6.8	8.5	.2	0.0	0.2	0.4	0.6	0.7	0.9	1.1	1.3	1.4	1.6	
10.3	1.7	3.4	5.1	6.9	8.6	.3	0.1	0.2	0.4	0.6	0.8	0.9	1.1	1.3	1.5	1.6	
10.4	1.7	3.5	5.2	6.9	8.7	.4	0.1	0.2	0.4	0.6	0.8	0.9	1.1	1.3	1.5	1.6	
10.5	1.8	3.5	5.3	7.0	8.8	.5	0.1	0.3	0.4	0.6	0.8	1.0	1.1	1.3	1.5	1.7	
10.6	1.8	3.5	5.3	7.1	8.8	.6	0.1	0.3	0.5	0.6	0.8	1.0	1.2	1.3	1.5	1.7	
10.7	1.8	3.6	5.4	7.2	8.9	.7	0.1	0.3	0.5	0.6	0.8	1.0	1.2	1.3	1.5	1.7	
10.8	1.8	3.6	5.4	7.2	9.0	.8	0.1	0.3	0.5	0.7	0.8	1.0	1.2	1.4	1.5	1.7	
10.9	1.9	3.7	5.5	7.3	9.1	.9	0.2	0.3	0.5	0.7	0.9	1.0	1.2	1.4	1.6	1.7	
11.0	1.8	3.6	5.5	7.3	9.1	.0	0.0	0.2	0.4	0.6	0.8	1.0	1.1	1.3	1.5	1.7	1.3 (0.1) 3.8 (0.2) 6.3 (0.3) 8.9 (0.4) 11.4 (0.5) 14.0 (0.6) 16.5 (0.7) 19.0 (0.8) 21.6 (0.9) 24.1 (1.0) 26.7 (1.1) 29.2 (1.2) 31.7 (1.3) 34.3
11.1	1.8	3.7	5.5	7.4	9.2	.1	0.0	0.2	0.4	0.6	0.8	1.0	1.2	1.4	1.6	1.7	
11.2	1.8	3.7	5.6	7.4	9.3	.2	0.0	0.2	0.4	0.6	0.8	1.0	1.2	1.4	1.6	1.8	
11.3	1.9	3.8	5.6	7.5	9.4	.3	0.1	0.2	0.4	0.6	0.8	1.0	1.2	1.4	1.6	1.8	
11.4	1.9	3.8	5.7	7.6	9.5	.4	0.1	0.3	0.5	0.7	0.8	1.0	1.2	1.4	1.6	1.8	
11.5	1.9	3.8	5.8	7.7	9.6	.5	0.1	0.3	0.5	0.7	0.9	1.1	1.2	1.4	1.6	1.8	
11.6	1.9	3.9	5.8	7.7	9.7	.6	0.1	0.3	0.5	0.7	0.9	1.1	1.3	1.5	1.6	1.8	
11.7	2.0	3.9	5.9	7.8	9.8	.7	0.1	0.3	0.5	0.7	0.9	1.1	1.3	1.5	1.7	1.9	
11.8	2.0	4.0	5.9	7.9	9.9	.8	0.2	0.3	0.5	0.7	0.9	1.1	1.3	1.5	1.7	1.9	
11.9	2.0	4.0	6.0	8.0	10.0	.9	0.2	0.4	0.6	0.7	0.9	1.1	1.3	1.5	1.7	1.9	
12.0	2.0	4.0	6.0	8.0	10.0	.0	0.0	0.2	0.4	0.6	0.8	1.0	1.2	1.5	1.7	1.9	
12.1	2.0	4.0	6.0	8.0	10.1	.1	0.0	0.2	0.4	0.6	0.9	1.1	1.3	1.5	1.7	1.9	
12.2	2.0	4.0	6.1	8.1	10.1	.2	0.0	0.2	0.5	0.7	0.9	1.1	1.3	1.5	1.7	1.9	
12.3	2.0	4.1	6.1	8.2	10.2	.3	0.1	0.3	0.5	0.7	0.9	1.1	1.3	1.5	1.7	1.9	
12.4	2.1	4.1	6.2	8.3	10.3	.4	0.1	0.3	0.5	0.7	0.9	1.1	1.3	1.5	1.7	2.0	
12.5	2.1	4.2	6.3	8.3	10.4	.5	0.1	0.3	0.5	0.7	0.9	1.1	1.4	1.6	1.8	2.0	1.2 (0.1) 3.5 (0.2) 5.8 (0.3) 8.1 (0.4) 10.5 (0.5) 12.8 (0.6) 15.1 (0.7) 17.4 (0.8) 19.8 (0.9) 22.1 (1.0) 24.4 (1.1) 26.7 (1.2) 29.1 (1.3) 31.4 (1.4) 33.7 (1.5) 36.0
12.6	2.1	4.2	6.3	8.4	10.5	.6	0.1	0.3	0.5	0.7	1.0	1.2	1.4	1.6	1.8	2.0	
12.7	2.1	4.3	6.4	8.5	10.6	.7	0.1	0.4	0.6	0.8	1.0	1.2	1.4	1.6	1.8	2.0	
12.8	2.2	4.3	6.4	8.6	10.7	.8	0.2	0.4	0.6	0.8	1.0	1.2	1.4	1.6	1.8	2.0	
12.9	2.2	4.3	6.5	8.6	10.8	.9	0.2	0.4	0.6	0.8	1.0	1.2	1.4	1.6	1.9	2.1	
13.0	2.1	4.3	6.5	8.6	10.8	.0	0.0	0.2	0.4	0.7	0.9	1.1	1.3	1.6	1.8	2.0	
13.1	2.2	4.3	6.5	8.7	10.9	.1	0.0	0.2	0.5	0.7	0.9	1.1	1.4	1.6	1.8	2.0	
13.2	2.2	4.4	6.6	8.8	11.0	.2	0.0	0.3	0.5	0.7	0.9	1.2	1.4	1.6	1.8	2.1	
13.3	2.2	4.4	6.6	8.9	11.1	.3	0.1	0.3	0.5	0.7	1.0	1.2	1.4	1.6	1.9	2.1	
13.4	2.2	4.5	6.7	8.9	11.2	.4	0.1	0.3	0.5	0.8	1.0	1.2	1.4	1.7	1.9	2.1	
13.5	2.3	4.5	6.8	9.0	11.3	.5	0.1	0.3	0.6	0.8	1.0	1.2	1.5	1.7	1.9	2.1	
13.6	2.3	4.5	6.8	9.1	11.3	.6	0.1	0.4	0.6	0.8	1.0	1.3	1.5	1.7	1.9	2.2	
13.7	2.3	4.6	6.9	9.2	11.4	.7	0.2	0.4	0.6	0.8	1.1	1.3	1.5	1.7	2.0	2.2	
13.8	2.3	4.6	6.9	9.2	11.5	.8	0.2	0.4	0.6	0.9	1.1	1.3	1.5	1.8	2.0	2.2	
13.9	2.4	4.7	7.0	9.3	11.6	.9	0.2	0.4	0.7	0.9	1.1	1.3	1.6	1.8	2.0	2.2	
14.0	2.3	4.6	7.0	9.3	11.6	.0	0.0	0.2	0.5	0.7	1.0	1.2	1.4	1.7	1.9	2.2	1.1 (0.1) 3.2 (0.2) 5.3 (0.3) 7.5 (0.4) 9.6 (0.5) 11.7 (0.6) 13.9 (0.7) 16.0 (0.8) 18.1 (0.9) 20.3 (1.0) 22.4 (1.1) 24.5 (1.2) 26.7 (1.3) 28.8 (1.4) 30.9 (1.5) 33.1 (1.6) 35.2
14.1	2.3	4.7	7.0	9.4	11.7	.1	0.0	0.3	0.5	0.7	1.0	1.2	1.5	1.7	2.0	2.2	
14.2	2.3	4.7	7.1	9.4	11.8	.2	0.0	0.3	0.5	0.8	1.0	1.3	1.5	1.7	2.0	2.2	
14.3	2.4	4.8	7.1	9.5	11.9	.3	0.1	0.3	0.6	0.8	1.0	1.3	1.5	1.8	2.0	2.2	
14.4	2.4	4.8	7.2	9.6	12.0	.4	0.1	0.3	0.6	0.8	1.1	1.3	1.5	1.8	2.0	2.3	
14.5	2.4	4.8	7.3	9.7	12.1	.5	0.1	0.4	0.6	0.8	1.1	1.3	1.6	1.8	2.1	2.3	
14.6	2.4	4.9	7.3	9.7	12.2	.6	0.1	0.4	0.6	0.9	1.1	1.4	1.6	1.8	2.1	2.3	
14.7	2.5	4.9	7.4	9.8	12.3	.7	0.2	0.4	0.7	0.9	1.1	1.4	1.6	1.9	2.1	2.3	
14.8	2.5	5.0	7.4	9.9	12.4	.8	0.2	0.4	0.7	0.9	1.2	1.4	1.6	1.9	2.1	2.4	
14.9	2.5	5.0	7.5	10.0	12.5	.9	0.2	0.5	0.7	0.9	1.2	1.4	1.7	1.9	2.2	2.4	
15.0	2.5	5.0	7.5	10.0	12.5	.0	0.0	0.3	0.5	0.8	1.0	1.3	1.5	1.8	2.1	2.3	
15.1	2.5	5.0	7.5	10.0	12.6	.1	0.0	0.3	0.5	0.8	1.1	1.3	1.6	1.8	2.1	2.4	
15.2	2.5	5.0	7.6	10.1	12.6	.2	0.1	0.3	0.6	0.8	1.1	1.3	1.6	1.9	2.1	2.4	
15.3	2.5	5.1	7.6	10.2	12.7	.3	0.1	0.3	0.6	0.9	1.1	1.4	1.6	1.9	2.1	2.4	
15.4	2.6	5.1	7.7	10.3	12.8	.4	0.1	0.4	0.6	0.9	1.1	1.4	1.7	1.9	2.2	2.4	
15.5	2.6	5.2	7.8	10.3	12.9	.5	0.1	0.4	0.6	0.9	1.2	1.4	1.7	1.9	2.2	2.5	
15.6	2.6	5.2	7.8	10.4	13.0	.6	0.2	0.4	0.7	0.9	1.2	1.4	1.7	2.0	2.2	2.5	
15.7	2.6	5.3	7.9	10.5	13.1	.7	0.2	0.4	0.7	1.0	1.2	1.5	1.7	2.0	2.2	2.5	
15.8	2.7	5.3	7.9	10.6	13.2	.8	0.2	0.5	0.7	1.0	1.2	1.5	1.8	2.0	2.3	2.5	
15.9	2.7	5.3	8.0	10.6	13.3	.9	0.2	0.5	0.7	1.0	1.3	1.5	1.8	2.0	2.3	2.6	
	10′	20′	30′	40′	50′		0′	1′	2′	3′	4′	5′	6′	7′	8′	9′	

The Double-Second-Difference correction (Corr.) is always to be added to the tabulated altitude.

INTERPOLATION TABLE

Dec. Inc.	Altitude Difference (d) Tens 10'	20'	30'	40'	50'	Decimals	Units 0'	1'	2'	3'	4'	5'	6'	7'	8'	9'	Double Second Diff. and Corr.
16.0	2.6	5.3	8.0	10.6	13.3	.0	0.0	0.3	0.5	0.8	1.1	1.4	1.6	1.9	2.2	2.5	
16.1	2.7	5.3	8.0	10.7	13.4	.1	0.0	0.3	0.6	0.9	1.1	1.4	1.7	2.0	2.2	2.5	
16.2	2.7	5.4	8.1	10.8	13.5	.2	0.1	0.3	0.6	0.9	1.2	1.4	1.7	2.0	2.3	2.5	1.0 0.1
16.3	2.7	5.4	8.1	10.9	13.6	.3	0.1	0.4	0.6	0.9	1.2	1.5	1.7	2.0	2.3	2.6	3.0 0.2
16.4	2.7	5.5	8.2	10.9	13.7	.4	0.1	0.4	0.7	0.9	1.2	1.5	1.8	2.0	2.3	2.6	4.9 0.3
16.5	2.8	5.5	8.3	11.0	13.8	.5	0.1	0.4	0.7	1.0	1.2	1.5	1.8	2.1	2.3	2.6	6.9 0.4
16.6	2.8	5.5	8.3	11.1	13.8	.6	0.2	0.4	0.7	1.0	1.3	1.5	1.8	2.1	2.4	2.6	8.9 0.5
16.7	2.8	5.6	8.4	11.2	13.9	.7	0.2	0.5	0.7	1.0	1.3	1.6	1.8	2.1	2.4	2.7	10.8 0.6
16.8	2.8	5.6	8.4	11.2	14.0	.8	0.2	0.5	0.8	1.0	1.3	1.6	1.9	2.1	2.4	2.7	12.8 0.7
16.9	2.9	5.7	8.5	11.3	14.1	.9	0.2	0.5	0.8	1.1	1.3	1.6	1.9	2.2	2.4	2.7	14.8 0.8 16.7 0.9
17.0	2.8	5.6	8.5	11.3	14.1	.0	0.0	0.3	0.6	0.9	1.2	1.5	1.7	2.0	2.3	2.6	18.7 1.0
17.1	2.8	5.7	8.5	11.4	14.2	.1	0.0	0.3	0.6	0.9	1.2	1.5	1.8	2.1	2.4	2.7	20.7 1.1
17.2	2.8	5.7	8.6	11.4	14.3	.2	0.1	0.3	0.6	0.9	1.2	1.5	1.8	2.1	2.4	2.7	22.7 1.2
17.3	2.9	5.8	8.6	11.5	14.4	.3	0.1	0.4	0.7	1.0	1.3	1.5	1.8	2.1	2.4	2.7	24.6 1.3
17.4	2.9	5.8	8.7	11.6	14.5	.4	0.1	0.4	0.7	1.0	1.3	1.6	1.9	2.2	2.4	2.7	26.6 1.4
17.5	2.9	5.8	8.8	11.7	14.6	.5	0.1	0.4	0.7	1.0	1.3	1.6	1.9	2.2	2.5	2.8	28.6 1.5
17.6	2.9	5.9	8.8	11.7	14.7	.6	0.2	0.5	0.8	1.0	1.3	1.6	1.9	2.2	2.5	2.8	30.5 1.6
17.7	3.0	5.9	8.9	11.8	14.8	.7	0.2	0.5	0.8	1.1	1.4	1.7	2.0	2.2	2.5	2.8	32.5 1.7
17.8	3.0	6.0	8.9	11.9	14.9	.8	0.2	0.5	0.8	1.1	1.4	1.7	2.0	2.3	2.6	2.9	34.5
17.9	3.0	6.0	9.0	12.0	15.0	.9	0.3	0.6	0.8	1.1	1.4	1.7	2.0	2.3	2.6	2.9	
18.0	3.0	6.0	9.0	12.0	15.0	.0	0.0	0.3	0.6	0.9	1.2	1.5	1.8	2.2	2.5	2.8	
18.1	3.0	6.0	9.0	12.0	15.1	.1	0.0	0.3	0.6	1.0	1.3	1.6	1.9	2.2	2.5	2.8	0.9 0.1
18.2	3.0	6.0	9.1	12.1	15.1	.2	0.1	0.4	0.7	1.0	1.3	1.6	1.9	2.2	2.5	2.8	2.8 0.2
18.3	3.0	6.1	9.1	12.2	15.2	.3	0.1	0.4	0.7	1.0	1.3	1.6	1.9	2.3	2.6	2.9	4.6 0.3
18.4	3.1	6.1	9.2	12.3	15.3	.4	0.1	0.4	0.7	1.0	1.4	1.7	2.0	2.3	2.6	2.9	6.5 0.4
18.5	3.1	6.2	9.3	12.3	15.4	.5	0.2	0.5	0.8	1.1	1.4	1.7	2.0	2.3	2.6	2.9	8.3 0.5
18.6	3.1	6.2	9.3	12.4	15.5	.6	0.2	0.5	0.8	1.1	1.4	1.7	2.0	2.3	2.7	3.0	10.2 0.6
18.7	3.1	6.3	9.4	12.5	15.6	.7	0.2	0.5	0.8	1.1	1.4	1.8	2.1	2.4	2.7	3.0	12.0 0.7
18.8	3.2	6.3	9.4	12.6	15.7	.8	0.2	0.6	0.9	1.2	1.5	1.8	2.1	2.4	2.7	3.0	13.9 0.8
18.9	3.2	6.3	9.5	12.6	15.8	.9	0.3	0.6	0.9	1.2	1.5	1.8	2.1	2.4	2.7	3.1	15.7 0.9 17.6 1.0
19.0	3.1	6.3	9.5	12.6	15.8	.0	0.0	0.3	0.6	1.0	1.3	1.6	1.9	2.3	2.6	2.9	19.4 1.1
19.1	3.2	6.3	9.5	12.7	15.9	.1	0.0	0.4	0.7	1.0	1.3	1.7	2.0	2.3	2.6	3.0	21.3 1.2
19.2	3.2	6.4	9.6	12.8	16.0	.2	0.1	0.4	0.7	1.0	1.4	1.7	2.0	2.3	2.7	3.0	23.1 1.3
19.3	3.2	6.4	9.6	12.9	16.1	.3	0.1	0.4	0.7	1.1	1.4	1.7	2.0	2.4	2.7	3.0	25.0 1.4
19.4	3.2	6.5	9.7	12.9	16.2	.4	0.1	0.5	0.8	1.1	1.4	1.8	2.1	2.4	2.7	3.1	26.8 1.5 28.7 1.6
19.5	3.3	6.5	9.8	13.0	16.3	.5	0.2	0.5	0.8	1.1	1.5	1.8	2.1	2.4	2.8	3.1	30.5 1.7
19.6	3.3	6.5	9.8	13.1	16.3	.6	0.2	0.5	0.8	1.2	1.5	1.8	2.1	2.5	2.8	3.1	32.3 1.8
19.7	3.3	6.6	9.9	13.2	16.4	.7	0.2	0.6	0.9	1.2	1.5	1.9	2.2	2.5	2.8	3.2	34.2
19.8	3.3	6.6	9.9	13.2	16.5	.8	0.3	0.6	0.9	1.2	1.6	1.9	2.2	2.5	2.9	3.2	
19.9	3.4	6.7	10.0	13.3	16.6	.9	0.3	0.6	0.9	1.3	1.6	1.9	2.2	2.6	2.9	3.2	
20.0	3.3	6.6	10.0	13.3	16.6	.0	0.0	0.3	0.7	1.0	1.4	1.7	2.0	2.4	2.7	3.1	
20.1	3.3	6.7	10.0	13.4	16.7	.1	0.0	0.4	0.7	1.1	1.4	1.7	2.1	2.4	2.8	3.1	0.9 0.1
20.2	3.3	6.7	10.1	13.4	16.8	.2	0.1	0.4	0.8	1.1	1.4	1.8	2.1	2.5	2.8	3.1	2.6 0.2
20.3	3.4	6.8	10.1	13.5	16.9	.3	0.1	0.4	0.8	1.1	1.5	1.8	2.2	2.5	2.8	3.2	4.4 0.3
20.4	3.4	6.8	10.2	13.6	17.0	.4	0.1	0.5	0.8	1.2	1.5	1.8	2.2	2.5	2.9	3.2	6.2 0.4
20.5	3.4	6.8	10.3	13.7	17.1	.5	0.2	0.5	0.9	1.2	1.5	1.9	2.2	2.6	2.9	3.2	7.9 0.5
20.6	3.4	6.9	10.3	13.7	17.2	.6	0.2	0.5	0.9	1.2	1.6	1.9	2.3	2.6	2.9	3.3	9.7 0.6
20.7	3.5	6.9	10.4	13.8	17.3	.7	0.2	0.6	0.9	1.3	1.6	1.9	2.3	2.6	3.0	3.3	11.4 0.7
20.8	3.5	7.0	10.4	13.9	17.4	.8	0.3	0.6	1.0	1.3	1.6	2.0	2.3	2.7	3.0	3.3	13.2 0.8
20.9	3.5	7.0	10.5	14.0	17.5	.9	0.3	0.6	1.0	1.3	1.7	2.0	2.4	2.7	3.0	3.4	14.9 0.9 16.7 1.0
21.0	3.5	7.0	10.5	14.0	17.5	.0	0.0	0.4	0.7	1.1	1.4	1.8	2.1	2.5	2.9	3.2	18.5 1.1
21.1	3.5	7.0	10.5	14.0	17.6	.1	0.0	0.4	0.8	1.1	1.5	1.8	2.2	2.5	2.9	3.3	20.2 1.2
21.2	3.5	7.0	10.6	14.1	17.6	.2	0.1	0.4	0.8	1.1	1.5	1.9	2.2	2.6	2.9	3.3	22.0 1.3
21.3	3.5	7.1	10.6	14.2	17.7	.3	0.1	0.5	0.8	1.2	1.5	1.9	2.3	2.6	3.0	3.3	23.7 1.4
21.4	3.6	7.1	10.7	14.3	17.8	.4	0.1	0.5	0.9	1.2	1.6	1.9	2.3	2.7	3.0	3.4	25.5 1.5 27.3 1.6
21.5	3.6	7.2	10.8	14.3	17.9	.5	0.2	0.5	0.9	1.3	1.6	2.0	2.3	2.7	3.0	3.4	29.0 1.7
21.6	3.6	7.2	10.8	14.4	18.0	.6	0.2	0.6	0.9	1.3	1.6	2.0	2.4	2.7	3.1	3.4	30.8 1.8
21.7	3.6	7.3	10.9	14.5	18.1	.7	0.3	0.6	1.0	1.3	1.7	2.0	2.4	2.8	3.1	3.5	32.5 1.9
21.8	3.7	7.3	10.9	14.6	18.2	.8	0.3	0.6	1.0	1.4	1.7	2.1	2.4	2.8	3.2	3.5	34.3
21.9	3.7	7.3	11.0	14.6	18.3	.9	0.3	0.7	1.0	1.4	1.8	2.1	2.5	2.8	3.2	3.5	
22.0	3.6	7.3	11.0	14.6	18.3	.0	0.0	0.4	0.7	1.1	1.5	1.9	2.2	2.6	3.0	3.4	0.8 0.1
22.1	3.7	7.3	11.0	14.7	18.4	.1	0.0	0.4	0.8	1.2	1.5	1.9	2.3	2.7	3.0	3.4	2.5 0.2
22.2	3.7	7.4	11.1	14.8	18.5	.2	0.1	0.4	0.8	1.2	1.6	1.9	2.3	2.7	3.1	3.4	4.2 0.3
22.3	3.7	7.4	11.1	14.9	18.6	.3	0.1	0.5	0.9	1.2	1.6	2.0	2.4	2.7	3.1	3.5	5.9 0.4
22.4	3.7	7.5	11.2	14.9	18.7	.4	0.1	0.5	0.9	1.3	1.6	2.0	2.4	2.8	3.1	3.5	7.6 0.5
22.5	3.8	7.5	11.3	15.0	18.8	.5	0.2	0.6	0.9	1.3	1.7	2.1	2.4	2.8	3.2	3.6	9.3 0.6
22.6	3.8	7.5	11.3	15.1	18.8	.6	0.2	0.6	1.0	1.3	1.7	2.1	2.5	2.8	3.2	3.6	11.0 0.7
22.7	3.8	7.6	11.4	15.2	18.9	.7	0.3	0.6	1.0	1.4	1.8	2.1	2.5	2.9	3.3	3.6	12.7 0.8
22.8	3.8	7.6	11.4	15.2	19.0	.8	0.3	0.7	1.0	1.4	1.8	2.2	2.5	2.9	3.3	3.7	14.4 0.9
22.9	3.9	7.7	11.5	15.3	19.1	.9	0.3	0.7	1.1	1.5	1.8	2.2	2.6	3.0	3.3	3.7	16.1 1.0 17.8 1.1
23.0	3.8	7.6	11.5	15.3	19.1	.0	0.0	0.4	0.8	1.2	1.6	2.0	2.3	2.7	3.1	3.5	19.5 1.2
23.1	3.8	7.7	11.5	15.4	19.2	.1	0.0	0.4	0.8	1.2	1.6	2.0	2.4	2.8	3.2	3.6	21.2 1.3
23.2	3.8	7.7	11.6	15.4	19.3	.2	0.1	0.5	0.9	1.3	1.6	2.0	2.4	2.8	3.2	3.6	22.8 1.4
23.3	3.9	7.8	11.6	15.5	19.4	.3	0.1	0.5	0.9	1.3	1.7	2.1	2.5	2.9	3.3	3.6	24.5 1.5
23.4	3.9	7.8	11.7	15.6	19.5	.4	0.2	0.5	0.9	1.3	1.7	2.1	2.5	2.9	3.3	3.7	26.2 1.6 27.9 1.7
23.5	3.9	7.8	11.8	15.7	19.6	.5	0.2	0.6	1.0	1.4	1.8	2.2	2.5	2.9	3.3	3.7	29.6 1.8
23.6	3.9	7.9	11.8	15.7	19.7	.6	0.2	0.6	1.0	1.4	1.8	2.2	2.6	3.0	3.4	3.8	31.3 1.9
23.7	4.0	7.9	11.9	15.8	19.8	.7	0.3	0.7	1.1	1.4	1.8	2.2	2.6	3.0	3.4	3.8	33.0 2.0
23.8	4.0	8.0	11.9	15.9	19.9	.8	0.3	0.7	1.1	1.5	1.9	2.3	2.7	3.1	3.4	3.8	34.7
23.9	4.0	8.0	12.0	16.0	20.0	.9	0.4	0.7	1.1	1.5	1.9	2.3	2.7	3.1	3.5	3.9	
	10'	20'	30'	40'	50'		0'	1'	2'	3'	4'	5'	6'	7'	8'	9'	

Dec. Inc.	Altitude Difference (d) Tens 10'	20'	30'	40'	50'	Decimals	Units 0'	1'	2'	3'	4'	5'	6'	7'	8'	9'	Double Second Diff. and Corr.
24.0	4.0	8.0	12.0	16.0	20.0	.0	0.0	0.4	0.8	1.2	1.6	2.0	2.4	2.9	3.3	3.7	0.8 0.1
24.1	4.0	8.0	12.0	16.0	20.1	.1	0.0	0.4	0.9	1.3	1.7	2.1	2.5	2.9	3.3	3.7	2.5 0.2
24.2	4.0	8.0	12.1	16.1	20.1	.2	0.1	0.5	0.9	1.3	1.7	2.1	2.5	2.9	3.3	3.8	4.1 0.3
24.3	4.0	8.1	12.1	16.2	20.2	.3	0.1	0.5	0.9	1.3	1.8	2.2	2.6	3.0	3.4	3.8	5.8 0.4
24.4	4.1	8.1	12.2	16.3	20.3	.4	0.2	0.6	1.0	1.4	1.8	2.2	2.6	3.0	3.4	3.8	7.4 0.5
24.5	4.1	8.2	12.3	16.3	20.4	.5	0.2	0.6	1.0	1.4	1.8	2.2	2.7	3.1	3.5	3.9	9.1 0.6
24.6	4.1	8.2	12.3	16.4	20.5	.6	0.2	0.7	1.1	1.5	1.9	2.3	2.7	3.1	3.5	3.9	10.7 0.7
24.7	4.1	8.3	12.4	16.5	20.6	.7	0.3	0.7	1.1	1.5	1.9	2.3	2.7	3.1	3.6	4.0	12.3 0.8
24.8	4.2	8.3	12.4	16.6	20.7	.8	0.3	0.7	1.1	1.6	2.0	2.4	2.8	3.2	3.6	4.0	14.0 0.9
24.9	4.2	8.3	12.5	16.6	20.8	.9	0.4	0.8	1.2	1.6	2.0	2.4	2.8	3.2	3.6	4.0	15.6 1.0 17.3 1.1
25.0	4.1	8.3	12.5	16.6	20.8	.0	0.0	0.4	0.8	1.3	1.7	2.1	2.5	3.0	3.4	3.8	18.9 1.2
25.1	4.2	8.3	12.5	16.7	20.9	.1	0.0	0.5	0.9	1.3	1.7	2.2	2.6	3.0	3.4	3.9	20.6 1.3
25.2	4.2	8.4	12.6	16.8	21.0	.2	0.1	0.5	0.9	1.4	1.8	2.2	2.6	3.1	3.5	3.9	22.2 1.4
25.3	4.2	8.4	12.6	16.9	21.1	.3	0.1	0.6	1.0	1.4	1.8	2.3	2.7	3.1	3.5	4.0	23.9 1.5
25.4	4.2	8.5	12.7	16.9	21.2	.4	0.2	0.6	1.0	1.4	1.9	2.3	2.7	3.1	3.6	4.0	25.5 1.6
25.5	4.3	8.5	12.8	17.0	21.3	.5	0.2	0.6	1.1	1.5	1.9	2.3	2.8	3.2	3.6	4.0	27.2 1.7
25.6	4.3	8.5	12.8	17.1	21.3	.6	0.3	0.7	1.1	1.5	2.0	2.4	2.8	3.2	3.7	4.1	28.8 1.8
25.7	4.3	8.6	12.9	17.2	21.4	.7	0.3	0.7	1.1	1.6	2.0	2.4	2.8	3.3	3.7	4.1	30.4 1.9
25.8	4.3	8.6	12.9	17.2	21.5	.8	0.3	0.8	1.2	1.6	2.0	2.5	2.9	3.3	3.7	4.2	32.1 2.0
25.9	4.4	8.7	13.0	17.3	21.6	.9	0.4	0.8	1.2	1.7	2.1	2.5	2.9	3.4	3.8	4.2	33.7 2.1 35.4
26.0	4.3	8.6	13.0	17.3	21.6	.0	0.0	0.4	0.9	1.3	1.8	2.2	2.6	3.1	3.5	4.0	0.8 0.1
26.1	4.3	8.7	13.0	17.4	21.7	.1	0.0	0.5	0.9	1.4	1.8	2.3	2.7	3.1	3.6	4.0	2.4 0.2
26.2	4.3	8.7	13.1	17.4	21.8	.2	0.1	0.5	1.0	1.4	1.9	2.3	2.7	3.2	3.6	4.1	4.0 0.3
26.3	4.4	8.8	13.1	17.5	21.9	.3	0.1	0.6	1.0	1.5	1.9	2.3	2.8	3.2	3.7	4.1	5.7 0.4
26.4	4.4	8.8	13.2	17.6	22.0	.4	0.2	0.6	1.1	1.5	1.9	2.4	2.8	3.3	3.7	4.2	7.3 0.5
26.5	4.4	8.8	13.3	17.7	22.1	.5	0.2	0.7	1.1	1.5	2.0	2.4	2.9	3.3	3.8	4.2	8.9 0.6
26.6	4.4	8.9	13.3	17.7	22.2	.6	0.3	0.7	1.1	1.6	2.0	2.5	2.9	3.4	3.8	4.2	10.5 0.7
26.7	4.5	8.9	13.4	17.8	22.3	.7	0.3	0.8	1.2	1.6	2.1	2.5	3.0	3.4	3.8	4.3	12.1 0.8
26.8	4.5	9.0	13.4	17.9	22.4	.8	0.4	0.8	1.2	1.7	2.1	2.6	3.0	3.4	3.9	4.3	13.7 0.9
26.9	4.5	9.0	13.5	18.0	22.5	.9	0.4	0.8	1.3	1.7	2.2	2.6	3.0	3.5	3.9	4.4	15.4 1.0 17.0 1.1
27.0	4.5	9.0	13.5	18.0	22.5	.0	0.0	0.5	0.9	1.4	1.8	2.3	2.7	3.2	3.7	4.1	18.6 1.2
27.1	4.5	9.0	13.5	18.0	22.6	.1	0.0	0.5	1.0	1.4	1.9	2.3	2.8	3.3	3.7	4.2	20.2 1.3
27.2	4.5	9.0	13.6	18.1	22.6	.2	0.1	0.5	1.0	1.5	1.9	2.4	2.8	3.3	3.8	4.2	21.8 1.4
27.3	4.5	9.1	13.6	18.2	22.7	.3	0.1	0.6	1.1	1.5	2.0	2.4	2.9	3.3	3.8	4.3	23.4 1.5
27.4	4.6	9.1	13.7	18.3	22.8	.4	0.2	0.6	1.1	1.6	2.0	2.5	2.9	3.4	3.8	4.3	25.1 1.6
27.5	4.6	9.2	13.8	18.3	22.9	.5	0.2	0.7	1.1	1.6	2.1	2.5	3.0	3.4	3.9	4.4	26.7 1.7
27.6	4.6	9.2	13.8	18.4	23.0	.6	0.3	0.7	1.2	1.6	2.1	2.6	3.0	3.5	3.9	4.4	28.3 1.8
27.7	4.6	9.3	13.9	18.5	23.1	.7	0.3	0.8	1.2	1.7	2.2	2.6	3.1	3.5	4.0	4.4	29.9 1.9
27.8	4.7	9.3	13.9	18.6	23.2	.8	0.4	0.8	1.3	1.7	2.2	2.7	3.1	3.6	4.0	4.5	31.5 2.0
27.9	4.7	9.3	14.0	18.6	23.3	.9	0.4	0.9	1.3	1.8	2.2	2.7	3.2	3.6	4.1	4.5	33.1 2.1 34.7
28.0	4.6	9.3	14.0	18.6	23.3	.0	0.0	0.5	0.9	1.4	1.9	2.4	2.8	3.3	3.8	4.3	0.8 0.1
28.1	4.7	9.3	14.0	18.7	23.4	.1	0.0	0.5	1.0	1.5	1.9	2.4	2.9	3.4	3.8	4.3	2.4 0.2
28.2	4.7	9.4	14.1	18.8	23.5	.2	0.1	0.6	1.0	1.5	2.0	2.5	2.9	3.4	3.9	4.4	4.0 0.3
28.3	4.7	9.4	14.1	18.9	23.6	.3	0.1	0.6	1.1	1.6	2.0	2.5	3.0	3.5	3.9	4.4	5.6 0.4
28.4	4.7	9.5	14.2	18.9	23.7	.4	0.2	0.7	1.1	1.6	2.1	2.6	3.0	3.5	4.0	4.5	7.2 0.5
28.5	4.8	9.5	14.3	19.0	23.8	.5	0.2	0.7	1.2	1.7	2.1	2.6	3.1	3.6	4.0	4.5	8.8 0.6
28.6	4.8	9.5	14.3	19.1	23.8	.6	0.3	0.8	1.2	1.7	2.2	2.7	3.1	3.6	4.1	4.6	10.4 0.7
28.7	4.8	9.6	14.4	19.2	23.9	.7	0.3	0.8	1.3	1.8	2.2	2.7	3.2	3.7	4.1	4.6	12.0 0.8
28.8	4.8	9.6	14.4	19.2	24.0	.8	0.4	0.9	1.3	1.8	2.3	2.8	3.2	3.7	4.2	4.7	13.6 0.9
28.9	4.9	9.7	14.5	19.3	24.1	.9	0.4	0.9	1.4	1.9	2.3	2.8	3.3	3.8	4.2	4.7	15.2 1.0 16.8 1.1
29.0	4.8	9.6	14.5	19.3	24.1	.0	0.0	0.5	1.0	1.5	2.0	2.5	2.9	3.4	3.9	4.4	18.4 1.2
29.1	4.8	9.7	14.5	19.4	24.2	.1	0.0	0.5	1.0	1.5	2.0	2.5	3.0	3.5	4.0	4.5	20.0 1.3
29.2	4.8	9.7	14.6	19.4	24.3	.2	0.1	0.6	1.1	1.6	2.1	2.6	3.0	3.5	4.0	4.5	21.6 1.4
29.3	4.9	9.8	14.6	19.5	24.4	.3	0.1	0.6	1.1	1.6	2.1	2.6	3.1	3.6	4.1	4.6	23.2 1.5
29.4	4.9	9.8	14.7	19.6	24.5	.4	0.2	0.7	1.2	1.7	2.2	2.7	3.1	3.6	4.1	4.6	24.8 1.6
29.5	4.9	9.8	14.8	19.7	24.6	.5	0.2	0.7	1.2	1.7	2.2	2.7	3.2	3.7	4.2	4.7	26.4 1.7
29.6	4.9	9.9	14.8	19.7	24.7	.6	0.3	0.8	1.3	1.8	2.3	2.8	3.2	3.7	4.2	4.7	28.0 1.8
29.7	5.0	9.9	14.9	19.8	24.8	.7	0.3	0.8	1.3	1.8	2.3	2.8	3.3	3.8	4.3	4.8	29.6 1.9
29.8	5.0	10.0	14.9	19.9	24.9	.8	0.4	0.9	1.4	1.9	2.4	2.9	3.3	3.8	4.3	4.8	31.2 2.0
29.9	5.0	10.0	15.0	20.0	25.0	.9	0.4	0.9	1.4	1.9	2.4	2.9	3.4	3.9	4.4	4.9	32.8 2.1 34.4
30.0	5.0	10.0	15.0	20.0	25.0	.0	0.0	0.5	1.0	1.5	2.0	2.5	3.0	3.6	4.1	4.6	0.8 0.1
30.1	5.0	10.0	15.0	20.0	25.1	.1	0.1	0.6	1.1	1.6	2.1	2.6	3.1	3.6	4.1	4.6	2.4 0.2
30.2	5.0	10.0	15.1	20.1	25.1	.2	0.1	0.6	1.1	1.6	2.1	2.6	3.2	3.7	4.2	4.7	4.0 0.3
30.3	5.0	10.1	15.1	20.2	25.2	.3	0.2	0.7	1.2	1.7	2.2	2.7	3.2	3.7	4.2	4.7	5.6 0.4
30.4	5.1	10.1	15.2	20.3	25.3	.4	0.2	0.7	1.2	1.7	2.2	2.7	3.3	3.8	4.3	4.8	7.2 0.5
30.5	5.1	10.2	15.3	20.3	25.4	.5	0.3	0.8	1.3	1.8	2.3	2.8	3.3	3.8	4.3	4.8	8.8 0.6
30.6	5.1	10.2	15.3	20.4	25.5	.6	0.3	0.8	1.3	1.8	2.3	2.8	3.4	3.9	4.4	4.9	10.4 0.7
30.7	5.1	10.3	15.4	20.5	25.6	.7	0.4	0.9	1.4	1.9	2.4	2.9	3.4	3.9	4.4	4.9	12.0 0.8
30.8	5.2	10.3	15.4	20.6	25.7	.8	0.4	0.9	1.4	1.9	2.4	2.9	3.5	4.0	4.5	5.0	13.6 0.9
30.9	5.2	10.3	15.5	20.6	25.8	.9	0.5	1.0	1.5	2.0	2.5	3.0	3.5	4.0	4.5	5.0	15.2 1.0 16.8 1.1
31.0	5.1	10.3	15.5	20.6	25.8	.0	0.0	0.5	1.0	1.6	2.1	2.6	3.1	3.7	4.2	4.7	18.4 1.2
31.1	5.2	10.3	15.5	20.7	25.9	.1	0.1	0.6	1.1	1.6	2.2	2.7	3.2	3.7	4.3	4.8	20.0 1.3
31.2	5.2	10.4	15.6	20.8	26.0	.2	0.1	0.6	1.2	1.7	2.2	2.7	3.3	3.8	4.3	4.8	21.6 1.4
31.3	5.2	10.4	15.6	20.9	26.1	.3	0.2	0.7	1.2	1.7	2.3	2.8	3.3	3.8	4.4	4.9	23.2 1.5
31.4	5.2	10.5	15.7	20.9	26.2	.4	0.2	0.7	1.3	1.8	2.3	2.8	3.4	3.9	4.4	4.9	24.8 1.6
31.5	5.3	10.5	15.8	21.0	26.3	.5	0.3	0.8	1.3	1.8	2.4	2.9	3.4	3.9	4.5	5.0	26.4 1.7
31.6	5.3	10.5	15.8	21.1	26.3	.6	0.3	0.8	1.4	1.9	2.4	2.9	3.5	4.0	4.5	5.0	28.0 1.8
31.7	5.3	10.6	15.9	21.2	26.4	.7	0.4	0.9	1.4	1.9	2.5	3.0	3.5	4.0	4.6	5.1	29.6 1.9
31.8	5.3	10.6	15.9	21.2	26.5	.8	0.4	0.9	1.5	2.0	2.5	3.0	3.6	4.1	4.6	5.1	31.2 2.0
31.9	5.4	10.7	16.0	21.3	26.6	.9	0.5	1.0	1.5	2.0	2.6	3.1	3.6	4.1	4.7	5.2	32.8 2.1 34.4
	10'	20'	30'	40'	50'		0'	1'	2'	3'	4'	5'	6'	7'	8'	9'	

The Double-Second-Difference correction (Corr.) is always to be added to the tabulated altitude.

36°, 324° L.H.A. LATITUDE SAME NAME AS DECLINATION

N. Lat. {L.H.A. greater than 180°......Zn=Z; L.H.A. less than 180°............Zn=360°−Z}

Dec.	30° Hc	d	Z	31° Hc	d	Z	32° Hc	d	Z	33° Hc	d	Z	34° Hc	d	Z	35° Hc	d	Z	36° Hc	d	Z	37° Hc	d	Z	Dec.
°	° ′	′	°	° ′	′	°	° ′	′	°	° ′	′	°	° ′	′	°	° ′	′	°	° ′	′	°	° ′	′	°	°
0	44 28.7	+41.7	124.5	43 54.3	+42.6	125.3	43 19.3	+43.4	126.1	42 43.6	+44.2	126.9	42 07.3	+45.0	127.6	41 30.4	+45.8	128.3	40 52.9	+46.5	129.0	40 14.9	+47.2	129.6	0
1	45 10.4	41.3	123.5	44 36.9	42.2	124.4	44 02.7	43.0	125.2	43 27.8	43.9	125.9	42 52.3	44.6	126.7	42 16.2	45.3	127.4	41 39.4	46.1	128.1	41 02.1	46.8	128.8	1
2	45 51.7	40.6	122.5	45 19.1	41.5	123.3	44 45.7	42.5	124.2	44 11.7	43.3	125.0	43 36.9	44.2	125.8	43 01.5	45.0	126.5	42 25.5	45.7	127.3	41 48.9	46.4	128.0	2
3	46 32.3	40.1	121.4	46 00.6	41.0	122.3	45 28.2	41.9	123.2	44 55.0	42.8	124.0	44 21.1	43.6	124.8	43 46.5	44.4	125.6	43 11.2	45.3	126.4	42 35.3	46.0	127.1	3
4	47 12.4	39.4	120.3	46 41.6	40.4	121.3	46 10.1	41.4	122.1	45 37.8	42.3	123.0	45 04.7	43.2	123.9	44 30.9	44.1	124.7	43 56.5	44.8	125.5	43 21.3	45.6	126.3	4
5	47 51.8	+38.7	119.2	47 22.0	+39.8	120.2	46 51.5	+40.7	121.1	46 20.1	+41.7	122.0	45 47.9	+42.6	122.9	45 15.0	+43.5	123.7	44 41.3	+44.4	124.6	44 06.9	+45.2	125.4	5
6	48 30.5	38.1	118.1	48 01.8	39.1	119.1	47 32.2	40.2	120.0	47 01.8	41.1	120.9	46 30.5	42.1	121.9	45 58.5	43.0	122.7	45 25.7	43.8	123.6	44 52.1	44.7	124.4	6
7	49 08.6	37.3	116.9	48 40.9	38.5	117.9	48 12.4	39.5	118.9	47 42.9	40.6	119.9	47 12.6	41.5	120.8	46 41.5	42.4	121.7	46 09.5	43.4	122.6	45 36.8	44.2	123.5	7
8	49 45.9	36.5	115.7	49 19.4	37.7	116.7	48 51.9	38.8	117.8	48 23.5	39.8	118.8	47 54.1	40.9	119.7	47 23.9	41.9	120.7	46 52.9	42.8	121.6	46 21.0	43.8	122.5	8
9	50 22.4	35.8	114.5	49 57.1	36.9	115.5	49 30.7	38.1	116.6	49 03.3	39.2	117.6	48 35.0	40.3	118.6	48 05.8	41.3	119.6	47 35.7	42.3	120.6	47 04.8	43.2	121.5	9
10	50 58.2	+34.9	113.2	50 34.0	+36.1	114.3	50 08.8	+37.3	115.4	49 42.5	+38.5	116.5	49 15.3	+39.6	117.5	48 47.1	+40.6	118.5	48 18.0	+41.6	119.5	47 48.0	+42.6	120.5	10
11	51 33.1	34.0	111.9	51 10.1	35.3	113.0	50 46.1	36.5	114.2	50 21.0	37.7	115.3	49 54.9	38.8	116.4	49 27.7	40.0	117.4	48 59.6	41.0	118.4	48 30.6	42.0	119.4	11
12	52 07.1	33.1	110.6	51 45.4	34.4	111.7	51 22.6	35.7	112.9	50 58.7	36.9	114.1	50 33.7	38.1	115.2	50 07.7	39.2	116.3	49 40.6	40.4	117.3	49 12.6	41.4	118.3	12
13	52 40.2	32.1	109.2	52 19.8	33.5	110.4	51 58.3	34.8	111.6	51 35.6	36.1	112.8	51 11.8	37.3	113.9	50 46.9	38.5	115.1	50 21.0	39.6	116.2	49 54.0	40.8	117.2	13
14	53 12.3	31.1	107.8	52 53.3	32.5	109.0	52 33.1	33.9	110.3	52 11.7	35.2	111.5	51 49.1	36.5	112.7	51 25.4	37.8	113.8	51 00.6	39.0	115.0	50 34.8	40.0	116.1	14
15	53 43.4	+30.0	106.4	53 25.8	+31.5	107.6	53 07.0	+32.9	108.9	52 46.9	+34.3	110.2	52 25.6	+35.7	111.4	52 03.2	+36.9	112.6	51 39.6	+38.1	113.8	51 14.8	+39.4	114.9	15
16	54 13.4	29.0	104.9	53 57.3	30.5	106.2	53 39.9	32.0	107.5	53 21.2	33.4	108.8	53 01.3	34.7	110.1	52 40.1	36.0	111.3	52 17.7	37.3	112.5	51 54.2	38.5	113.7	16
17	54 42.4	27.8	103.4	54 27.8	29.4	104.7	54 11.9	30.8	106.1	53 54.6	32.3	107.4	53 36.0	33.7	108.7	53 16.1	35.1	110.0	52 55.0	36.5	111.2	52 32.7	37.7	112.4	17
18	55 10.2	26.6	101.8	54 57.2	28.2	103.2	54 42.7	29.8	104.6	54 26.9	31.3	106.0	54 09.7	32.8	107.3	53 51.2	34.2	108.6	53 31.5	35.5	109.9	53 10.4	36.9	111.1	18
19	55 36.8	25.3	100.3	55 25.4	27.0	101.7	55 12.5	28.6	103.1	54 58.2	30.2	104.5	54 42.5	31.7	105.9	54 25.4	33.2	107.2	54 07.0	34.6	108.5	53 47.3	36.0	109.8	19
20	56 02.1	+24.1	98.6	55 52.4	+25.7	100.1	55 41.1	+27.4	101.5	55 28.4	+29.0	103.0	55 14.2	+30.6	104.4	54 58.6	+32.1	105.8	54 41.6	+33.6	107.1	54 23.3	+35.0	108.5	20
21	56 26.2	22.7	97.0	56 18.1	24.5	98.5	56 08.5	26.2	100.0	55 57.4	27.8	101.4	55 44.8	29.4	102.9	55 30.7	31.0	104.3	55 15.2	32.5	105.7	54 58.3	34.0	107.1	21
22	56 48.9	21.4	95.3	56 42.6	23.1	96.8	56 34.7	24.9	98.3	56 25.2	26.6	99.8	56 14.2	28.3	101.3	56 01.7	29.9	102.8	55 47.7	31.5	104.2	55 32.3	33.0	105.6	22
23	57 10.3	19.9	93.6	57 05.7	21.8	95.1	56 59.6	23.5	96.7	56 51.8	25.3	98.2	56 42.5	26.9	99.7	56 31.6	28.6	101.2	56 19.2	30.3	102.7	56 05.3	31.8	104.1	23
24	57 30.2	18.5	91.8	57 27.5	20.3	93.4	57 23.1	22.1	95.0	57 17.1	23.9	96.5	57 09.4	25.7	98.1	57 00.2	27.4	99.6	56 49.5	29.0	101.1	56 37.1	30.8	102.6	24
25	57 48.7	+16.9	90.1	57 47.8	+18.8	91.7	57 45.2	+20.7	93.2	57 41.0	+22.5	94.8	57 35.1	+24.3	96.4	57 27.6	+26.1	97.9	57 18.5	+27.8	99.5	57 07.9	+29.4	101.0	25
26	58 05.6	15.3	88.3	58 06.6	17.2	89.9	58 05.9	19.1	91.5	58 03.5	21.0	93.1	57 59.4	22.9	94.7	57 53.7	24.7	96.3	57 46.3	26.5	97.8	57 37.3	28.3	99.4	26
27	58 20.9	13.8	86.4	58 23.8	15.7	88.0	58 25.0	17.7	89.7	58 24.5	19.6	91.3	58 22.3	21.4	92.9	58 18.4	23.3	94.5	58 12.8	25.1	96.1	58 05.6	26.9	97.7	27
28	58 34.7	12.1	84.6	58 39.5	14.1	86.2	58 42.7	16.0	87.8	58 44.1	18.0	89.5	58 43.7	20.0	91.1	58 41.7	21.8	92.8	58 37.9	23.7	94.4	58 32.5	25.5	96.0	28
29	58 46.8	10.5	82.7	58 53.6	12.5	84.3	58 58.7	14.4	86.0	59 02.1	16.3	87.6	59 03.7	18.3	89.3	59 03.5	20.3	91.0	59 01.6	22.2	92.6	58 58.0	24.1	94.3	29
30	58 57.3	+8.8	80.8	59 06.1	+10.7	82.4	59 13.1	+12.8	84.1	59 18.4	+14.8	85.8	59 22.0	+16.7	87.4	59 23.8	+18.7	89.1	59 23.8	+20.7	90.8	59 22.1	+22.5	92.5	30
31	59 06.1	7.0	78.8	59 16.8	9.1	80.5	59 25.9	11.0	82.2	59 33.2	13.0	83.9	59 38.7	15.1	85.6	59 42.5	17.0	87.3	59 44.5	19.0	89.0	59 44.6	21.0	90.7	31
32	59 13.1	5.3	76.9	59 25.9	7.3	78.6	59 36.9	9.3	80.2	59 46.2	11.3	81.9	59 53.8	13.3	83.6	59 59.5	15.4	85.3	60 03.5	17.4	87.1	60 05.6	19.4	88.8	32
33	59 18.4	3.6	75.0	59 33.2	5.5	76.6	59 46.2	7.6	78.3	59 57.5	9.6	80.0	60 07.1	11.6	81.7	60 14.9	13.7	83.4	60 20.9	15.7	85.2	60 25.0	17.8	86.9	33
34	59 22.0	+1.8	73.0	59 38.7	3.8	74.6	59 53.8	5.7	76.3	60 07.1	7.8	78.0	60 18.7	9.9	79.7	60 28.6	11.8	81.4	60 36.6	13.9	83.2	60 42.8	16.0	85.0	34
35	59 23.8	0.0	71.0	59 42.5	+2.0	72.7	59 59.5	+4.0	74.3	60 14.9	+6.0	76.0	60 28.6	+8.0	77.7	60 40.4	+10.1	79.4	60 50.5	+12.2	81.2	60 58.8	+14.2	83.0	35
36	59 23.8	−1.7	69.1	59 44.5	+0.1	70.7	60 03.5	2.1	72.3	60 20.9	4.1	74.0	60 36.6	6.2	75.7	60 50.5	8.3	77.4	61 02.7	10.3	79.2	61 13.0	12.5	81.0	36
37	59 22.1	3.5	67.1	59 44.6	−1.6	68.7	60 05.6	+0.4	70.3	60 25.0	2.4	72.0	60 42.8	4.3	73.7	60 58.8	6.4	75.4	61 13.0	8.5	77.1	61 25.5	10.6	78.9	37
38	59 18.6	5.3	65.2	59 43.0	3.4	66.7	60 06.0	−1.5	68.3	60 27.4	+0.4	69.9	60 47.1	2.5	71.6	61 05.2	4.5	73.3	61 21.5	6.6	75.1	61 36.1	8.6	76.9	38
39	59 13.3	7.0	63.2	59 39.6	5.2	64.7	60 04.5	3.3	66.3	60 27.8	−1.3	67.9	60 49.6	+0.6	69.6	61 09.7	2.6	71.3	61 28.1	4.7	73.0	61 44.7	6.8	74.8	39
40	59 06.3	−8.7	61.3	59 34.4	−6.9	62.8	60 01.2	−5.1	64.3	60 26.5	−3.3	65.9	60 50.2	−1.3	67.5	61 12.3	+0.7	69.2	61 32.8	+2.7	70.9	61 51.5	+4.9	72.7	40
41	58 57.6	10.5	59.3	59 27.5	8.7	60.8	59 56.1	6.9	62.3	60 23.2	5.0	63.9	60 48.9	3.1	65.5	61 13.0	−1.2	67.1	61 35.5	+0.9	68.8	61 56.4	2.9*	70.6	41
42	58 47.1	12.0	57.4	59 18.8	10.4	58.9	59 49.2	8.7	60.3	60 18.2	6.9	61.8	60 45.8	5.0	63.4	61 11.8	3.0	65.0	61 36.4	−1.1*	66.7	61 59.3	+0.9*	68.4	42
43	58 35.1	13.8	55.6	59 08.4	12.1	56.9	59 40.5	10.4	58.4	60 11.3	8.7	59.8	60 40.8	6.9	61.4	61 08.8	5.0	63.0	61 35.3	3.1	64.6	62 00.2	−1.1	66.3	43
44	58 21.3	15.3	53.7	58 56.3	13.8	55.0	59 30.1	12.1	56.4	60 02.6	10.4	57.9	60 33.9	8.7	59.4	61 03.8	6.9	60.9	61 32.2	5.0	62.5	61 59.1	3.0	64.2	44
45	58 06.0	−16.9	51.9	58 42.5	−15.3	53.2	59 18.0	−13.9	54.5	59 52.2	−12.2	55.9	60 25.2	−10.5	57.3	60 56.9	−8.7	58.9	61 27.2	−6.8	60.4	61 56.1	−5.0	62.1	45
46	57 49.1	18.4	50.1	58 27.2	17.0	51.3	59 04.1	15.4	52.6	59 40.0	13.9	53.9	60 14.7	12.2	55.4	60 48.2	10.5	56.8	61 20.4	8.8	58.4	61 51.1	6.9	59.9	46
47	57 30.7	19.9	48.3	58 10.2	18.5	49.5	58 48.7	17.1	50.7	59 26.1	15.5	52.0	60 02.5	14.0	53.4	60 37.7	12.4	54.8	61 11.6	10.6	56.3	61 44.2	8.8	57.8	47
48	57 10.8	21.3	46.5	57 51.7	20.0	47.7	58 31.6	18.6	48.9	59 10.6	17.2	50.1	59 48.5	15.6	51.5	60 25.3	14.0	52.8	61 01.0	12.4	54.3	61 35.4	10.7	55.8	48
49	56 49.5	22.7	44.8	57 31.7	21.4	45.9	58 13.0	20.1	47.1	58 53.4	18.7	48.3	59 32.9	17.4	49.5	60 11.3	15.8	50.9	60 48.6	14.2	52.2	61 24.7	12.5	53.7	49
50	56 26.8	−24.0	43.1	57 10.3	−22.9	44.2	57 52.9	−21.6	45.3	58 34.7	−20.3	46.4	59 15.5	−18.9	47.7	59 55.5	−17.5	48.9	60 34.4	−16.0	50.3	61 12.2	−14.4	51.7	50
51	56 02.8	25.3	41.5	56 47.4	24.2	42.5	57 31.3	23.0	43.5	58 14.4	21.8	44.6	58 56.6	20.4	45.8	59 38.0	19.1	47.0	60 18.4	17.6	48.3	60 57.8	16.1	49.7	51
52	55 37.5	26.6	39.9	56 23.2	25.5	40.8	57 08.3	24.4	41.8	57 52.6	23.2	42.9	58 36.2	22.0	44.0	59 18.9	20.6	45.2	60 00.8	19.3	46.4	60 41.7	17.9	47.7	52
53	55 10.9	27.8	38.3	55 57.7	26.8	39.2	56 43.9	25.7	40.2	57 29.4	24.6	41.2	58 14.2	23.4	42.2	58 58.3	22.2	43.3	59 41.5	20.9	44.5	60 23.8	19.5	45.7	53
54	54 43.1	28.9	36.7	55 30.9	27.9	37.6	56 18.2	27.0	38.5	57 04.8	25.9	39.5	57 50.8	24.8	40.5	58 36.1	23.7	41.5	59 20.6	22.4	42.7	60 04.3	21.1	43.8	54
55	54 14.2	−30.0	35.2	55 03.0	−29.1	36.1	55 51.2	−28.2	36.9	56 38.9	−27.2	37.8	57 26.0	−26.2	38.8	58 12.4	−25.0	39.8	58 58.2	−23.9	40.8	59 43.2	−22.7	42.0	55
56	53 44.2	31.1	33.8	54 33.9	30.3	34.5	55 23.0	29.3	35.4	56 11.7	28.4	36.2	56 59.8	27.4	37.1	57 47.4	26.4	38.1	58 34.3	25.3	39.1	59 20.5	24.1	40.1	56
57	53 13.1	32.1	32.3	54 03.6	31.3	33.1	54 53.7	30.5	33.8	55 43.3	29.6	34.6	56 32.4	28.7	35.5	57 21.0	27.7	36.4	58 09.0	26.7	37.3	58 56.4	25.7	38.4	57
58	52 41.0	33.0	30.9	53 32.3	32.3	31.6	54 23.2	31.5	32.3	55 13.7	30.7	33.1	56 03.7	29.8	33.9	56 53.3	29.0	34.8	57 42.3	28.0	35.7	58 30.7	26.9	36.6	58
59	52 08.0	34.0	29.5	53 00.0	33.3	30.2	53 51.7	32.6	30.9	54 43.0	31.8	31.6	55 33.9	31.0	32.4	56 24.3	30.1	33.2	57 14.3	29.3	34.0	58 03.8	28.4	34.9	59
60	51 34.0	−34.9	28.2	52 26.7	−34.2	28.8	53 19.1	−33.6	29.5	54 11.2	−32.9	30.1	55 02.9	−32.1	30.9	55 54.2	−31.3	31.6	56 45.0	−30.4	32.4	57 35.4	−29.5	33.3	60
61	50 59.1	35.7	26.9	51 52.5	35.1	27.5	52 45.5	34.4	28.1	53 38.3	33.8	28.7	54 30.8	33.1	29.4	55 22.9	32.4	30.1	56 14.6	31.6	30.9	57 05.9	30.8	31.6	61
62	50 23.4	36.5	25.6	51 17.4	36.0	26.2	52 11.1	35.4	26.7	53 04.5	34.8	27.3	53 57.7	34.2	28.0	54 50.5	33.4	28.6	55 43.0	32.7	29.3	56 35.1	32.0	30.1	62
63	49 46.9	37.3	24.4	50 41.4	36.8	24.9	51 35.7	36.2	25.4	52 29.7	35.6	26.0	53 23.5	35.0	26.6	54 17.1	34.5	27.2	55 10.3	33.8	27.9	56 03.1	33.0	28.5	63
64	49 09.6	38.1	23.2	50 04.6	37.5	23.7	50 59.5	37.1	24.2	51 54.1	36.5	24.7	52 48.5	35.9	25.2	53 42.6	35.3	25.8	54 36.5	34.7	26.4	55 30.1	34.1	27.1	64
65	48 31.5	−38.7	22.0	49 27.1	−38.3	22.5	50 22.4	−37.8	22.9	51 17.6	−37.3	23.4	52 12.6	−36.8	23.9	53 07.3	−36.3	24.5	54 01.8	−35.7	25.0	54 56.0	−35.1	25.6	65
66	47 52.8	39.4	20.9	48 48.8	39.0	21.3	49 44.6	38.5	21.7	50 40.3	38.1	22.2	51 35.8	37.7	22.6	52 31.0	37.1	23.1	53 26.1	36.6	23.7	54 20.9	36.0	24.2	66
67	47 13.4	40.0	19.8	48 09.8	39.6	20.1	49 06.1	39.3	20.5	50 02.2	38.8	21.0	50 58.1	38.3	21.4	51 53.9	37.9	21.9	52 49.5	37.4	22.3	53 44.9	36.9	22.9	67
68	46 33.4	40.6	18.7	47 30.2	40.3	19.0	48 26.8	39.9	19.4	49 23.4	39.6	19.8	50 19.8	39.2	20.2	51 16.0	38.7	20.6	52 12.1	38.3	21.1	53 08.0	37.8	21.5	68
69	45 52.8	41.3	17.6	46 49.9	40.9	17.9	47 46.9	40.5	18.3	48 43.8	40.2	18.6	49 40.6	39.8	19.0	50 37.3	39.4	19.4	51 33.8	39.0	19.8	52 30.2	38.6	20.2	69
70	45 11.5	−41.7	16.6	46 09.0	−41.5	16.9	47 06.4	−41.2	17.2	48 03.6	−40.8	17.5	49 00.8	−40.5	17.8	49 57.9	−40.2	18.2	50 54.8	−39.8	18.6	51 51.6	−39.4	19.0	70
71	44 29.8	42.3	15.6	45 27.5	42.0	15.8	46 25.2	41.7	16.1	47 22.8	41.4	16.4	48 20.3	41.1	16.7	49 17.7	40.8	17.1	50 15.0	40.4	17.4	51 12.2	40.1	17.8	71
72	43 47.5	42.8	14.6	44 45.5	42.5	14.8	45 43.5	42.3	15.1	46 41.4	42.0	15.4	47 39.2	41.7	15.6	48 36.9	41.4	15.9	49 34.6	41.1	16.3	50 32.1	40.8	16.6	72
73	43 04.7	43.3	13.6	44 03.0	43.1	13.8	45 01.2	42.8	14.1	45 59.4	42.6	14.3	46 57.5	42.3	14.6	47 55.5	42.0	14.9	48 53.5	41.8	15.2	49 51.3	41.4	15.5	73
74	42 21.4	43.7	12.7	43 19.9	43.5	12.9	44 18.4	43.3	13.1	45 16.8	43.0	13.3	46 15.2	42.8	13.6	47 13.5	42.6	13.8	48 11.7	42.3	14.1	49 09.9	42.1	14.3	74
75	41 37.7	−44.1	11.7	42 36.4	−43.9	11.9	43 35.1	−43.7	12.1	44 33.8	−43.6	12.3	45 32.4	−43.4	12.5	46 30.9	−43.1	12.8	47 29.4	−42.9	13.0	48 27.8	−42.7	13.3	75
76	40 53.6	44.6	10.8	41 52.5	44.4	11.0	42 51.4	44.3	11.2	43 50.2	44.0	11.4	44 49.0	43.8	11.6	45 47.8	43.7	11.8	46 46.5	43.5	12.0	47 45.1	43.2	12.2	76
77	40 09.0	44.9	10.0	41 08.1	44.8	10.1	42 07.1	44.6	10.3	43 06.2	44.5	10.4	44 05.2	44.4	10.6	45 04.1	44.1	10.8	46 03.0	43.9	11.0	47 01.9	43.7	11.2	77
78	39 24.1	45.4	9.1	40 23.3	45.2	9.2	41 22.5	45.1	9.4	42 21.7	44.9	9.5	43 20.8	44.7	9.7	44 20.0	44.6	9.8	45 19.1	44.5	10.0	46 18.2	44.3	10.2	78
79	38 38.7	45.7	8.3	39 38.1	45.6	8.4	40 37.4	45.4	8.5	41 36.8	45.3	8.6	42 36.1	45.2	8.8	43 35.4	45.1	8.9	44 34.6	44.9	9.1	45 33.9	44.8	9.2	79
80	37 53.0	−46.0	7.4	38 52.5	−45.9	7.5	39 52.0	−45.8	7.6	40 51.5	−45.7	7.8	41 50.9	−45.6	7.9	42 50.3	−45.4	8.0	43 49.7	−45.3	8.1	44 49.1	−45.2	8.3	80
81	37 07.0	46.3	6.6	38 06.6	46.2	6.7	39 06.2	46.1	6.8	40 05.8	46.1	6.9	41 05.3	45.9	7.0	42 04.9	45.8	7.1	43 04.4	45.7	7.2	44 03.9	45.6	7.4	81
82	36 20.7	46.7	5.8	37 20.4	46.6	5.9	38 20.0	46.4	6.0	39 19.7	46.4	6.1	40 19.4	46.3	6.2	41 19.0	46.2	6.3	42 18.7	46.2	6.4	43 18.3	46.1	6.5	82
83	35 34.0	46.9	5.1	36 33.8	46.9	5.1	37 33.6	46.9	5.2	38 33.3	46.7	5.3	39 33.1	46.7	5.3	40 32.8	46.6	5.4	41 32.5	46.5	5.5	42 32.2	46.4	5.6	83
84	34 47.1	47.2	4.3	35 46.9	47.1	4.3	36 46.7	47.1	4.4	37 46.6	47.1	4.5	38 46.4	47.0	4.5	39 46.2	46.9	4.6	40 46.0	46.9	4.7	41 45.8	46.8	4.7	84
85	33 59.9	−47.5	3.5	34 59.8	−47.5	3.6	35 59.6	−47.4	3.6	36 59.5	−47.3	3.7	37 59.4	−47.3	3.7	38 59.3	−47.3	3.8	39 59.1	−47.2	3.8	40 59.0	−47.2	3.9	85
86	33 12.4	47.8	2.8	34 12.3	47.7	2.8	35 12.2	47.6	2.9	36 12.2	47.7	2.9	37 12.1	47.6	3.0	38 12.0	47.6	3.0	39 11.9	47.5	3.0	40 11.8	47.5	3.1	86
87	32 24.6	47.9	2.1	33 24.6	48.0	2.1	34 24.6	48.0	2.1	35 24.5	47.9	2.2	36 24.5	47.9	2.2	37 24.4	47.8	2.2	38 24.4	47.9	2.2	39 24.3	47.8	2.3	87
88	31 36.7	48.3	1.4	32 36.6	48.2	1.4	33 36.6	48.2	1.4	34 36.6	48.2	1.4	35 36.6	48.2	1.4	36 36.6	48.2	1.5	37 36.5	48.1	1.5	38 36.5	48.1	1.5	88
89	30 48.4	48.4	0.7	31 48.4	48.4	0.7	32 48.4	48.4	0.7	33 48.4	48.4	0.7	34 48.4	48.4	0.7	35 48.4	48.4	0.7	36 48.4	48.4	0.7	37 48.4	48.4	0.7	89
90	30 00.0	−48.6	0.0	31 00.0	−48.6	0.0	32 00.0	−48.7	0.0	33 00.0	−48.7	0.0	34 00.0	−48.7	0.0	35 00.0	−48.7	0.0	36 00.0	−48.7	0.0	37 00.0	−48.7	0.0	90
	30°			31°			32°			33°			34°			35°			36°			37°			

36°, 324° L.H.A. LATITUDE SAME NAME AS DECLINATION

LATITUDE CONTRARY NAME TO DECLINATION L.H.A. 36°, 324°

Dec.	30° Hc	30° d	30° Z	31° Hc	31° d	31° Z	32° Hc	32° d	32° Z	33° Hc	33° d	33° Z	34° Hc	34° d	34° Z	35° Hc	35° d	35° Z	36° Hc	36° d	36° Z	37° Hc	37° d	37° Z	Dec.
°	° ′	′	°	° ′	′	°	° ′	′	°	° ′	′	°	° ′	′	°	° ′	′	°	° ′	′	°	° ′	′	°	°
0	44 28.7	-42.4	124.5	43 54.3	-43.1	125.3	43 19.3	-44.0	126.1	42 43.6	-44.7	126.9	42 07.3	-45.4	127.6	41 30.4	-46.1	128.3	40 52.9	-46.8	129.0	40 14.9	-47.4	129.6	0
1	43 46.3	42.8	125.5	43 11.2	43.6	126.3	42 35.3	44.3	127.0	41 58.9	45.1	127.8	41 21.9	45.9	128.5	40 44.3	46.5	129.1	40 06.1	47.1	129.8	39 27.5	47.8	130.4	1
2	43 03.5	43.2	126.5	42 27.6	44.1	127.2	41 51.0	44.8	127.9	41 13.8	45.5	128.6	40 36.0	46.2	129.3	39 57.8	46.9	130.0	39 19.0	47.5	130.6	38 39.7	48.1	131.2	2
3	42 20.3	43.8	127.4	41 43.5	44.5	128.1	41 06.2	45.2	128.8	40 28.3	45.9	129.5	39 49.8	46.5	130.2	39 10.9	47.2	130.8	38 31.5	47.8	131.4	37 51.6	48.4	132.0	3
4	41 36.5	44.1	128.4	40 59.0	44.8	129.0	40 21.0	45.6	129.7	39 42.4	46.3	130.3	39 03.3	46.9	131.0	38 23.7	47.5	131.6	37 43.7	48.1	132.2	37 03.2	48.7	132.7	4
5	40 52.4	-44.6	129.3	40 14.2	-45.3	129.9	39 35.4	-45.9	130.6	38 56.1	-46.5	131.2	38 16.4	-47.2	131.8	37 36.2	-47.8	132.3	36 55.6	-48.4	132.9	36 14.5	-48.9	133.4	5
6	40 07.8	44.9	130.1	39 28.9	45.6	130.8	38 49.5	46.3	131.4	38 09.6	46.9	132.0	37 29.2	47.5	132.5	36 48.4	48.1	133.1	36 07.2	48.6	133.6	35 25.6	49.2	134.2	6
7	39 22.9	45.4	131.0	38 43.3	46.0	131.6	38 03.2	46.6	132.2	37 22.7	47.2	132.8	36 41.7	47.8	133.3	36 00.3	48.3	133.8	35 18.6	48.9	134.4	34 36.4	49.4	134.9	7
8	38 37.5	45.7	131.8	37 57.3	46.4	132.4	37 16.6	47.0	133.0	36 35.5	47.6	133.5	35 53.9	48.0	134.1	35 12.0	48.6	134.6	34 29.7	49.1	135.1	33 47.0	49.6	135.5	8
9	37 51.8	46.0	132.7	37 10.9	46.6	133.2	36 29.6	47.2	133.8	35 47.9	47.7	134.3	35 05.9	48.4	134.8	34 23.4	48.9	135.3	33 40.6	49.4	135.8	32 57.4	49.8	136.2	9
10	37 05.8	-46.4	133.5	36 24.3	-46.9	134.0	35 42.4	-47.5	134.5	35 00.2	-48.1	135.0	34 17.5	-48.5	135.5	33 34.5	-49.0	136.0	32 51.2	-49.5	136.4	32 07.6	-50.1	136.9	10
11	36 19.4	46.6	134.3	35 37.4	47.3	134.8	34 54.9	47.7	135.3	34 12.1	48.3	135.8	33 29.0	48.9	136.2	32 45.5	49.3	136.7	32 01.7	49.8	137.1	31 17.5	50.2	137.5	11
12	35 32.8	47.0	135.0	34 50.1	47.5	135.5	34 07.2	48.1	136.0	33 23.8	48.5	136.5	32 40.1	49.0	136.9	31 56.2	49.5	137.4	31 11.9	50.0	137.8	30 27.3	50.4	138.2	12
13	34 45.8	47.2	135.8	34 02.6	47.7	136.3	33 19.1	48.3	136.7	32 35.3	48.8	137.2	31 51.1	49.2	137.6	31 06.7	49.8	138.0	30 21.9	50.1	138.4	29 36.9	50.6	138.8	13
14	33 58.6	47.5	136.5	33 14.9	48.0	137.0	32 30.8	48.5	137.4	31 46.5	49.0	137.9	31 01.9	49.5	138.3	30 16.9	49.9	138.7	29 31.8	50.4	139.0	28 46.3	50.7	139.4	14
15	33 11.1	-47.7	137.3	32 26.9	-48.3	137.7	31 42.3	-48.7	138.1	30 57.5	-49.2	138.5	30 12.4	-49.6	138.9	29 27.0	-50.0	139.3	28 41.4	-50.5	139.7	27 55.6	-50.9	140.0	15
16	32 23.4	48.0	138.0	31 38.6	48.5	138.4	30 53.6	48.9	138.8	30 08.3	49.4	139.2	29 22.8	49.9	139.6	28 37.0	50.3	139.9	27 50.9	50.6	140.3	27 04.7	51.1	140.6	16
17	31 35.4	48.3	138.7	30 50.1	48.6	139.1	30 04.7	49.2	139.5	29 18.9	49.6	139.9	28 32.9	50.0	140.2	27 46.7	50.4	140.6	27 00.3	50.9	140.9	26 13.6	51.2	141.2	17
18	30 47.1	48.4	139.4	30 01.5	48.9	139.8	29 15.5	49.3	140.2	28 29.3	49.7	140.5	27 42.9	50.2	140.8	26 56.3	50.6	141.1	26 09.4	50.9	141.5	25 22.4	51.3	141.8	18
19	29 58.7	48.6	140.1	29 12.6	49.1	140.5	28 26.2	49.5	140.8	27 39.6	50.0	141.1	26 52.7	50.3	141.5	26 05.7	50.7	141.8	25 18.5	51.1	142.1	24 31.1	51.5	142.3	19
20	29 10.1	-48.9	140.8	28 23.5	-49.3	141.1	27 36.7	-49.7	141.4	26 49.6	-50.1	141.8	26 02.4	-50.5	142.1	25 15.0	-50.9	142.4	24 27.4	-51.2	142.6	23 39.6	-51.6	142.9	20
21	28 21.2	49.0	141.4	27 34.2	49.5	141.8	26 47.0	49.9	142.1	25 59.5	50.2	142.4	25 11.9	50.6	142.7	24 24.1	51.0	142.9	23 36.2	51.4	143.2	22 48.0	51.7	143.5	21
22	27 32.2	49.2	142.1	26 44.7	49.6	142.4	25 57.1	50.0	142.7	25 09.3	50.4	143.0	24 21.3	50.8	143.3	23 33.1	51.1	143.5	22 44.8	51.5	143.8	21 56.3	51.8	144.0	22
23	26 43.0	49.4	142.7	25 55.1	49.8	143.0	25 07.1	50.2	143.3	24 18.9	50.5	143.6	23 30.5	50.8	143.8	22 42.0	51.2	144.1	21 53.3	51.5	144.3	21 04.5	51.9	144.6	23
24	25 53.6	49.6	143.4	25 05.3	49.9	143.6	24 16.9	50.3	143.9	23 28.4	50.7	144.2	22 39.7	51.1	144.4	21 50.8	51.4	144.7	21 01.8	51.7	144.9	20 12.6	52.0	145.1	24
25	25 04.0	-49.7	144.0	24 15.4	-50.1	144.2	23 26.6	-50.4	144.5	22 37.7	-50.8	144.8	21 48.6	-51.1	145.0	20 59.4	-51.4	145.2	20 10.1	-51.8	145.4	19 20.6	-52.1	145.6	25
26	24 14.3	49.8	144.6	23 25.3	50.2	144.8	22 36.2	50.6	145.1	21 46.9	50.9	145.3	20 57.5	51.2	145.5	20 08.0	51.6	145.8	19 18.3	51.9	146.0	18 28.5	52.1	146.2	26
27	23 24.5	50.0	145.2	22 35.1	50.3	145.4	21 45.6	50.7	145.7	20 56.0	51.0	145.9	20 06.3	51.4	146.1	19 16.4	51.6	146.3	18 26.4	51.8	146.5	17 36.4	52.3	146.7	27
28	22 34.5	50.2	145.8	21 44.8	50.5	146.0	20 54.9	50.8	146.2	20 05.0	51.1	146.5	19 14.9	51.4	146.7	18 24.8	51.8	146.8	17 34.5	52.1	147.0	16 44.1	52.3	147.2	28
29	21 44.3	50.2	146.4	20 54.3	50.6	146.6	20 04.1	50.9	146.8	19 13.9	51.2	147.0	18 23.5	51.5	147.2	17 33.0	51.8	147.4	16 42.4	52.1	147.5	15 51.8	52.4	147.7	29
30	20 54.1	-50.4	147.0	20 03.7	-50.7	147.2	19 13.2	-51.0	147.4	18 22.7	-51.4	147.6	17 32.0	-51.6	147.7	16 41.2	-51.9	147.9	15 50.3	-52.2	148.1	14 59.4	-52.5	148.2	30
31	20 03.7	50.5	147.6	19 13.0	50.8	147.8	18 22.2	51.1	147.9	17 31.3	51.4	148.1	16 40.4	51.7	148.3	15 49.3	52.0	148.4	14 58.1	52.2	148.6	14 06.9	52.5	148.7	31
32	19 13.2	50.5	148.1	18 22.2	50.9	148.3	17 31.1	51.2	148.5	16 39.9	51.5	148.6	15 48.7	51.8	148.8	14 57.3	52.1	148.9	14 05.9	52.4	149.1	13 14.4	52.6	149.2	32
33	18 22.7	50.7	148.7	17 31.3	50.9	148.9	16 39.9	51.2	149.0	15 48.4	51.5	149.2	14 56.9	51.9	149.3	14 05.2	52.1	149.5	13 13.5	52.3	149.6	12 21.8	52.7	149.7	33
34	17 32.0	50.8	149.3	16 40.4	51.1	149.4	15 48.7	51.4	149.6	14 56.9	51.7	149.7	14 05.0	51.9	149.8	13 13.1	52.2	150.0	12 21.2	52.5	150.1	11 29.1	52.7	150.2	34
35	16 41.2	-50.9	149.8	15 49.3	-51.2	150.0	14 57.3	-51.4	150.1	14 05.2	-51.7	150.2	13 13.1	-51.9	150.4	12 20.9	-52.2	150.5	11 28.7	-52.5	150.6	10 36.4	-52.7	150.7	35
36	15 50.3	50.9	150.4	14 58.1	51.2	150.5	14 05.9	51.5	150.6	13 13.5	51.7	150.8	12 21.2	52.1	150.9	11 28.7	52.3	151.0	10 36.2	52.5	151.1	9 43.7	52.8	151.2	36
37	14 59.4	51.1	150.9	14 06.9	51.3	151.1	13 14.4	51.6	151.2	12 21.8	51.9	151.3	11 29.1	52.1	151.4	10 36.4	52.3	151.5	9 43.7	52.6	151.6	8 50.9	52.8	151.6	37
38	14 08.3	51.1	151.5	13 15.6	51.4	151.6	12 22.8	51.6	151.7	11 29.9	51.8	151.8	10 37.0	52.1	151.9	9 44.1	52.4	152.0	8 51.1	52.6	152.0	7 58.1	52.8	152.1	38
39	13 17.2	51.1	152.0	12 24.2	51.4	152.1	11 31.2	51.7	152.2	10 38.1	52.0	152.3	9 44.9	52.2	152.4	8 51.7	52.4	152.5	7 58.5	52.6	152.5	7 05.3	52.9	152.6	39
40	12 26.1	-51.3	152.5	11 32.8	-51.5	152.6	10 39.5	-51.8	152.7	9 46.1	-51.9	152.8	8 52.7	-52.2	152.9	7 59.3	-52.4	153.0	7 05.9	-52.7	153.0	6 12.4	-52.9	153.1	40
41	11 34.8	51.3	153.1	10 41.3	51.5	153.2	9 47.7	51.7	153.2	8 54.2	52.1	153.3	8 00.5	52.2	153.4	7 06.9	52.5	153.4	6 13.2	52.7	153.5	5 19.5	52.9	153.5	41
42	10 43.5	51.3	153.6	9 49.8	51.6	153.7	8 56.0	51.9	153.8	8 02.1	52.0	153.8	7 08.3	52.3	153.9	6 14.4	52.5	153.9	5 20.5	52.7	154.0	4 26.6	53.0	154.0	42
43	9 52.2	51.4	154.1	8 58.2	51.6	154.2	8 04.1	51.8	154.3	7 10.1	52.1	154.3	6 16.0	52.3	154.4	5 21.9	52.5	154.4	4 27.8	52.8	154.5	3 33.6	52.9	154.5	43
44	9 00.8	51.4	154.7	8 06.6	51.7	154.7	7 12.3	51.8	154.8	6 18.0	52.1	154.8	5 23.7	52.3	154.9	4 29.4	52.6	154.9	3 35.0	52.7	154.9	2 40.7	53.0	155.0	44
45	8 09.4	-51.5	155.2	7 14.9	-51.7	155.2	6 20.4	-51.9	155.3	5 25.9	-52.2	155.3	4 31.4	-52.4	155.4	3 36.8	-52.6	155.4	2 42.3	-52.8	155.4	1 47.7	-53.0	155.4	45
46	7 17.9	51.5	155.7	6 23.2	51.8	155.7	5 28.5	52.0	155.8	4 33.7	52.1	155.8	3 39.0	52.4	155.8	2 44.2	52.5	155.9	1 49.5	52.8	155.9	0 54.7	53.0	155.9	46
47	6 26.4	51.6	156.2	5 31.4	51.7	156.3	4 36.5	51.9	156.3	3 41.6	52.2	156.3	2 46.6	52.3	156.3	1 51.7	52.6	156.4	0 56.7	52.8	156.4	0 01.7	-52.9	156.4	47
48	5 34.8	51.6	156.7	4 39.7	51.8	156.8	3 44.6	52.0	156.8	2 49.4	52.2	156.8	1 54.3	52.4	156.8	0 59.1	52.6	156.8	0 03.9	-52.8	156.8	0 51.2	+53.0	23.2	48
49	4 43.2	51.5	157.2	3 47.9	51.8	157.3	2 52.6	52.0	157.3	1 57.2	52.2	157.3	1 01.9	52.4	157.3	0 06.5	-52.6	157.3	0 48.9	+52.7	22.7	1 44.2	53.0	22.7	49
50	3 51.7	-51.7	157.7	2 56.1	-51.8	157.8	2 00.6	-52.0	157.8	1 05.0	-52.2	157.8	0 09.5	-52.4	157.8	0 46.1	+52.6	22.2	1 41.6	+52.8	22.2	2 37.2	+52.9	22.2	50
51	3 00.0	51.6	158.3	2 04.3	51.8	158.3	1 08.6	52.0	158.3	0 12.8	-52.2	158.3	0 42.9	+52.4	21.7	1 38.7	52.5	21.7	2 34.4	52.8	21.7	3 30.1	53.0	21.8	51
52	2 08.4	51.6	158.8	1 12.5	51.8	158.8	0 16.6	-52.1	158.8	0 39.4	+52.2	21.2	1 35.3	52.4	21.2	2 31.2	52.6	21.2	3 27.2	52.7	21.3	4 23.1	52.9	21.3	52
53	1 16.8	51.7	159.3	0 20.7	-51.9	159.3	0 35.5	+52.0	20.7	1 31.6	52.2	20.7	2 27.7	52.4	20.7	3 23.8	52.6	20.8	4 19.9	52.7	20.8	5 16.0	52.9	20.8	53
54	0 25.1	-51.6	159.8	0 31.2	+51.8	20.2	1 27.5	52.0	20.2	2 23.8	52.2	20.2	3 20.1	52.3	20.2	4 16.4	52.5	20.3	5 12.6	52.7	20.3	6 08.9	52.9	20.3	54
55	0 26.5	+51.7	19.7	1 23.0	+51.8	19.7	2 19.5	+52.0	19.7	3 16.0	+52.1	19.7	4 12.4	+52.4	19.8	5 08.9	+52.5	19.8	6 05.3	+52.7	19.8	7 01.8	+52.8	19.9	55
56	1 18.2	51.6	19.2	2 14.8	51.8	19.2	3 11.5	52.0	19.2	4 08.1	52.2	19.2	5 04.8	52.3	19.3	6 01.4	52.5	19.3	6 58.0	52.7	19.3	7 54.6	52.9	19.4	56
57	2 09.8	51.6	18.7	3 06.6	51.8	18.7	4 03.5	51.9	18.7	5 00.3	52.1	18.7	5 57.1	52.3	18.8	6 53.9	52.4	18.8	7 50.7	52.6	18.9	8 47.5	52.7	18.9	57
58	3 01.4	51.6	18.2	3 58.4	51.8	18.2	4 55.4	52.0	18.2	5 52.4	52.1	18.2	6 49.4	52.2	18.3	7 46.3	52.5	18.3	8 43.3	52.6	18.4	9 40.2	52.8	18.4	58
59	3 53.0	51.6	17.7	4 50.2	51.7	17.7	5 47.4	51.9	17.7	6 44.5	52.1	17.7	7 41.6	52.3	17.8	8 38.8	52.4	17.8	9 35.9	52.5	17.9	10 33.0	52.7	17.9	59
60	4 44.6	+51.6	17.2	5 41.9	+51.8	17.2	6 39.3	+51.8	17.2	7 36.6	+52.0	17.2	8 33.9	+52.2	17.3	9 31.2	+52.3	17.3	10 28.4	+52.5	17.4	11 25.7	+52.6	17.4	60
61	5 36.2	51.5	16.6	6 33.7	51.7	16.7	7 31.1	51.9	16.7	8 28.6	52.0	16.7	9 26.1	52.1	16.8	10 23.5	52.3	16.8	11 20.9	52.5	16.9	12 18.3	52.6	17.0	61
62	6 27.7	51.5	16.1	7 25.4	51.6	16.2	8 23.0	51.8	16.2	9 20.6	52.0	16.2	10 18.2	52.1	16.3	11 15.8	52.2	16.3	12 13.4	52.3	16.4	13 10.9	52.5	16.5	62
63	7 19.2	51.5	15.6	8 17.0	51.6	15.6	9 14.8	51.8	15.7	10 12.6	51.9	15.7	11 10.3	52.1	15.8	12 08.0	52.2	15.8	13 05.7	52.4	15.9	14 03.4	52.5	16.0	63
64	8 10.7	51.5	15.1	9 08.6	51.6	15.1	10 06.6	51.7	15.2	11 04.5	51.8	15.2	12 02.4	51.9	15.3	13 00.2	52.2	15.3	13 58.1	52.3	15.4	14 55.9	52.4	15.5	64
65	9 02.2	+51.4	14.6	10 00.2	+51.6	14.6	10 58.3	+51.6	14.7	11 56.3	+51.8	14.7	12 54.3	+52.0	14.8	13 52.4	+52.0	14.8	14 50.4	+52.2	14.9	15 48.3	+52.4	15.0	65
66	9 53.6	51.3	14.0	10 51.8	51.4	14.1	11 49.9	51.6	14.1	12 48.1	51.8	14.2	13 46.3	51.8	14.2	14 44.4	52.0	14.3	15 42.6	52.1	14.4	16 40.7	52.2	14.5	66
67	10 44.9	51.3	13.5	11 43.2	51.4	13.6	12 41.5	51.6	13.6	13 39.9	51.6	13.7	14 38.1	51.8	13.7	15 36.4	52.0	13.8	16 34.7	52.0	13.9	17 32.9	52.2	13.9	67
68	11 36.2	51.2	13.0	12 34.6	51.4	13.0	13 33.1	51.5	13.1	14 31.5	51.6	13.1	15 29.9	51.8	13.2	16 28.4	51.8	13.3	17 26.7	52.0	13.3	18 25.1	52.1	13.4	68
69	12 27.4	51.2	12.5	13 26.0	51.3	12.5	14 24.6	51.4	12.6	15 23.1	51.6	12.6	16 21.7	51.6	12.7	17 20.2	51.8	12.7	18 18.7	51.9	12.8	19 17.2	52.0	12.9	69
70	13 18.6	+51.1	11.9	14 17.3	+51.2	12.0	15 16.0	+51.3	12.0	16 14.7	+51.4	12.1	17 13.3	+51.6	12.1	18 12.0	+51.6	12.2	19 10.6	+51.8	12.3	20 09.2	+51.9	12.4	70
71	14 09.7	51.0	11.4	15 08.5	51.1	11.4	16 07.3	51.3	11.5	17 06.1	51.4	11.5	18 04.9	51.5	11.6	19 03.6	51.6	11.7	20 02.4	51.7	11.8	21 01.1	51.8	11.8	71
72	15 00.7	51.0	10.8	15 59.6	51.1	10.9	16 58.6	51.1	10.9	17 57.5	51.2	11.0	18 56.4	51.3	11.1	19 55.2	51.5	11.1	20 54.1	51.6	11.2	21 52.9	51.7	11.3	72
73	15 51.7	50.8	10.3	16 50.7	51.0	10.3	17 49.7	51.1	10.4	18 48.7	51.2	10.5	19 47.7	51.3	10.5	20 46.7	51.4	10.6	21 45.7	51.5	10.7	22 44.6	51.6	10.7	73
74	16 42.5	50.8	9.7	17 41.7	50.8	9.8	18 40.8	51.0	9.8	19 39.9	51.1	9.9	20 39.0	51.2	10.0	21 38.1	51.3	10.0	22 37.2	51.3	10.1	23 36.2	51.5	10.2	74
75	17 33.3	+50.7	9.2	18 32.5	+50.8	9.2	19 31.8	+50.8	9.3	20 31.0	+50.9	9.3	21 30.2	+51.0	9.4	22 29.4	+51.1	9.5	23 28.5	+51.3	9.5	24 27.7	+51.3	9.6	75
76	18 24.0	50.6	8.6	19 23.3	50.7	8.7	20 22.6	50.8	8.7	21 21.9	50.9	8.8	22 21.2	51.0	8.8	23 20.5	51.0	8.9	24 19.8	51.1	9.0	25 19.0	51.2	9.1	76
77	19 14.6	50.5	8.1	20 14.0	50.6	8.1	21 13.4	50.6	8.2	22 12.8	50.7	8.2	23 12.2	50.8	8.3	24 11.5	50.9	8.3	25 10.9	51.0	8.4	26 10.2	51.1	8.5	77
78	20 05.1	50.3	7.5	21 04.6	50.4	7.5	22 04.0	50.6	7.6	23 03.5	50.6	7.6	24 03.0	50.6	7.7	25 02.4	50.8	7.8	26 01.9	50.8	7.8	27 01.3	50.9	7.9	78
79	20 55.4	50.3	6.9	21 55.0	50.3	6.9	22 54.6	50.3	7.0	23 54.1	50.5	7.0	24 53.6	50.6	7.1	25 53.2	50.6	7.2	26 52.7	50.7	7.2	27 52.2	50.8	7.3	79
80	21 45.7	+50.1	6.3	22 45.3	+50.2	6.4	23 44.9	+50.3	6.4	24 44.6	+50.3	6.5	25 44.2	+50.4	6.5	26 43.8	+50.4	6.6	27 43.4	+50.5	6.6	28 43.0	+50.6	6.7	80
81	22 35.8	50.0	5.7	23 35.5	50.0	5.8	24 35.2	50.1	5.8	25 34.9	50.2	5.9	26 34.6	50.2	5.9	27 34.2	50.3	6.0	28 33.9	50.4	6.0	29 33.6	50.4	6.1	81
82	23 25.8	49.8	5.1	24 25.5	50.0	5.2	25 25.3	50.0	5.2	26 25.1	50.0	5.2	27 24.8	50.1	5.3	28 24.5	50.2	5.3	29 24.3	50.2	5.4	30 24.0	50.3	5.4	82
83	24 15.6	49.7	4.5	25 15.5	49.7	4.5	26 15.3	49.8	4.6	27 15.1	49.8	4.6	28 14.9	49.9	4.7	29 14.7	49.9	4.7	30 14.5	50.0	4.8	31 14.3	50.0	4.8	83
84	25 05.3	49.6	3.9	26 05.2	49.6	3.9	27 05.1	49.6	4.0	28 04.9	49.7	4.0	29 04.8	49.7	4.0	30 04.6	49.8	4.1	31 04.5	49.8	4.1	32 04.3	49.9	4.2	84
85	25 54.9	+49.4	3.3	26 54.8	+49.4	3.3	27 54.7	+49.4	3.3	28 54.6	+49.5	3.4	29 54.5	+49.5	3.4	30 54.4	+49.5	3.4	31 54.3	+49.6	3.5	32 54.2	+49.6	3.5	85
86	26 44.3	49.2	2.6	27 44.2	49.2	2.7	28 44.1	49.3	2.7	29 44.1	49.3	2.7	30 44.0	49.3	2.7	31 43.9	49.4	2.8	32 43.9	49.4	2.8	33 43.8	49.4	2.8	86
87	27 33.5	49.0	2.0	28 33.4	49.1	2.0	29 33.4	49.1	2.0	30 33.4	49.1	2.0	31 33.3	49.1	2.1	32 33.3	49.1	2.1	33 33.3	49.1	2.1	34 33.2	49.2	2.1	87
88	28 22.5	48.9	1.3	29 22.5	48.9	1.3	30 22.5	48.8	1.4	31 22.5	48.8	1.4	32 22.4	48.9	1.4	33 22.4	48.9	1.4	34 22.4	48.9	1.4	35 22.4	48.9	1.4	88
89	29 11.4	48.6	0.7	30 11.4	48.6	0.7	31 11.3	48.7	0.7	32 11.3	48.7	0.7	33 11.3	48.7	0.7	34 11.3	48.7	0.7	35 11.3	48.7	0.7	36 11.3	48.7	0.7	89
90	30 00.0	+48.4	0.0	31 00.0	+48.4	0.0	32 00.0	+48.4	0.0	33 00.0	+48.4	0.0	34 00.0	+48.4	0.0	35 00.0	+48.4	0.0	36 00.0	+48.4	0.0	37 00.0	+48.4	0.0	90
	30°			31°			32°			33°			34°			35°			36°			37°			

S. Lat. { L.H.A. greater than 180°......Zn=180°−Z
L.H.A. less than 180°............Zn=180°+Z

LATITUDE SAME NAME AS DECLINATION L.H.A. 144°, 216°

36°, 324° L.H.A. LATITUDE SAME NAME AS DECLINATION

N. Lat. { L.H.A. greater than 180°......Zn=Z ; L.H.A. less than 180°............Zn=360°−Z }

Dec.	38° Hc	d	Z	39° Hc	d	Z	40° Hc	d	Z	41° Hc	d	Z
°	° ′	′	°	° ′	′	°	° ′	′	°	° ′	′	°
0	39 36.4	+47.8	130.3	38 57.4	+48.4	130.9	38 17.8	+49.0	131.5	37 37.9	+49.5	132.1
1	40 24.2	47.4	129.5	39 45.8	48.1	130.1	39 06.8	48.8	130.8	38 27.4	49.3	131.4
2	41 11.6	47.2	128.7	40 33.9	47.7	129.4	39 55.6	48.4	130.0	39 16.7	49.1	130.6
3	41 58.8	46.7	127.9	41 21.6	47.5	128.6	40 44.0	48.1	129.2	40 05.8	48.7	129.9
4	42 45.5	46.4	127.0	42 09.1	47.1	127.7	41 32.1	47.7	128.4	40 54.5	48.4	129.1
5	43 31.9	+45.9	126.1	42 56.2	+46.7	126.9	42 19.8	+47.4	127.6	41 42.9	+48.1	128.3
6	44 17.8	45.5	125.2	43 42.9	46.2	126.0	43 07.2	47.1	126.8	42 31.0	47.7	127.5
7	45 03.3	45.1	124.3	44 29.1	45.9	125.1	43 54.3	46.6	125.9	43 18.7	47.4	126.7
8	45 48.4	44.6	123.4	45 15.0	45.5	124.2	44 40.9	46.2	125.1	44 06.1	47.0	125.8
9	46 33.0	44.1	122.4	46 00.5	44.9	123.3	45 27.1	45.8	124.1	44 53.1	46.6	125.0
10	47 17.1	+43.6	121.4	46 45.4	+44.5	122.3	46 12.9	+45.3	123.2	45 39.7	+46.1	124.1
11	48 00.7	43.0	120.4	47 29.9	43.9	121.3	46 58.2	44.9	122.3	46 25.8	45.7	123.2
12	48 43.7	42.4	119.4	48 13.8	43.4	120.3	47 43.1	44.3	121.3	47 11.5	45.2	122.2
13	49 26.1	41.8	118.3	48 57.2	42.8	119.3	48 27.4	43.8	120.3	47 56.7	44.7	121.2
14	50 07.9	41.1	117.2	49 40.0	42.2	118.2	49 11.2	43.2	119.2	48 41.4	44.2	120.2
15	50 49.0	+40.5	116.0	50 22.2	+41.6	117.1	49 54.4	+42.6	118.2	49 25.6	+43.6	119.2
16	51 29.5	39.7	114.8	51 03.8	40.8	116.0	50 37.0	41.9	117.1	50 09.2	42.9	118.1
17	52 09.2	39.0	113.6	51 44.6	40.2	114.8	51 18.9	41.3	115.9	50 52.1	42.4	117.0
18	52 48.2	38.1	112.4	52 24.8	39.3	113.6	52 00.2	40.5	114.8	51 34.5	41.7	115.9
19	53 26.3	37.3	111.1	53 04.1	38.6	112.3	52 40.7	39.8	113.6	52 16.2	40.9	114.7
20	54 03.6	+36.4	109.8	53 42.7	+37.7	111.1	53 20.5	+39.0	112.3	52 57.1	+40.3	113.5
21	54 40.0	35.5	108.4	54 20.4	36.8	109.7	53 59.5	38.2	111.0	53 37.4	39.4	112.3
22	55 15.5	34.4	107.0	54 57.2	35.9	108.4	54 37.7	37.2	109.7	54 16.8	38.6	111.0
23	55 49.9	33.4	105.6	55 33.1	34.9	107.0	55 14.9	36.3	108.3	54 55.4	37.7	109.7
24	56 23.3	32.3	104.1	56 08.0	33.8	105.5	55 51.2	35.4	106.9	55 33.1	36.7	108.3
25	56 55.6	+31.1	102.5	56 41.8	+32.8	104.0	56 26.6	+34.2	105.5	56 09.8	+35.8	106.9
26	57 26.7	30.0	101.0	57 14.6	31.5	102.5	57 00.8	33.2	104.0	56 45.6	34.7	105.5
27	57 56.7	28.6	99.3	57 46.1	30.4	100.9	57 34.0	32.0	102.4	57 20.3	33.6	104.0
28	58 25.3	27.3	97.7	58 16.5	29.1	99.3	58 06.0	30.8	100.9	57 53.9	32.4	102.4
29	58 52.6	26.0	96.0	58 45.6	27.7	97.6	58 36.8	29.5	99.2	58 26.3	31.3	100.8
30	59 18.6	+24.4	94.2	59 13.3	+26.3	95.9	59 06.3	+28.1	97.5	58 57.6	+29.9	99.2
31	59 43.0	23.0	92.4	59 39.6	24.9	94.1	59 34.4	26.8	95.8	59 27.5	28.6	97.5
32	60 06.0	21.4	90.6	60 04.5	23.3	92.3	60 01.2	25.3	94.0	59 56.1	27.1	95.7
33	60 27.4	19.7	88.7	60 27.8	21.8	90.4	60 26.5	23.7	92.2	60 23.2	25.7	94.0
34	60 47.1	18.1	86.7	60 49.6	20.1	88.5	60 50.2	22.1	90.3	60 48.9	24.1	92.1
35	61 05.2	+16.3	84.8	61 09.7	+18.4	86.6	61 12.3	+20.5	88.4	61 13.0	+22.5	90.2
36	61 21.5	14.6	82.8	61 28.1	16.6	84.6	61 32.8	18.7	86.4	61 35.5	20.9	88.3
37	61 36.1	12.7	80.7	61 44.7	14.9	82.6	61 51.5	17.0	84.4	61 56.4	19.0	86.3
38	61 48.8	10.8	78.7	61 59.6	12.9	80.5	62 08.5	15.1	82.4	62 15.4	17.3	84.3
39	61 59.6	8.9	76.6	62 12.5	11.1	78.4	62 23.6	13.2	80.3	62 32.7	15.4	82.2
40	62 08.5	+6.9	74.5	62 23.6	+9.1	76.3	62 36.8	+11.3	78.2	62 48.1	+13.5	80.1
41	62 15.4	5.0	72.4	62 32.7	7.2•	74.2	62 48.1	9.3•	76.1	63 01.6	11.5•	78.0
42	62 20.4	3.0•	70.2	62 39.9	5.1•	72.0	62 57.4	7.3•	73.9	63 13.1	9.5•	75.8
43	62 23.4	+1.0•	68.1	62 45.0	3.1•	69.9	63 04.7	5.3•	71.7	63 22.6	7.5•	73.6
44	62 24.4	−1.0•	65.9	62 48.1	+1.1•	67.7	63 10.0	3.2•	69.5	63 30.1	5.4•	71.4
45	62 23.4	−3.0	63.7	62 49.2	−1.0•	65.5	63 13.2	+1.1•	67.3	63 35.5	+3.3•	69.1
46	62 20.4	4.9•	61.6	62 48.2	3.0•	63.3	63 14.3	−0.9•	65.1	63 38.8	+1.1•	66.9
47	62 15.5	7.0•	59.4	62 45.2	5.0•	61.1	63 13.4	3.0•	62.8	63 39.9	−0.9•	64.6
48	62 08.5	8.9	57.3	62 40.2	7.0•	58.9	63 10.4	5.1•	60.6	63 39.0	3.0•	62.4
49	61 59.6	10.8	55.2	62 33.2	9.1	56.8	63 05.3	7.1•	58.4	63 36.0	5.2•	60.1
50	61 48.8	−12.7	53.1	62 24.1	−10.9	54.6	62 58.2	−9.1•	56.2	63 30.8	−7.2•	57.9
51	61 36.1	14.6	51.1	62 13.2	12.9	52.5	62 49.1	11.2	54.1	63 23.6	9.3•	55.7
52	61 21.5	16.3	49.0	62 00.3	14.7	50.4	62 37.9	13.0	51.9	63 14.3	11.3•	53.5
53	61 05.2	18.0	47.0	61 45.6	16.5	48.4	62 24.9	15.0	49.8	63 03.0	13.3	51.3
54	60 47.2	19.8	45.1	61 29.1	18.4	46.4	62 09.9	16.7	47.7	62 49.7	15.1	49.2
55	60 27.4	−21.4	43.1	61 10.7	−20.0	44.4	61 53.2	−18.6	45.7	62 34.6	−17.1	47.1
56	60 06.0	22.9	41.3	60 50.7	21.6	42.4	61 34.6	20.3	43.7	62 17.5	18.9	45.0
57	59 43.1	24.5	39.4	60 29.1	23.3	40.5	61 14.3	22.0	41.7	61 58.6	20.6	43.0
58	59 18.6	25.9	37.6	60 05.8	24.8	38.7	60 52.3	23.6	39.8	61 38.0	22.3	41.0
59	58 52.7	27.3	35.9	59 41.0	26.2	36.9	60 28.7	25.1	37.9	61 15.7	24.0	39.0
60	58 25.4	−28.7	34.1	59 14.8	−27.7	35.1	60 03.6	−26.7	36.1	60 51.7	−25.5	37.1
61	57 56.7	29.9	32.5	58 47.1	29.0	33.4	59 36.9	28.0	34.3	60 26.2	27.0	35.3
62	57 26.8	31.1	30.9	58 18.1	30.3	31.7	59 08.9	29.4	32.6	59 59.2	28.4	33.5
63	56 55.7	32.3	29.3	57 47.8	31.5	30.0	58 39.5	30.6	30.9	59 30.8	29.8	31.7
64	56 23.4	33.4	27.7	57 16.3	32.7	28.5	58 08.9	31.9	29.2	59 01.0	31.1	30.0
65	55 50.0	−34.5	26.3	56 43.6	−33.7	26.9	57 37.0	−33.1	27.6	58 29.9	−32.3	28.4
66	55 15.5	35.4	24.8	56 09.9	34.9	25.4	57 03.9	34.2	26.1	57 57.6	33.5	26.8
67	54 40.1	36.4	23.4	55 35.0	35.8	24.0	56 29.7	35.2	24.6	57 24.1	34.5	25.2
68	54 03.7	37.3	22.0	54 59.2	36.8	22.6	55 54.5	36.2	23.1	56 49.6	35.7	23.7
69	53 26.4	38.1	20.7	54 22.4	37.6	21.2	55 18.3	37.2	21.7	56 13.9	36.6	22.3
70	52 48.3	−39.0	19.4	53 44.8	−38.6	19.9	54 41.1	−38.1	20.4	55 37.3	−37.6	20.9
71	52 09.3	39.7	18.2	53 06.2	39.3	18.6	54 03.0	38.9	19.0	54 59.7	38.5	19.5
72	51 29.6	40.5	17.0	52 26.9	40.1	17.3	53 24.1	39.7	17.7	54 21.2	39.3	18.2
73	50 49.1	41.1	15.8	51 46.8	40.8	16.1	52 44.4	40.5	16.5	53 41.9	40.2	16.9
74	50 08.0	41.8	14.6	51 06.0	41.5	15.0	52 03.9	41.2	15.3	53 01.7	40.8	15.6
75	49 26.2	−42.4	13.5	50 24.5	−42.2	13.8	51 22.7	−41.9	14.1	52 20.9	−41.6	14.4
76	48 43.8	43.0	12.4	49 42.3	42.8	12.7	50 40.8	42.5	13.0	51 39.3	42.3	13.3
77	48 00.8	43.6	11.4	48 59.5	43.3	11.6	49 58.3	43.2	11.9	50 57.0	42.9	12.1
78	47 17.2	44.1	10.4	48 16.2	43.9	10.6	49 15.1	43.7	10.8	50 14.1	43.6	11.0
79	46 33.1	44.6	9.4	47 32.3	44.5	9.6	48 31.4	44.2	9.7	49 30.5	44.1	9.9
80	45 48.5	−45.1	8.4	46 47.8	−44.9	8.6	47 47.2	−44.8	8.7	48 46.4	−44.6	8.9
81	45 03.4	45.5	7.5	46 02.9	45.4	7.6	47 02.4	45.3	7.8	48 01.8	45.1	7.9
82	44 17.9	46.0	6.6	45 17.5	45.8	6.7	46 17.1	45.8	6.8	47 16.7	45.7	6.9
83	43 31.9	46.3	5.7	44 31.7	46.3	5.8	45 31.3	46.1	5.9	46 31.0	46.1	6.0
84	42 45.6	46.8	4.8	43 45.4	46.7	4.9	44 45.2	46.6	5.0	45 44.9	46.5	5.1
85	41 58.8	−47.1	4.0	42 58.7	−47.1	4.0	43 58.6	−47.0	4.1	44 58.4	−46.9	4.2
86	41 11.7	47.4	3.1	42 11.6	47.4	3.2	43 11.6	47.4	3.2	44 11.5	47.4	3.3
87	40 24.3	47.8	2.3	41 24.2	47.7	2.4	42 24.2	47.7	2.4	43 24.1	47.7	2.4
88	39 36.5	48.1	1.5	40 36.5	48.1	1.5	41 36.5	48.1	1.6	42 36.4	48.0	1.6
89	38 48.4	48.4	0.8	39 48.4	48.4	0.8	40 48.4	48.4	0.8	41 48.4	48.4	0.8
90	38 00.0	−48.7	0.0	39 00.0	−48.7	0.0	40 00.0	−48.7	0.0	41 00.0	−48.7	0.0
	38°			39°			40°			41°		

Dec.	42° Hc	d	Z	43° Hc	d	Z	44° Hc	d	Z	45° Hc	d	Z
°	° ′	′	°	° ′	′	°	° ′	′	°	° ′	′	°
0	36 57.4	+50.1	132.6	36 16.6	+50.6	133.2	35 35.3	+51.2	133.7	34 53.6	+51.7	134.2
1	37 47.5	49.9	132.0	37 07.2	50.4	132.5	36 26.5	50.9	133.1	35 45.3	51.4	133.6
2	38 37.4	49.6	131.2	37 57.6	50.2	131.8	37 17.4	50.7	132.4	36 36.7	51.2	133.0
3	39 27.0	49.4	130.5	38 47.8	49.9	131.1	38 08.1	50.5	131.7	37 27.9	51.0	132.3
4	40 16.4	49.0	129.8	39 37.7	49.7	130.4	38 58.6	50.2	131.0	38 18.9	50.8	131.6
5	41 05.4	+48.8	129.0	40 27.4	+49.3	129.7	39 48.8	+50.0	130.3	39 09.7	+50.5	131.0
6	41 54.2	48.4	128.2	41 16.7	49.1	128.9	40 38.8	49.6	129.6	40 00.2	50.3	130.3
7	42 42.6	48.0	127.4	42 05.8	48.7	128.2	41 28.4	49.4	128.9	40 50.5	50.0	129.5
8	43 30.6	47.8	126.6	42 54.5	48.4	127.4	42 17.8	49.1	128.1	41 40.5	49.7	128.8
9	44 18.4	47.3	125.8	43 42.9	48.1	126.6	43 06.9	48.7	127.3	42 30.2	49.4	128.1
10	45 05.7	+46.9	124.9	44 31.0	+47.7	125.7	43 55.6	+48.4	126.5	43 19.6	+49.1	127.3
11	45 52.6	46.5	124.0	45 18.7	47.3	124.9	44 44.0	48.1	125.7	44 08.7	48.7	126.5
12	46 39.1	46.1	123.1	46 06.0	46.8	124.0	45 32.1	47.6	124.8	44 57.4	48.4	125.7
13	47 25.2	45.6	122.2	46 52.8	46.5	123.1	46 19.7	47.2	124.0	45 45.8	48.0	124.8
14	48 10.8	45.0	121.2	47 39.3	45.9	122.1	47 06.9	46.8	123.1	46 33.8	47.6	124.0
15	48 55.8	+44.6	120.2	48 25.2	+45.5	121.2	47 53.7	+46.3	122.1	47 21.4	+47.1	123.1
16	49 40.4	44.0	119.2	49 10.7	44.9	120.2	48 40.0	45.9	121.2	48 08.5	46.8	122.1
17	50 24.4	43.4	118.1	49 55.6	44.4	119.2	49 25.9	45.3	120.2	48 55.3	46.2	121.2
18	51 07.8	42.7	117.0	50 40.0	43.8	118.1	50 11.2	44.8	119.2	49 41.5	45.7	120.2
19	51 50.5	42.1	115.9	51 23.8	43.1	117.0	50 56.0	44.2	118.1	50 27.2	45.2	119.2
20	52 32.6	+41.4	114.7	52 06.9	+42.6	115.9	51 40.2	+43.6	117.1	51 12.4	+44.6	118.2
21	53 14.0	40.6	113.5	52 49.5	41.8	114.8	52 23.8	42.9	115.9	51 57.0	44.0	117.1
22	53 54.6	39.9	112.3	53 31.3	41.0	113.6	53 06.7	42.2	114.8	52 41.0	43.3	116.0
23	54 34.5	39.0	111.0	54 12.3	40.3	112.3	53 48.9	41.5	113.6	53 24.3	42.7	114.8
24	55 13.5	38.1	109.7	54 52.6	39.5	111.0	54 30.4	40.8	112.4	54 07.0	41.9	113.6
25	55 51.6	+37.2	108.3	55 32.1	+38.5	109.7	55 11.2	+39.8	111.1	54 48.9	+41.2	112.4
26	56 28.8	36.2	106.9	56 10.6	37.7	108.4	55 51.0	39.1	109.8	55 30.1	40.3	111.1
27	57 05.0	35.2	105.5	56 48.3	36.6	106.9	56 30.1	38.1	108.4	56 10.4	39.5	109.8
28	57 40.2	34.0	104.0	57 24.9	35.6	105.5	57 08.2	37.1	107.0	56 49.9	38.5	108.4
29	58 14.2	32.9	102.4	58 00.5	34.6	104.0	57 45.3	36.0	105.5	57 28.4	37.6	107.0
30	58 47.1	+31.7	100.8	58 35.1	+33.3	102.4	58 21.3	+35.0	104.0	58 06.0	+36.5	105.6
31	59 18.8	30.4	99.2	59 08.4	32.1	100.8	58 56.3	33.8	102.4	58 42.5	35.5	104.1
32	59 49.2	29.0	97.5	59 40.5	30.8	99.2	59 30.1	32.5	100.8	59 18.0	34.2	102.5
33	60 18.2	27.6	95.7	60 11.3	29.5	97.4	60 02.6	31.3	99.2	59 52.2	33.0	100.9
34	60 45.8	26.0	93.9	60 40.8	28.0	95.7	60 33.9	29.9	97.4	60 25.2	31.7	99.2
35	61 11.8	+24.6	92.0	61 08.8	+26.5	93.9	61 03.8	+28.4	95.7	60 56.9	+30.3	97.5
36	61 36.4	22.9	90.1	61 35.3	24.9	92.0	61 32.2	26.9	93.8	61 27.2	28.9	95.7
37	61 59.3	21.1	88.2	62 00.2	23.2	90.1	61 59.1	25.3	91.9	61 56.1	27.3	93.8
38	62 20.4	19.5	86.2	62 23.4	21.6	88.1	62 24.4	23.7	90.0	62 23.4	25.8	91.9
39	62 39.9	17.5	84.1	62 45.0	19.7	86.1	62 48.1	21.9	88.0	62 49.2	24.0	89.9
40	62 57.4	+15.7	82.0	63 04.7	+17.9	84.0	63 10.0	+20.1	86.0	63 13.2	+22.3	87.9
41	63 13.1	13.8•	79.9	63 22.6	16.0	81.9	63 30.1	18.2	83.9	63 35.5	20.4	85.9
42	63 26.9	11.7•	77.7	63 38.6	14.0•	79.7	63 48.3	16.2	81.7	63 55.9	18.5	83.7
43	63 38.6	9.7•	75.5	63 52.6	11.9•	77.5	64 04.5	14.3•	79.5	64 14.4	16.5•	81.5
44	63 48.3	7.6•	73.3	64 04.5	9.9•	75.3	64 18.8	12.1•	77.3	64 30.9	14.5•	79.3
45	63 55.9	+5.5•	71.1	64 14.4	+7.8•	73.0	64 30.9	+10.1•	75.0	64 45.4	+12.4•	77.1
46	64 01.4	3.4•	68.8	64 22.2	5.6•	70.7	64 41.0	7.9•	72.7	64 57.8	10.2•	74.8
47	64 04.8	+1.2•	66.5	64 27.8	3.4•	68.4	64 48.9	5.7•	70.4	65 08.0	8.0•	72.4
48	64 06.0	−1.0•	64.2	64 31.2	+1.2•	66.1	64 54.6	3.4•	68.0	65 16.0	5.8•	70.1
49	64 05.0	3.1•	61.9	64 32.4	−1.0•	63.8	64 58.0	+1.2•	65.7	65 21.8	3.5•	67.7
50	64 01.9	−5.2•	59.6	64 31.4	−3.1•	61.4	64 59.2	−1.0•	63.3	65 25.3	+1.2•	65.3
51	63 56.7	7.4•	57.4	64 28.3	5.4•	59.1	64 58.2	3.2•	61.0	65 26.5	−1.1•	62.9
52	63 49.3	9.4•	55.1	64 22.9	7.5•	56.8	64 55.0	5.5•	58.6	65 25.4	3.4•	60.5
53	63 39.9	11.5•	52.9	64 15.4	9.6•	54.5	64 49.5	7.7•	56.3	65 22.0	5.6•	58.1
54	63 28.4	13.5•	50.7	64 05.8	11.8•	52.3	64 41.8	9.9•	53.9	65 16.4	7.9•	55.7
55	63 14.9	−15.5	48.5	63 54.0	−13.7•	50.0	64 31.9	−11.9•	51.6	65 08.5	−10.1•	53.3
56	62 59.4	17.3	46.4	63 40.3	15.8•	47.8	64 20.0	14.1•	49.4	64 58.4	12.3•	51.0
57	62 42.1	19.2	44.3	63 24.5	17.7	45.7	64 05.9	16.1	47.1	64 46.1	14.3•	48.7
58	62 22.9	21.0	42.2	63 06.8	19.5	43.5	63 49.8	18.0	44.9	64 31.8	16.5•	46.4
59	62 01.9	22.7	40.2	62 47.3	21.3	41.5	63 31.8	19.9	42.8	64 15.3	18.4	44.2
60	61 39.2	−24.3	38.2	62 26.0	−23.1	39.4	63 11.9	−21.8	40.7	63 56.9	−20.3	42.0
61	61 14.9	25.9	36.3	62 02.9	24.8	37.4	62 50.1	23.5	38.6	63 36.6	22.2	39.9
62	60 49.0	27.4	34.5	61 38.1	26.3	35.5	62 26.6	25.1	36.6	63 14.4	23.9	37.8
63	60 21.6	28.9	32.7	61 11.8	27.8	33.6	62 01.5	26.8	34.7	62 50.5	25.6	35.8
64	59 52.7	30.2	30.9	60 44.0	29.3	31.8	61 34.7	28.3	32.8	62 24.9	27.3	33.8
65	59 22.5	−31.5	29.2	60 14.7	−30.7	30.0	61 06.4	−29.8	30.9	61 57.6	−28.8	31.9
66	58 51.0	32.7	27.5	59 44.0	31.9	28.3	60 36.6	31.1	29.2	61 28.8	30.2	30.0
67	58 18.3	34.0	25.9	59 12.1	33.2	26.7	60 05.5	32.4	27.4	60 58.6	31.7	28.3
68	57 44.3	35.0	24.4	58 38.9	34.4	25.0	59 33.1	33.7	25.8	60 26.9	32.9	26.5
69	57 09.3	36.1	22.9	58 04.5	35.5	23.5	58 59.4	34.9	24.1	59 54.0	34.2	24.8
70	56 33.2	−37.0	21.4	57 29.0	−36.5	22.0	58 24.5	−35.9	22.6	59 19.8	−35.4	23.2
71	55 56.2	38.1	20.0	56 52.5	37.6	20.5	57 48.6	37.1	21.1	58 44.4	36.4	21.6
72	55 18.1	38.8	18.6	56 14.9	38.4	19.1	57 11.5	38.0	19.6	58 08.0	37.5	20.1
73	54 39.2	39.7	17.3	55 36.5	39.4	17.7	56 33.5	38.9	18.2	57 30.5	38.5	18.7
74	53 59.5	40.6	16.0	54 57.1	40.2	16.4	55 54.6	39.8	16.8	56 52.0	39.5	17.2
75	53 18.9	−41.3	14.8	54 16.9	−41.0	15.1	55 14.8	−40.7	15.5	56 12.5	−40.2	15.9
76	52 37.6	42.0	13.5	53 35.9	41.7	13.9	54 34.1	41.4	14.2	55 32.3	41.2	14.6
77	51 55.6	42.7	12.4	52 54.2	42.4	12.7	53 52.7	42.2	13.0	54 51.1	41.9	13.3
78	51 12.9	43.3	11.3	52 11.8	43.1	11.5	53 10.5	42.8	11.8	54 09.2	42.6	12.0
79	50 29.6	43.9	10.2	51 28.7	43.8	10.4	52 27.7	43.6	10.6	53 26.6	43.3	10.9
80	49 45.7	−44.5	9.1	50 44.9	−44.3	9.3	51 44.1	−44.1	9.5	52 43.3	−44.0	9.7
81	49 01.2	45.0	8.1	50 00.6	44.9	8.2	51 00.0	44.7	8.4	51 59.3	44.5	8.6
82	48 16.2	45.5	7.1	49 15.7	45.4	7.2	50 15.3	45.3	7.4	51 14.8	45.2	7.5
83	47 30.7	46.0	6.1	48 30.3	45.9	6.2	49 30.0	45.8	6.3	50 29.6	45.7	6.5
84	46 44.7	46.5	5.1	47 44.4	46.3	5.2	48 44.2	46.3	5.3	49 43.9	46.2	5.5
85	45 58.2	−46.8	4.2	46 58.1	−46.8	4.3	47 57.9	−46.8	4.4	48 57.7	−46.7	4.5
86	45 11.4	47.3	3.3	46 11.3	47.3	3.4	47 11.1	47.1	3.5	48 11.0	47.1	3.5
87	44 24.1	47.7	2.5	45 24.0	47.6	2.5	46 24.0	47.6	2.6	47 23.9	47.6	2.6
88	43 36.4	48.0	1.6	44 36.4	48.0	1.7	45 36.4	48.0	1.7	46 36.3	47.9	1.7
89	42 48.4	48.4	0.8	43 48.4	48.4	0.8	44 48.4	48.4	0.8	45 48.4	48.4	0.8
90	42 00.0	−48.7	0.0	43 00.0	−48.7	0.0	44 00.0	−48.7	0.0	45 00.0	−48.7	0.0
	42°			43°			44°			45°		

36°, 324° L.H.A. LATITUDE SAME NAME AS DECLINATION

LATITUDE CONTRARY NAME TO DECLINATION L.H.A. 36°, 324°

Dec.	38° Hc	d	Z	39° Hc	d	Z	40° Hc	d	Z	41° Hc	d	Z	42° Hc	d	Z	43° Hc	d	Z	44° Hc	d	Z	45° Hc	d	Z	Dec.
°	° ′	′	°	° ′	′	°	° ′	′	°	° ′	′	°	° ′	′	°	° ′	′	°	° ′	′	°	° ′	′	°	°
0	39 36.4	-48.1	130.3	38 57.4	-48.7	130.9	38 17.8	-49.2	131.5	37 37.9	-49.9	132.1	36 57.4	-50.3	132.6	36 16.6	-50.9	133.2	35 35.3	-51.3	133.7	34 53.6	-51.8	134.2	0
1	38 48.3	48.4	131.0	38 08.7	49.0	131.6	37 28.6	49.6	132.2	36 48.0	50.0	132.8	36 07.1	50.6	133.3	35 25.7	51.1	133.8	34 44.0	51.6	134.3	34 01.8	52.0	134.8	1
2	37 59.9	48.7	131.8	37 19.7	49.3	132.4	36 39.0	49.7	132.9	35 58.0	50.3	133.5	35 16.5	50.8	134.0	34 34.6	51.2	134.5	33 52.4	51.7	135.0	33 09.8	52.1	135.4	2
3	37 11.2	48.9	132.5	36 30.4	49.4	133.1	35 49.3	50.1	133.6	35 07.7	50.6	134.1	34 25.7	51.0	134.6	33 43.4	51.5	135.1	33 00.7	51.9	135.6	32 17.7	52.4	136.0	3
4	36 22.3	49.2	133.3	35 41.0	49.8	133.8	34 59.2	50.2	134.3	34 17.1	50.7	134.8	33 34.7	51.2	135.3	32 51.9	51.6	135.7	32 08.8	52.1	136.2	31 25.3	52.4	136.6	4
5	35 33.1	-49.5	134.0	34 51.2	-49.9	134.5	34 09.0	-50.4	135.0	33 26.4	-50.9	135.4	32 43.5	-51.4	135.9	32 00.3	-51.8	136.3	31 16.7	-52.2	136.8	30 32.9	-52.7	137.2	5
6	34 43.6	49.7	134.7	34 01.3	50.2	135.1	33 18.6	50.7	135.6	32 35.5	51.1	136.1	31 52.1	51.5	136.5	31 08.5	52.0	136.9	30 24.5	52.4	137.3	29 40.2	52.7	137.7	6
7	33 53.9	49.9	135.3	33 11.1	50.4	135.8	32 27.9	50.8	136.3	31 44.4	51.3	136.7	31 00.6	51.7	137.1	30 16.5	52.1	137.5	29 32.1	52.5	137.9	28 47.5	52.9	138.3	7
8	33 04.0	50.1	136.0	32 20.7	50.5	136.5	31 37.1	51.0	136.9	30 53.1	51.4	137.3	30 08.9	51.9	137.7	29 24.4	52.3	138.1	28 39.6	52.6	138.4	27 54.6	53.0	138.8	8
9	32 13.9	50.3	136.7	31 30.2	50.8	137.1	30 46.1	51.2	137.5	30 01.7	51.6	137.9	29 17.0	52.0	138.3	28 32.1	52.4	138.6	27 47.0	52.8	139.0	27 01.6	53.1	139.3	9
10	31 23.6	-50.5	137.3	30 39.4	-50.9	137.7	29 54.9	-51.4	138.1	29 10.1	-51.8	138.5	28 25.0	-52.1	138.8	27 39.7	-52.5	139.2	26 54.2	-52.9	139.5	26 08.5	-53.3	139.8	10
11	30 33.1	50.6	137.9	29 48.5	51.1	138.3	29 03.5	51.5	138.7	28 18.3	51.9	139.1	27 32.9	52.3	139.4	26 47.2	52.6	139.7	26 01.3	53.0	140.1	25 15.2	53.3	140.4	11
12	29 42.5	50.9	138.6	28 57.4	51.3	138.9	28 12.0	51.6	139.3	27 26.4	52.0	139.6	26 40.6	52.4	140.0	25 54.6	52.8	140.3	25 08.3	53.1	140.6	24 21.9	53.5	140.9	12
13	28 51.6	51.0	139.2	28 06.1	51.4	139.5	27 20.4	51.8	139.9	26 34.4	52.2	140.2	25 48.2	52.5	140.5	25 01.8	52.9	140.8	24 15.2	53.2	141.1	23 28.4	53.5	141.4	13
14	28 00.6	51.1	139.8	27 14.7	51.5	140.1	26 28.6	51.9	140.4	25 42.2	52.2	140.7	24 55.7	52.6	141.0	24 08.9	52.9	141.3	23 22.0	53.3	141.6	22 34.9	53.6	141.9	14
15	27 09.5	-51.3	140.3	26 23.2	-51.7	140.7	25 36.7	-52.1	141.0	24 50.0	-52.4	141.3	24 03.1	-52.8	141.6	23 16.0	-53.1	141.8	22 28.7	-53.4	142.1	21 41.3	-53.7	142.3	15
16	26 18.2	51.5	140.9	25 31.5	51.8	141.2	24 44.6	52.1	141.5	23 57.6	52.6	141.8	23 10.3	52.8	142.1	22 22.9	53.2	142.3	21 35.3	53.5	142.6	20 47.6	53.8	142.8	16
17	25 26.7	51.5	141.5	24 39.7	51.9	141.8	23 52.5	52.3	142.1	23 05.0	52.6	142.3	22 17.5	53.0	142.6	21 29.7	53.2	142.8	20 41.8	53.5	143.1	19 53.8	53.8	143.3	17
18	24 35.2	51.7	142.1	23 47.8	52.1	142.3	23 00.2	52.4	142.6	22 12.4	52.7	142.9	21 24.5	53.0	143.1	20 36.5	53.4	143.3	19 48.3	53.7	143.5	19 00.0	54.0	143.8	18
19	23 43.5	51.8	142.6	22 55.7	52.1	142.9	22 07.8	52.5	143.1	21 19.7	52.8	143.4	20 31.5	53.1	143.6	19 43.1	53.4	143.8	18 54.6	53.7	144.0	18 06.0	54.0	144.2	19
20	22 51.7	-52.0	143.2	22 03.6	-52.3	143.4	21 15.3	-52.6	143.7	20 26.9	-52.9	143.9	19 38.4	-53.2	144.1	18 49.7	-53.5	144.3	18 00.9	-53.7	144.5	17 12.0	-54.0	144.7	20
21	21 59.7	52.0	143.7	21 11.3	52.3	143.9	20 22.7	52.6	144.2	19 34.0	53.0	144.4	18 45.2	53.3	144.6	17 56.2	53.5	144.8	17 07.2	53.9	145.0	16 18.0	54.1	145.1	21
22	21 07.7	52.1	144.2	20 19.0	52.5	144.5	19 30.1	52.8	144.7	18 41.0	53.0	144.9	17 51.9	53.3	145.1	17 02.7	53.7	145.2	16 13.3	53.9	145.4	15 23.9	54.2	145.6	22
23	20 15.6	52.2	144.8	19 26.5	52.5	145.0	18 37.3	52.8	145.2	17 48.0	53.1	145.4	16 58.6	53.4	145.5	16 09.0	53.6	145.7	15 19.4	53.9	145.9	14 29.7	54.2	146.0	23
24	19 23.4	52.4	145.3	18 34.0	52.6	145.5	17 44.5	52.9	145.7	16 54.9	53.2	145.9	16 05.2	53.5	146.0	15 15.4	53.8	146.2	14 25.5	54.0	146.3	13 35.5	54.3	146.5	24
25	18 31.0	-52.3	145.8	17 41.4	-52.7	146.0	16 51.6	-53.0	146.2	16 01.7	-53.3	146.3	15 11.7	-53.5	146.5	14 21.6	-53.8	146.6	13 31.5	-54.1	146.8	12 41.2	-54.3	146.9	25
26	17 38.7	52.5	146.3	16 48.7	52.8	146.5	15 58.6	53.1	146.7	15 08.4	53.3	146.8	14 18.2	53.6	147.0	13 27.8	53.8	147.1	12 37.4	54.1	147.2	11 46.9	54.3	147.3	26
27	16 46.2	52.6	146.8	15 55.9	52.8	147.0	15 05.5	53.1	147.2	14 15.1	53.4	147.3	13 24.6	53.7	147.4	12 34.0	53.9	147.5	11 43.3	54.1	147.7	10 52.6	54.4	147.8	27
28	15 53.6	52.6	147.3	15 03.1	52.9	147.5	14 12.4	53.1	147.6	13 21.7	53.4	147.8	12 30.9	53.6	147.9	11 40.1	53.9	148.0	10 49.2	54.2	148.1	9 58.2	54.4	148.2	28
29	15 01.0	52.7	147.8	14 10.2	53.0	148.0	13 19.3	53.2	148.1	12 28.3	53.5	148.2	11 37.3	53.8	148.3	10 46.2	54.0	148.4	9 55.0	54.2	148.5	9 03.8	54.4	148.6	29
30	14 08.3	-52.7	148.3	13 17.2	-53.0	148.5	12 26.1	-53.3	148.6	11 34.8	-53.5	148.7	10 43.5	-53.7	148.8	9 52.2	-54.0	148.9	9 00.8	-54.2	149.0	8 09.4	-54.5	149.1	30
31	13 15.6	52.8	148.8	12 24.2	53.0	148.9	11 32.8	53.3	149.1	10 41.3	53.6	149.2	9 49.8	53.8	149.2	8 58.2	54.1	149.3	8 06.6	54.3	149.4	7 14.9	54.5	149.5	31
32	12 22.8	52.9	149.3	11 31.2	53.1	149.4	10 39.5	53.4	149.5	9 47.7	53.5	149.6	8 56.0	53.9	149.7	8 04.1	54.0	149.8	7 12.3	54.3	149.8	6 20.4	54.5	149.9	32
33	11 29.9	52.9	149.8	10 38.1	53.2	149.9	9 46.1	53.4	150.0	8 54.2	53.7	150.1	8 02.1	53.8	150.1	7 10.1	54.1	150.2	6 18.0	54.3	150.3	5 25.9	54.5	150.3	33
34	10 37.0	52.9	150.3	9 44.9	53.2	150.4	8 52.7	53.4	150.4	8 00.5	53.6	150.5	7 08.3	53.9	150.6	6 16.0	54.1	150.6	5 23.7	54.3	150.7	4 31.4	54.6	150.7	34
35	9 44.1	-53.0	150.8	8 51.7	-53.2	150.8	7 59.3	-53.4	150.9	7 06.9	-53.7	151.0	6 14.4	-53.9	151.0	5 21.9	-54.1	151.1	4 29.4	-54.4	151.1	3 36.8	-54.5	151.2	35
36	8 51.1	53.0	151.2	7 58.5	53.2	151.3	7 05.9	53.5	151.4	6 13.2	53.7	151.4	5 20.5	53.9	151.5	4 27.8	54.2	151.5	3 35.0	54.3	151.5	2 42.3	54.6	151.6	36
37	7 58.1	53.0	151.7	7 05.3	53.3	151.8	6 12.4	53.5	151.8	5 19.5	53.7	151.9	4 26.6	54.0	151.9	3 33.6	54.1	151.9	2 40.7	54.4	152.0	1 47.7	54.6	152.0	37
38	7 05.1	53.1	152.2	6 12.0	53.3	152.2	5 18.9	53.5	152.3	4 25.8	53.8	152.3	3 32.6	53.9	152.4	2 39.5	54.2	152.4	1 46.3	54.4	152.4	0 53.1	-54.5	152.4	38
39	6 12.0	53.1	152.6	5 18.7	53.3	152.7	4 25.4	53.6	152.7	3 32.0	53.7	152.8	2 38.7	54.0	152.8	1 45.3	54.2	152.8	0 51.9	-54.3	152.8	0 01.4	+54.6	27.2	39
40	5 18.9	-53.1	153.1	4 25.4	-53.4	153.2	3 31.8	-53.5	153.2	2 38.3	-53.8	153.2	1 44.7	-54.0	153.2	0 51.1	-54.1	153.2	0 02.4	+54.4	26.8	0 56.0	+54.6	26.8	40
41	4 25.8	53.2	153.6	3 32.0	53.3	153.6	2 38.3	53.6	153.6	1 44.5	53.8	153.7	0 50.7	-53.9	153.7	0 03.0	+54.2	26.3	0 56.8	54.4	26.3	1 50.6	54.6	26.3	41
42	3 32.6	53.1	154.0	2 38.7	53.4	154.1	1 44.7	53.6	154.1	0 50.7	-53.7	154.1	0 03.2	+54.0	25.9	0 57.2	54.2	25.9	1 51.2	54.4	25.9	2 45.2	54.5	25.9	42
43	2 39.5	53.2	154.5	1 45.3	53.4	154.5	0 51.1	-53.5	154.5	0 03.0	+53.8	25.5	0 57.2	54.0	25.5	1 51.4	54.2	25.5	2 45.6	54.3	25.5	3 39.7	54.5	25.5	43
44	1 46.3	53.2	155.0	0 51.9	-53.3	155.0	0 02.4	+53.6	25.0	0 56.8	53.8	25.0	1 51.2	54.0	25.0	2 45.6	54.1	25.0	3 39.9	54.3	25.1	4 34.2	54.6	25.1	44
45	0 53.1	-53.2	155.4	0 01.4	+53.4	24.6	0 56.0	+53.6	24.6	1 50.6	+53.8	24.6	2 45.2	+53.9	24.6	3 39.7	+54.1	24.6	4 34.2	+54.4	24.6	5 28.8	+54.5	24.7	45
46	0 00.1	+53.1	24.1	0 54.8	53.4	24.1	1 49.6	53.6	24.1	2 44.4	53.7	24.1	3 39.1	53.9	24.2	4 33.8	54.2	24.2	5 28.6	54.3	24.2	6 23.3	54.5	24.3	46
47	0 53.2	53.2	23.6	1 48.2	53.4	23.6	2 43.2	53.5	23.7	3 38.1	53.7	23.7	4 33.0	54.0	23.7	5 28.0	54.1	23.7	6 22.9	54.3	23.8	7 17.8	54.4	23.8	47
48	1 46.4	53.2	23.2	2 41.6	53.3	23.2	3 36.7	53.5	23.2	4 31.8	53.8	23.2	5 27.0	54.0	23.3	6 22.1	54.1	23.3	7 17.2	54.2	23.4	8 12.2	54.5	23.4	48
49	2 39.6	53.1	22.7	3 34.9	53.3	22.7	4 30.2	53.6	22.8	5 25.6	53.7	22.8	6 20.9	53.9	22.8	7 16.2	54.0	22.9	8 11.4	54.3	22.9	9 06.7	54.4	23.0	49
50	3 32.7	+53.2	22.2	4 28.2	+53.4	22.3	5 23.8	+53.5	22.3	6 19.3	+53.7	22.3	7 14.8	+53.8	22.4	8 10.2	+54.1	22.4	9 05.7	+54.2	22.5	10 01.1	+54.4	22.6	50
51	4 25.9	53.1	21.8	5 21.6	53.3	21.8	6 17.3	53.4	21.8	7 13.0	53.6	21.9	8 08.6	53.8	21.9	9 04.3	54.0	22.0	9 59.9	54.1	22.1	10 55.5	54.3	22.1	51
52	5 19.0	53.1	21.3	6 14.9	53.2	21.3	7 10.7	53.5	21.4	8 06.6	53.6	21.4	9 02.4	53.8	21.5	9 58.3	53.9	21.6	10 54.0	54.2	21.6	11 49.8	54.3	21.7	52
53	6 12.1	53.1	20.8	7 08.1	53.3	20.9	8 04.2	53.4	20.9	9 00.2	53.6	21.0	9 56.2	53.8	21.0	10 52.2	53.9	21.1	11 48.2	54.1	21.2	12 44.1	54.5	21.3	53
54	7 05.2	53.0	20.4	8 01.4	53.2	20.4	8 57.6	53.4	20.5	9 53.8	53.6	20.5	10 50.0	53.7	20.6	11 46.1	53.9	20.7	12 42.3	54.0	20.7	13 38.4	54.2	20.8	54
55	7 58.2	+53.0	19.9	8 54.6	+53.2	20.0	9 51.0	+53.4	20.0	10 47.4	+53.5	20.1	11 43.7	+53.7	20.1	12 40.0	+53.9	20.2	13 36.3	+54.0	20.3	14 32.6	+54.1	20.4	55
56	8 51.2	53.0	19.4	9 47.8	53.1	19.5	10 44.4	53.3	19.5	11 40.9	53.5	19.6	12 37.4	53.6	19.7	13 33.9	53.9	19.8	14 30.3	54.0	19.8	15 26.7	54.2	19.9	56
57	9 44.2	52.9	19.0	10 40.9	53.1	19.0	11 37.7	53.2	19.1	12 34.4	53.4	19.1	13 31.0	53.6	19.2	14 27.7	53.7	19.3	15 24.3	53.9	19.4	16 20.9	54.0	19.5	57
58	10 37.1	52.9	18.5	11 34.0	53.1	18.5	12 30.9	53.2	18.6	13 27.8	53.3	18.7	14 24.6	53.5	18.8	15 21.4	53.7	18.8	16 18.2	53.8	18.9	17 14.9	54.0	19.0	58
59	11 30.0	52.9	18.0	12 27.1	53.0	18.1	13 24.1	53.2	18.1	14 21.1	53.4	18.2	15 18.1	53.5	18.3	16 15.1	53.6	18.4	17 12.0	53.8	18.5	18 08.9	53.9	18.6	59
60	12 22.9	+52.8	17.5	13 20.1	+53.0	17.6	14 17.3	+53.1	17.7	15 14.5	+53.2	17.7	16 11.6	+53.4	17.8	17 08.7	+53.5	17.9	18 05.8	+53.7	18.0	19 02.8	+53.9	18.1	60
61	13 15.7	52.7	17.0	14 13.1	52.8	17.1	15 10.4	53.0	17.2	16 07.7	53.2	17.3	17 05.0	53.3	17.3	18 02.2	53.5	17.4	18 59.5	53.6	17.5	19 56.7	53.7	17.6	61
62	14 08.4	52.7	16.5	15 05.9	52.9	16.6	16 03.4	53.0	16.7	17 00.9	53.1	16.8	17 58.3	53.3	16.9	18 55.7	53.4	17.0	19 53.1	53.6	17.1	20 50.4	53.7	17.2	62
63	15 01.1	52.6	16.0	15 58.8	52.7	16.1	16 56.4	52.9	16.2	17 54.0	53.1	16.3	18 51.6	53.2	16.4	19 49.1	53.4	16.5	20 46.7	53.4	16.6	21 44.1	53.7	16.7	63
64	15 53.7	52.6	15.5	16 51.5	52.7	15.6	17 49.3	52.8	15.7	18 47.1	52.9	15.8	19 44.8	53.1	15.9	20 42.5	53.2	16.0	21 40.1	53.4	16.1	22 37.8	53.5	16.2	64
65	16 46.3	+52.5	15.0	17 44.2	+52.6	15.1	18 42.1	+52.8	15.2	19 40.0	+52.9	15.3	20 37.9	+53.0	15.4	21 35.7	+53.2	15.5	22 33.5	+53.3	15.6	23 31.3	+53.4	15.7	65
66	17 38.8	52.4	14.5	18 36.8	52.6	14.6	19 34.9	52.6	14.7	20 32.9	52.8	14.8	21 30.9	52.9	14.9	22 28.9	53.0	15.0	23 26.8	53.2	15.1	24 24.7	53.4	15.2	66
67	18 31.2	52.3	14.0	19 29.4	52.4	14.1	20 27.5	52.6	14.2	21 25.7	52.7	14.3	22 23.8	52.9	14.4	23 21.9	53.0	14.5	24 20.0	53.1	14.6	25 18.1	53.2	14.7	67
68	19 23.5	52.2	13.5	20 21.8	52.3	13.6	21 20.1	52.5	13.7	22 18.4	52.6	13.8	23 16.7	52.7	13.9	24 14.9	52.9	14.0	25 13.1	53.0	14.1	26 11.3	53.1	14.2	68
69	20 15.7	52.1	13.0	21 14.1	52.3	13.1	22 12.6	52.4	13.2	23 11.0	52.5	13.2	24 09.4	52.6	13.3	25 07.8	52.7	13.5	26 06.1	52.9	13.6	27 04.4	53.0	13.7	69
70	21 07.8	+52.0	12.4	22 06.4	+52.1	12.5	23 05.0	+52.2	12.6	24 03.5	+52.4	12.7	25 02.0	+52.5	12.8	26 00.5	+52.6	12.9	26 59.0	+52.7	13.0	27 57.4	+52.9	13.2	70
71	21 59.8	52.0	11.9	22 58.5	52.1	12.0	23 57.2	52.2	12.1	24 55.9	52.3	12.2	25 54.5	52.4	12.3	26 53.1	52.5	12.4	27 51.7	52.7	12.5	28 50.3	52.7	12.6	71
72	22 51.8	51.8	11.4	23 50.6	51.9	11.5	24 49.4	52.0	11.5	25 48.2	52.1	11.6	26 46.9	52.3	11.7	27 45.6	52.4	11.8	28 44.4	52.5	12.0	29 43.0	52.7	12.1	72
73	23 43.6	51.7	10.8	24 42.5	51.8	10.9	25 41.4	51.9	11.0	26 40.3	52.0	11.1	27 39.2	52.1	11.2	28 38.0	52.3	11.3	29 36.9	52.3	11.4	30 35.7	52.4	11.5	73
74	24 35.3	51.5	10.3	25 34.3	51.7	10.3	26 33.3	51.8	10.4	27 32.3	51.9	10.5	28 31.3	52.0	10.6	29 30.3	52.1	10.7	30 29.2	52.2	10.8	31 28.1	52.3	11.0	74
75	25 26.8	+51.5	9.7	26 26.0	+51.5	9.8	27 25.1	+51.6	9.9	28 24.2	+51.7	10.0	29 23.3	+51.8	10.1	30 22.4	+51.9	10.2	31 21.4	+52.1	10.3	32 20.4	+52.2	10.4	75
76	26 18.3	51.3	9.1	27 17.5	51.4	9.2	28 16.7	51.5	9.3	29 15.9	51.6	9.4	30 15.1	51.7	9.5	31 14.3	51.8	9.6	32 13.5	51.8	9.7	33 12.6	52.0	9.8	76
77	27 09.6	51.1	8.5	28 08.9	51.3	8.6	29 08.2	51.4	8.7	30 07.5	51.5	8.8	31 06.8	51.5	8.9	32 06.1	51.6	9.0	33 05.3	51.8	9.1	34 04.6	51.8	9.2	77
78	28 00.7	51.0	8.0	29 00.2	51.0	8.0	29 59.6	51.1	8.1	30 59.0	51.2	8.2	31 58.3	51.4	8.3	32 57.7	51.4	8.4	33 57.1	51.5	8.5	34 56.4	51.6	8.6	78
79	28 51.7	50.9	7.4	29 51.2	51.0	7.4	30 50.7	51.0	7.5	31 50.2	51.1	7.6	32 49.7	51.1	7.7	33 49.1	51.3	7.8	34 48.6	51.3	7.9	35 48.0	51.4	7.9	79
80	29 42.6	+50.6	6.7	30 42.2	+50.7	6.8	31 41.7	+50.8	6.9	32 41.3	+50.9	7.0	33 40.8	+51.0	7.0	34 40.4	+51.0	7.1	35 39.9	+51.1	7.2	36 39.4	+51.2	7.3	80
81	30 33.2	50.5	6.1	31 32.9	50.6	6.2	32 32.5	50.7	6.3	33 32.2	50.7	6.3	34 31.8	50.8	6.4	35 31.4	50.9	6.5	36 31.0	51.0	6.6	37 30.6	51.0	6.7	81
82	31 23.7	50.3	5.5	32 23.5	50.3	5.6	33 23.2	50.4	5.6	34 22.9	50.5	5.7	35 22.6	50.5	5.8	36 22.3	50.6	5.8	37 22.0	50.7	5.9	38 21.6	50.8	6.0	82
83	32 14.0	50.1	4.9	33 13.8	50.2	4.9	34 13.6	50.2	5.0	35 13.4	50.2	5.0	36 13.1	50.4	5.1	37 12.9	50.4	5.2	38 12.7	50.4	5.2	39 12.4	50.5	5.3	83
84	33 04.1	49.9	4.2	34 04.0	49.9	4.3	35 03.8	50.0	4.3	36 03.6	50.1	4.3	37 03.5	50.1	4.4	38 03.3	50.1	4.5	39 03.1	50.2	4.5	40 02.9	50.3	4.6	84
85	33 54.0	+49.7	3.5	34 53.9	+49.7	3.5	35 53.8	+49.8	3.6	36 53.7	+49.8	3.7	37 53.6	+49.8	3.7	38 53.4	+49.9	3.8	39 53.3	+49.9	3.8	40 53.2	+49.9	3.9	85
86	34 43.7	49.5	2.9	35 43.6	49.5	2.9	36 43.6	49.5	2.9	37 43.5	49.5	3.0	38 43.4	49.6	3.0	39 43.3	49.6	3.1	40 43.2	49.7	3.1	41 43.1	49.7	3.1	86
87	35 33.2	49.2	2.2	36 33.1	49.3	2.2	37 33.1	49.2	2.2	38 33.0	49.3	2.3	39 33.0	49.3	2.3	40 32.9	49.4	2.3	41 32.9	49.3	2.4	42 32.8	49.4	2.4	87
88	36 22.4	48.9	1.5	37 22.4	48.9	1.5	38 22.3	49.0	1.5	39 22.3	49.0	1.5	40 22.3	49.0	1.5	41 22.3	49.0	1.6	42 22.2	49.1	1.6	43 22.2	49.1	1.6	88
89	37 11.3	48.7	0.7	38 11.3	48.7	0.7	39 11.3	48.7	0.8	40 11.3	48.7	0.8	41 11.3	48.7	0.8	42 11.3	48.7	0.8	43 11.3	48.7	0.8	44 11.3	48.7	0.8	89
90	38 00.0	+48.4	0.0	39 00.0	+48.4	0.0	40 00.0	+48.4	0.0	41 00.0	+48.4	0.0	42 00.0	+48.4	0.0	43 00.0	+48.4	0.0	44 00.0	+48.4	0.0	45 00.0	+48.4	0.0	90
	38°			39°			40°			41°			42°			43°			44°			45°			

S. Lat. {L.H.A. greater than 180°......Zn=180°−Z
L.H.A. less than 180°...........Zn=180°+Z

LATITUDE SAME NAME AS DECLINATION L.H.A. 144°, 216°

INTERPOLATION TABLE

Dec. Inc.	Altitude Difference (d) Tens 10′	20′	30′	40′	50′	Decimals	Units 0′	1′	2′	3′	4′	5′	6′	7′	8′	9′
28.0	4.6	9.3	14.0	18.6	23.3	.0	0.0	0.5	0.9	1.4	1.9	2.4	2.8	3.3	3.8	4.3
28.1	4.7	9.3	14.0	18.7	23.4	.1	0.0	0.5	1.0	1.5	1.9	2.4	2.9	3.4	3.8	4.3
28.2	4.7	9.4	14.1	18.8	23.5	.2	0.1	0.6	1.0	1.5	2.0	2.5	2.9	3.4	3.9	4.4
28.3	4.7	9.4	14.1	18.9	23.6	.3	0.1	0.6	1.1	1.6	2.0	2.5	3.0	3.5	3.9	4.4
28.4	4.7	9.5	14.2	18.9	23.7	.4	0.2	0.7	1.1	1.6	2.1	2.6	3.0	3.5	4.0	4.5
28.5	4.8	9.5	14.3	19.0	23.8	.5	0.2	0.7	1.2	1.7	2.1	2.6	3.1	3.6	4.0	4.5
28.6	4.8	9.5	14.3	19.1	23.8	.6	0.3	0.8	1.2	1.7	2.2	2.7	3.1	3.6	4.1	4.6
28.7	4.8	9.6	14.4	19.2	23.9	.7	0.3	0.8	1.3	1.8	2.2	2.7	3.2	3.7	4.1	4.6
28.8	4.8	9.6	14.4	19.2	24.0	.8	0.4	0.9	1.3	1.8	2.3	2.8	3.2	3.7	4.2	4.7
28.9	4.9	9.7	14.5	19.3	24.1	.9	0.4	0.9	1.4	1.9	2.3	2.8	3.3	3.8	4.2	4.7
29.0	4.8	9.6	14.5	19.3	24.1	.0	0.0	0.5	1.0	1.5	2.0	2.5	2.9	3.4	3.9	4.4
29.1	4.8	9.7	14.5	19.4	24.2	.1	0.0	0.5	1.0	1.5	2.0	2.5	3.0	3.5	4.0	4.5
29.2	4.8	9.7	14.6	19.4	24.3	.2	0.1	0.6	1.1	1.6	2.1	2.6	3.0	3.5	4.0	4.5
29.3	4.9	9.8	14.6	19.5	24.4	.3	0.1	0.6	1.1	1.6	2.1	2.6	3.1	3.6	4.1	4.6
29.4	4.9	9.8	14.7	19.6	24.5	.4	0.2	0.7	1.2	1.7	2.2	2.7	3.1	3.6	4.1	4.6
29.5	4.9	9.8	14.8	19.7	24.6	.5	0.2	0.7	1.2	1.7	2.2	2.7	3.2	3.7	4.2	4.7
29.6	4.9	9.9	14.8	19.7	24.7	.6	0.3	0.8	1.3	1.8	2.3	2.8	3.2	3.7	4.2	4.7
29.7	5.0	9.9	14.9	19.8	24.8	.7	0.3	0.8	1.3	1.8	2.3	2.8	3.3	3.8	4.3	4.8
29.8	5.0	10.0	14.9	19.9	24.9	.8	0.4	0.9	1.4	1.9	2.4	2.9	3.3	3.8	4.3	4.8
29.9	5.0	10.0	15.0	20.0	25.0	.9	0.4	0.9	1.4	1.9	2.4	2.9	3.4	3.9	4.4	4.9
30.0	5.0	10.0	15.0	20.0	25.0	.0	0.0	0.5	1.0	1.5	2.0	2.5	3.0	3.6	4.1	4.6
30.1	5.0	10.0	15.0	20.0	25.1	.1	0.1	0.6	1.1	1.6	2.1	2.6	3.1	3.6	4.1	4.6
30.2	5.0	10.0	15.1	20.1	25.1	.2	0.1	0.6	1.1	1.6	2.1	2.6	3.2	3.7	4.2	4.7
30.3	5.0	10.1	15.1	20.2	25.2	.3	0.2	0.7	1.2	1.7	2.2	2.7	3.2	3.7	4.2	4.7
30.4	5.1	10.1	15.2	20.3	25.3	.4	0.2	0.7	1.2	1.7	2.2	2.7	3.3	3.8	4.3	4.8
30.5	5.1	10.2	15.3	20.3	25.4	.5	0.3	0.8	1.3	1.8	2.3	2.8	3.3	3.8	4.3	4.8
30.6	5.1	10.2	15.3	20.4	25.5	.6	0.3	0.8	1.3	1.8	2.3	2.8	3.4	3.9	4.4	4.9
30.7	5.1	10.3	15.4	20.5	25.6	.7	0.4	0.9	1.4	1.9	2.4	2.9	3.4	3.9	4.4	4.9
30.8	5.2	10.3	15.4	20.6	25.7	.8	0.4	0.9	1.4	1.9	2.4	2.9	3.5	4.0	4.5	5.0
30.9	5.2	10.3	15.5	20.6	25.8	.9	0.5	1.0	1.5	2.0	2.5	3.0	3.5	4.0	4.5	5.0
31.0	5.1	10.3	15.5	20.6	25.8	.0	0.0	0.5	1.0	1.6	2.1	2.6	3.1	3.7	4.2	4.7
31.1	5.2	10.3	15.5	20.7	25.9	.1	0.1	0.6	1.1	1.6	2.2	2.7	3.2	3.7	4.3	4.8
31.2	5.2	10.4	15.6	20.8	26.0	.2	0.1	0.6	1.2	1.7	2.2	2.7	3.3	3.8	4.3	4.8
31.3	5.2	10.4	15.6	20.9	26.1	.3	0.2	0.7	1.2	1.7	2.3	2.8	3.3	3.8	4.4	4.9
31.4	5.2	10.5	15.7	20.9	26.2	.4	0.2	0.7	1.3	1.8	2.3	2.8	3.4	3.9	4.4	4.9
31.5	5.3	10.5	15.8	21.0	26.3	.5	0.3	0.8	1.3	1.8	2.4	2.9	3.4	3.9	4.5	5.0
31.6	5.3	10.5	15.8	21.1	26.3	.6	0.3	0.8	1.4	1.9	2.4	2.9	3.5	4.0	4.5	5.0
31.7	5.3	10.6	15.9	21.2	26.4	.7	0.4	0.9	1.4	1.9	2.5	3.0	3.5	4.0	4.6	5.1
31.8	5.3	10.6	15.9	21.2	26.5	.8	0.4	0.9	1.5	2.0	2.5	3.0	3.6	4.1	4.6	5.1
31.9	5.4	10.7	16.0	21.3	26.6	.9	0.5	1.0	1.5	2.0	2.6	3.1	3.6	4.1	4.7	5.2
32.0	5.3	10.6	16.0	21.3	26.6	.0	0.0	0.5	1.1	1.6	2.2	2.7	3.2	3.8	4.3	4.9
32.1	5.3	10.7	16.0	21.4	26.7	.1	0.1	0.6	1.1	1.7	2.2	2.8	3.3	3.8	4.4	4.9
32.2	5.3	10.7	16.1	21.4	26.8	.2	0.1	0.6	1.2	1.7	2.3	2.8	3.4	3.9	4.4	5.0
32.3	5.4	10.8	16.1	21.5	26.9	.3	0.2	0.7	1.2	1.8	2.3	2.9	3.4	4.0	4.5	5.0
32.4	5.4	10.8	16.2	21.6	27.0	.4	0.2	0.8	1.3	1.8	2.4	2.9	3.5	4.0	4.5	5.1
32.5	5.4	10.8	16.3	21.7	27.1	.5	0.3	0.8	1.4	1.9	2.4	3.0	3.5	4.1	4.6	5.1
32.6	5.4	10.9	16.3	21.7	27.2	.6	0.3	0.9	1.4	1.9	2.5	3.0	3.6	4.1	4.7	5.2
32.7	5.5	10.9	16.4	21.8	27.3	.7	0.4	0.9	1.5	2.0	2.5	3.1	3.6	4.2	4.7	5.3
32.8	5.5	11.0	16.4	21.9	27.4	.8	0.4	1.0	1.5	2.1	2.6	3.1	3.7	4.2	4.8	5.3
32.9	5.5	11.0	16.5	22.0	27.5	.9	0.5	1.0	1.6	2.1	2.7	3.2	3.7	4.3	4.8	5.4
33.0	5.5	11.0	16.5	22.0	27.5	.0	0.0	0.6	1.1	1.7	2.2	2.8	3.3	3.9	4.5	5.0
33.1	5.5	11.0	16.5	22.0	27.6	.1	0.1	0.6	1.2	1.7	2.3	2.8	3.4	4.0	4.5	5.1
33.2	5.5	11.0	16.6	22.1	27.6	.2	0.1	0.7	1.2	1.8	2.3	2.9	3.5	4.0	4.6	5.1
33.3	5.5	11.1	16.6	22.2	27.7	.3	0.2	0.7	1.3	1.8	2.4	3.0	3.5	4.1	4.6	5.2
33.4	5.6	11.1	16.7	22.3	27.8	.4	0.2	0.8	1.3	1.9	2.5	3.0	3.6	4.1	4.7	5.2
33.5	5.6	11.2	16.8	22.3	27.9	.5	0.3	0.8	1.4	2.0	2.5	3.1	3.6	4.2	4.7	5.3
33.6	5.6	11.2	16.8	22.4	28.0	.6	0.3	0.9	1.5	2.0	2.6	3.1	3.7	4.2	4.8	5.4
33.7	5.6	11.3	16.9	22.5	28.1	.7	0.4	0.9	1.5	2.1	2.6	3.2	3.7	4.3	4.9	5.4
33.8	5.7	11.3	16.9	22.6	28.2	.8	0.4	1.0	1.6	2.1	2.7	3.2	3.8	4.4	4.9	5.5
33.9	5.7	11.3	17.0	22.6	28.3	.9	0.5	1.1	1.6	2.2	2.7	3.3	3.9	4.4	5.0	5.5
34.0	5.6	11.3	17.0	22.6	28.3	.0	0.0	0.6	1.1	1.7	2.3	2.9	3.4	4.0	4.6	5.2
34.1	5.7	11.3	17.0	22.7	28.4	.1	0.1	0.6	1.2	1.8	2.4	2.9	3.5	4.1	4.7	5.2
34.2	5.7	11.4	17.1	22.8	28.5	.2	0.1	0.7	1.3	1.8	2.4	3.0	3.6	4.1	4.7	5.3
34.3	5.7	11.4	17.1	22.9	28.6	.3	0.2	0.7	1.3	1.9	2.5	3.0	3.6	4.2	4.8	5.3
34.4	5.7	11.5	17.2	22.9	28.7	.4	0.2	0.8	1.4	2.0	2.5	3.1	3.7	4.3	4.8	5.4
34.5	5.8	11.5	17.3	23.0	28.8	.5	0.3	0.9	1.4	2.0	2.6	3.2	3.7	4.3	4.9	5.5
34.6	5.8	11.5	17.3	23.1	28.8	.6	0.3	0.9	1.5	2.1	2.6	3.2	3.8	4.4	4.9	5.5
34.7	5.8	11.6	17.4	23.2	28.9	.7	0.4	1.0	1.6	2.1	2.7	3.3	3.9	4.4	5.0	5.6
34.8	5.8	11.6	17.4	23.2	29.0	.8	0.5	1.0	1.6	2.2	2.8	3.3	3.9	4.5	5.1	5.6
34.9	5.9	11.7	17.5	23.3	29.1	.9	0.5	1.1	1.7	2.2	2.8	3.4	4.0	4.5	5.1	5.7
35.0	5.8	11.6	17.5	23.3	29.1	.0	0.0	0.6	1.2	1.8	2.4	3.0	3.5	4.1	4.7	5.3
35.1	5.8	11.7	17.5	23.4	29.2	.1	0.1	0.7	1.2	1.8	2.4	3.0	3.6	4.2	4.8	5.4
35.2	5.8	11.7	17.6	23.4	29.3	.2	0.1	0.7	1.3	1.9	2.5	3.1	3.7	4.3	4.9	5.4
35.3	5.9	11.8	17.6	23.5	29.4	.3	0.2	0.8	1.4	2.0	2.5	3.1	3.7	4.3	4.9	5.5
35.4	5.9	11.8	17.7	23.6	29.5	.4	0.2	0.8	1.4	2.0	2.6	3.2	3.8	4.4	5.0	5.6
35.5	5.9	11.8	17.8	23.7	29.6	.5	0.3	0.9	1.5	2.1	2.7	3.3	3.8	4.4	5.0	5.6
35.6	5.9	11.9	17.8	23.7	29.7	.6	0.4	0.9	1.5	2.1	2.7	3.3	3.9	4.5	5.1	5.7
35.7	6.0	11.9	17.9	23.8	29.8	.7	0.4	1.0	1.6	2.2	2.8	3.4	4.0	4.6	5.1	5.7
35.8	6.0	12.0	17.9	23.9	29.9	.8	0.5	1.1	1.7	2.2	2.8	3.4	4.0	4.6	5.2	5.8
35.9	6.0	12.0	18.0	24.0	30.0	.9	0.5	1.1	1.7	2.3	2.9	3.5	4.1	4.7	5.3	5.9
	10′	20′	30′	40′	50′		0′	1′	2′	3′	4′	5′	6′	7′	8′	9′

Double Second Diff. and Corr. (28.0–29.9 and 30.0–31.9):

Double Second Diff.	Corr.
0.8	
	0.1
2.4	
	0.2
4.0	
	0.3
5.6	
	0.4
7.2	
	0.5
8.8	
	0.6
10.4	
	0.7
12.0	
	0.8
13.6	
	0.9
15.2	
	1.0
16.8	
	1.1
18.4	
	1.2
20.0	
	1.3
21.6	
	1.4
23.2	
	1.5
24.8	
	1.6
26.4	
	1.7
28.0	
	1.8
29.6	
	1.9
31.2	
	2.0
32.8	
	2.1
34.4	

Double Second Diff. and Corr. (32.0–33.9):

Double Second Diff.	Corr.
0.8	
	0.1
2.4	
	0.2
4.0	
	0.3
5.7	
	0.4
7.3	
	0.5
8.9	
	0.6
10.5	
	0.7
12.1	
	0.8
13.7	
	0.9
15.4	
	1.0
17.0	
	1.1
18.6	
	1.2
20.2	
	1.3
21.8	
	1.4
23.4	
	1.5
25.1	
	1.6
26.7	
	1.7
28.3	
	1.8
29.9	
	1.9
31.5	
	2.0
33.1	
	2.1
34.7	

Double Second Diff. and Corr. (34.0–35.9):

Double Second Diff.	Corr.
0.8	
	0.1
2.5	
	0.2
4.1	
	0.3
5.8	
	0.4
7.4	
	0.5
9.1	
	0.6
10.7	
	0.7
12.3	
	0.8
14.0	
	0.9
15.6	
	1.0
17.3	
	1.1
18.9	
	1.2
20.6	
	1.3
22.2	
	1.4
23.9	
	1.5
25.5	
	1.6
27.2	
	1.7
28.8	
	1.8
30.4	
	1.9
32.1	
	2.0
33.7	
	2.1
35.4	

Dec. Inc.	Altitude Difference (d) Tens 10′	20′	30′	40′	50′	Decimals	Units 0′	1′	2′	3′	4′	5′	6′	7′	8′	9′
36.0	6.0	12.0	18.0	24.0	30.0	.0	0.0	0.6	1.2	1.8	2.4	3.0	3.6	4.3	4.9	5.5
36.1	6.0	12.0	18.0	24.0	30.1	.1	0.1	0.7	1.3	1.9	2.5	3.1	3.7	4.3	4.9	5.5
36.2	6.0	12.0	18.1	24.1	30.1	.2	0.1	0.7	1.3	1.9	2.6	3.2	3.8	4.4	5.0	5.6
36.3	6.0	12.1	18.1	24.2	30.2	.3	0.2	0.8	1.4	2.0	2.6	3.2	3.8	4.4	5.0	5.7
36.4	6.1	12.1	18.2	24.3	30.3	.4	0.2	0.9	1.5	2.1	2.7	3.3	3.9	4.5	5.1	5.7
36.5	6.1	12.2	18.3	24.3	30.4	.5	0.3	0.9	1.5	2.1	2.7	3.3	4.0	4.6	5.2	5.8
36.6	6.1	12.2	18.3	24.4	30.5	.6	0.4	1.0	1.6	2.2	2.8	3.4	4.0	4.6	5.2	5.8
36.7	6.1	12.3	18.4	24.5	30.6	.7	0.4	1.0	1.6	2.3	2.9	3.5	4.1	4.7	5.3	5.9
36.8	6.2	12.3	18.4	24.6	30.7	.8	0.5	1.1	1.7	2.3	2.9	3.5	4.1	4.7	5.4	6.0
36.9	6.2	12.3	18.5	24.6	30.8	.9	0.5	1.2	1.8	2.4	3.0	3.6	4.2	4.8	5.4	6.0
37.0	6.1	12.3	18.5	24.6	30.8	.0	0.0	0.6	1.2	1.9	2.5	3.1	3.7	4.4	5.0	5.6
37.1	6.2	12.3	18.5	24.7	30.9	.1	0.1	0.7	1.3	1.9	2.6	3.2	3.8	4.4	5.1	5.7
37.2	6.2	12.4	18.6	24.8	31.0	.2	0.1	0.7	1.4	2.0	2.6	3.2	3.9	4.5	5.1	5.7
37.3	6.2	12.4	18.6	24.9	31.1	.3	0.2	0.8	1.4	2.1	2.7	3.3	3.9	4.6	5.2	5.8
37.4	6.2	12.5	18.7	24.9	31.2	.4	0.2	0.9	1.5	2.1	2.7	3.4	4.0	4.6	5.2	5.9
37.5	6.3	12.5	18.8	25.0	31.3	.5	0.3	0.9	1.6	2.2	2.8	3.4	4.1	4.7	5.3	5.9
37.6	6.3	12.5	18.8	25.1	31.3	.6	0.4	1.0	1.6	2.2	2.9	3.5	4.1	4.7	5.4	6.0
37.7	6.3	12.6	18.9	25.2	31.4	.7	0.4	1.1	1.7	2.3	2.9	3.6	4.2	4.8	5.4	6.1
37.8	6.3	12.6	18.9	25.2	31.5	.8	0.5	1.1	1.7	2.4	3.0	3.6	4.2	4.9	5.5	6.1
37.9	6.4	12.7	19.0	25.3	31.6	.9	0.6	1.2	1.8	2.4	3.1	3.7	4.3	4.9	5.6	6.2
38.0	6.3	12.6	19.0	25.3	31.6	.0	0.0	0.6	1.3	1.9	2.6	3.2	3.8	4.5	5.1	5.8
38.1	6.3	12.7	19.0	25.4	31.7	.1	0.1	0.7	1.3	2.0	2.6	3.3	3.9	4.6	5.2	5.8
38.2	6.3	12.7	19.1	25.4	31.8	.2	0.1	0.8	1.4	2.1	2.7	3.3	4.0	4.6	5.3	5.9
38.3	6.4	12.8	19.1	25.5	31.9	.3	0.2	0.8	1.5	2.1	2.8	3.4	4.0	4.7	5.3	6.0
38.4	6.4	12.8	19.2	25.6	32.0	.4	0.3	0.9	1.5	2.2	2.8	3.5	4.1	4.7	5.4	6.0
38.5	6.4	12.8	19.3	25.7	32.1	.5	0.3	1.0	1.6	2.2	2.9	3.5	4.2	4.8	5.5	6.1
38.6	6.4	12.9	19.3	25.7	32.2	.6	0.4	1.0	1.7	2.3	3.0	3.6	4.2	4.9	5.5	6.2
38.7	6.5	12.9	19.4	25.8	32.3	.7	0.4	1.1	1.7	2.4	3.0	3.7	4.3	4.9	5.6	6.2
38.8	6.5	13.0	19.4	25.9	32.4	.8	0.5	1.2	1.8	2.4	3.1	3.7	4.4	5.0	5.6	6.3
38.9	6.5	13.0	19.5	26.0	32.5	.9	0.6	1.2	1.9	2.5	3.1	3.8	4.4	5.1	5.7	6.4
39.0	6.5	13.0	19.5	26.0	32.5	.0	0.0	0.7	1.3	2.0	2.6	3.3	3.9	4.6	5.3	5.9
39.1	6.5	13.0	19.5	26.0	32.6	.1	0.1	0.7	1.4	2.0	2.7	3.4	4.0	4.7	5.3	6.0
39.2	6.5	13.0	19.6	26.1	32.6	.2	0.1	0.8	1.4	2.1	2.8	3.4	4.1	4.7	5.4	6.1
39.3	6.5	13.1	19.6	26.2	32.7	.3	0.2	0.9	1.5	2.2	2.8	3.5	4.1	4.8	5.5	6.1
39.4	6.6	13.1	19.7	26.3	32.8	.4	0.3	0.9	1.6	2.2	2.9	3.6	4.2	4.9	5.5	6.2
39.5	6.6	13.2	19.8	26.3	32.9	.5	0.3	1.0	1.6	2.3	3.0	3.6	4.3	4.9	5.6	6.3
39.6	6.6	13.2	19.8	26.4	33.0	.6	0.4	1.1	1.7	2.4	3.0	3.7	4.3	5.0	5.7	6.3
39.7	6.6	13.3	19.9	26.5	33.1	.7	0.5	1.1	1.8	2.4	3.1	3.8	4.4	5.1	5.7	6.4
39.8	6.7	13.3	19.9	26.6	33.2	.8	0.5	1.2	1.8	2.5	3.2	3.8	4.5	5.1	5.8	6.5
39.9	6.7	13.3	20.0	26.6	33.3	.9	0.6	1.3	1.9	2.6	3.2	3.9	4.5	5.2	5.9	6.5
40.0	6.6	13.3	20.0	26.6	33.3	.0	0.0	0.7	1.3	2.0	2.7	3.4	4.0	4.7	5.4	6.1
40.1	6.7	13.3	20.0	26.7	33.4	.1	0.1	0.7	1.4	2.1	2.8	3.4	4.1	4.8	5.5	6.1
40.2	6.7	13.4	20.1	26.8	33.5	.2	0.1	0.8	1.5	2.2	2.8	3.5	4.2	4.9	5.5	6.2
40.3	6.7	13.4	20.1	26.9	33.6	.3	0.2	0.9	1.6	2.2	2.9	3.6	4.3	4.9	5.6	6.3
40.4	6.7	13.5	20.2	26.9	33.7	.4	0.3	0.9	1.6	2.3	3.0	3.6	4.3	5.0	5.7	6.3
40.5	6.8	13.5	20.3	27.0	33.8	.5	0.3	1.0	1.7	2.4	3.0	3.7	4.4	5.1	5.7	6.4
40.6	6.8	13.5	20.3	27.1	33.8	.6	0.4	1.1	1.8	2.4	3.1	3.8	4.5	5.1	5.8	6.5
40.7	6.8	13.6	20.4	27.2	33.9	.7	0.5	1.1	1.8	2.5	3.2	3.8	4.5	5.2	5.9	6.5
40.8	6.8	13.6	20.4	27.2	34.0	.8	0.5	1.2	1.9	2.6	3.2	3.9	4.6	5.3	5.9	6.6
40.9	6.9	13.7	20.5	27.3	34.1	.9	0.6	1.3	2.0	2.6	3.3	4.0	4.7	5.3	6.0	6.7
41.0	6.8	13.6	20.5	27.3	34.1	.0	0.0	0.7	1.4	2.1	2.8	3.5	4.1	4.8	5.5	6.2
41.1	6.8	13.7	20.5	27.4	34.2	.1	0.1	0.8	1.5	2.1	2.8	3.5	4.2	4.9	5.6	6.3
41.2	6.8	13.7	20.6	27.4	34.3	.2	0.1	0.8	1.5	2.2	2.9	3.6	4.3	5.0	5.7	6.4
41.3	6.9	13.8	20.6	27.5	34.4	.3	0.2	0.9	1.6	2.3	3.0	3.7	4.4	5.0	5.7	6.4
41.4	6.9	13.8	20.7	27.6	34.5	.4	0.3	1.0	1.7	2.4	3.0	3.7	4.4	5.1	5.8	6.5
41.5	6.9	13.8	20.8	27.7	34.6	.5	0.3	1.0	1.7	2.4	3.1	3.8	4.5	5.2	5.9	6.6
41.6	6.9	13.9	20.8	27.7	34.7	.6	0.4	1.1	1.8	2.5	3.2	3.9	4.6	5.3	5.9	6.6
41.7	7.0	13.9	20.9	27.8	34.8	.7	0.5	1.2	1.9	2.6	3.3	3.9	4.6	5.3	6.0	6.7
41.8	7.0	14.0	20.9	27.9	34.9	.8	0.6	1.2	1.9	2.6	3.3	4.0	4.7	5.4	6.1	6.8
41.9	7.0	14.0	21.0	28.0	35.0	.9	0.6	1.3	2.0	2.7	3.4	4.1	4.8	5.5	6.2	6.8
42.0	7.0	14.0	21.0	28.0	35.0	.0	0.0	0.7	1.4	2.1	2.8	3.5	4.2	5.0	5.7	6.4
42.1	7.0	14.0	21.0	28.0	35.1	.1	0.1	0.8	1.5	2.2	2.9	3.6	4.3	5.0	5.7	6.4
42.2	7.0	14.0	21.1	28.1	35.1	.2	0.1	0.8	1.6	2.3	3.0	3.7	4.4	5.1	5.8	6.5
42.3	7.0	14.1	21.1	28.2	35.2	.3	0.2	0.9	1.6	2.3	3.0	3.8	4.5	5.2	5.9	6.6
42.4	7.1	14.1	21.2	28.3	35.3	.4	0.3	1.0	1.7	2.4	3.1	3.8	4.5	5.2	5.9	6.7
42.5	7.1	14.2	21.3	28.3	35.4	.5	0.4	1.1	1.8	2.5	3.2	3.9	4.6	5.3	6.0	6.7
42.6	7.1	14.2	21.3	28.4	35.5	.6	0.4	1.1	1.8	2.5	3.3	4.0	4.7	5.4	6.1	6.8
42.7	7.1	14.3	21.4	28.5	35.6	.7	0.5	1.2	1.9	2.6	3.3	4.0	4.7	5.5	6.2	6.9
42.8	7.2	14.3	21.4	28.6	35.7	.8	0.6	1.3	2.0	2.7	3.4	4.1	4.8	5.5	6.2	6.9
42.9	7.2	14.3	21.5	28.6	35.8	.9	0.6	1.3	2.1	2.8	3.5	4.2	4.9	5.6	6.3	7.0
43.0	7.1	14.3	21.5	28.6	35.8	.0	0.0	0.7	1.4	2.2	2.9	3.6	4.3	5.1	5.8	6.5
43.1	7.2	14.3	21.5	28.7	35.9	.1	0.1	0.8	1.5	2.2	3.0	3.7	4.4	5.1	5.9	6.6
43.2	7.2	14.4	21.6	28.8	36.0	.2	0.1	0.9	1.6	2.3	3.0	3.8	4.5	5.2	5.9	6.7
43.3	7.2	14.4	21.6	28.9	36.1	.3	0.2	0.9	1.7	2.4	3.1	3.8	4.6	5.3	6.0	6.7
43.4	7.2	14.5	21.7	28.9	36.2	.4	0.3	1.0	1.7	2.5	3.2	3.9	4.6	5.4	6.1	6.8
43.5	7.3	14.5	21.8	29.0	36.3	.5	0.4	1.1	1.8	2.5	3.3	4.0	4.7	5.4	6.2	6.9
43.6	7.3	14.5	21.8	29.1	36.3	.6	0.4	1.2	1.9	2.6	3.3	4.1	4.8	5.5	6.2	7.0
43.7	7.3	14.6	21.9	29.2	36.4	.7	0.5	1.2	2.0	2.7	3.4	4.1	4.9	5.6	6.3	7.0
43.8	7.3	14.6	21.9	29.2	36.5	.8	0.6	1.3	2.0	2.8	3.5	4.2	4.9	5.7	6.4	7.1
43.9	7.4	14.7	22.0	29.3	36.6	.9	0.7	1.4	2.1	2.8	3.6	4.3	5.0	5.7	6.5	7.2
	10′	20′	30′	40′	50′		0′	1′	2′	3′	4′	5′	6′	7′	8′	9′

Double Second Diff. and Corr. (36.0–37.9):

Double Second Diff.	Corr.
0.8	
	0.1
2.5	
	0.2
4.2	
	0.3
5.9	
	0.4
7.6	
	0.5
9.3	
	0.6
11.0	
	0.7
12.7	
	0.8
14.4	
	0.9
16.1	
	1.0
17.8	
	1.1
19.5	
	1.2
21.2	
	1.3
22.8	
	1.4
24.5	
	1.5
26.2	
	1.6
27.9	
	1.7
29.6	
	1.8
31.3	
	1.9
33.0	
	2.0
34.7	

Double Second Diff. and Corr. (38.0–39.9):

Double Second Diff.	Corr.
0.9	
	0.1
2.6	
	0.2
4.4	
	0.3
6.2	
	0.4
7.9	
	0.5
9.7	
	0.6
11.4	
	0.7
13.2	
	0.8
14.9	
	0.9
16.7	
	1.0
18.5	
	1.1
20.2	
	1.2
22.0	
	1.3
23.7	
	1.4
25.5	
	1.5
27.3	
	1.6
29.0	
	1.7
30.8	
	1.8
32.5	
	1.9
34.3	

Double Second Diff. and Corr. (40.0–41.9):

Double Second Diff.	Corr.
0.9	
	0.1
2.8	
	0.2
4.6	
	0.3
6.5	
	0.4
8.3	
	0.5
10.2	
	0.6
12.0	
	0.7
13.9	
	0.8
15.7	
	0.9
17.6	
	1.0
19.4	
	1.1
21.3	
	1.2
23.1	
	1.3
25.0	
	1.4
26.8	
	1.5
28.7	
	1.6
30.5	
	1.7
32.3	
	1.8
34.2	

Double Second Diff. and Corr. (42.0–43.9):

Double Second Diff.	Corr.
1.0	
	0.1
3.0	
	0.2
4.9	
	0.3
6.9	
	0.4
8.9	
	0.5
10.8	
	0.6
12.8	
	0.7
14.8	
	0.8
16.7	
	0.9
18.7	
	1.0
20.7	
	1.1
22.7	
	1.2
24.6	
	1.3
26.6	
	1.4
28.6	
	1.5
30.5	
	1.6
32.5	
	1.7
34.5	

The Double-Second-Difference correction (Corr.) is always to be added to the tabulated altitude.

INTERPOLATION TABLE

Dec. Inc.	Tens 10′	20′	30′	40′	50′	Decimals	Units 0′	1′	2′	3′	4′	5′	6′	7′	8′	9′	Double Second Diff. and Corr.
44.0	7.3	14.6	22.0	29.3	36.6	.0	0.0	0.7	1.5	2.2	3.0	3.7	4.4	5.2	5.9	6.7	1.1 0.1
44.1	7.3	14.7	22.0	29.4	36.7	.1	0.1	0.8	1.6	2.3	3.0	3.8	4.5	5.3	6.0	6.7	3.2 0.2
44.2	7.3	14.7	22.1	29.4	36.8	.2	0.1	0.9	1.6	2.4	3.1	3.9	4.6	5.3	6.1	6.8	5.3 0.3
44.3	7.4	14.8	22.1	29.5	36.9	.3	0.2	1.0	1.7	2.4	3.2	3.9	4.7	5.4	6.2	6.9	7.5 0.4
44.4	7.4	14.8	22.2	29.6	37.0	.4	0.3	1.0	1.8	2.5	3.3	4.0	4.7	5.5	6.2	7.0	9.6 0.5
44.5	7.4	14.8	22.3	29.7	37.1	.5	0.4	1.1	1.9	2.6	3.3	4.1	4.8	5.6	6.3	7.0	11.7 0.6
44.6	7.4	14.9	22.3	29.7	37.2	.6	0.4	1.2	1.9	2.7	3.4	4.2	4.9	5.6	6.4	7.1	13.9 0.7
44.7	7.5	14.9	22.4	29.8	37.3	.7	0.5	1.3	2.0	2.7	3.5	4.2	5.0	5.7	6.5	7.2	16.0 0.8
44.8	7.5	15.0	22.4	29.9	37.4	.8	0.6	1.3	2.1	2.8	3.6	4.3	5.0	5.8	6.5	7.3	18.1 0.9
44.9	7.5	15.0	22.5	30.0	37.5	.9	0.7	1.4	2.2	2.9	3.6	4.4	5.1	5.9	6.6	7.3	20.3 1.0
45.0	7.5	15.0	22.5	30.0	37.5	.0	0.0	0.8	1.5	2.3	3.0	3.8	4.5	5.3	6.1	6.8	22.4 1.1
45.1	7.5	15.0	22.5	30.0	37.6	.1	0.1	0.8	1.6	2.4	3.1	3.9	4.6	5.4	6.1	6.9	24.5 1.2
45.2	7.5	15.0	22.6	30.1	37.6	.2	0.2	0.9	1.7	2.4	3.2	3.9	4.7	5.5	6.2	7.0	26.7 1.3
45.3	7.5	15.1	22.6	30.2	37.7	.3	0.2	1.0	1.7	2.5	3.3	4.0	4.8	5.5	6.3	7.1	28.8 1.4
45.4	7.6	15.1	22.7	30.3	37.8	.4	0.3	1.1	1.8	2.6	3.3	4.1	4.9	5.6	6.4	7.1	30.9 1.5
45.5	7.6	15.2	22.8	30.3	37.9	.5	0.4	1.1	1.9	2.7	3.4	4.2	4.9	5.7	6.4	7.2	33.1 1.6
45.6	7.6	15.2	22.8	30.4	38.0	.6	0.5	1.2	2.0	2.7	3.5	4.2	5.0	5.8	6.5	7.3	35.2
45.7	7.6	15.3	22.9	30.5	38.1	.7	0.5	1.3	2.0	2.8	3.6	4.3	5.1	5.8	6.6	7.4	
45.8	7.7	15.3	22.9	30.6	38.2	.8	0.6	1.4	2.1	2.9	3.6	4.4	5.2	5.9	6.7	7.4	
45.9	7.7	15.3	23.0	30.6	38.3	.9	0.7	1.4	2.2	3.0	3.7	4.5	5.2	6.0	6.7	7.5	
46.0	7.6	15.3	23.0	30.6	38.3	.0	0.0	0.8	1.5	2.3	3.1	3.9	4.6	5.4	6.2	7.0	1.2 0.1
46.1	7.7	15.3	23.0	30.7	38.4	.1	0.1	0.9	1.6	2.4	3.2	4.0	4.7	5.5	6.3	7.1	3.5 0.2
46.2	7.7	15.4	23.1	30.8	38.5	.2	0.2	0.9	1.7	2.5	3.3	4.0	4.8	5.6	6.4	7.1	5.8 0.3
46.3	7.7	15.4	23.1	30.9	38.6	.3	0.2	1.0	1.8	2.6	3.3	4.1	4.9	5.7	6.4	7.2	8.1 0.4
46.4	7.7	15.5	23.2	30.9	38.7	.4	0.3	1.1	1.9	2.6	3.4	4.2	5.0	5.7	6.5	7.3	10.5 0.5
46.5	7.8	15.5	23.3	31.0	38.8	.5	0.4	1.2	1.9	2.7	3.5	4.3	5.0	5.8	6.6	7.4	12.8 0.6
46.6	7.8	15.5	23.3	31.1	38.8	.6	0.5	1.2	2.0	2.8	3.6	4.3	5.1	5.9	6.7	7.4	15.1 0.7
46.7	7.8	15.6	23.4	31.2	38.9	.7	0.5	1.3	2.1	2.9	3.6	4.4	5.2	6.0	6.7	7.5	17.4 0.8
46.8	7.8	15.6	23.4	31.2	39.0	.8	0.6	1.4	2.2	2.9	3.7	4.5	5.3	6.0	6.8	7.6	19.8 0.9
46.9	7.9	15.7	23.5	31.3	39.1	.9	0.7	1.5	2.2	3.0	3.8	4.6	5.3	6.1	6.9	7.7	22.1 1.0
47.0	7.8	15.6	23.5	31.3	39.1	.0	0.0	0.8	1.6	2.4	3.2	4.0	4.7	5.5	6.3	7.1	24.4 1.1
47.1	7.8	15.7	23.5	31.4	39.2	.1	0.1	0.9	1.7	2.5	3.2	4.0	4.8	5.6	6.4	7.2	26.7 1.2
47.2	7.8	15.7	23.6	31.4	39.3	.2	0.2	0.9	1.7	2.5	3.3	4.1	4.9	5.7	6.5	7.3	29.1 1.3
47.3	7.9	15.8	23.6	31.5	39.4	.3	0.2	1.0	1.8	2.6	3.4	4.2	5.0	5.8	6.6	7.4	31.4 1.4
47.4	7.9	15.8	23.7	31.6	39.5	.4	0.3	1.1	1.9	2.7	3.5	4.3	5.1	5.9	6.6	7.4	33.7 1.5 36.0
47.5	7.9	15.8	23.8	31.7	39.6	.5	0.4	1.2	2.0	2.8	3.6	4.4	5.1	5.9	6.7	7.5	1.3 0.1
47.6	7.9	15.9	23.8	31.7	39.7	.6	0.5	1.3	2.1	2.8	3.6	4.4	5.2	6.0	6.8	7.6	3.8 0.2
47.7	8.0	15.9	23.9	31.8	39.8	.7	0.6	1.3	2.1	2.9	3.7	4.5	5.3	6.1	6.9	7.7	6.3 0.3
47.8	8.0	16.0	23.9	31.9	39.9	.8	0.6	1.4	2.2	3.0	3.8	4.6	5.4	6.2	7.0	7.8	8.9 0.4
47.9	8.0	16.0	24.0	32.0	40.0	.9	0.7	1.5	2.3	3.1	3.9	4.7	5.5	6.3	7.0	7.8	11.4 0.5
48.0	8.0	16.0	24.0	32.0	40.0	.0	0.0	0.8	1.6	2.4	3.2	4.0	4.8	5.7	6.5	7.3	14.0 0.6
48.1	8.0	16.0	24.0	32.0	40.1	.1	0.1	0.9	1.7	2.5	3.3	4.1	4.9	5.7	6.5	7.4	16.5 0.7
48.2	8.0	16.0	24.1	32.1	40.1	.2	0.2	1.0	1.8	2.6	3.4	4.2	5.0	5.8	6.6	7.4	19.0 0.8
48.3	8.0	16.1	24.1	32.2	40.2	.3	0.2	1.1	1.9	2.7	3.5	4.3	5.1	5.9	6.7	7.5	21.6 0.9
48.4	8.1	16.1	24.2	32.3	40.3	.4	0.3	1.1	1.9	2.7	3.6	4.4	5.2	6.0	6.8	7.6	24.1 1.0
48.5	8.1	16.2	24.3	32.3	40.4	.5	0.4	1.2	2.0	2.8	3.6	4.4	5.3	6.1	6.9	7.7	26.7 1.1
48.6	8.1	16.2	24.3	32.4	40.5	.6	0.5	1.3	2.1	2.9	3.7	4.5	5.3	6.1	7.0	7.8	29.2 1.2
48.7	8.1	16.3	24.4	32.5	40.6	.7	0.6	1.4	2.2	3.0	3.8	4.6	5.4	6.2	7.0	7.8	31.7 1.3
48.8	8.2	16.3	24.4	32.6	40.7	.8	0.6	1.5	2.3	3.1	3.9	4.7	5.5	6.3	7.1	7.9	34.3
48.9	8.2	16.3	24.5	32.6	40.8	.9	0.7	1.5	2.3	3.2	4.0	4.8	5.6	6.4	7.2	8.0	
49.0	8.1	16.3	24.5	32.6	40.8	.0	0.0	0.8	1.6	2.5	3.3	4.1	4.9	5.8	6.6	7.4	1.4 0.1
49.1	8.2	16.3	24.5	32.7	40.9	.1	0.1	0.9	1.7	2.6	3.4	4.2	5.0	5.9	6.7	7.5	4.2 0.2
49.2	8.2	16.4	24.6	32.8	41.0	.2	0.2	1.0	1.8	2.6	3.5	4.3	5.1	5.9	6.8	7.6	7.1 0.3
49.3	8.2	16.4	24.6	32.9	41.1	.3	0.2	1.1	1.9	2.7	3.5	4.4	5.2	6.0	6.8	7.7	9.9 0.4
49.4	8.2	16.5	24.7	32.9	41.2	.4	0.3	1.2	2.0	2.8	3.6	4.5	5.3	6.1	6.9	7.8	12.7 0.5
49.5	8.3	16.5	24.8	33.0	41.3	.5	0.4	1.2	2.1	2.9	3.7	4.5	5.4	6.2	7.0	7.8	15.5 0.6
49.6	8.3	16.5	24.8	33.1	41.3	.6	0.5	1.3	2.1	3.0	3.8	4.6	5.4	6.3	7.1	7.9	18.4 0.7
49.7	8.3	16.6	24.9	33.2	41.4	.7	0.6	1.4	2.2	3.1	3.9	4.7	5.5	6.4	7.2	8.0	21.2 0.8
49.8	8.3	16.6	24.9	33.2	41.5	.8	0.7	1.5	2.3	3.1	4.0	4.8	5.6	6.4	7.3	8.1	24.0 0.9
49.9	8.4	16.7	25.0	33.3	41.6	.9	0.7	1.6	2.4	3.2	4.0	4.9	5.7	6.5	7.3	8.2	26.8 1.0
50.0	8.3	16.6	25.0	33.3	41.6	.0	0.0	0.8	1.7	2.5	3.4	4.2	5.0	5.9	6.7	7.6	29.7 1.1
50.1	8.3	16.7	25.0	33.4	41.7	.1	0.1	0.9	1.8	2.6	3.5	4.3	5.1	6.0	6.8	7.7	32.5 1.2
50.2	8.3	16.7	25.1	33.4	41.8	.2	0.2	1.0	1.9	2.7	3.5	4.4	5.2	6.1	6.9	7.7	35.3
50.3	8.4	16.8	25.1	33.5	41.9	.3	0.3	1.1	1.9	2.8	3.6	4.5	5.3	6.1	7.0	7.8	
50.4	8.4	16.8	25.2	33.6	42.0	.4	0.3	1.2	2.0	2.9	3.7	4.5	5.4	6.2	7.1	7.9	
50.5	8.4	16.8	25.3	33.7	42.1	.5	0.4	1.3	2.1	2.9	3.8	4.6	5.5	6.3	7.2	8.0	1.6 0.1
50.6	8.4	16.9	25.3	33.7	42.2	.6	0.5	1.3	2.2	3.0	3.9	4.7	5.6	6.4	7.2	8.1	4.8 0.2
50.7	8.5	16.9	25.4	33.8	42.3	.7	0.6	1.4	2.3	3.1	4.0	4.8	5.6	6.5	7.3	8.2	8.0 0.3
50.8	8.5	17.0	25.4	33.9	42.4	.8	0.7	1.5	2.4	3.2	4.0	4.9	5.7	6.6	7.4	8.2	11.2 0.4
50.9	8.5	17.0	25.5	34.0	42.5	.9	0.8	1.6	2.4	3.3	4.1	5.0	5.8	6.6	7.5	8.3	14.5 0.5
51.0	8.5	17.0	25.5	34.0	42.5	.0	0.0	0.9	1.7	2.6	3.4	4.3	5.1	6.0	6.9	7.7	17.7 0.6
51.1	8.5	17.0	25.5	34.0	42.6	.1	0.1	0.9	1.8	2.7	3.5	4.4	5.2	6.1	7.0	7.8	20.9 0.7
51.2	8.5	17.0	25.6	34.1	42.6	.2	0.2	1.0	1.9	2.7	3.6	4.5	5.3	6.2	7.0	7.9	24.1 0.8
51.3	8.5	17.1	25.6	34.2	42.7	.3	0.3	1.1	2.0	2.8	3.7	4.5	5.4	6.3	7.1	8.0	27.3 0.9
51.4	8.6	17.1	25.7	34.3	42.8	.4	0.3	1.2	2.1	2.9	3.8	4.6	5.5	6.4	7.2	8.1	30.5 1.0
51.5	8.6	17.2	25.8	34.3	42.9	.5	0.4	1.3	2.1	3.0	3.9	4.7	5.6	6.4	7.3	8.2	33.7 1.1
51.6	8.6	17.2	25.8	34.4	43.0	.6	0.5	1.4	2.2	3.1	3.9	4.8	5.7	6.5	7.4	8.2	36.9
51.7	8.6	17.3	25.9	34.5	43.1	.7	0.6	1.5	2.3	3.2	4.0	4.9	5.8	6.6	7.5	8.3	
51.8	8.7	17.3	25.9	34.6	43.2	.8	0.7	1.5	2.4	3.3	4.1	5.0	5.8	6.7	7.6	8.4	
51.9	8.7	17.3	26.0	34.6	43.3	.9	0.8	1.6	2.5	3.3	4.2	5.1	5.9	6.8	7.6	8.5	
	10′	20′	30′	40′	50′		0′	1′	2′	3′	4′	5′	6′	7′	8′	9′	

Dec. Inc.	Tens 10′	20′	30′	40′	50′	Decimals	Units 0′	1′	2′	3′	4′	5′	6′	7′	8′	9′	Double Second Diff. and Corr.
52.0	8.6	17.3	26.0	34.6	43.3	.0	0.0	0.9	1.7	2.6	3.5	4.4	5.2	6.1	7.0	7.9	1.8 0.1
52.1	8.7	17.3	26.0	34.7	43.4	.1	0.1	1.0	1.8	2.7	3.6	4.5	5.3	6.2	7.1	8.0	5.5 0.2
52.2	8.7	17.4	26.1	34.8	43.5	.2	0.2	1.0	1.9	2.8	3.7	4.5	5.4	6.3	7.2	8.0	9.1 0.3
52.3	8.7	17.4	26.1	34.9	43.6	.3	0.3	1.1	2.0	2.9	3.8	4.6	5.5	6.4	7.3	8.1	12.8 0.4
52.4	8.7	17.5	26.2	34.9	43.7	.4	0.3	1.2	2.1	3.0	3.8	4.7	5.6	6.5	7.3	8.2	16.5 0.5
52.5	8.8	17.5	26.3	35.0	43.8	.5	0.4	1.3	2.2	3.1	3.9	4.8	5.7	6.6	7.4	8.3	20.1 0.6
52.6	8.8	17.5	26.3	35.1	43.8	.6	0.5	1.4	2.3	3.1	4.0	4.9	5.8	6.6	7.5	8.4	23.8 0.7
52.7	8.8	17.6	26.4	35.2	43.9	.7	0.6	1.5	2.4	3.2	4.1	5.0	5.9	6.7	7.6	8.5	27.4 0.8
52.8	8.8	17.6	26.4	35.2	44.0	.8	0.7	1.6	2.4	3.3	4.2	5.1	5.9	6.8	7.7	8.6	31.1 0.9
52.9	8.9	17.7	26.5	35.3	44.1	.9	0.8	1.7	2.5	3.4	4.3	5.2	6.0	6.9	7.8	8.7	34.7
53.0	8.8	17.6	26.5	35.3	44.1	.0	0.0	0.9	1.8	2.7	3.6	4.5	5.3	6.2	7.1	8.0	2.1 0.1
53.1	8.8	17.7	26.5	35.4	44.2	.1	0.1	1.0	1.9	2.8	3.7	4.5	5.4	6.3	7.2	8.1	6.2 0.2
53.2	8.8	17.7	26.6	35.4	44.3	.2	0.2	1.1	2.0	2.9	3.7	4.6	5.5	6.4	7.3	8.2	10.4 0.3
53.3	8.9	17.8	26.6	35.5	44.4	.3	0.3	1.2	2.1	2.9	3.8	4.7	5.6	6.5	7.4	8.3	14.5 0.4
53.4	8.9	17.8	26.7	35.6	44.5	.4	0.4	1.2	2.1	3.0	3.9	4.8	5.7	6.6	7.5	8.4	18.6 0.5
53.5	8.9	17.8	26.8	35.7	44.6	.5	0.4	1.3	2.2	3.1	4.0	4.9	5.8	6.7	7.6	8.5	22.8 0.6
53.6	8.9	17.9	26.8	35.7	44.7	.6	0.5	1.4	2.3	3.2	4.1	5.0	5.9	6.8	7.7	8.6	26.9 0.7
53.7	9.0	17.9	26.9	35.8	44.8	.7	0.6	1.5	2.4	3.3	4.2	5.1	6.0	6.9	7.8	8.6	31.1 0.8
53.8	9.0	18.0	26.9	35.9	44.9	.8	0.7	1.6	2.5	3.4	4.3	5.2	6.1	7.0	7.8	8.7	35.2
53.9	9.0	18.0	27.0	36.0	45.0	.9	0.8	1.7	2.6	3.5	4.4	5.3	6.2	7.0	7.9	8.8	
54.0	9.0	18.0	27.0	36.0	45.0	.0	0.0	0.9	1.8	2.7	3.6	4.5	5.4	6.4	7.3	8.2	2.4 0.1
54.1	9.0	18.0	27.0	36.0	45.1	.1	0.1	1.0	1.9	2.8	3.7	4.6	5.5	6.4	7.4	8.3	7.2 0.2
54.2	9.0	18.0	27.1	36.1	45.1	.2	0.2	1.1	2.0	2.9	3.8	4.7	5.6	6.5	7.4	8.4	12.0 0.3
54.3	9.0	18.1	27.1	36.2	45.2	.3	0.3	1.2	2.1	3.0	3.9	4.8	5.7	6.6	7.5	8.4	16.8 0.4
54.4	9.1	18.1	27.2	36.3	45.3	.4	0.4	1.3	2.2	3.1	4.0	4.9	5.8	6.7	7.6	8.5	21.6 0.5
54.5	9.1	18.2	27.3	36.3	45.4	.5	0.5	1.4	2.3	3.2	4.1	5.0	5.9	6.8	7.7	8.6	26.4 0.6
54.6	9.1	18.2	27.3	36.4	45.5	.6	0.5	1.5	2.4	3.3	4.2	5.1	6.0	6.9	7.8	8.7	31.2 0.7
54.7	9.1	18.3	27.4	36.5	45.6	.7	0.6	1.5	2.5	3.4	4.3	5.2	6.1	7.0	7.9	8.8	36.0
54.8	9.2	18.3	27.4	36.6	45.7	.8	0.7	1.6	2.5	3.5	4.4	5.3	6.2	7.1	8.0	8.9	
54.9	9.2	18.3	27.5	36.6	45.8	.9	0.8	1.7	2.6	3.5	4.5	5.4	6.3	7.2	8.1	9.0	
55.0	9.1	18.3	27.5	36.6	45.8	.0	0.0	0.9	1.8	2.8	3.7	4.6	5.5	6.5	7.4	8.3	2.9 0.1
55.1	9.2	18.3	27.5	36.7	45.9	.1	0.1	1.0	1.9	2.9	3.8	4.7	5.6	6.6	7.5	8.4	8.6 0.2
55.2	9.2	18.4	27.6	36.8	46.0	.2	0.2	1.1	2.0	3.0	3.9	4.8	5.7	6.7	7.6	8.5	14.4 0.3
55.3	9.2	18.4	27.6	36.9	46.1	.3	0.3	1.2	2.1	3.1	4.0	4.9	5.8	6.8	7.7	8.6	20.2 0.4
55.4	9.2	18.5	27.7	36.9	46.2	.4	0.4	1.3	2.2	3.1	4.1	5.0	5.9	6.8	7.8	8.7	25.9 0.5
55.5	9.3	18.5	27.8	37.0	46.3	.5	0.5	1.4	2.3	3.2	4.2	5.1	6.0	6.9	7.9	8.8	31.7 0.6
55.6	9.3	18.5	27.8	37.1	46.3	.6	0.6	1.5	2.4	3.3	4.3	5.2	6.1	7.0	8.0	8.9	37.5
55.7	9.3	18.6	27.9	37.2	46.4	.7	0.6	1.6	2.5	3.4	4.3	5.3	6.2	7.1	8.0	9.0	
55.8	9.3	18.6	27.9	37.2	46.5	.8	0.7	1.7	2.6	3.5	4.4	5.4	6.3	7.2	8.1	9.1	
55.9	9.4	18.7	28.0	37.3	46.6	.9	0.8	1.8	2.7	3.6	4.5	5.5	6.4	7.3	8.2	9.2	
56.0	9.3	18.6	28.0	37.3	46.6	.0	0.0	0.9	1.9	2.8	3.8	4.7	5.6	6.6	7.5	8.5	3.6 0.1
56.1	9.3	18.7	28.0	37.4	46.7	.1	0.1	1.0	2.0	2.9	3.9	4.8	5.7	6.7	7.6	8.6	10.9 0.2
56.2	9.3	18.7	28.1	37.4	46.8	.2	0.2	1.1	2.1	3.0	4.0	4.9	5.8	6.8	7.7	8.7	18.2 0.3
56.3	9.4	18.8	28.1	37.5	46.9	.3	0.3	1.2	2.2	3.1	4.0	5.0	5.9	6.9	7.8	8.8	25.5 0.4
56.4	9.4	18.8	28.2	37.6	47.0	.4	0.4	1.3	2.3	3.2	4.1	5.1	6.0	7.0	7.9	8.9	32.8 0.5
56.5	9.4	18.8	28.3	37.7	47.1	.5	0.5	1.4	2.4	3.3	4.2	5.2	6.1	7.1	8.0	8.9	40.1
56.6	9.4	18.9	28.3	37.7	47.2	.6	0.6	1.5	2.4	3.4	4.3	5.3	6.2	7.2	8.1	9.0	
56.7	9.5	18.9	28.4	37.8	47.3	.7	0.7	1.6	2.5	3.5	4.4	5.4	6.3	7.3	8.2	9.1	
56.8	9.5	19.0	28.4	37.9	47.4	.8	0.8	1.7	2.6	3.6	4.5	5.5	6.4	7.3	8.3	9.2	
56.9	9.5	19.0	28.5	38.0	47.5	.9	0.8	1.8	2.7	3.7	4.6	5.6	6.5	7.4	8.4	9.3	
57.0	9.5	19.0	28.5	38.0	47.5	.0	0.0	1.0	1.9	2.9	3.8	4.8	5.7	6.7	7.7	8.6	5.0 0.1
57.1	9.5	19.0	28.5	38.0	47.6	.1	0.1	1.1	2.0	3.0	3.9	4.9	5.8	6.8	7.8	8.7	15.0 0.2
57.2	9.5	19.0	28.6	38.1	47.6	.2	0.2	1.1	2.1	3.1	4.0	5.0	5.9	6.9	7.9	8.8	25.0 0.3
57.3	9.5	19.1	28.6	38.2	47.7	.3	0.3	1.2	2.2	3.2	4.1	5.1	6.0	7.0	8.0	8.9	35.1
57.4	9.6	19.1	28.7	38.3	47.8	.4	0.4	1.3	2.3	3.3	4.2	5.2	6.1	7.1	8.0	9.0	
57.5	9.6	19.2	28.8	38.3	47.9	.5	0.5	1.4	2.4	3.4	4.3	5.3	6.2	7.2	8.1	9.1	
57.6	9.6	19.2	28.8	38.4	48.0	.6	0.6	1.5	2.5	3.4	4.4	5.4	6.3	7.3	8.2	9.2	
57.7	9.6	19.3	28.9	38.5	48.1	.7	0.7	1.6	2.6	3.5	4.5	5.5	6.4	7.4	8.3	9.3	
57.8	9.7	19.3	28.9	38.6	48.2	.8	0.8	1.7	2.7	3.6	4.6	5.6	6.5	7.5	8.4	9.4	
57.9	9.7	19.3	29.0	38.6	48.3	.9	0.9	1.8	2.8	3.7	4.7	5.7	6.6	7.6	8.5	9.5	
58.0	9.6	19.3	29.0	38.6	48.3	.0	0.0	1.0	1.9	2.9	3.9	4.9	5.8	6.8	7.8	8.8	8.2 0.1
58.1	9.7	19.3	29.0	38.7	48.4	.1	0.1	1.1	2.0	3.0	4.0	5.0	5.9	6.9	7.9	8.9	24.6 0.2
58.2	9.7	19.4	29.1	38.8	48.5	.2	0.2	1.2	2.1	3.1	4.1	5.1	6.0	7.0	8.0	9.0	41.0
58.3	9.7	19.4	29.1	38.9	48.6	.3	0.3	1.3	2.2	3.2	4.2	5.2	6.1	7.1	8.1	9.1	
58.4	9.7	19.5	29.2	38.9	48.7	.4	0.4	1.4	2.3	3.3	4.3	5.3	6.2	7.2	8.2	9.2	
58.5	9.8	19.5	29.3	39.0	48.8	.5	0.5	1.5	2.4	3.4	4.4	5.4	6.3	7.3	8.3	9.3	
58.6	9.8	19.5	29.3	39.1	48.8	.6	0.6	1.6	2.5	3.5	4.5	5.5	6.4	7.4	8.4	9.4	
58.7	9.8	19.6	29.4	39.2	48.9	.7	0.7	1.7	2.6	3.6	4.6	5.6	6.5	7.5	8.5	9.5	
58.8	9.8	19.6	29.4	39.2	49.0	.8	0.8	1.8	2.7	3.7	4.7	5.7	6.6	7.6	8.6	9.6	
58.9	9.9	19.7	29.5	39.3	49.1	.9	0.9	1.9	2.8	3.8	4.8	5.8	6.7	7.7	8.7	9.7	
59.0	9.8	19.6	29.5	39.3	49.1	.0	0.0	1.0	2.0	3.0	4.0	5.0	5.9	6.9	7.9	8.9	16.2 0.1
59.1	9.8	19.7	29.5	39.4	49.2	.1	0.1	1.1	2.1	3.1	4.1	5.1	6.0	7.0	8.0	9.0	48.6
59.2	9.8	19.7	29.6	39.4	49.3	.2	0.2	1.2	2.2	3.2	4.2	5.2	6.1	7.1	8.1	9.1	
59.3	9.9	19.8	29.6	39.5	49.4	.3	0.3	1.3	2.3	3.3	4.3	5.3	6.2	7.2	8.2	9.2	
59.4	9.9	19.8	29.7	39.6	49.5	.4	0.4	1.4	2.4	3.4	4.4	5.4	6.3	7.3	8.3	9.3	
59.5	9.9	19.8	29.8	39.7	49.6	.5	0.5	1.5	2.5	3.5	4.5	5.5	6.4	7.4	8.4	9.4	0.0 0.0
59.6	9.9	19.9	29.8	39.7	49.7	.6	0.6	1.6	2.6	3.6	4.6	5.6	6.5	7.5	8.5	9.5	48.2
59.7	10.0	19.9	29.9	39.8	49.8	.7	0.7	1.7	2.7	3.7	4.7	5.7	6.6	7.6	8.6	9.6	
59.8	10.0	20.0	29.9	39.9	49.9	.8	0.8	1.8	2.8	3.8	4.8	5.8	6.7	7.7	8.7	9.7	
59.9	10.0	20.0	30.0	40.0	50.0	.9	0.9	1.9	2.9	3.9	4.9	5.9	6.8	7.8	8.8	9.8	
	10′	20′	30′	40′	50′		0′	1′	2′	3′	4′	5′	6′	7′	8′	9′	

The Double-Second-Difference correction (Corr.) is always to be added to the tabulated altitude.

Supplemental Reading List

Blewitt, Mary. *Celestial Navigation for Yachtsmen*. Tuckahoe, N.Y.: John De Graff, Inc., 1971.

Bowditch, Nathaniel (original author). *American Practical Navigator,* Pub. No. 9. Washington, D.C.: U.S. Government Printing Office, 1977.

Buchanek, Jack, and Bergin, Edward J. *Piloting Navigation with the Pocket Calculator*. Blue Ridge Summit, Pa.: Tab Books, 1976.

Cruising. New York: Time-Life Books, 1975.

Hobbs, Richard R. *Marine Navigation 2: Celestial and Electronic*. Annapolis, Md.: Naval Institute Press, 1974.

Maloney, Elbert S. *Chapman Piloting, Seamanship, and Small Boat Handling*. 53rd ed. New York: Motor Boating and Sailing, 1977.

————. *Dutton's Navigation and Piloting*. 13th ed. Annapolis, Md.: Naval Institute Press, 1978.

Mixter, George W. *Primer of Navigation*. 4th ed. Princeton, N.J.: D. Van Nostrand Company, Inc., 1960.

Navigation. New York: Time-Life Books, 1975.

Racing. New York: Time-Life Books, 1975.

Shufeldt, H. H., and Dunlap, G. D. *Piloting and Dead Reckoning*. Annapolis, Md.: Naval Institute Press, 1970.